Rembrandt
THE LATE WORKS

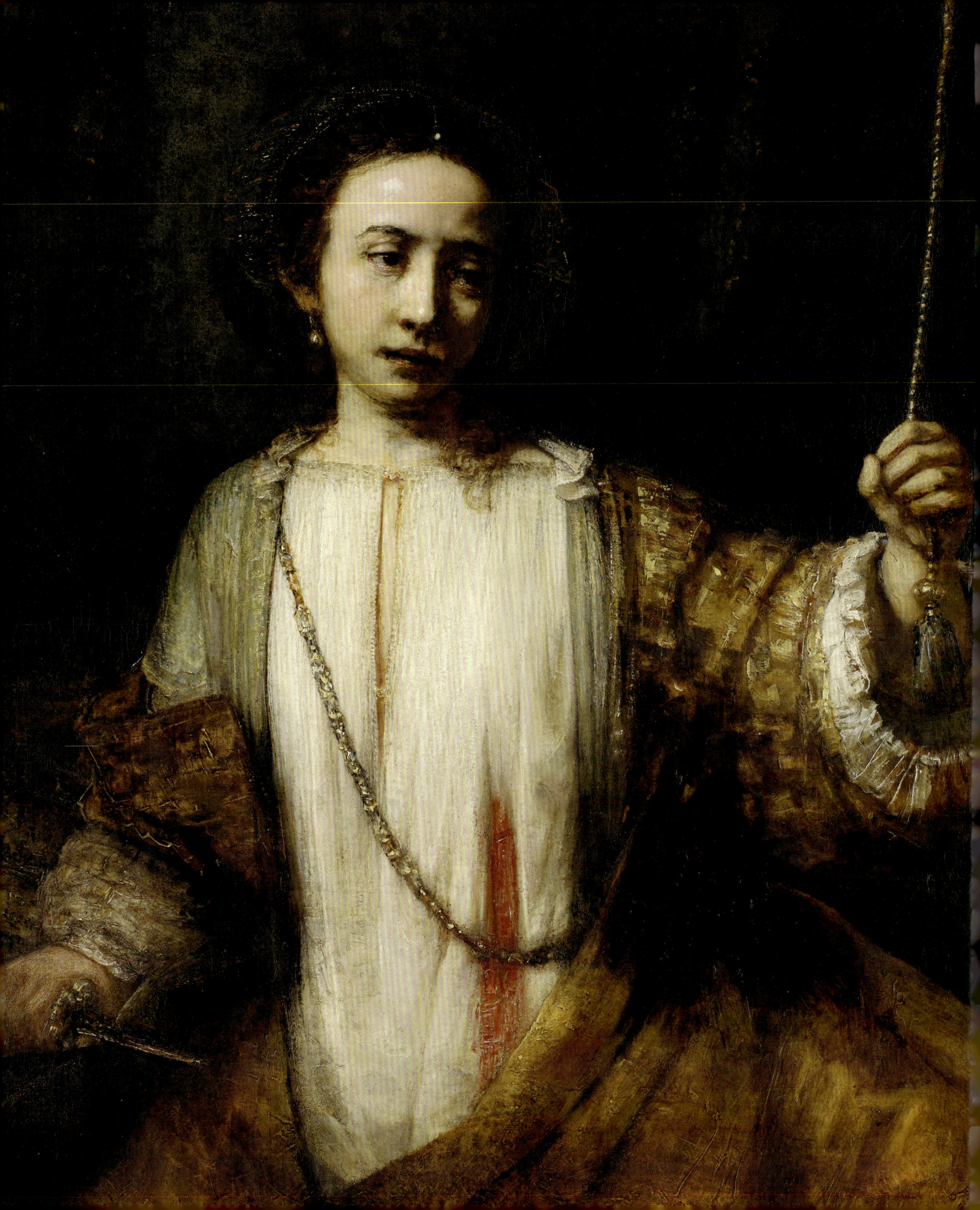

Rembrandt
THE LATE WORKS

Jonathan Bikker and Gregor J. M. Weber

Marjorie E. Wieseman and Erik Hinterding

WITH CONTRIBUTIONS BY

Marijn Schapelhouman and Anna Krekeler

EDITORIAL CONSULTANT

Christopher White

PUBLISHED BY NATIONAL GALLERY COMPANY, LONDON

IN ASSOCIATION WITH THE RIJKSMUSEUM, AMSTERDAM

DISTRIBUTED BY YALE UNIVERSITY PRESS

This book is published on the occasion of the exhibition
Rembrandt: The Late Works
at the National Gallery, London
15 October 2014 – 18 January 2015
AND
Late Rembrandt
at the Rijksmuseum, Amsterdam
12 February – 17 May 2015

First published in Great Britain in 2014 by
National Gallery Company Limited
in association with the Rijksmuseum, Amsterdam

National Gallery Company Limited
St Vincent House
30 Orange Street
London WC2H 7HH
www.nationalgallery.co.uk

ISBN 978 1 85709 557 9 HB
ISBN 978 1 85709 558 6 PB

British Library Cataloguing in Publication Data
A catalogue record is available from the British Library
Library of Congress Control Number 2014944965

All works illustrated are by Rembrandt unless otherwise indicated. Comparative illustrations are denoted as figures. All other numbered illustrations denote works in the exhibition.

All measurements give height before width.

Publisher JAN GREEN
Project Editor SARAH DERRY
Editor JOHANNA STEPHENSON
Designer PHILIP LEWIS
Picture Researcher ANNA SIEBERT
Production JANE HYNE and PENNY LE TISSIER
Translations WORDWORKERS, UTRECHT and MICHAEL HOYLE, AMSTERDAM

Designed and typeset in DTL Elzevir

Origination by AltaImage, London
Printed and bound in Italy by Conti TipoColor

FRONT COVER
Detail from *The Sampling Officials of the Amsterdam Drapers' Guild*, known as '*The Syndics*' (cat. 56)

BACK COVER AND PAGE 8
Details from *A Woman bathing in a Stream* (cat. 95)

FRONTISPIECE
Detail from *Lucretia* (cat. 57)

PAGES 10–11
Detail from *Portrait of a Couple as Isaac and Rebecca*, known as '*The Jewish Bride*' (cat. 92)

PAGE 270
Detail from *Portrait of Margaretha de Geer, Wife of Jacob Trip* (cat. 40)

CONTENTS

SPONSOR'S FOREWORD

Shell is proud to be sponsoring this exceptional exhibition of works created by Rembrandt in his later years. As an Anglo-Dutch company with UK roots stretching back more than a century, it gives us great pleasure to join the National Gallery in bringing to London this stunning collection of works from such a celebrated and respected Dutch master.

Rembrandt was one of the true innovators of his time. His audacious techniques reframed perspectives on the use of colour and texture, while his pioneering approach to self portraiture continues to influence artists all over the world today.

Shell is full of passionate experts who, like Rembrandt, live and breathe curiosity and innovation. Nothing excites us more than finding new and inventive ways to use our technology. Some of the most innovative ideas arise from collaboration between diverse parties. I am therefore particularly proud that Shell scientists at our Amsterdam Technology Centre are working in partnership with National Gallery experts to analyse the molecular structure of red pigments used by Rembrandt and other seventeenth-century artists. Together they are investigating the chemistry behind some of the colour changes that develop over time, which can help inform how the paintings are best preserved for future generations.

This exhibition is not just an outstanding and historic collection of art. It is a study in innovation, and a reminder of what is possible when conventions are challenged and imagination set free.

We hope you enjoy it.

Ben van Beurden
CHIEF EXECUTIVE OFFICER
ROYAL DUTCH SHELL

SPONSORED BY

FOREWORD

The National Gallery and the Rijksmuseum have been discussing the possibility of mounting an exhibition devoted to Rembrandt's late work for over two decades and there can be no more fitting subject for the first great international loan exhibition to be held at the Rijksmuseum since its triumphant re-opening in 2013. Rembrandt after all is not only the greatest figure in Dutch art of the Golden Age – probably indeed the most famous of all Dutchmen – but he is to The Netherlands what Shakespeare is to England. That Rembrandt's work is superbly represented in the Rijksmuseum is hardly surprising; it is also true that Rembrandt always had a strong presence in the National Gallery and indeed works by him have formed an important part of English collections since the seventeenth century.

One way in which Rembrandt's late work may be defined is its independence from – even its opposition to – the prevailing and popular tendencies in Dutch art of his day. However his art was understood, it was always recognised as innovative and, although clearly more appreciated by his contemporaries than has often been supposed, it has been rediscovered with amazement by successive generations of artists and admired in many different ways by art lovers in every century since his death.

No great European painter, with the exception of Dürer, has achieved so much as a printmaker, and the intriguing parallels and creative interplay between Rembrandt's etchings and paintings and of course his drawings (which do not always relate to either) is a major attraction in the exhibition, as also of this volume. This feature of the exhibition reflects the wide range of the Rijksmuseum's collections and curatorial expertise, while the National Gallery collection, though exclusively of paintings, holds several important examples of Rembrandt's late work. It speaks for the fruitful and complementary nature of such partnerships that, despite the differences in each institution's holdings, the experience of visitors to the exhibition at either venue will be greatly enhanced by our collaboration.

The concept of the exhibition was developed by Gregor J. M. Weber and Jonathan Bikker at the Rijksmuseum in collaboration with Marjorie E. Wieseman at the National Gallery, and with valuable contributions by Erik Hinterding, Marijn Schapelhouman and Anna Krekeler. In Amsterdam, we would like to thank Ernst van de Wetering, Peter Schatborn and Taco Dibbits for their advice. Both institutions would like to thank the authors for their outstanding contributions to the catalogue.

We are enormously grateful to the individuals and institutions who have agreed to lend their precious works to this exhibition. In London, we owe a special debt to the Rijksmuseum and the City of Amsterdam, without whose generosity no significant exhibition of Rembrandt's late works could be possible. We would like to thank Shell for their extraordinarily generous support of *Rembrandt: The Late Works*, and for their sponsorship of scientific research into Rembrandt's pigments.

Nicholas Penny
DIRECTOR, THE NATIONAL GALLERY, LONDON

Wim Pijbes
DIRECTOR, RIJKSMUSEUM, AMSTERDAM

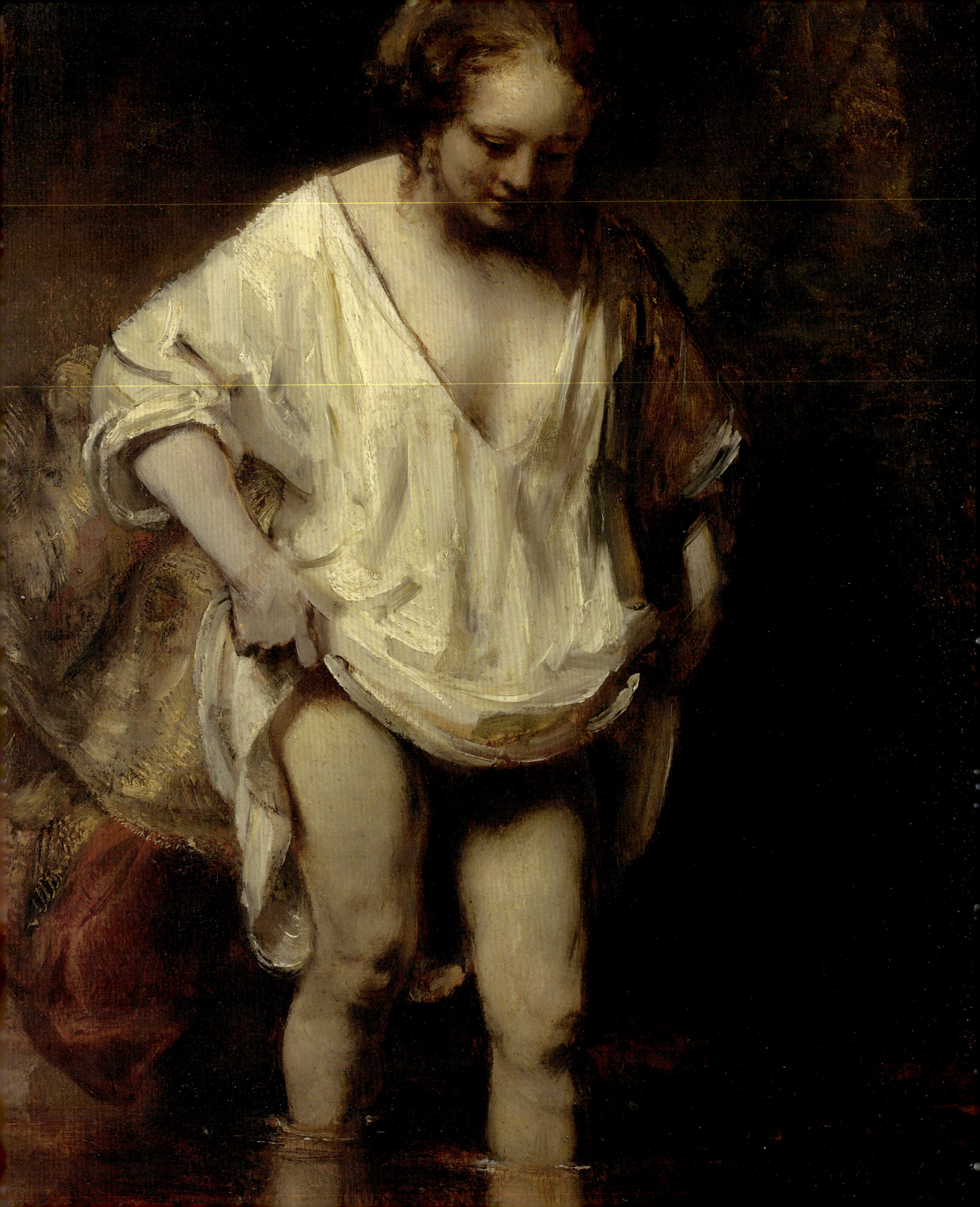

ACKNOWLEDGEMENTS

In preparing this exhibition and accompanying publication, we have had assistance from many institutions and individuals. We are especially grateful for the ongoing support and encouragement of our directors, Nicholas Penny at The National Gallery, London and Wim Pijbes at The Rijksmuseum, Amsterdam, who have backed this project generously and enthusiastically throughout its long gestation.

We would especially like to thank the many museums and private collectors who have so generously and graciously agreed to lend works from their collections to this exhibition. As this entails depriving themselves and their visitors of important and much-loved works for an extended period of time, we are most appreciative of the sacrifice such a loan represents. Several of the works in the exhibition have been recently cleaned or restored; we have benefited greatly from our colleagues' generosity in sharing their research, allowing us to examine works closely and observe treatments in process. In addition to colleagues at our own institutions, we are grateful to the following friends and colleagues who have assisted our work in a variety of ways:

Sébastien Allard, Stijn Alsteens, Heinrich Schulze Altcappenberg, Dita Amory, László Baán, Alfred and Isabel Bader, Christophe Becker, Rickard Becklén, Holm Bevers, Szilvia Bodnár, Christopher Brown, Julius Bryant, The Duke of Buccleuch and Queensberry, KBE, Edwin Buijsen, Cynthia Burlingham, Quentin Buvelot, An Van Camp, Thomas Campbell, Görel Cavalli-Björkman, Hugo Chapman, Peter van der Coelen, Patricia Collins, Leslie Cozzi, James Cuno, Marcus Dekiert, John Delancy, Lloyd DeWitt, Stephanie Dickey, Joris Dik, Blaise Ducos, Anna Eavis, Michael Eissenhauer, Albert J. Elen, Tony Ellwood, Ildikó Ember, Mark Evans, Sjarel Ex, Kaywin Feldman, Michiel Franken, Carina Fryklund, Silke Gatenbröcker, Melanie Gifford, Emilie Gordenker, Joan Gorman, Anne Harmssen, Craig Hartley, Babette Hartwieg, Laura Houliston, Koen Janssens, Susan Jenkins, Hildegard Kaul, Anna Keay, Timothy Knox, Thomas Kren, Bernd Küster, Frauke Laarmann-Westdijk, Friso Lammertse, Justus Lange, Claudia Laurenze-Landsberg, Christophe Leribault, Walter A. Liedtke, Bernd Wolfgang Lindemann, Jochen Luckhardt, Neil MacGregor, David Marquis, Jean-Luc Martinez, Ellen McAdam, Eva Michel, Norbert Middelkoop, Regina Moreira, Otto Naumann, Petria Noble, Patrick Noon, Magnus Olausson, Nadine Orenstein, Andrew Penny, The Trustees of the Penrhyn Settled Estates, Ann Philbin, Michiel Plomp, Vincent Pomarède, Timothy Potts, Earl A. Powell III, Rijksbureau voor Kunsthistorische Documentatie, The Hague, Sophie Renouard de Bussière, Martin Roth, Xavier Salmon, Gill Saunders, Olivia Savatier-Sjöholm, J.S.M. Savenije, Scott Schaefer, Marjan Scharloo, Peter Schatborn, Gary Schwartz, David Scrase, Michael Semff, Anja Ševčík, Kriste Sibul, Jhr Jan Six van Hillegom, Susanna Slöör, Eric Jan Sluijter, Geert van der Snickt, Stephen Somerville, Paul Spies, Philippa Stephenson, Yvonne Szafran, Matthew Teitelbaum, Simon Thurley, Colin D. Turner, Gerard Vaughan, Jaap van der Veen, Susanne Wagini, Sandra Webster-Cook, Ernst van de Wetering, Arthur K. Wheelock, Jr, Catherine Whistler, John Wilson, Anne T. Woollett, Allen Wright and those private lenders who wish to remain anonymous.

In the preparation of the catalogue, we have benefited greatly from Sir Christopher White's erudition and experience: he has provided guidance and advice with a gentle touch. The translators have done a superlative job of capturing the particular nuances of the original texts. The catalogue was elegantly designed by Philip Lewis, and patiently copyedited by Johanna Stephenson.

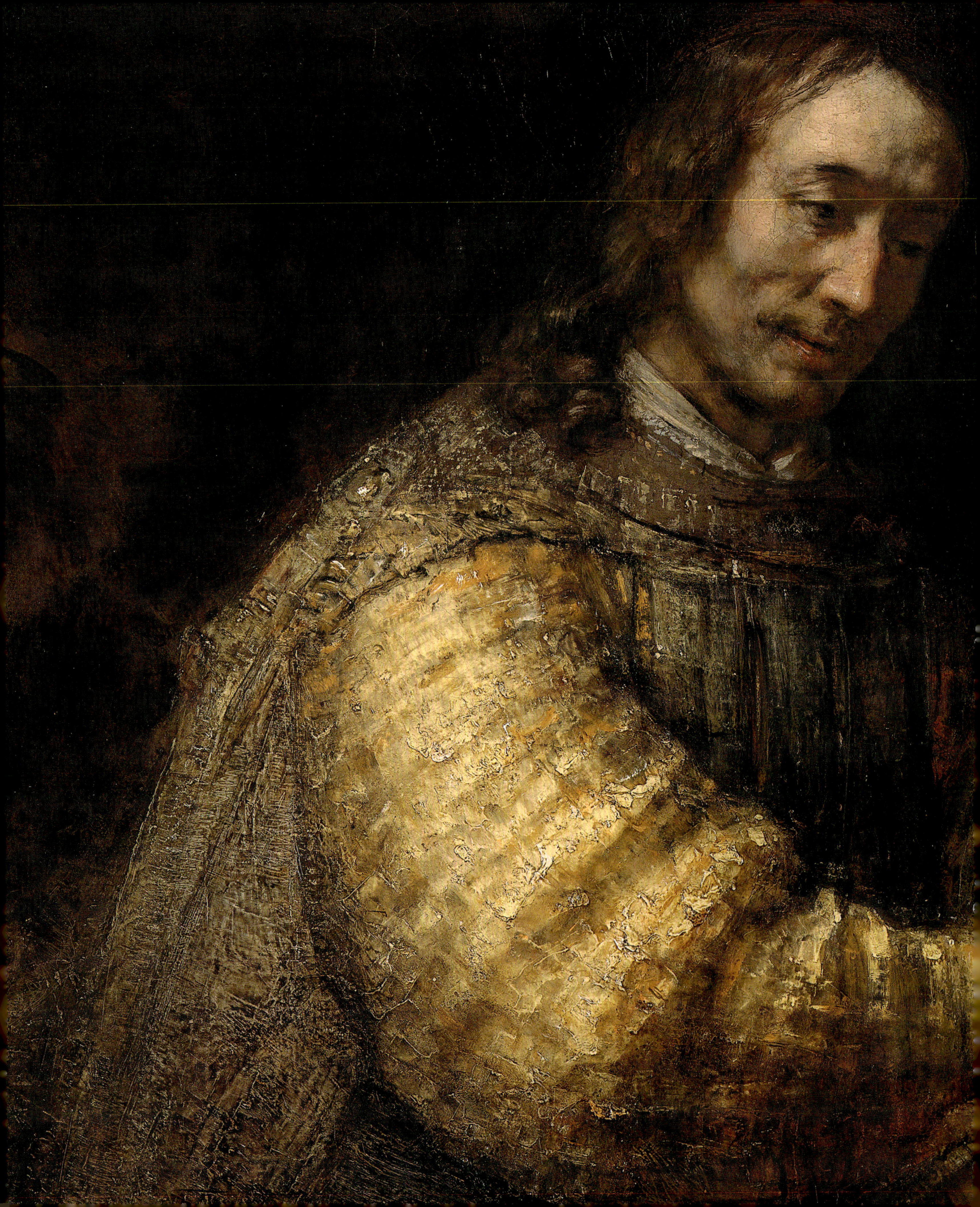

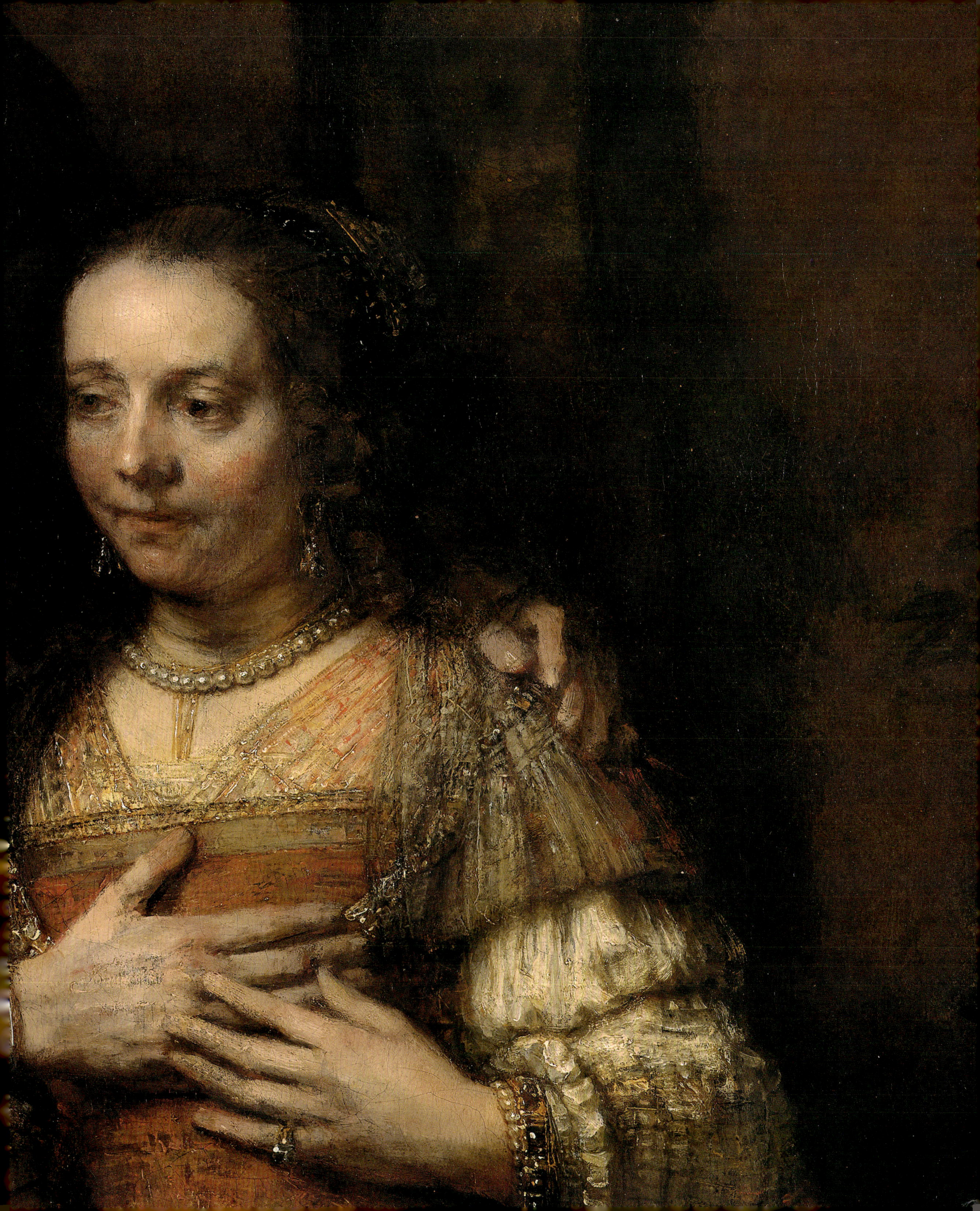

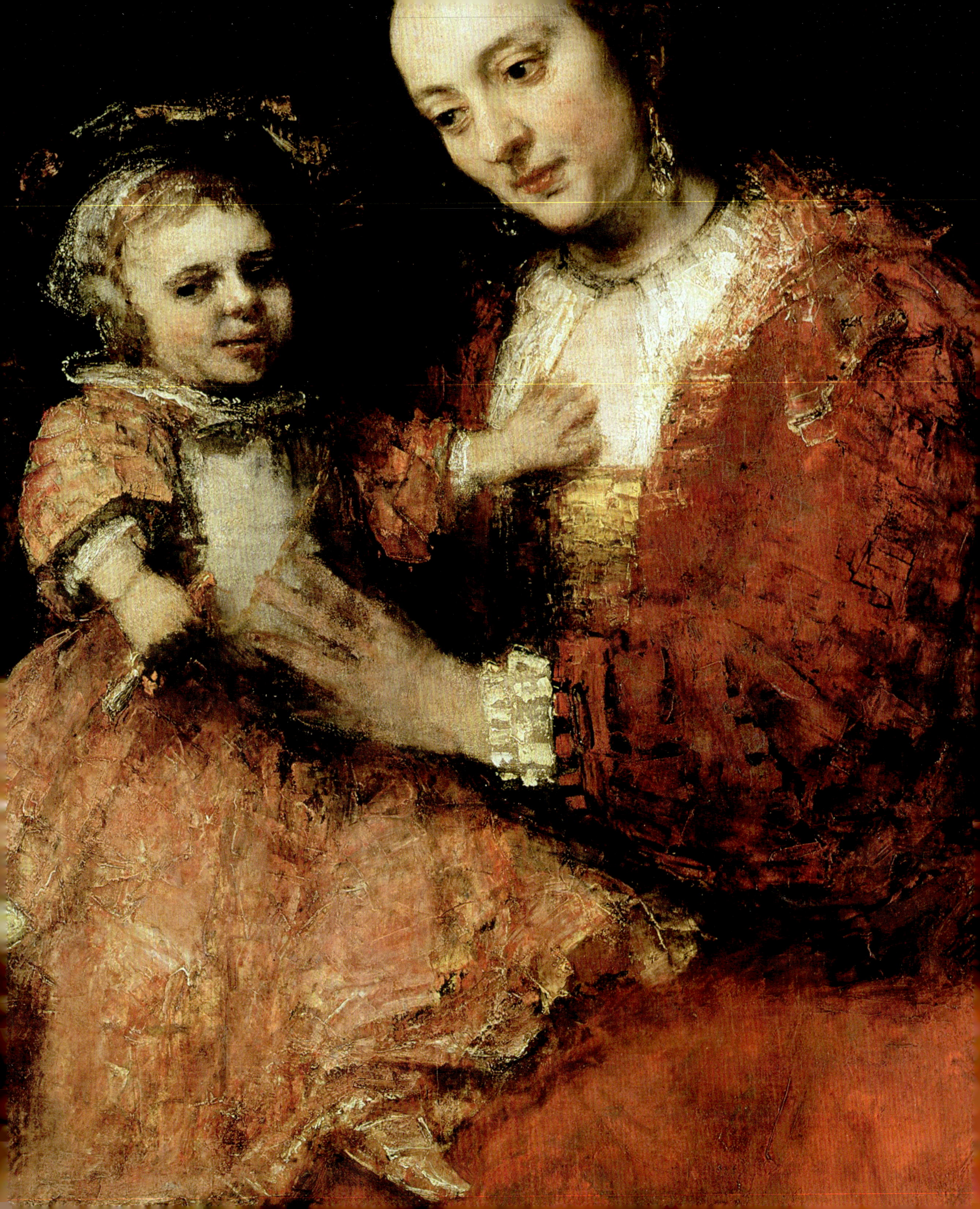

EXPLAINING LATE REMBRANDT

Jonathan Bikker and Gregor J. M. Weber

A SLEEVE SO thickly painted one could almost grab hold of it (cat. 92); a woman absorbed in troubled contemplation of her fate (cat. 112); shafts of heavenly light bursting into a scene of utter darkness (cat. 62). The enthralling climax of his spectacular artistry, Rembrandt's late work constitutes a distinct, although by no means rigidly uniform, phase of his career. Remarkably, this most daring and individualistic period of Rembrandt's creativity has never before been the subject of an exhibition. The chapters that follow explore the qualities that distinguish the master's work in roughly the last third of his life: an uncompromising exaltation of the humble, the mundane and even the ugly; an assiduous mining of the broadest possible range of visual sources for creative inspiration; a relentlessly experimental approach to expressive technique, whether in paintings, drawings or prints; an exceptional skill in rendering the effects of light; and a search to understand and represent humanity's most profound motivations and emotional states.

Never a conformist, Rembrandt throughout his career bucked all trends to produce powerfully engaging works of unparalleled individuality. Far from becoming complacent or falling into decline, he radically changed course in his later years and executed his most distinctive and daring drawings, etchings and paintings. Although some aspects of his late style were anticipated by such artists as Titian (active from about 1506; died 1576) and Frans Hals (1582/3–1666), Rembrandt's contemporaries must have looked in awe at the broadly painted and etched surfaces of his canvases and prints, the bold textural effects he was able to realise using unorthodox methods, and the complete unravelling of his protagonists' deepest thoughts and feelings. Unfortunately, the earliest recorded reactions to Rembrandt's late work date to long after the artist's death in 1669, and were penned by critics – a number of them practising artists – who embraced a style at the opposite end of the spectrum from his own. An example is Gerard de Lairesse (1640–1711), who in his youth had been an admirer of Rembrandt and even had his portrait painted by him (fig. 51), but in his theoretical treatise published in 1707 condemned the textured surfaces of the older artist's pictures, claiming that the objects depicted in a painting should 'appear rounded and raised by Art alone, and not by daubing'.[1] The vehemence of some of these writers' attacks on Rembrandt's late style, that of Arnold Houbraken (1660–1719) being foremost among them, is a good indication that this art made a deep impact on Rembrandt's contemporaries. If it had gone unnoticed, or had not been considered exceptional and out of the ordinary in its own time, Houbraken and others would certainly not have gone out of their way to criticise and even ridicule it later on.

The pronouncements of Rembrandt's earliest critics and biographers – not all of it negative, by the way – are discussed throughout the present book, as are the most salient aspects of Rembrandt's late work. The aim of this introductory essay is to examine why he made the radical transformation that resulted in his late style. But it is necessary at this point to identify when the late period began. The monumental brushstrokes that are an essential component of the broad handling of Rembrandt's late paintings first make their appearance in *Young Girl at a Window* of 1651 (fig. 1),[2] and the date of this painting is in close proximity to other milestones in the development of his late style, including the first depiction of an intensely meditative figure in his late work, and the first extensive use of drypoint.[3] The answer to when Rembrandt's late style began is easier to give than why it began, although art-historical discussions of the late period, for example

Detail from *Portrait of a Family* (cat. 94)

some of those that will be examined below, are often vague about its chronology, or only take the artist's very late works into consideration, without indicating how they differ from his slightly earlier ones.

None of Rembrandt's earliest critics and biographers offers an explanation for the evolution of his late style, but Roger de Piles (1635–1709), writing in 1699, did develop a theory to account for the late works of all artists. According to De Piles, every artist's career can be divided into three stages, or 'manners', as he called them: early, middle and late.[4] In the early phase of their careers, they follow their teachers' styles, while during the middle phase they form their own, only to degenerate into habit in their late and final phase. De Piles did not discuss Rembrandt's oeuvre in these terms, but he did apply this model to Titian's work, suggesting in addition that the Venetian master consciously developed a loose style late in life only because it was less fatiguing than the more meticulous manner he had employed during his prime.[5] For De Piles, therefore, the final phase of every artist's career was one of decline, and in Titian's case it was also clearly accompanied by physical deterioration.

Long before the French academician published his theory of the three manners, the late work of numerous individual artists had been viewed in a negative light, as merely the product of men plagued by the infirmities of old age, including shaky hands and impaired vision. Because he was very advanced in years when he developed it, Titian's late style in particular was often described in these terms. But Giorgio Vasari (1511–1574), in his biography of the great Venetian master, offers a positive assessment:

> It is true, however, that the method of work which he employed in these last pictures is no little different from the method of his youth ... and these last works are executed with bold strokes and dashed off with a broad and even coarse sweep of the brush, insomuch that from near little can be seen, but from a distance they appear perfect.... And this method, so used, is judicious, beautiful and astonishing, because it makes pictures appear alive and painted with great art, but conceals the labour.[6]

Vasari's biography of Titian would have been well known to seventeenth-century Dutch artists and connoisseurs, as Karel van Mander (1548–1606) included a translation of it in his *Schilder-Boeck* (*Book of Painting*) of 1604.[7] Significantly, the Dutch author gave great emphasis to Vasari's positive evaluation of Titian's late technique by paraphrasing the passage in the introductory chapters of his book.[8] Van Mander, moreover, made a laudatory addition to Vasari's complimentary text by way of a warning to young artists: begin with a fine technique, as only the greatest and most experienced artists can successfully employ the broad manner of painting.

A prerequisite to adopting this coarse style, therefore, was that the artist should be very experienced: he needed to have fully mastered the skill of painting finely detailed pictures before he could successfully employ a rough technique – through abbreviation and omission – to create the desired effect. In 1675 Joachim von Sandrart (1606–1688) advised young artists to practise delicate, smooth painting as they would naturally acquire the free, coarse technique in old age as their eyesight failed.[9] But this technique was definitely not seen as evidence of a decline in their *artistic* powers; on the contrary, the natural process of ageing would give them an individualistic, looser style. There was no suggestion that the work

FIG. 1
Young Girl at a Window, 1651
Oil on canvas, 78 × 63 cm
Nationalmuseum, Stockholm

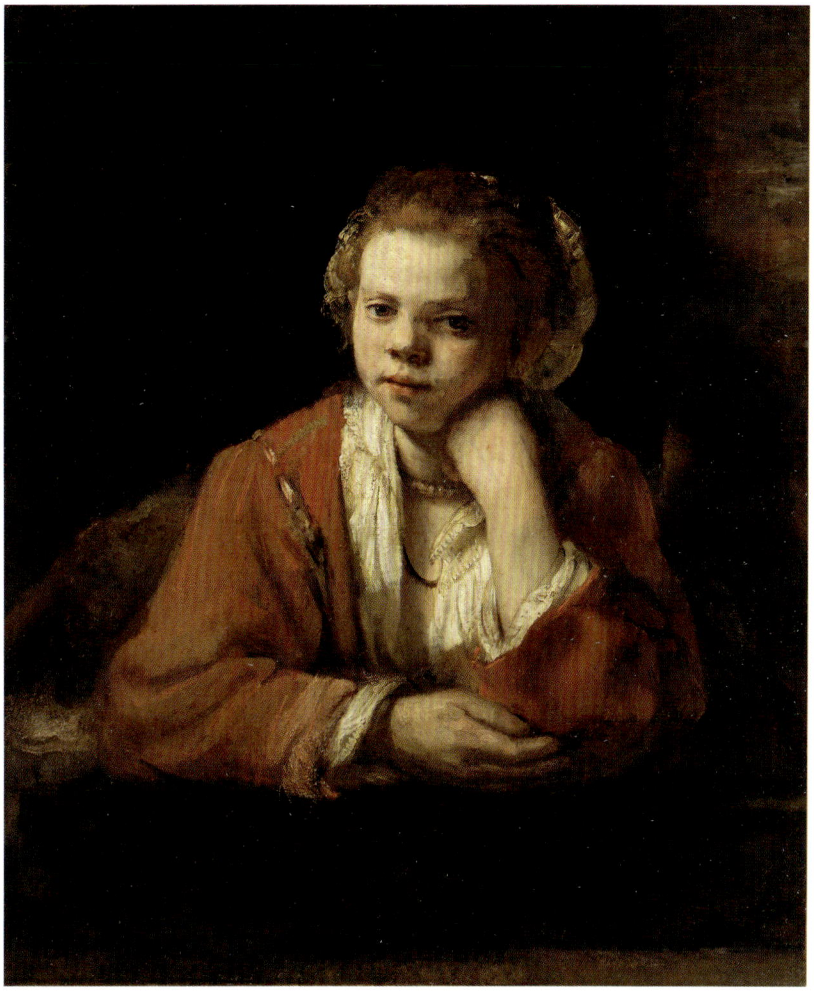

of ageing artists was lacking in creativity. The creative process in old age could be appreciated as a phase of maturity and experience; indeed, it was viewed as offering the opportunity for a new, expressive style. This extended not only to the form but also to the content of the mature artist's work. Since the time of Plato, Aristotle and Horace, edifying subjects, moralising writings and solemn epic poems had been considered most appropriate for the old, as sensuality and the passions were associated primarily with the young (and were seen as ridiculous and even disgraceful in older people). Not *pathos* but *ethos* determined the character of the art that was appropriate in old age.[10] The classical author Quintilian, whose textbook on rhetoric had a major, lasting influence, discussed both concepts in detail: *pathos* stood for agitated, impetuous passions while *ethos* denoted restrained, steadfast, ethical conduct. The former is temporary; the latter permanent.[11]

Rembrandt himself would have shared the idealised image of an aged artist as a figure of maturity and wisdom. In addition to van Mander's glowing elaboration of Vasari's assessment of Titian's late manner, Rembrandt was probably familiar with Cesare Ripa's (about 1555–1622) personification of '*disegno*', the drawing that is the foundation of all art, in his widely consulted *Iconologia*, which had been translated into Dutch in 1644. According to Ripa, *disegno* could be envisaged either as a young man, a mature man or an old man: the young man embodies the beauty of art, the mature man the dexterity and intellect, but the old man embodies the perfection that can only be achieved with the ripeness of old age.[12] Furthermore, rather than being subjects of mockery, the elderly artists sitting at their easels depicted by, among others, Rembrandt's former pupil Gerrit Dou (1613–1675) and his followers are wise and experienced men, accorded the same dignity as aged scholars (fig. 2).

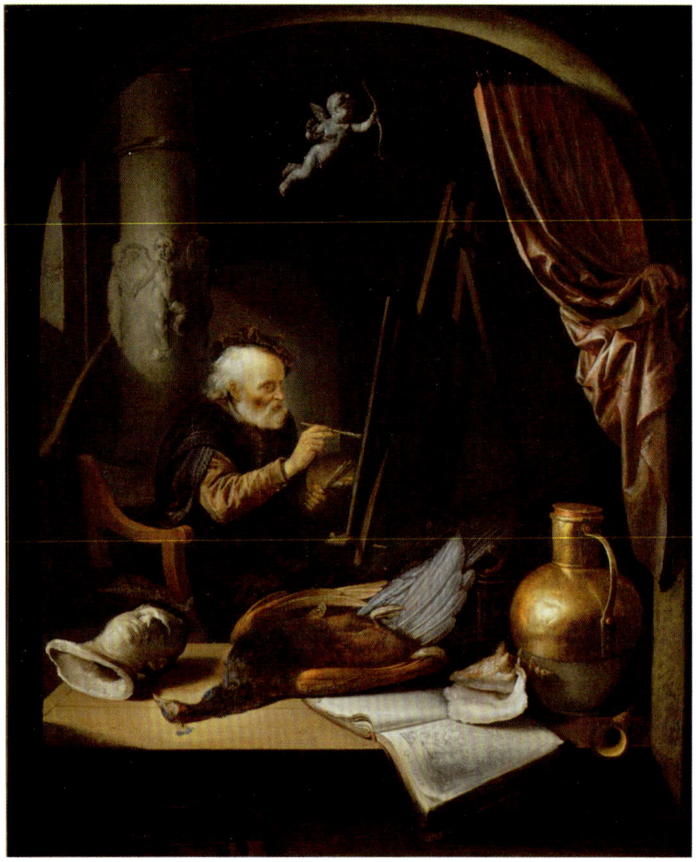

FIG. 2
GERRIT DOU (1613–1675)
An Artist in his Studio: An Allegory of the Art of Painting, 1649
Oil on panel, 68.2 × 53.5 cm
Johnny van Haeften Ltd, London

It is unlikely, however, that when he began the distinctive style that constitutes the culmination of his achievement Rembrandt would have identified himself with the truly elderly artists in these paintings. He was only 45 years old in 1651 and he had, moreover, only recently begun a relationship with the much younger Hendrickje Stoffels (1626–1663). Nor is it likely that his contemporaries would have viewed him as particularly old. The Dutch physician Johan van Beverwyck (1594–1647) set the beginning of old age at 50; for Jacob Cats (1577–1660), the author of a book on the subject, it began at 60.[13] While there can be no doubt that Rembrandt possessed the necessary artistic maturity to produce loosely executed works instilled with *ethos*, there is no reason to believe that he began to suffer from poor eyesight sometime around 1650, as Titian reportedly did in extreme old age, or that the Dutch artist's hands trembled, the affliction Nicolas Poussin (1594–1665) already complained about in his fifties.[14] At the same time as Rembrandt made some of his most broadly executed paintings, he was also making finely detailed etchings, and he was certainly capable of handling the paintbrush more precisely than was his wont if the need arose.[15]

Determining when Rembrandt's late period began and his particular circumstances at that moment were of little importance to the group of German critics who in the early 1900s concerned themselves for the first time since De Piles with defining a universal 'late style'. At the beginning of the twentieth century the search for specific rules governing the evolution of styles gave rise to a mythology of the aged artistic genius, driven to produce outstanding works in the face of his approaching death. Following the theories developed by Heinrich Wölfflin and Alois Riegl, style in art was interpreted as the expression of a certain cultural phase, the traits of a particular historical period. An artist's life, too, was broken down into the distinct stages – recalling those formulated by De Piles – of early, mature and late works, with rules governing their artistic expression. The concept of '*Altersstil*' (old age style) emerged to account for late-life creativity. As mostly German-speaking scholars addressed this issue, it has become standard practice to use the German word in publications in all languages. But is there actually such a thing as an *Altersstil* that consistently characterises the work of all great masters in their golden years? Are there similarities between the late works of Michelangelo (1475–1564), Titian, Rembrandt and Goya (1746–1828), or is this simply a myth, an art historian's fantasy? According to the authors who coined the term, the characteristics that defined *Altersstil* (recalling the observations made above) were a tendency towards abstraction and formal simplicity, combined with greater depth in the subjective and intellectual content. The assumption was that these characteristics can be identified in all art forms and eras.[16]

The nineteenth-century cult of genius, in addition to the ideological encumbrance of Rembrandt being claimed as a member of the Germanic people, resulted in his late work in particular being considered an example of *Altersstil* par excellence. The art historians Carl Neumann and Georg Simmel notably saw in him the confirmation of their theory that exceptional artists ascend at the end of their lives to a spiritual state that defies rational understanding; isolated from the world, they create artistic soliloquies, the full meanings of which others can only guess at.[17] With one foot in the afterlife, the spiritual content of their late works transcends the boundaries of what can be represented; these works therefore remain merely suggestion and mystery. Regarding form, there is an emphasis on the inchoate: sketchy works deliberately left unfinished. Goethe's maxim, that 'Ageing is a gradual withdrawal from appearances', is often invoked by these authors, and comparisons are made with the uninhibited art of 'primitive' peoples and children.[18] Many of the writings on Rembrandt from this period draw on these romantic notions, which have no objective basis, and these opinions still have an influence even today.[19]

The question of whether there is indeed an *Altersstil* that links the late works of artists such as Michelangelo, Titian, Rembrandt and Goya is not one that modern scholars would ask. Restricting a nuanced view of actual changes in the works of ageing artists to those whom the art historical canon considers towering geniuses is no longer permissible. The emphasis is instead on the individual circumstances in which each artist worked. The elements that link artists are explained more by the physical and mental capabilities that determine whether they are able to continue with their creative work into old age, rather than by a common style.[20] Recent research has therefore focused on questions concerning older artists' social circumstances and health, their self-representations and the strategies they used to market their works.[21]

The opposite of a universal old-age style to account for Rembrandt's late period was proposed in a popular monograph on the artist written in 1906 by the influential Dutch museum director Frederik Schmidt-Degener, who felt that the work of Holland's greatest artist was inextricably linked to his biography.[22] Schmidt-Degener drew a sharp line dividing Rembrandt's life into two periods, before and after 1642: with the death of his wife Saskia Uylenburgh (1612–1642) in that year, all joy and frivolity departed from Rembrandt's life for good. The artist's own intrinsic sombreness had been over-ruled by his wife's cheery disposition, but now that she was gone it resurfaced. Rembrandt stopped 'posing for the world' and withdrew himself to focus solely on being an artist.[23]

The year 1642 has also been viewed as a watershed in a more recent theory accounting for the development of Rembrandt's late style. Ernst van de Wetering in 2006 suggested that '*The Night Watch*' (fig. 97), which was completed in that year, caused Rembrandt to suffer

Detail from *Portrait of Gerard de Lairesse* (fig. 51)

an artistic crisis.[24] In this great civic guard piece Rembrandt pushed the pictorial language he had been developing in the previous twenty years too far, creating an overemphasis on action. He had no choice but to reinvent his approach to picture making. The most attractive aspect of Van de Wetering's theory is that, unlike the notion of *Altersstil* or Schmidt-Degener's romanticised biographical account, Rembrandt's stylistic development is not determined by external forces beyond his control, but comes of a self-conscious act.

This said, another, less personal explanation can be considered, namely that in an increasingly competitive art market Rembrandt sought to exploit the full potential of his fame – what we might now call his brand – by concentrating on the aspects of his art that were most closely associated with his reputation: his phenomenal rendering of texture and light, and his uncanny ability to penetrate the emotional profundities of his subjects. At the very moment his former pupils Govert Flinck (1615–1660) and Ferdinand Bol (1616–1680), who were among the most sought-after artists in Amsterdam, abandoned Rembrandt's style in favour of one based on the art of Peter Paul Rubens (1577–1640) and his followers, Rembrandt purged his own art of anything that might be reminiscent of the great Flemish painter. At the same time, he took the aspects of his own style that were already present in his early work to a whole new level, producing a body of unmistakably individualistic works, radically innovative in their technique, their unadulterated rendering of nature, their extremely nuanced representation of light and their profound exploration of the human soul. As Houbraken explained:

> As regards his method of painting (although contemptible in many ways) I have to conclude that he did as he did on purpose. Had he painted in a manner which followed that of anyone else, or laid his brush at the foot of any celebrated Italian, or at the feet of any other highfliers, the world would have recognised his borrowings by comparing the one with the other. By doing the very opposite he anticipated any unfavourable comparison, like Tiberius, as related by Tacitus, 'who always avoided anything that would give the people an opportunity to compare him with Augustus, knowing that his memory was fondly cherished by all.'[25]

By following his own path, rather than that of another artist, Rembrandt also placed a product on the market that was clearly different from all others, and immediately recognisable.

For accuracy, the artworks included in this volume are examples that are known for certain to be by Rembrandt; issues of originality and authenticity are not the goal of this study. To present the most sensitive and comprehensive coverage of the distinguishing features and achievements of Rembrandt's late oeuvre, works are grouped according to the themes and categories (in the broadest intellectual sense) that are fundamental to the understanding of Rembrandt's late period, and which appear not only in his paintings but also in his drawings and prints. These are the ideas or obsessions to which he continually returns, which excite his interest and stimulate his imagination, and which make his late work not simply distinctive but also innovative and extraordinary.

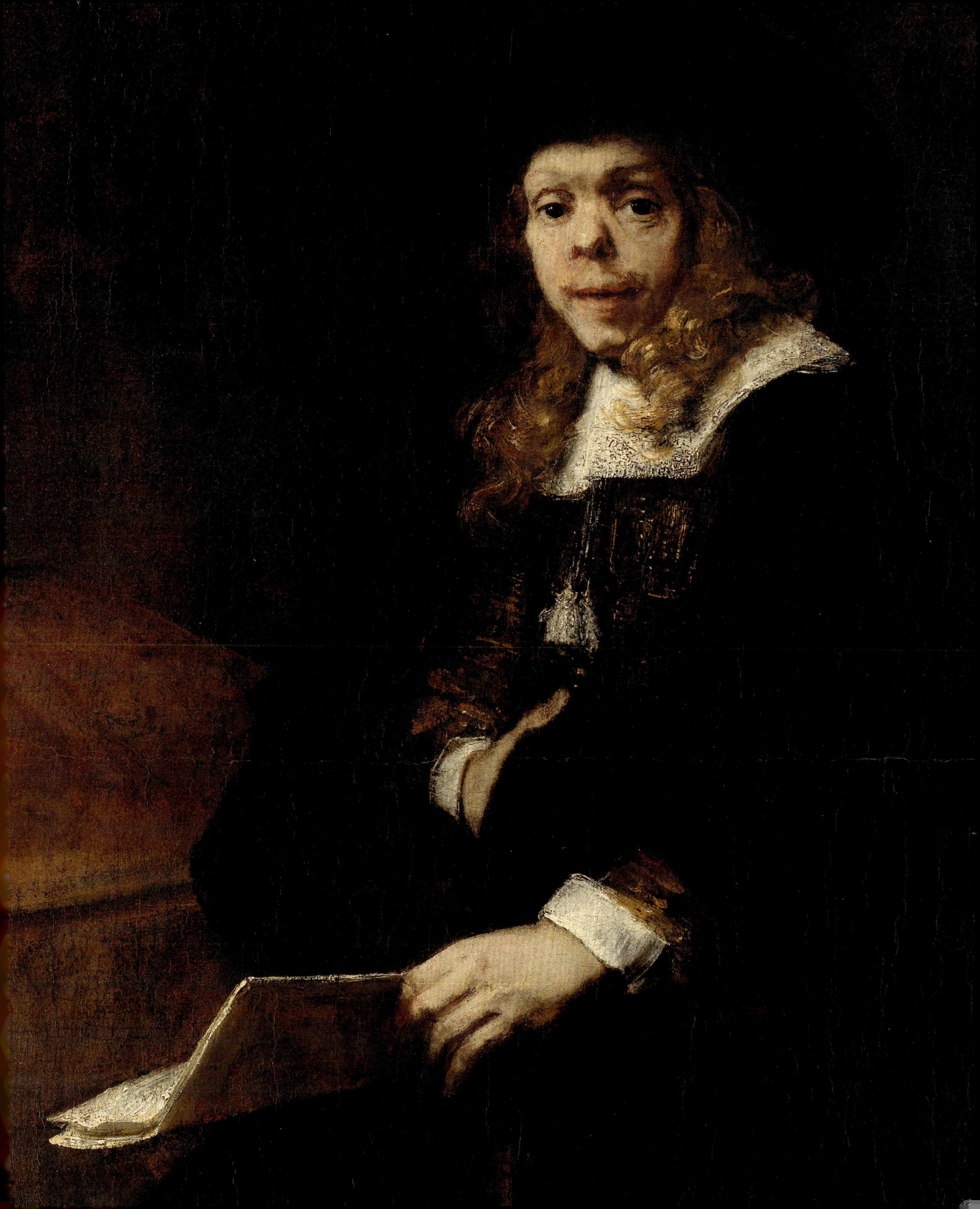

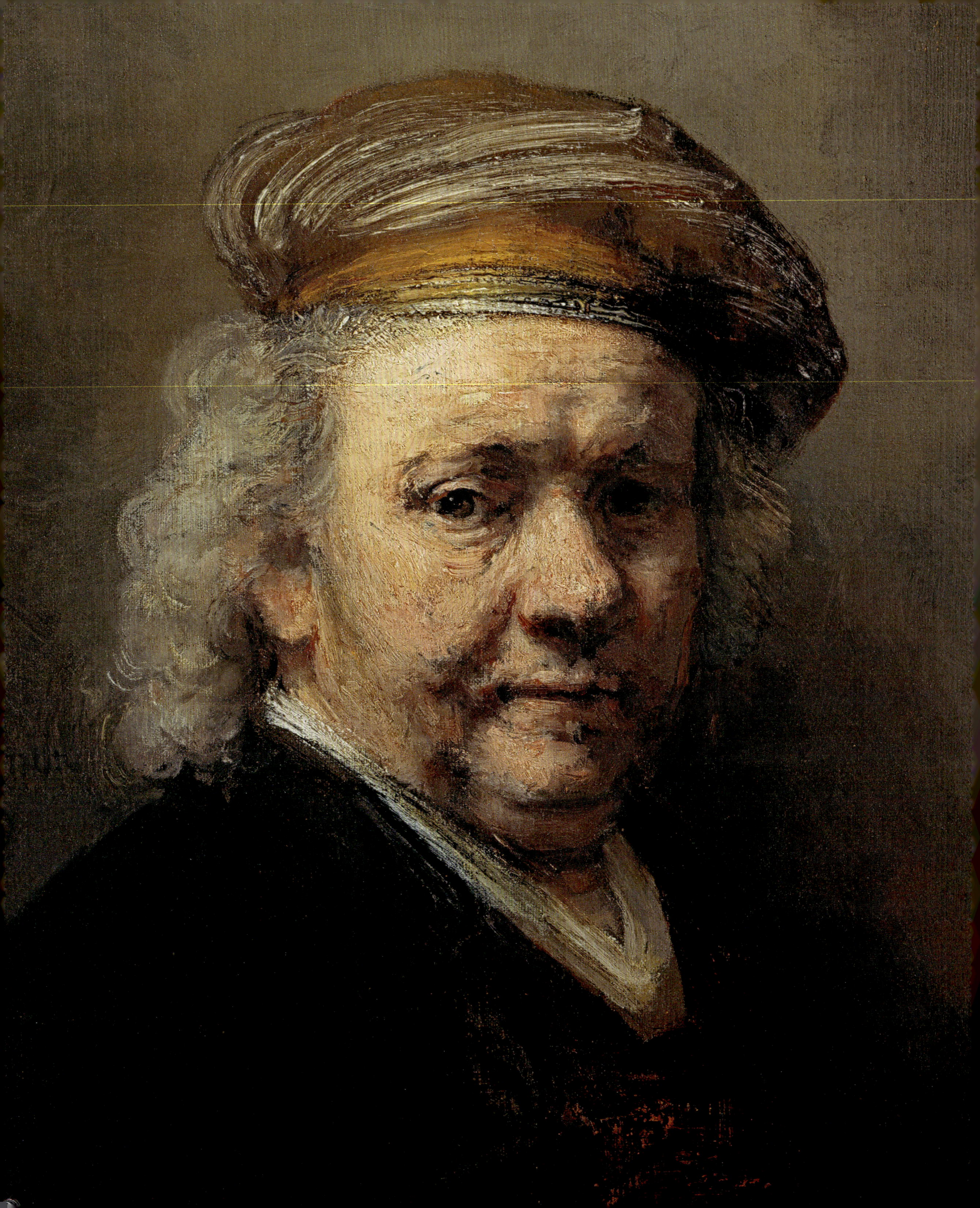

LATER LIFE AND CAREER

Jonathan Bikker

THE YEARS COVERED in this publication, roughly the last third of Rembrandt's life, were extremely tumultuous for the artist, marked by overwhelming professional setbacks – his bankruptcy in 1656 and the rejection of his painting from the Town Hall in 1662 – as well as profound personal losses – the death of his lover in 1663 and that of his son in 1668. The documents that record these traumatic events tell us little or nothing about how Rembrandt dealt with them, or about his personality in general. Nor are the early biographies of the artist very informative about this matter, and what they do say about Rembrandt's character cannot be taken at face value. The only insight into Rembrandt's personality in the later part of his life is provided by Arnold Houbraken, who wrote in the first volume of his artist biographies published in 1718: 'He [Rembrandt] spent the autumn of his life in the company of ordinary folk and practitioners of art' because – and here Houbraken quotes Rembrandt – '"If I want to relieve my spirit, then I should not seek honour, but freedom"'.[1] Houbraken's claim, however, was not based on the observations of those who knew Rembrandt in his later years, but was derived from earlier biographies of the artist: both Joachim von Sandrart in 1675 and Roger de Piles in 1699 already asserted that Rembrandt 'associated with the lower orders', and the latter writer even supplied the supposed quote from Rembrandt concerning his pursuit of freedom.[2] Von Sandrart implied that Rembrandt was seeking out his own kind, having described the artist in the beginning of his biography as 'merely someone sprung up from the flatland and but the son of a miller'.[3] While De Piles and Houbraken also mention that Rembrandt's father had been a miller, neither of these biographers suggest that his was a lowly occupation, and neither follows Von Sandrart in claiming that Rembrandt's association with 'ordinary folk' hampered his work. Although repeated by Houbraken from earlier biographies, he alone claimed that Rembrandt's association with ordinary people was an aspect of his later years, and there may be some truth to this.

Before making this statement, Houbraken tells the reader about Rembrandt's wife, hopelessly jumbling the facts, as he does often in his life of the artist. Without mentioning her name, Houbraken refers to a 1636 self-portrait etching, showing Rembrandt with his wife Saskia Uylenburgh, but mistakenly claims that she 'was a farm-girl from Raarep, or Ransdorp, in Waterland'.[4] Saskia in fact came from Friesland, and was by no means a farm-girl, but rather the youngest daughter of a former pensionary of the Court of Friesland and burgomaster of Leeuwarden. After her death in 1642, Rembrandt hired Geertje Dircks (1600/10–1656?), the unlettered widow of a ship's trumpeter, to care for his nine-month-old son Titus (1641–1668).[5] Unlike Saskia, Geertje, with whom Rembrandt soon became romantically involved, can be considered to come from an 'ordinary' background. Born on a farm in Edam, she had lived with her brother Pieter in Ransdorp, a small village close to Amsterdam, before entering Rembrandt's household. Houbraken, who may have been informed about Geertje by one of his teachers, Jacobus Leveck (1634–1675) or Samuel van Hoogstraten (1627–1678), both of whom had trained with Rembrandt, obviously mistook her for his wife. The relationship ended with a great deal of animosity in June 1649, resulting in Geertje suing Rembrandt for breaching his supposed promise to marry her. Rembrandt was forced by the court to pay her an annual allowance and to fund her confinement in the house of correction in Gouda.

Nor did Hendrickje Stoffels, the young woman who became Rembrandt's housekeeper and replaced the

Detail from *Self Portrait* (cat. 4)

middle-aged Geertje as his mistress, come from the higher echelons of Dutch society. Born and raised in the east of the country, her father had been an army sergeant and the official hunter at the castle in her home town. She was Rembrandt's companion from 1649 until her death from the plague in 1663. In Hendrickje's case, too, marriage was out of the question, for if he had wed her Rembrandt would have been obliged to turn over Saskia's half of their estate at the time of her death to his son Titus. Its value was estimated at more than 20,000 guilders.[6] When she was pregnant with their daughter Cornelia (1654–1685) in 1654, Hendrickje received a severe reprimand from the Reformed Church, of which she, but not Rembrandt, was an official member. On 25 June of that year, she was called before the church council and accused of 'whoredom', which in this instance meant fornication, and excluded from taking Communion.[7]

The ramifications of Rembrandt's common-law relationship with Hendrickje for his social status and career are difficult to assess, but it certainly did not have a positive effect. Rembrandt would have done better to marry a woman from the upper class, whose family connections could have provided new avenues of patronage. His shrewd pupils Ferdinand Bol and Govert Flinck did exactly that.[8] It has been suggested that Rembrandt's marital status, and specifically the Church's censure of Hendrickje, cost the artist the support and possibly the friendship of his admirer Jan Six (1618–1700), the wealthy young patrician whose portrait Rembrandt etched in 1647 (fig. 68) and painted in 1654 (cat. 101). Six's 1655 wedding to Margaretha Tulp (1634–1709), a daughter of the strict Calvinist physician and burgomaster Nicolaes Tulp (1593–1674), or his first municipal appointment in 1656 as Commissioner of Marital Affairs, may have led to his distancing himself from the morally lax artist.[9] Whether or not this was the case, however, another son-in-law of Nicolaes Tulp's, the physician Arnout Tholinx (1607–1679), had no qualms about commissioning the wayward Rembrandt to execute his painted portrait in 1656 as well as an etched one around the same time (cat. 43).[10]

Another event in Rembrandt's later years, his bankruptcy, also tarnished his reputation.[11] On 14 July 1656 the artist was granted *cessio bonorum*, a type of insolvency whereby he surrendered his property to the city authorities, who sold it and then assigned shares to his various creditors.[12] Only one of Rembrandt's early biographers, the Italian Filippo Baldinucci (1624–1697), mentions his bankruptcy, asserting that it resulted from Rembrandt's habit of buying back his own etchings all over Europe at great expense.[13] While there is no evidence supporting this far-fetched claim, the precise reasons for Rembrandt's financial debacle have never been fully understood. The likely causes, however, were the marked decrease in his production in the decade after 1642, the year in which '*The Night Watch*' was completed and his wife Saskia died, his overspending, among other things on his collection of art and naturalia, and, perhaps, risky investments in the art trade. Another factor, which was beyond Rembrandt's control, was the severe economic downturn caused by the First Anglo-Dutch War (1652–4).[14]

The artist's primary financial burden was the house on Sint Anthonisbreestraat that he had purchased in 1639 for the astronomical sum of 13,000 guilders.[15] The mortgage for the house was in the hands of its owner, Christoffel Thijs (1603–1680). By 1649 Thijs had recouped only 6,000 guilders, and Rembrandt stopped paying not only the principal sum but also the annual interest of 5 per cent and the real estate taxes.[16]

On 8 January 1653 Thijs demanded payment of the outstanding 8,400 guilders, which included the accumulated interest as well as the taxes he had been paying out of his own pocket. Rembrandt scrambled to borrow this sum and managed to arrange loans from three individuals totalling 9,380 guilders. He promised to repay the two largest loans within a year and pledged all his possessions as security.[17] Only 7,000 guilders went to Thijs, which covered the principal and meant that the deed of the property could be transferred to Rembrandt. He was still obliged to pay Thijs the arrears in interest and taxes, but what the artist did with the remaining 2,380 guilders is a mystery. Nor is it known, for example, what he did with the 3,150 guilders he borrowed from the surgeon Daniel Francen on 30 May 1656.[18] He may have had other debts that we do not know about, or he perhaps used the money to make investments, possibly in art, that ultimately did not perform. In the meantime he tried to raise the funds to pay back what he had borrowed by collecting outstanding debts and organising sales of his possessions at the Keizerskroon Inn, but as the details of these ventures are no longer known, their success cannot be determined.[19] Rembrandt also negotiated to purchase a more modest dwelling on Handboogstraat for 7,000 guilders, 3,000 of which was to be paid for in paintings and prints.[20] His intention was probably to sell his own house on Sint Anthonisbreestraat and use the profits to pay off his debts, but the deal to purchase the new house fell through. With none of these frantic fundraising measures having their desired effect, Rembrandt had no choice but to apply for *cessio bonorum*. Before doing so, however, he made an unethical, though at the time not illegal, manoeuvre by transferring the deed to his house to his 14-year-old son so that it could not be seized by his creditors. This strategy backfired, however, and through the intervention of the authorities the house was sold on 1 February 1658.[21] By this date the authorities had also held four of the six sales of Rembrandt's possessions, including his art collection, and the remaining two sales were scheduled for 20 December 1658.[22]

Despite the sometimes lucrative commissions Rembrandt was to receive in the coming years, his finances never recovered, and, in economic terms, he now belonged among the 'ordinary folk' with whom Houbraken says he associated. By August 1661, but perhaps already in 1658, the artist, Hendrickje, Titus and Cornelia moved to a small house at 184 Rozengracht, for which they paid an annual rent of 225 guilders.[23] The house was located in the Jordaan, a neighbourhood of mostly tradesmen and small retailers who provided goods and services to the rich elite living on the nearby fashionable canals: Prinsengracht, Keizersgracht and Herengracht. Numerous other artists lived in the area, by no means all of them as impoverished as Rembrandt. Govert Flinck, for example, lived a few canals away on the more exclusive Lauriersgracht, where he had purchased two adjacent houses for 10,000 guilders in 1644.[24]

Friends of Rembrandt also lived in the neighbourhood, including the apothecary Abraham Francen (1612–after 1672), whose first documented contact with the artist dates to 1653, when he was given power of attorney to collect Rembrandt's debts. Francen frequently acted as a witness on Rembrandt's behalf in the 1650s and 1660s in financial as well as personal matters. He also witnessed Titus's first will in 1655, vouched for him when he petitioned for legal independence in 1665 and was one of Cornelia's two guardians after Rembrandt's death.[25] According to a mid-eighteenth-century source, Francen, whose portrait Rembrandt etched around 1657 (cat. 103), was a passionate but impecunious collector.[26] His precarious financial state seems to be confirmed by his frequent changes of address in the Jordaan neighbourhood.[27] This notwithstanding, it was Francen's brother Daniel who lent Rembrandt the aforementioned 3,150 guilders in 1656.

Another friend was the painter Christiaen Dusart (1618–1682), who lived on Prinsengracht, around the corner from Rozengracht.[28] His first known contact with Rembrandt dates to 1661, when he witnessed Hendrickje's will. Dusart was relatively well off and could afford to lend Rembrandt 600 guilders in 1668, for which the artist volunteered a prized portfolio of Lucas van Leyden prints and drawings as collateral. Dusart became Cornelia's other guardian after Rembrandt's death in 1669.[29] The merchant and connoisseur Lodewijk van Ludick (1607–1669), with whom Rembrandt had had dealings since the 1640s, moved to Rozengracht sometime in or before 1666, but one suspects that he may no longer have been on friendly terms with the artist at the time.[30] Rembrandt's friendships with Francen, Dusart and possibly Van Ludick seem to confirm Houbraken's assertion that in the autumn of his life the artist sought out the company of others involved with art.[31]

At the end of 1660, Hendrickje and Titus formally established an enterprise 'in paintings, graphic arts, engravings and woodcuts, as well as prints, curios, and all related objects, which they began doing jointly more than two years ago'.[32] Their sole employee was Rembrandt, the purpose of the company being to keep his income out of the hands of creditors. While in the early 1650s Rembrandt had substantially increased his output of etchings, probably in an effort to stave off bankruptcy,[33] by the time the document formalising Hendrickje and Titus's company was drawn up, he had all but stopped producing the prints listed as among the items it marketed; there are only two etchings from 1659 (cat. 30, for example), none from 1660, one from 1661 (cat. 96), and then a final one produced in 1664.[34] It seems likely that after the sale of his house in 1658 Rembrandt no longer owned a printing press. Indeed, there would hardly have been room for one in the small Rozengracht dwelling. The new house was also too small to provide working space for the large number of apprentices Rembrandt had trained when living on Sint Anthonisbreestraat. According to Von Sandrart, that house had been filled 'with almost innumerable young people of good family, who came to him for instruction and tuition. Each paid him 100 florins a year', and Rembrandt also profited from selling their work.[35] The names of six pupils who received instruction from the master are known for the period 1648 to 1654,[36] but only two painters, Gottfried Kneller (1646–1723) and Arent de Gelder (1645–1727), are reported to have studied with him in the 1660s. However, there may have been many more, as the number of known pupils for all periods of Rembrandt's career seems quite limited in the light of Von Sandrart's claim. There are, moreover, a number of paintings datable to the 1660s that were more likely executed by members of Rembrandt's workshop than by the master himself. According to Houbraken, Rembrandt rented a warehouse on Bloemgracht during his early career in Amsterdam, where his pupils, 'in order to be able to paint from life without disturbing each other, made small cubicles, each one for himself, by setting up partitions of paper or oilcloth'.[37] It is tempting to speculate that this actually occurred after Rembrandt's move to Rozengracht, which is only one canal away from Bloemgracht. When the Sint Anthonisbreestraat house was sold in 1658 Rembrandt took with him 'several partitions in the attic

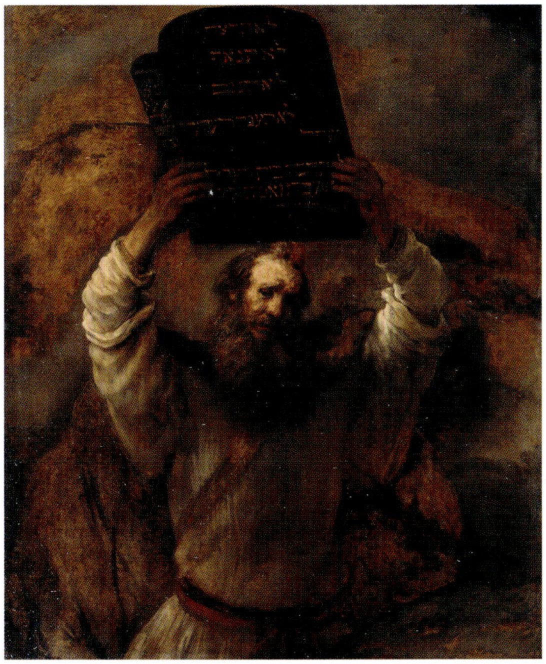

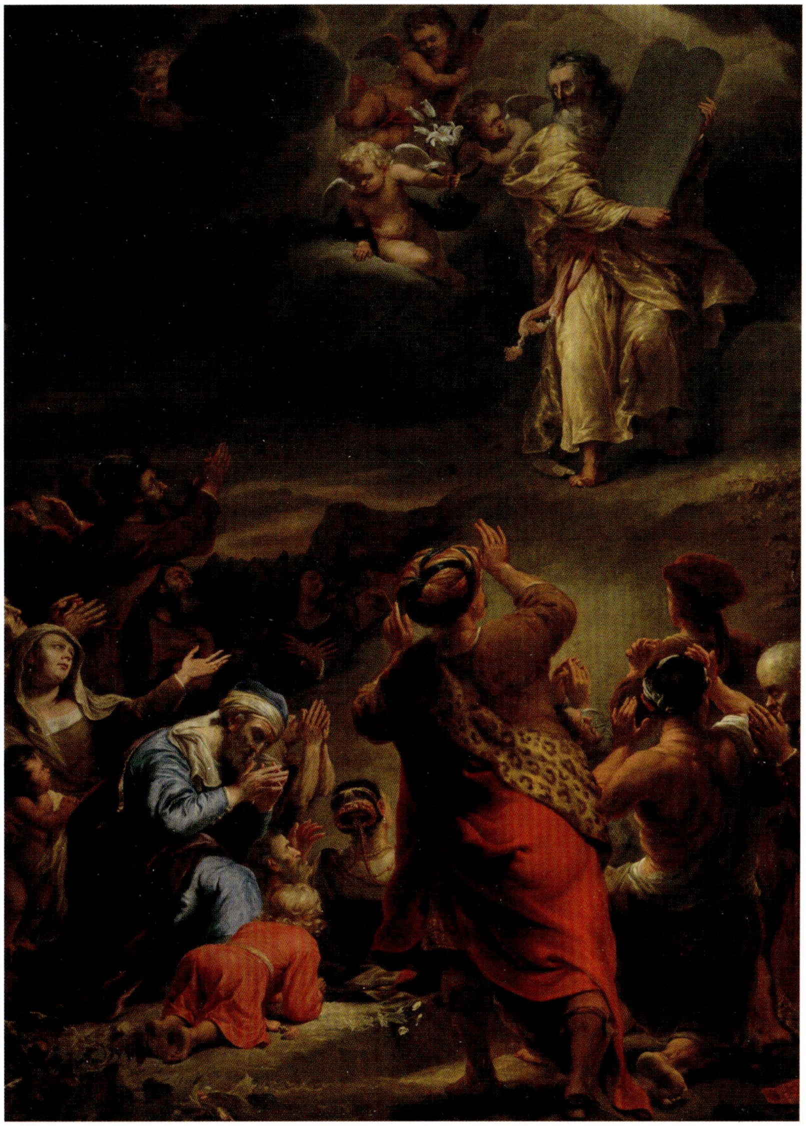

FIG. 3
Moses breaking the Tablets of the Law, 1659
Oil on canvas, 168.5 × 136.5 cm
Staatliche Museen zu Berlin, Gemäldegalerie

FIG. 4
FERDINAND BOL
(1616–1680)
Moses descends from Mount Sinai, about 1663
Oil on canvas, 423 × 284 cm
Royal Palace (formerly the Town Hall), Amsterdam

placed there for his apprentices',[38] conceivably to be used in the Bloemgracht warehouse.

At exactly the time Rembrandt's financial problems were coming to a head, exceptional opportunities had opened up for a few lucky artists in the form of lucrative contracts to decorate the rooms of Amsterdam's new Town Hall, which was officially inaugurated in the summer of 1655. It has been suggested that Rembrandt's 1659 *Moses breaking the Tablets of the Law* (fig. 3) was executed as a chimney-piece for the aldermen's chamber in the new Town Hall, later to be replaced by the painting by Ferdinand Bol that still hangs there (fig. 4).[39] According to this hypothesis, Rembrandt's painting, which is significantly smaller than Bol's picture, was subsequently cut down in size, but this has proven not to be the case and analysis of its iconography also indicates that it would not have been an appropriate work for this location.[40] None of the commissions for the Town Hall awarded in the second half of the 1650s went to Rembrandt, and it was probably no consolation whatsoever to him that his former pupils Ferdinand Bol and Govert Flinck did receive them. Both artists had abandoned Rembrandt's manner in favour of a brighter and more elegant Flemish Baroque style based, in their history paintings, on the example of Peter Paul Rubens. One of the reasons why the burgomasters who awarded the commissions favoured Bol and Flinck over Rembrandt was certainly their adoption of this international style of painting. Another reason was the good footing on which both artists stood with the burgomasters, one of whom,

FIG. 5
GOVERT FLINCK
(1615–1660)
Marcus Curius Dentatus refuses the Gifts of the Samnites, 1656
Oil on canvas, 485 × 377 cm
Royal Palace (formerly the Town Hall), Amsterdam

FIG. 6
JAN LIEVENS (1607–1674)
Brinio raised up on a Shield, 1661
Oil on canvas, 546 × 538 cm
Royal Palace (formerly the Town Hall), Amsterdam

FIG. 7
JACOB JORDAENS
(1593–1678)
A Roman Camp under Attack by Night, 1661–2
Oil on canvas, 550 × 550 cm
Royal Palace (formerly the Town Hall), Amsterdam

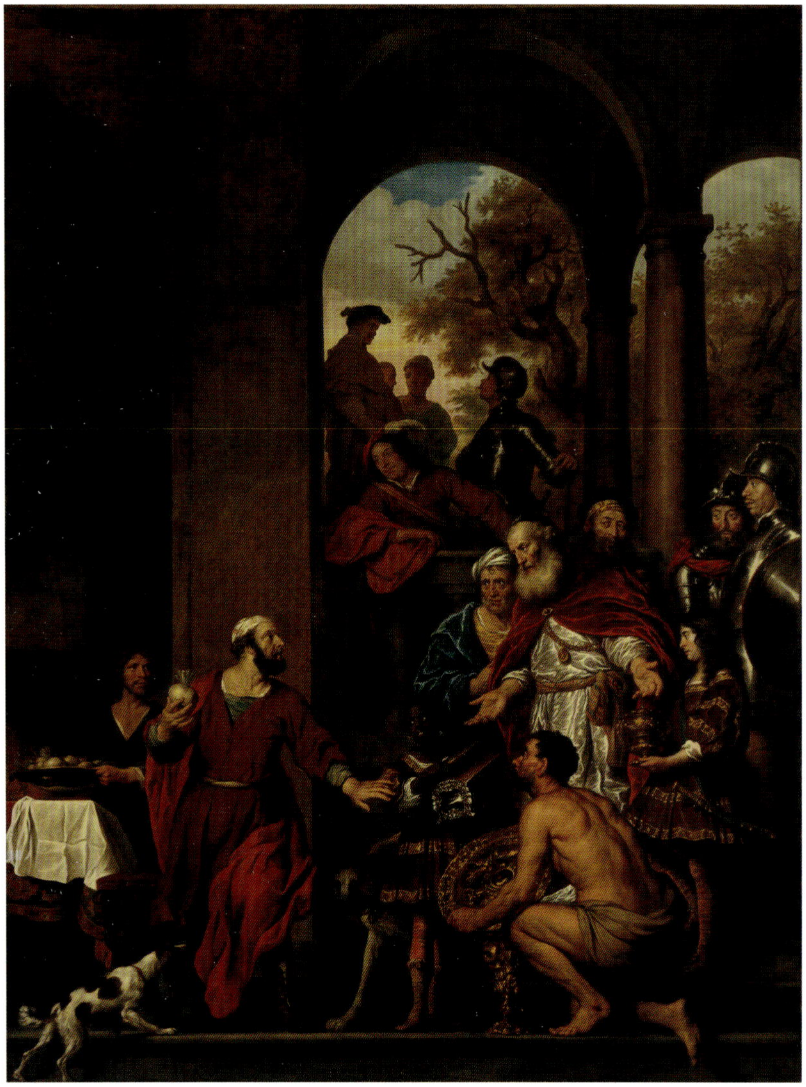

Hendrick Dircksz Spiegel (1598–1667), was the grandfather of Bol's wife. Houbraken informs us of Flinck's special friendship with the powerful brothers Cornelis (1599–1664) and Andries de Graeff (1611–1678): 'The latter often came to his house, and he was on such familiar terms with the former that in the evening, when he was too tired to go on painting, he would often call on him unannounced.'[41] Rembrandt, on the other hand, did not have this kind of connection with the De Graeffs; in fact, their relationship may very well have been one of animosity as Rembrandt and Andries de Graeff apparently quibbled in 1642 over the price of a painting the artist had executed for the future burgomaster.[42] Rembrandt, moreover, may have wished to maintain his liberty rather than pay court to the brothers. According to Von Sandrart, who prided himself on his own 'courtly comportment' during his years in Amsterdam (1637–45), Rembrandt could have increased his wealth significantly if he had associated with and been willing to please the right people, instead of fraternising with the lower classes.[43]

Cornelis de Graeff and another Flinck supporter, Joan Huydecoper (1599–1661), were two of Amsterdam's four burgomasters when on 28 November 1659, Flinck was awarded the prize contract to paint eight enormous canvases depicting scenes from the Batavian revolt, as well as four with related biblical and classical subjects, for the lunettes of the gallery surrounding the Citizens' Hall in the Amsterdam Town Hall.[44] Flinck, who had already earned 3,000 guilders for two chimney-pieces executed for the Town Hall in 1656 (fig. 5) and 1658, was to complete two paintings in the series annually, and was to receive 1,000 guilders for each work. Had Rembrandt received the commission instead, the 12,000 guilder total would have gone a long way to reversing his disastrous

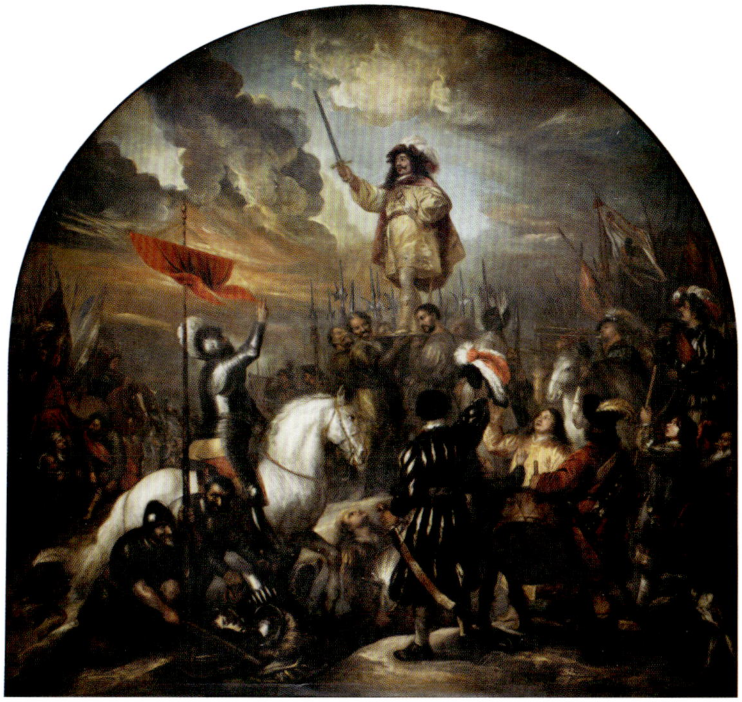

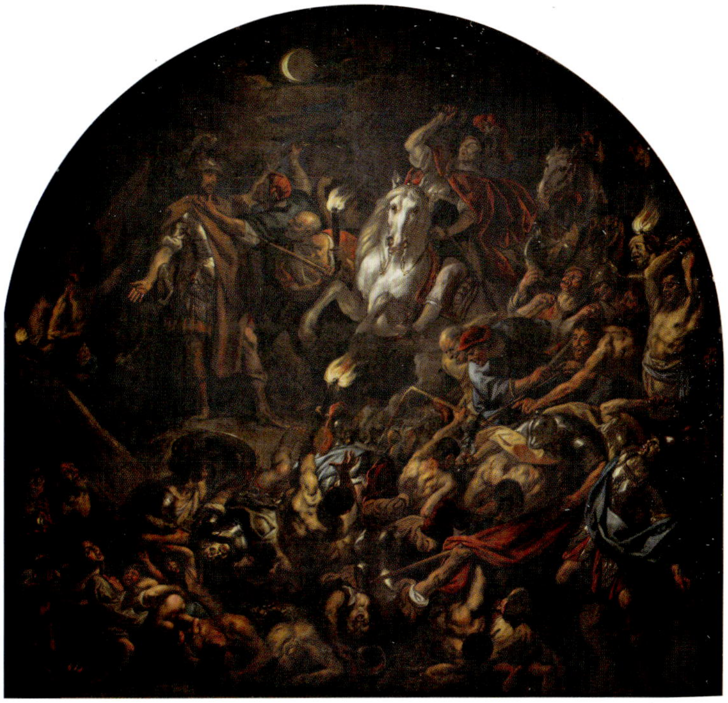

financial situation. As fate would have it, he did eventually secure a contract to paint one of the works in the series, *The Conspiracy of the Batavians under Claudius Civilis* (cat. 72): Flinck died of the plague on 2 February 1660 before he was able to begin work on the series and the burgomasters began to portion out the commission among other artists. On 13 January 1661, Jan Lievens (1607–1674) (fig. 6) and the Antwerp-based painter Jacob Jordaens (1593–1678) (fig. 7) were commissioned to execute one painting each for 1,200 guilders. Just over three months later Lievens was paid for his work, and in June 1661 Jordaens came to Amsterdam to deliver his painting. In November of the same year the Flemish artist provided two more works for the gallery. There is no municipal contract relating to Rembrandt's painting, but a compositional sketch (cat. 71) drawn on the back of a funeral announcement of 25 October 1661 indicates that he was working on it at that time.[45] It must have been installed sometime before 21 July 1662, the date of the preface to Melchior Fokkens's book on Amsterdam which includes a description of Rembrandt's painting *in situ*. Yet within a few months, on 24 September 1662, it was replaced by a painting of the theme Flinck had made in watercolour and charcoal as a temporary decoration for the August 1659 visit of Amalia van Solms to Amsterdam, now hastily reworked by Jürgen Ovens (1623–1678) (fig. 8). The next certain mention of Rembrandt's painting dates to 1734, when it was sold at an anonymous auction in Amsterdam to the merchant Nicolas Cohl (1674–1751), and made its way to Sweden by 1767.[46]

A possible explanation for the rejection of the *Claudius Civilis* is provided in a document recording an arrangement Rembrandt made on 28 August 1662 with Lodewijk van Ludick to repay a loan. According to this contract, 'Van Ludick shall enjoy a fourth part of all that the aforementioned Van Rijn shall come to profit by the painting delivered to the Town Hall and that for as much as he [Van Rijn] has to claim from it as here still may further profit in the repainting or otherwise benefit'.[47] Rembrandt, who apparently had not yet been paid for the painting, was perhaps negotiating with the burgomasters to receive extra payment for changes they or he wanted done to the work. However, the contracts given to Lievens and Jordaens among others stipulated that the artists would not be remunerated should their canvases require reworking. It was, perhaps, Rembrandt's insistence that he be given more money for alterations that led to the rejection of his painting and the hiring of Ovens for a mere 48 guilders to revamp Flinck's 1659 painting.[48] As attractive as this theory is, the possibility that the burgomasters considered Rembrandt's painting unsalvageable and, therefore, simply rejected it outright, cannot be excluded. One of the reasons for rejecting it

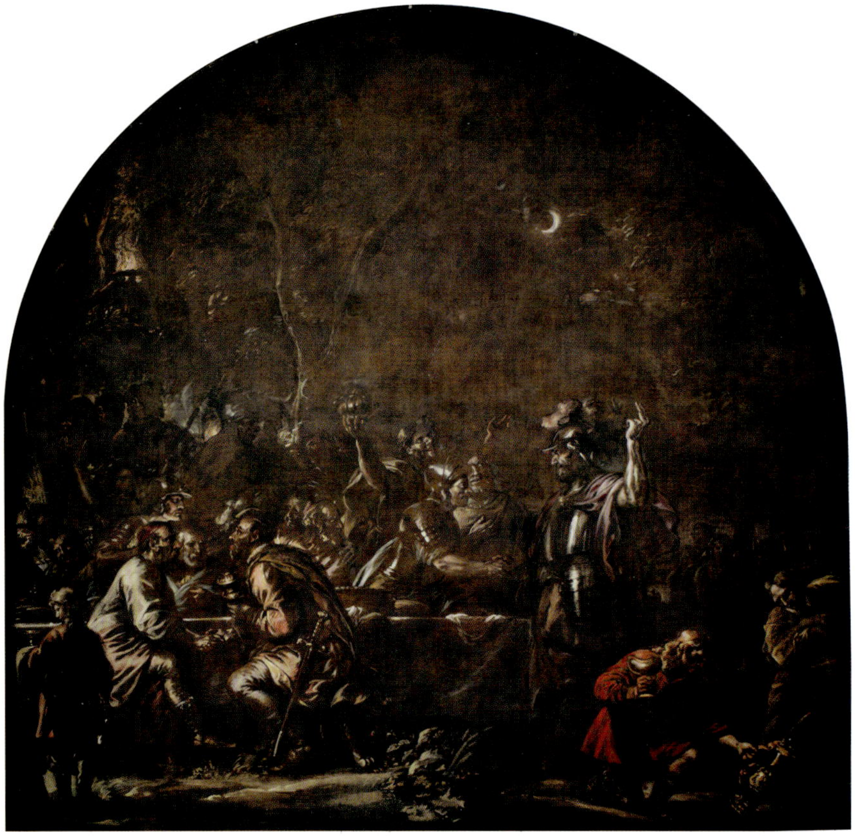

FIG. 8
GOVERT FLINCK
(1615–1660)
and JÜRGEN OVENS
(1623–1678)
The Conspiracy of the Batavians under Claudius Civilis, 1659/62
Oil on canvas, 550 × 550 cm
Royal Palace (formerly the Town Hall), Amsterdam

may have been the artist's shocking breach of decorum in depicting Claudius Civilis full face, with his grotesquely empty eyesocket in plain sight.[49] Another reason may have been the placement of the figures in a horizontal line, at a significant distance from the picture plane, so that approximately three quarters of the composition was given over to presumably unarticulated architecture and landscape elements cast in shadow.[50] This is in marked contrast to the paintings by Flinck/Ovens, Lievens, and especially Jordaens, in which figures occupy the immediate foreground and are scattered over more levels within the composition. Neither of these 'problems' with Rembrandt's painting could be easily remedied.

Rembrandt probably never saw a penny of the 1,200 guilders he was owed for the *Claudius Civilis*. Lodewijk van Ludick at any rate did not receive his quarter share, and sold the claim to the money Rembrandt owed him to Harmen Becker (about 1617–1678) at a loss.[51] A little over a month after the *Claudius Civilis* reworked by Ovens was installed in the Town Hall, Rembrandt's finances were so depleted he was forced to sell Saskia's grave in the Oude Kerk.[52]

Rembrandt may not have been the darling of the most powerful political figures in Amsterdam, among them men like Andries and Cornelis de Graeff, but he did not want for commissions during the 1650s and 1660s. According to Houbraken, patrons had to plead with him and pay him extra to get their paintings, which, because he was so busy, were a long time in the making.[53] Statistical analysis has shown that compared to the second half of the 1640s Rembrandt's production increased enormously in the remaining years of his career.[54] In the first half of the 1660s, when he was an 'employee' of Hendrickje and Titus's firm, the total surface area of his paintings equalled that of the first half of the 1630s, the period in which he moved to Amsterdam and established himself as the city's most sought-after artist. The total surface area of his history paintings in the first half of the 1660s did not lag too far behind that of the popular Ferdinand Bol, while the square metreage of his portraits actually exceeded that of his former pupil in the same period. Among Rembrandt's portrait sitters in these years were the merchant banker Frederik Rihel (cat. 53) and the wealthy industrialist Jacob Trip and his wife Margaretha de Geer (cats 39 and 40), people hardly on the fringes of society.[55] Another wealthy client was Jan Jacobsz Hinlopen (1626–1666), the first owner (and likely commissioner) of

Rembrandt's *Ahasuerus and Haman at the Feast of Esther* from 1660 (fig. 84).[56] Himself a town councillor, Hinlopen was married to a daughter of burgomaster Joan Huydecoper, and he was also related by marriage to Rembrandt's patrons Jan Six and Arnout Tholinx.[57]

Rembrandt's most important Amsterdam commissions in his later period, besides the failed project for the Town Hall, were for two group portraits. In the year he applied for *cessio bonorum*, he completed *The Anatomy Lesson of Dr Joan Deyman* (cat. 29) for the Surgeons' Guild. The commission was occasioned by Deyman's appointment to the post of Praelector Anatomiae in the previous year. He succeeded Dr Nicolaes Tulp, whose annual anatomy lesson was the subject of a 1632 portrait by Rembrandt (fig. 96).[58] No other paintings had been executed for the Guild in the intervening twenty-three years, which attests to the surgeons' undiminished faith in Rembrandt. Although not among the sitters, the medical professionals in Rembrandt's milieu, such as Arnout Tholinx and Abraham and Daniel Francen, may have played a role in securing the commission. While Nicolaes Tulp and his other son-in-law Jan Six may not have actively promoted the Surgeons' Guild's patronage of the artist, they apparently did not try to prevent it. Sadly reduced to a fragment by a fire in the early eighteenth century, the 1656 portrait had been executed on a monumental canvas of two and a half by three metres. Of almost equally impressive dimensions is the 1662 portrait of the sampling officials of the Amsterdam Drapers' Guild, known as *'The Syndics'* (cat. 56). This was Rembrandt's first depiction of a corporate body seated around a table, a frequently used compositional type in seventeenth-century Dutch portraiture, and one in which his competitors such as Ferdinand Bol, Jürgen Ovens and Bartholomeus van der Helst (1613–1670) (fig. 9) were well practised. The sampling officials may have turned to Rembrandt instead of one of these other artists not only because of his proven capabilities as a portraitist in general, but perhaps also on the recommendation of some of the civic guardsmen who had been portrayed in *'The Night Watch'*, eight of whom they probably would have known well through their involvement in the textile trade.[59]

It would be interesting to know what kind of prices Rembrandt charged for his late portraits, especially the very large *Anatomy Lesson*, *'Syndics'* and *Portrait of Frederik Rihel on Horseback*, but unfortunately documents that might shed light on this subject have not survived, or

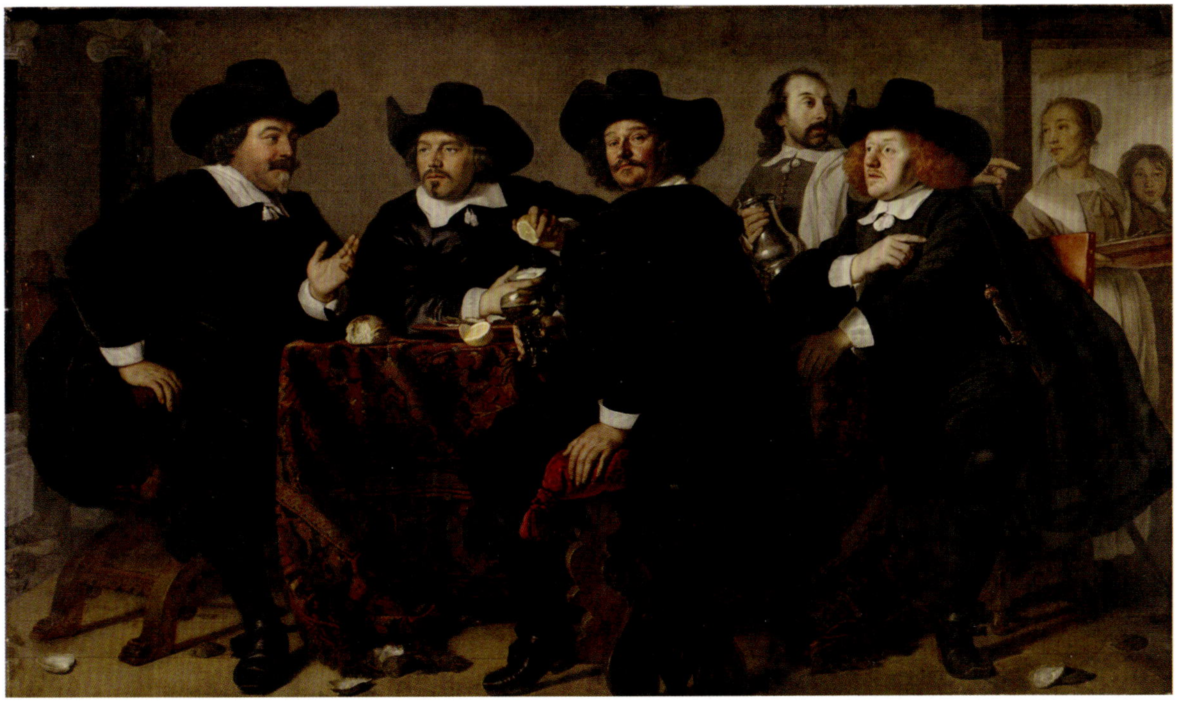

FIG. 9
BARTHOLOMEUS VAN DER HELST
(1613–1670)
Governors of the Kloveniersdoelen, 1655
Oil on canvas, 171 × 283 cm
Amsterdam Museum

have not as yet been discovered.[60] In addition to the 1,200 guilders he was supposed to receive for the *Claudius Civilis*, the fee for one other late history painting is known. A document dated 28 August 1662 mentions a *Nativity* and a *Circumcision* Rembrandt had painted for Lodewijk van Ludick, valued at 600 guilders.[61] The latter work has been convincingly identified as the small painting (56.5 × 75 cm) now in Washington (fig. 10).[62] The no longer traceable *Nativity* would have been a pendant to this work and would have had the same dimensions. Equivalent to the annual salary of a trained artisan, 300 guilders was an exceptionally high price for a work of this size painted for a private collector.

In addition to the patronage he received from Amsterdam citizens and institutions, several foreign clients placed orders with Rembrandt during his later career. The best known example is the Sicilian nobleman Don Antonio Ruffo (1610/11–1678), for whom the Dutch artist painted three historical portraits, the 1653 *Aristotle with a Bust of Homer* (fig. 69), a no longer extant *Alexander the Great*, which was delivered in 1661, and the 1663 *Homer* (fig. 71), for which he received 500 guilders apiece.[63] Rembrandt's fame also spread to northern Italy: in 1666 he was commissioned by the nobleman Francesco Maria Sauli to paint modelli for two altar-pieces for a church in Genoa.[64] The agreed rate was 1,200 guilders but, as happened frequently in his career,

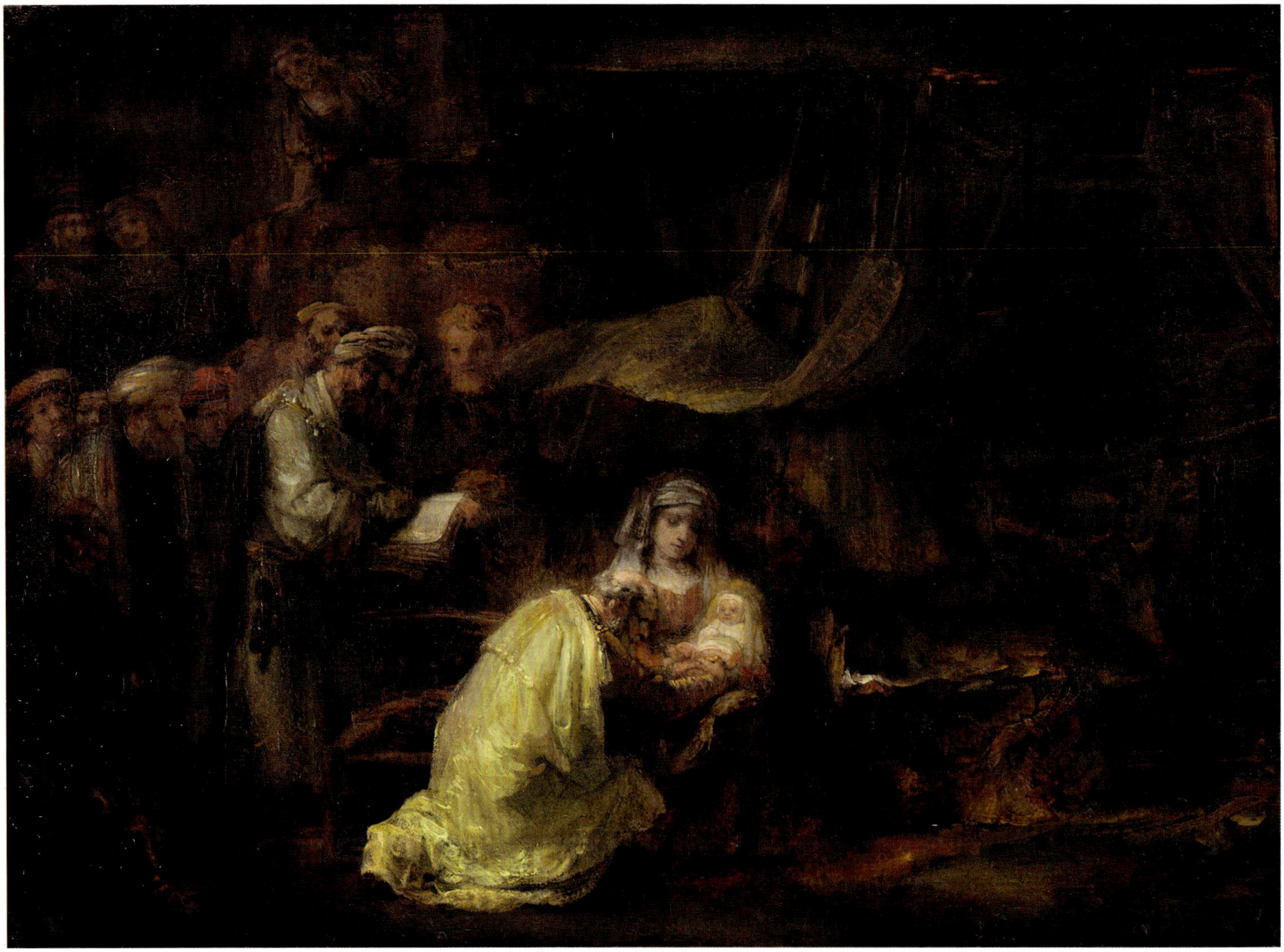

FIG. 10
The Circumcision, 1661
Oil on canvas, 56.5 × 75 cm
National Gallery of Art, Washington (Widener Collection)

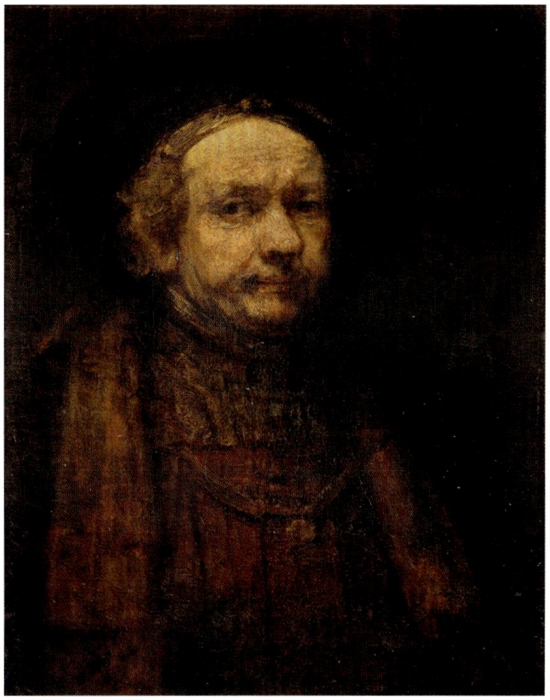

FIG. 11
Self Portrait, about 1669
Oil on canvas, 71 × 54.2 cm
Galleria degli Uffizi, Florence

Rembrandt later wanted more money, amounting to 3,000 guilders.[65] In the end he was paid only 1,023.15 guilders, and the commission to paint the altarpieces themselves was not forthcoming, possibly because of his outrageous demand for more than twice the agreed fee for the modelli, or because of the complaints about the length of time it took him to produce the designs. Another work by Rembrandt, his *Self Portrait* from around 1669 now in the Uffizi (fig. 11), was possibly obtained directly from the artist in Amsterdam by an Italian collector, Cosimo III de' Medici (1642–1723). His visit to Rembrandt's studio in the winter of 1667 was recorded by one of the members of his retinue, who referred to the artist as '*Reinbrant, pittore famoso*' (Rembrandt, the famous painter).[66] On that occasion, the artist had no finished works on hand to show the prince, but Cosimo returned to Amsterdam in 1669 and may have purchased or commissioned the work at that time.[67]

There is also reason to believe that two paintings by Rembrandt were sold to clients in France in the 1660s. The banker and art dealer Everhard Jabach (1618–1695), who hailed from Cologne but lived in Paris from 1638 onwards, may have been the original owner of Rembrandt's *Self Portrait as the Apostle Paul* (cat. 111).[68] Between 1646 and 1680 Jabach was a partner in a trading company based in Amsterdam together with four citizens of that city who were related to him by marriage.[69] He also had important ties to the Amsterdam art world, and may well have met Rembrandt on a number of occasions, beginning in 1637. When the art dealer Gerrit Uylenburgh (about 1625–1679) went bankrupt in 1675, Jabach, who had given him paintings on consignment, was his principal creditor.[70] Uylenburgh, who himself had paintings by Rembrandt in his stock and lived near the artist in the 1660s, was the eldest son of the art dealer Hendrick Uylenburgh (about 1587–1661), whose cousin Saskia had married Rembrandt in 1634, and for whom Rembrandt ran a studio in the early 1630s. It is tempting to think that Jabach imported more paintings by Rembrandt into France, among them the 1660 *Self Portrait at the Easel*, which was first recorded in the collection of Louis XIV in 1683.[71]

The high prices Rembrandt charged and received for his paintings during his late period attest to his undiminished reputation, at least in some circles. Despite his economic and personal hardships, he retained faith in his own stature as an artist and in the quality of his work. When confronted in 1654 by the Portuguese-Jewish merchant Diego d'Andrade (1608–1660) with the accusation that a portrait of a young woman he had executed was not a good likeness, rather than retouching the work or returning the deposit of 75 guilders demanded by the claimant, Rembrandt requested payment in full before he would finish the work or if the claimant refused to pay him that the painters' guild be allowed to determine whether the portrait resembled the sitter.[72] Rembrandt

Detail from *Self Portrait as the Apostle Paul* (cat.111)

had a somewhat similar dispute with Ruffo over the *Alexander* he sent to him in 1661.[73] The nobleman was dissatisfied with the fact that several pieces of canvas had been used and claimed that the seams were visible. He wanted either a refund or to have the *Homer* free of charge. Rembrandt responded that the seams would not be visible if the painting was hung in better light, but offered to paint a new version of the *Alexander* if Ruffo would bear the shipping costs.

Based on these disputes with D'Andrade and Ruffo, and the earlier disagreement with Andries de Graeff over the price of a painting, as well as Von Sandrart's claim that Rembrandt was not willing to please the right people, a few scholars have painted a picture of Rembrandt as a stubborn, unaccommodating social outcast whose abrasive personality contributed in large measure to his financial malaise.[74] However, other artists had disagreements with their patrons over the price of their work; and can Rembrandt really be accused of acting unreasonably in his disputes with D'Andrade and Ruffo?[75] It is not known how the former controversy was resolved, but we do know that Ruffo did not in the end return the *Alexander* to the artist.

Despite the lucrative contract from Sauli for the modelli and the fact that Rembrandt continued to paint until his death in 1669, his last years appear to have been particularly bleak financially. A 1666 document informs us that his landlord was taking legal action because the artist had stopped paying the rent.[76] Personal tragedy also befell Rembrandt in 1668, when Titus fell ill on a trip to Leiden and died, at the age of 27. Only a few months earlier Titus had married a cousin, Magdalena van Loo (1641–1669), who was pregnant with their daughter Titia (1669–1715) at the time of his death. In the last year of his life, Rembrandt had only his daughter Cornelia with him, and his financial situation was so desperate that it was only by using her savings that he could pay the bills.[77]

Rembrandt's late life was fraught with heartbreaking personal losses and unrelenting financial setbacks. Yet it was under these dreadful circumstances that he produced his greatest work. Faced with such overwhelming financial worries, a lesser artist would have adapted his style to the prevailing taste. But instead of compromising, Rembrandt remained undaunted in the pursuit of his radical technical innovations, his naturalistic depiction of the world, and his portrayal of the most profound human emotions. Perhaps Houbraken was correct in stating that it was not honour but freedom that the artist sought in the autumn of his life.

OVERLEAF
Detail from *The Conspiracy of the Batavians under Claudius Civilis* (cat. 72)

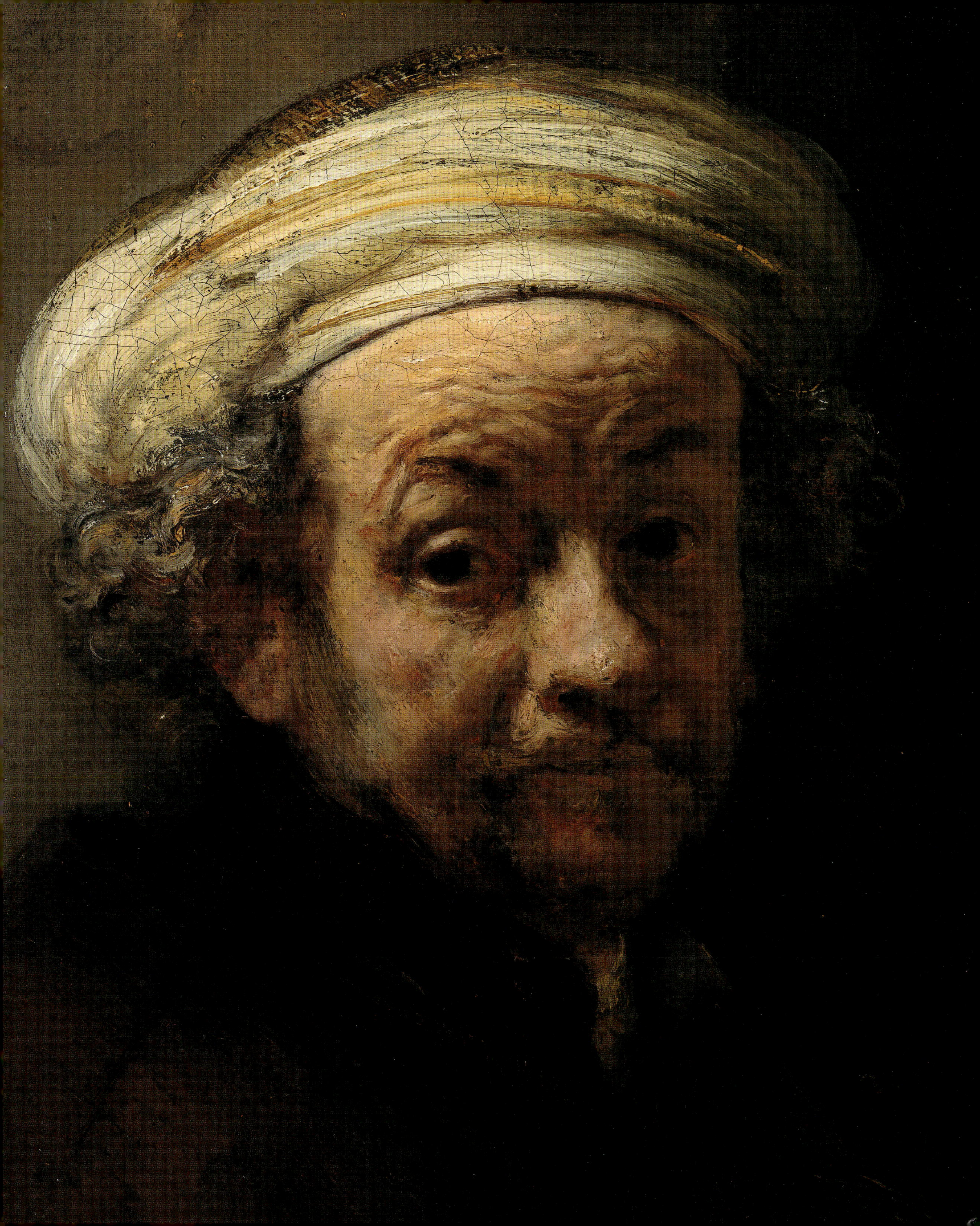

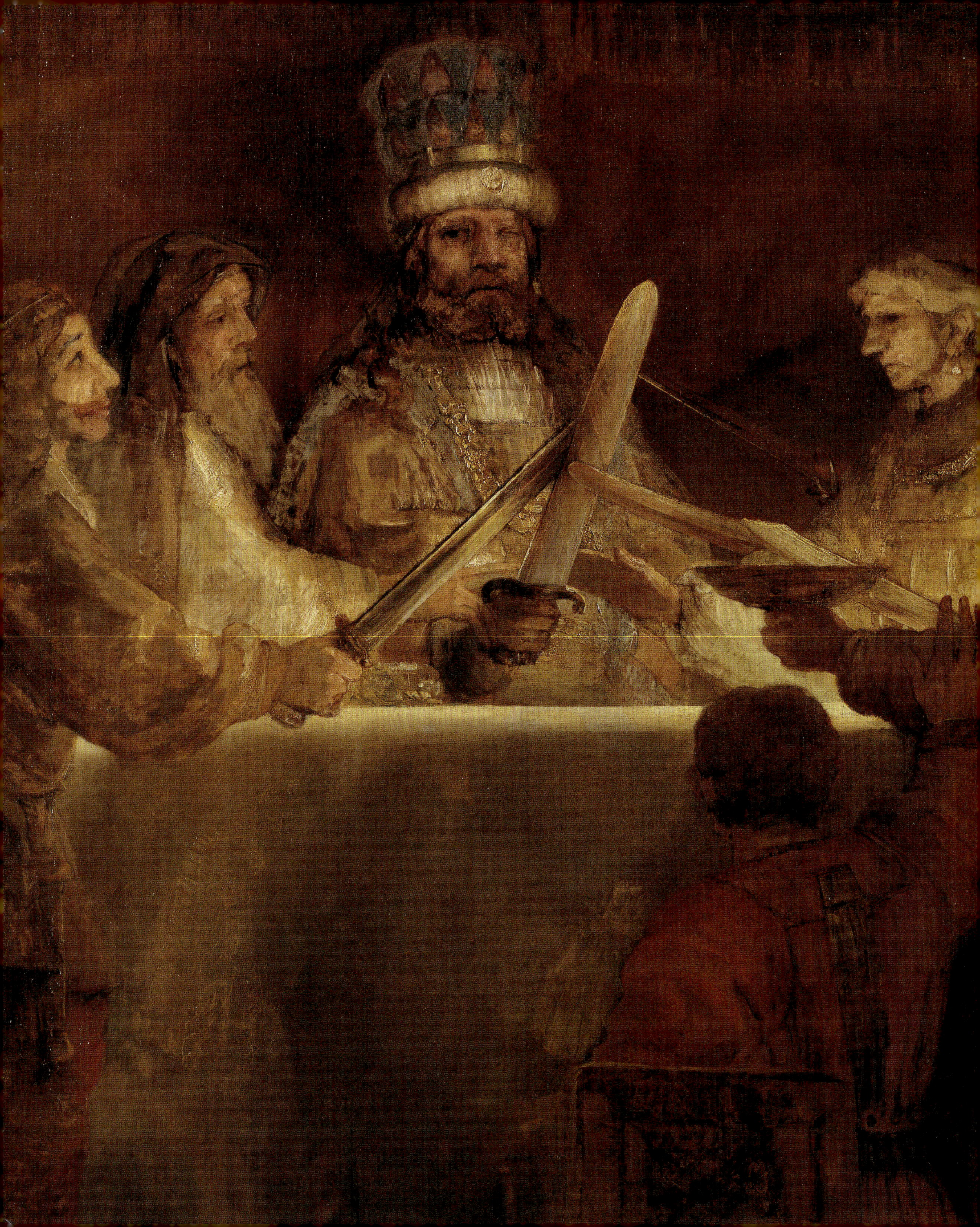

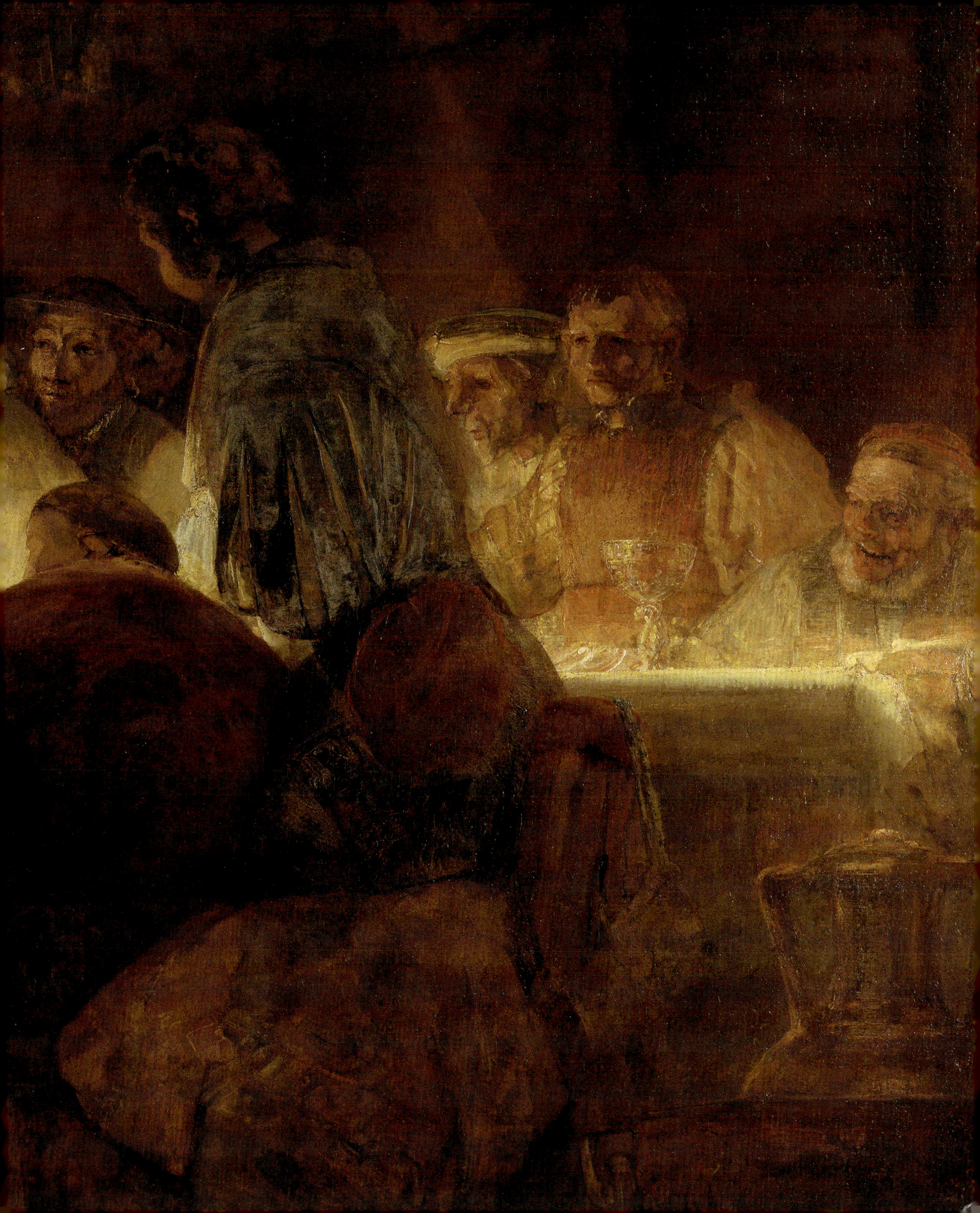

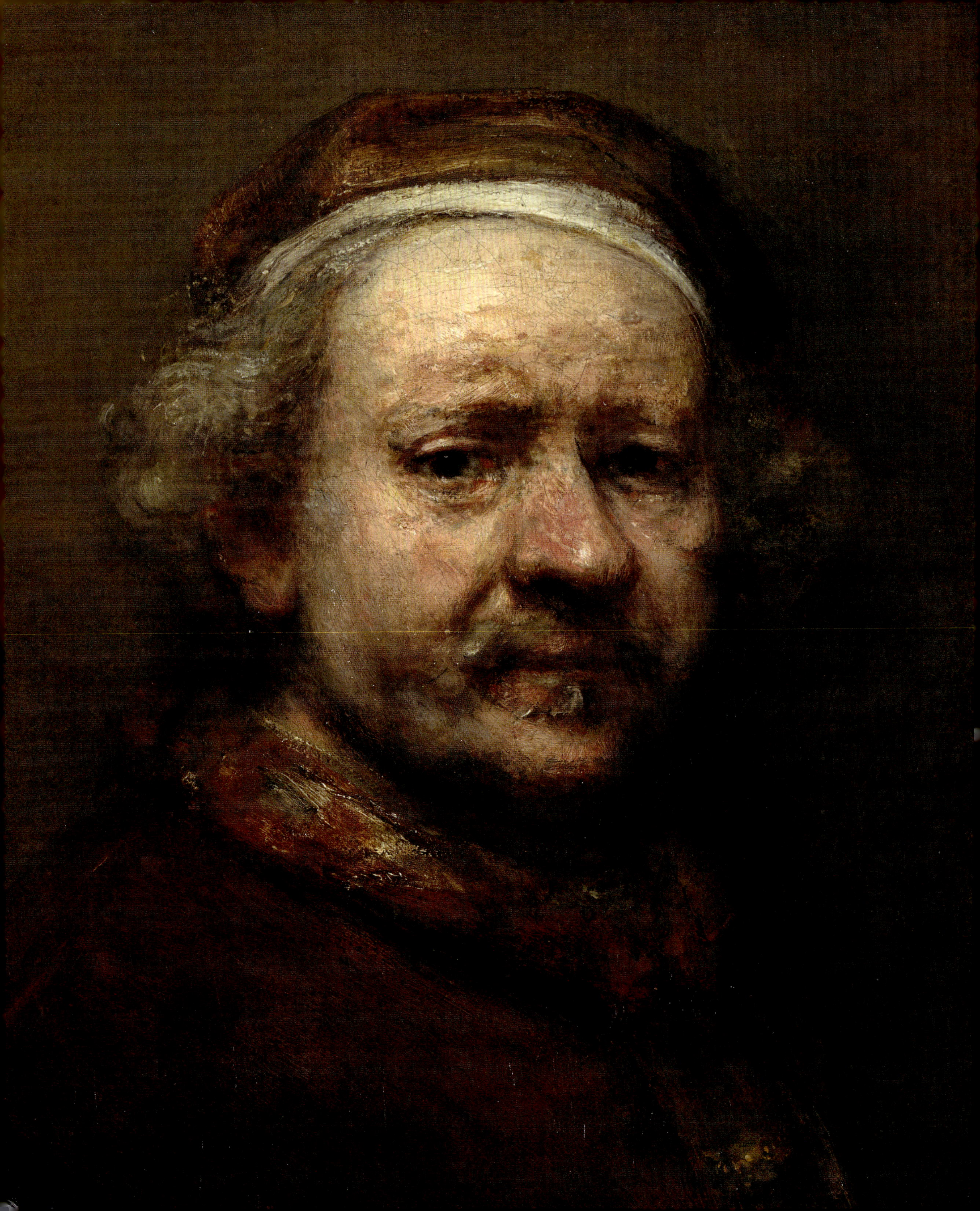

THE LATE SELF PORTRAITS

Marjorie E. Wieseman

THE EIGHTY OR SO self portraits that Rembrandt made over the course of his career are probably the most immediately recognisable part of his wide-ranging oeuvre. His distinctive snub features and electric curls are easily spotted in paintings, drawings and prints, commanding admiration for the uncompromising and often audacious ways in which he presented his singular visage to the world.[1] With relentless curiosity we probe these silent images for clues to Rembrandt 'the man', holding them up against the events that marked his personal and professional life – mounting fame and artistic success, personal tragedy, economic debacle and, eventually, the looming spectre of senescence – in an effort to read the self portraits as a coherent pictorial autobiography.[2] But to assume that an autobiographical structure can explain what drove this tirelessly inventive artist to devote roughly a tenth of his entire painted and etched oeuvre[3] to recording his own features is at best a hopeful fallacy: ever the wilful artist, Rembrandt obdurately resists any semblance of a tidy, predictable progression. The simple fact that he painted his largest and most grandiose self portrait – the Frick *Self Portrait* of 1658 (fig. 12) – in the same year as the last of the public auctions ensuing from the *cessio bonorum* (a debtor's voluntary surrender of goods to his creditors) of two years earlier should confound any effort to view the self portraits as directly autobiographical. Each of them was made in response to a specific set of circumstances and although the intensity of Rembrandt's interest in the subject rarely wavered, certainly his immediate concerns and priorities for making them evolved over the course of his career. Boldly independent, recording his features with unprecedented objectivity and a remarkably unfettered technique, Rembrandt's self portraits draw from but rarely conform to the long tradition of self portraiture and artists' portraits in Northern European art.[4] And far from settling into complacency as he aged, producing routine likenesses to satisfy wealthy collectors, the self portraits Rembrandt painted in his final years are among the most thoughtful and inventive creations of his entire career.

Rembrandt's self portraits can be roughly grouped into three chronological clusters. The youthful self portraits typically reveal an artist brimming with passion and brash enthusiasm, mugging with abandon or subjecting his features to a sharp blaze of illumination and in general paying little heed to social or artistic conventions (fig. 13). The painted self portraits of the 1630s and 1640s are less overtly radical. Many seem designed to further – or at least acknowledge – his own rising status as one of Amsterdam's most respected painters, and to advance the dignity of the profession (and his own place within it) by incorporating sophisticated references to prominent artists of the past (fig. 14). By contrast, many of the 15 or so painted self portraits produced during the final decades – between about 1652 and his death in 1669 – show Rembrandt focusing on more internally motivated concerns: achieving a realistic and sympathetic rendering of old age, now extending its merciless reach across his own face and body, and reflecting upon his profession and his own place within it.

Determining what Rembrandt's self portraits are 'about' – if indeed they are 'about' anything – is not a simple matter. Seduced by the compelling (if deceptive) honesty of these images, critics and historians have proposed many different, and often conflicting, theories to explain the motivation and intent behind them. Most often at issue is whether – or the extent to which – Rembrandt's self portraits indicate that he consciously searched inwardly for self-knowledge and an understanding

Detail from *Self Portrait at the Age of 63* (cat. 3)

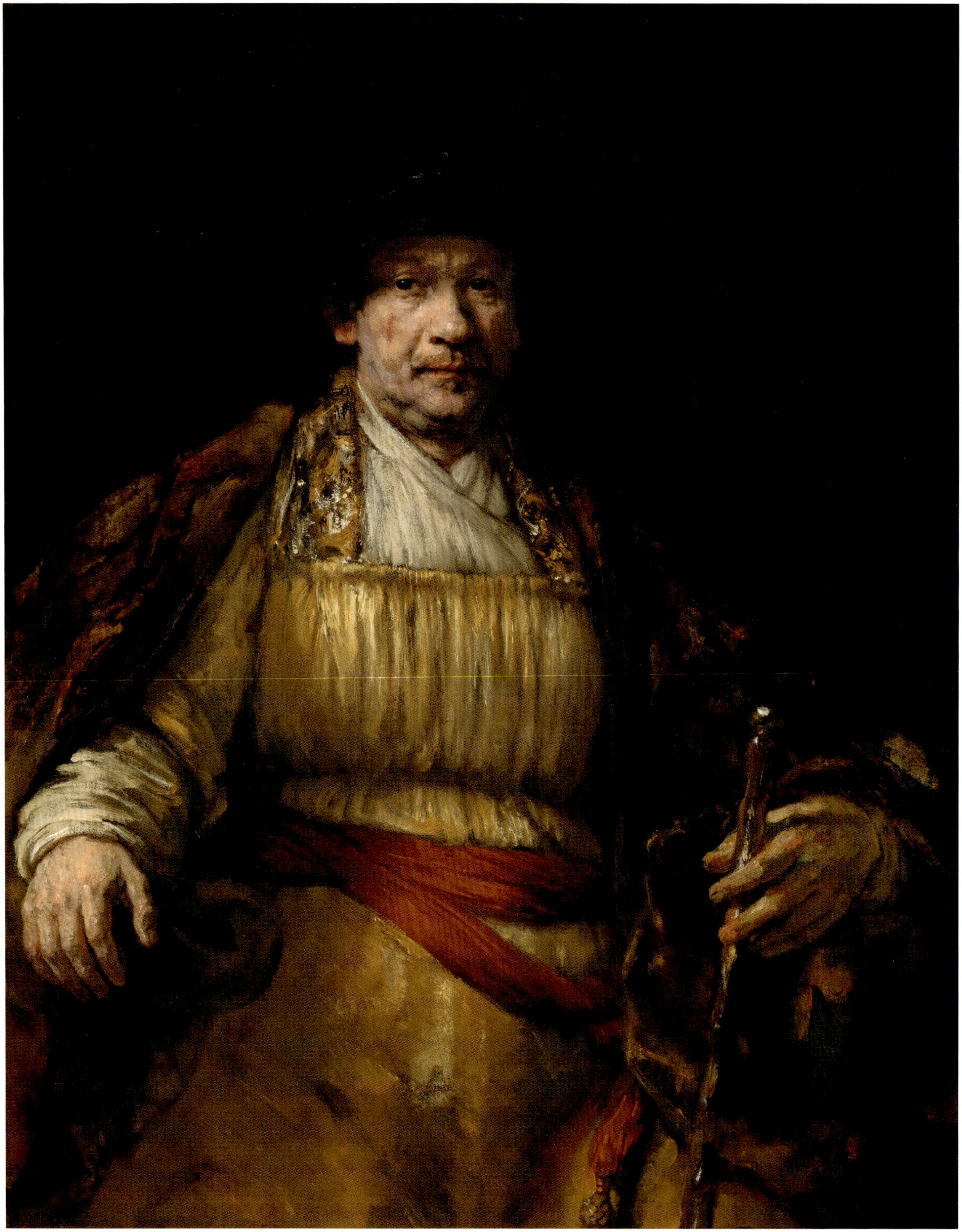

FIG. 12
Self Portrait, 1658
Oil on canvas, 133.7 × 103.8 cm
The Frick Collection,
New York

FIG. 13
Self Portrait, about 1628
Oil on panel, 22.6 × 19.7 cm
Rijksmuseum, Amsterdam.
Purchased with the support
of the Vereniging Rembrandt,
the Stichting tot Bevordering
van de Belangen van het
Rijksmuseum and the
Ministry of CRM (Culture,
Recreation and Social Welfare)

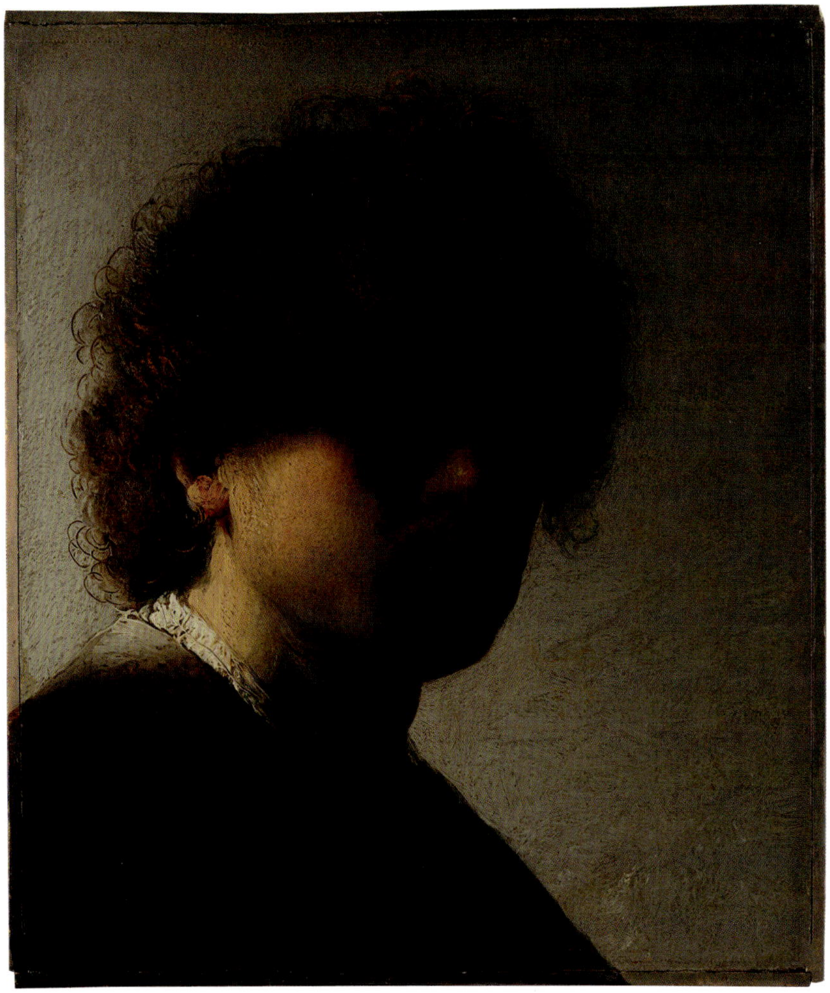

of his own identity, that he constructed and outwardly projected a unique sense of self, and in so doing documented his evolving ideas about his role as an artist.[5] An opposing view argues that such a degree of introspection and self-awareness was unheard of in the seventeenth century, and that Rembrandt considered his self portraits primarily as a marketable commodity, satisfying the demands of an art-loving clientele by providing a recognisable likeness of a renowned painter, by his own hand and in his characteristic style.[6] The one need not (and surely does not) preclude the other, however. Individually or as a group, the self portraits can be both personal, reflecting an 'inward-looking and deeply engaged artistic personality', and performative, demonstrating Rembrandt's keen and calculating awareness of the precise image he was crafting for public consumption.[7]

There does seem to be ample evidence to suggest that consciously looking inwards to attain an understanding of what makes each individual unique was, if not widespread in the seventeenth-century Dutch Republic, certainly a growing preoccupation among the intellectually curious – which Rembrandt most assuredly was. Most often cited in this context are the influential *Essais* of Michel de Montaigne (1533–1592), in which the author used a remarkably frank and honest examination of his own life and innermost thoughts to reflect on the broader human condition.[8] Moreover, the Protestant emphasis on individual responsibility for salvation encouraged self-examination and a scrutiny of all aspects of one's life. For an artist like Rembrandt, whose very existence was so inextricably bound up with his art, any consideration of his own identity and place in the world would necessarily have extended to an examination of his identity as an artist, and indeed a number of self portraits show him reflecting upon this issue. To cite a relatively early example, in the *Self Portrait at the Age of 34* (fig. 14) Rembrandt – then nearing the peak of his popular success – conspicuously positioned himself amidst

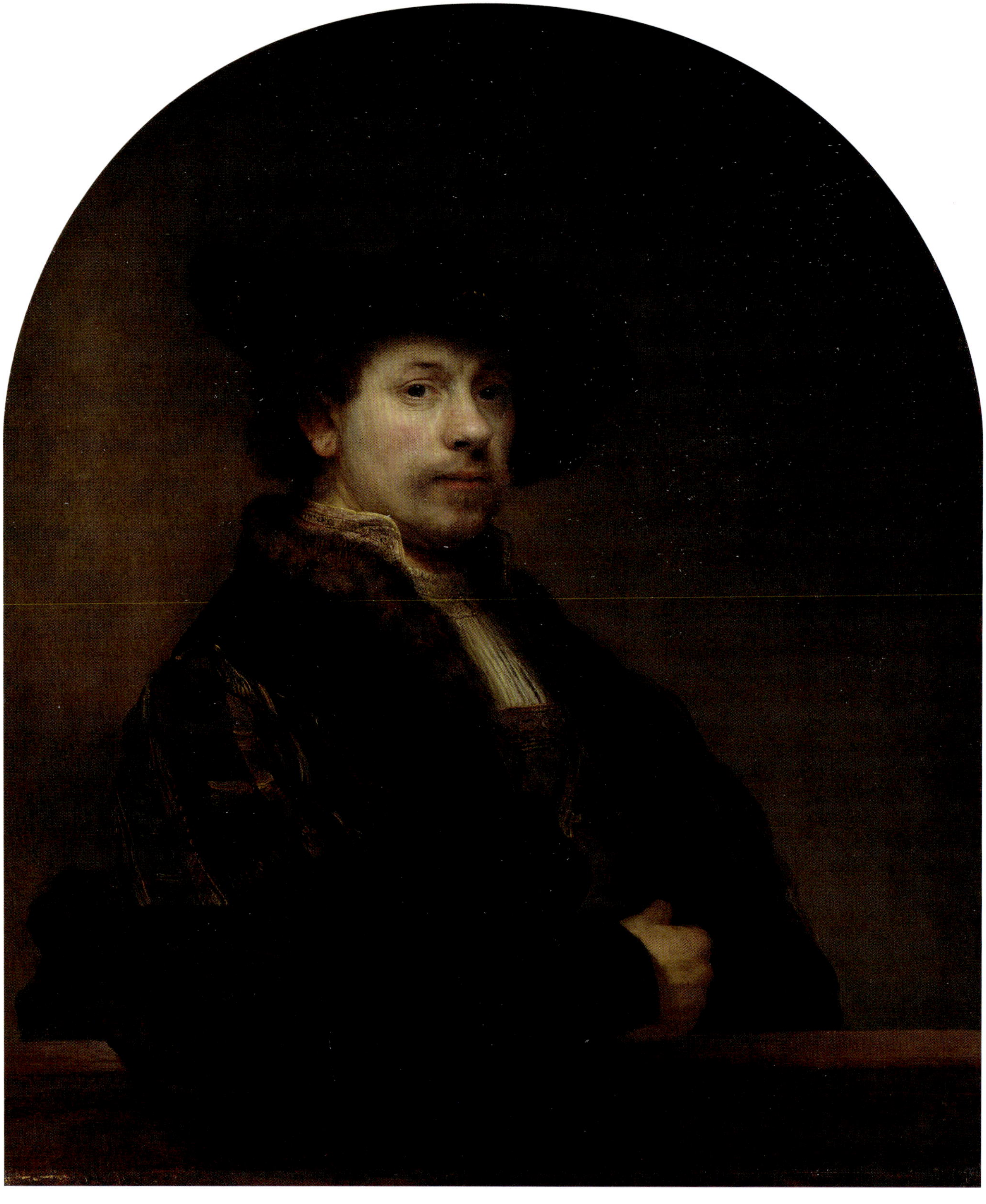

FIG. 14
Self Portrait at the Age of 34,
1640
Oil on canvas, 102 × 80 cm
The National Gallery, London

great artists of the previous century, such as Raphael (1483–1520), Titian, Dürer (1471–1528) and Lucas van Leyden (1494–1533), through the deliberate choice of sixteenth-century garments and a particular swaggering pose.[9] In self portraits of the 1650s and 1660s, references to artistic practice and the artist's status become more personal and more considered, a transformation that seems to suggest a natural progression in Rembrandt's search for self-knowledge. Older, wiser, no longer driven to make a name for himself but instead considering where talent, ambition and fate had carried him, Rembrandt now synthesises and interprets a lifetime of experience. Although he expressed these emerging preoccupations with unprecedented sensitivity and candour, this development was not unique to Rembrandt. Modern gerontologists have observed that any tendencies towards introspection typically become more pronounced in old age. While in youth we focus on acquiring knowledge and experience (consider Rembrandt's youthful experiments with light and exaggerated facial expression) and look to others to help gauge what is important (Rembrandt's concern to be accepted by elite society), experience enhances the ability to analyse and interpret human motivations and intentions and to make decisions based on those experiences, rendering external influences far less significant.[10]

However much he may have been engaged in a search for self-knowledge, Rembrandt was without question an astute and persistent self-promoter, eager to ensure that his likeness was readily available to collectors through both paintings and prints. Even during his lifetime, his self portraits could be found in prestigious collections throughout Europe; it is not without significance that no self portraits are listed in the inventory of his possessions drawn up in 1656.[11] The contemporary demand for likenesses of Rembrandt executed 'in his style' also prompted the production of copies and close variants of authentic self portraits by pupils and artists in the master's orbit.[12] Rembrandt cannot have been unaware of or unresponsive to the public demand for his self portraits, and in all likelihood responded by consciously shaping how he presented himself, through conspicuous references to the art of the past, choice of dress[13] and, in many cases, by introducing subtle links to the more highly regarded genre of history painting. Yet it is difficult to believe that such deliberate, complex and inventive works as the self portraits were made with the idea of marketability uppermost in the artist's mind. Rembrandt devoted scarcely less thought or artistry to his self portraits than to a history piece, and from both a theoretical and technical point of view, it is instructive to consider them in that context. The technical complexity of these works, and the often quite extensive adjustments he made during the painting process in order to achieve a particular expressive effect, will be considered in detail below. But just as importantly (and equally revealing), the self portraits are an integral part of Rembrandt's lifelong fascination for the representation of character and human passions, which in turn enabled him to imbue historical narrative with unprecedented immediacy and humanity.[14]

From the outset of his career Rembrandt was keenly aware of the value that seventeenth-century art lovers placed on an artist's ability to depict a wide range of human passions and emotions.[15] In assiduously developing this facility, he followed (consciously or unconsciously) the advice of art theorists such as Karel van Mander and Franciscus Junius (1545–1602), who exhorted painters to mine the depths of their own emotions for inspiration: only by experiencing comparable emotions could artists empathise with their

FIG. 15
Self Portrait at the Window, drawing on an Etching Plate, 1648
Etching and drypoint, 16 × 13 cm
Rijksmuseum, Amsterdam. Bequest of Mr and Mrs De Bruijn-van der Leeuw, Muri, Switzerland

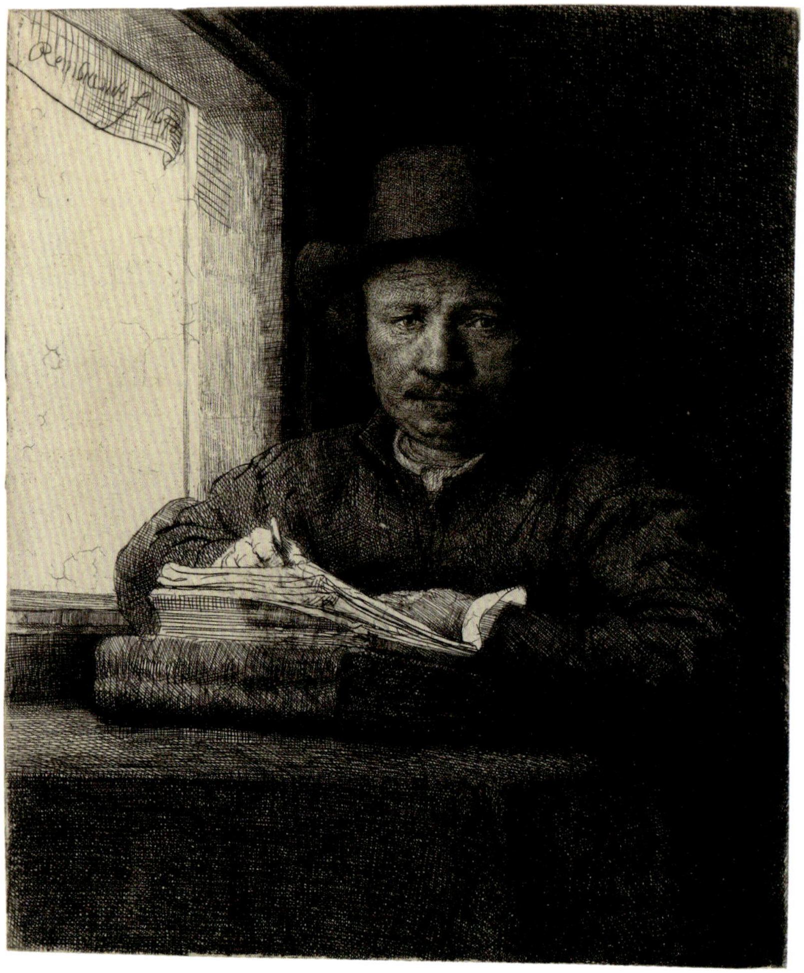

subjects; only by studying the effects of those emotions upon physical attitude and facial expression could they convincingly represent these emotions in their paintings and achieve the ultimate goal of moving the beholder.[16] Significantly, Samuel van Hoogstraten – who was, after all, Rembrandt's pupil – explicitly exhorted artists to mimic actors, enacting various roles before a mirror in order to study the passions and comprehend their impact on outward appearance.[17]

While in the early years of his career Rembrandt explored the external display of fleeting passions in both figural studies and historical scenes (figs 78, 80), in maturity the extroversion and volatility of those youthful exercises was transformed into an intensive investigation of the inner life of his subject, whether it concerned a historical figure or his own self. As his conception of historical themes evolved towards the inwardly directed single figures that dominate his late works (see, for example, cats 57, 112 and 113), Rembrandt's self portraits followed a parallel path: they too become more inwardly directed and subtly, profoundly expressive. Indeed, we can imagine that in his later years Rembrandt – a mature man and an experienced artist – was himself well on the way to becoming a historical figure.[18] In these late self portraits he turned his experienced and intensely inquisitive eye, mind and hand to the consideration of his own ageing flesh, the emotional onslaughts of his tumultuous personal life and his uncertain professional status, venturing bold experiments in presentation, finish and the balance of light and shadow to achieve unique expressive effect.

In 1652, after a hiatus of about seven years, Rembrandt returned to painting self portraits. It is not clear why he had abandoned the practice during these years, which saw a general falling off in his productivity

1
Self Portrait, drawing on an Etching Plate, 1658
Etching, 11.8 × 6.4 cm
Only state
Graphische Sammlung Albertina, Vienna
(DG 1930/562)

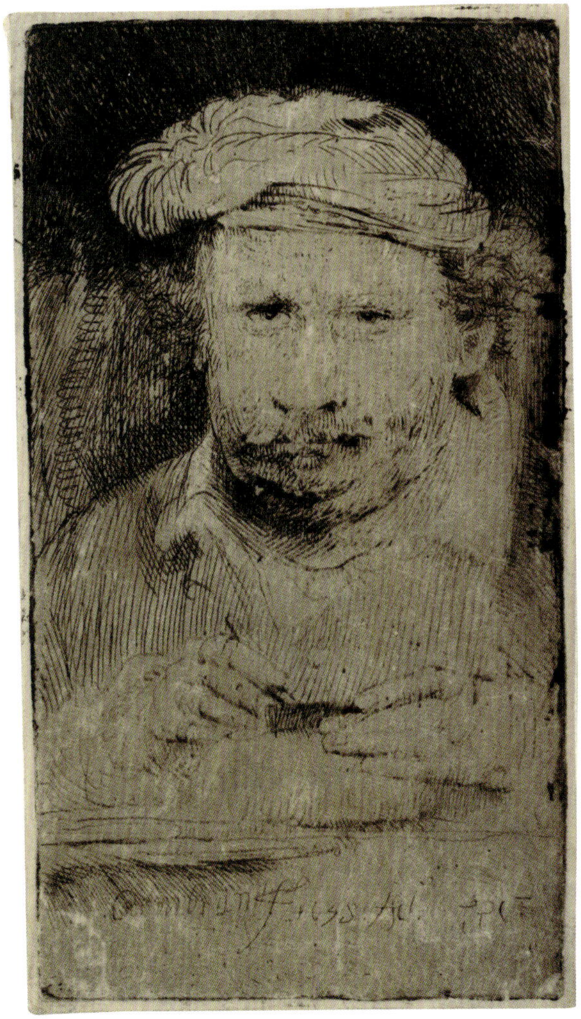

overall. Certainly it was a period beset by domestic crises: his first wife, Saskia Uylenburgh, had died in 1642, apparently after a prolonged illness; and he was the object of a bitter lawsuit brought by his former mistress (and nursemaid to his son Titus), Geertje Dircks. More importantly, perhaps, it has been argued that by the early 1640s Rembrandt may have felt he had taken his exploration of external drama and illusionism as far as he could, and was seeking new approaches to art-making that would enable him to achieve an evocation of a more profound realism, 'so convincingly natural as to surpass the formulaic art of classical antiquity and its successors'.[19] One can almost sense Rembrandt during these years trying to find the right means and techniques with which to make his vision manifest.

Presaged, perhaps, by the *Self Portrait at the Window, drawing on an Etching-Plate* of 1648 (fig. 15), in which he portrays himself actively practising his craft, a number of the late self portraits show Rembrandt grappling with how best to represent his intense relationship with the art of painting. There is a long tradition in Northern art of painters depicting themselves before an easel, usually as an elegant and learned gentleman painter with poised brush,[20] but characteristically, rather than adopting this well-worn formula, Rembrandt explored more oblique ways of expressing his visceral engagement with his profession. Even the portraits in which he does depict himself before an easel (fig. 19, cats 20 and 58) challenge preconceived notions of how and why a painter might represent himself at work.[21]

The imposing *Self Portrait* of 1652 in the Kunsthistorisches Museum, Vienna (fig. 16), assumes a grander format than nearly all of Rembrandt's earlier self portraits. Standing with his hands on his hips, thumbs tucked into the sash binding his waist, and holding the

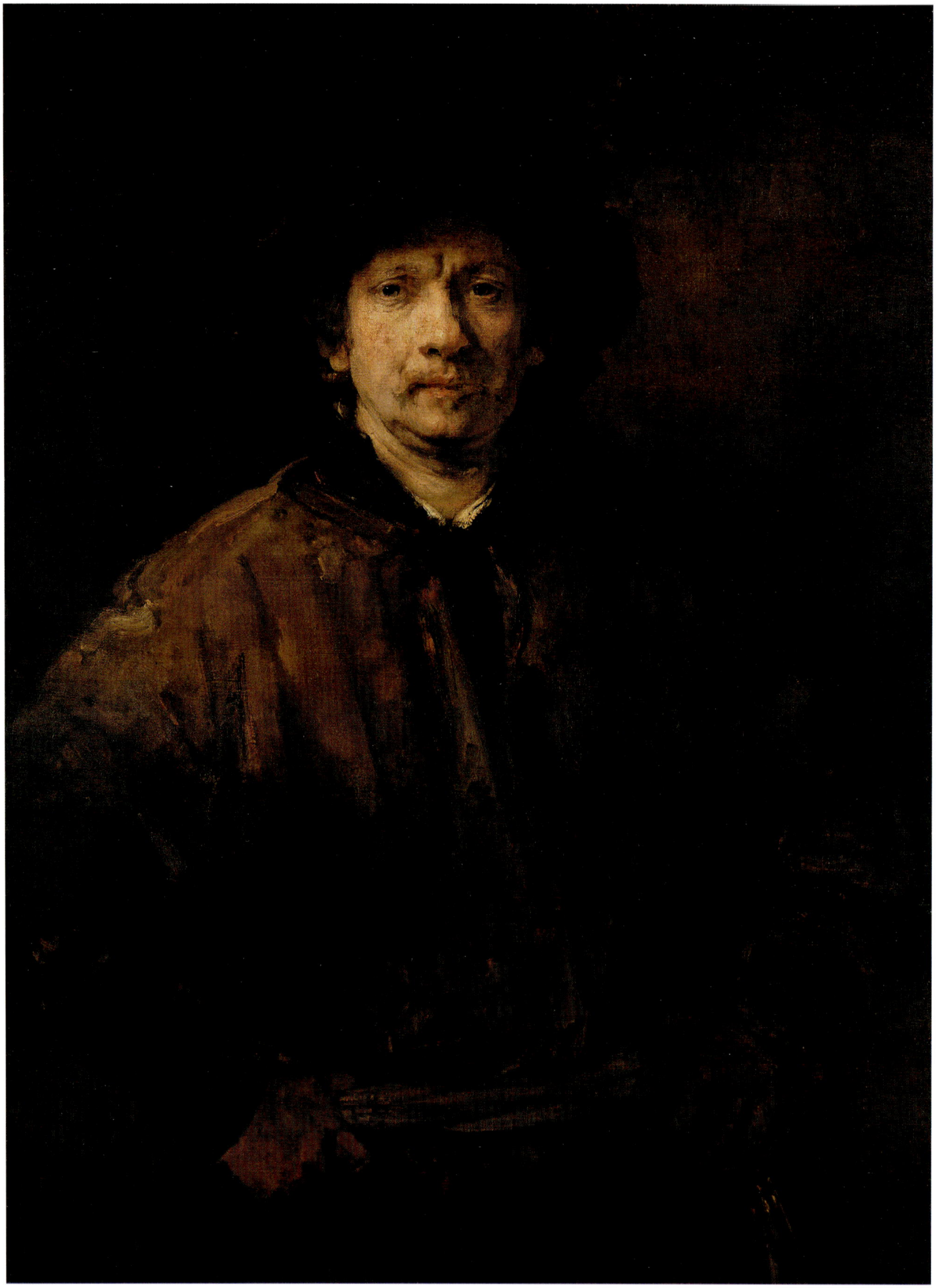

FIG. 16
Self Portrait, 1652
Oil on canvas, 112.1 × 81 cm
Kunsthistorisches Museum,
Vienna

viewer with a level gaze, he cuts a sober, direct and authoritative figure. The face, which receives the strongest illumination within the painting, is rendered with flat, even and fairly thick brushstrokes that also reflect and absorb the light striking the canvas from without, increasing the visual impact of the composition. By contrast, the hands and garments, more thinly painted, with free, at times almost chaotic brushstrokes, seem almost to dissolve into the background. Rembrandt wears practical, contemporary 'studio attire' consisting of a brown *tabbaard* (robe) over a black doublet and an old-fashioned soft beret, the latter a familiar attribute of painters in both portraits and genre paintings.[22] Some writers have seen in this deliberate informality both a disdain for social decorum and evidence of a self-confidence unprecedented in Dutch self portraiture.[23] But it has also been suggested that Rembrandt's choice of such homely garments might, paradoxically, have been intended to convey a degree of humility and respect for the art of painting: notable painters of the past, such as Dürer, were said to have worn their paint-stained working clothes in public as a badge of honour.[24]

An almost diametrically opposed vision of the artist is presented in the imposing Frick *Self Portrait* of 1658 (fig. 12). Here Rembrandt seems to claim for himself the same regal title awarded to the Greek painter Apelles, the 'Prince of Painters'.[25] He sits solidly in a throne-like chair, his generously draped figure filling the entire width of the picture. The silver-knobbed walking stick held loosely, almost delicately, in his left hand was a fashionable accessory in the seventeenth century (compare the *Portrait of Jacob Trip*, cat. 39), but here also recalls both a painter's maulstick and a ruler's sceptre. As in his history paintings, Rembrandt's flamboyant garb is a dazzling amalgam of sixteenth-century historical dress and exotic oriental elements, designed to express wealth and power of fabled magnitude. Despite the princely allusions and the grandeur of his dress, Rembrandt made no attempt to ennoble his rugged, ageing face: shaded by the brim of his black beret, the fall of light emphasises the furrow between his brows and the heavy jowls that sag unevenly to his neck. Cloaked in shadow, his dark eyes fix us with a steady gaze but a disconcertingly unreadable expression. The remarkably varied and complex application of paint across the surface of the canvas – smooth parallel strokes for the pleats of his gown, broad swathes over his thighs, riotous swirls and dabs for the gilt-encrusted bands over his shoulders, criss-crossed slashes of white for the sleeves – is unified by a masterful orchestration of light and shadow that draws our attention to the head, chest and right (painting) hand of the artist. This showy likeness was created amidst the sales of Rembrandt's possessions following the *cessio bonorum*, a proud statement conceived in defiance of the debilitating loss of the material props of his livelihood and professional reputation.

In precisely the same year – 1658 – Rembrandt etched the intimate and ephemeral *Self Portrait, drawing on an Etching Plate* (cat. 1), a diminutive print, known in only two impressions. Lightly etched, with deftly scribbled lines, the likeness is as casual and spontaneous as a snapshot. Yet Rembrandt signed and dated the plate and printed it on expensive Japanese paper, suggesting his satisfaction with the image as complete. Staring intently into the mirror before him, Rembrandt's figure is bathed in strong light, which blurs and flattens his already broad features; by contrast, his hands, wielding etching needle and copper plate with practised delicacy, are made almost ethereal by the light.

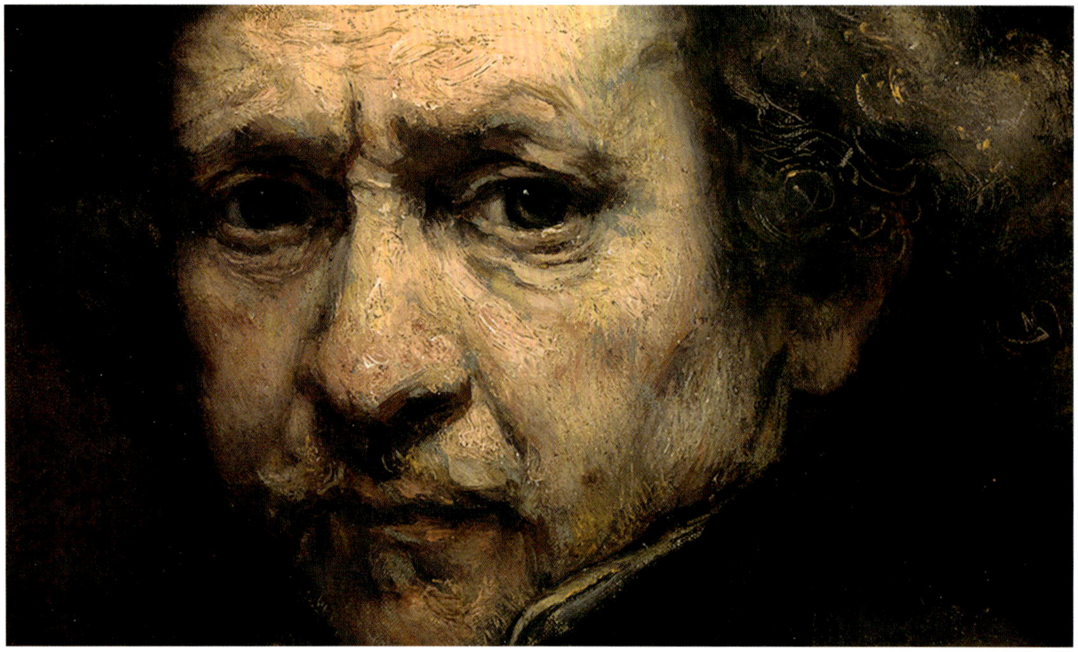

Detail from *Self Portrait* (cat. 2)

2
Self Portrait, 1659
Oil on canvas, 84.5 × 66 cm
National Gallery of Art, Washington

The contrast between this ghostly apparition and the more formally composed, solid and substantial image of a decade earlier (fig. 15) could not be more striking. Similarly, the painted Vienna and Frick self portraits could hardly be more different in their depiction of a seventeenth-century painter – the one a proud member of the humble artisan class, the other commandeering for himself a prominent place in history – yet both suggest an awareness of the complex social status of artists at this time. The self portraits in which Rembrandt makes no overt reference to his profession nonetheless also convey his passionate engagement with the art and craft of painting. The deceptively simple *Self Portrait* of 1659 in the National Gallery of Art in Washington (cat. 2) is painted in such a free and direct manner that it might be considered unfinished, yet Rembrandt signed and dated the work, indicating that he felt it had reached a sufficient level of completion.[26] The flesh of the face is rendered with a broad and fluent vocabulary of layered flecks and dabs of opaque paint, with areas of the light greyish imprimatura and transparent brown underpaint left exposed. Creamy swirls of paint in the brow give the face its slightly quizzical expression; thick horizontal strokes emphasise the heavy folds of flesh at the upper and lower eyelids, while thinner brushstrokes evoke the slack, depleted flesh of his jowls where they droop loosely over the stiff standing collar of his coat. The highly expressive and at times unorthodox brushwork is an insistent reminder of the artist's presence: the painting is its own advertisement of the maker's artistry. The audacity of Rembrandt's technique is particularly evident when this painting is compared with his other self portraits of similar date, the *Self Portrait* of about 1657 in Edinburgh (fig. 17) and the *Self Portrait* of 1660 in New York (fig. 18), which are by comparison quite finely and meticulously painted.

Although the brushwork in the Washington *Self Portrait* appears entirely spontaneous, X-radiographs show that Rembrandt made several changes to the painting as he worked: he originally depicted himself wearing a white 'painter's cap', but replaced this with a soft black beret.[27] The change reveals the artist's concern for the balance of light and dark within the composition: in the final image, our eye is not distracted by a bright white cap but is instead drawn to what is now the lightest part of the composition, the master's illuminated face, framed by his dark beret. But perhaps in making this alteration Rembrandt also debated the connotations of wearing a mundane, workman-like head covering (presumably part of his habitual studio attire – see fig. 19),[28] electing ultimately to replace it with a hat bearing more elevated historic connotations in order to distance himself, however slightly, from appearing physically engaged in artisanal labour.

X-radiographs also reveal that Rembrandt made this same modification, from a white 'painter's cap' to a dark or coloured headcovering, in three other self portraits (fig. 18, cats 3 and 4).[29] In the *Self Portrait at the Easel* of

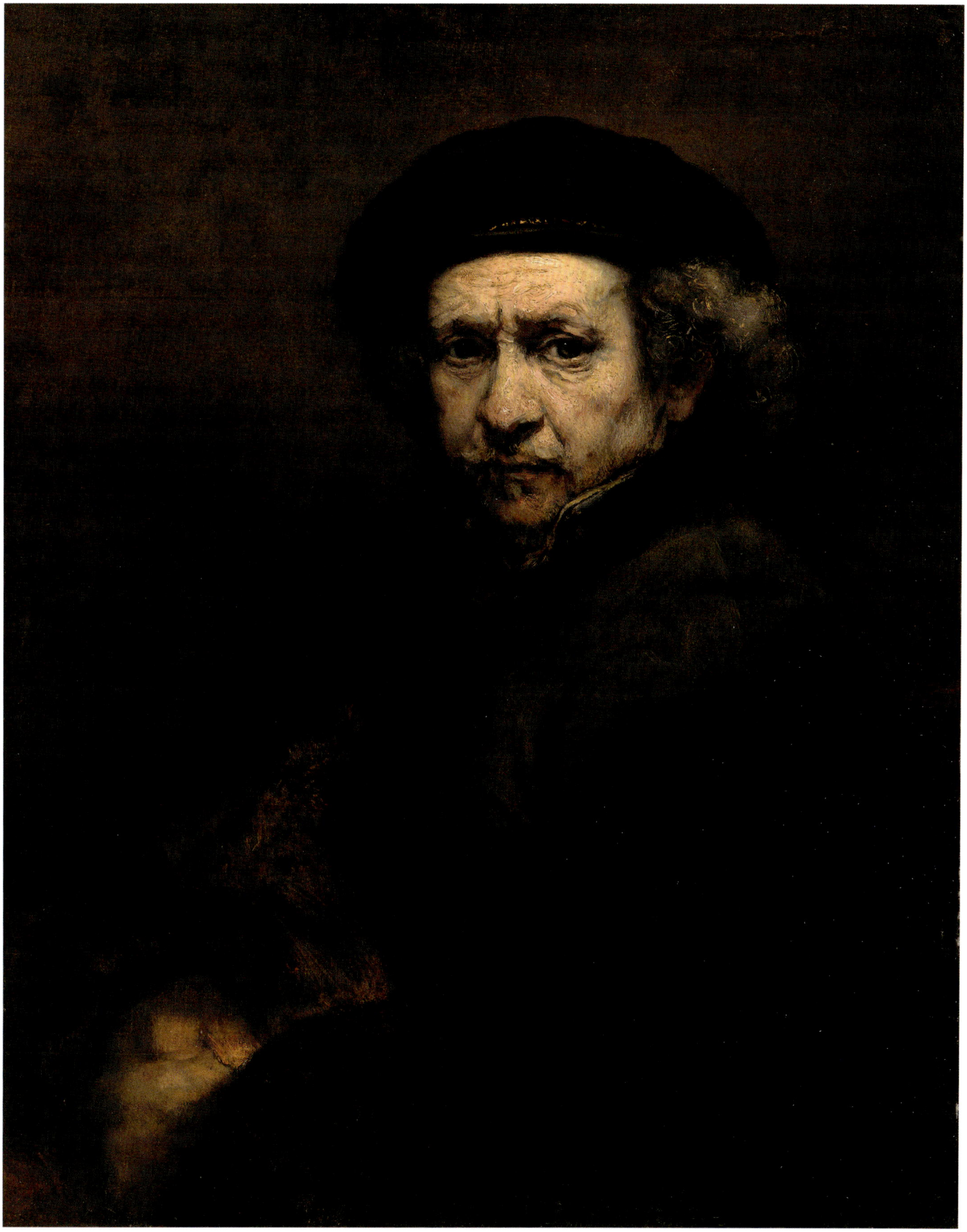

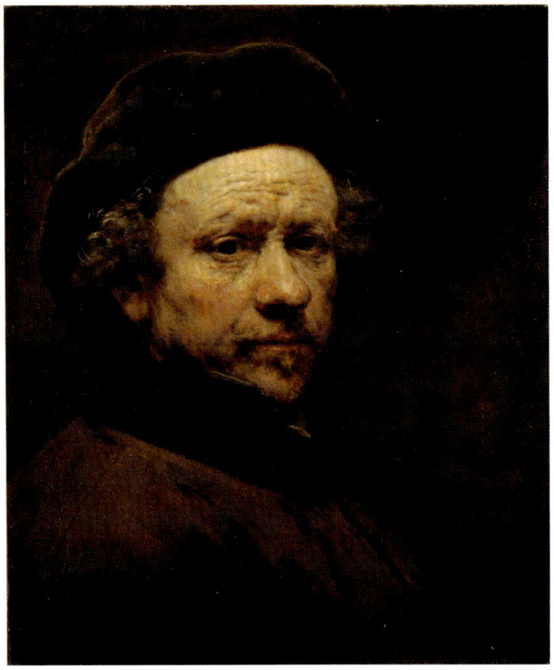

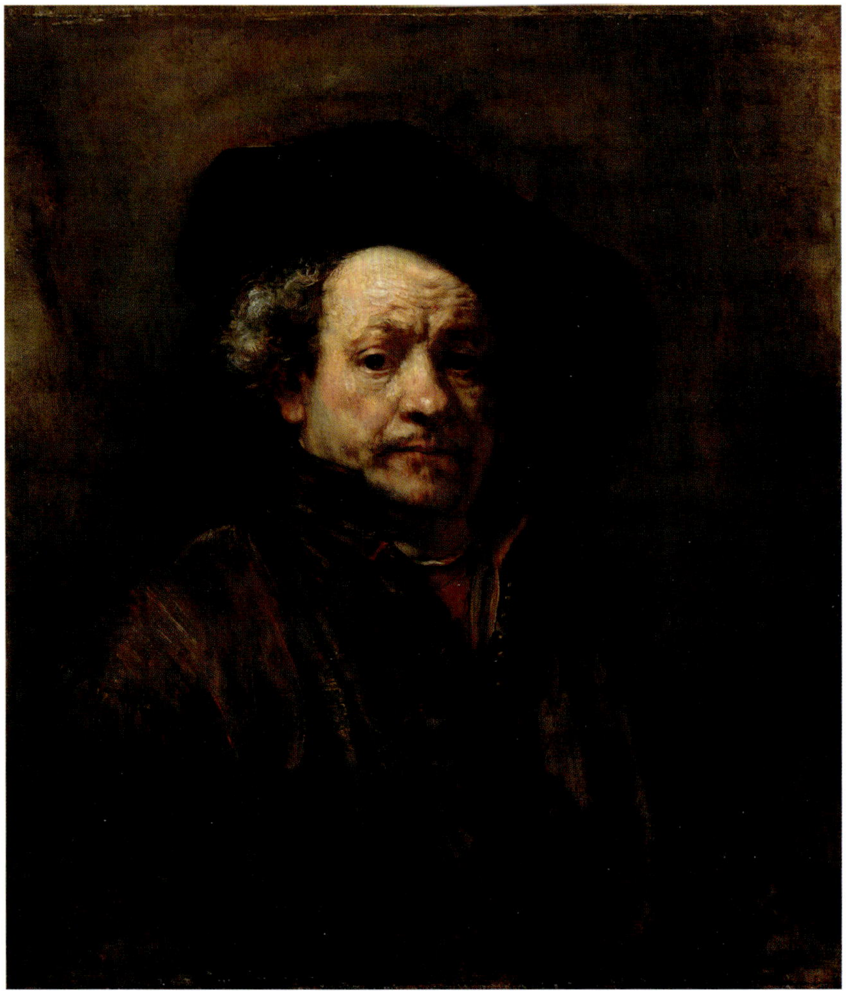

1660 in the Louvre (fig. 19), on the other hand, X-radiographs show a large reserve left around the head, which suggests that he initially intended to represent himself wearing a dark beret and then changed it to a white cap.[30] The Louvre self portrait is the first in which Rembrandt depicts himself as painter with all the accoutrements of his craft: a painting propped on an easel just visible at the right edge of the canvas, a maulstick in his right hand and a fistful of brushes and a colour-laden palette in his left. The switch to a mundane white cap is entirely in keeping with the artist's slightly scruffy appearance (fancy pseudo-historical garments notwithstanding) and his decision – finally, at the age of 54 – to present himself as a painter at home in his studio, fully immersed in his craft.

Rembrandt subsequently depicted himself before an easel on two other occasions: in the *Self Portrait as Zeuxis* of about 1662 (cat. 20), in the Wallraf-Richartz-Museum, Cologne, and in the magisterial *Self Portrait with Two Circles* (cat. 58) at Kenwood House, London. The Cologne *Self Portrait* shows a maniacally grinning Rembrandt in the guise of the Greek painter Zeuxis (active in the fifth century BC), who was lauded for his ability not only to depict reality with perfect illusionism, but indeed to surpass it.[31] It is, unusually, one of only two self portraits in which Rembrandt adopted such a historical guise for himself, despite being so thoroughly devoted to depicting complex personalities from history, mythology and the Bible in his other works. His only other is the *Self Portrait as the Apostle Paul*, painted in 1661 (cat. 111).[32] This poignant, almost wistful image was part of the series of late religious portraits Rembrandt executed between about 1657 and 1662, profoundly moving studies in contemplation and prayerfulness representing men and women inspired by faith, beset by doubt, or pleading for deliverance.[33] Whether Rembrandt viewed this painting primarily as a self portrait, or as an image of the apostle that just happened to draw on his

FIG. 17
Self Portrait, Aged 51, about 1657
Oil on canvas, 53 × 43 cm
National Gallery of Scotland, Edinburgh. Bridgewater Loan, 1945

FIG. 18
Self Portrait, 1660
Oil on canvas, 81 × 67.6 cm
The Metropolitan Museum of Art, New York.
Bequest of Benjamin Altman, 1913

FIG. 19
Self Portrait at the Easel, 1660
Oil on canvas, 111 × 85 cm
Musée du Louvre, Paris

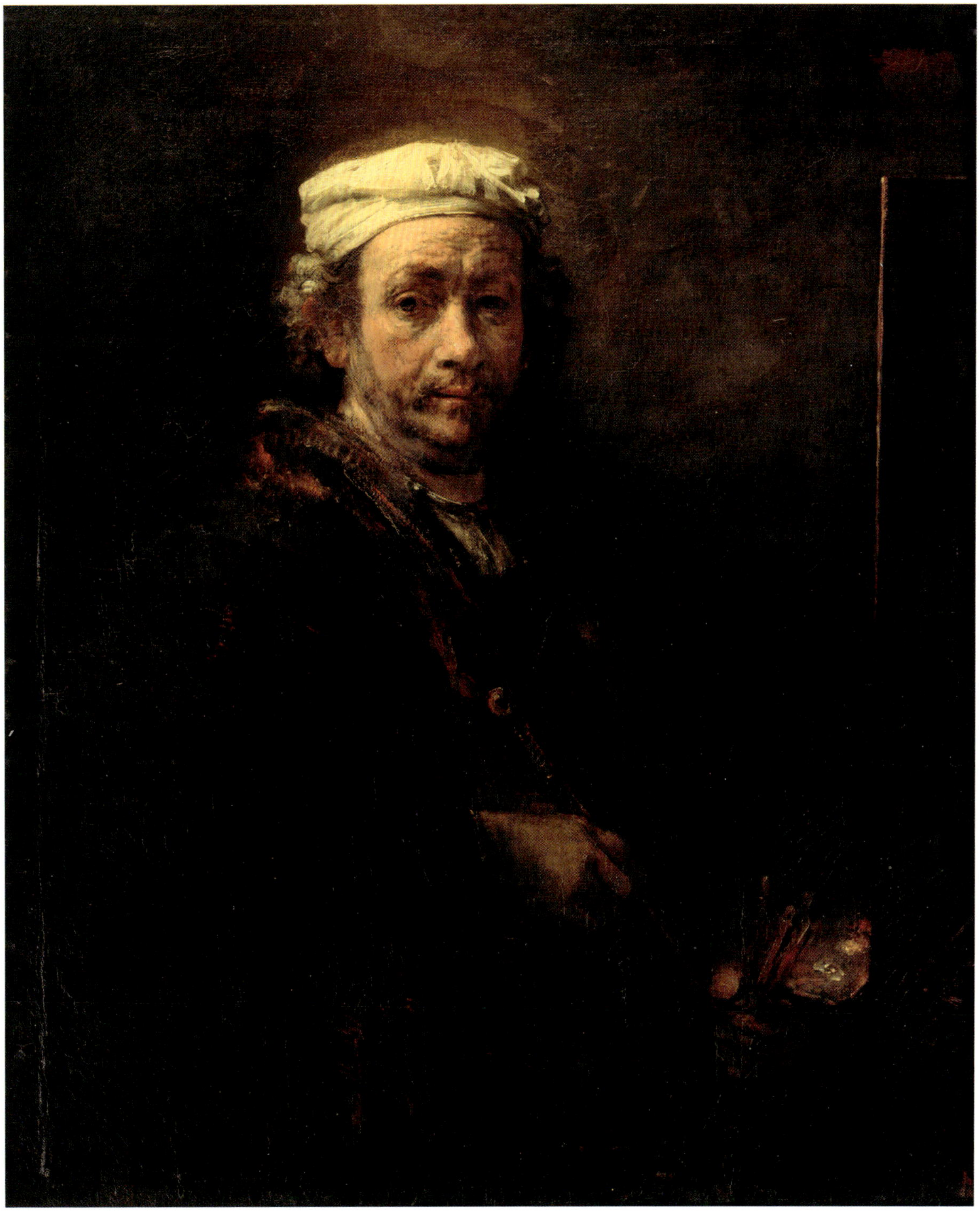

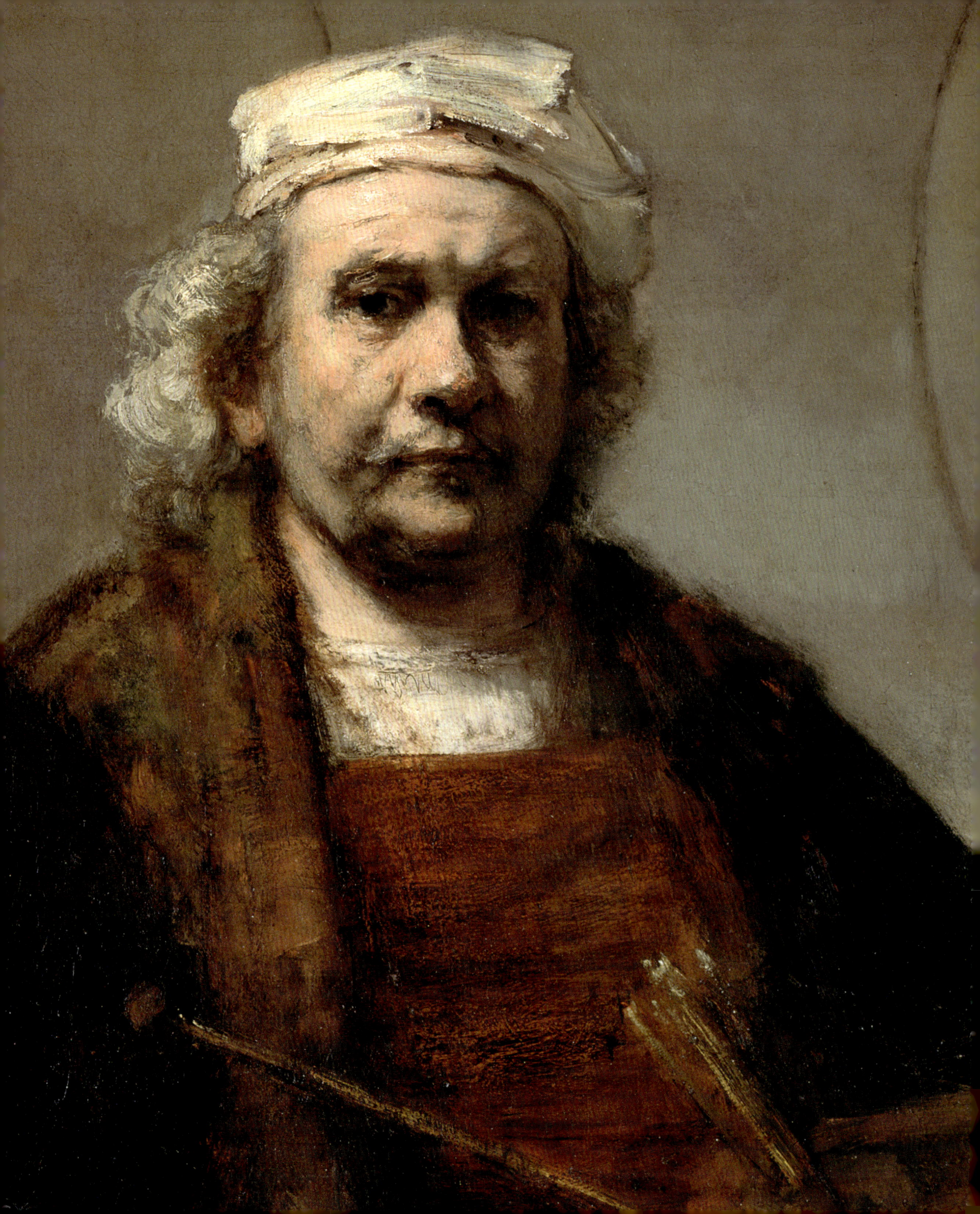

Detail from *Self Portrait with Two Circles* (cat. 58)

own features, is not clear; what is significant is the fact that he chose to identify himself specifically with the apostle Paul. It has been convincingly argued that Paul – by reputation an indefatigable, non-conforming and yet immensely humble man – was the apostle with whom Rembrandt identified most closely, and with one facet of the apostle's complex identity in particular:

> ... the apostle Paul with whom Rembrandt identified was that flawed human, the man who once was Saul, the man who somehow, on the way to Damascus, had found favor in God's eye. He had received the gift of grace that he did not deserve, and the realization of that gift continued to bewilder and amaze him until his dying days.[34]

The fact that Rembrandt chose to depict this revered saint with his own features, giving them a quizzical, almost helpless expression, may suggest that he empathised particularly strongly with the feeling of being the unworthy recipient of a great and onerous gift – in Rembrandt's case the difficult and mysterious gift of artistic talent. Almost as if to demonstrate the very magnitude of this gift, the entire composition was painted rapidly, wet-in-wet. The astonishing range in scale and form of the brushstrokes shows Rembrandt's stunning command of technique. For the forehead, most fully in the light, he applied thick paint using a mix of relatively short, comma-like strokes and longer, rippled strokes to accentuate the brow's deep furrows; in the nose, cheeks and chin, a more subtle but no less complex layering of colours and textures conjures up the merciless imperfections of ageing flesh.

In the *Self Portrait with Two Circles* (cat. 58), probably painted between 1665 and 1669, Rembrandt returned to a more direct consideration of his identity as an artist. As in the *Self Portrait at the Easel* (fig. 19), and the *Self Portrait as Zeuxis* (cat. 20), he represents himself as painter at work: standing solidly before an easel (the edge of the canvas or panel is visible as a slim, slightly angled strip at the right edge of the painting), a modest linen cap pulled down over his whitened curls, he is armed with the painter's requisites of palette, brushes and maulstick. Inscribed on the light-coloured wall behind him are two simple arcs. Rembrandt wears a vaguely historicising costume: a *tabbaard* (loose robe) worn over a red *borstlap* (bib) and a shirt in sixteenth-century style.[35] Over the shirt but lost beneath the *borstlap* is the ghostly suggestion of a gold chain, reminiscent of the chains awarded to artists by wealthy patrons as a mark of prestige and favour, usually flaunted but here tucked aside with brusque nonchalance.[36]

Both technically and iconographically, *Self Portrait with Two Circles* is the most complex and enigmatic of all Rembrandt's self portraits. The painting appears unfinished: the crisp highlights of the white cap have been applied with a few swift strokes of the loaded brush, leaving the initial outline in dark paint still visible; the right hand, resting on his hip, is barely blocked in and the left, holding palette, brushes and maulstick, is suggested with a flurry of rapid brushstrokes.[37] However, X-radiographs show that even at this early stage Rembrandt had already made significant alterations to the composition, revealing subtle changes in self-presentation. He initially positioned himself turned more to the right, his proper left hand raised as if touching brush to canvas, and in his other hand holding palette, maulstick and several more brushes: presumably he was precisely recording his reflection in the mirror before him as he composed the picture. By turning the figure slightly more towards the viewer, and transferring palette,

3
Self Portrait at the Age of 63, 1669
Oil on canvas, 86 × 70.5 cm
The National Gallery, London

brushes and maulstick to the opposite (proper left) hand, Rembrandt not only avoided the difficulties inherent in the direct transcription of a mirrored reflection, by which he would seem to be painting left-handed,[38] but he also shifted the emphasis of the painting away from an image of an artist at work (captured in the act of creating this very painting) to a more objective image of a painter pure and simple. Our attention gravitates not towards the action of painting, but to the likeness that has been created: we recognise Rembrandt as the creator of this work *not* because we see him in the act of painting, but because in this figure, drawn with utmost skill and supreme confidence, we find unmistakable evidence of his signature handiwork. Although the painting is not signed, it is easy to imagine that Rembrandt was well satisfied with it: the swiftly sketched forms tantalise and engage, inviting the viewer to complete them for him- or herself.[39] And surely Rembrandt must have enjoyed the serendipitous conceit of the painter's fingers becoming virtually indistinguishable from the tools of his craft, in the quickly, eloquently dashed forms of the hand holding palette, brushes and maulstick.[40]

The most curious aspect of the painting – and the one that has inspired the most critical debate – are the two (partial) circles on the wall behind the figure, which have been variously interpreted as representing the two hemispheres from a large world map; as cabbalistic signs or references to an Aristotelian world view; as representing *ars* and *exercitatio* (theory and practice); or as simply having been added to balance the slightly off-centre figure and emphasise the underlying geometrical structure of the composition. Perhaps the most promising argument centres on a familiar theme in the history of art, described by Vasari, Van Mander and others, of the ability to draw a perfect circle freehand – as the young Giotto (about 1267–1337) was reputed to have done – as the ultimate proof of an artist's skill.[41] The closed form of a complete circle also represented eternity. The circles in the Kenwood painting, however, are not complete; nor are they drawn with a single, fluent line, but rather with a succession of shorter overlapping strokes. These differences might argue against viewing the circles as allusions to legendary manifestations of artistic skill,[42] but on the other hand they are precisely in keeping with the painting's distinctive bravura execution. These are not Giotto's perfect circles, they are Rembrandt's; in not only delineating form but bearing the signature touch of the artist, they surpass the simpler efforts of those earlier masters.[43]

In the final year of his life Rembrandt painted three self portraits, all rather modest in comparison to the triumphant *Self Portrait with Two Circles* of a few years earlier: the *Self Portrait at the Age of 63* in the National Gallery (cat. 3), the *Self Portrait* in the Uffizi (fig. 11)[44] and the *Self Portrait* in the Mauritshuis (cat. 4). Rembrandt appears palpably frailer in the London painting, his skin pasty, his hands gently clasped; even his wiry hair seems to lack its customary vigour. Yet the conception and execution of the painting reveals no slackening of interest or ability: the paint is applied with great sensitivity, varying from a thin, glaze-like treatment of the darker areas of the costume and background to a thick, almost sculptural build-up of paint in the highlighted areas of the face. Here the paint is worked wet-in-wet, once again using a complex layering of different strokes and dabs of colour – offset by patches of the exposed greyish-brown ground – to simulate the appearance of old, roughened and pockmarked flesh. In the tip of the nose and the earlobe Rembrandt made a few short scratches in the wet paint to bring precise accents of light and texture to these

4
Self Portrait, 1669
Oil on canvas, 65.4 × 60.2 cm
Royal Picture Gallery
Mauritshuis, The Hague

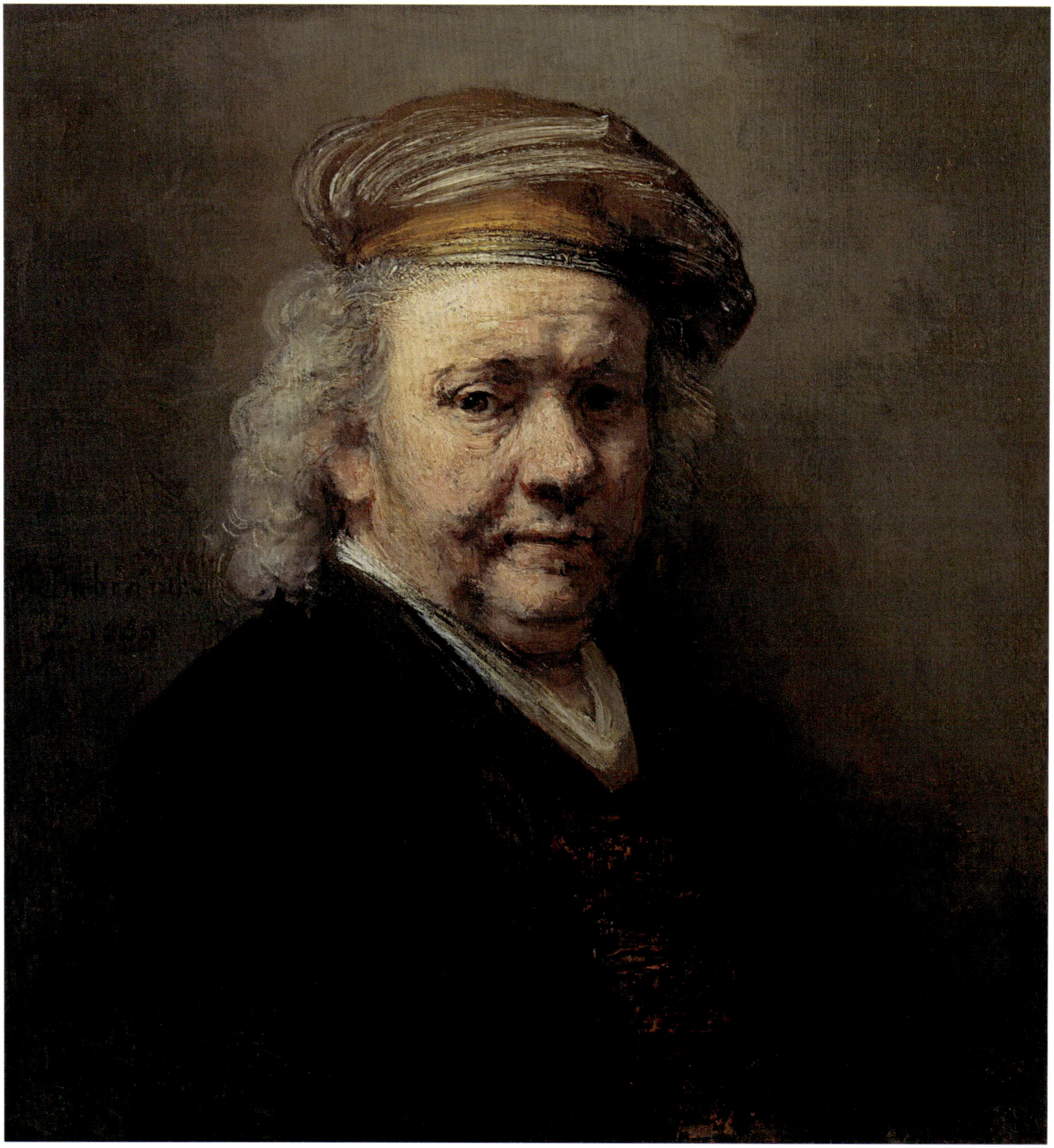

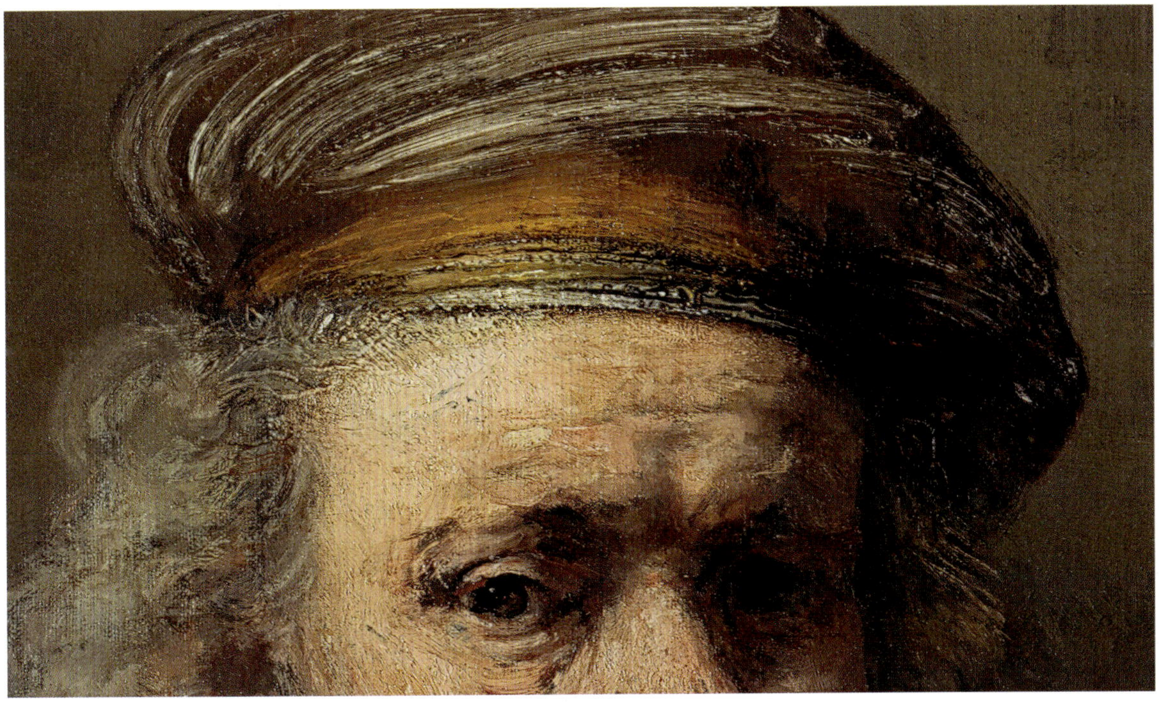

Detail from *Self Portrait* (cat. 4)

areas. His fur-trimmed doublet reflects fashions of the early to mid-fifteenth century, apparently inspired by engraved portraits of illustrious Netherlandish painters such as Dirck Bouts (1400?–1475) and Rogier van der Weyden (about 1399–1464).[45] In choosing a garment with such specific, recognisable associations, he once again placed himself in the tradition of his famous predecessors.

As in other late self portraits, X-radiographs of the *Self Portrait at the Age of 63* reveal that Rembrandt made changes as he worked, adjusting the compositional focus and the balance of light and dark. His hat was originally larger, extending further above his head and to the right; it was also entirely white, probably a painter's cap similar to that worn in the *Self Portrait with Two Circles*. The hands were originally open (not clasped) and holding a single brush. By making these simple modifications Rembrandt arrived at a quieter image, which harbours its energy in the magnificently painted head enveloped in a gentle luminosity, and at the same time imposed a discreet distance between the reality of his reflected image (a painter at work) and the conceit of the painted likeness, the master's hand revealed in his characteristic style.

The bust-length painting in the Mauritshuis (cat. 4) is believed to be Rembrandt's final self portrait. His face is slack and puffy, the likeness unsparing: with a thick swipe of paint Rembrandt emphasised the pouch of flesh under his right eye, and with almost clinical detachment observed how his sagging jowls now gathered in a weighty swag beneath his chin. As in the *Self Portrait at the Age of 63*, in the highlighted areas of the face, hair and beret he worked wet-in-wet, layering different colours, textures and consistencies of paint with bold assurance; in other areas he applied the paint more thinly, often leaving the underlayers exposed.[46] Once again, X-radiographs and pentimenti visible to the naked eye show that even in this simple composition, realised at the very end of his life, Rembrandt made a number of changes as he worked. He seems to have first depicted himself wearing an open coat and a red *borstlap* – similar to the combination worn in the *Self Portrait with Two Circles* – but then covered the red with a layer of black paint; hints of red now simmer through this upper layer. And once again, he changed his hat: X-radiographs indicate that he first painted himself with the now-familiar white painter's cap, then scraped away much of the white paint before laying down a layer of reddish brown underpaint, over which he dragged broad strokes of grey, orange and yellow before finally adding a few quick scratches in the wet paint to decorate the lower band of this fanciful beret. These impulsive changes and creative touches are as characteristic and as natural to Rembrandt at the close of his career as they were at the beginning, vivid evidence that his technical prowess, emotional insight and inventive power only deepened as he aged.

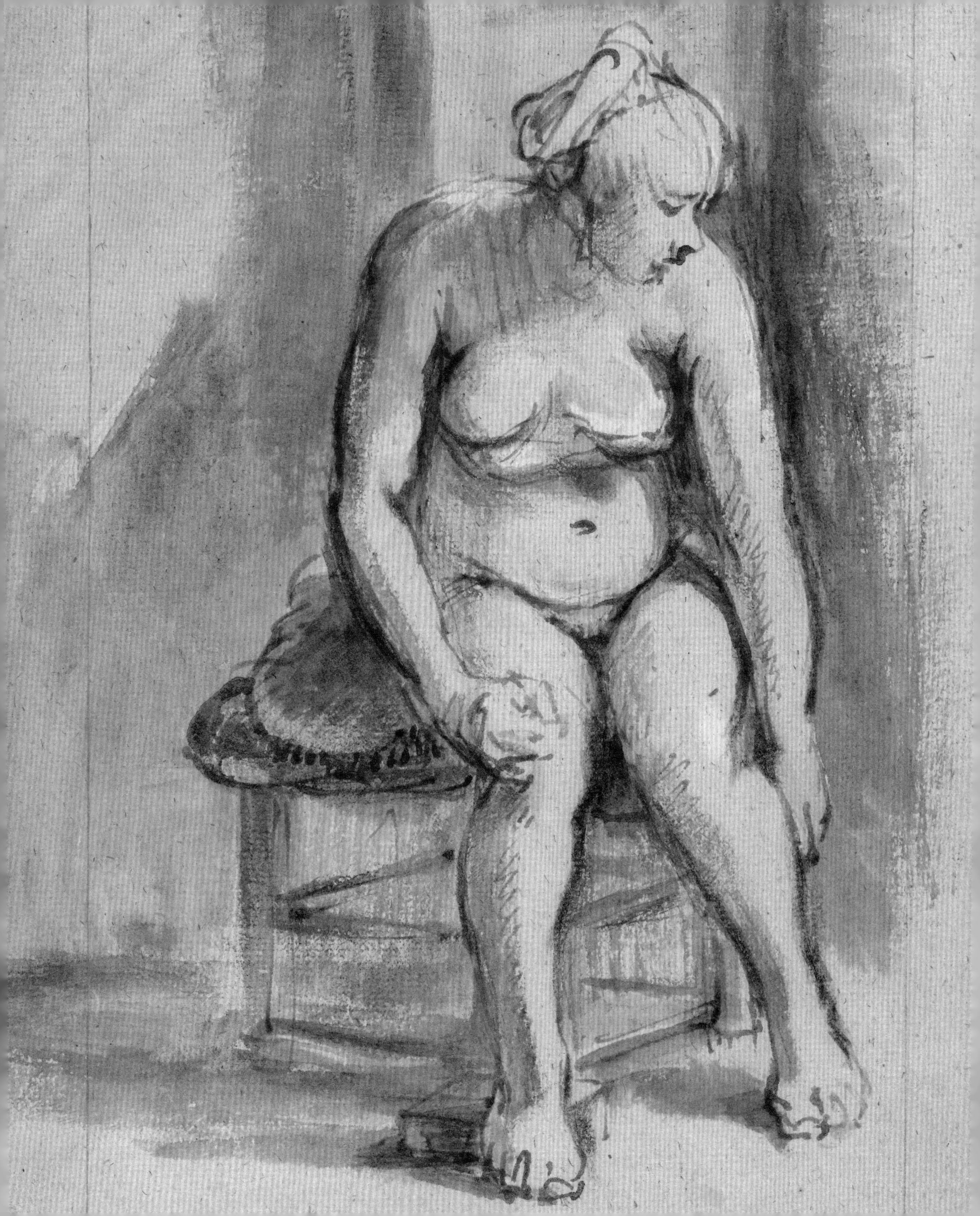

OBSERVATION OF EVERYDAY LIFE

Gregor J. M. Weber

'Naer het leven'

On 1 May 1664 in Amsterdam, Elsje Christiaens was condemned to death. The 18-year-old Danish girl had arrived in Holland only the previous month, looking for work as a maid. Two weeks later she was still unable to pay the rent for her room and a fight with her landlady ensued; the landlady fell down the cellar steps and died. The sentence required that Christiaens be bound to a stake and strangled to death; her head was then struck with the hatchet with which she had attacked her landlady. Her corpse was subsequently taken to the Volewijk gallows field to the north of Amsterdam, where it was bound to a stake with the hatchet hanging above her head as a warning to others. The young Danish woman's fate would undoubtedly have been the talk of the town because this was the first time in 21 years that a woman had been executed in this manner.

Rembrandt, then aged about 58, went by boat to the scene so that he could record the event with his drawing instruments. He drew the agonised body on location; three sketches from different viewpoints have survived (see cats 5 and 6).[1] The draughtsman thus became a reporter, noting the figure tied to the gallows, the slumped body devoid of all life. Rembrandt did not balk at capturing such an unhappy, pathetic creature on paper. Using quill and brush to record the horrific spectacle, he simply reproduced what he saw unflinchingly, without frills and with no regard for preconceptions of beauty or ugliness. For him such a reproduction of an appalling real-life event was part of the artist's task; that he should be drawing the unpleasant as well as the beautiful was for Rembrandt a self-evident artistic concept.

He felt the same need to document current events when Amsterdam's Town Hall burned down on the night of 6–7 July 1652. Two days later he was at the scene, drawing the ruins, including the safety measures taken to prop up the structure (fig. 20). He made a note on the sheet: 'the Town Hall of Amsterdam seen from the Waag [weighing house] / after it had burned down / 9 July / 1652 Rembrandt van Rijn'.

Rembrandt's eye, so alert to the world around him, informed his art from the very beginning and he maintained this interest into old age. The starting point for his pictorial vision remained the real world around him, with all its peculiarities, its randomness and defects, its ordinariness and its anomalies. In the language of the time such observational studies were termed *naer het leven* or *nae 't leven* (from life). This was the term Rembrandt himself used, as can be seen in the inventory of the contents of his house on Jodenbreestraat, made at the time of his bankruptcy in July 1656. In compiling the inventory the representative of Amsterdam's Desolate Boedelkamer, the official organisation responsible for dealing with bankrupts, undoubtedly received help from the artist himself: much of the information reveals such a familiarity with the objects that it can only have come from Rembrandt. A number of artworks were described as *'naer 't leven'*, including, among others, *'een Ossie naer 't leven van Rembrant'* (an ox from life by Rembrandt), *'twee hasewinden nae 't leven vanden selven'* (two greyhounds from life by the same person [Rembrandt]), *'een dito [kunstboeck] vol teeckeninge van Rembrant bestaende in beesten nae 't leven'* (a ditto [artbook] full of drawings by Rembrandt consisting of animals from life), *'een paert nae 't leven vanden selven'* (a horse from life by the same person [Rembrandt]) and *'een vissie nae 't leven'* (a fish from life).

The inventory also included landscapes and townscapes that were *'naer 't leven'*, by Rembrandt and others. A third category lists *tronies* (studies of heads) from life; there is even one described as *'Christus tronie nae 't leven'* (Christ's head from life). A fourth group is specified as

Detail from *Nude Woman seated by a Stove* (cat. 19)

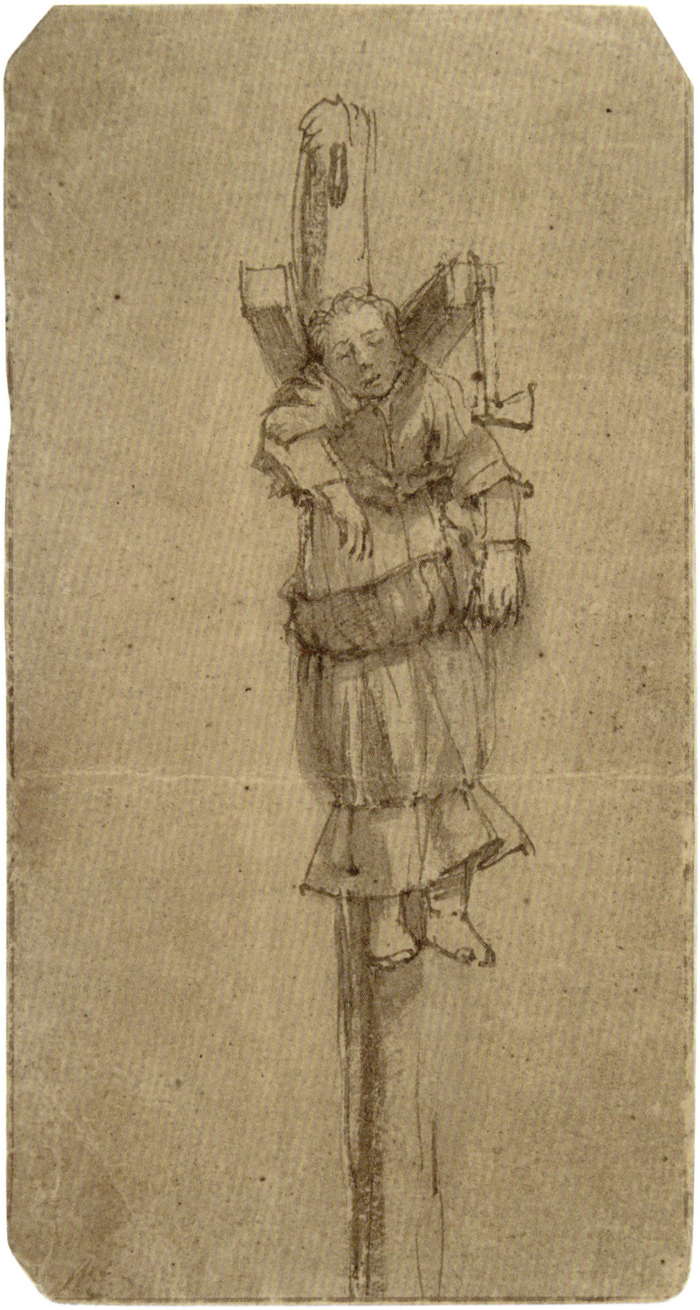

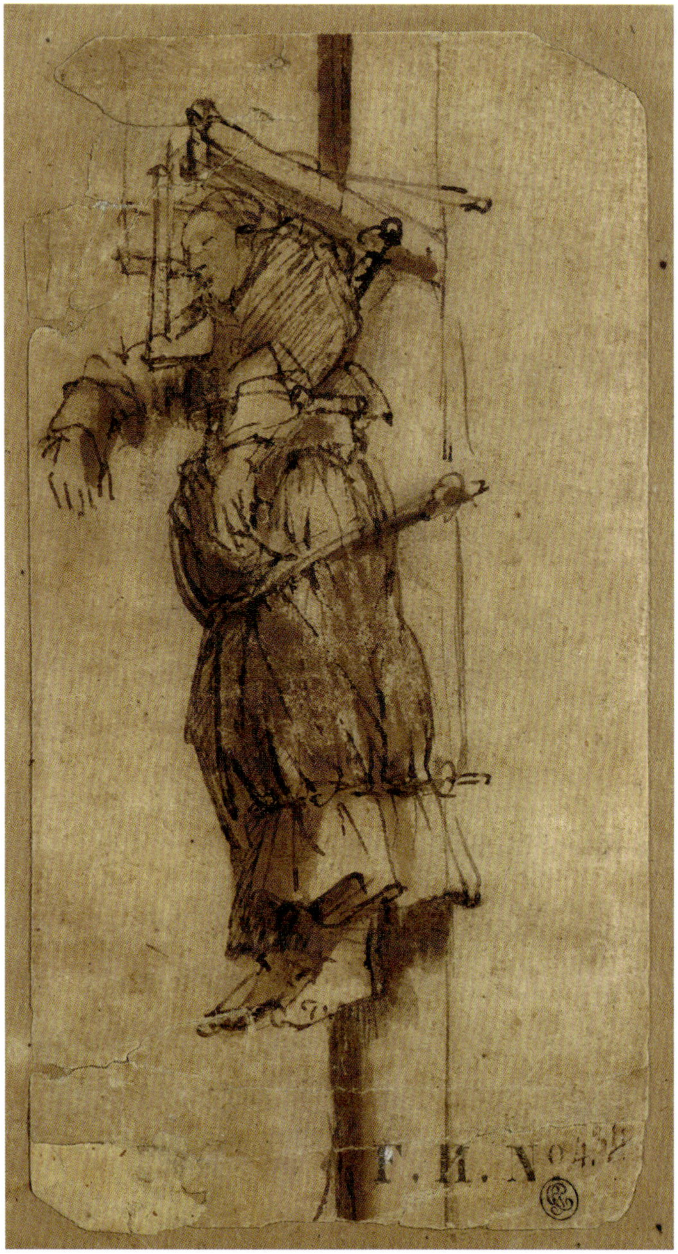

5
Elsje Christiaens hanging on the Gibbet, 1664
Pen and brush and brown ink, 17.2 × 9 cm
The Metropolitan Museum of Art, New York

6
Elsje Christiaens hanging on the Gibbet, in three-quarter Profile, 1664
Pen and brush and brown ink, 15.8 × 8.1 cm
The Metropolitan Museum of Art, New York

being objects *'op 't leven afgegoten'* (cast from life), such as *'een moor'* (a Moor), numerous *'handen en tronies'* (hands and heads), *'17 handen en armen'* (17 hands and arms) and eight items of unspecified *'pleijster werck'* (plaster work), as well as natural objects such as sea snails and other aquatic creatures. A lion and a bull were *'op het leven gebouceert'* (modelled from life) by Rembrandt's own hands, as was a *'naeckt vrouwtie gemodelt nae't leven'* (nude woman modelled from life).[2]

The use of the term *'naer 't leven'* here is entirely in line with the language of the time. *'Leven'* was a general term referring to all natural phenomena, both living and dead. Karel van Mander gave the expression a specific interpretation in his *Schilder-Boeck* of 1604, when he contrasted it with artistic production *'uyt den gheest'* (from the mind or imagination). *'Naer 't leven'* meant pictorial representations based on empirical observation and was embedded in a naturalistic concept of art.[3] 'From life' meant the depiction of real-life objects from direct observation: portraits and studies of heads, landscapes, animals and plants, and even objects whose shape was transmitted directly in the form of a cast, rather than being reproduced in another medium using a pencil or paintbrush. That Rembrandt's inventory included a drawing of Christ's head 'from life' has led to considerable debate. It most likely meant that Rembrandt used a Jewish model from among his neighbours for this study.[4]

Rembrandt's bankruptcy in 1656 forced him to sell a great deal, but of course he continued to draw and was still producing studies of natural objects 'from life' after this date. His drawing of a lion, for example – certainly not a familiar sight in Amsterdam – is dated stylistically to 1660–5 at the earliest (cat. 7).

He dated his painting of a slaughtered ox 1655 (fig. 22), a year before the bankruptcy inventory. It is no longer possible to ascertain whether this work is the one listed in the inventory as *'een Ossie naer 't leven van Rembrant'*, but this impressive painting is in keeping with the idea of recording nature directly, warts and all, entirely in the spirit of *'naer 't leven'*. The partly gutted carcass hangs heavily upside down from a gallows-like contraption, its extremities stretched out. The colour scheme is not dominated by red flesh but rather by the yellow tones of the sinew, skin and fat. Rembrandt has applied the colours thickly so that he is not just painting, but as it were modelling the flesh itself on the surface of the painting. The brushstrokes follow the texture of the variously stretched, clenched, smooth and gristly bones and tendons, flesh and fat. The work gives the effect of Rembrandt having painted the flesh 'from life', as if cast from a real animal, as described for other natural objects in his inventory.[5] The concept of 'from life', from the real world, could hardly be illustrated more starkly. Its size, and the way it is presented, give the painting the feel of a

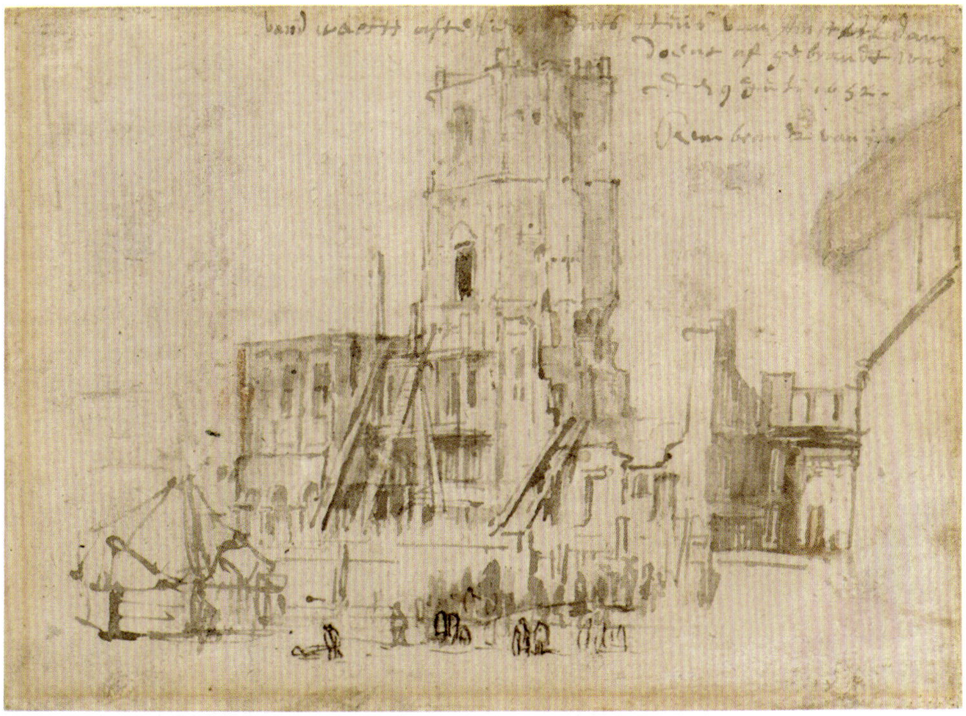

FIG. 20
Amsterdam's Old Town Hall after the Fire, 9 July 1652
Pen and brown ink, some red chalk, 15 × 20.1 cm
Museum Het Rembrandthuis, Amsterdam

portrait, albeit one of a dead and disembowelled animal. Rembrandt emphasises the subject's value as an image by introducing an arched shape at the top: he had used an arch in previous decades for sacred images such as his *Passion* series, *Saint John The Baptist Preaching*, *The Visitation* and *Christ and the Adulteress*, as well as in portraits of identified individuals such as the preacher Cornelis Anslo.

There was already a long tradition of the slaughtered animal as a theme: a century earlier, Pieter Aertsen (1507/8–1575) and Joachim Beuckelaer (active 1560–1574) were painting market and kitchen scenes with similar slaughtered animals, in the case of Beuckelaer as the sole object in the foreground (fig. 21). Rembrandt also owned '*een ossie nae 't leven*' by his teacher Pieter Lastman (1583–1633), a painting now unfortunately lost. The theme was usually incorporated in genre scenes of daily life, with figures in action, such as in the popular almanacs (annual calendars) to illustrate November, the 'month for slaughtering', where they would be accompanied by a text giving a moralistic message, reminding the reader to think of his own mortality and how he would be assessed by God on Judgement Day.[6] But here Rembrandt dispensed with the usual narrative details and presented the suspended carcass in isolation: the pictorial staging elevates a commonplace theme into a bold symbol of life and death.

The landscape drawings form another large group of works in the inventory labelled '*naer 't leven*'. Rembrandt committed many of them to paper during his walks in

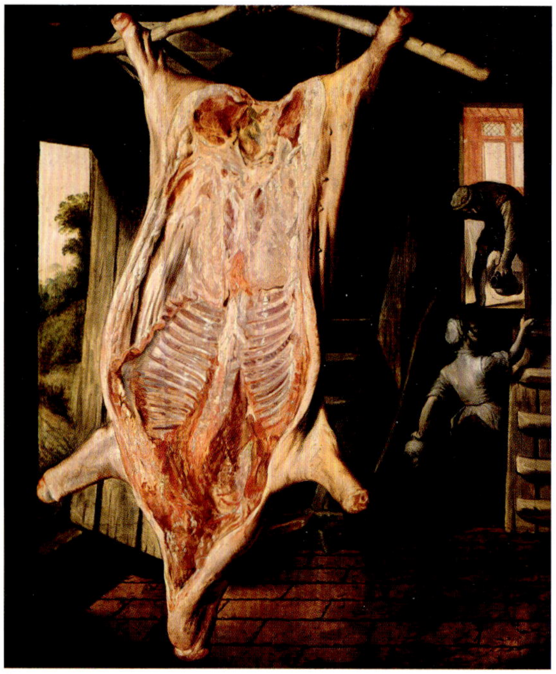

FIG. 21
JOACHIM BEUCKELAER
(active 1560–1574)
The Slaughtered Pig, 1563
Oil on panel, 114 × 83 cm
Wallraf-Richartz-Museum & Fondation Corboud, Cologne

FIG. 22
The Slaughtered Ox, 1655
Oil on panel, 94 × 69 cm
Musée du Louvre, Paris

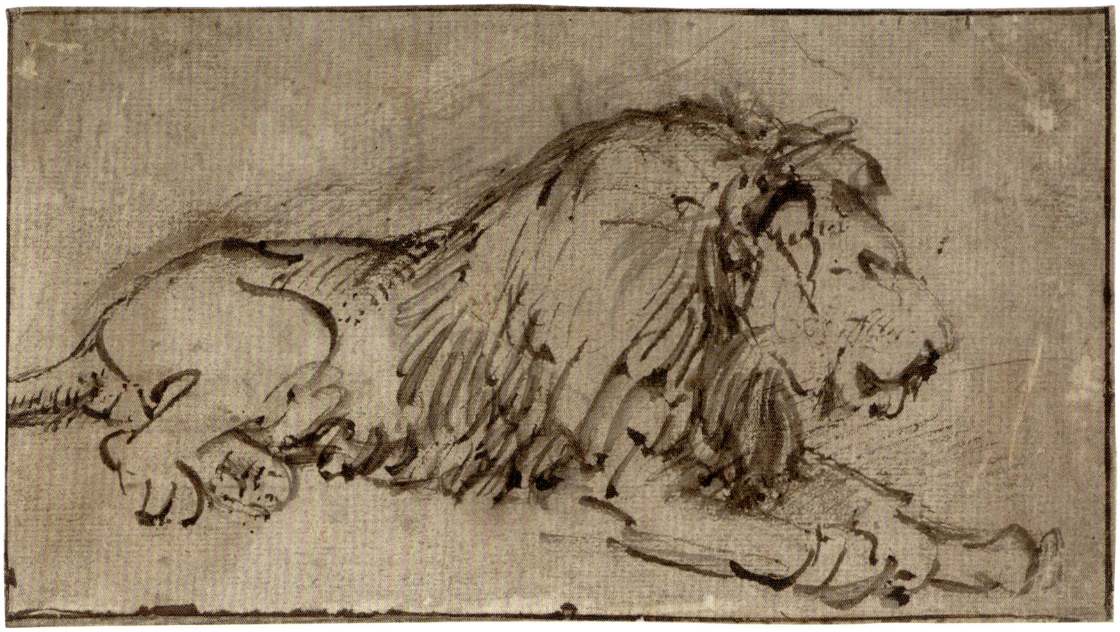

7
Recumbent Lion, facing Right, about 1660–5
Pen and brown ink, 12.2 × 21.2 cm
Rijksmuseum, Amsterdam

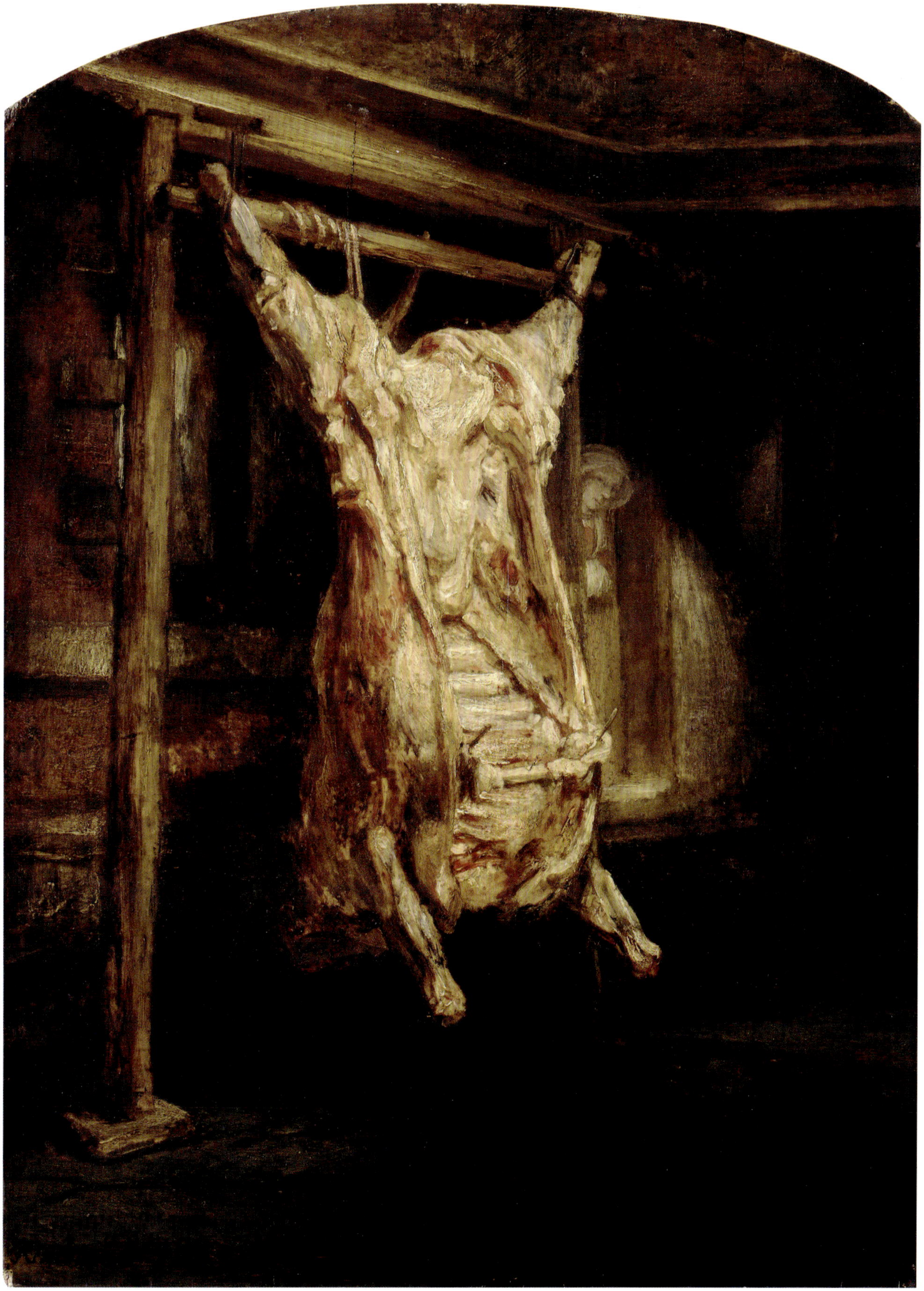

8
The Amstelveenseweg outside Amsterdam, about 1660–2
Pen and brush in brown ink, 13.5 × 20.4 cm
Rijksmuseum, Amsterdam

9
Farmhouse on a River, about 1652 or 1653?
Pen and brown ink, 12 × 22.6 cm
Museum Boijmans Van Beuningen, Rotterdam

the countryside around Amsterdam. Previously a painter primarily of the human figure in portraits and history paintings, he first started to focus on landscapes shortly before 1640. After about twelve years or so he largely lost interest in the theme, but in the meantime had produced a dozen or so paintings (all of which he probably kept for himself), as well as around two hundred drawings and some 32 etchings with landscape themes. Many of his drawings – views of farmhouses, churches, polders and canals – were actually produced in the countryside. A number can be linked precisely to specific locations and viewpoints using old maps.[7] For example, Rembrandt often stopped on the Amstelveenseweg to draw a scene from life. One of his last landscape drawings (cat. 8), dated around 1660–2, was produced on this route, looking towards Amstelveen: the broad road in the centre is separated from the footpath on the right by small stakes. On the far right, close to the tree with the S-shaped trunk, an earthwork slopes upwards. This small dyke is of a type used there up to the end of the nineteenth century, protecting the land on the left from flooding. Here and there, tall wooden entrance gates leading to the farmhouses beyond are lightly sketched on the rough '*kardoespapier*' (cartridge paper) in between the trees on the left and the right. A drawing produced about ten years earlier (cat. 9) shows – based on rather less evidence – a group of peasant houses on the Sloterweg looking towards Amsterdam. Another drawing of the

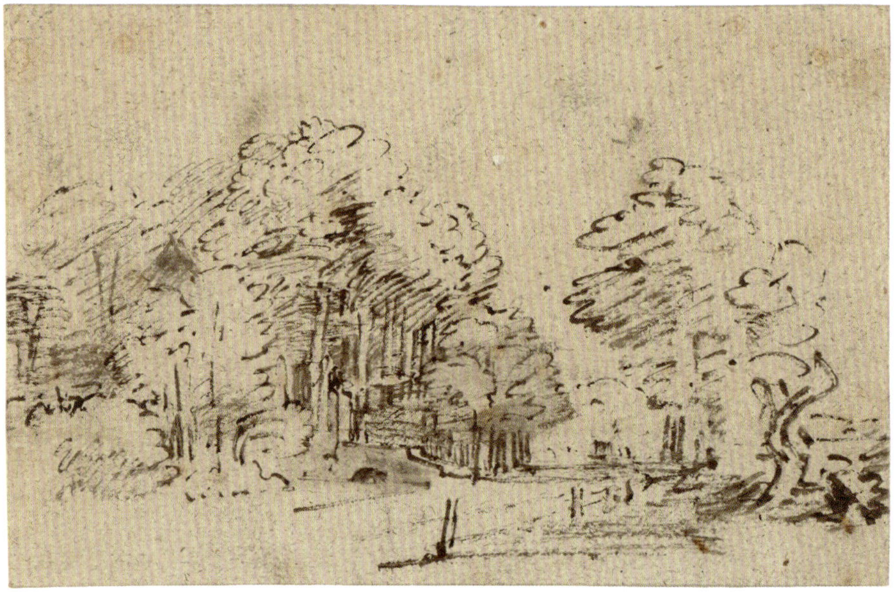

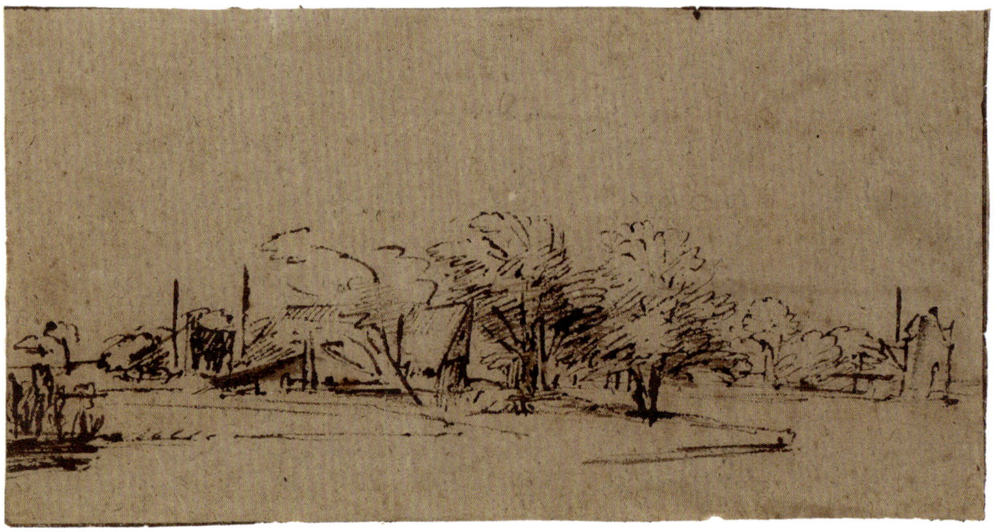

10
Clump of Trees with a Vista, 1652
Drypoint, 15.6 × 21.1 cm
First state of two
Ashmolean Museum, Oxford (WA 1855.425)

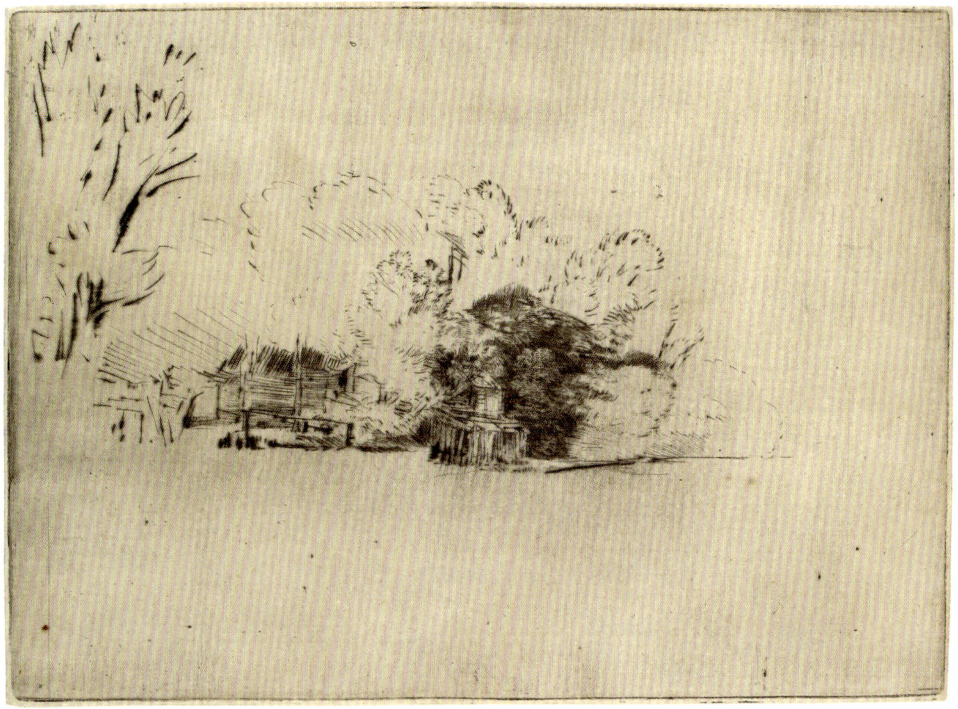

11
Clump of Trees with a Vista, 1652
Drypoint, 12.4 × 21.1 cm
Second state of two
The Fitzwilliam Museum, Cambridge (AD.12.39-388)

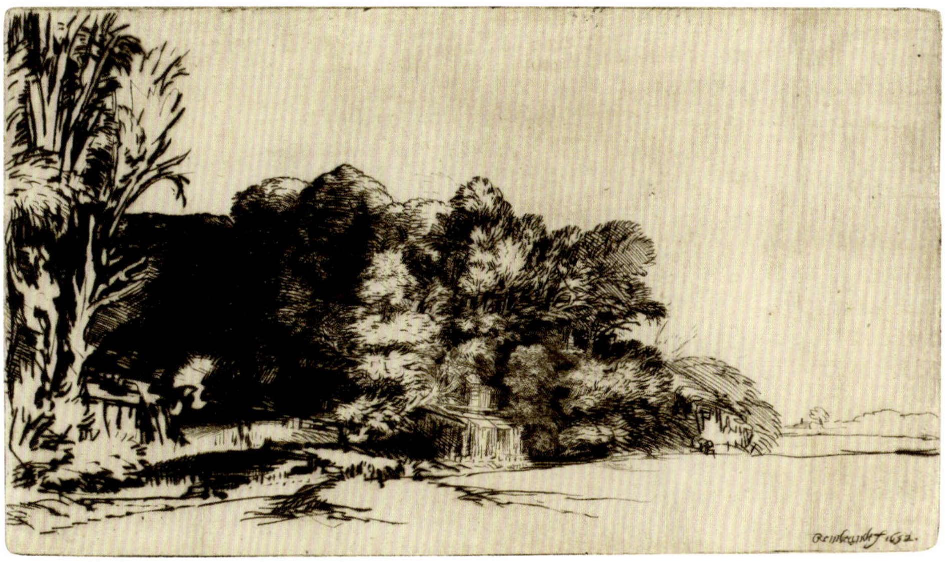

same subject has a viewpoint somewhat closer to the houses.[8] In this way, we are able to witness Rembrandt's rambles with his sketchbook in his hand.

Back at home, these drawings served as a treasure trove of motifs for his prints of landscape scenes. Rembrandt used the technique of drypoint etching for the 1652 sheet *Clump of Trees with a Vista* (cats 10 and 11): he scratched powerful incisions directly on the plate for the lines depicting the tree in the foreground on the left, applying the point more gently for the trees and the distant view on the right. The raised burrs of his most deeply scratched marks give the black of the lines a velvety texture (see p. 153). It has been suggested that Rembrandt produced these drypoint etchings first-hand, on location. However, this is not very likely; in this particular case he printed a first version of the sheet (cat. 10) in his studio before working on it further (including trimming the bottom of the copper etching plate), then adding his signature and date and printing it again (cat. 11).

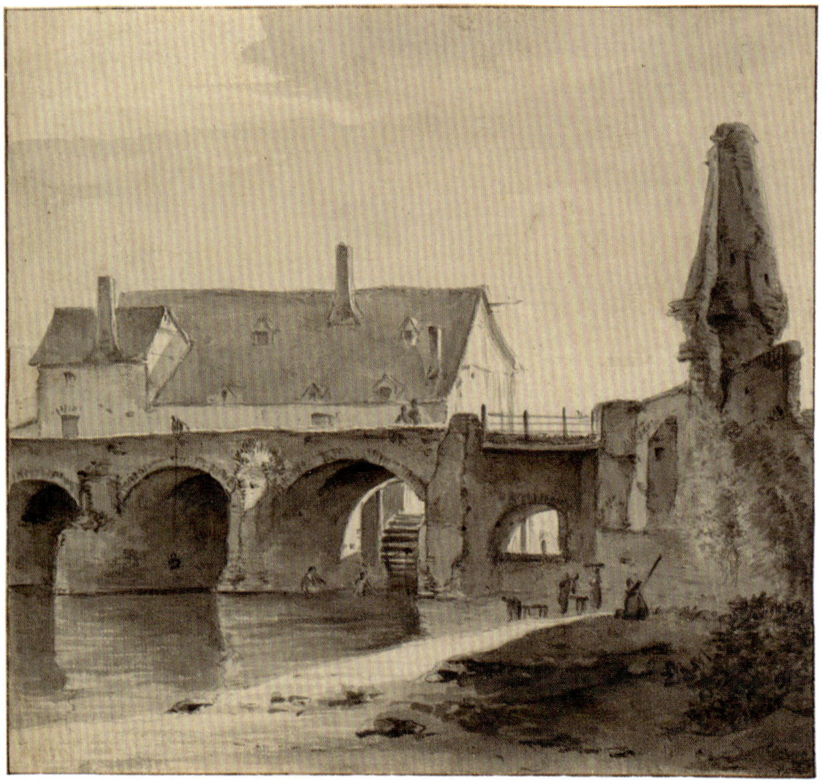

FIG. 23
WILLEM SCHELLINKS
(1627–1678)
The Pont-Neuf in Angers, 1646
Pen and wash on paper,
19.2 × 19.8 cm
Koninklijke Musea voor
Schone Kunsten van Belgie,
Brussels

Inns offered a break on such walks and a place to pass the time. The sketch for *The Ringball Player* (cat. 12), an etching produced the following year, in 1654, may have been created in such a place.[9] Here Rembrandt experimented with a highly unconventional composition: he drew the viewer's attention to a man in the dark foreground relaxing at a table, one leg stretched out along the bench. Beyond a partition, in the bright light, a ringball player is driving the ball with his club, while two more gentlemen can be seen through a gap. Because this etching is not a complete, detailed depiction of either a tavern scene or a ringball alley, the picture appears fragmented and random – like a snapshot *'naer 't leven'*.

'Schilderachtig'

Since it was first used in Karel van Mander's *Schilder-Boeck* of 1604, the term *'schilderachtig'* (picturesque) came into common usage to describe pictures that gave a particularly lifelike reproduction of natural objects.[10] The poet Gerbrand Adriaensz Bredero (1585–1618) was already applying the term in this sense, as if its meaning were obvious, in the foreword to his 1618 book of songs *Geestigh liedt-boexcken* when he explained the concept behind his own poems: '… as a painter, I have followed the picturesque [*schilderachtig*], saying that "the best painters are those who come closest to life"'.[11] Bredero described his didactic purpose in much the same way in the foreword to his play *De Spaansche Brabander* in the same year: 'For I place before your eyes here, nakedly and *schilderachtig*, the abuses of this modern, depraved world.'[12] The term encompassed the real world in its unadorned state, with its visible signs of ugliness, decay, poverty and old age. When the landscape artist Willem Schellinks (1627–1678) travelled through France in 1664, he noted certain bridges as being *'schilderachtig'* in his diary, and described a hermit's cottage on a rock next to a river as 'very *schilderachtig* and pleasing'. He recorded some of these buildings, such as the winding medieval bridge in *Pont-Neuf at Angers* (fig. 23).[13]

12
The Ringball Player, 1654
Etching, 9.5 × 14.3 cm
First state of two
Rijksmuseum, Amsterdam
(RP-P-OB-215)

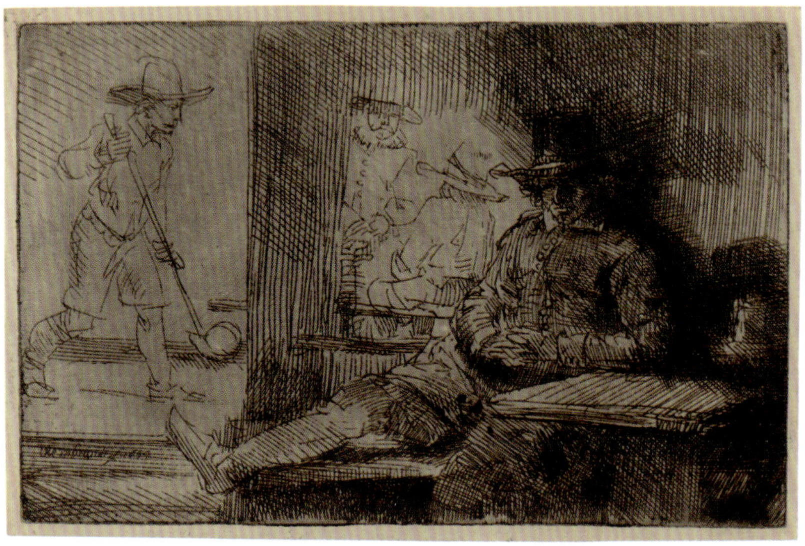

Rembrandt's choice of subjects for his landscapes indicate that he adhered to precisely this definition of '*schilderachtig*' right into old age, not only with regard to his choice of landscapes and buildings, but also, for example, in his portrayals of the aged and the poor, and of unusual and exotic items of clothing. The definition of 'picturesque' ascribed to him by the contemporary man of letters Andries Pels (1631–1681) is well known: 'He scoured the entire city, on bridges and in odd corners, in the New and North markets, for armour, helmets, Japanese daggers, furs and rags which he found *schilderachtig*.'[14] This was intended as a criticism, for by now a new, quite different definition of 'picturesque' had gained prominence. In 1671, two years after Rembrandt's death, Jan de Bisschop (1628–1671) published his illustrations of exemplary antique sculpture in two volumes. In the foreword to the volume *Paradigmata*, he argued that '*schilderachtig*' referred exclusively to that which was '*voor de konst verkieselijck*' (to be preferred in art). In his view, this could only mean subjects that are beautiful, intact and unblemished:

> For it is clearly an error of judgement to believe … that what is more *schilderachtig* … is a malformed, old, wrinkled person rather than a well-formed, fresh and youthful one; a dilapidated or unsuitable building rather than a new one built according to the rules of art; a beggar and peasant rather than a nobleman and a king; a dry, crooked and ill-clothed tree rather than a green one, thick-crowned.[15]

The situation had been turned on its head: no longer was the real world in all its manifestations being termed '*schilderachtig*', specifically including the unusual, the abnormal and indeed the ugly; the definition was now restricted to those things that were by their very nature beautiful. Underlying this was the conviction that beauty alone could remain beautiful in art, whereas ugliness could never become beautiful through art. In 1707 the classically orientated artist and theorist Gerard de Lairesse explained that both beauty and ugliness have power over people, the former delighting and enchanting

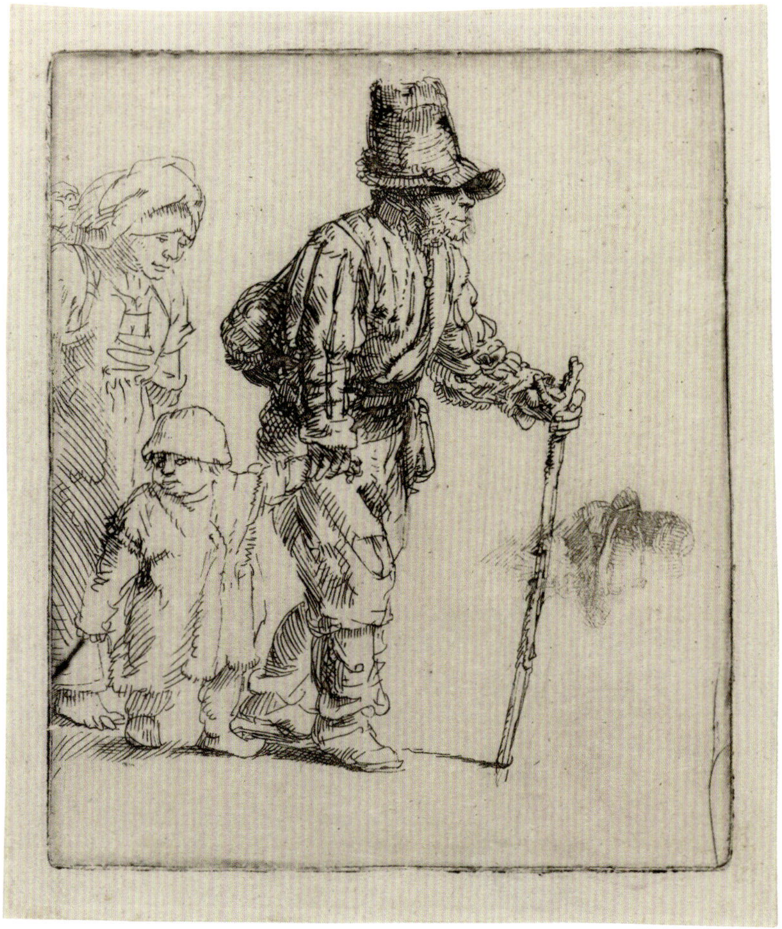

13
Peasant Family on the Tramp, about 1652
Etching, 11.3 × 9.3 cm
First state of three
Rijksmuseum, Amsterdam
(RP-P-OB-220)

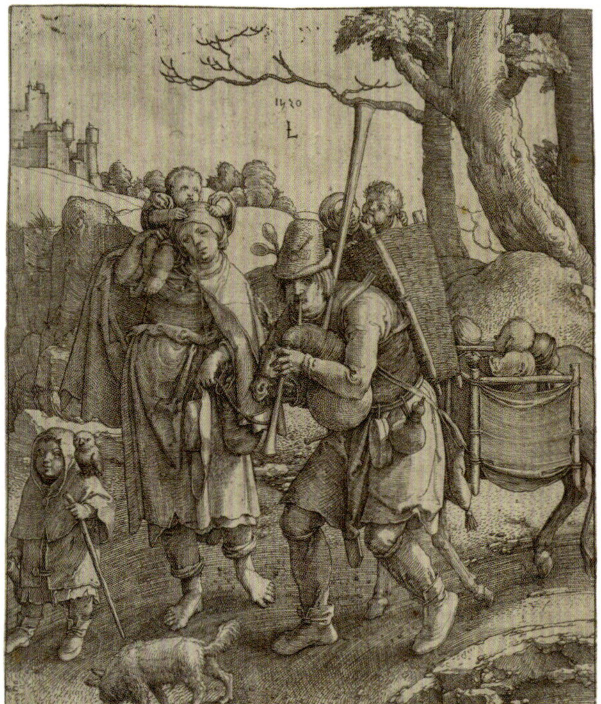

FIG. 24
LUCAS VAN LEYDEN
(died 1533)
The Beggars ('*Owlglass*'), 1520
Etching and engraving, 17.4 × 14.1 cm
Rijksmuseum, Amsterdam

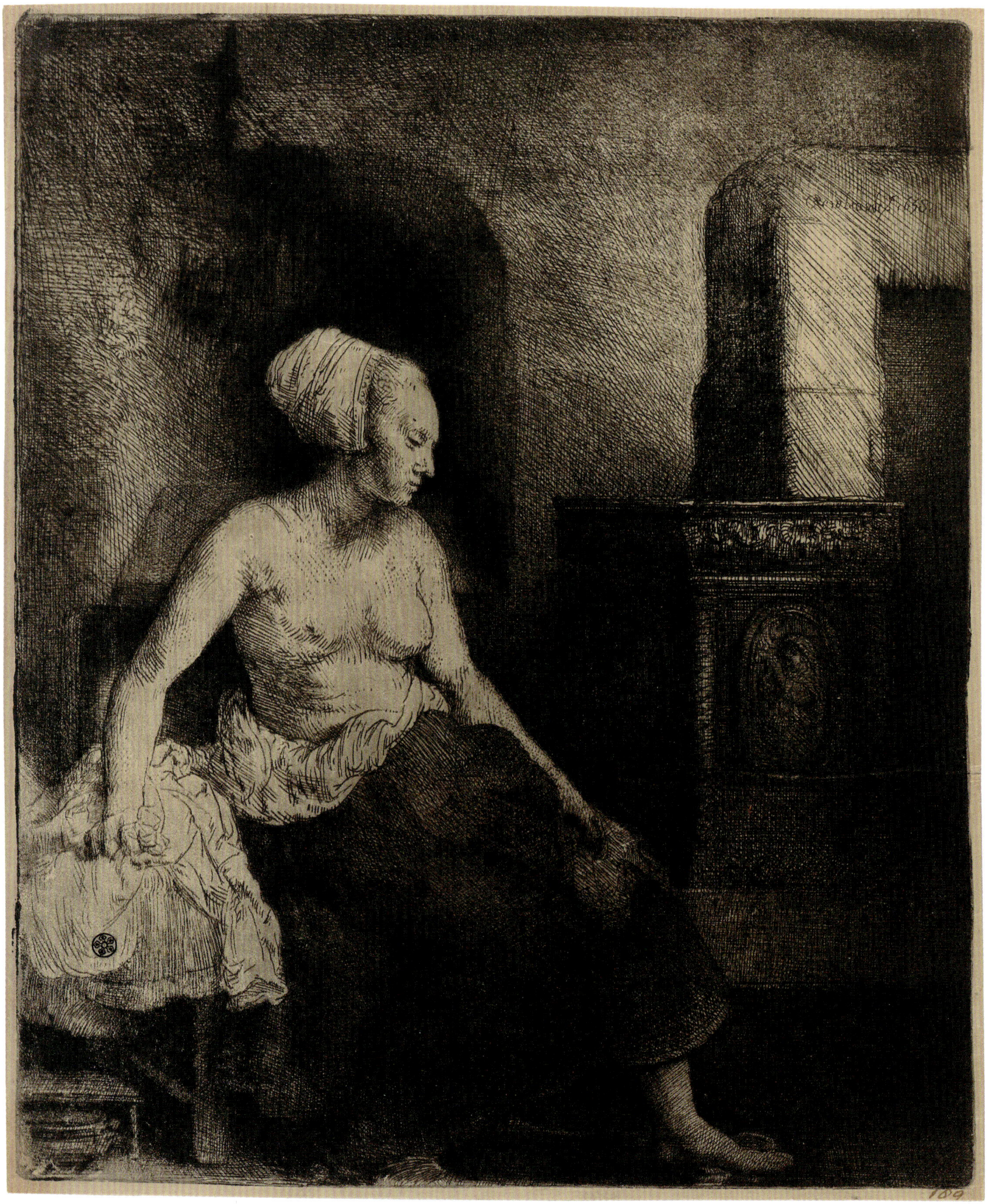

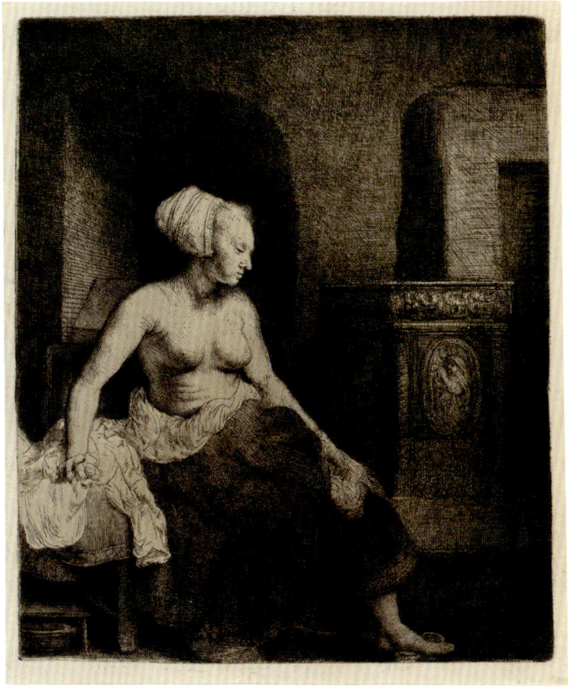

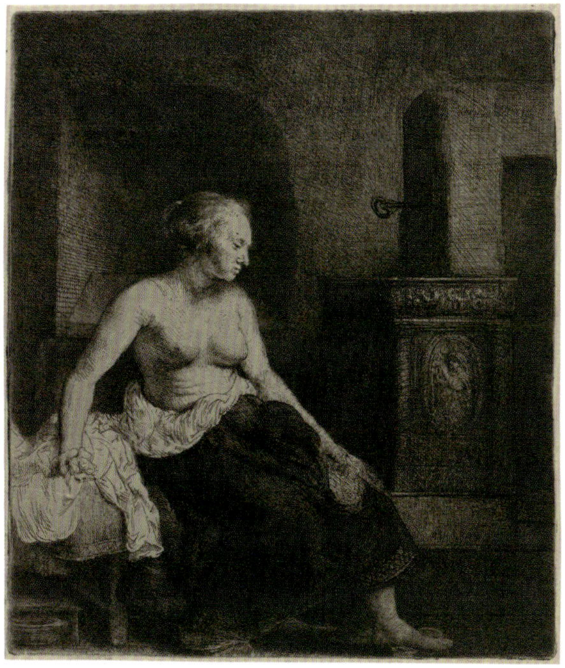

14
Woman sitting half-dressed beside a Stove, 1658
Etching and drypoint,
22.8 × 18.7 cm
First state of seven
Rijksmuseum, Amsterdam
(RP-P-1962-73)

15
Woman sitting half-dressed beside a Stove, 1658
Etching and drypoint,
22.8 × 18.7 cm
Third state of seven
The Fitzwilliam Museum,
Cambridge (AD.12.39-74)

16
Woman sitting half-dressed beside a Stove, 1658
Etching and drypoint,
22.8 × 18.7 cm
Sixth state of seven
Rijksmuseum, Amsterdam
(RP-P-OB-258)

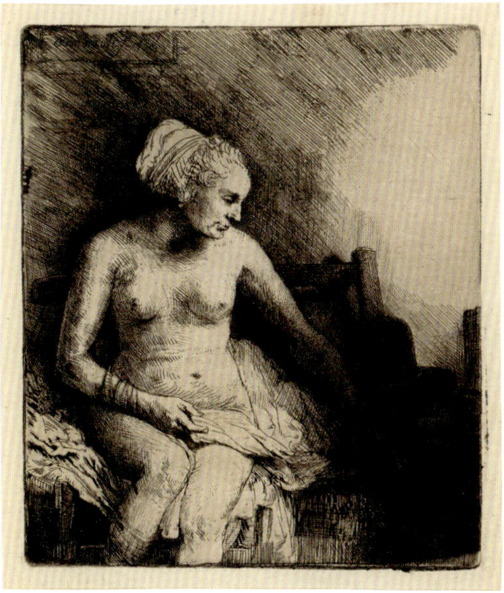

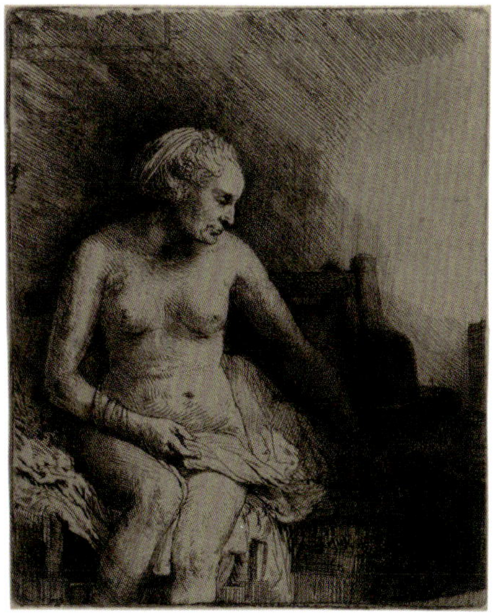

17
Woman at the Bath, with a Hat beside her, 1658
Etching and drypoint,
15.6 × 12.9 cm
First state of two
The Fitzwilliam Museum,
Cambridge (AD.12.39-160)

18
Woman at the Bath, with a Hat beside her, 1658
Etching and drypoint,
15.6 × 12.9 cm
Second state of two
Rijksmuseum, Amsterdam
(RP-P-OB-262)

19
Nude Woman seated by a Stove, about 1661–2
Pen and brush in brown ink with black chalk and white bodycolour, 29.2 × 17.5 cm
Rijksmuseum, Amsterdam

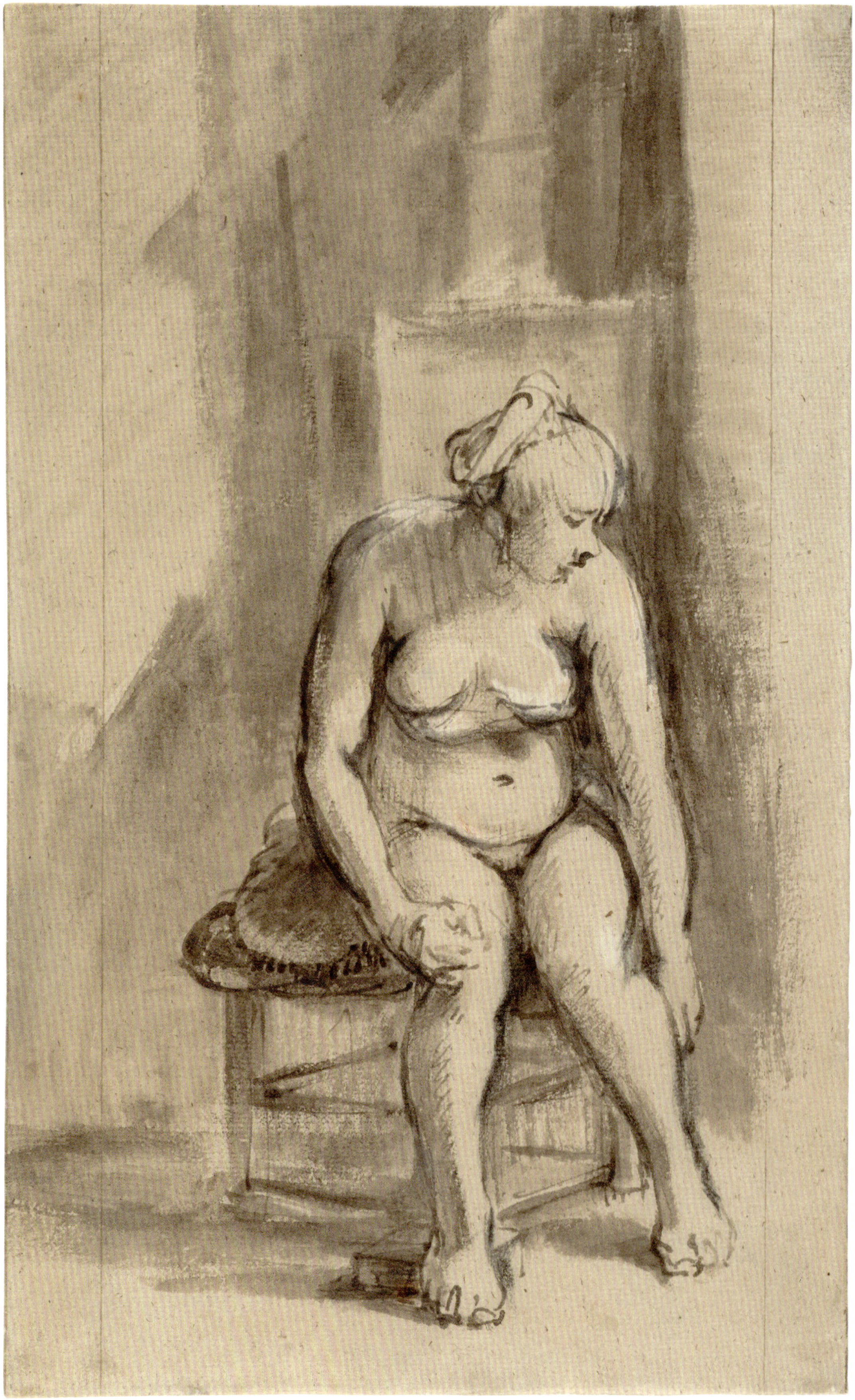

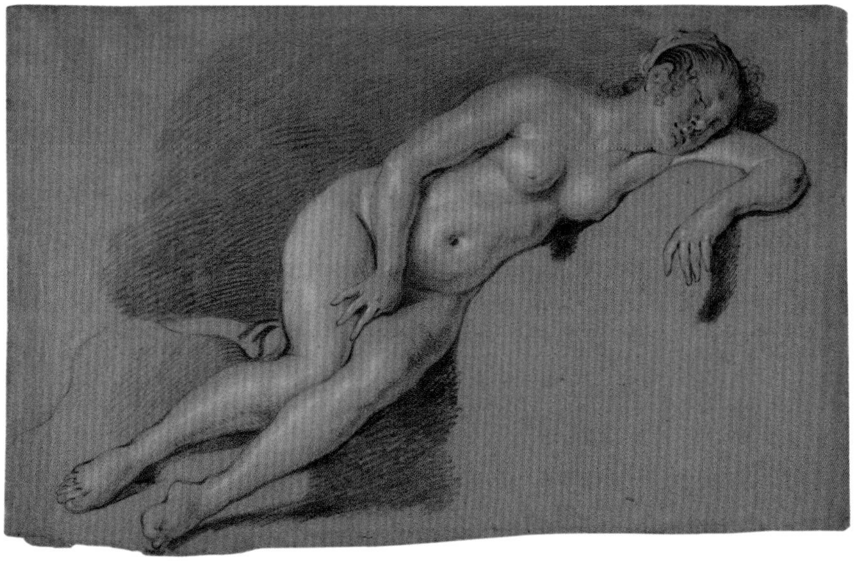

FIG. 25
GOVERT FLINCK
(1615–1660)
Reclining Female Nude,
about 1650
Black chalk, heightened with white, on blue paper,
27.1 × 41.1 cm
The Metropolitan Museum of Art, New York

them and the latter being disgusting and abhorrent to them: 'Therefore it cannot be denied that the picturesque, which is the most beautiful and the most exquisite, means nothing other than that which is worthy of being painted, while that which is worst and ugly is least deserving of this honour.'[16] For him – as for De Bisschop – unworthy and ugly subjects included crooked trees, angular mountains, dilapidated buildings, beggars and cripples.

Rembrandt portrayed precisely such subjects in his landscape compositions and in the many etchings with ragged figures from the 1630s. A later example, his *Peasant Family on the Tramp* of about 1652 (cat. 13), shows a motley group of figures: the man with his slit doublet (a fashion dating from the early sixteenth century) and high hat, pulling by the hand a small boy with a round, thickly padded body, who looks as if he might have come from a Bruegel painting. The peasant woman carries a baby on her back, its little head just visible. We can undoubtedly see evidence of Rembrandt's admiration for the graphic art of Lucas van Leyden (fig. 24) here.[17] De Bisschop's principles would also seem to preclude 'a nude woman with a fat, swollen belly, sagging breasts, wrinkled garters around her legs and many more such deformities'[18] (fig. 95) as a model for a mythical beauty such as Leda or Danaë. Although De Bisschop did not specifically mention his name, it was clear to any reader that Rembrandt's art was meant as the precautionary counterexample.

In fact, Rembrandt and his pupils would practise drawing from life models as a means of studying form and improving their artistic understanding.[19] While other artists would make their models pose in appropriate roles for famous historical or mythological scenes, Rembrandt deliberately made a direct reproduction of the model in front of him. An etching of 1658 shows a woman with a nude upper body sitting unostentatiously in homely surroundings, in front of a stove. This composition must have been particularly important to Rembrandt as he produced the print in a total of seven states (among them cats 14–16). The model's pose (in mirror image) recalls Rembrandt's painting of Bathsheba of 1654 (cat. 112), but this etching is no more than a picture of a model patiently performing her task in the studio. For the sixth state of the print (cat. 16) Rembrandt removed the model's white bonnet, thus integrating her head more fully into the dark background. This does not detract in any way from the feeling of an authentic portrayal of the scene as it actually appeared.

Another etching was produced in 1658, this time with an entirely nude female model (cats 17 and 18). Rembrandt drew her individual features with even more emphasis as she sits, huddled, with her neck stretched forward. A man's hat is on the bench beside her. This picture, too, was clearly drawn 'from life': it is definitely based on Rembrandt's particular concept of the 'picturesque', unfettered by the classical ideal of 'beauty'. He adhered to the same principle in two other etchings of female models, in 1658 (cat. 35) and 1661,[20] at the same time portraying them in poses associated with specific art-historical types. He followed the same principle in his drawings, depicting his subjects without idealising them. One such example is a study of about 1661–2 showing a female model in front of a stove (cat. 19).

It may be no coincidence that Rembrandt produced three etchings of female nudes in 1658, the year in which two of his former pupils, Govert Flinck and Ferdinand Bol, had joined up with three other Amsterdam artists to draw and paint female nude models. They had long since developed a more pleasing, idealising style that was a clear departure from Rembrandt's radical naturalism (fig. 25). From this perspective, Rembrandt's sheets also seem like a deliberate statement speaking out against the younger generation's conception of art.[21]

'Alles uit zig zelf te weten'[22]

The German artist and man of letters Joachim von Sandrart, who lived and worked in Amsterdam in the 1640s, also used the term 'picturesque' to describe Rembrandt's notion of art nearly thirty years later: 'he painted … generally simple things that were easily understood, things that just appealed to him and were *schilderachtig* (as the Dutch say), which were nevertheless full of characteristic motifs sought directly from nature'.[23] This creativity based directly on real-life examples also meant renouncing the artistic rules stipulated by a classical conception of art. In the words of Von Sandrart,

> Thus [Rembrandt] remained true to the practice he had adopted and did not shrink from opposing and disputing our artistic rules, such as those for the anatomy and measurements of human limbs, the rules of perspective and the value of antique statues, Raphael's draughtsmanship and sound training, or the academies that are vital to our profession, professing that you should commit to nature and nature alone, and not to any other rules …[24]

This criticism is representative of a whole series of authors who rebuked Rembrandt for his abandonment of the rules and his independently minded desire to work things out for himself. As Arnold Houbraken put it in 1718, 'He does not feel an obligation to any grounding, guidelines or rules; instead he professes to have found out everything by himself!'[25] Rembrandt acquired the status of an adversary of the rule-driven academic art establishment, becoming an idiosyncratic 'art heretic' and the most prominent counterexample for these art theorists.[26] In addition to all the faults listed by Von Sandrart, Houbraken mentioned one more:

> Rembrandt did not want to conform to anyone else's rules, even less to follow the famous examples of those who had attained eternal renown by selecting beautiful subjects; instead he was content to imitate life as it appeared before him without making any kind of selection at all.[27]

In the opinion of Houbraken and others, Rembrandt's fault lay in his unwillingness or inability to select and portray the most beautiful elements in nature, a notion of beauty that could be acquired through the study of classical models, for example, as described by De Bisschop and Lairesse. The Greek artist Zeuxis (active in the late fifth century BC) was frequently cited as proof of the importance of selecting the most beautiful elements when creating a work of art. According to legend, Zeuxis was given the task of painting a picture of Helen of Troy, the exceptionally beautiful woman who had sparked off the Trojan War. He chose the five most beautiful women in Croton as models and then selected the most perfect part of each woman's body, which he combined to create his ideal image of Helen (fig. 26). However, in 1604 Karel van Mander had related a very different anecdote about this same Zeuxis, based on the classical source Marcus Verrius Flaccus, in which Zeuxis

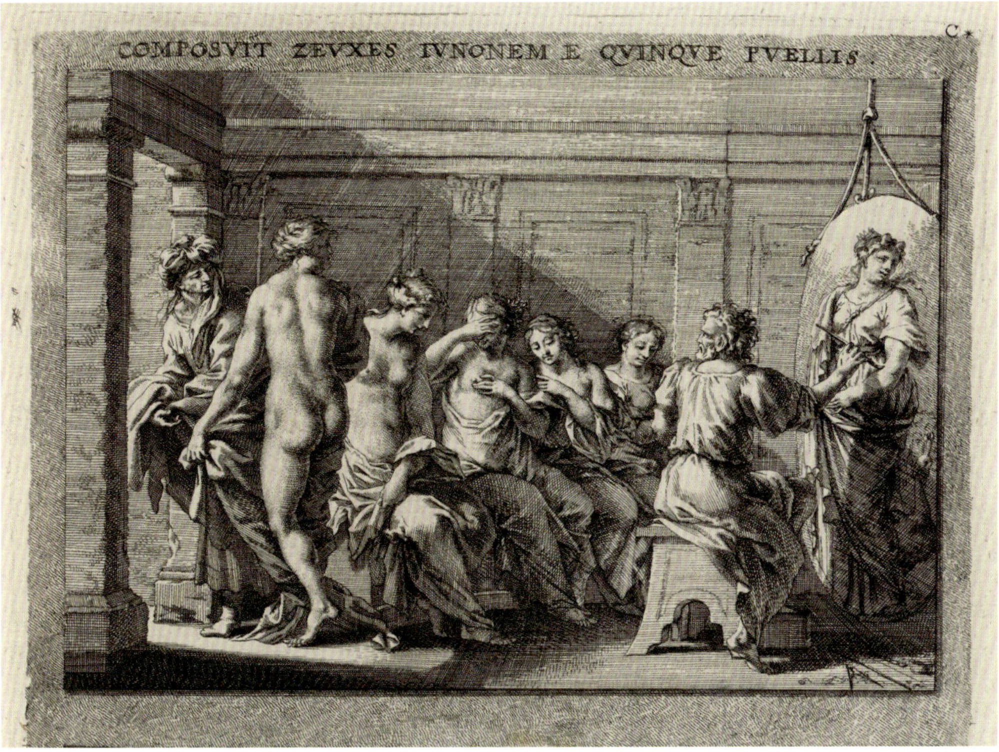

FIG. 26
JOHANN J. VON SANDRART (1655–1698)
after JOACHIM VON SANDRART (1606–1688)
Zeuxis Painting Helen of Troy, based on the Women of Croton, 1683
From J. von Sandrart, *Teutsche Academie … Academia Nobilissimae Artis Pictoriae*, 1683, plate C*, 1 (opposite p. 50)
Engraving, 13.5 × 19.1 cm

> was supposed to have died from excessive laughing, to such an extent that he choked, when he was painting a wrinkled, comical old woman from life … Hereupon a poet composed this verse: 'Why are you laughing so excessively? Or are you intent on imitating the artist who died of laughter?'[28]

So did Zeuxis, the prime example of an idealising conception of art, also paint an amusing and imperfect old woman?

Rembrandt evidently appreciated this interpretation of the classical reference, as he painted a self portrait in the role of Zeuxis. He turns towards the viewer with a laugh, mouth slightly open, eyes twinkling and eyebrows raised (cat. 20).[29] He is standing in front of a portrait of a person with a prominent chin and hook nose, decked out in gold jewellery. Unfortunately the edges of the painting were later defaced, but an auction catalogue of 1758 still described the scene as *Rembrandt Painting an Old Woman*. In addition, his pupil Arent de Gelder painted his own self portrait in the same role (fig. 27) – no doubt aware of Rembrandt's example.[30] In his version the narrative is complete with the laughing artist himself, his painting and the sitter for the portrait, the old woman. De Gelder even depicted her holding an orange in her hand, perhaps a reference to the judgement of Paris. According to this classical myth, Paris gave Aphrodite the golden apple to indicate that he chose her above Hera and Athena as the fairest goddess of them all; in return Aphrodite promised Paris the most beautiful mortal woman, Helen of Troy.

It is not known whether the ageing Rembrandt wanted his self portrait as Zeuxis to be understood as an argument against the criticisms from the camp of the classicists. His painting probably dates from 1662, before the texts by Jan de Bisschop, Joachim von Sandrart, Gerard de Lairesse and Arnold Houbraken appeared in print. However, Rembrandt would certainly have noticed that he was missing out on many prestigious commissions, such as the painting of the Oranjezaal in the Huis ten Bosch or the large-scale paintings for the new Amsterdam Town Hall. His former colleagues and pupils such as Jan Lievens, Govert Flinck and Ferdinand Bol were being given commissions for the Town Hall and it was only when Flinck unexpectedly died in February 1660 that Rembrandt was assigned one of his own (see cats 71–2). For reasons that are still unknown, this work, *The Conspiracy of the Batavians under Claudius Civilis*, Rembrandt's largest painting, was taken down from its place in the Town Hall before September 1662. We know from a document dated 28 August 1662 that he had not received any remuneration at that time but there may have been a '*verschildering*' (reworking) planned.[31] We do

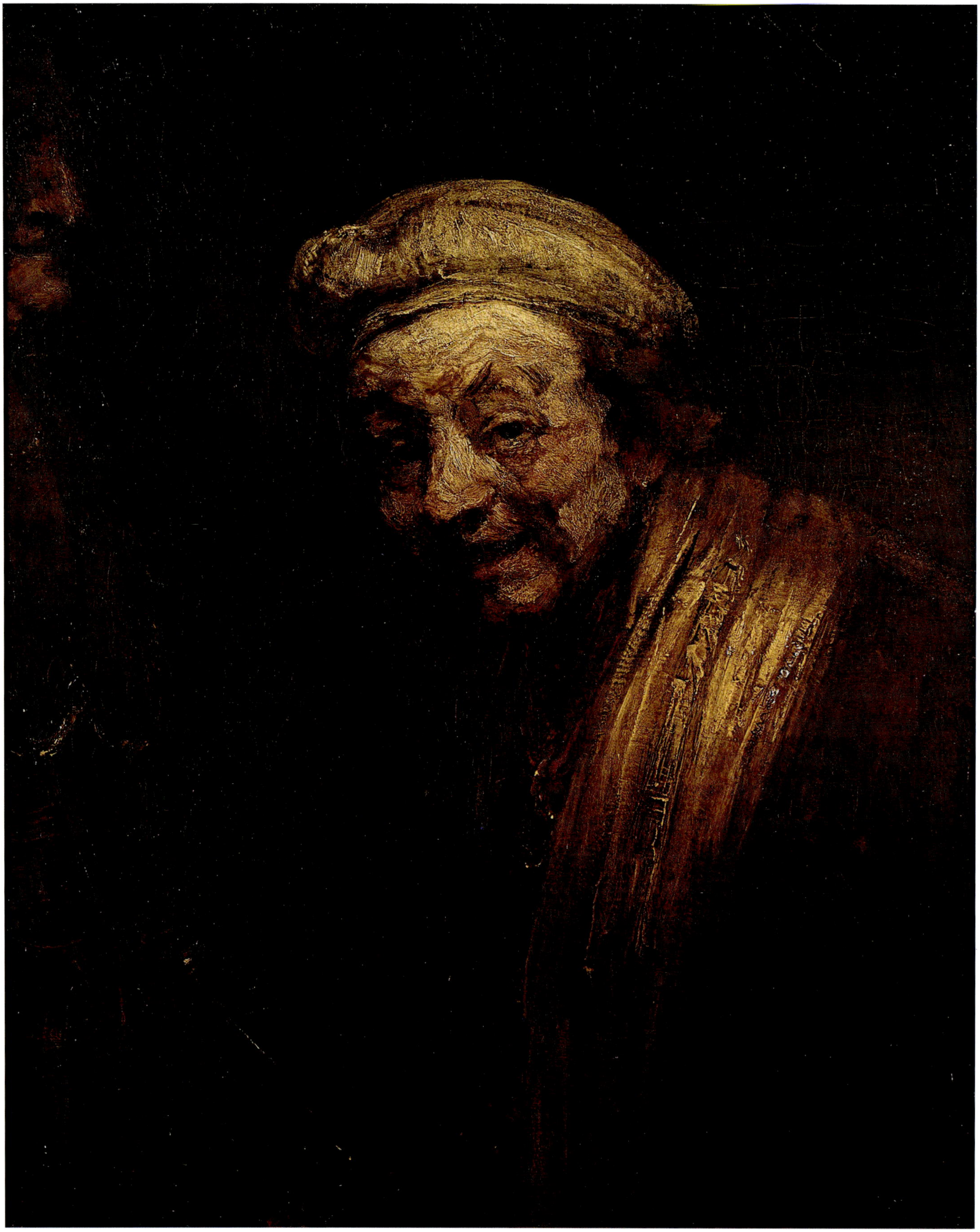

20
Self Portrait as Zeuxis,
about 1662
Oil on canvas, 82.5 × 65 cm
Wallraf-Richartz-Museum &
Fondation Corboud, Cologne

not know whether this was at Rembrandt's request or (more plausibly) because of criticism from the mayors of Amsterdam who had commissioned the work. However, considering the picture itself, a more convincing reason could be the changed views on what style was appropriate in such a location. Rembrandt's rough, gnomish Batavians are not portrayed in even a remotely classical style (as they are in the paintings by his colleagues), but instead as extremely '*schilderachtig*'. The one-eyed Claudius Civilis clearly shows his entire face, including his blind eye (instead of hiding it by having his head turned): this picture was true to the concept of '*naer 't leven*'. Rembrandt's principle of always giving an unadulterated portrayal of nature may therefore have led to the rejection of the picture. In this context, his self portrait as Zeuxis could have been a deliberate statement of his opinion that an artist could still be 'classical' with an ugly physiognomy and an unheroic laugh.

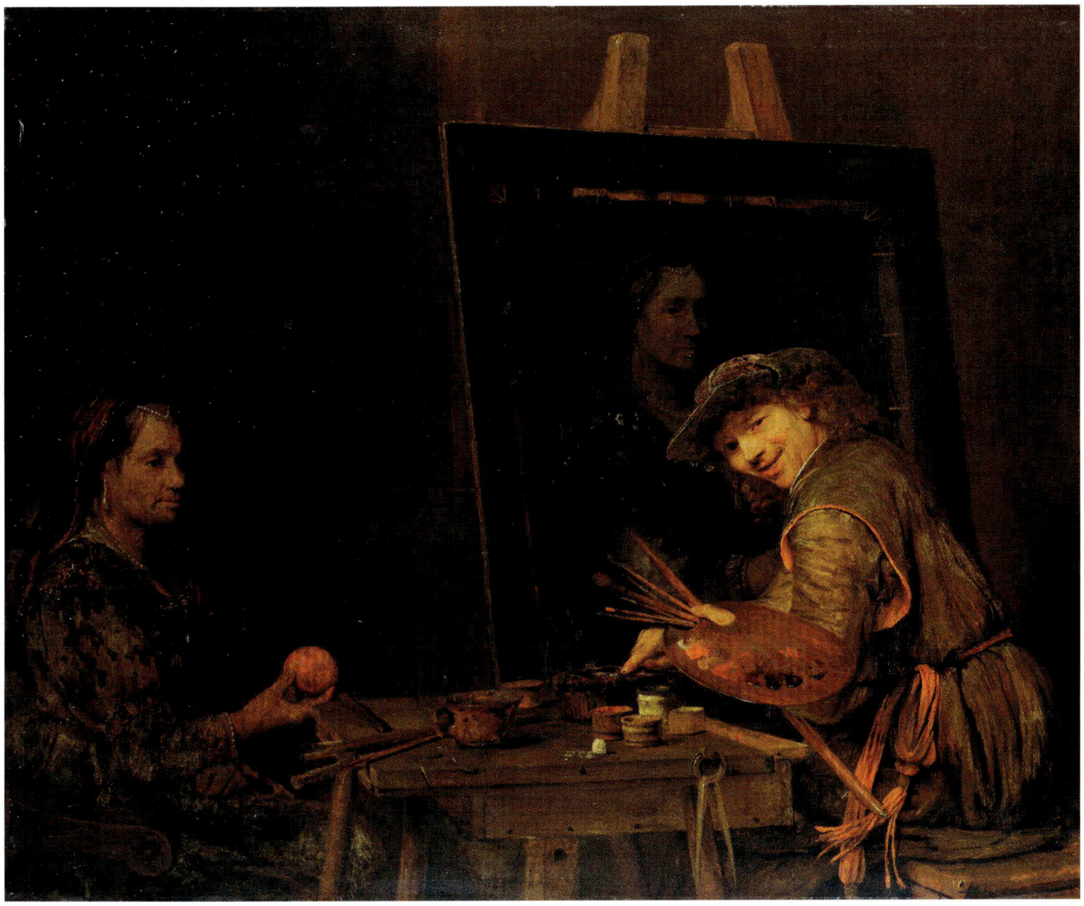

FIG. 27
ARENT DE GELDER
(1645–1727)
Self Portrait as Zeuxis, 1685
Oil on canvas, 142 × 169 cm
Städelsches Kunstinstitut,
Frankfurt am Main

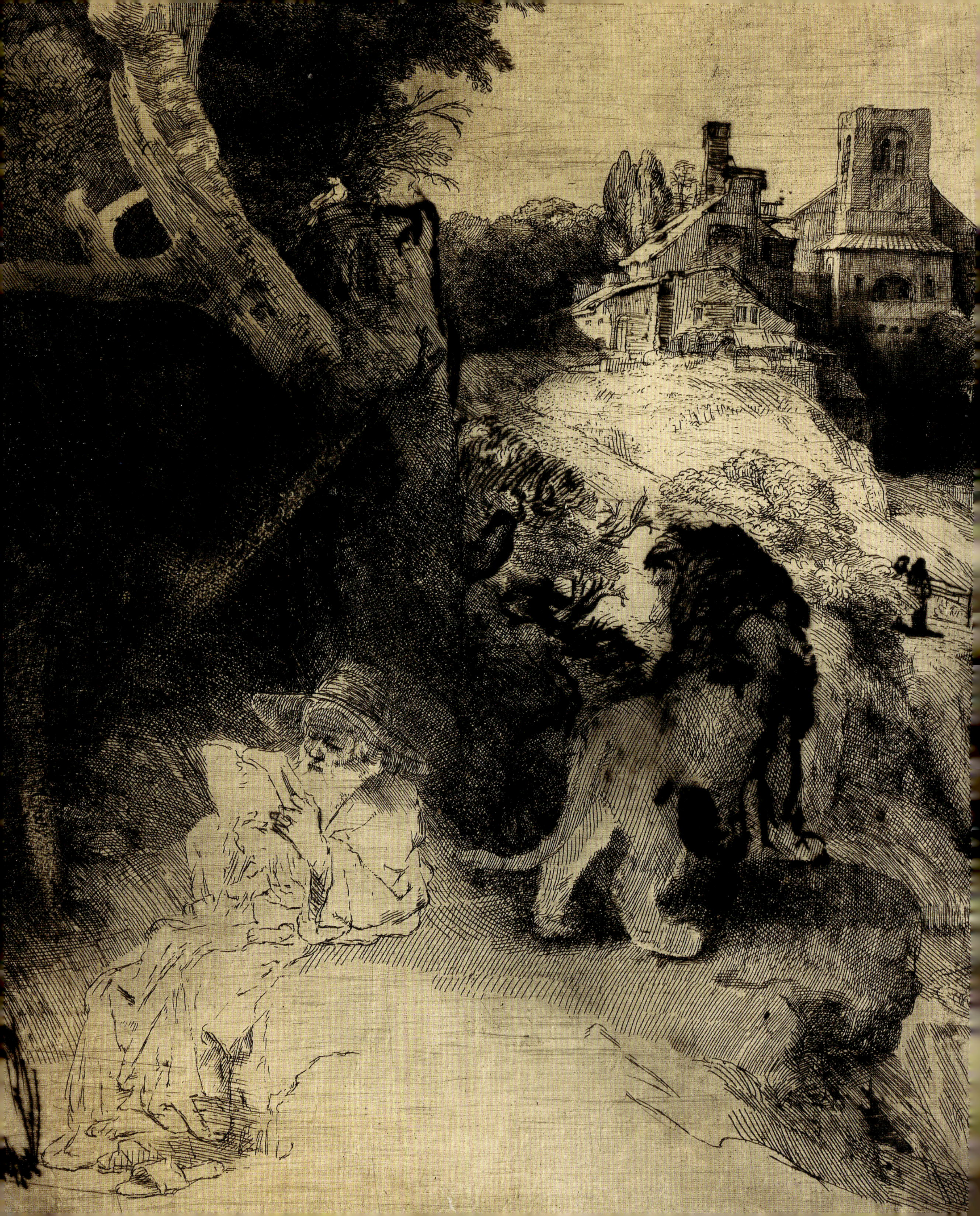

EMULATION

Jonathan Bikker

ROGER DE PILES'S claims about Rembrandt's working methods published in 1699 can be added to the litany of accusations explored in the previous chapter that the artist only followed nature and did so unselectively: 'we must not think to find Correctness of Design, nor a Gusto of the Antique in his Works. He us'd to say, he aim'd at nothing more than to imitate Living Nature, making that Nature consist only in things Created, such as they appear'. The French author's criticism differed on one point from that launched by, among others, Joachim von Sandrart and Arnold Houbraken, however, as unlike them he mentions Rembrandt's great passion for collecting in this context: 'tho' he pretended to despise Antiquity, and to form to himself a new Manner, he was very curious in getting the fine Designs, that came out of Italy, and had a great Collection of them; as also of Italian Prints'.[1] The only problem was that 'he made little or no use of them'.[2] The image of Rembrandt as 'the first heretic of painting', who flouted the rules of art by refusing to follow the example set by his illustrious predecessors, had a long life that eventually shed its negative connotations to become regarded as a defining aspect of the artist's defiant individualism; when, at the beginning of the nineteenth century, Rembrandt's use of the work of other artists as models was first published, loud protests were launched by those who viewed the discovery of these borrowings as malicious attacks on the Dutch genius's originality.[3] Nowadays, of course, it is a well-known and accepted fact that Rembrandt adopted and reworked motifs and compositions from other artists. Indeed, the number of formal sources scholars had discovered for Rembrandt's drawings, prints and paintings grew to such proportions that by 1977 it took a 142-page book just to list them all.[4] Not only is the number of these sources staggering, their diversity is impressive, even when the more dubious proposals are not considered. This holds true for Rembrandt's late period as much as for earlier moments in his career. De Piles probably would have been shocked if he had known how varied Rembrandt's sources actually were in his later years.

Given the often-discussed similarities between Rembrandt's late painting technique and that used by Titian in his final years, it comes as no surprise that the Dutch artist also made use of the Venetian's compositions. The best-known Titian prototypes informing Rembrandt's oeuvre are the *Portrait of a Man with a Quilted Sleeve* from around 1512,[5] which in the seventeenth century was mistakenly assumed to represent the Renaissance poet Lodovico Ariosto (1474–1533), and the *Flora* of about 1515–20 now in the Uffizi (fig. 28). Both works were in the collection of the diplomat Alfonso López (1582–1649) in Amsterdam in the 1630s, and their initial impact on the Dutch artist also dates to that period: the 'Ariosto' was a source for a 1639 self-portrait etching and the 1640 painted *Self Portrait at the Age of 34* in the National Gallery, London (fig. 14), while by 1635 the *Flora* had already served this function for Rembrandt's painting of the same theme, also in London.[6] A 1641 *Flora* by Rembrandt is also indebted to Titian's example, but the version of the theme by the Dutch artist that comes closest to this Venetian model is a painting in New York (fig. 29) from around 1654. The latter picture is the only one to show the figure wearing the white chemise with voluminous sleeves of Titian's *Flora*, and the profile view as well as the positioning of the hands, especially the extended right one holding flowers, are also quite similar. By the time the New York version was made, Titian's *Flora* had not been on view in Amsterdam for some 13 years, as López moved with his collection to

Detail from *Saint Jerome reading in an Italianate Landscape* (cat. 23)

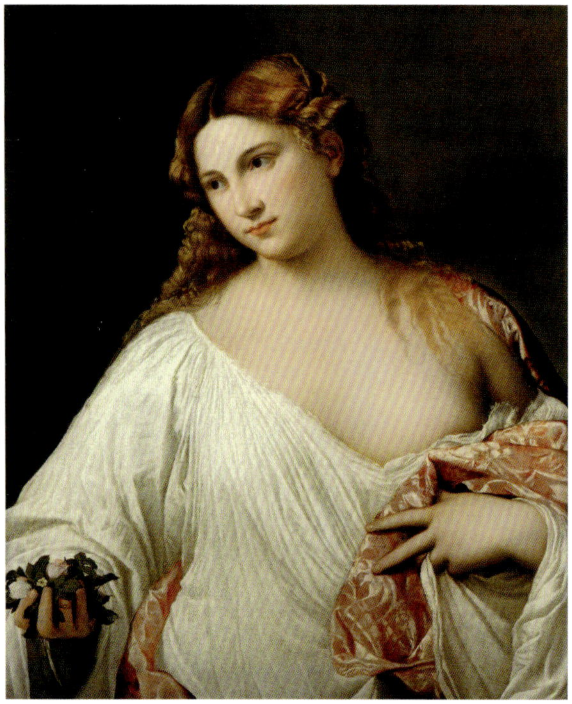

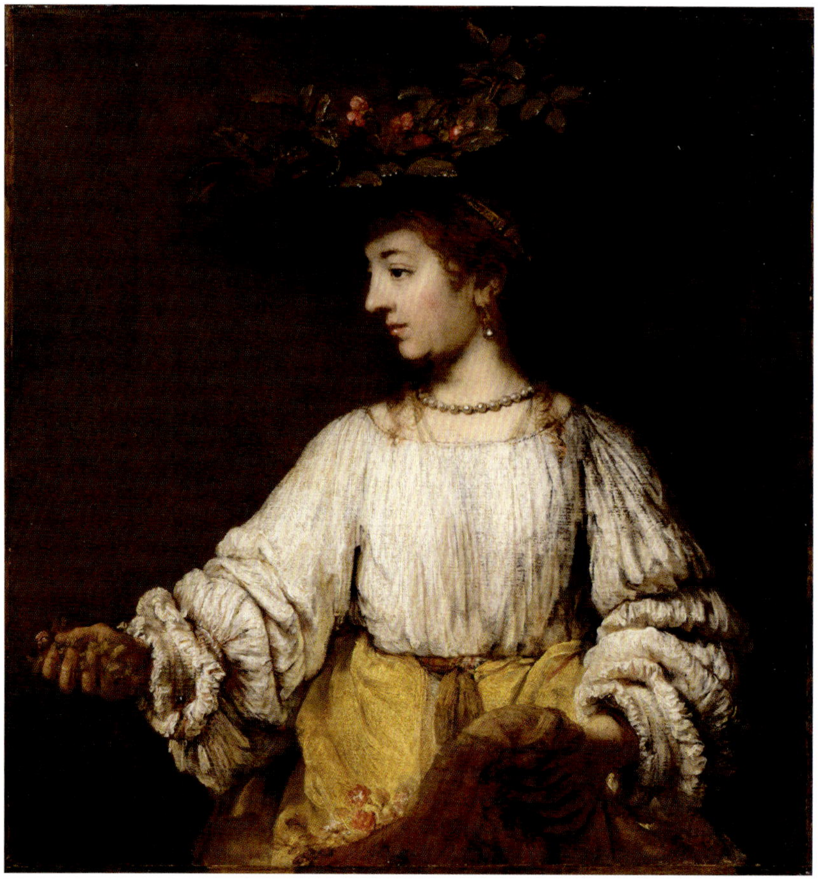

FIG. 28
TITIAN (died 1576)
Flora, about 1515–20
Oil on canvas, 79.7 × 63.5 cm
Galleria degli Uffizi, Florence

FIG. 29
Flora, about 1654
Oil on canvas, 100 × 91.8 cm
The Metropolitan Museum of Art, New York.
Gift of Archer M. Huntington, in memory of his father, Collis Potter Huntington, 1926

Paris in 1641. Rembrandt may have relied on the print Joachim von Sandrart made after Titian's painting around 1640, which, however, shows a mirror image of the composition, or perhaps a no longer extant sketch by his own hand.

Such a drawing (fig. 30) has survived of another painting owned by López, Raphael's *Portrait of Baldassare Castiglione*, which the diplomat purchased at the sale of Lucas van Uffelen's collection in Amsterdam on 9 April 1639. Apparently Rembrandt made his quick pen sketch in the sale room, as the price fetched by the painting as well as the total amount generated by the auction is recorded on the sheet itself. Like the *Flora* by Titian, Raphael's composition was put to immediate use but continued to have reverberations in Rembrandt's oeuvre long after the painting itself was no longer present in Amsterdam. The *Portrait of Baldassare Castiglione* was also one of the Dutch artist's models for the above-mentioned 1639 etched self portrait, as well as the painted one of 1640 now in London.[7] Twenty years after Raphael's painting appeared in the Van Uffelen sale, and after Rembrandt was first inspired by it, he turned to it again for his 1659 *Self Portrait* in Washington (cat. 2).[8] He must have derived the profile view of his body from his own sketch, where it is more pronounced than in the original, but the folded hands were possibly remembered from Raphael's painting as Rembrandt's drawing hardly indicates them and he did not incorporate this element into his 1639 and 1640 self portraits. The Castiglione pose was employed once again in Rembrandt's 1669 *Self Portrait* in London (cat. 3), but this time the figure is reversed so that the artist turns to the right, which is Rembrandt's usual orientation in his self portraits.[9] While the X-radiograph of the London *Self Portrait* indicates that Rembrandt began with a different pose, the X-radiograph and autoradiographs[10] for Rembrandt's *Man with a Magnifying Glass* (The Metropolitan Museum of Art, New York) from the beginning of the 1660s suggest the reverse.[11] In the latter case he first planned to use the pose of the Raphael portrait, but moved away from it in the final version of his painting. After his re-use of it in 1659, the pose had become such an integral part of Rembrandt's own artistic vocabulary that making reference to his drawn copy would have been unnecessary.

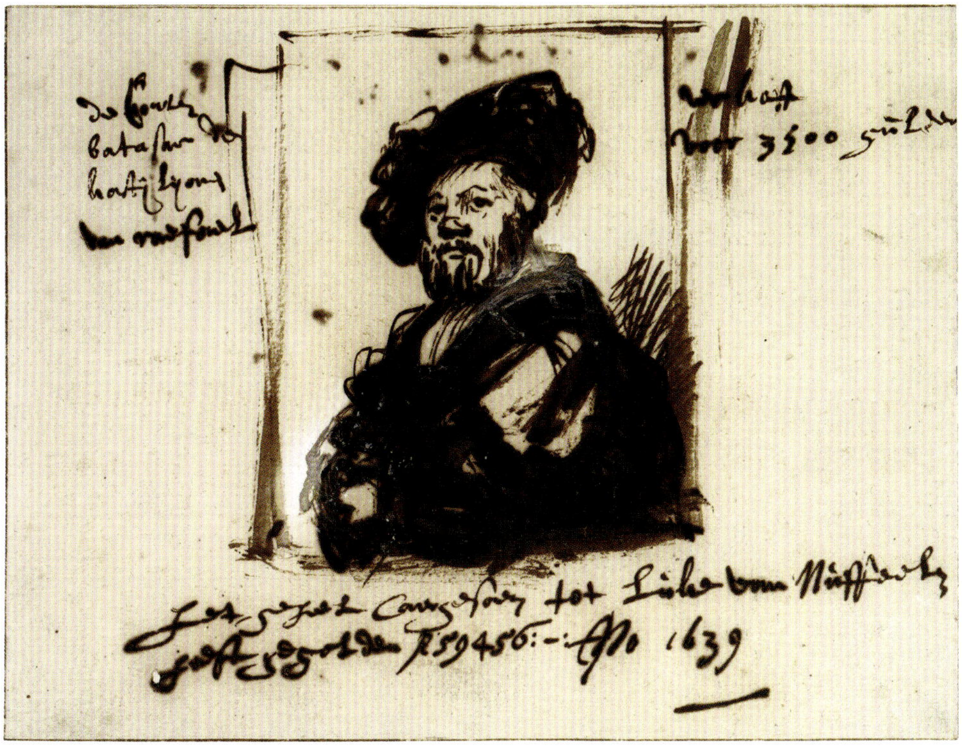

FIG. 30
Portrait of Baldassare Castiglione (after RAPHAEL), 1639
Pen and brown ink with white highlights, 16.3 × 20.7 cm
Graphische Sammlung Albertina, Vienna

Unlike Titian's *Flora* and Raphael's *Portrait of Baldassare Castiglione*, the visually most readily apparent model for Rembrandt's majestic *Juno* (cat. 21) in the Hammer Museum is a painting the Dutch artist most likely never saw: Titian's *Portrait of a Lady*, known as *'La Schiavona'* (fig. 31), which was certainly in Italy throughout the seventeenth century and was not reproduced in print.[12] In addition to the monumental, frontal pose of the *Juno*, such costume elements as the square neckline and the hairnet with strings of pearls recall Titian's portrait. Although *'La Schiavona'* could not have been his model, another sixteenth-century Venetian portrait of a woman probably was, as they often feature three-quarter-length frontal poses.[13] A no longer traceable work attributed to Bonifazio de' Pitati (known as Bonifazio Veronese, 1487–1553), which shows the woman in such a pose, has also been put forward as a possible candidate.[14] Like the *Juno*, the woman in this portrait has a commanding presence not only because of her frontality, but also because her robust body fills much of the picture space. In addition, she has a square neckline with pendant necklace and her left hand rests on a table in the same manner as the *Juno*.

An X-radiograph of the Hammer Museum painting (fig. 32) shows a fundamental modification: the figure's right arm was initially painted in the same position as her left, with both hands resting on a balustrade or ledge that ran the entire width of the picture.[15] The original composition with both arms at her sides would, therefore, have been even closer to the portrait attributed to Bonifazio as well as to other sixteenth-century Venetian portraits. Not only was the figure's right arm raised in the final design, but she was also given a sceptre, a standard element of Juno's iconography in the seventeenth century. Because the peacock – Juno's requisite attribute – appears to have been wedged into the lower left corner as if it were an afterthought, the possibility exists that the Hammer Museum painting was not begun as a representation of the goddess of marriage and wealth. The crown and the spectacular jewelled band holding her ermine cloak together were perhaps also later additions. According to a document drafted on 29 August 1665 the picture's probable first owner, Harmen Becker, had reportedly

FIG. 31
TITIAN (died 1576)
Portrait of a Lady
(*'La Schiavona'*), about 1510–12
Oil on canvas, 119.2 × 100.4 cm
The National Gallery,
London

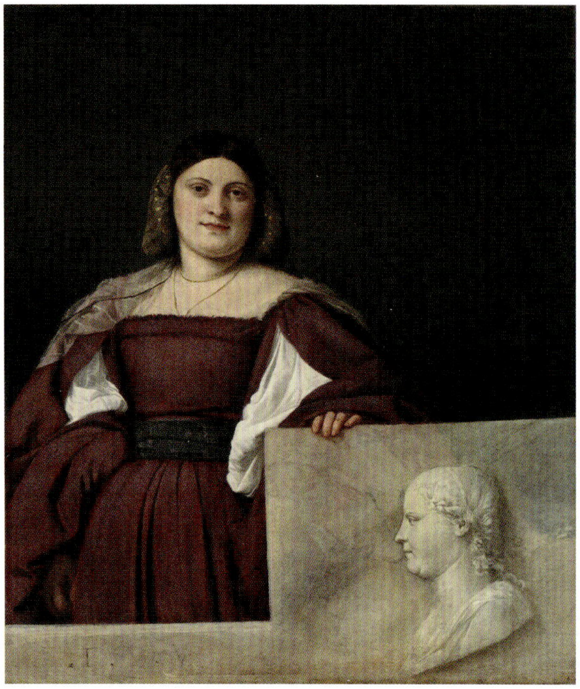

21
Juno, about 1662–5
Oil on canvas, 127 × 123.8 cm
Hammer Museum,
Los Angeles

FIG. 32
Composite X-radiograph
of *Juno* (cat. 21)
Taken in 1977, Harvard
University for the
Hammer Museum,
Los Angeles

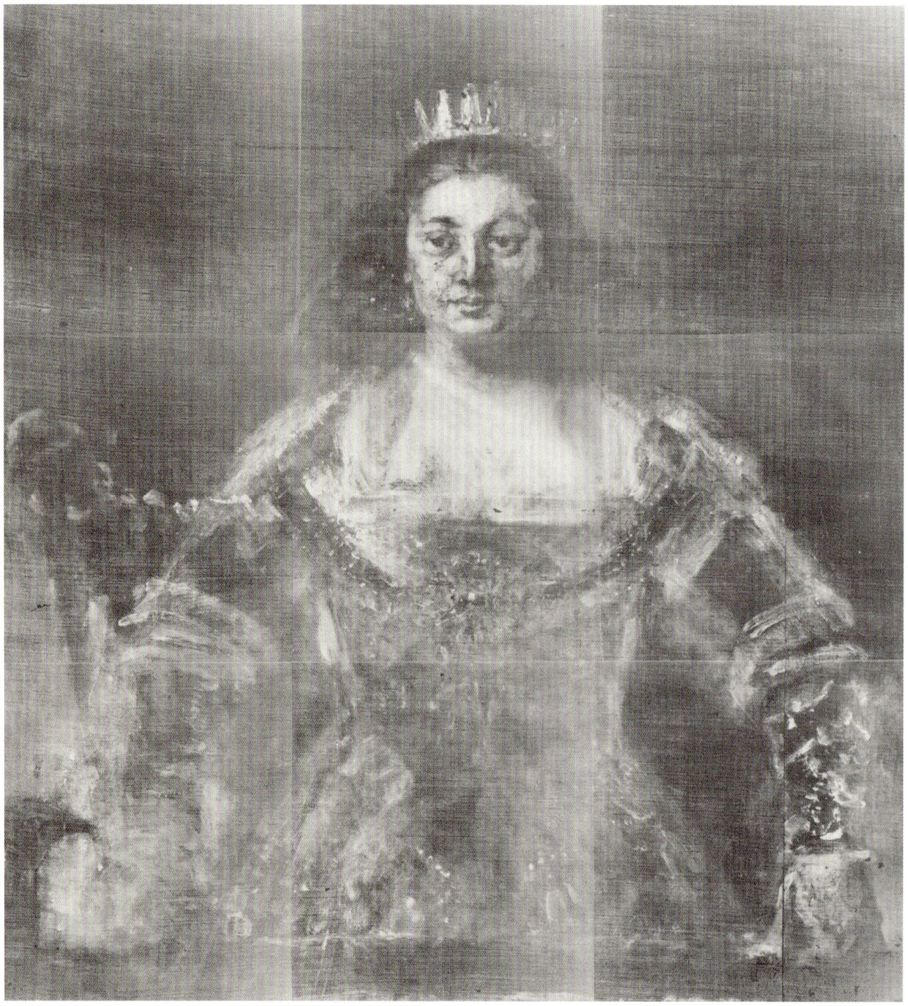

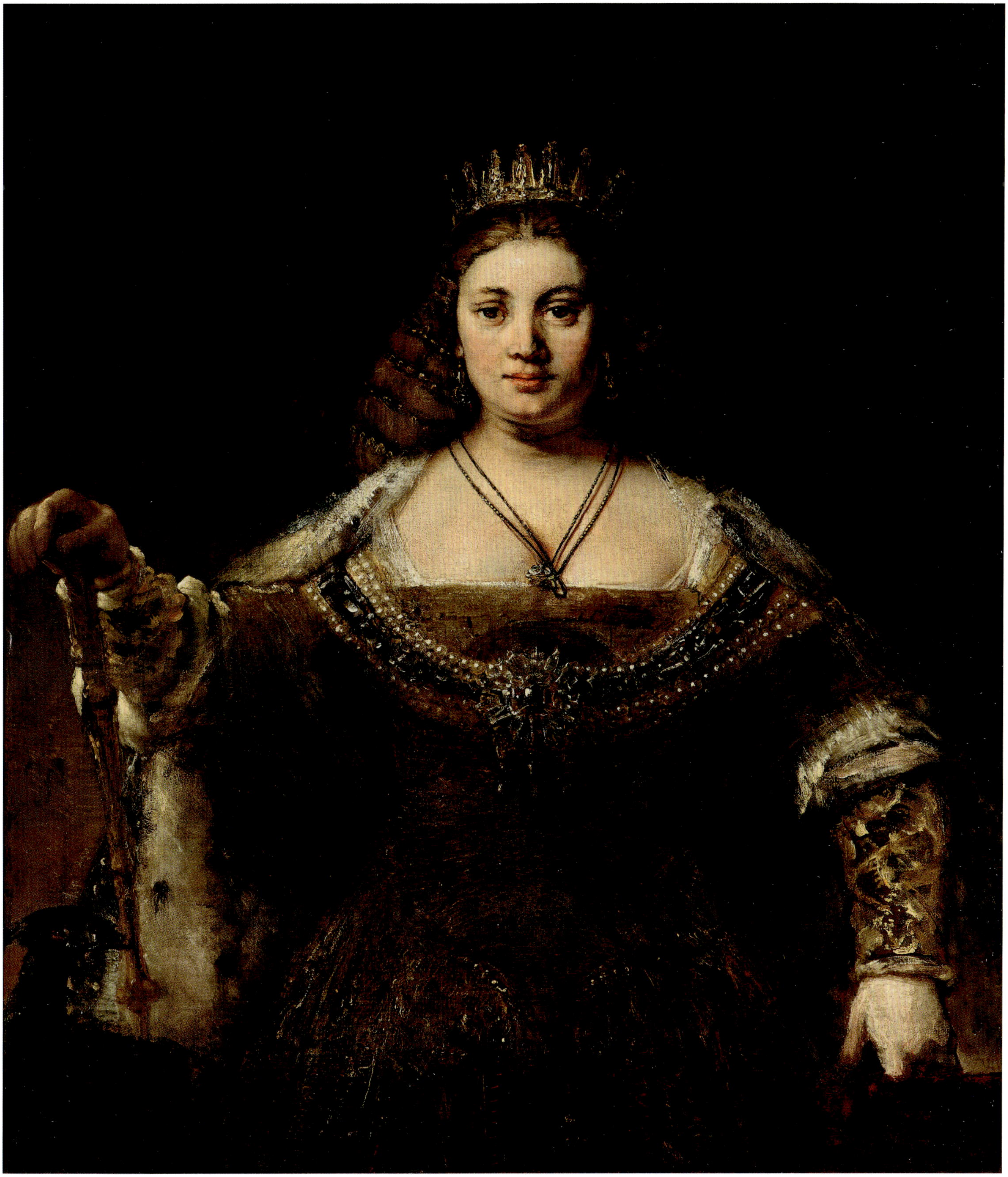

told Rembrandt to finish the *Juno* about a year and a half earlier, in the spring of 1664.[16] The work on the painting that still needed to be done was, perhaps, its transformation from a *tronie* (a fanciful, often exotic bust or half-length figure) *à la* sixteenth-century Venetian portraiture, to the Roman Queen of Heaven.

In addition to large-scale, single-figure paintings by Titian and artists in his circle that Rembrandt could have seen in a number of Dutch collections,[17] landscapes executed on paper by or after the Venetian master had a powerful impact on the Dutch artist in the later part of his career. The inventory of Rembrandt's possessions drawn up on the occasion of his insolvency in 1656 (see p. 22) lists 'One ditto [book] very large, with almost all the works of Titian', which would have included engravings and woodcut reproductions of his landscapes as well as, perhaps, some of his original landscape drawings. Two drawn copies by Rembrandt of Titian's landscape drawings have been preserved, as well as a landscape drawing in the style of the Titian circle artist Domenico Campagnola (1500–1564) that he retouched.[18] The upright format and diagonal division of Titian's *Saint Jerome reading in a Landscape*, engraved by Cornelis Cort (1533–1578) in 1565 (fig. 33), inspired Rembrandt's etching of the theme (cats 22–3) of around 1653. A rare preparatory drawing for this print (fig. 34) exists, which, despite having the same dimensions, was not followed to the letter.[19] The general layout of the composition is the same and the thick strokes of the reed pen used in the lion and the tree have been translated into drypoint. On the other hand, the buildings in the background are different, and, more significantly, the division of light and dark has been reversed. While brown wash casts the foreground of the drawing in shadow, in the etching this section of the composition was boldly left blank, thereby suggesting the intensity of the Mediterranean sun. The alternating bands of light and shade, the latter created by dense parallel hatching and crosshatching as well as drypoint, give greater emphasis in the etching to the diagonal sweep derived from Titian's design. Rembrandt also made changes to the tree against which Jerome leans, which may have been prompted by further study of Titian's example. The size of the stump has been reduced in comparison to the drawing, while that of the branch sprouting from it has increased dramatically. The monumental proportions and triumphant upward thrust of the branch recall the gnarly tree growing at an impossible angle out of a boulder in Cort's engraving after Titian.[20]

The Italianate architecture in the background of Rembrandt's *Saint Jerome*, as well as that in the

FIG. 33
CORNELIS CORT (1533–1578)
after TITIAN (died 1576)
Saint Jerome reading in a Landscape, 1565
Engraving, 31.5 × 25.5 cm
Rijksmuseum, Amsterdam

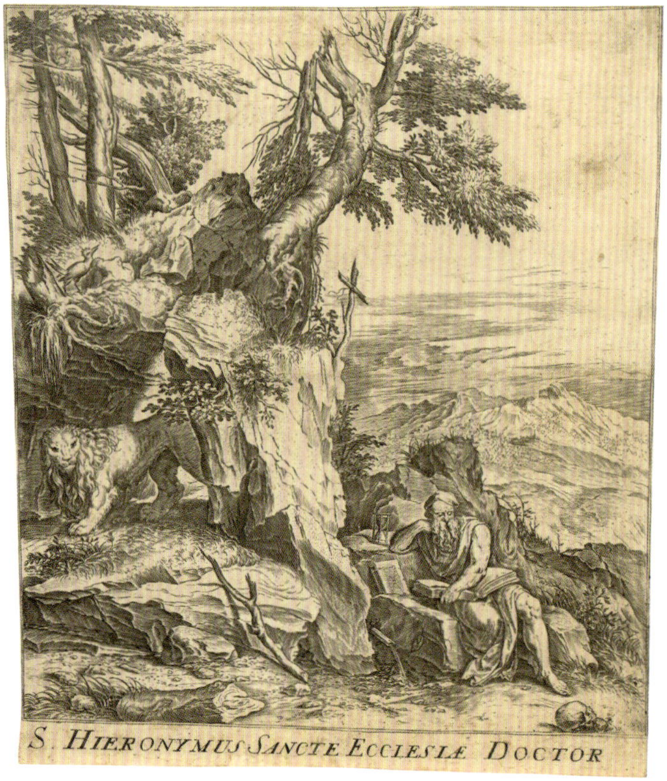

FIG. 34
Saint Jerome reading in an Italianate Landscape, about 1653
Pen and brown ink, with brown wash and white bodycolour, 26 × 20.4 cm
Kunsthalle, Kupferstichkabinett, Hamburg

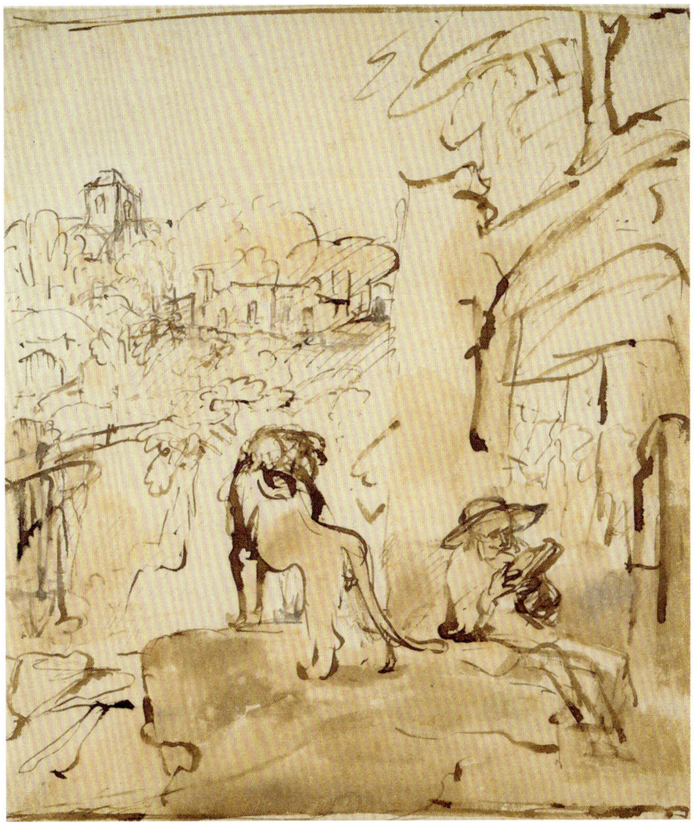

22
Saint Jerome reading in an Italianate Landscape, about 1653
Etching and drypoint, 25.9 × 21 cm
First state of two
Rijksmuseum, Amsterdam (RP-P-OB-184)

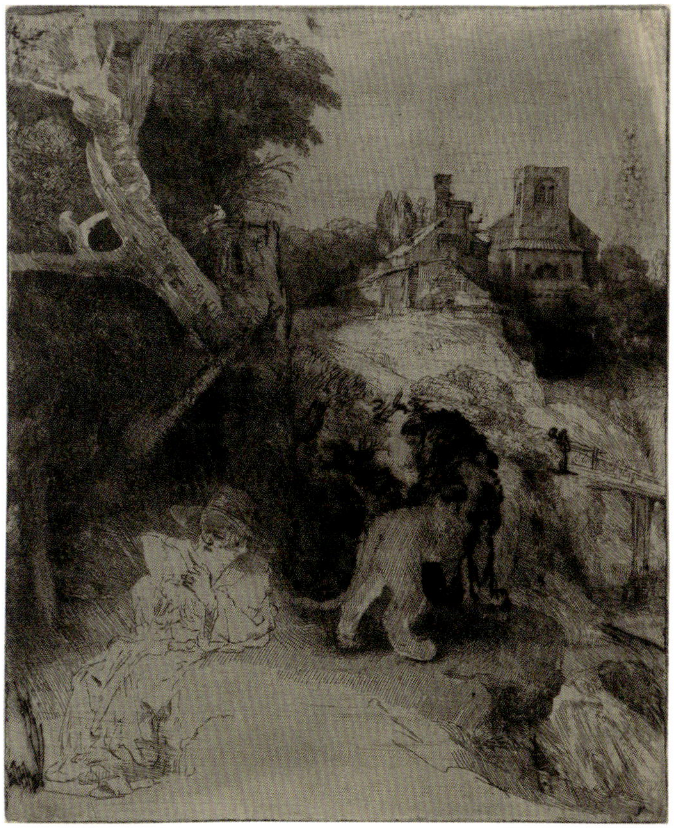

23
Saint Jerome reading in an Italianate Landscape, about 1653
Etching and drypoint, 25.9 × 21 cm
Second state of two
The Fitzwilliam Museum, Cambridge (AD.12.39-376)

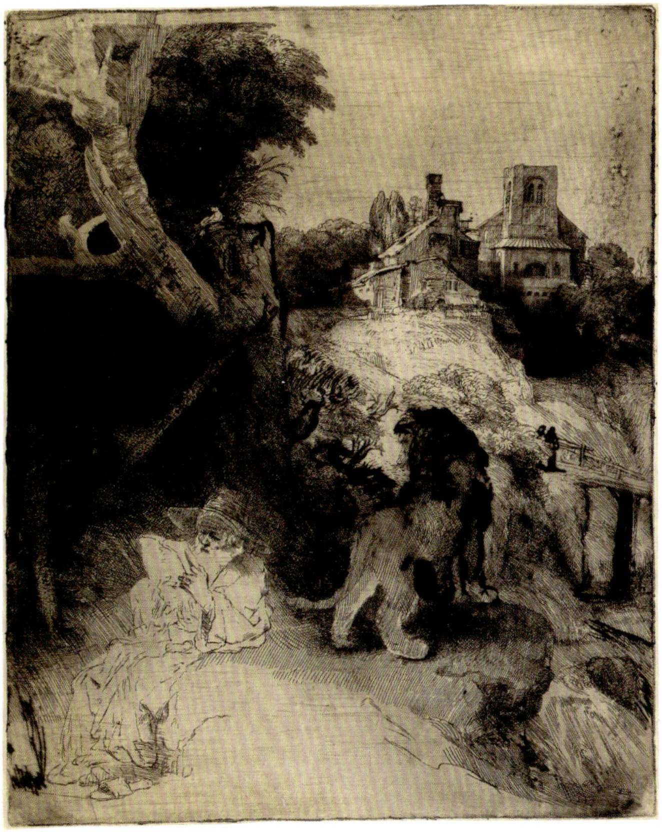

FIG. 35
ALESSANDRO MORETTO
(1498–1554)
Christ and the Woman of Samaria, about 1515–20
Oil on canvas, 38.8 × 31.2 cm
Accademia Carrara, Bergamo. Bequest of Giovanni Morelli, 1891

backgrounds of his 1657 *Saint Francis beneath a Tree, praying* (cat. 66) and his 1658 *Christ and the Woman of Samaria* (cat. 24) are loosely based on prints and possibly a painting by artists in Titian's circle.[21] The structures on the hill in the *Christ and the Woman of Samaria*, especially the circular temple, somewhat resemble those in a painting of this theme attributed to the sixteenth-century Brescian artist Alessandro Moretto (1498–1554; fig. 35). The Samaritan woman's pose in Rembrandt's etching is also similar, and it has been suggested therefore that the painting attributed to Moretto may be a smaller version of one described in Rembrandt's 1656 inventory as 'A large picture of "The Samaritan Woman" by Giorgione, of which a half share belongs to Pieter [de] la Tombe'.[22] Be this as it may, the most impressive aspects of Rembrandt's design – Christ's humble pose as he asks the woman for water and the veil of darkness covering her face, symbolising that she has not yet recognised the Messiah – appear to be without precedent.

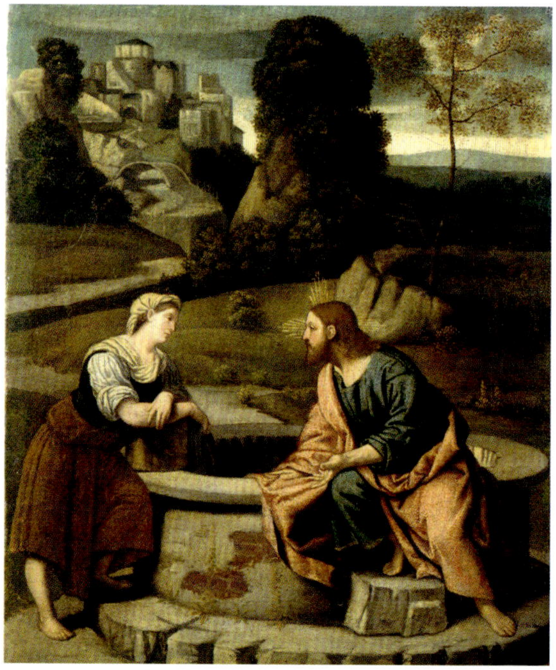

24
Christ and the Woman of Samaria, 1658
Etching and drypoint, 12.6 × 16 cm
Third state of five
The Fitzwilliam Museum, Cambridge (AD.12.39-63)

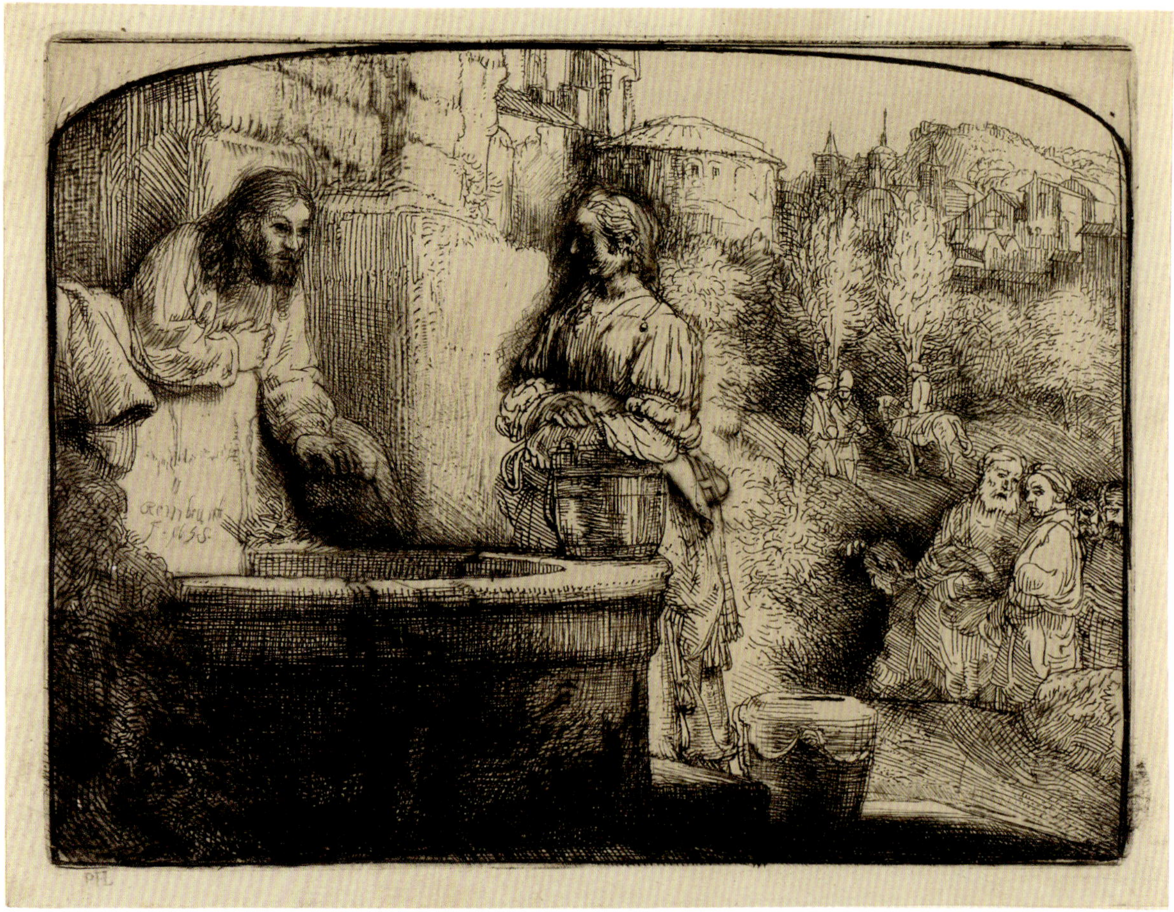

It may have astonished Von Sandrart, who criticised Rembrandt for paying no heed to Raphael's draughtsmanship, and De Piles, who saw none of Raphael's 'good taste' in the Dutchman's work, that Rembrandt did in fact express an interest in this High Renaissance master's designs during his late period.[23] The lingering influence of Raphael's *Portrait of Baldassare Castiglione* on Rembrandt's portraits has already been discussed, but the Dutch artist also studied multi-figured, classical compositions by Raphael and his circle. An example is the sketch *Homer reciting Verses* (cat. 25) that Rembrandt made in 1652 for Jan Six's *Pandora* album, an *album amicorum* (album of friends or friendship book). Six, who had made a 20-month grand tour of Italy beginning in 1641, may very well have seen the painting on which this sketch was based, namely Raphael's fresco *Apollo on Parnassus* in the Stanza della Segnatura in the Vatican.[24] Rembrandt's sketch is a reworking of the left side of the *Parnassus*, which he would have known from Marcantonio Raimondi's reproductive engraving (fig. 36).[25] Homer, who is the central figure on this side of the engraving, has been retained in the same position, while the scribe eagerly listening to him on the left now sits at his feet on the right. The other classical authors and the muses in Raphael's assembly have been stripped of their individual identities to become anonymous members of Homer's attentive audience. Rembrandt also made use of Raphael's placement of the figures on two levels, and he kept two of the trees to the right of the classical bard as well.

Judging from one of the few seventeenth-century Dutch statements about artistic emulation, made in

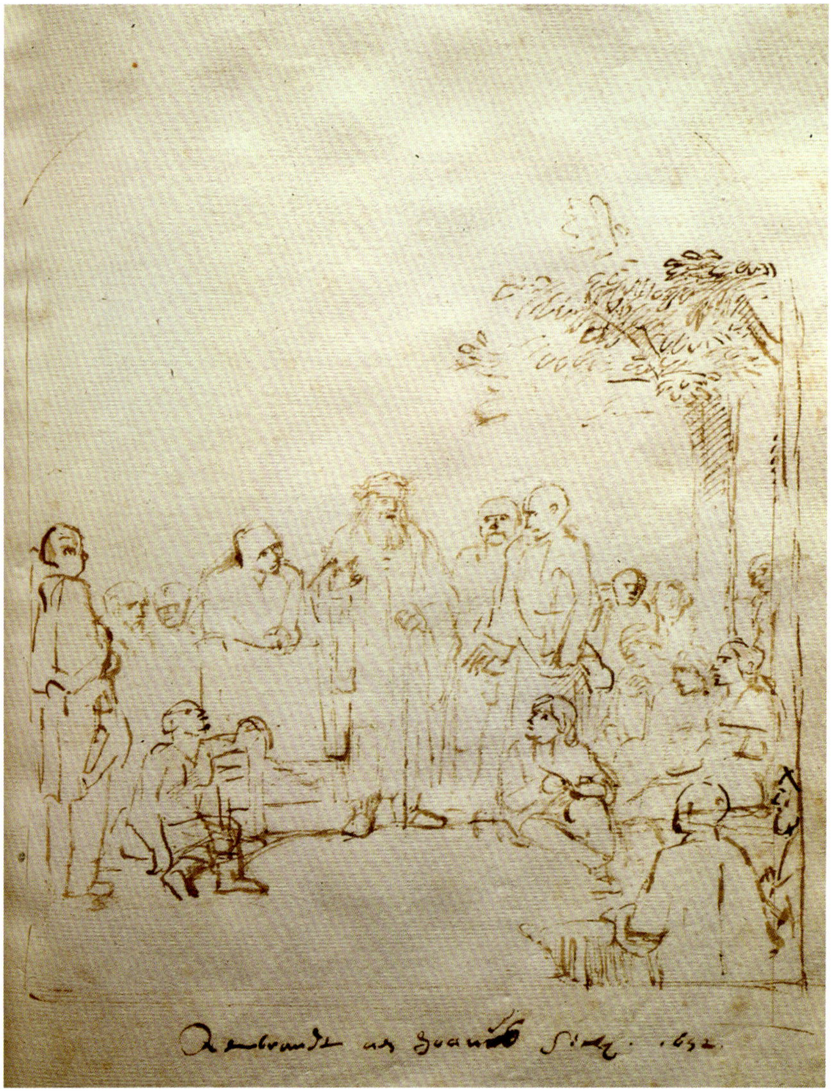

25
Homer reciting Verses
(*'Pandora'*, *Album Amicorum Jan Six*, fol. 40r), 1652
Pen and brush and brown ink, with white bodycolour,
19 × 14 cm
Six Collection, Amsterdam

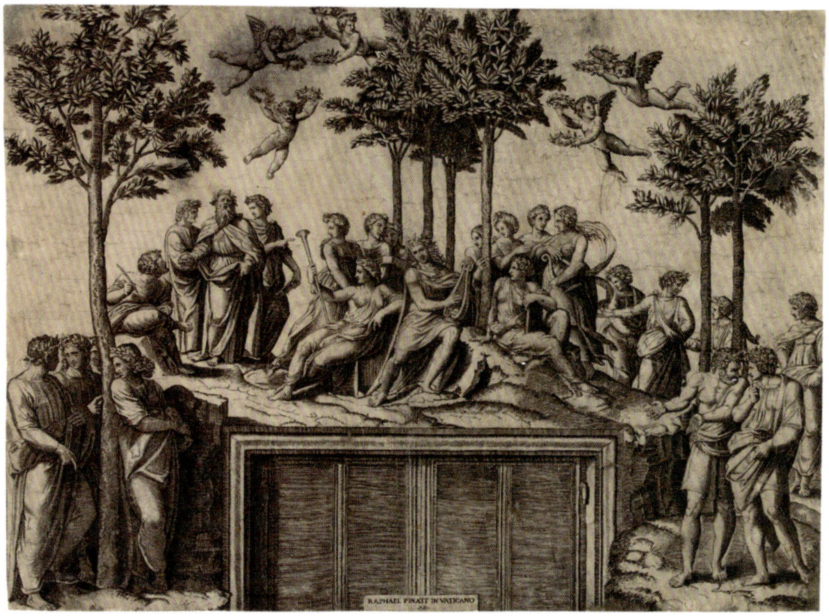

FIG. 36
MARCANTONIO RAIMONDI (1480–1534)
after RAPHAEL (1483–1520)
Apollo and the Muses on Mount Parnassus, about 1517–20
Engraving, 34.4 × 46.4 cm
Rijksmuseum, Amsterdam

1678 by Samuel van Hoogstraten, the way in which Rembrandt made use of Raphael's composition in his *Homer reciting Verses* would have met with critical approval. Van Hoogstraten saw nothing wrong with 'composing verses based on a familiar tune', but advised prospective artists to be vigilant in choosing a different subject.[26] Although derived from Raphael's *Parnassus*, the subject of the 1652 drawing is different. There is, however, no connection to the fresco's subject matter in the next step in the evolution of Raphael's composition within Rembrandt's oeuvre, the etching *Christ preaching*, known as *'La Petite Tombe'* (cat. 26).[27] Instead of Homer standing on a mound reciting his verses to a throng of avid listeners arranged in a semicircle, in the print it is Christ standing on a platform addressing an equally attentive crowd organised in a similar layout. In both works, the area beneath the speaker has been left blank and a figure sits at either side of his feet. The poses of some of the members of Christ's audience, including most conspicuously the man seen from behind on the left, can also be traced back to the *Homer reciting Verses*. While the *Christ preaching* is clearly related to Rembrandt's 1652 drawing, its ultimate derivation from the *Parnassus* is not at all obvious. In fact, the reference contained in Rembrandt's etching to another fresco by Raphael in the Stanza della Segnatura is more readily apparent: the figure of Christ is a mirror-image quotation of Raphael's Christ seated in Glory in the *Disputà*.

A drawing in Haarlem (cat. 27) is another example of Rembrandt's interest in Raphael, or at least his circle, as it reproduces a sheet attributed to one of his pupils, Polidoro da Caravaggio (about 1499–1543; fig. 37).[28] Rembrandt probably owned the Italian sketch, and may have regarded it as a work by Raphael himself. The drawing's classical design, like that of the *Parnassus*, appears to be what intrigued the Dutch artist. However, while retaining its symmetrical composition, he made some small modifications to the figures. For example, the seated mourner, who appears to be a man in the original, has become a woman; the figure no longer holds a hand before his face, but rather rests the side of her head upon it. The positions of the right hands of the two

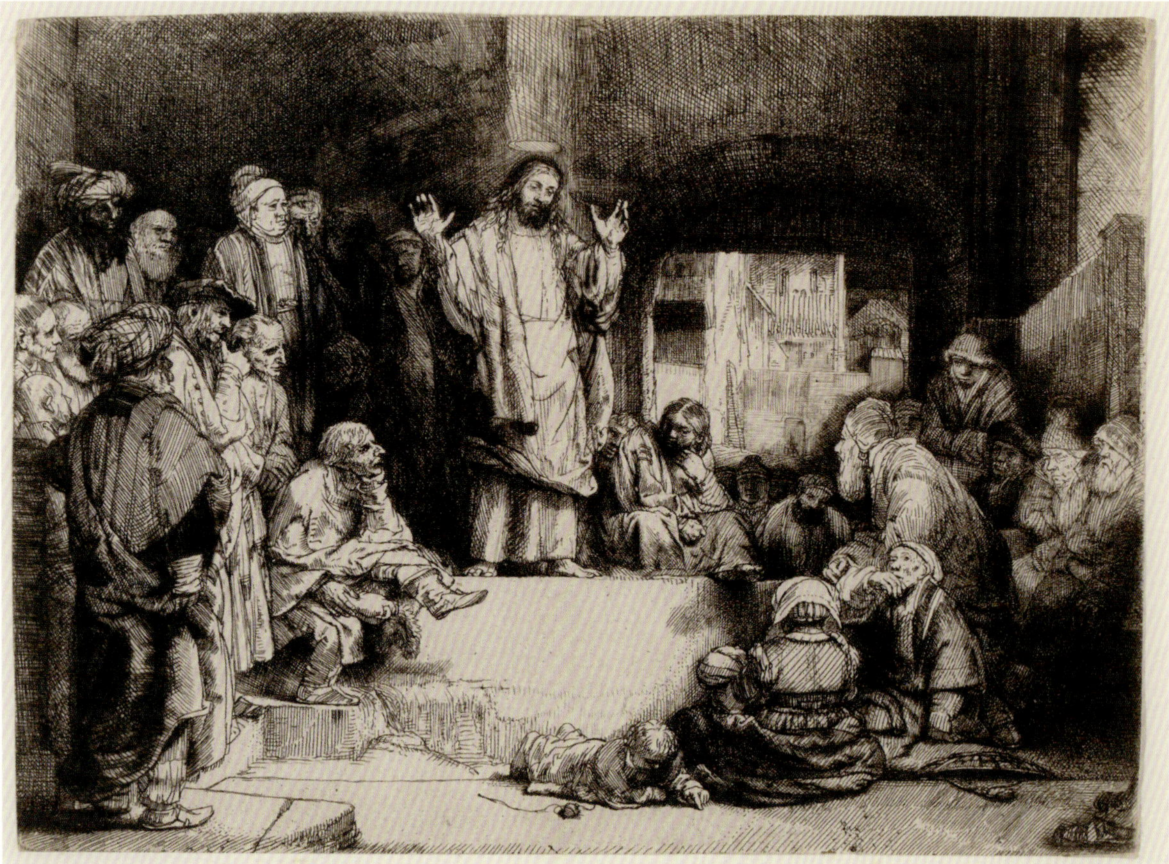

26
Christ preaching
(*'La Petite Tombe'*), about 1657
Etching and drypoint,
15.5 × 20.7 cm
First state of two
Victoria and Albert Museum, London (CAI 642)

FIG. 37
POLIDORO DA CARAVAGGIO
(about 1499–1543)
The Entombment,
about 1520–43
Brown ink and brown wash, heightened with white gouache, on cream antique laid paper, framing lines in black ink,
11.7 × 18.3 cm
Harvard Art Museums/Fogg Museum, Cambridge, MA.
Bequest of Charles A. Loeser

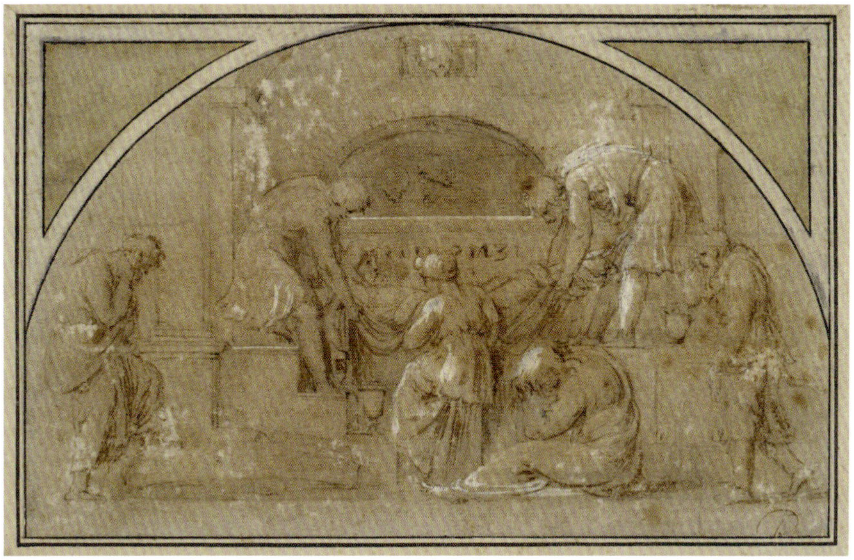

27
The Entombment of Christ
(after POLIDORO DA CARAVAGGIO), about 1657–8
Pen and brush in brown ink, white heightening, yellow and red chalk, 18.1 × 28.4 cm
Teylers Museum, Haarlem

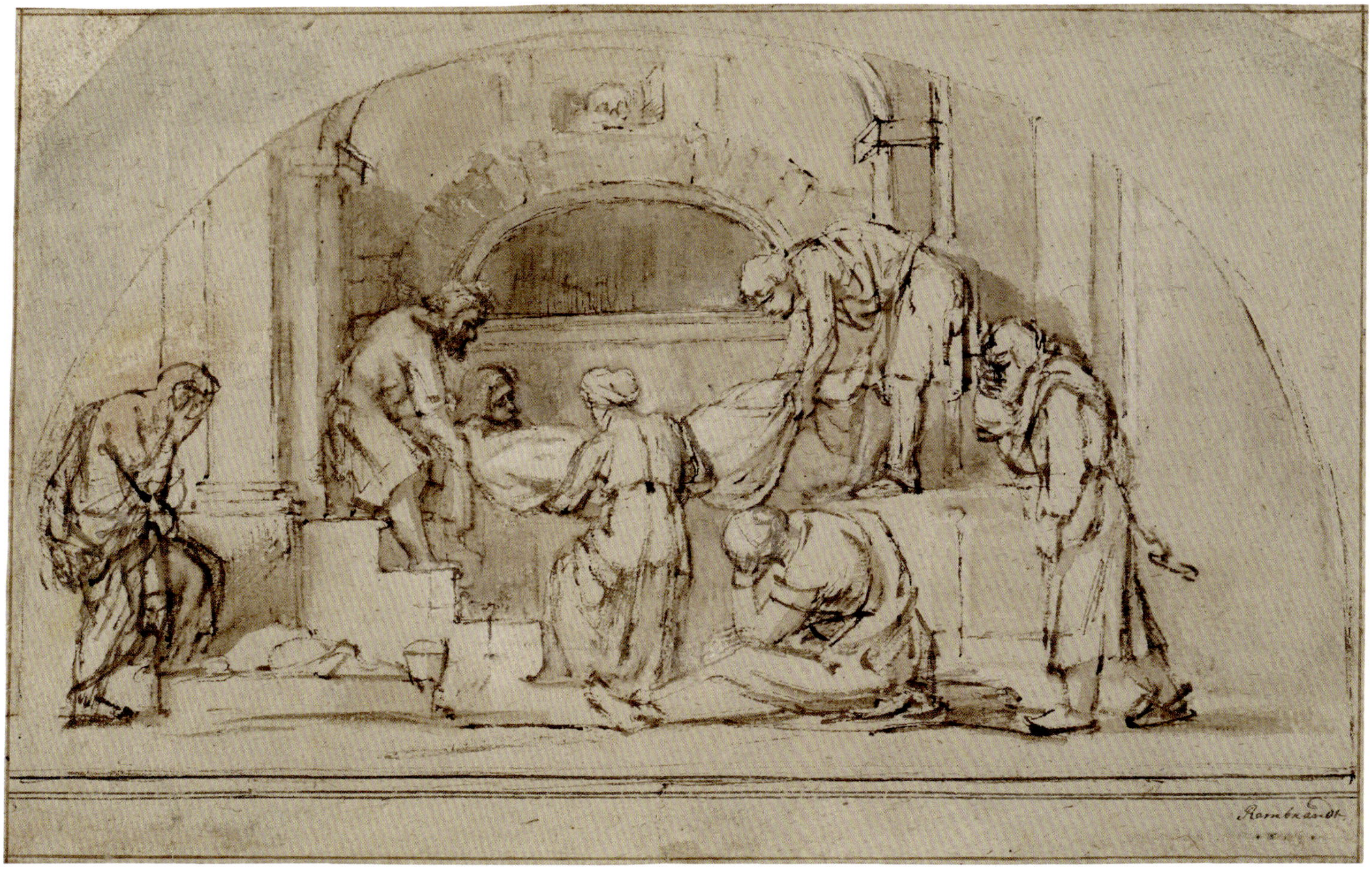

28
Design for the Frame of 'The Anatomy Lesson of Dr Joan Deyman', about 1656
Reed pen and brown ink, 10.9 × 13.2 cm
Amsterdam Museum

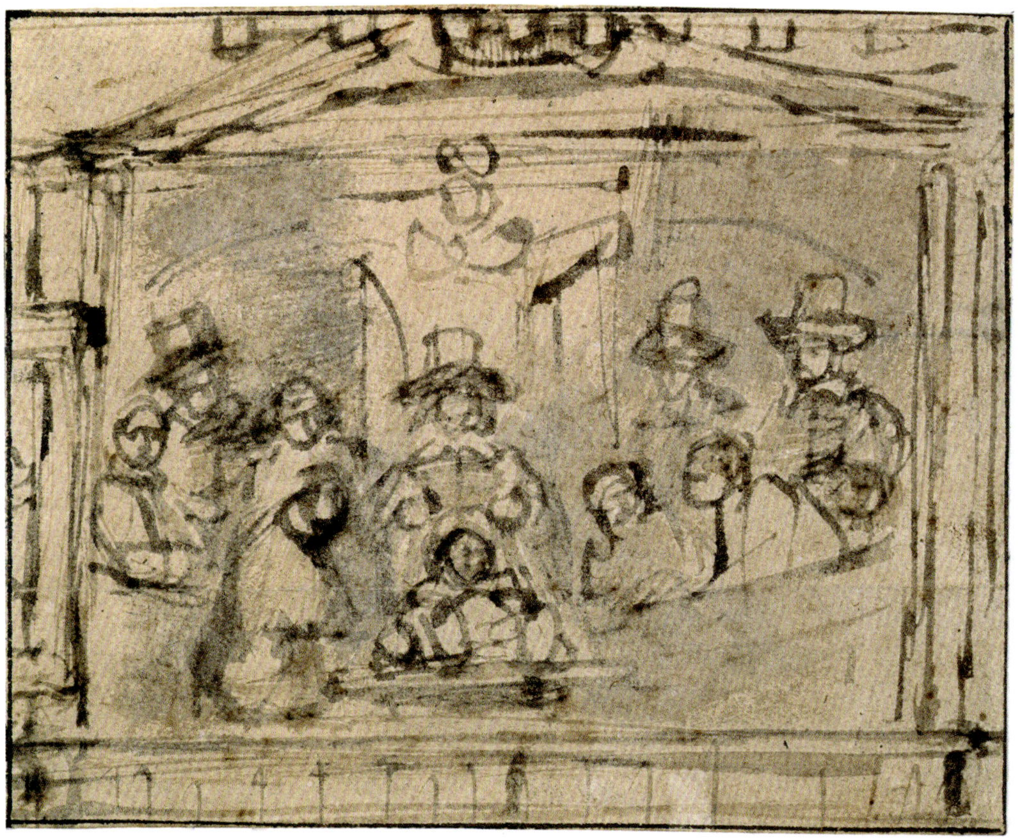

mourners framing the scene on either side have also been changed so that they now use them to cover their faces. A more important alteration is the introduction of greater depth to the relief-like composition by way of shadows applied with the brush. Rembrandt possibly made this copy of the Raphaelesque drawing while he was pondering the composition for his etching *The Entombment* (cats 80–1).[29] Whether or not this was the case, in the end he only incorporated the high wall, double arch and skulls into the print.[30]

The classical symmetry characterising the works by Raphael and his circle that the Dutch master had studied in the early 1650s reappears in Rembrandt's most unclassical work from his late period, the 1656 *Anatomy Lesson of Dr Joan Deyman* (cat. 29). Much of the painting, which would have measured about 245 by 300 cm, was destroyed in a fire in 1723, but its original appearance is known from a reed pen drawing Rembrandt had executed in order to demonstrate how the painting should be framed and hung in the anatomy theatre of the Amsterdam Surgeons' Guild (cat. 28). The fragment only shows part of Dr Joan Deyman, assisted by Gijsbrecht Matthijsz Calcoen, dissecting the brain of the newly executed criminal Joris Fonteijn, who also went by the moniker 'Black John' ('Zwarte Jan'). In the drawing, the corpse, Dr Deyman and a broad pilaster behind him form a monumental central axis with eight doctors arranged to either side in two ascending diagonals. By placing Deyman in the centre of the composition Rembrandt returned to the traditional format of the anatomy lesson, which he himself had abandoned in his only other work in this genre, the highly acclaimed *Anatomy Lesson of Dr Nicolaes Tulp* of 1632 (fig. 96).[31] This notwithstanding, none of the earlier portraits shows the corpse facing the viewer in bold foreshortening with its feet jutting out of the picture plane. Rembrandt's inspiration for the symmetrical arrangement of his sitters and the strong perpendicular positioning of the corpse probably came from the frontispiece to Andreas Vesalius's 1543 *De Humani Corporis Fabrica* (fig. 38), which also contains illustrations of dissected brains that he would have consulted.[32] In the frontispiece, however, the corpse is placed at a much safer and less confrontational distance from the viewer than in Rembrandt's painting, which lends support to the suggestion of some scholars that the Dutch artist followed another source for this aspect of his composition. Of the many possible prototypes, an etching after the *Lamentation over the Body of Christ by the*

29
The Anatomy Lesson of
Dr Joan Deyman, 1656
Oil on canvas, 100 × 134 cm
Amsterdam Museum

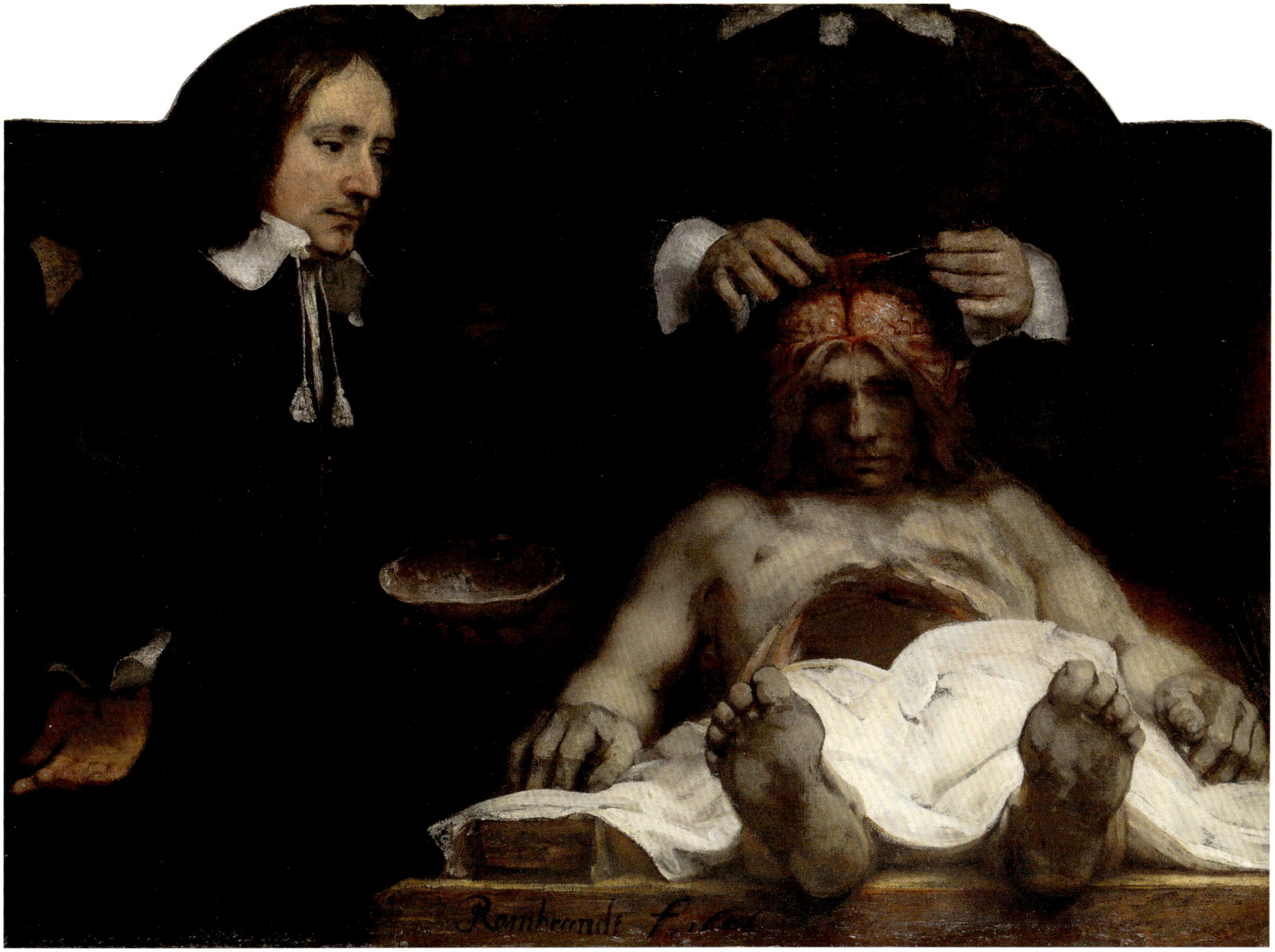

Three Marys (fig. 39) by Orazio Borgianni (1575–1616) is the best candidate.[33]

The symmetrical design of *The Anatomy Lesson of Dr Joan Deyman* and the accomplished foreshortening of the corpse are features on which classicist critics such as Von Sandrart, De Piles and Houbraken could not fault Rembrandt. Had they known the painting, however, they surely would have objected to the shockingly gruesome presentation of the cadaver's disembowelled torso and flayed cranium, not to mention the dirty soles of the feet thrust into the beholder's face. It may be argued that it is in the nature of the genre of the anatomy lesson that these gory details be represented, but Rembrandt pushed this aspect to its limits. No greater contrast can be imagined than with the *Anatomy Lesson of Dr Frederik Ruysch* painted by Adriaen Backer (1635–1684) in 1670 (fig. 40).[34] The corpse in this work is also shown in foreshortening, but has the idealised appearance of a Greek god and its head, not its feet, is closest to the picture plane so that the viewer is not unsettled by the delicate incision in the thigh, now at a safe and comfortable distance in the background.

The 1656 inventory of Rembrandt's studio lists individual albums of the works on paper by or after the major Italian Renaissance artists Raphael, Titian and Michelangelo. There was also an album containing prints

FIG. 38
JAN STEFAN VAN CALCAR
(1499–about 1546/50)
Frontispiece to Andreas Vesalius, *De Humani Corporis Fabrica*, Basle 1543
Woodcut, 35 × 25 cm
Rijksmuseum, Amsterdam

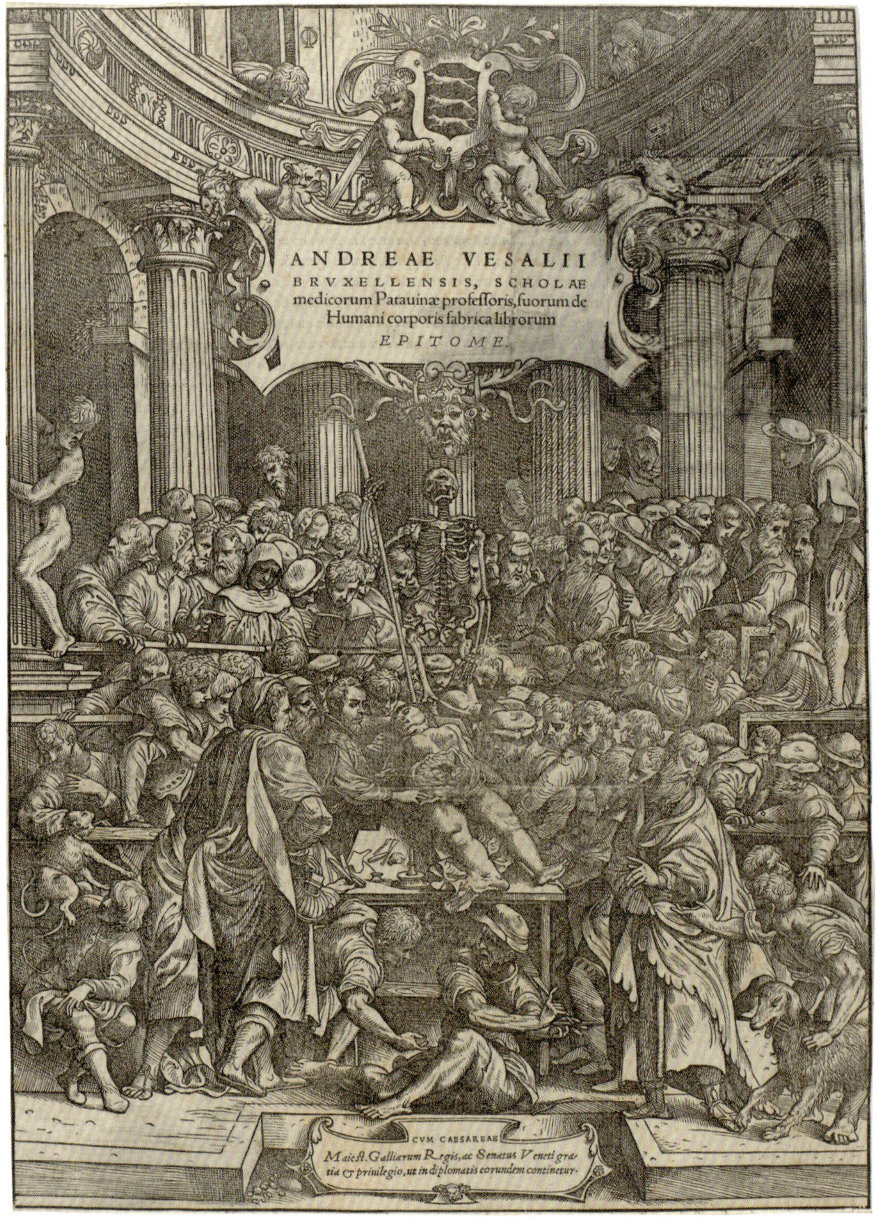

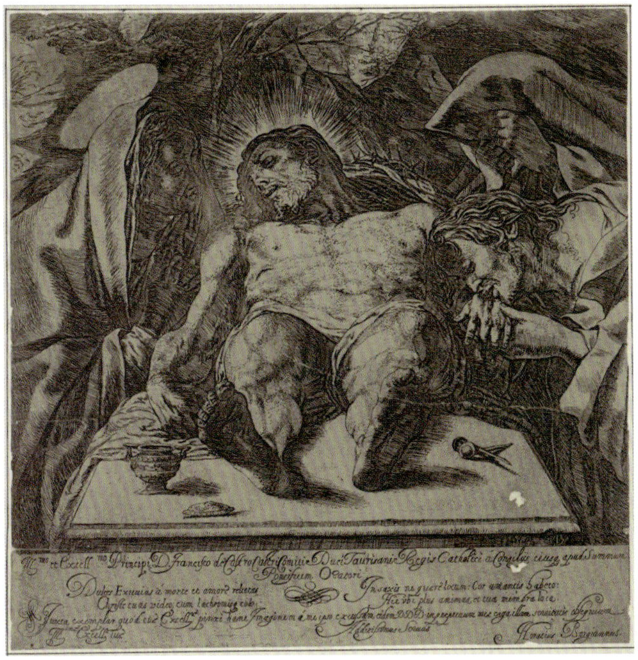

FIG. 39
ORAZIO BORGIANNI
(1575–1616)
Lamentation over the Body of Christ by the Three Marys, 1615
Etching, 23.4 × 22.4 cm
The Metropolitan Museum of Art, New York

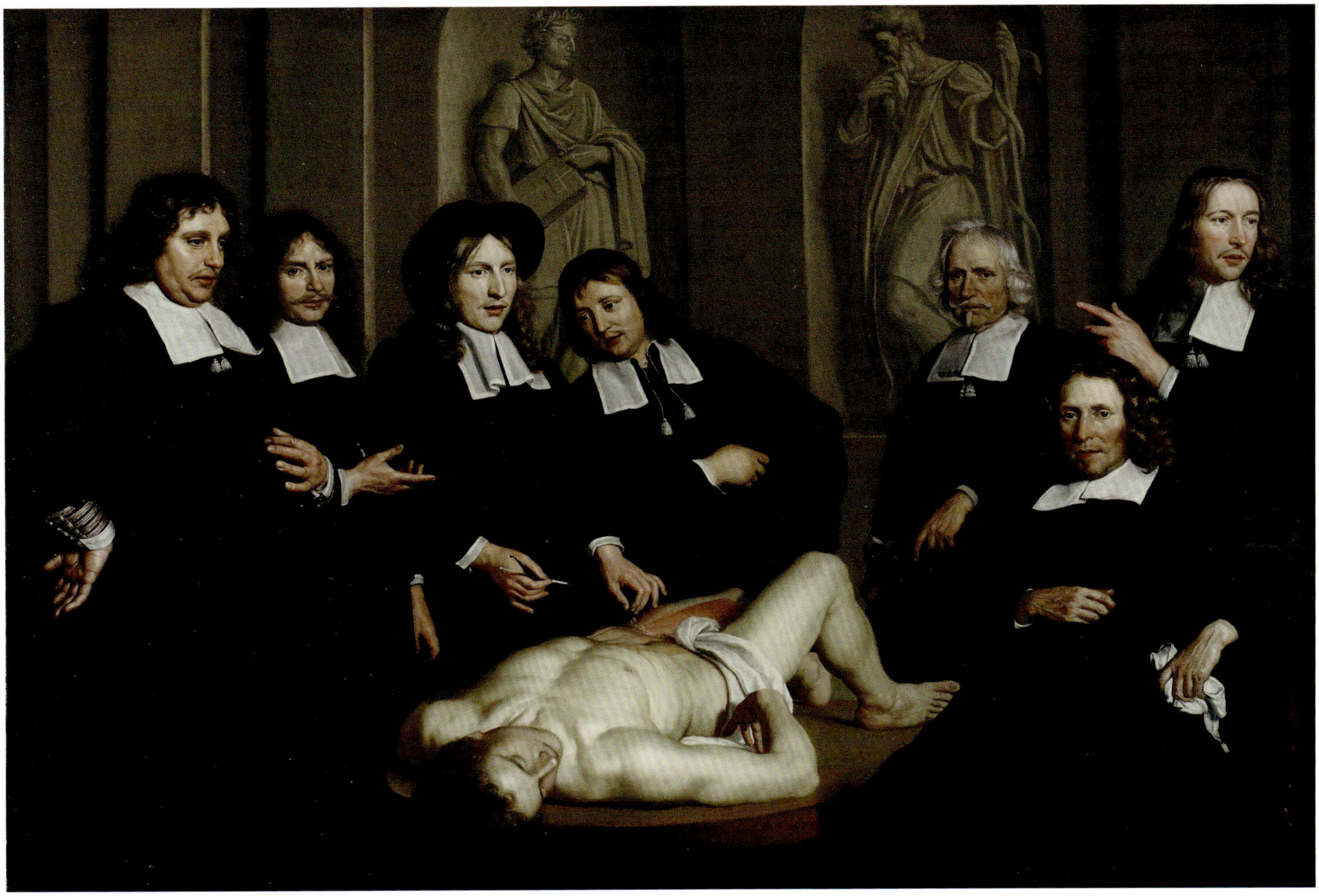

FIG. 40
ADRIAEN BACKER
(1635–1684)
The Anatomy Lesson of Dr Frederik Ruysch, 1670
Oil on canvas, 168 × 244 cm
Amsterdam Museum

FIG. 41
ANNIBALE CARRACCI
(1560–1609)
Jupiter and Antiope, 1592
Etching, 15.1 × 22.4 cm
Rijksmuseum, Amsterdam

by or after the later Italian artists Annibale (1560–1609), Agostino (1557–1602) and Ludovico Carracci (1555–1619), Guido Reni (1575–1642) and the Spanish artist Jusepe de Ribera (1591–1652), who was active in Italy.[35] Not all of Annibale Carracci's work was contained in that album, however, as there was another containing 'erotica by Raphael, Rosso, Annibale Carracci, and Giulio Bonasone'.[36] Although his more famous brother is named, the album probably included Agostino Carracci's notorious series the *Lascivie* (*Lusts*), but it may have also contained a 1592 etching by Annibale of a lecherous Jupiter disguised as a satyr staring at the crotch of a naked, sleeping Antiope (fig. 41). Annibale's print served as the model for Rembrandt's 1659 etching of the same subject (cat. 30), but the Dutch master made a number of important changes to the design in order to outdo the erotic appeal of his prototype. By omitting extraneous details such as the cupid holding a bow and the landscape in the background, and by cropping the figure of Antiope on the left, Rembrandt achieved a far greater sense of immediacy in his version. The position of the nude's proper left arm has also been altered so that it is now raised above her head. Ultimately derived from the marble *Sleeping Ariadne* in the Vatican, this was a popular pose with a number of seventeenth-century Dutch artists.[37] In Rembrandt's print, however, it is more powerfully suggestive of sexual abandon, as the nude's right arm is also raised, her head is thrust further back and her lips are sensuously parted. Light and shade also play a large part in stirring up in the viewer the same desire that drove the Roman god. The dark shadow cast on the curtain behind the bed accentuates Antiope's naked torso, but more importantly, the position of the shadow cast by Annibale's Jupiter has been changed so that it falls not on the nude's legs but on her buttocks and sex, making the object of the god's lust appear all the more intriguing. And as the shadow is cast by Jupiter's own body, it also works as a metaphor of his impending possession of the sleeping beauty.

In addition to the Italian masters discussed here, Rembrandt was keenly interested in the art of his Dutch predecessors during his late period. According to the seventeenth-century Italian writer Filippo Baldinucci, who had his information from a former pupil of Rembrandt, Bernhard Keil (1624–1687), the Dutch master

> deserves great praise for a certain goodness of his, extravagant though it be, namely that, for the sake of the great esteem in which he held his art, whenever things produced by great men of those parts were offered for sale, he bid so high at the outset that no one else came forward to bid.[38]

Other early accounts specifically mention one Dutch artist in particular, Lucas van Leyden, for whose work

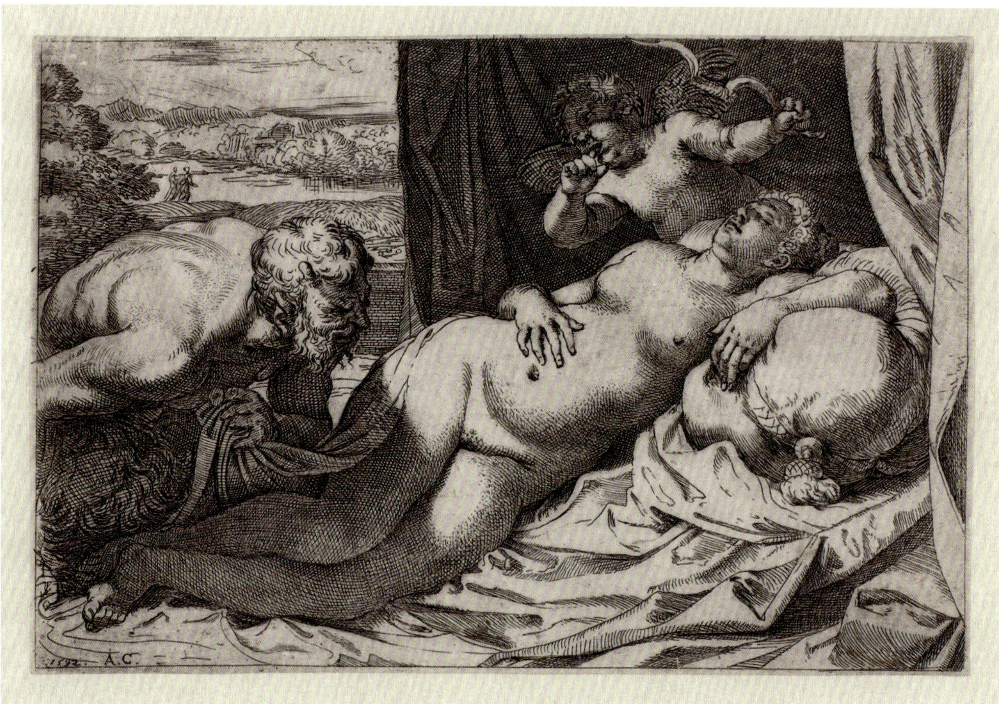

30
Jupiter and Antiope, 1659
Etching and drypoint,
13.8 × 20.5 cm
Second state of three
The Fitzwilliam Museum,
Cambridge (AD.12.39-159)

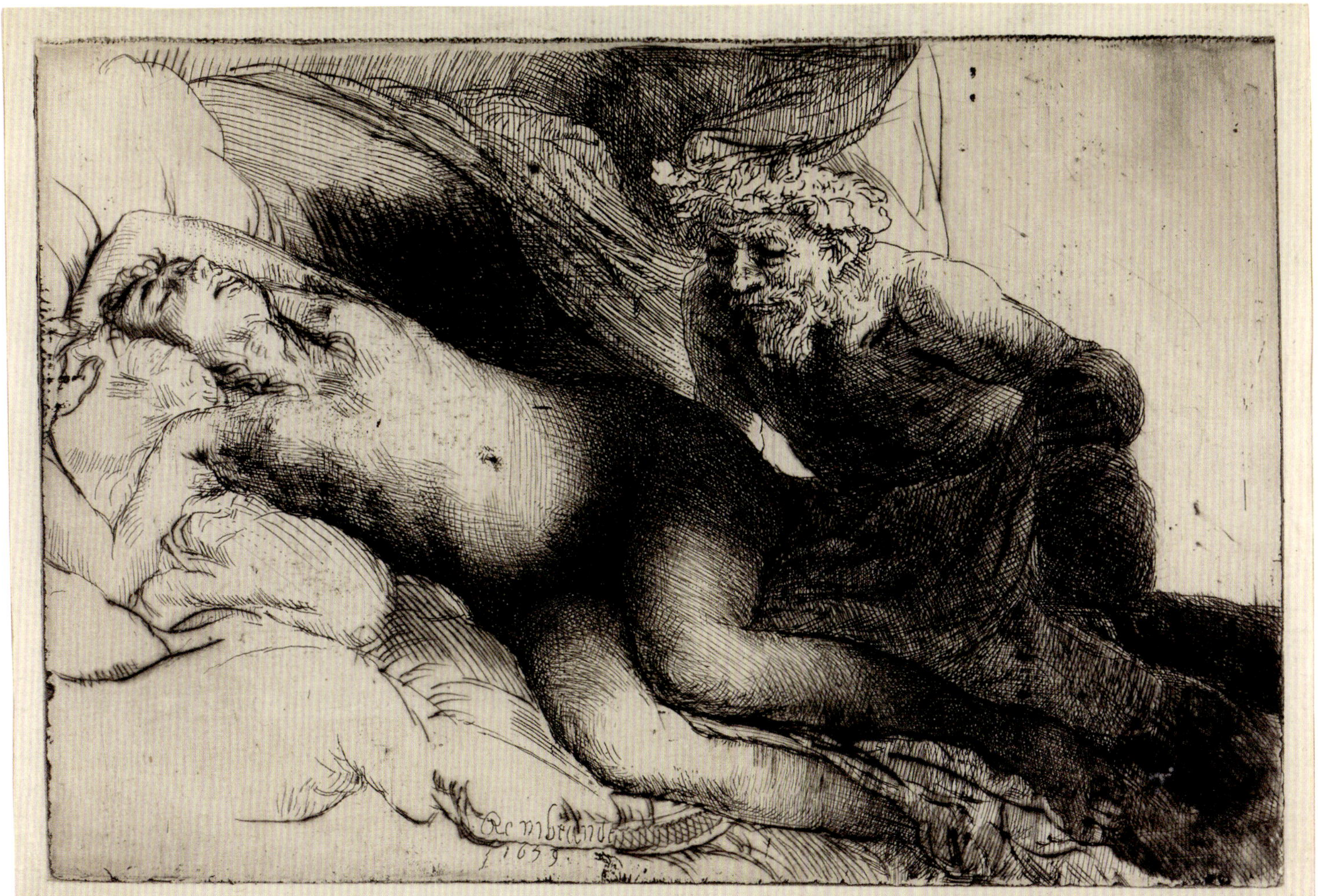

Detail from *Christ presented to the People* (*Ecce Homo*) (cat. 31)

Rembrandt was willing to part with substantial amounts of money. Von Sandrart, for example, commented:

> I am assured by the renowned artist Mr Johann Ulrich Mayr that he saw his master Mr Rembrandt bid 1,400 guilders at a public auction for 14 fine impressions of prints by this artist including the Ecce homo, St Paul's journey to Damascus, the large Crucifixion and the dance of Mary Magdalen.[39]

Rembrandt's 1656 inventory includes two albums with prints by Lucas, one containing woodcuts and the other engravings 'including duplicates and single sheets'.[40] As the greatest seventeenth-century Dutch printmaker he may well have considered himself to be the artistic heir of Lucas van Leyden, who was not only the greatest Dutch graphic artist of the previous century, but was born in the same town.

The culmination of Rembrandt's lifelong engagement with Lucas's work was his use of the large *Ecce Homo* (fig. 42), one of the 14 sheets by the sixteenth-century artist for which, according to Von Sandrart, he shelled out 1,400 guilders, as the prototype for his even larger print of the same subject from 1655 (cats 31–2).[41] Rembrandt would have been familiar with Karel van Mander's praise of the 'diverse peoples' in Lucas's print and the 'wondrously modern and well-executed buildings/ all being so utterly well-observed in accordance with the perspectives of Art and proportion'.[42] Indeed, it is precisely the swarming mob in the foreground and the podium upon which the group including Pontius Pilate and Christ stand, as well as certain elements of the architectural setting, that Rembrandt adopted for his own print. The similarities in the grouping of the figures and the placement of the steps leading up to the platform become even more apparent when Rembrandt's composition is viewed in reverse, that is, in the direction he himself would have had before him as he composed the design on the copper plate.[43] Unlike his model, however, Rembrandt's composition is symmetrical and closed on three sides .[44] The figures of Christ and his jailers, moreover, have been placed significantly closer to the viewer. In the sixth of the eight states, Rembrandt moved even further away from Lucas's design by eliminating the animated crowd in the foreground (cat. 32).[45] While this radical intervention was born of necessity – the lavish burr produced by the drypoint technique had almost vanished by then – as a consequence the beholder takes on the role of the people to whom Pilate posed the fateful question: 'Whom will ye that I release unto you? Barabbas, or Jesus which is called Christ?' (Matthew 27: 17).[46]

A work by the lesser-known sixteenth-century Flemish artist Dirck Vellert (about 1480/85– about

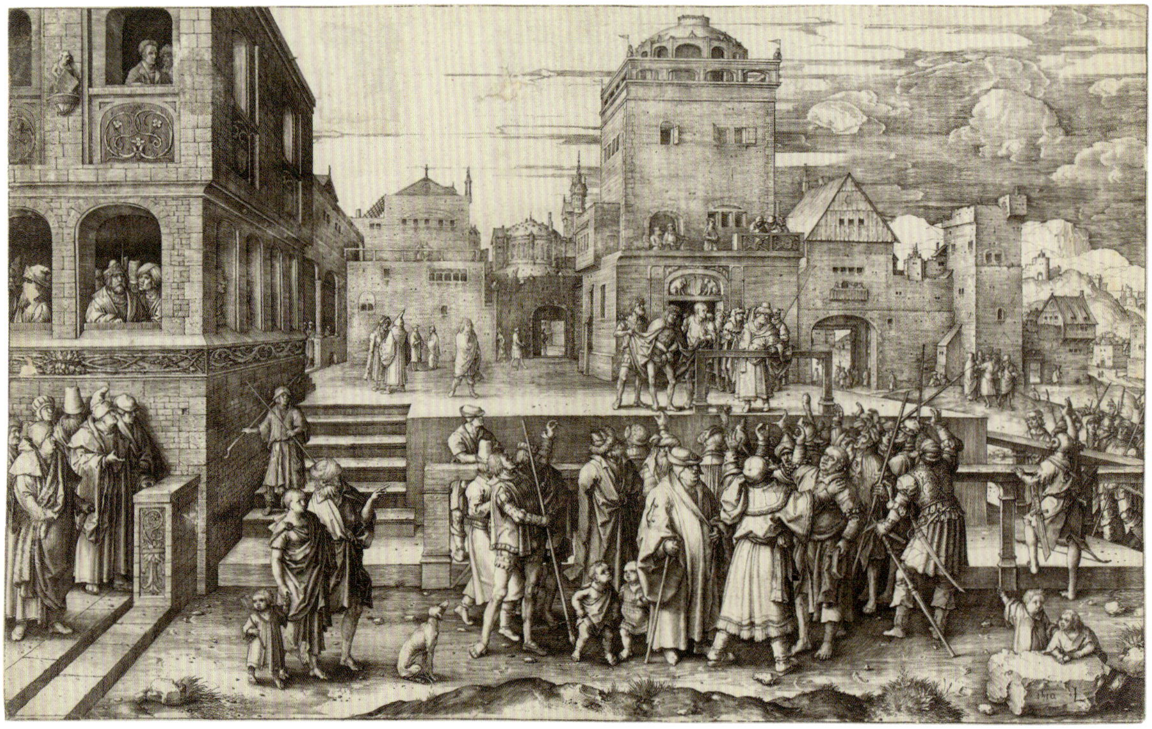

FIG. 42
LUCAS VAN LEYDEN
(1494–1533)
Ecce Homo, 1510
Engraving, 28.5 × 45.2 cm
Rijksmuseum, Amsterdam

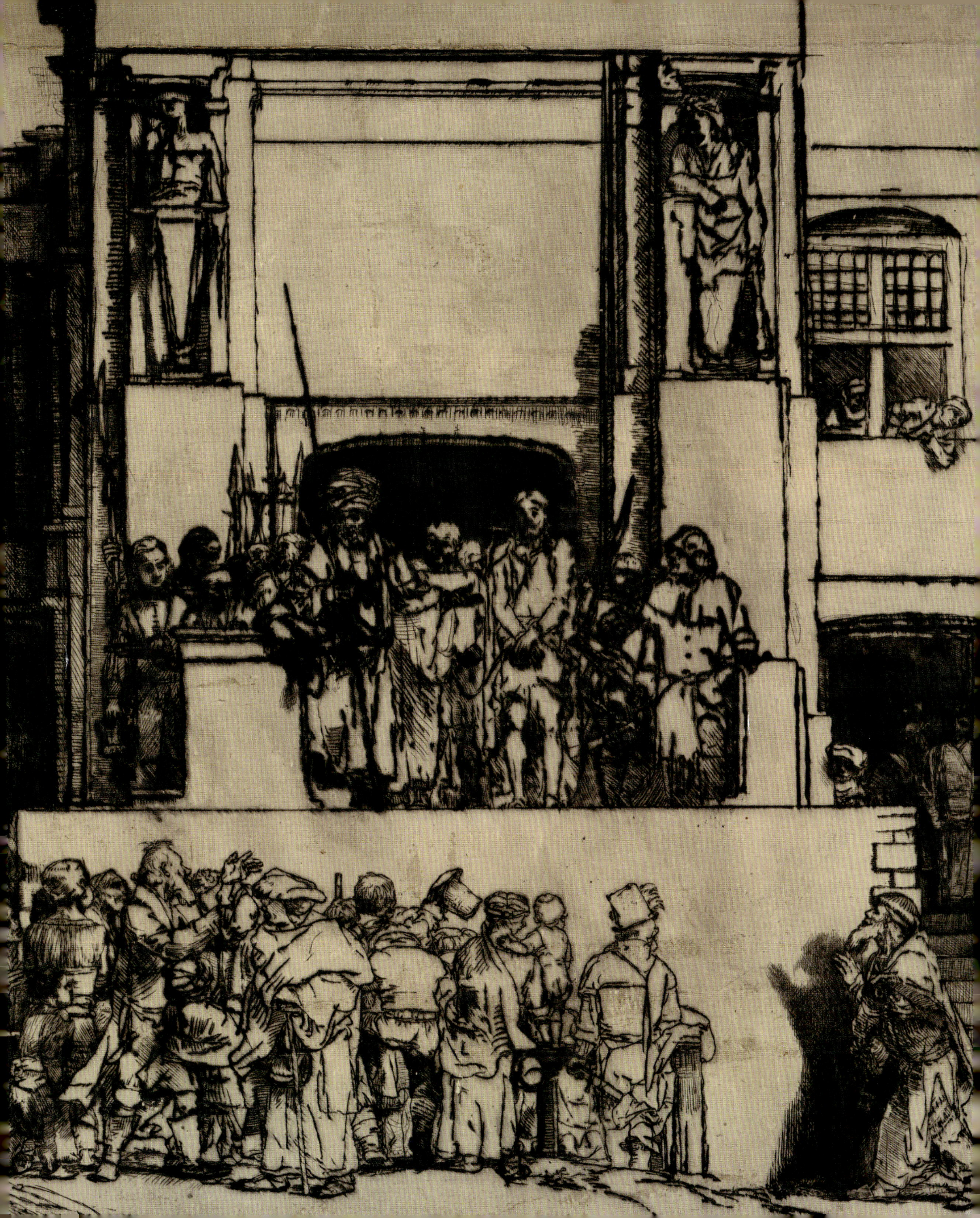

31
Christ presented to the People (*Ecce Homo*), 1655
Drypoint, 38.3 × 45.5 cm
First state of eight
The British Museum, London (1848,0911.38)

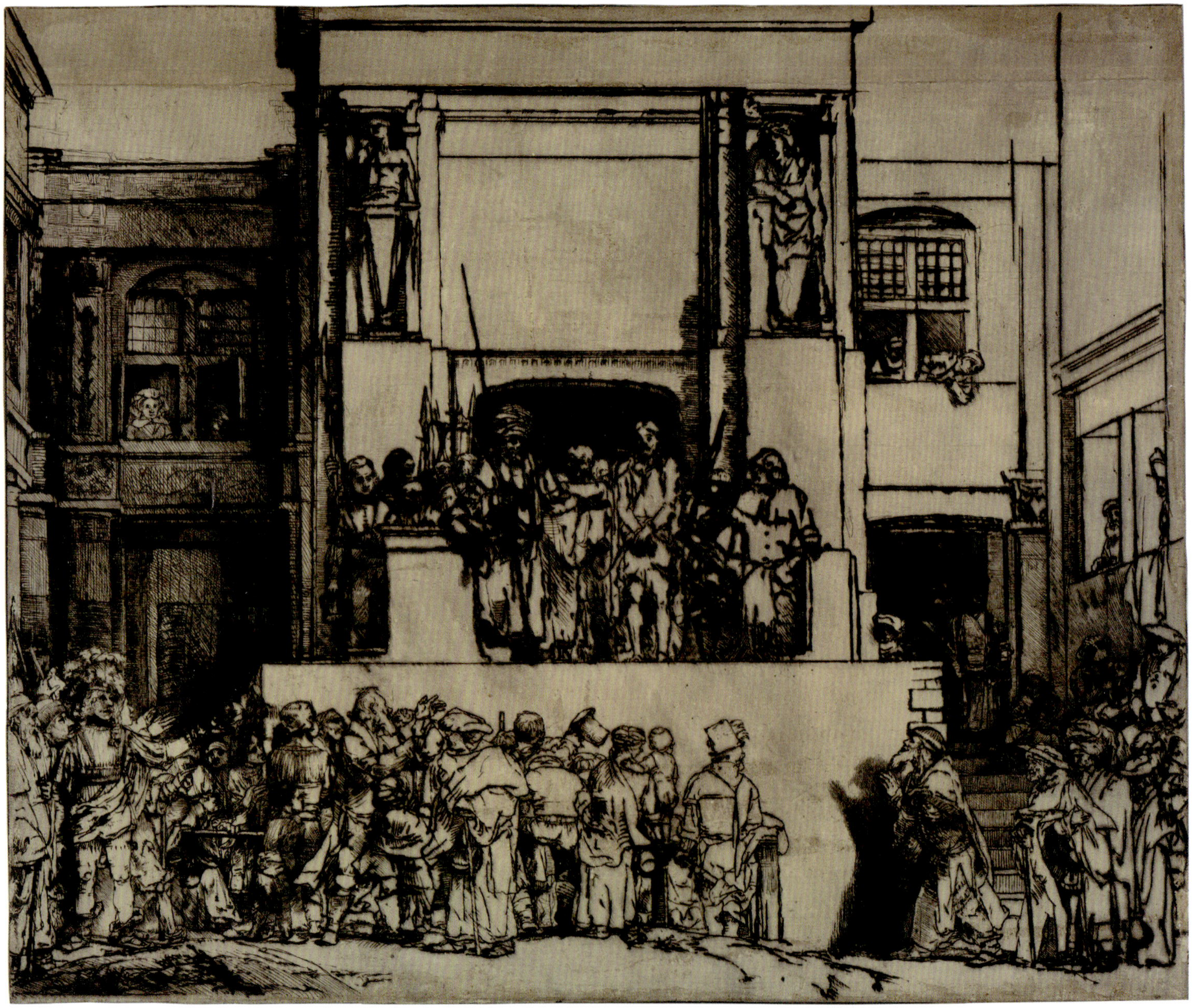

32
Christ presented to the People (*Ecce Homo*), 1655
Drypoint, 35.8 × 45.5 cm
Sixth state of eight
The British Museum, London (1848,0724.17)

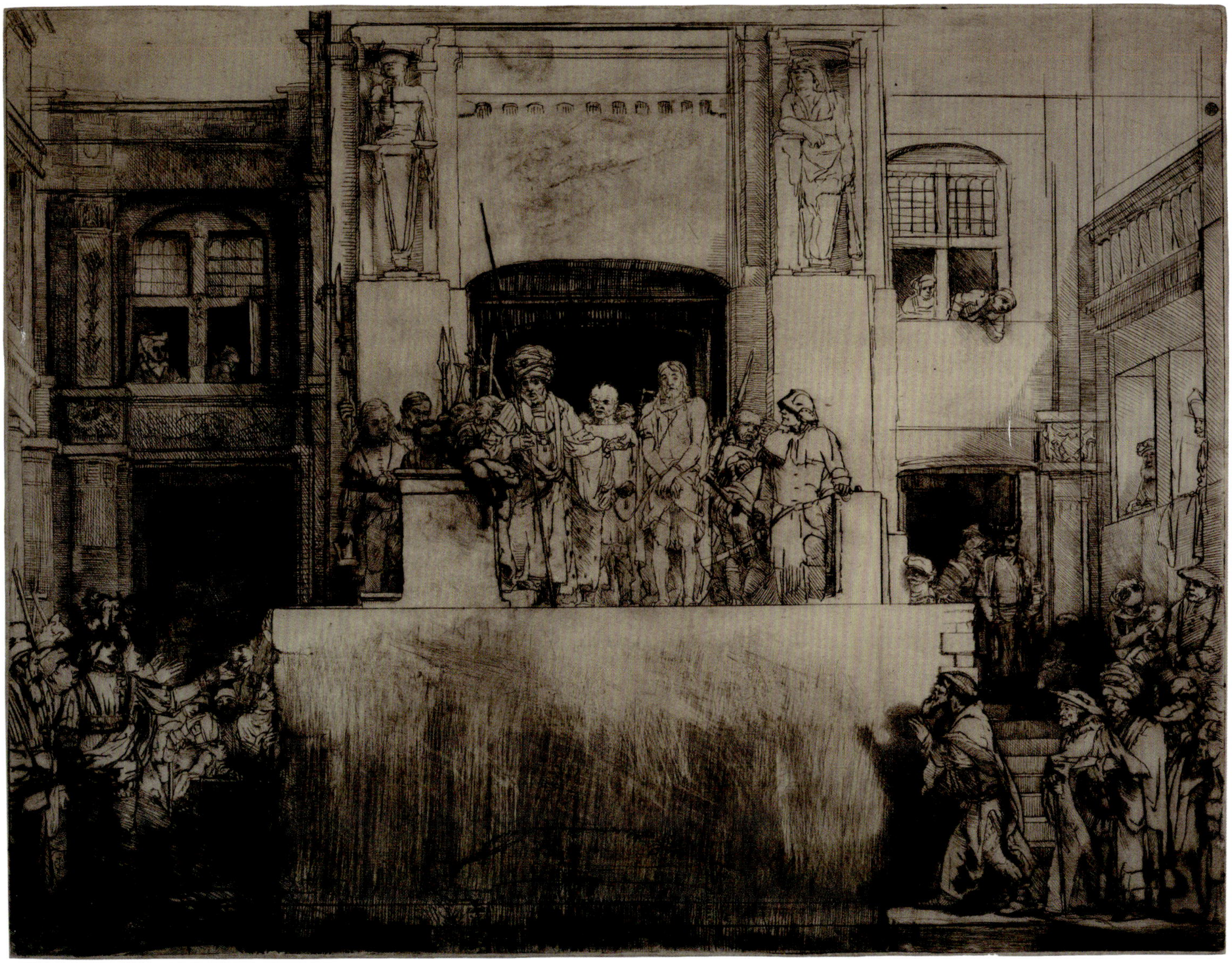

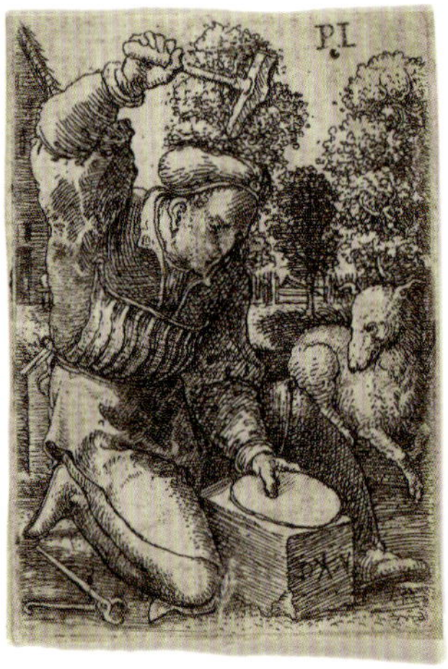

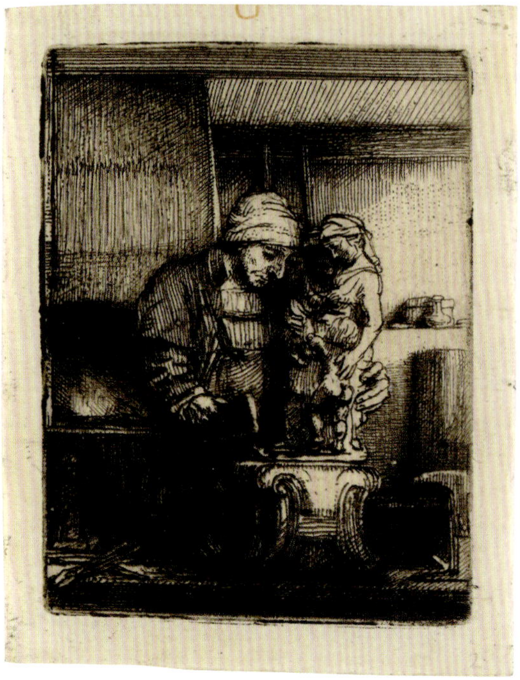

FIG. 43
DIRCK JACOBSZ VELLERT
(about 1480/85– about 1547)
The Smith, about 1520–30
Etching and engraving,
5.8 × 3.9 cm
The Metropolitan Museum of Art, New York. Purchase, Joseph Pulitzer Bequest, 1917

33
The Goldsmith, 1655
Etching and drypoint,
7.7 × 5.6 cm
First state of three
Ashmolean Museum, Oxford (WA 1855.349)

1547), of far more modest proportions than Lucas's *Ecce Homo*, also served as a model for one of Rembrandt's late prints. Vellert's tiny etching of a smith (fig. 43) was the prototype for Rembrandt's 1655 *Goldsmith* (cat. 33).[47] Not only are the two artisans similarly engrossed in their hammering, but they also wear comparable apparel, including an apron with smocking, and even have similar facial features, most notably their beak-like noses. However, the scene in Rembrandt's slightly larger etching with drypoint has been moved indoors and a metal statuette of a woman with two children, symbolising Charity, has been added. The sculptor tenderly caresses his work, with his left hand mirroring how the mother affectionately holds her children. Rembrandt's print, therefore, is a charming evocation of the artist's love of his creation.

Rembrandt's most exotic source of inspiration during his later years came from seventeenth-century Indian Mughal miniatures, which he reproduced in at least 23 pen-and-wash drawings.[48] These are not copies in the strictest sense of the word, as he not only executed them in a different medium, but also introduced perspective and shading, and changed some of the details. The originals were probably kept in the album listed in the 1656 inventory as containing 'curious drawings in miniature as well as woodcuts and engravings on copper of various costumes'.[49] Indeed, Rembrandt would probably have collected these miniatures as examples of exotic Near Eastern dress that could be used to lend authenticity to his biblical scenes.[50] For instance, the feathered headgear worn by the figure at the upper left in the *Christ preaching* (cat. 26) resembles that in a number of these miniatures, as do the slippers worn by some of the other figures in this and other works with biblical subjects.[51] Most of Rembrandt's copies show only one or two figures. An exception is a scene of four sheiks conversing, seated cross-legged on the ground (fig. 44), which served as the model for the Dutch master's 1656 etching *Abraham entertaining the Angels* (cat. 34). In addition to the general design, some of the details in the etching, such as the impressive squared white beard worn by the figure of God, the jug carried by Abraham on the right, and the dish, were inspired by this model.

Rembrandt's engagement with the work of other artists during his late period was intense and his sources were quite diverse, as were the ends to which they were put. While some of his models, such as the Indian Mughal miniatures, mostly provided motifs to be incorporated into independent compositions, others, such as Annibale Carracci's *Jupiter and Antiope* (fig. 41), spurred Rembrandt on to an artistic competition whereby the prototype was surpassed, but remained recognisable. Yet another category of emulation is formed by those works, such as the *Christ preaching* (cat. 26), that are at a second remove from the prototype, in this instance Raphael's *Parnassus* (fig. 36). In these cases Rembrandt fully integrated an element found in the work of another artist he had studied into his own artistic vision. Staunch classicist critics like Roger de Piles may have failed to recognise that Rembrandt did indeed make use of 'the fine Designs, that came out of Italy', not only because they lacked access to the Dutch master's complete oeuvre, but also because the influence those works exerted on him was so integrally combined with, and expressed through, those aspects of his style that they considered reprehensible.

FIG. 44
Four Orientals seated under a Tree, about 1656–61
Pen and brown ink with brown and grey wash, touched with white and with some scraping-out, on oriental paper prepared with pale brown wash, 19.4 × 12.4 cm
The British Museum, London

34
Abraham entertaining the Angels, 1656
Etching and drypoint, 15.9 × 13.1 cm
Only state
The Fitzwilliam Museum, Cambridge (AD.12.39-71)

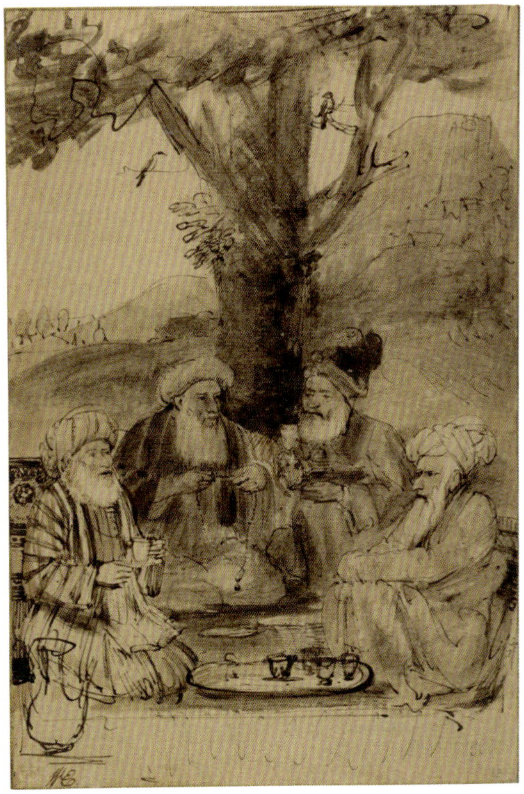

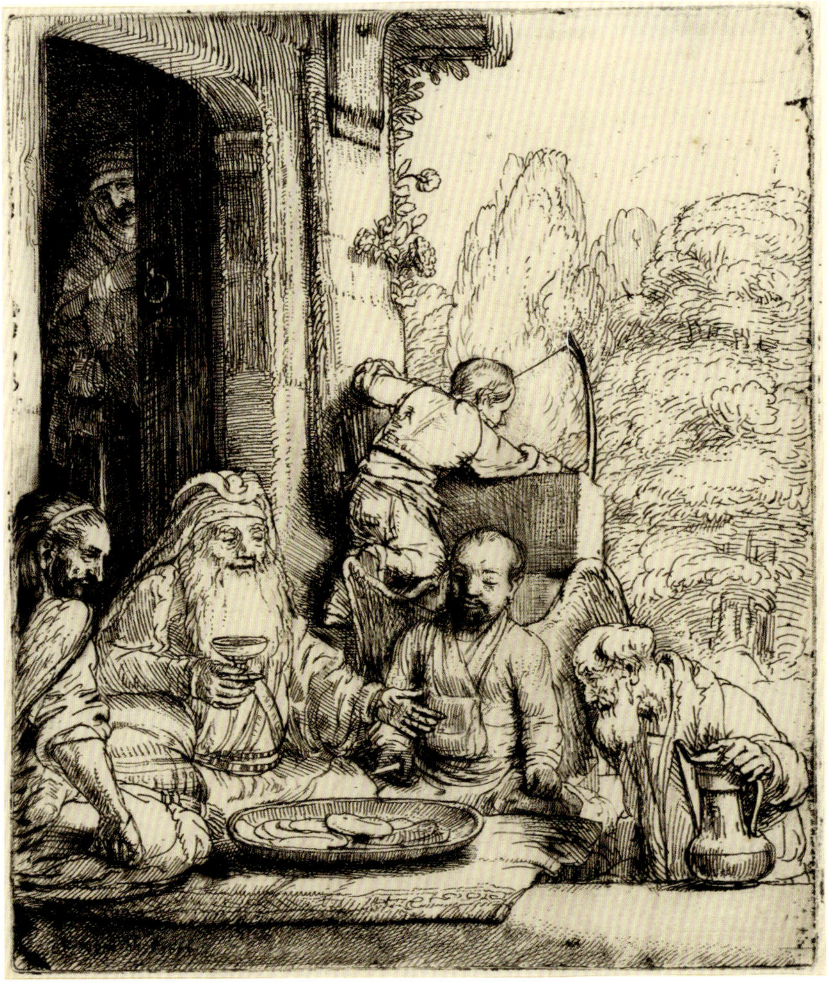

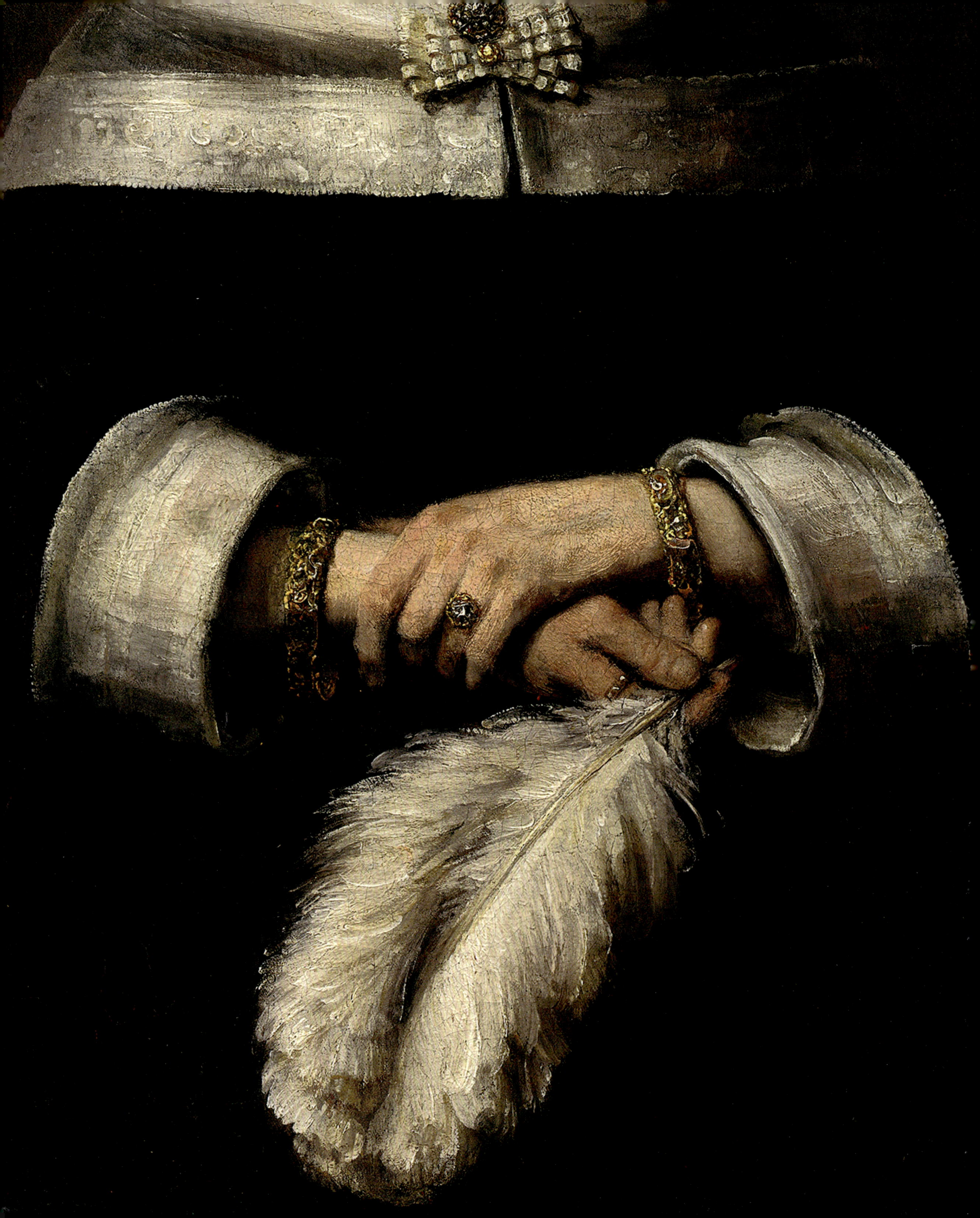

ARTISTIC CONVENTIONS

Marjorie E. Wieseman

THROUGHOUT HIS CAREER Rembrandt pushed against the boundaries of what was thought acceptable and appropriate in art. Whether depicting landscapes or historical subjects, in paintings, drawings or prints, as a mature artist he was no more likely to accept the prevailing norms than he had been in his fiery youth. As Filippo Baldinucci famously observed, 'his mind was very different from other people as well as his behaviour, and as unusual was also his manner of rendering'.[1]

Rembrandt's apparent rejection of accepted artistic conventions – rules based on a classical understanding of draughtsmanship, perspective, proportion, anatomy, beauty and symmetry – belied his thorough understanding of those rules, which in turn served as a springboard for his own, typically more thoughtful and inventive approach. This independence manifested itself in a variety of ways: in some instances Rembrandt blatantly defied artistic norms, but in others (portraiture, for example) he seems to test them more gently. For such avowed classicists as Baldinucci (as well as Jan de Bisschop, Andries Pels, Joachim von Sandrart, Arnold Houbraken and others), it was Rembrandt's depiction of the human form, particularly nudes, that constituted his most egregious transgression against all that was beautiful in art. For example, in conceiving the mysterious and poetic image of a reclining woman seen from behind, of 1658 (cat. 35), Rembrandt would undoubtedly been aware of the distinguished tradition of the pose: from sixteenth-century German and Venetian engravings to Northern examples by Abraham Bloemaert (1564–1651) and others, countless artists had traced the same classically elegant contours.[2] Rather than restricting his attention to the idealised proportions and linear grace of the figure, as so many had done before him, Rembrandt softened and blurred forms, enhancing the image's sensual appeal by emphasising the mystery inherent in a figure that guards its privacy and anonymity by turning its back to the viewer. The woman's body is cloaked in shadow; shaded contours beg an exploratory touch to better understand shape and form. The enigma of the model's skin colour only enhances the allure: is this a white woman, her body subsumed by dense shadow; or a black woman, her skin burnished with subtle highlights?[3] Similarly, in his beautifully observed drawing of a reclining nude (cat. 36) Rembrandt added a distinctive twist to the rich tradition of classical and Renaissance studies of women in similar poses by focusing on the extraordinary physicality of his model, the irrefutable (and somewhat ungainly) weightiness of her slumped and slumbering body.

When it came to commissioned portraits, Rembrandt was forced to negotiate a very different set of conventions and expectations, including the delicate dance between artist and patron; nevertheless, he was able to endow each likeness with his distinctive stamp. The seventeenth-century Dutch Republic fostered a culture particularly receptive to the development of diverse and innovative portrait types.[4] Superseding the traditional portrait clientele of the nobility and wealthy urban patriciate, from the late sixteenth century the Dutch Republic boasted an expanding – and increasingly ambitious and self-confident – middle class comprised of civic officials, merchants and professionals, who commissioned portraits to assert their newly won social and political status. The bustling capital city of Amsterdam was home to an especially dynamic population of wealthy merchants and magistrates, who actively encouraged competitive innovation in individual and family portraits, eventually defining their own set of traditions and conventions. The conventions guiding official public portraits of individuals and groups, on the other hand

Detail from *Portrait of a Lady with an Ostrich-Feather Fan* (cat. 38)

35
Reclining Female Nude
(*'La Négresse couchée'*), 1658
Etching and drypoint,
8.1 × 15.8 cm
Second state of six
The Fitzwilliam Museum,
Cambridge (AD.12.39-163)

36
Nude Woman resting on
a Cushion, about 1661–2
Pen and brush in brown ink
with white bodycolour,
13.6 × 28.3 cm
Rijksmuseum, Amsterdam
(RP-T-1917-1)

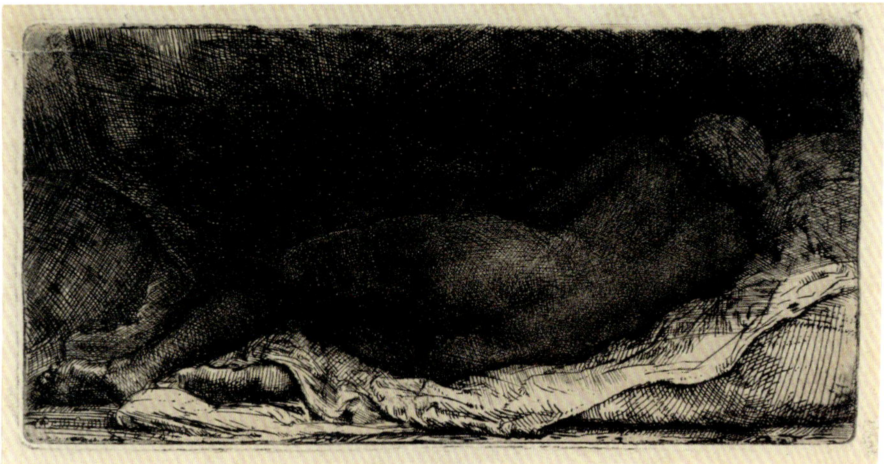

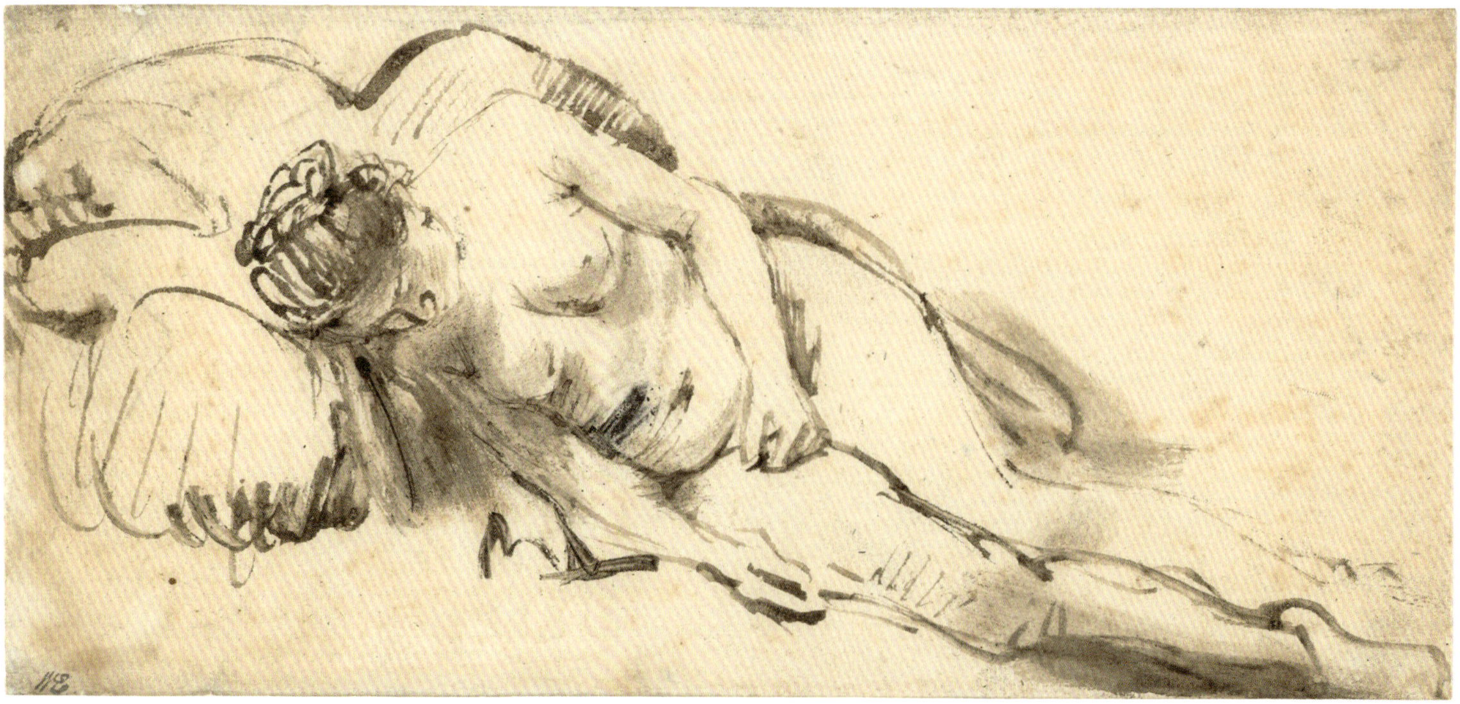

– local bureaucrats and administrators, regents of charitable institutions and officers of professional guilds and civic militia companies – remained more static throughout the century, relying on traditional compositional formats to invest them with the dignity and gravitas expected of public officials.

It was as a portraitist that the young Rembrandt first made a name for himself when in 1631 he moved to Amsterdam and began working for the painter and art dealer Hendrick Uylenburgh. Although he had painted few (if any) formal portraits before his move, the unprecedented immediacy and vitality of such large-scale works as the *Portrait of Nicolaes Ruts* of 1631 (The Frick Collection, New York) must have astonished Rembrandt's contemporaries in Amsterdam. Just one year later he won a prestigious commission to paint a distinguished group of Amsterdam surgeons as they observed an anatomy lesson given by their praelector, Dr Nicolaes Tulp (fig. 96). Here, too, Rembrandt infused an established portrait type (a group portrait in the form of an anatomy lesson) with a novel intensity that wholly engages the viewer in the drama of the moment.

Although Rembrandt was a prolific, inventive portraitist in both paintings and prints, his production was not consistent over the course of his career. After an initial burst of productivity – portraits comprised over half of all the paintings he made between 1631 and 1634 – his production of painted portraits dropped off sharply. Indeed, from the mid-1630s, his reputation secured, he seems to have accepted portrait commissions only exceptionally, devoting his energies to the more prestigious and ambitious field of history painting.[5] Apart from a brief flurry around 1639–42, he painted only a handful of portraits in the 12 years between the completion of his ground-breaking militia company portrait, '*The Night Watch*' (fig. 97), in 1642 and the *Portrait of Jan Six* (cat. 101) in 1654. His production of etched portraits was similarly sporadic, clustered in the years 1633–41 and 1646–7. From the mid-1650s portraits once again formed a significant part of his painted and graphic oeuvre; it is certainly conceivable that straitened financial circumstances led him to take on more portrait commissions during these years. In the final phase of his career, Rembrandt turned his hand to nearly every category of portraiture, producing intimate likenesses of friends and family, finely wrought portrait prints, individual portraits of men and women, pendant portraits, two incomparably moving portraits of a couple and a family group (cats 92 and 94), official group portraits for prominent Amsterdam institutions, and even a rare example of an equestrian portrait. In taking on these challenges he was continually engaged with the traditions and conventions of portraiture, walking a narrow line between the expectations of his clients (some of whom appear to have had very specific ideas about how they wished to be portrayed) and his own creative impulse.

The majority of Rembrandt's portrait commissions during these years came not from the most elite ranks of Amsterdam society, the powerful burgomasters and city officials, but from merchants and theologians, scholars and wealthy art lovers, friends, neighbours and professional contacts.[6] Various reasons have been proposed for his failure to garner consistent support from the top echelons of Amsterdam society. It is entirely possible that his notorious intransigence and allegedly abrasive personality, coupled with his unorthodox lifestyle, played a significant role. Just how inflexible Rembrandt could be is demonstrated in a document of 1654 in which a client brought suit against him for failing to deliver a recognisable likeness of the subject. Rembrandt, for his

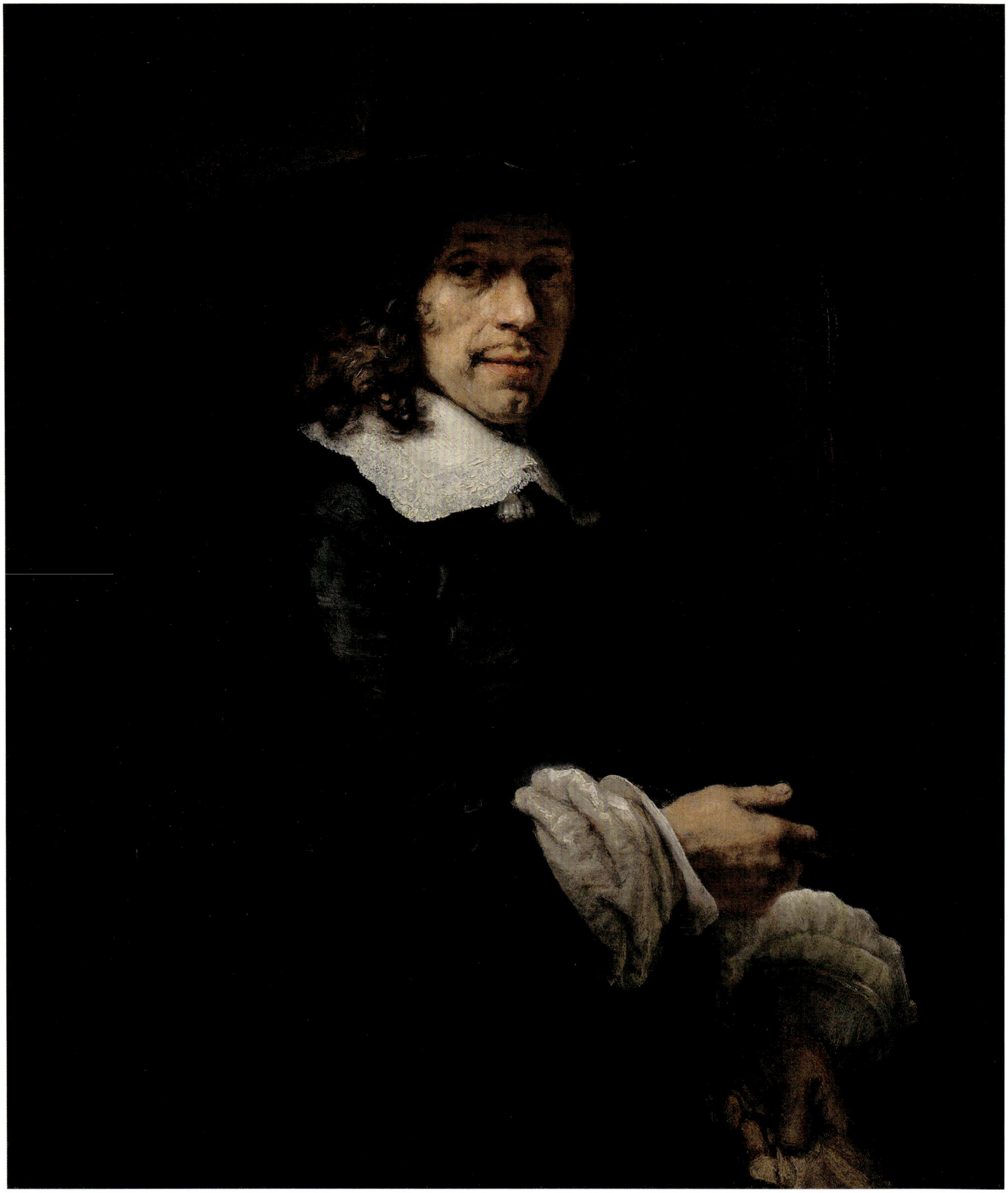

37
Portrait of a Gentleman with a Tall Hat and Gloves, about 1656–8
Oil on canvas, 99.5 × 82.5 cm
National Gallery of Art, Washington

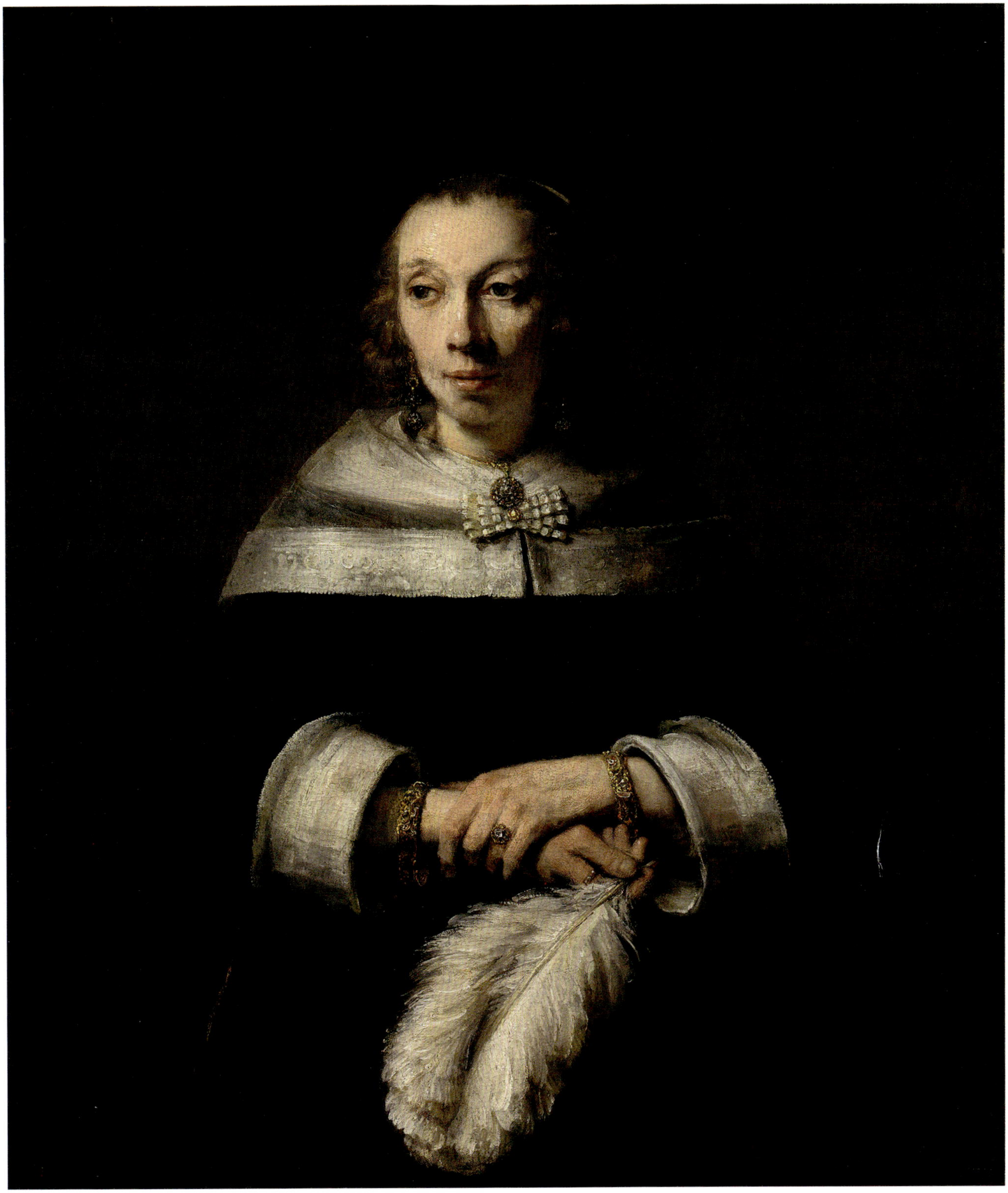

38
Portrait of a Lady with an Ostrich-Feather Fan, about 1656–8
Oil on canvas, 99.5 × 83 cm
National Gallery of Art, Washington

part, refused to finish the portrait until he had been paid, and left it 'to the judgment of the board of the St Lucas' Guild whether the painting is a likeness of the girl or not'. If the client was still not satisfied with his work, Rembrandt would keep the portrait and auction it off for his own benefit.[7] Such high-handed disregard for convention would not have won favour with seventeenth-century Amsterdam society, which operated via a system of *maagschappen*, closely knit social networks of families with their associated friends, clients and suppliers.[8] Business and personal transactions within these networks relied heavily on honour, trust and the impeccable reputation of the participants. Many of Rembrandt's contemporaries and former pupils, such as Jacob Backer (1609–1651), Ferdinand Bol, Govert Flinck and Bartholomeus van der Helst, successfully insinuated themselves into one or another of these *maagschappen*, and as a result were virtually guaranteed a steady stream of commissions, both public and private, from within the network. Rembrandt's refusal to yield to social convention may well have cost him entrée into this comfortable world; he still received commissions based on his reputation as a great artist, but fulfilling one commission did not automatically lead to others from within the network.

Moreover, his distinctive manner of painting – rough, painterly and decidedly idiosyncratic – was completely unlike the smooth, flowing style, informed by the Van Dyckian courtly elegance and Francophile taste that dominated fashionable portraiture in Amsterdam in the second half of the seventeenth century. Former Rembrandt pupils Bol, Flinck and Nicolaes Maes (1634–1693), as well as Van der Helst and Abraham van den Tempel (1622/3–1672), supplied just this sort of aspirational portrait to their sophisticated clientele, who valued the cosmopolitan and aristocratic associations of the style. Clarity of form, an accurate but flattering likeness and a respectful, even reverential detailing of material prosperity were key to the success of their portraits (see figs 45–6, 49). Rembrandt's bluntly challenging work would not have appealed to every potential client looking to have his or her features immortalised. Describing Nicolaes Maes's rejection of his master's tenebrous manner in favour of a brighter palette and more fluid application of paint, Arnold Houbraken explained that Maes had deliberately transformed his portrait-painting style because he 'saw that young women in particular took more pleasure in white than in brown'.[9] Still, Rembrandt did not lack sitters in his later years and devoted clients were rewarded with an insightful likeness that was at the same time a striking work of art, which through the artist's skilful brushwork, masterful orchestration of light and shade and his willingness to sacrifice precise form and specific detail for overall effect, was invested with a remarkable living presence.

Pendant portraits of a married couple, that of the husband typically placed to the left and the wife to the right, are among the most common portrait types during the period, frequently commissioned on the occasion of a couple's marriage or to commemorate some other life event. Rembrandt approached this most conventional format with a fresh eye, particularly in suggesting the relationship between the sitters. Although we no longer know the identities of the couple depicted in Rembrandt's poignant portraits of about 1656–8 in the National Gallery of Art, Washington (cats 37–8), we nonetheless have a sense of their personalities. The man regards the viewer with a hint of a smile; his body is turned sharply to the right and his right arm reaches across his body towards his wife, establishing a link between the two portraits. The woman, however, holds herself aloof. Her hooded gaze avoids contact with either her husband or the viewer; she makes no reciprocal outward gesture, but clasps her hands almost protectively before her waist.[10] In the portrait of the woman especially, Rembrandt's strong and varied brushwork evokes a real personality: her pale, haunted face is starkly modelled; her splendid jewellery is painted with thick impasto; and the single ostrich feather she holds is deftly rendered with richly layered strokes that evoke all the quivering delicacy of the original. Fans like these feature regularly in portraits of fashionable Dutch ladies, but rarely are they invested with such a vivid presence. Even the most cursory comparison with routinely fashionable likenesses such as Van der Helst's portraits of Louis de Geer and Jeanne Parmentier (figs 45–6) makes plain the insight and immediacy of Rembrandt's finely honed observation.

Numerous portraits exist of the wealthy Dordrecht merchant Jacob Trip (about 1576–1661) and his wife Margaretha de Geer (1583–1672): the Dordrecht painter Jacob Gerritsz Cuyp (1594–1652) painted the couple in 1649 and 1651, his son Aelbert Cuyp (1620–1691) in 1652, and Nicolaes Maes made no fewer than eight portraits of one or the other of them between 1655 and 1669. These works make it possible to appreciate the singularity of Rembrandt's likenesses (cats 39–40).[11] Maes's pendants of about 1660 (figs 47–8), which probably slightly pre-date Rembrandt's, depict the couple with stately poses and old-fashioned garments that are virtually mirror images of each other. Meticulous detailing of papery flesh and fur-trimmed garments fixes the images with cool, almost scientific precision. Rembrandt, on the other hand, honours the advanced age of his sitters (in 1661 Jacob was about 85 years old and Margaretha was 78) by using a light, suggestive touch to evoke and echo their corporeal fragility. Unusually, Jacob, painted in the year of his death, is dressed in rather idiosyncratic garments that would only have been worn indoors: a loose robe, a nightcap, and a simple white shawl in place of a starched collar.[12] His elegant walking stick now seems more a necessity of age than a stylish accessory. His garments allude to his wealth and status (echoes of costly padded silk robes imported from Japan) and mature wisdom (the robe is reminiscent of the *tabbaard*, a garment traditionally worn by scholars, clerics and the elderly); Trip himself possesses all the gravity of an Old Testament patriarch. The portrait is more quickly, economically and directly painted than its pendant; this fact, together with the sitter's static pose, has led to the suggestion that it might have been created posthumously from a painted likeness rather than the live model.[13] Alternatively, Trip's declining health may have hastened the execution of the portrait.

Rather than being positioned in a deferential half-turn towards her husband (as was customary in pendant

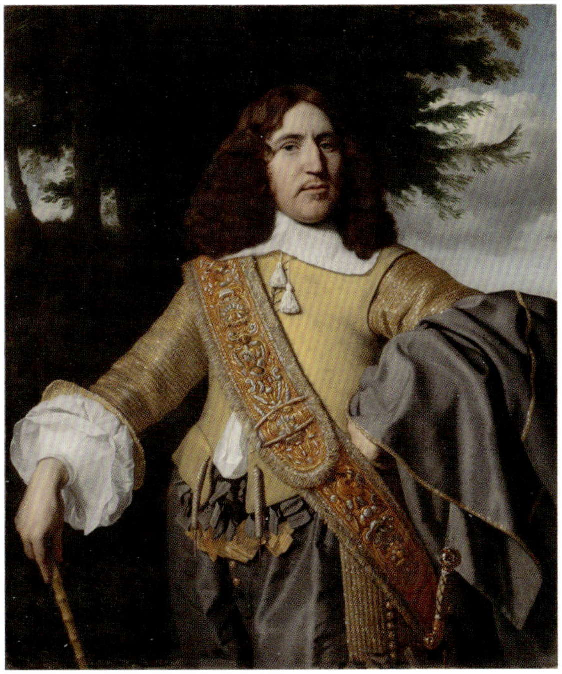

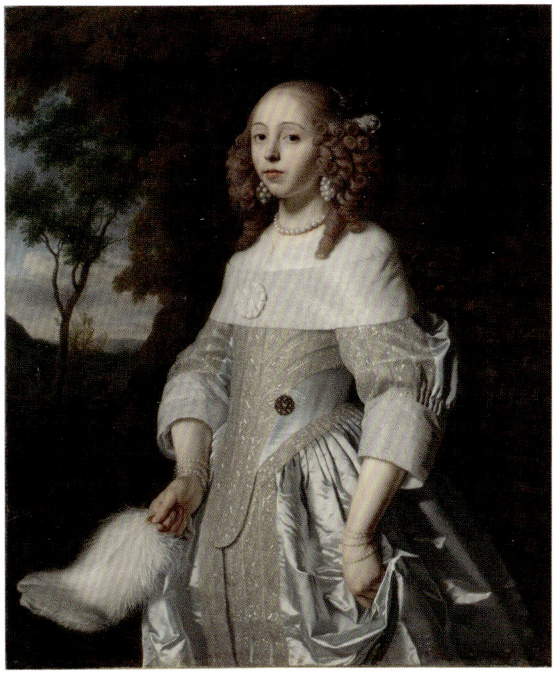

FIG. 45
BARTHOLOMEUS VAN DER HELST (1613–1670)
Portrait of Louis de Geer, 1656
Oil on canvas, 110 × 91 cm
Nationalmuseum, Stockholm

FIG. 46
BARTHOLOMEUS VAN DER HELST (1613–1670)
Portrait of Jeanne Parmentier, 1656
Oil on canvas, 110 × 91 cm
Nationalmuseum, Stockholm

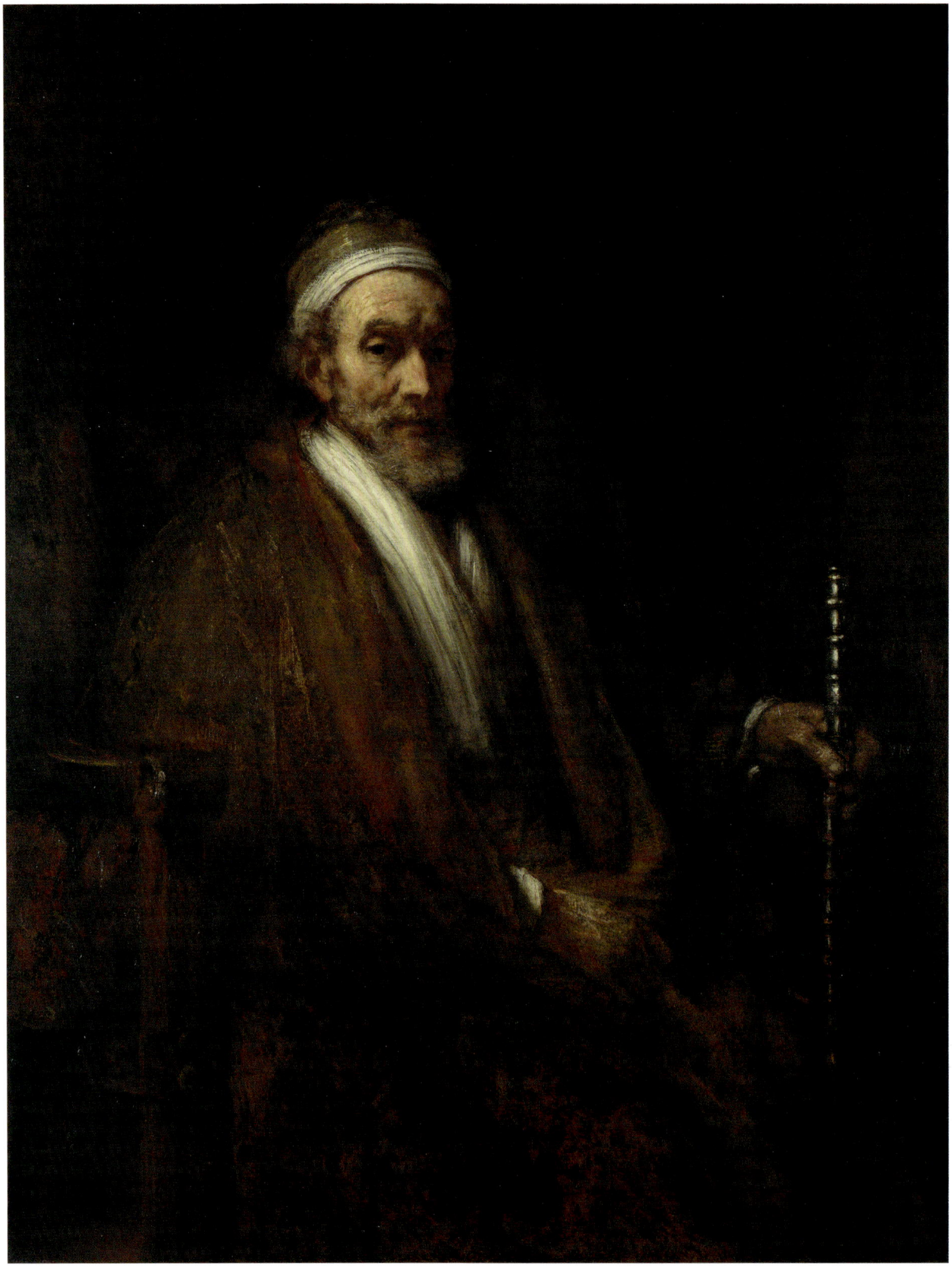

39
Portrait of Jacob Trip, about 1661
Oil on canvas, 130.5 × 97 cm
The National Gallery, London

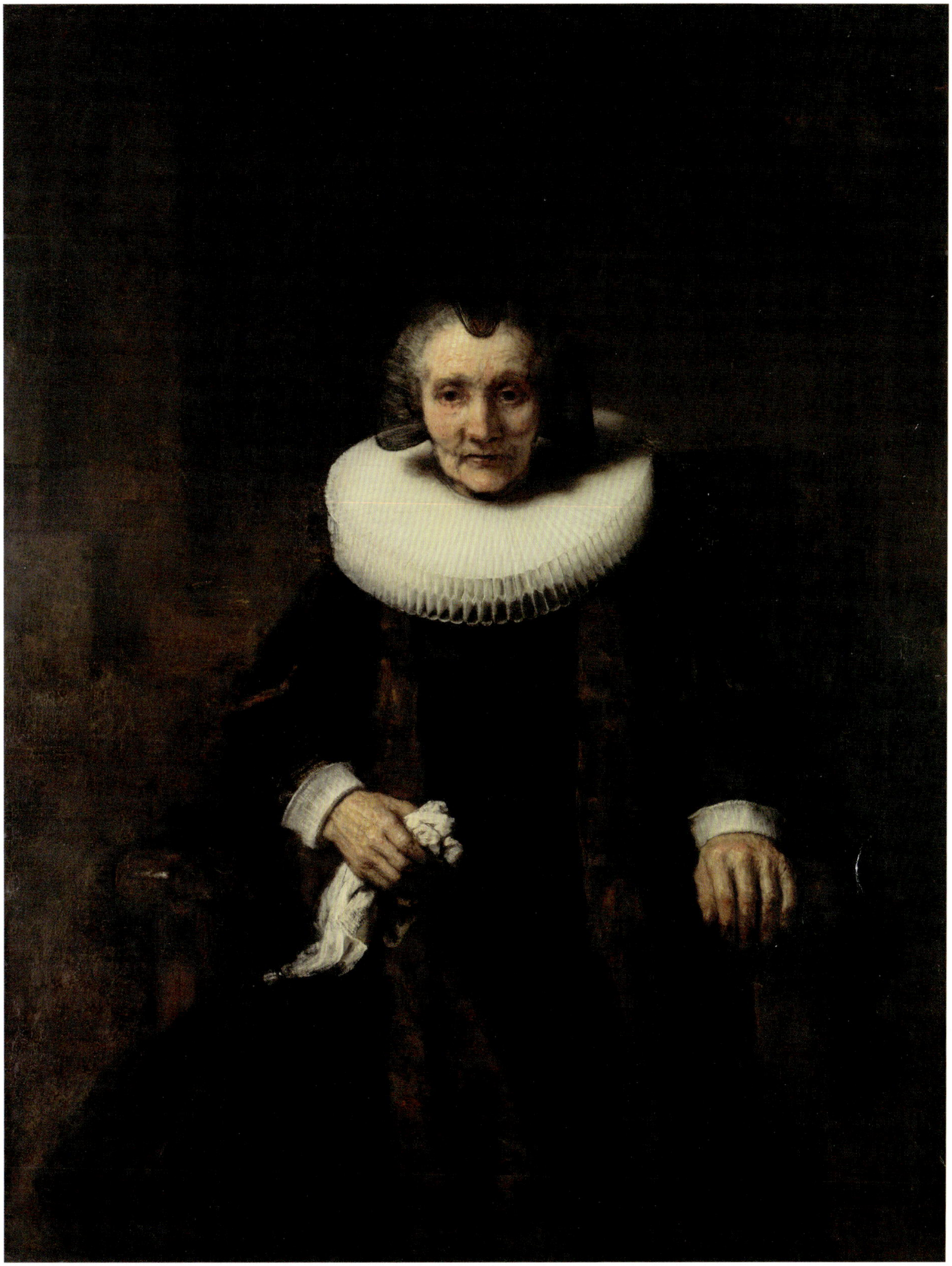

40
Portrait of Margaretha de Geer, Wife of Jacob Trip, about 1661
Oil on canvas, 130.5 × 97.5 cm
The National Gallery, London

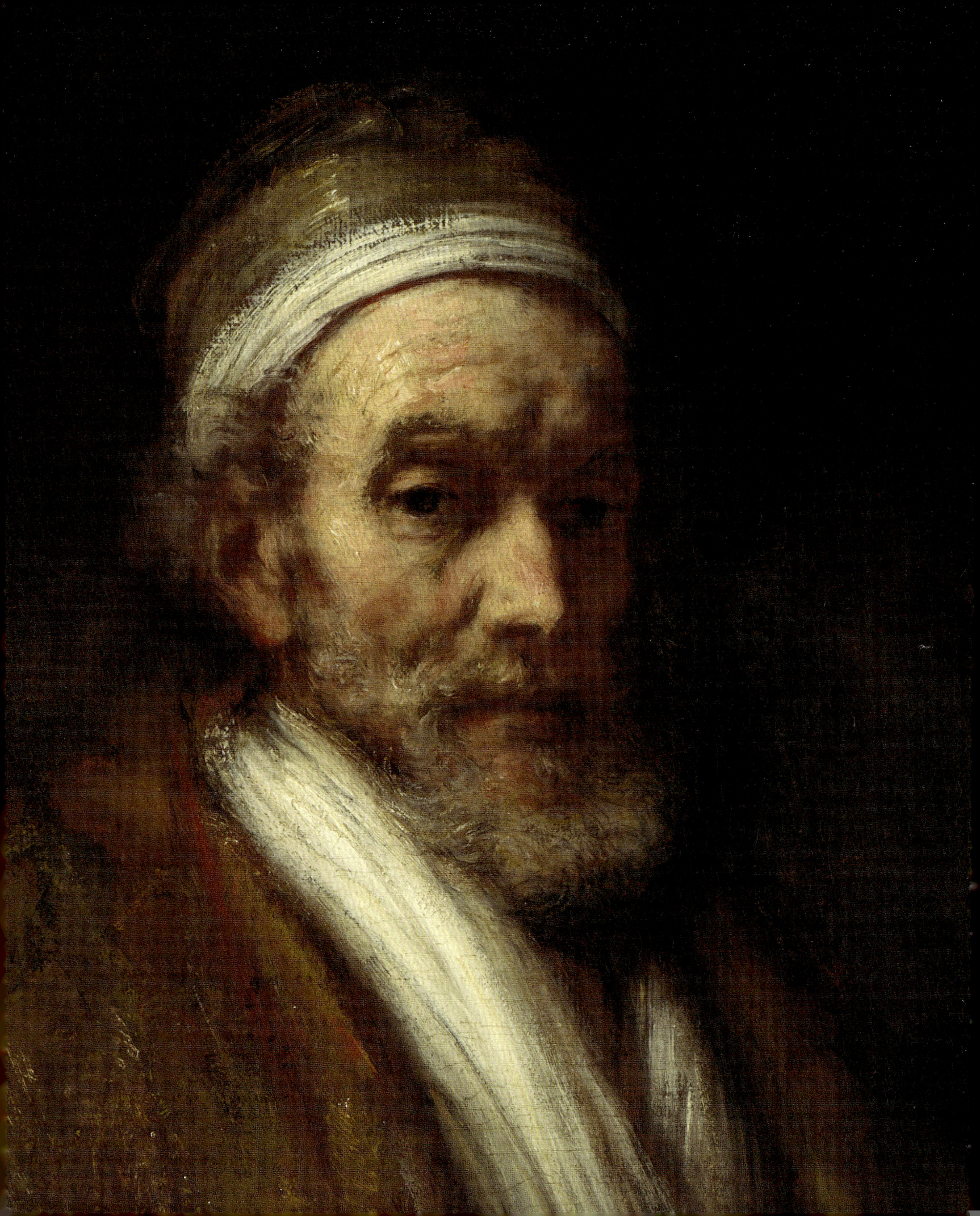

Detail from *Portrait of Jacob Trip* (cat. 39)

pairs), Margaretha de Geer is posed fully frontally and peers out at the viewer with a rheumy but disconcertingly beady-eyed stare (cat. 40). She, too, wears informal and quite old fashioned garments; her white handkerchief is probably a conservative fashion accessory rather than a sign of recent bereavement.[14] The paint here is more deliberately worked than in the companion portrait, and X-radiographs show numerous changes to the composition.[15] Most notably, Rembrandt repeatedly changed the position of the sitter's left hand, from initially resting passively in her lap to grasping the arm of her chair. Her hands are large, almost masculine, enhancing the impression of steely determination. Margaretha's regal bearing leaves no doubt as to her authority and iron will; after Jacob's death she continued for more than a decade as matriarch of one of the most powerful and influential dynasties in the United Provinces.

FIG. 47
NICOLAES MAES
(1634–1693)
Portrait of Jacob Trip, about 1660
Oil on canvas, 88 × 68 cm
Szépművészeti Múzeum, Budapest

FIG. 48
NICOLAES MAES
(1634–1693)
Portrait of Margaretha de Geer, about 1660
Oil on canvas, 88 × 68 cm
Szépművészeti Múzeum, Budapest

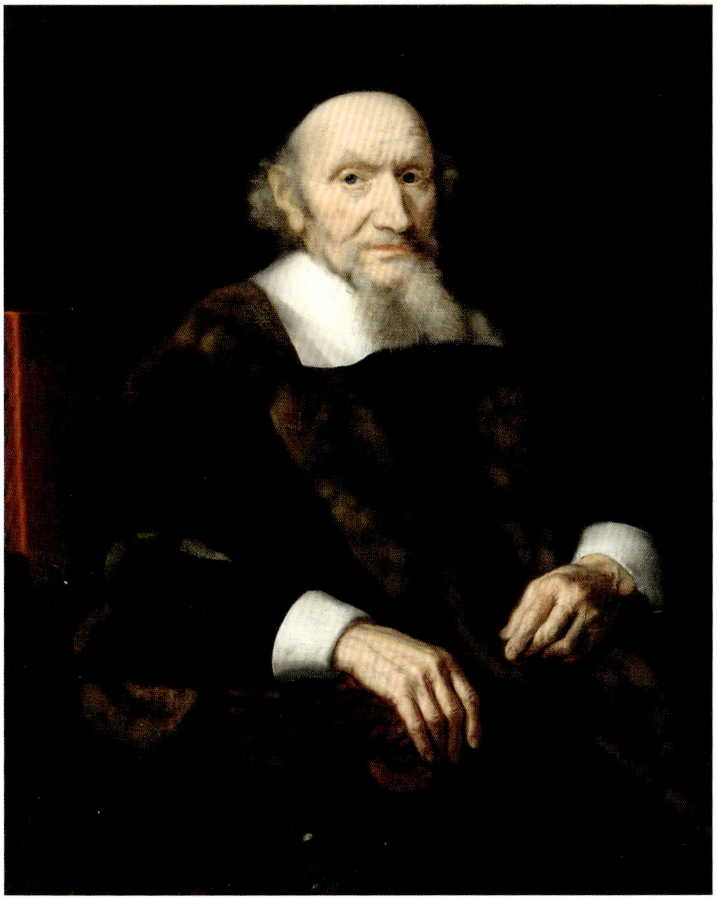

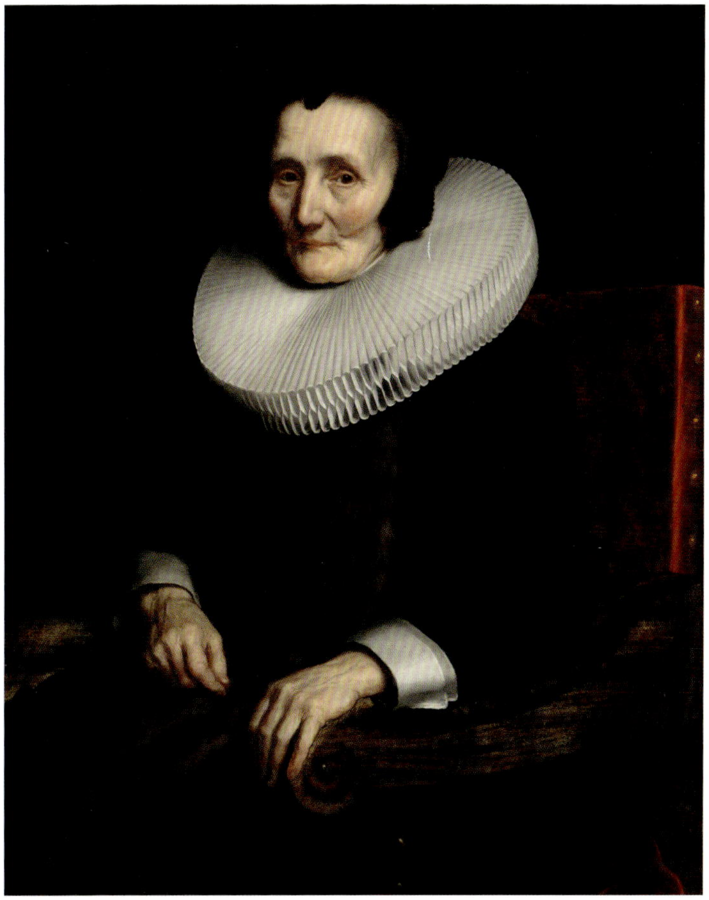

41
Portrait of Catrina Hooghsaet, 1657
Oil on canvas, 126 × 98.5 cm
Penrhyn Castle, Gwynedd

Detail from *Portrait of Catrina Hooghsaet* (cat. 41)

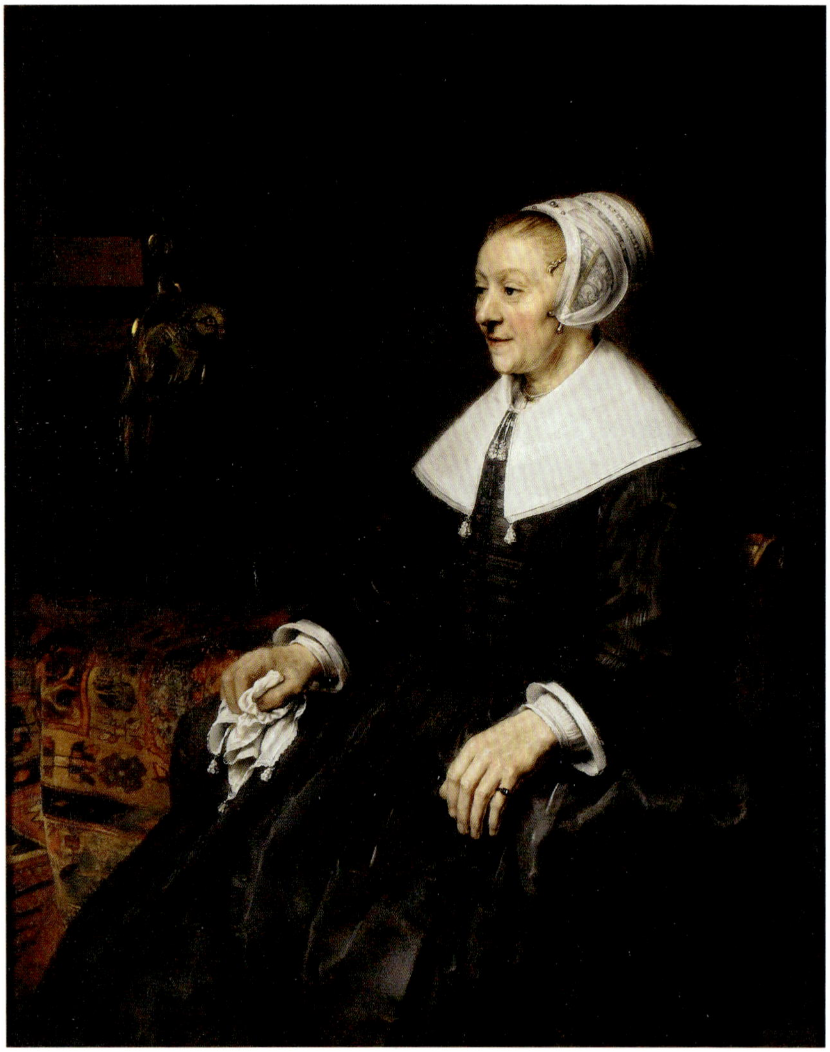

In painting the *Portrait of Catrina Hooghsaet* (cat. 41) Rembrandt faced an equally strong personality. Although Catrina (1607–1685) was married to her second husband when this portrait was painted (1657), it has no conventional pendant.[16] The marriage was apparently not a success, and for many years Catrina lived apart from her husband with a parrot for company. She was, by all accounts, an independent and spirited woman – not least in taking the initiative to commission a portrait of herself. She may well have had a key role in determining the look of the portrait, as the unusually fine degree of detail is more reminiscent of Rembrandt's work of the 1630s than the late 1650s, and the selection of accessories is also unusual. Catrina belonged to a Mennonite sect that forbade extravagant dress; in Rembrandt's portrait her wealth is effectively and appropriately suggested by her crisp, pristine linen, her large handkerchief and the carefully described intricacy of her gauzy cap, its multiple layers held in place with decorative gold hairpins and 'head irons'.[17] As with the portrait of Margaretha de Geer, X-radiographs reveal that Rembrandt considerably reworked parts of this composition. Catrina's left arm originally extended down by her side and her right was held closely against her waist. Further alterations were undertaken at the left side of the painting: at first there were objects – a box or basket, and perhaps a book – stacked on the table, and a swag of drapery at upper left; these were later replaced by the parrot swinging from a circular perch suspended from the branch of a tree. The image of Catrina's favoured companion (a 'parrot in a cage' is mentioned specifically in a codicil to her will, drawn up in December 1657) appears to have been added after the portrait was completed; whether by Rembrandt or by another hand is not certain.

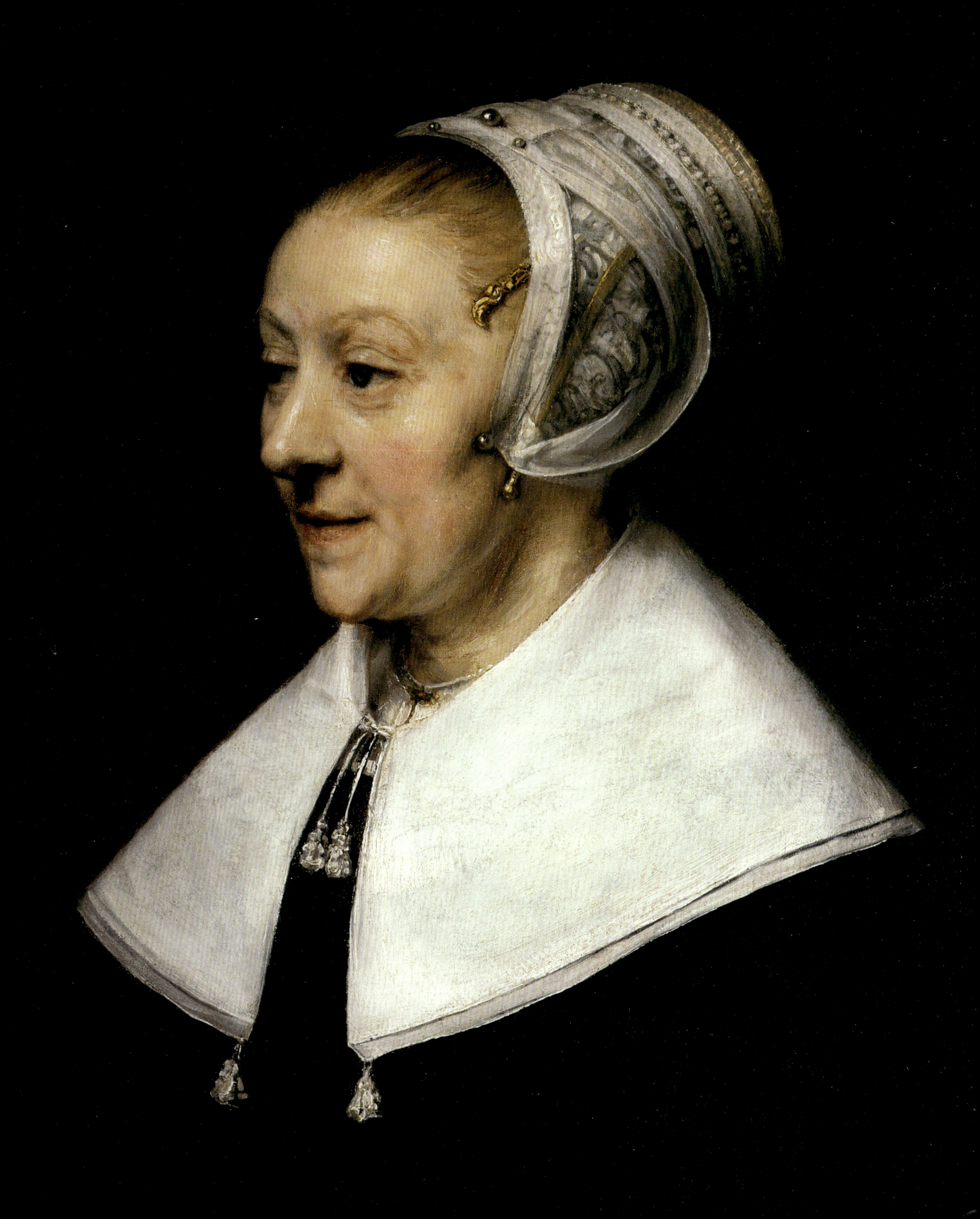

FIG. 49
ABRAHAM LAMBERTSZ VAN DEN TEMPEL
(1622–1672)
Portrait of Jacquemijna Le Pla, about 1666
Oil on canvas, 114.9 × 92.3 cm
Otto Naumann Ltd, New York

42
Portrait of a Lady with a Lap Dog, about 1662/1665
Oil on canvas, 81.3 × 64.1 cm
Art Gallery of Ontario, Toronto

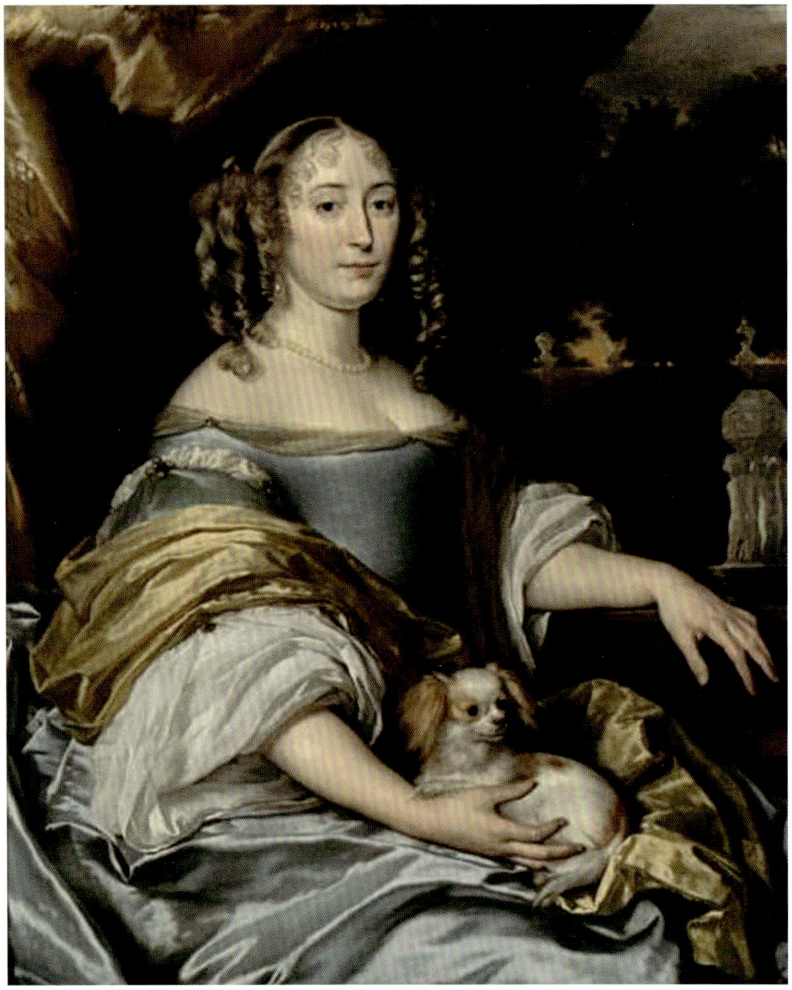

If the *Portrait of Catrina Hooghsaet* seems a little old-fashioned in its detailed technique and the conservatism of the sitter's dress, the *Portrait of a Lady with a Lap Dog* (cat. 42) shows Rembrandt confronting the very latest trends in portraiture. This simple but lush composition exhibits all the requisite features of stylish portraits of women in the early 1660s: colourful silks, a plush fur mantle, sparkling jewels, an elaborate coiffure and the frivolous accessory of a diminutive lap dog, but they are rendered with Rembrandt's signature brushwork, a startling departure from the smooth, flowing style typical for contemporary portraits of this type (fig. 49). The extraordinary variation in paint application – loose, looping strokes evoking the billows of the young woman's gown and finer touches picking out the details of her jewellery – the seriousness of her gaze and the harmonious way in which the folds of her fur wrap mimic the gesture of her hands as she tenderly cradles her pet, contribute to an exceptionally thoughtful and compelling likeness that demonstrates how Rembrandt effortlessly transformed the fashion of the moment.

Rembrandt's later portraits of men confronted the conventions of the genre in equally unexpected ways. This is certainly true of the half-dozen etched portraits he made between about 1655 and 1658.[18] Portrait prints, published as commercial ventures, book illustrations or independent works of art, and available at a wide range of price and quality, were phenomenally popular in the seventeenth-century Dutch Republic. Typically, they featured an image accompanied by a piece of text containing biographical data and/or an inscribed dedication or literary tribute. They appealed not only to the sitter's close associates, but also to collectors who assembled 'paper galleries' of military heroes, rulers,

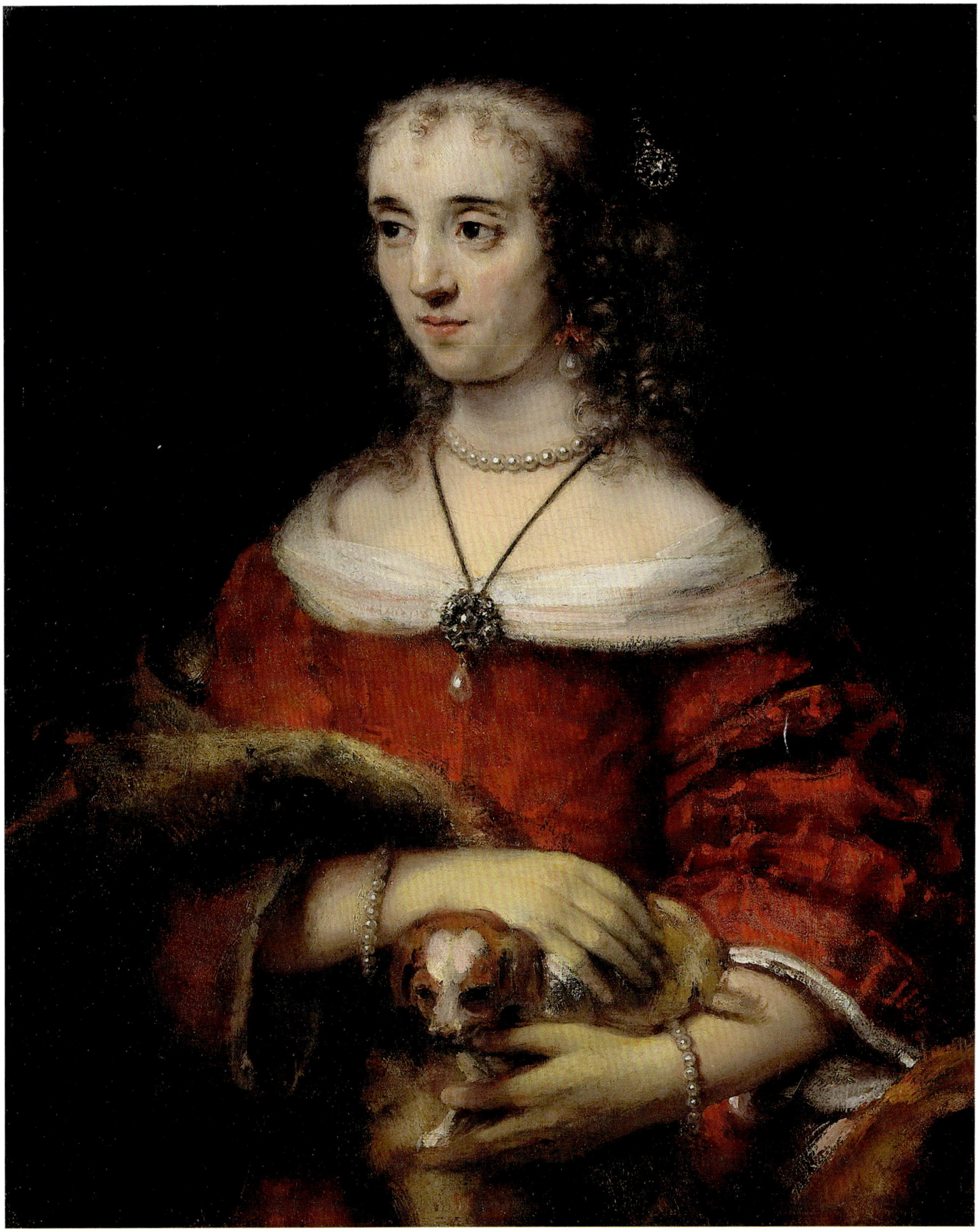

43
Portrait of Arnout Tholinx, about 1656
Etching, engraving and drypoint, 19.8 × 14.9 cm
First state of two
The British Museum, London (F,6.68)

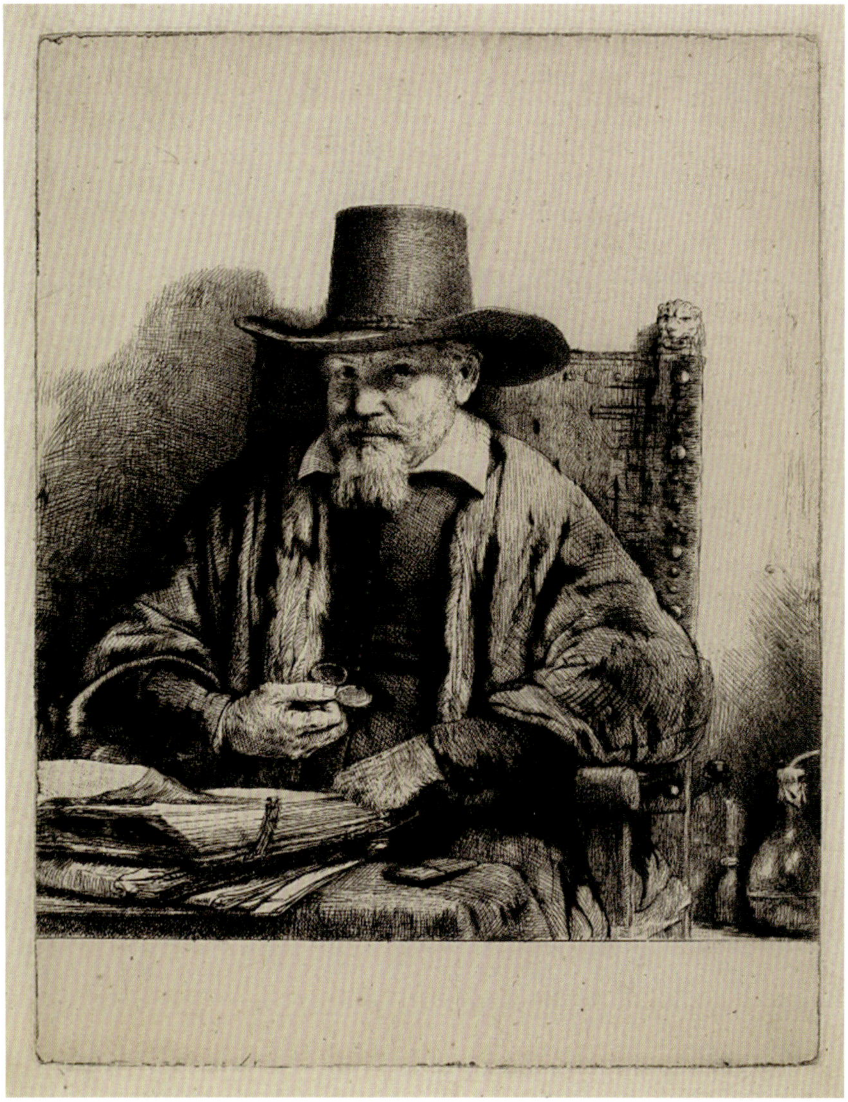

theologians, beautiful women, and so forth. Prints of prominent persons were usually engraved, the durability of the technique ensuring greater commercial distribution. Perhaps not surprisingly, Rembrandt's 17 portrait prints adhere to virtually none of these conventions: he depicted no rulers, heroes or beautiful women; most bear no inscriptions, not even the name of the sitter; and perhaps most significantly, nearly all are executed in the more versatile and responsive, but inherently fragile (and commercially unviable) techniques of etching and drypoint.

Rembrandt's etched portraits of the 1650s all depict individuals with whom he had some personal or professional affiliation: a print seller, Clement de Jonghe; a collector, Abraham Francen; a silversmith, Johannes Lutma; a calligrapher, Lieven Willemsz van Coppenol; two auctioneers, Thomas Jacobsz Haringh and Pieter Haringh; and a relative of one of his most devoted patrons, Arnout Tholinx. Tholinx (1607–1679), a physician, became Jan Six's brother-in-law in 1655, and it was undoubtedly this connection that led him to commission both a portrait in oils and a portrait print (cats 43–4) from Rembrandt in the following year.[19] Settled in his massive chair, spectacles grasped carefully between two fingers, he glances up from his perusal of a weighty volume. Bottles in the corner behind his chair allude to his profession, and the tall hat shading his eyes confers formal dignity. Impressions of this print are extremely rare; this, together with the abundant use of drypoint in the shadows, suggests that the copper plate became the property of the sitter and that few prints were ever pulled from it.

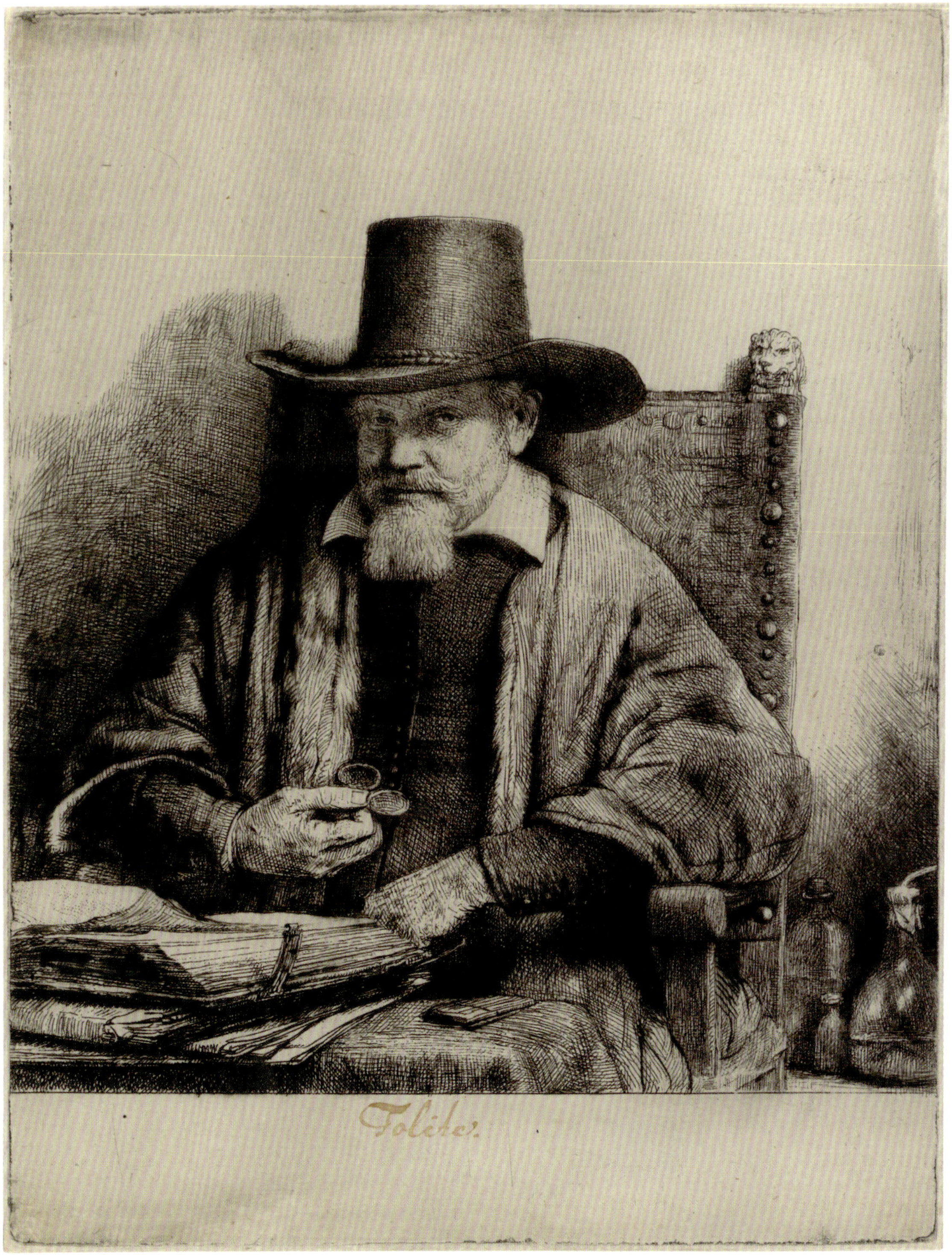

44
Portrait of Arnout Tholinx,
about 1656
Etching, engraving and
drypoint, 19.8 × 14.9 cm
Second state of two
Rijksmuseum, Amsterdam
(RP-P-OB-577)

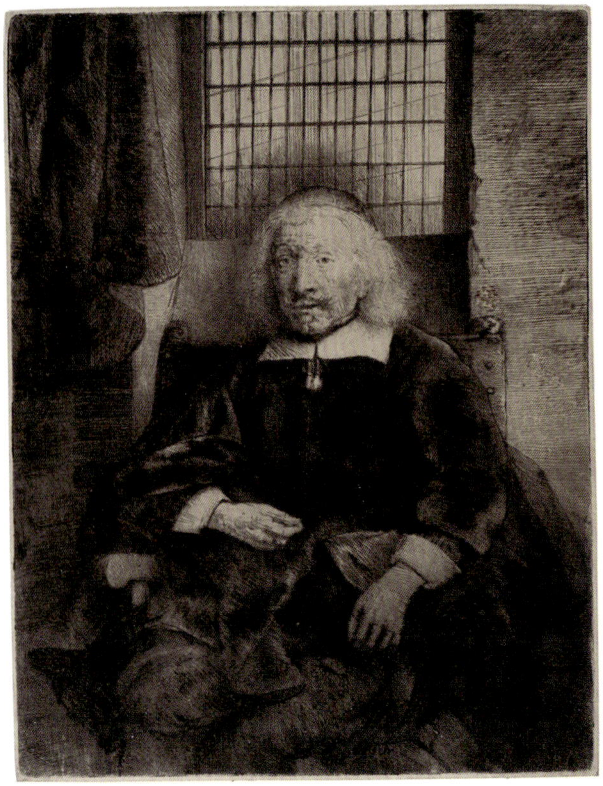

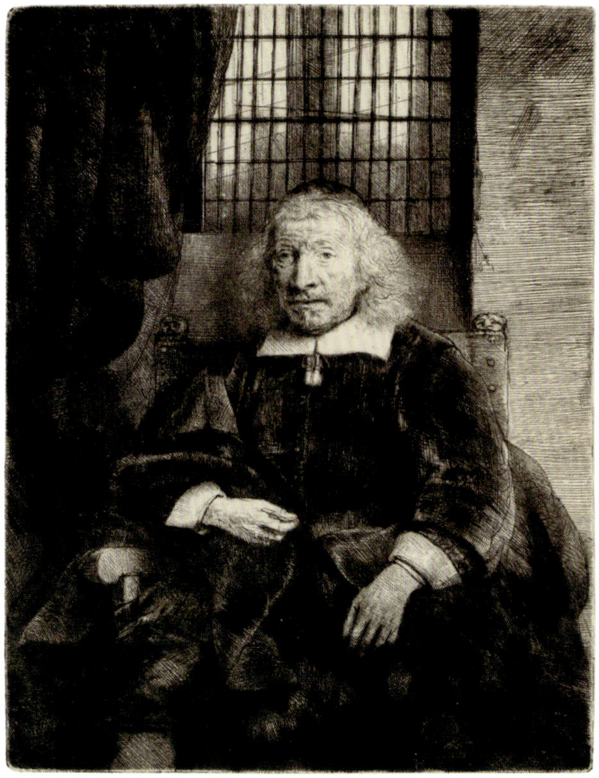

45
Thomas Jacobsz Haringh
(*'Old Haringh'*), about 1655
Drypoint with touches
of burin(?), 19.5 × 15 cm
First state of three
Graphische Sammlung
Albertina, Vienna
(DG1926/445)

46 and detail, opposite
Thomas Jacobsz Haringh
(*'Old Haringh'*), about 1655
Drypoint with touches
of burin(?), 19.5 × 15 cm
Third state of three
Ashmolean Museum,
Oxford (WA 1855.288)

FIG. 50
Portrait of Pieter Haringh
(*'Young Haringh'*), about 1655
Etching, engraving and
drypoint, 19.5 × 14.6 cm
Rijksmuseum, Amsterdam

Rembrandt's associations with Thomas Jacobsz Haringh (about 1586/7–1660) and Pieter Haringh (1609–1685) were forged under less pleasurable circumstances. As the official receiver for the orphans' court in Amsterdam, Pieter ('Young Haringh', fig. 50) was auctioneer at the voluntary sales of Rembrandt's possessions in 1655–6; his distant relative Thomas ('Old Haringh', cats 45–6) had the unenviable task of organising the forced sales of the artist's possessions held between 1656 and 1658. It has been suggested that the portraits were gifts from the artist, made in the hope of influencing favourable outcomes from the auctions.[20] Unusually, the prints are executed exclusively in drypoint, resulting in intensely rich, velvety blacks that anticipate the deep inking made possible with the introduction of the mezzotint technique.[21] Rembrandt's fine hatching with the drypoint needle produced far more subtle and delicate effects, however, as can be seen in Thomas Haringh's face and the silvery backlit cloud of his hair.

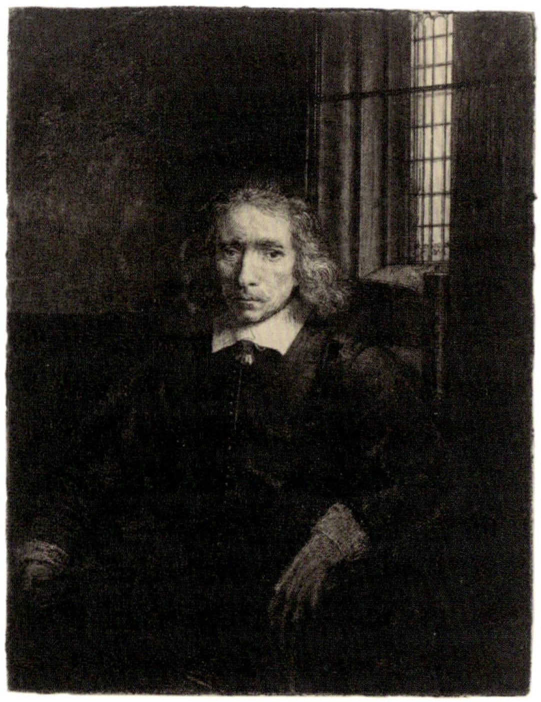

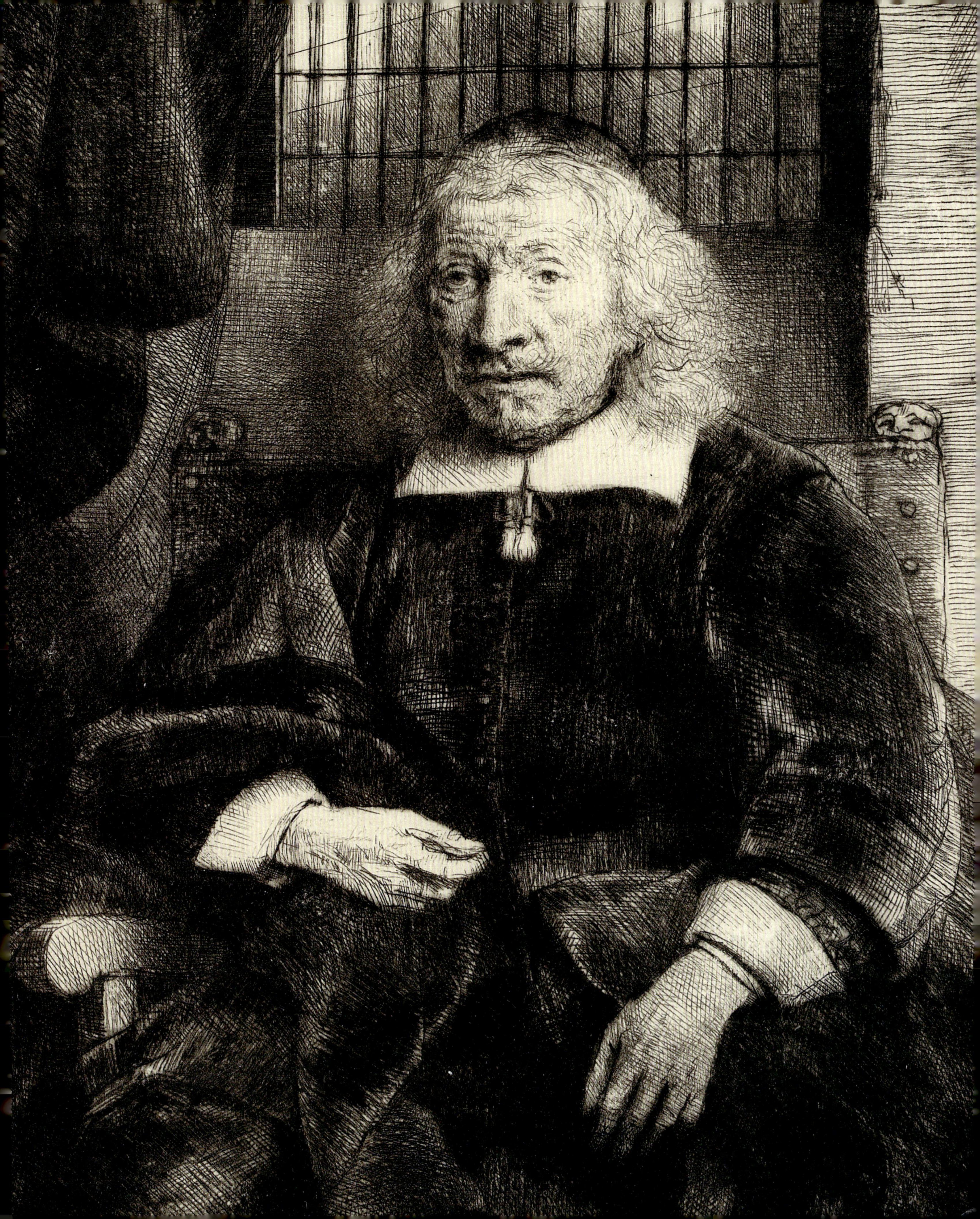

47
Portrait of Johannes Lutma, 1656
Etching, engraving and drypoint, 19.7 × 15 cm
First state of four
The Fitzwilliam Museum, Cambridge (AD.12.39-428)

48
Portrait of Johannes Lutma, 1656
Etching, engraving and drypoint, 19.7 × 15 cm
Second state of four
The Fitzwilliam Museum, Cambridge (AD.12.39-419)

Like Thomas Haringh, the silversmith Johannes Lutma (about 1584–1669) was already an elderly man when Rembrandt etched his portrait (cats 47–8). He depicts the master craftsman with the tools of his trade at his side, but with his squinting eyes nearly shut: apparently Lutma suffered problems with his eyesight, although in 1656 – the year of Rembrandt's print – declared that he had been cured of blindness.[22] In the first state of the print (cat. 47) the sitter is silhouetted against a vague, luminous background; in the second state (cat. 48) Rembrandt closed the space with a shadowy wall pierced by a deep window embrasure, creating an intimate, atmospheric effect similar to that in the Haringh portraits. Once again, the image is built up of a dense hatching of uniformly fine lines, here and there strengthened with the addition of drypoint.

Detail from *Portrait of Johannes Lutma* (cat. 47)

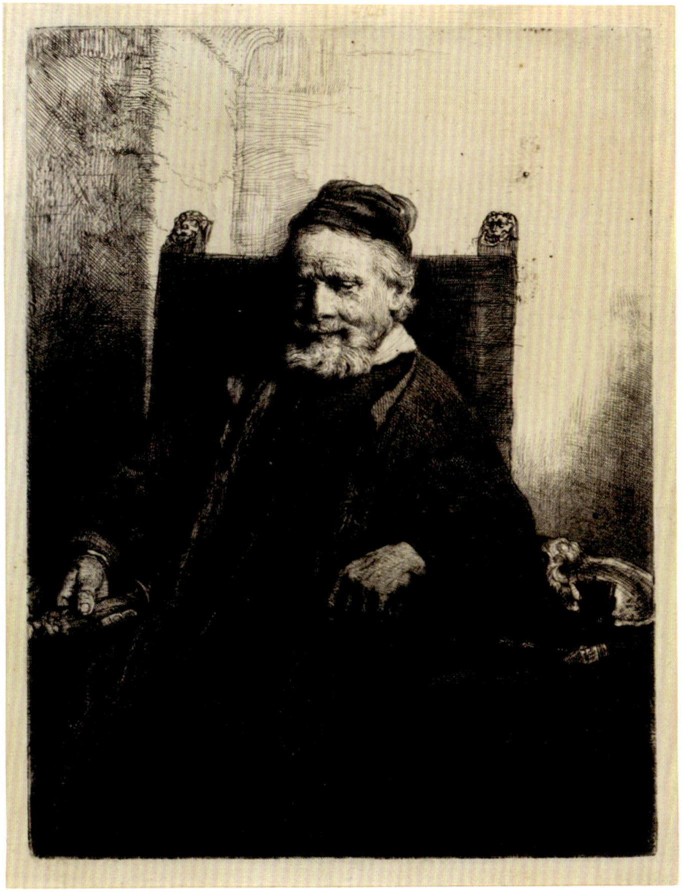

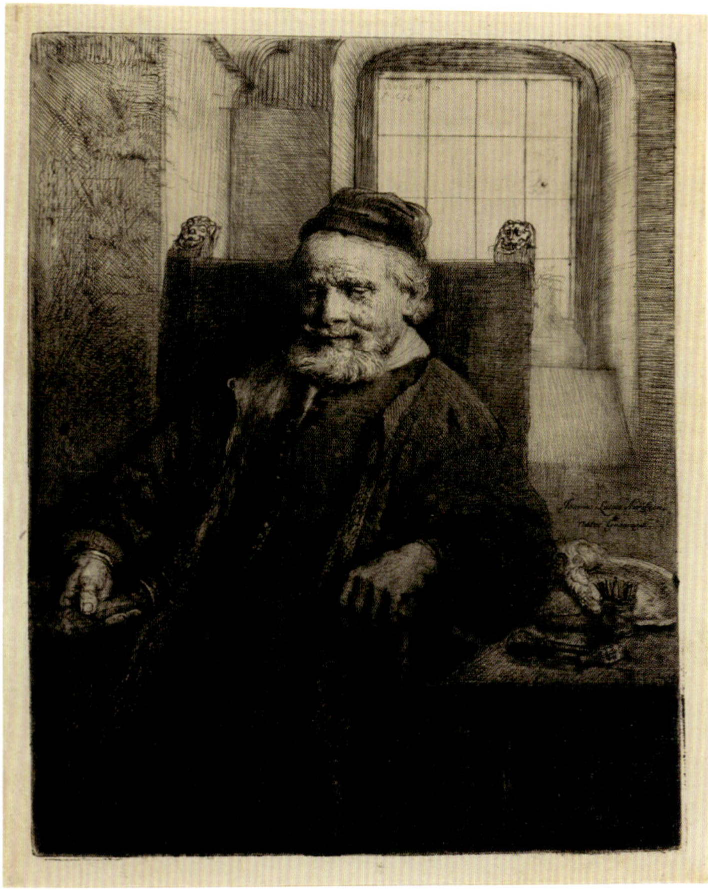

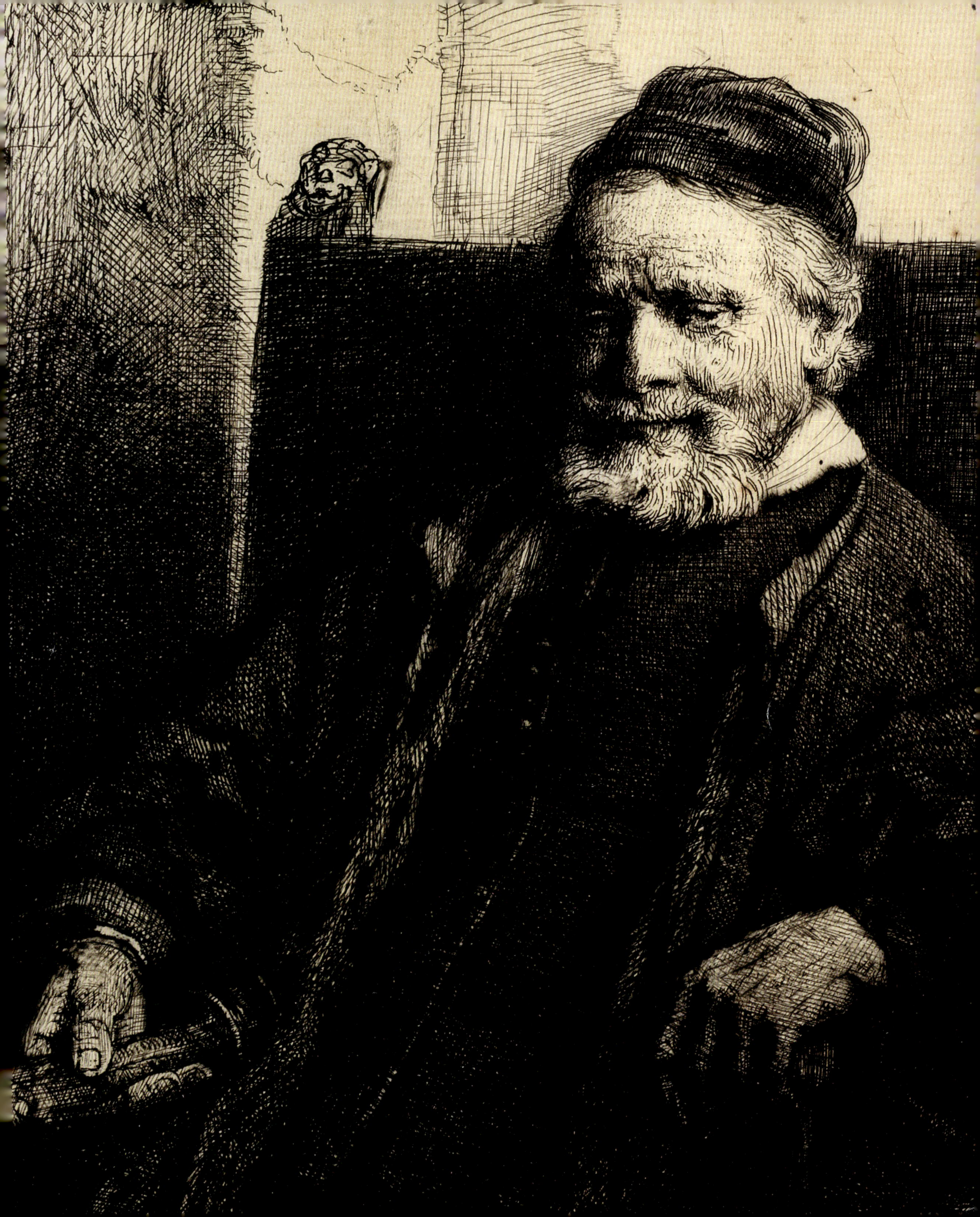

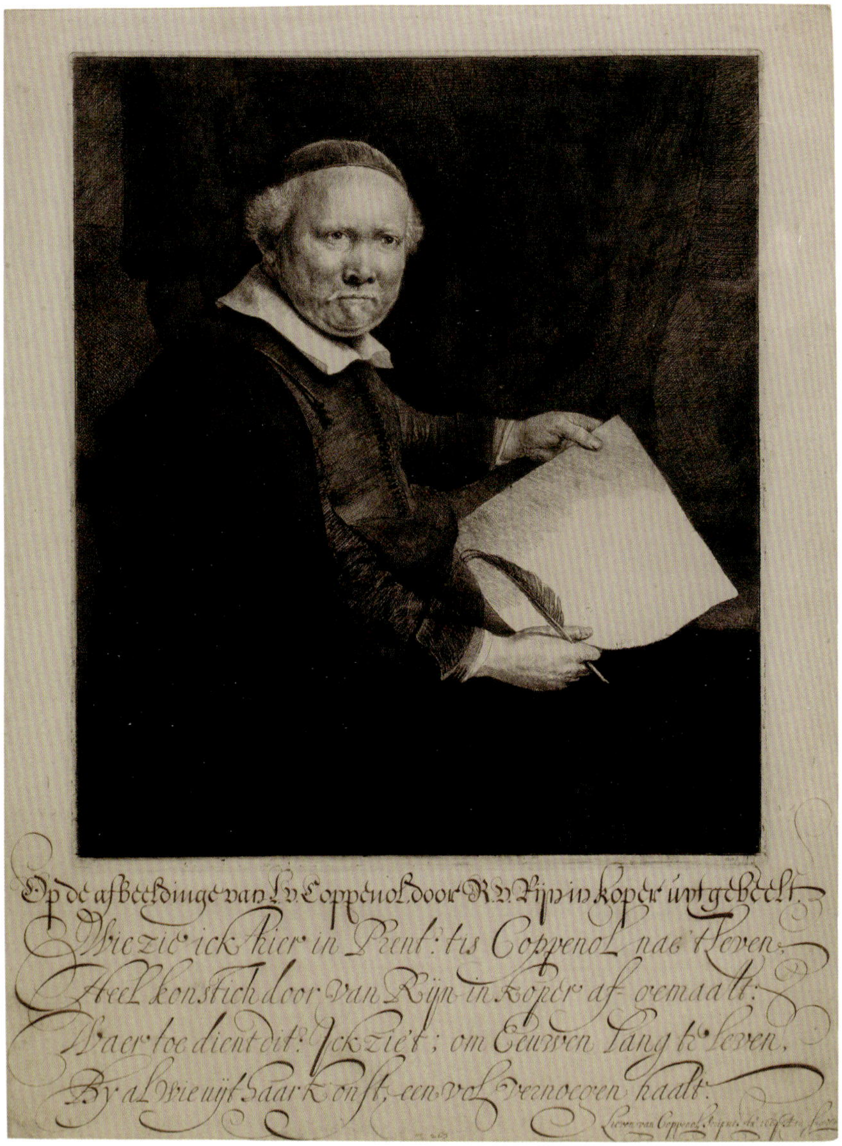

49
Portrait of the Calligrapher Lieven Willemsz van Coppenol ('The Large Coppenol'), 1658
Etching, engraving and drypoint, 34 × 29 cm
Seventh state of nine
British Museum, London
(F,6.65)

The commission to portray the pathologically vain calligrapher Lieven Willemsz van Coppenol (1598–after 1671) must have posed a different sort of challenge: within a very short span of time Rembrandt made two etchings, a drawing and a small portrait in oils of Coppenol.[23] The first of the etched portraits was probably that known as the '*Small Coppenol*' (cat. 51), which shows the calligrapher at his desk within a domestic interior. The young boy – Coppenol's grandson Antonius – probably alludes to his earlier post as a schoolmaster, which he had been forced to give up following an attack of mental illness. A quick, fluid pen-and-ink sketch (cat. 50) was made in preparation for this print. For whatever reason – whether artist or client were dissatisfied with this first image – Rembrandt made a second etching almost immediately (the '*Large Coppenol*', his largest portrait print; cat. 49), this time preceded by a painted sketch on panel at the same scale as the print.[24] Again seated at his desk, Coppenol tips a large blank sheet of paper towards the viewer, as if inviting closer inspection. Many surviving impressions of the print have an unusually large margin at the bottom: Coppenol sent examples of his penmanship to literary notables throughout the Netherlands, inviting poems in praise of his skill, which he then painstakingly copied in the space beneath his own printed likeness, as seen in an impression now in the British Museum (cat. 49).

The uniquely personal and expressive power of Rembrandt's late style is fully realised in three paintings that were probably his final commissioned portraits, two of unidentified men (cats 52 and 102) and one of the painter and art theorist Gerard de Lairesse (fig. 51). Born in Liège, Lairesse came to Amsterdam around 1665 to work for the art dealer Gerrit Uylenburgh, Hendrick Uylenburgh's son, and it was probably through Uylenburgh that Rembrandt encountered his ambitious younger colleague. Lairesse's misshapen facial features were most likely the result of hereditary syphilis;[25] rather than shying away from his hideous physiognomy, Rembrandt carved his features with bold, impartial strokes. With his long, blond locks flowing over his shoulders, Lairesse presents an elegant figure, acknowledging the viewer with eager confidence. The origins of this engaging and candid portrait are not known; indeed, it seems unlikely that the young painter would have been able to afford Rembrandt's fees. Perhaps the likeness was painted out of friendship, although it is difficult to imagine such a large, formal portrait having been done gratis for a relatively recent acquaintance.[26] What makes the portrait even more fascinating is the stark contrast between Rembrandt's characteristically brooding and pastose manner, and the smooth, colourful style of academic classicism championed by Lairesse as both painter and theorist. Of Rembrandt, Lairesse later said:

> I do not want to deny that I once had a special preference for his manner; but at that time I had hardly begun to understand the infallible rules of art. I found it necessary to recant my error and repudiate his; since his was based on nothing but light and fantastic conceits, without models, and which had no firm foundation on which to stand.[27]

The other two portraits in this group, both dated 1667, are each outstanding examples of Rembrandt's willingness to see beyond the conventions of the day, to manipulate technique and finish to achieve the most expressive effect. While the *Portrait of an Elderly Man* in the Mauritshuis (cat. 102) is almost uniformly broad in its treatment,[28] the *Portrait of a Blond Man* (cat. 52) shows impressive variation in paint application. The

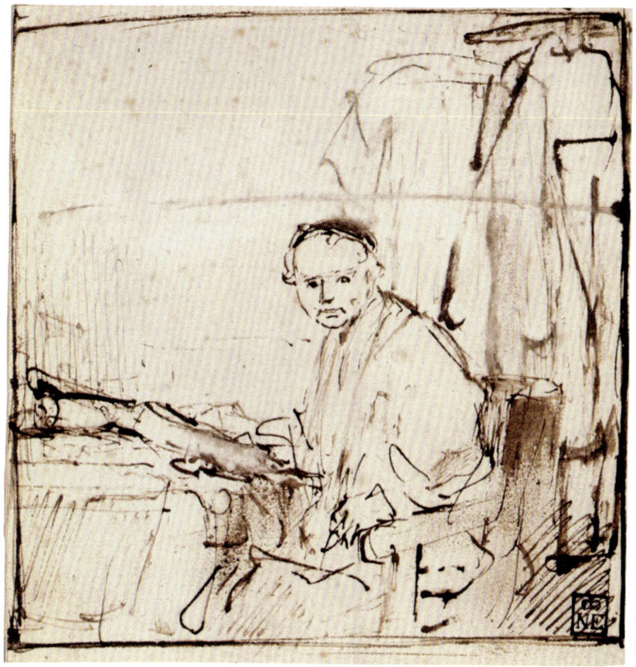

50
Sketch for the Portrait of Lieven Willemsz van Coppenol ('The Smaller Plate'), about 1658
Pen and brown ink, brown wash, with white heightening, 16.2 × 15.1 cm
Szépművészeti Múzeum, Budapest

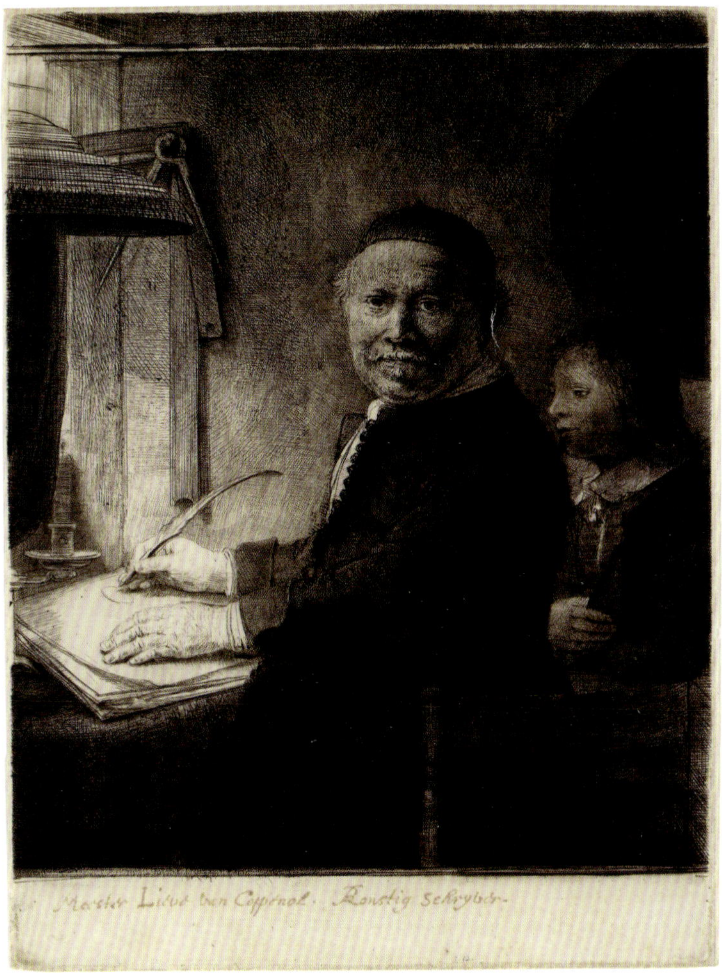

51
Portrait of the Calligrapher Lieven Willemsz van Coppenol ('The Smaller Plate'), about 1658
Etching, engraving and drypoint, 25.8 × 19 cm
Third state of seven
Ashmolean Museum, Oxford (WA1855.289)

FIG. 51
Portrait of Gerard de Lairesse,
about 1665–7
Oil on canvas, 112.4 × 87.6 cm
The Metropolitan Museum
of Art, New York,
Robert Lehman Collection

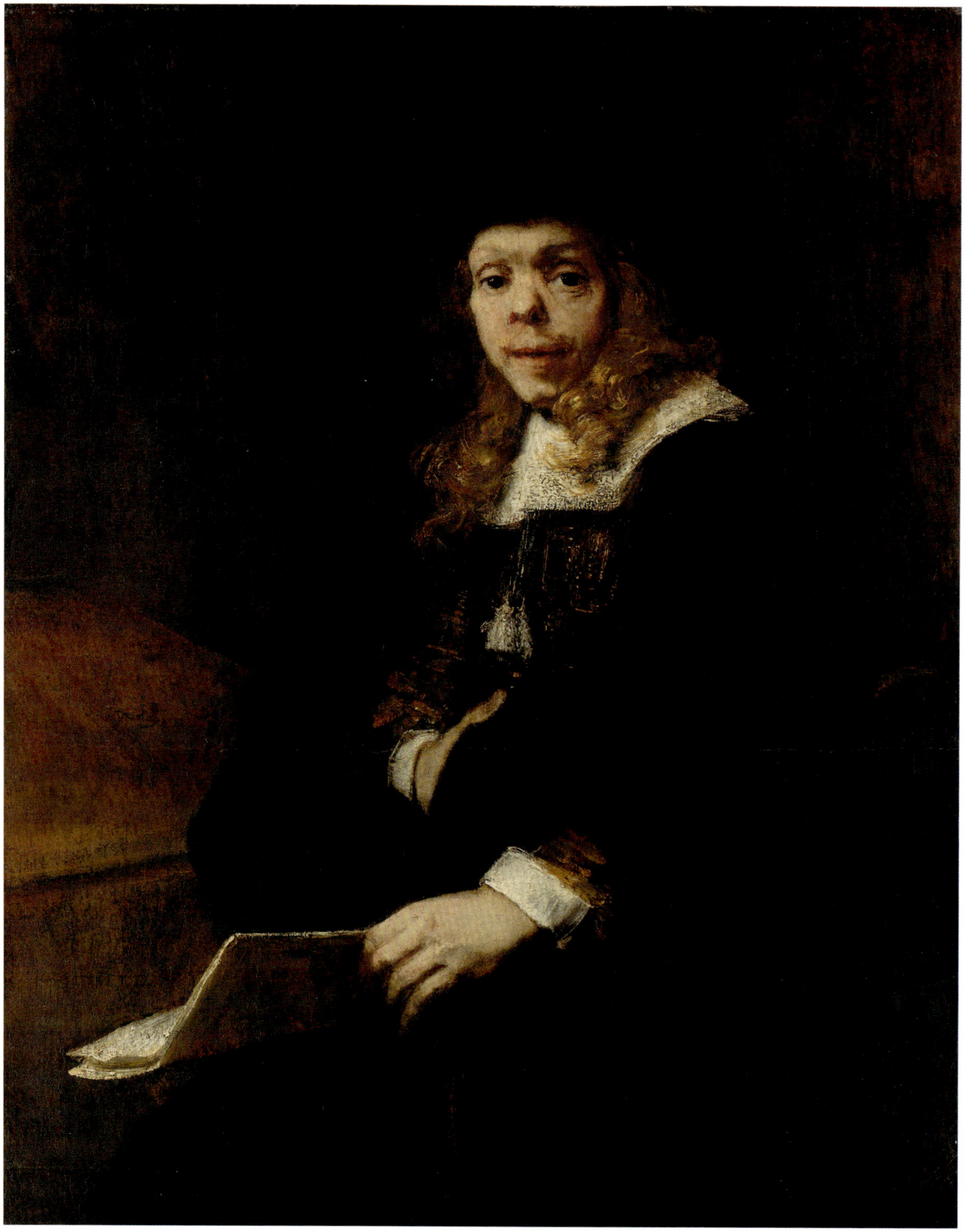

52
Portrait of a Blond Man, 1667
Oil on canvas, 108.9 × 92.7 cm
National Gallery of Victoria,
Melbourne

53
Portrait of Frederik Rihel on Horseback, about 1663
Oil on canvas, 294.5 × 241 cm
The National Gallery, London

most detailed brushwork is reserved for the treatment of the face and head: the flesh is built up with thin, densely layered brushstrokes that seem almost chaotic when viewed close up, but are extraordinarily effective from a distance. In the eyebrows and moustache the artist occasionally allowed the dark underpainting to shimmer through, to recreate the effect of the shadows cast by light hair against fair skin. While the majority of Dutch portraits rely on a carefully balanced composition to create an impression of solidity and aplomb, here the man's figure lists slightly off-centre and his right hand is cut off by the edge of the picture, infusing the composition with liveliness and a sense of impending movement.[29]

Rembrandt's *Portrait of Frederik Rihel on Horseback* (cat. 53) of about 1663[30] occupies a singular place in his oeuvre: not only is it the only equestrian portrait he painted, it is also one of just two life-sized equestrian portraits of ordinary citizens (that is, not stadtholders or members of the nobility) known to have been painted in the Netherlands in the seventeenth century.[31] Rembrandt's client may have encouraged him to attempt this unusual format. Frederik Rihel (1621–1681), a wealthy Amsterdam businessman, was an avid and accomplished horseman; his horse is shown performing a levade, a movement that required great control and balance on the part of both horse and rider. In 1660 Rihel had been part of the prestigious honour guard that provided a ceremonial escort for Mary, Princess of Orange (1631–1660), and the young Prince William III (1650–1702) on their visit to Amsterdam, and Rembrandt's painting is assumed to commemorate that event. As a native of Strasbourg, Rihel may have felt less constrained by the traditions of Dutch bourgeois portraiture and considerably more affinity with the pomp and grandeur of aristocratic traditions that prevailed in other European countries. In directing Rembrandt to portray him astride his horse, and on such a large scale, he may have wished to be considered not in the company of his fellow citizens, but on a level with contemporary English and European rulers, who were routinely portrayed in imposing equestrian state portraits by artists such as Titian, Rubens, Van Dyck (1599–1641) and Velázquez (1599–1660).[32] Although the painting of the horse has on occasion been dismissed as the work of another hand, the sketchiness of the form may be Rembrandt's deliberate attempt to divert attention to Rihel's face and splendid costume, necessarily placed well above the viewer's direct line of vision. Thick clots and swirls of white, yellow and red paint capture the light to give glittering texture to Rihel's rich costume and the horse's trappings, while the remainder of the dusky outdoor scene is relatively thinly painted.

In the final years of his career Rembrandt received at least two commissions for public group portraits from Amsterdam institutions: another anatomy lesson for the Surgeons' Guild in 1656, and in 1662 a portrait of the sampling officials of the Drapers' Guild. In both instances he had to contend with particularly entrenched formal and iconographic traditions. In *The Anatomy Lesson of Dr Joan Deyman* (cat. 29) the challenge was clear: to create a painting that was demonstrably different from his *Anatomy Lesson of Dr Nicolaes Tulp* (fig. 96) of 24 years earlier, but at least its equal in dramatic impact.[33]

The group portrait of the sampling officials of the Amsterdam Drapers' Guild – more commonly known as '*The Syndics*' or '*The Staalmeesters*' – presented its own unique challenge (cat. 56). With rare exception, seventeenth-century group portraits of administrative officials tended to be conservative and static, as the

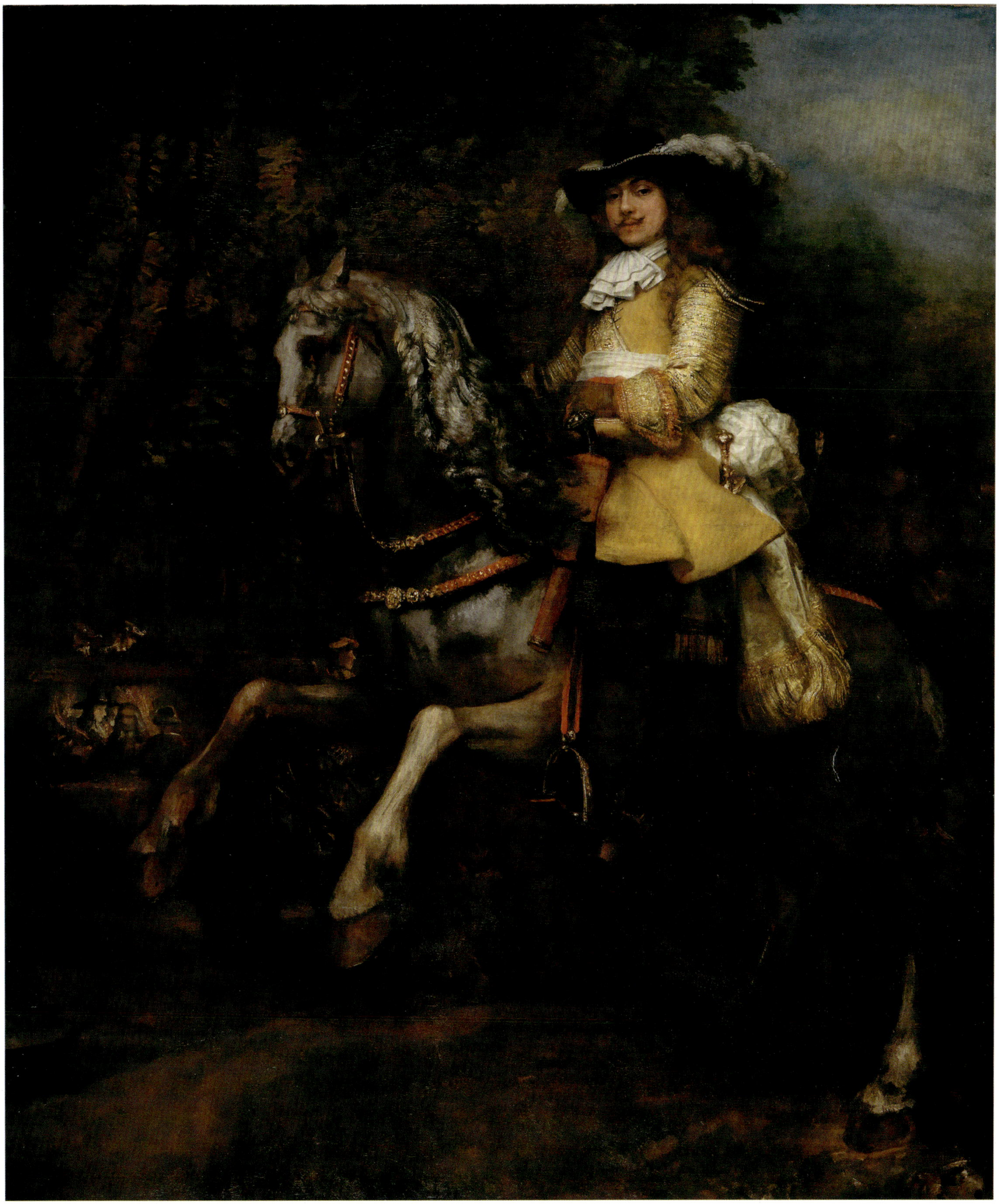

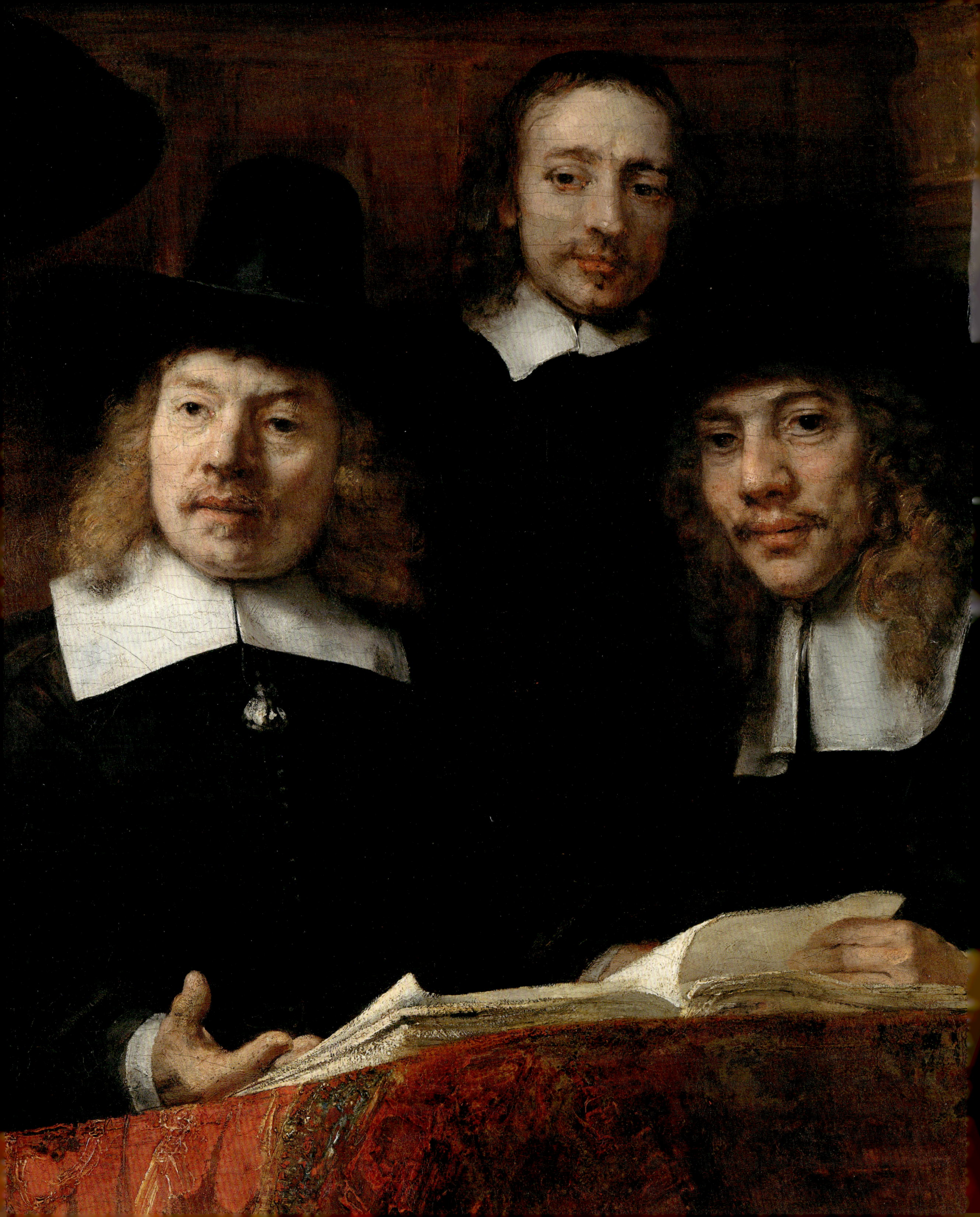

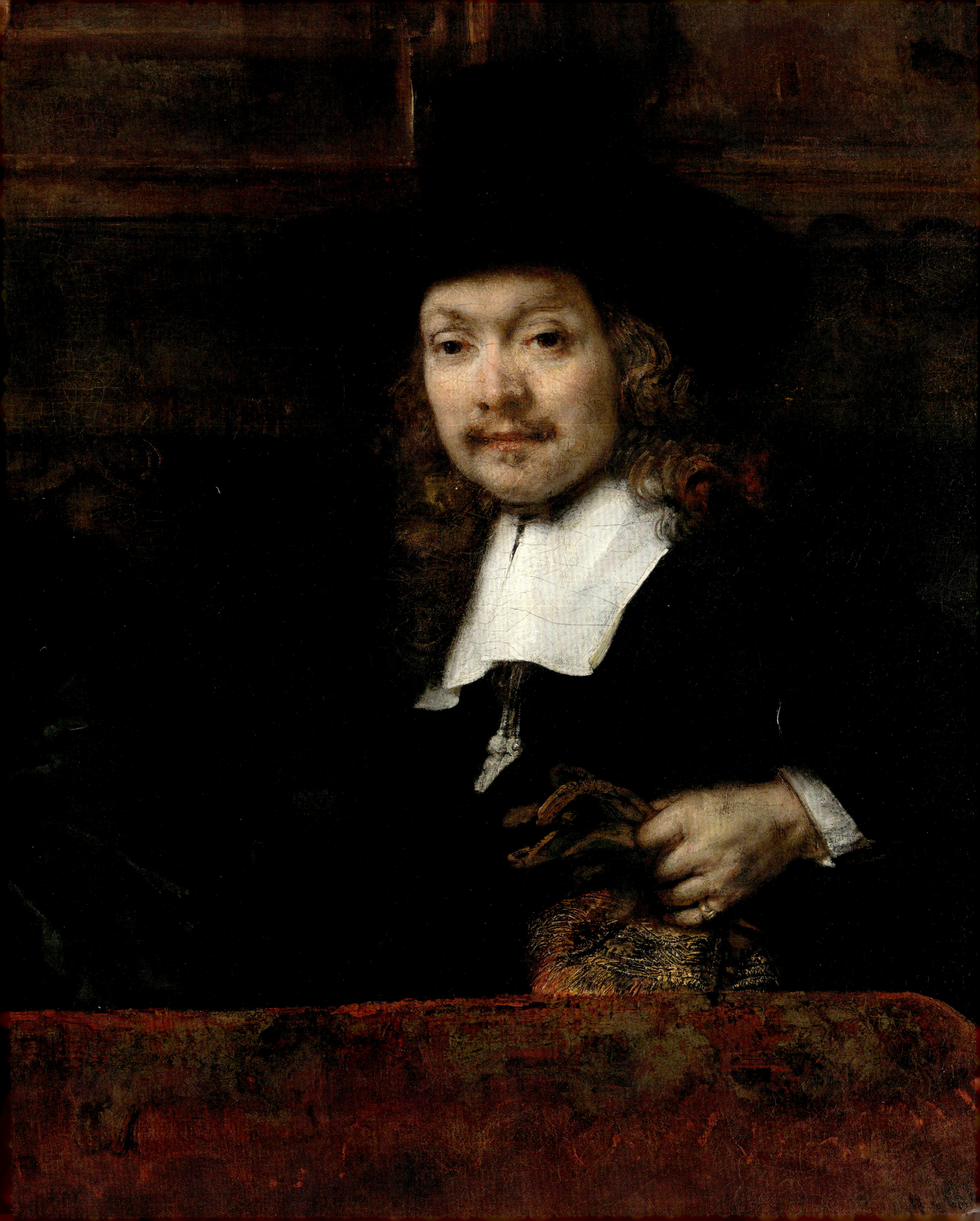

PAGES 126–127
Detail from *The Sampling Officials of the Amsterdam Drapers' Guild*, known as '*The Syndics*' (cat. 56)

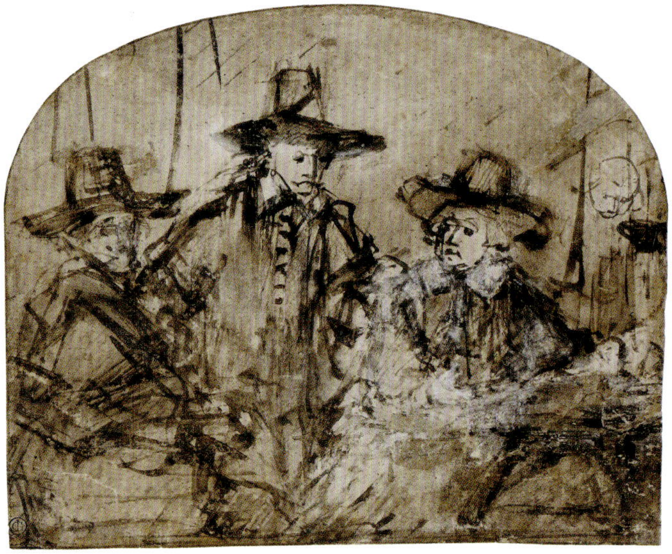

FIG. 52 (see cat. 68)
Three Syndics, about 1661–2
Reed pen, brush and brown ink with white bodycolour, 17.3 × 20.5 cm
Staatliche Museen zu Berlin, Kupferstichkabinett

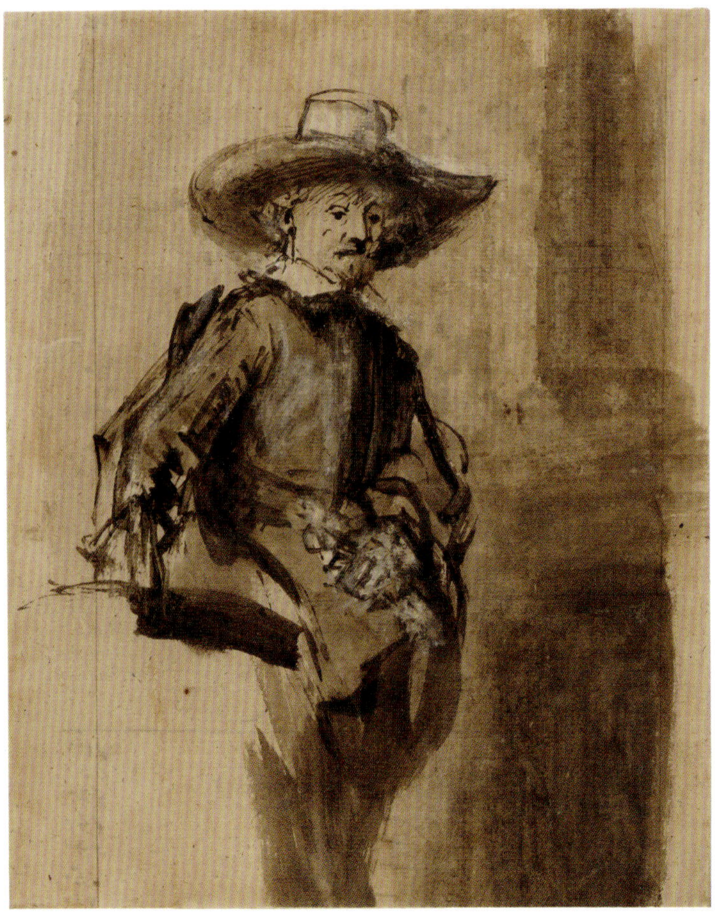

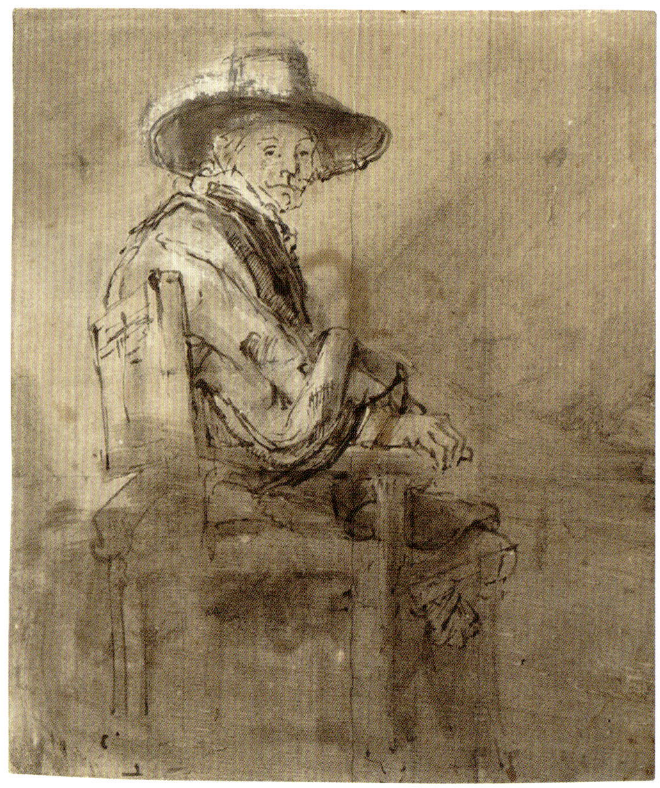

54
Standing Syndic: Volkert Jansz, about 1661–2
Reed pen, brush and brown ink, corrected and heightened with white, 22.5 × 17.5 cm
Museum Boijmans Van Beuningen, Rotterdam

55
Seated Syndic: Jacob van Loon, about 1661–2
Reed pen, brush and brown ink with white bodycolour, 19.5 × 16 cm
Rijksmuseum, Amsterdam

options for respectfully enlivening a scene of worthy individuals seated around a table were fairly limited. Working within these narrow parameters, Rembrandt nonetheless created a work of extraordinary power and immediacy. Syndics were charged with monitoring the quality of dyed woollen cloth produced and traded in Amsterdam, thereby safeguarding the reputation of an important sector of the city's economy. Rembrandt's depiction of the five individuals is intentionally uniform, their respective ranks (apart from that of their servant, who stands to the rear) indistinguishable, intimating that they acted with a single voice. The figures are slightly larger than life, and Rembrandt's decision to show them from a low vantage point – presumably taking into account the painting's final position in the syndics' office in the headquarters of the Drapers' Guild – only enhances their imposing stature. His characteristically loose and expressive technique varies considerably throughout the painting, with some areas, such as the faces of the sitters, elaborated more than others. The highlighted corner of the table carpet in the extreme foreground grabs our attention, not only because of its vivid colours, but also because of the textural variation in the dabbed, swirled, scraped and layered application of the paint surface.

The compressed space vibrates with restrained energy, thanks to the varied heights and angles of the syndics' heads and the gestures of their hands; the

56
The Sampling Officials of the Amsterdam Drapers' Guild, known as '*The Syndics*', 1662
Oil on canvas, 191.5 × 279 cm
Rijksmuseum, Amsterdam

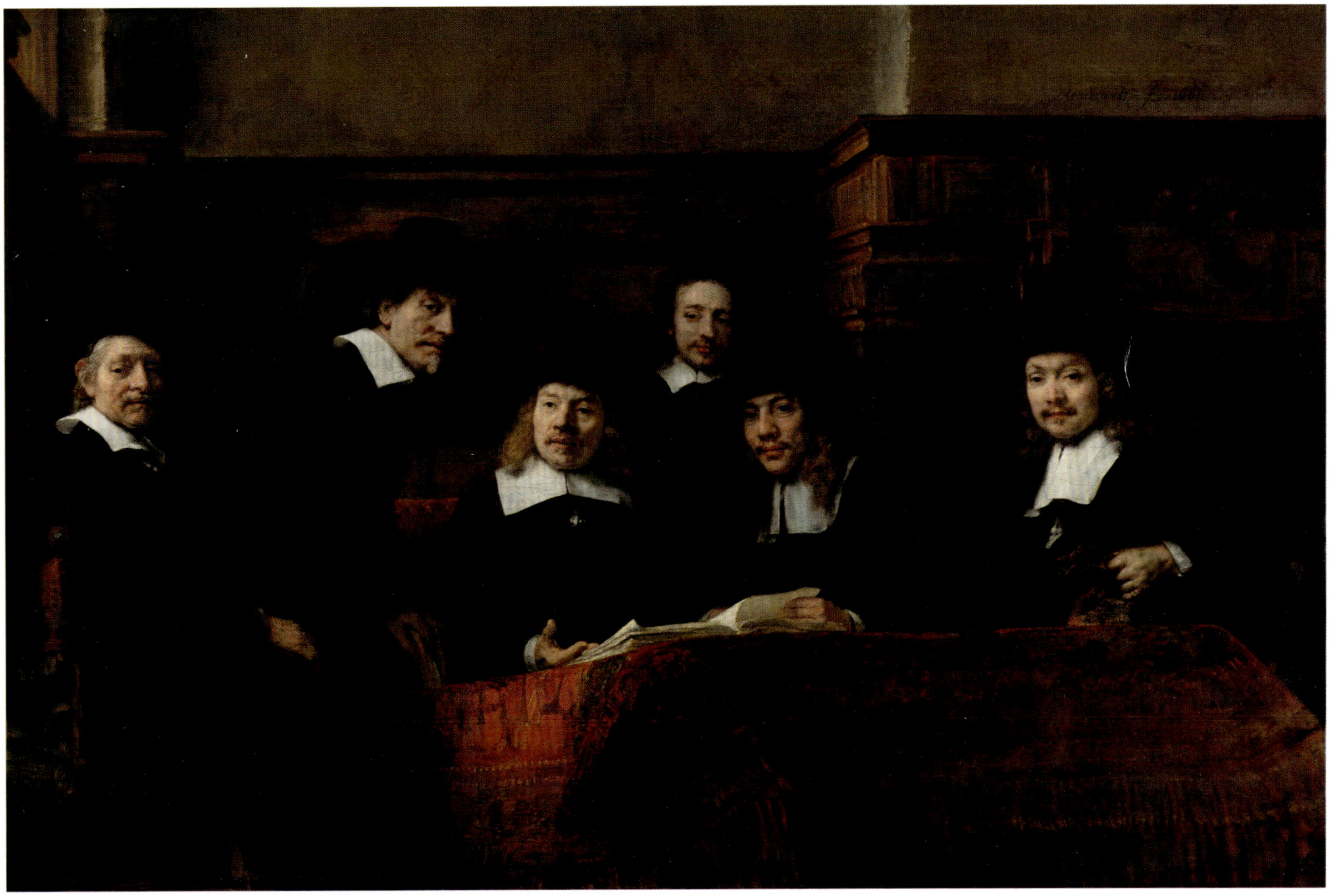

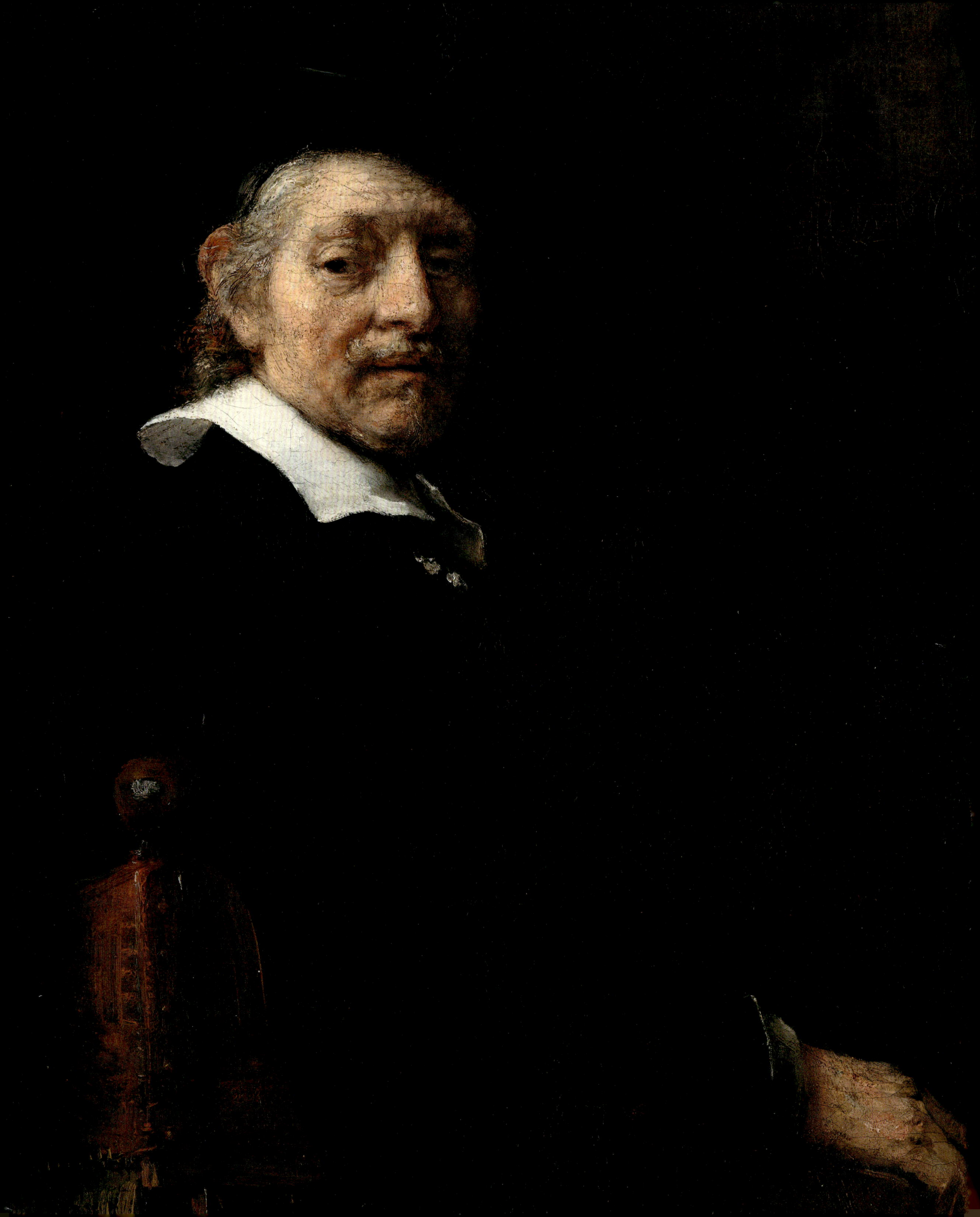

Detail from *The Sampling Officials of the Amsterdam Drapers' Guild*, known as *'The Syndics'* (cat. 56)

movement of the second man from the left (Volckert Jansz) as he rises from (or prepares to settle into) his chair; and perhaps most of all, the tension generated by the four men who gaze directly at the viewer. Neither welcoming nor dismissive, they make it incumbent upon the viewer to justify his or her presence at this solemn gathering. Throughout the seventeenth century other Amsterdam artists, from Werner van den Valckert (about 1585–after 1635) and Cornelis van der Voort (1576–1624) to Jacob Backer and Ferdinand Bol, had used this technique to involve the viewer in the scene, but it was almost always at the expense of the unity between the figures within the composition.[34] By clustering the figures more closely and eliminating unnecessary compositional details, and by adjusting his painterly technique to harness the light and focus the viewer's attention, Rembrandt manages to preserve the intimacy and integrity of the syndics' gathering.

Although *'The Syndics'* appears to present a near-perfect balance of light and shadow, energy and stillness, internal communication and external address, X-radiographs and macro XRF (X-ray fluorescence analysis) scans (figs 55–6), as well as three pen-and-wash drawings (fig. 52 or cat. 68, cats 54–5) reveal the enormous effort the artist expended in achieving this effect.[35] The steward (Frans Hendricksz Bel) was repositioned several times before Rembrandt was satisfied with the result, and finding the right arrangement for the three figures at the left gave him no end of difficulty (see pp. 141–3 below). Reflecting an earlier grouping of the figures, the Berlin sheet (fig. 52) shows Volckert Jansz standing between Jacob van Loon, seated at far left, and the syndics' chairman, Willem van Doeyenburg, seated at the head of the table. Although he ultimately rejected the pose, Rembrandt made an additional study of Volckert Jansz standing (cat. 54). A third drawing (cat. 55) shows the elderly Jacob van Loon in a pose that evidently satisfied Rembrandt, as it is repeated, unaltered, in the finished painting.

Governed by convention, the whims of fashion and a demand for verisimilitude, commissioned portraits inevitably limit an artist's ability to assert his creative independence and all too often succumb to bland compositional formulae. In part because of this, theoreticians like Van Mander regarded portraiture merely as a lucrative distraction from an artist's highest calling, that of history painting ('… most artists in order to sweeten their purse or partly to maintain themselves have often gone down this side road of the arts [that is to say copying from life] without time or appetite to explore History and the world of the imagination to the highest perfection').[36] Lairesse remarked on how portrait painters were held hostage to a client's whims: 'It has often seemed strange to me how someone can give up his freedom to become a slave'.[37] One never senses that Rembrandt regarded the art of portraiture as a necessary burden, however; rather, when he did take on a commission, he welcomed the challenge of working creatively within its strictures. Of all aspects of his oeuvre, the portraits are probably the most 'conventional', yet his sensitivity to individual personality and his extraordinary skill with brush and etching needle invest each likeness with haunting insight, liveliness and depth.

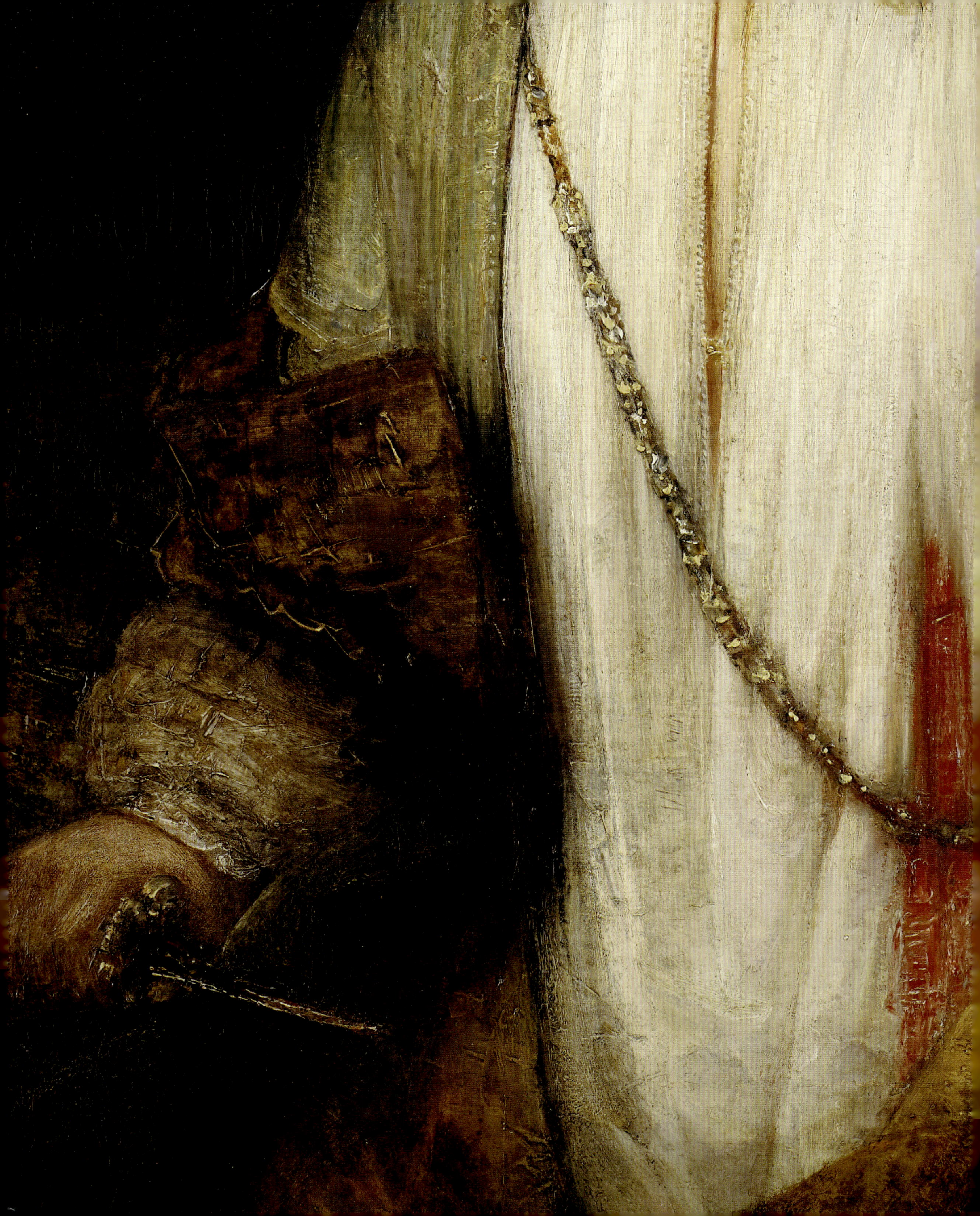

EXPERIMENTAL TECHNIQUE
THE PAINTINGS

Jonathan Bikker and Anna Krekeler

WHETHER IN HIS PAINTINGS, etchings or drawings, Rembrandt's exhilarating technique is arguably the most distinctive and intriguing feature of his late work. Indeed, the first time his late period was mentioned as such in the literature, it was in the context of his handling of the brush rather than his approach to subject matter or his pictorial influences. In his biography of the artist published in 1718, Arnold Houbraken pointed out, rather derisively, that when Rembrandt's late pictures were viewed up close it looked like the paint had been smeared on with a bricklayer's trowel.[1] Although his tone is mocking, Houbraken's *Life* of Rembrandt serves as a useful starting point for the exploration of the master's late painting techniques, especially when augmented by his description of the methods Rembrandt passed on to his last documented pupil, Arent de Gelder, and the observations of other early critics on Rembrandt's technique. While the latter only speak of the master's work in general, it is often apparent from their descriptions that they had his late pictures in mind. One example is the 1685 statement by the French theoretician André Félibien (1619–1695): 'often he simply used broad strokes of the brush, layering thick colours one on top of another, without blurring and blending them together'.[2] With a few exceptions, such a characterisation can only relate to the free brushwork of Rembrandt's paintings from the 1650s and 1660s. Further on in his text Félibien admits that not all of the Dutch artist's works were executed in this '*manière grossière*' (rough manner), but he makes abundantly clear – to a far greater degree in fact than Houbraken or any other early critic – how remarkable Rembrandt's late style is: 'All his pictures are painted in an extraordinary manner, and are quite different from those that seem so polished, in which category most Netherlandish painters fall.'[3]

In addition to the sweeping, unmodulated brushstrokes and thick application of paint that Félibien cites as characteristic of Rembrandt's late work, Houbraken mentions his use of the butt-end of the brush to score the surface of his paintings, his use of the palette knife and his tendency to sculpt with paint and to make changes during the painting process. The Dutch author also raises the question of finish in many of the late works. As well as likening the brushwork in Rembrandt's late paintings to the laying down of mortar with a bricklayer's trowel, elsewhere in his *Life* of the artist he describes the paint as being smeared on with a '*ruwe teerkwast*' (rough tar brush).[4] This description readily calls to mind *The Conspiracy of the Batavians under Claudius Civilis* (cat. 72), where a couple of very broad swathes of paint are enough to conjure up a face (see detail on p. 135 overleaf). This painting, the largest Rembrandt ever executed, was created for one of the lunettes in the large gallery surrounding the central hall of the Amsterdam Town Hall, where it would have been viewed from a considerable distance.

Individual brushstrokes are also visible in late works by Rembrandt of far more modest dimensions. In the Getty *Apostle Bartholomew* (cat. 109), for example, alternating short and long strokes of the brush, as well as daubs and flicks of buttery paint in a variety of pinks, reds, oranges and yellows, are clearly apparent when the saint's face is viewed close up. Félibien must have had such works in mind when he described Rembrandt's '*manière grossière*', and had his imaginary interlocutor remark that he had recently seen a painting by the master, 'in which all of the colours are separated, and the brushstrokes are so extraordinarily thick, that a face has something hideous about it, when viewed a little closer'.[5] Félibien responds to his friend's misgivings by falling

Detail from *Lucretia* (cat. 57)

Detail from *Self Portrait with Two Circles* (cat. 58)

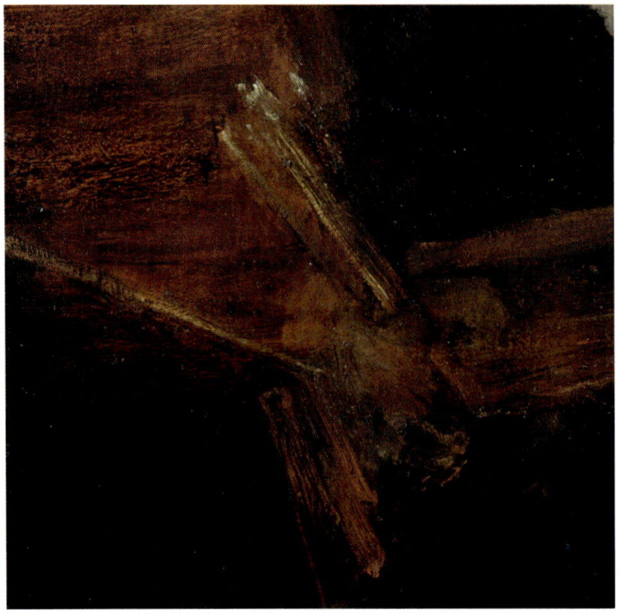

Detail from *The Conspiracy of the Batavians under Claudius Civilis* (cat. 72)

back on what by the late seventeenth century had become a topos in discussions of the 'rough' manner, namely that such works are meant to be seen from an appropriate distance. This truism had a classical source in the form of the Roman poet Horace's observation that in both poetry and painting, 'there is a kind which appeals to you more when you stand near and others when you step back further'.[6] The point was also almost invariably made in sixteenth- and seventeenth-century texts on Titian and Frans Hals, Rembrandt's great forerunners in the broad handling of the brush; Houbraken gives this an amusing twist when he describes Rembrandt pulling away visitors who want to see his paintings up close with the words 'the smell of the paint would bother you'.[7]

A few early commentators, including Félibien and Rembrandt's former pupil Samuel van Hoogstraten, went beyond merely stating that broadly painted works should be viewed from afar to explain the effect distance has on visual perception. For example, Van Hoogstraten in his 1678 treatise on painting advised artists not to waste their time on fine details when painting a work that is meant to be hung high on a wall, but 'to take with liberty brushes, so many as can be held in one hand, and let each stroke be single, leaving the colours almost unmixed in many places; for the distance and the thickness of the air will cause many things, that are in reality not assimilated, to seem to blend'.[8] In addition to the 'thickness of the air', the viewer's imagination was recognised to play a significant role in completing the illusion, as Van Hoogstraten pointed out in his discussion of draughtsmanship: 'a rough sketch can often create such a great impression on beholders that they can see more in it than is actually there'.[9] The French writer Roger de Piles later echoed and expanded this notion when he explained that rough sketches, Rembrandt's among them, had greater spirit and are more pleasing than neatly finished drawings, because 'the Imagination supplies all the Parts which are wanting, or are not finish'd, and each Man sees it according to his own Goût'.[10] In another publication, the same author compared the rough and fine manners of painting (*'le style ferme'* and *'le style poli'*), stating that the latter 'leaves no employment for the spectator's imagination, which pleases itself in discovering and finishing things which it ascribes to the artist, though, in fact, they proceed only from itself'.[11]

At times Rembrandt provides so little visual information that much is required of the viewer's imagination. In his *Portrait of Jan Six* (cat. 101), for example, the gold braid on the scarlet cloak is composed of nothing more than broad smudges and daubs of thinly applied yellow paint, and the glove worn on the sitter's left hand is suggested with equal economy, leaving a good deal of the ground layer exposed. In the case of the *Self Portrait with Two Circles* (cat. 58 and detail, above), the viewer actually sees things that are not really there, most notably the hand holding the palette, maulstick and brushes. According to Houbraken, in his final years Rembrandt was 'so quick to change and move on to other things' that he left 'many things only half finished'.[12] When pressed on the issue, Rembrandt would say in justification:

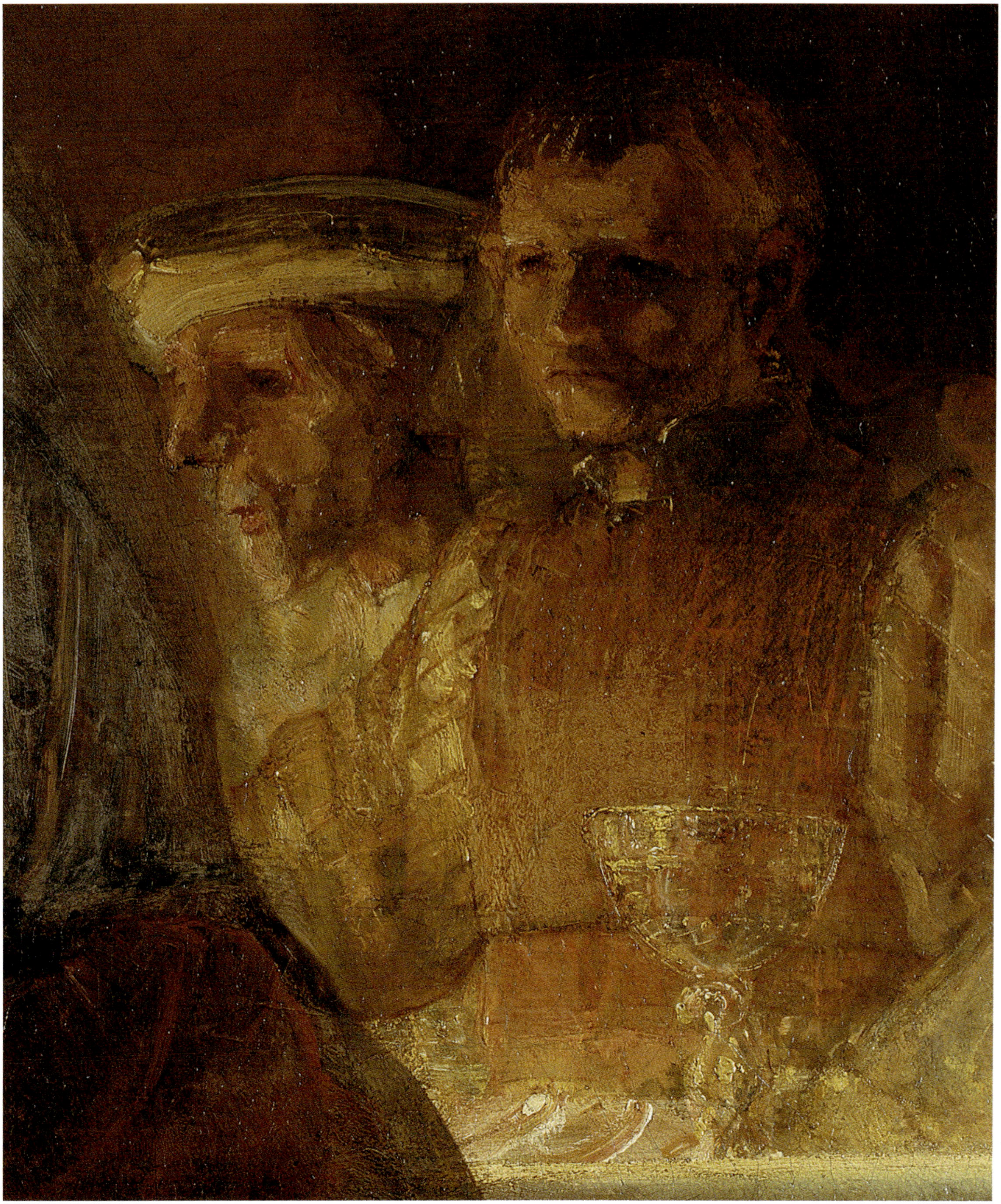

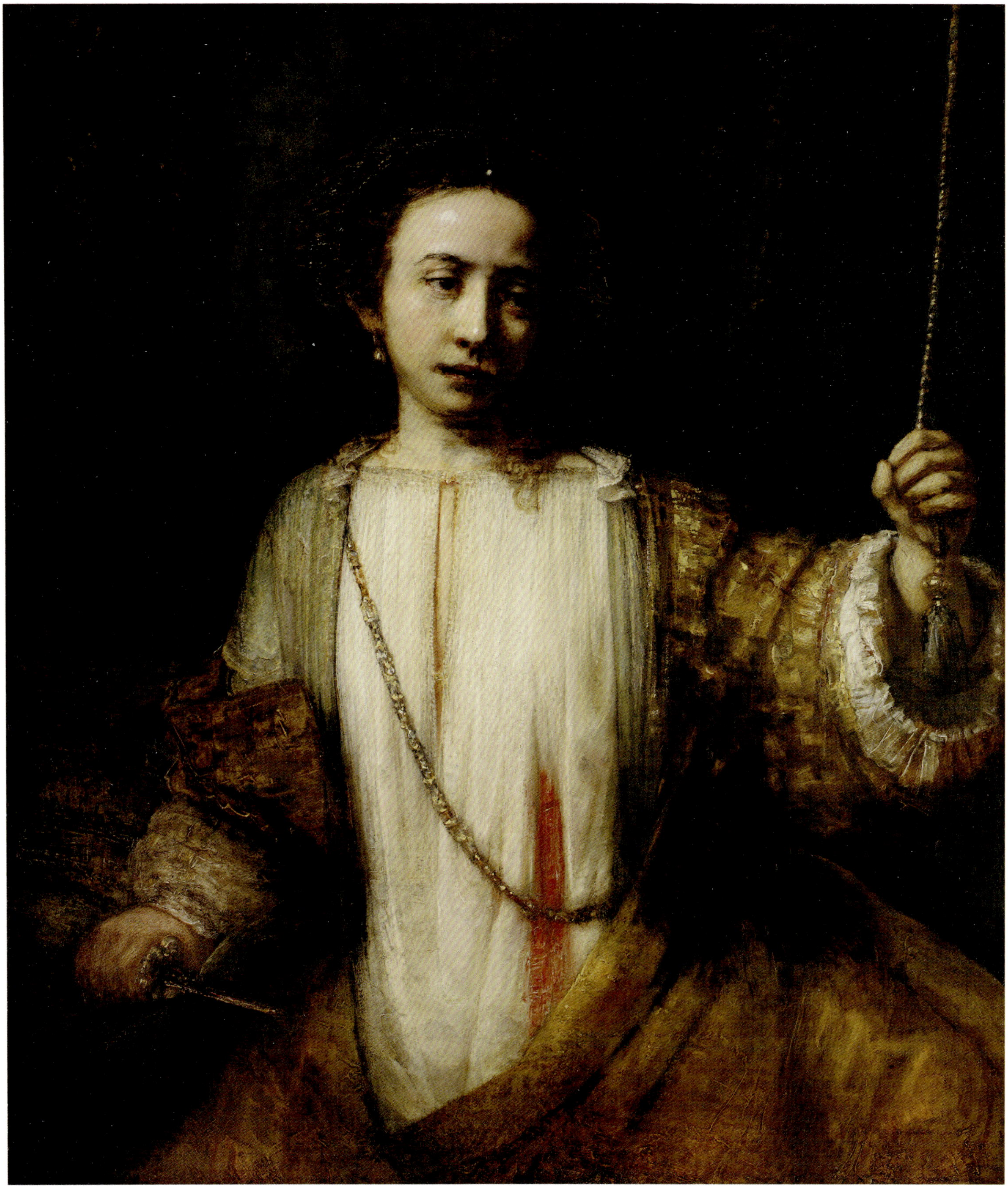

57
Lucretia, 1666
Oil on canvas, 110.2 × 92.3 cm
Minneapolis Institute of Arts, Minneapolis

'a work is complete if in it the master's intentions have been realised'.[13] While there can be no doubt that the master realised his intentions in the *Portrait of Jan Six*, which we know was delivered to the patron, the question of whether he also did so in the Kenwood House picture must remain open.[14]

Unlike Houbraken, for whom the *non finito* (seemingly unfinished) late works were evidence of Rembrandt's capriciousness, Van Hoogstraten viewed this quality in a positive light. Although not specifically in reference to his former teacher, he placed it in the context of a story told by Pliny the Elder concerning Apelles' judgement of the 'immensely laborious and infinitely meticulous' manner of his fellow artist, Protogenes. Apelles considered Protogenes' work to be on the same level or even superior to his own in all respects except one: 'he [Apelles] knew when to take his hand away from a picture'.[15] Van Hoogstraten maintained that this is the reason 'why great masters also sometimes left unfinished things that were fortuitously apt when first laid in' and advised: 'It may be, for instance, that the ground on your canvas or panel may be opportune in the colouring and, with the aid of a few daubs, may make your task easier'.[16] It is hard to imagine that the former Rembrandt pupil would not have had his teacher's late paintings in mind when he wrote this passage, as they are prime examples of this method. Often, as in the cases of *Lucretia* (cat. 57) and the *Self Portrait with Two Circles* (cat. 58), the ground layer and/or a freely brushed underpainting is left exposed in the part of the face cast in shadow. One of the most exhilarating uses of the underlying layers occurs in the Timken Museum's *Apostle Bartholomew* (cat. 108), where a brown undermodelling is incorporated into the lower parts of the sleeve and hand, as well as the cloak. A darker brown was applied with a dry brush on top of this layer to create contour lines and modelling. The same approach was taken in the apostle's face, where a brown underpaint was left exposed on both sides of the figure's right eye, and, most extraordinarily, in the entire right eyebrow (see details, overleaf). Rather than paint this on top of the flesh tones, as he did with the figure's left eyebrow, to create the right brow Rembrandt applied the flesh tones around the underlying brown layer.

Van Hoogstraten may very well have had the concept of *sprezzatura* in mind when he associated Pliny's tale of Apelles and Protogenes with this technique of incorporating the ground layer and first lay-in into a painting's final design. *Sprezzatura* was defined by Baldassare Castiglione (1478–1529) in *Il libro del cortegiano* (*The Book of the Courtier*) of 1528 as the ability to perform difficult tasks with an apparent ease that masks the effort and artistry involved.[17] Significantly, Castiglione's starting point for this definition was also Apelles' censure of Protogenes' inability to recognise when his paintings were finished. *The Book of the Courtier* was well known in seventeenth-century Dutch intellectual circles. As the author of his own manual of courtly conduct and a friend of the Dutch translator of Castiglione's book, Van Hoogstraten would have known it well.[18] Another learned figure with a special interest in the book was none other than Rembrandt's patron Jan Six, to whom the 1662 Dutch translation was dedicated, and whose library at the time of his death contained three Italian editions as well as a French translation of the book.[19] Six's nonchalant pose in Rembrandt's portrait (cat. 101) was probably intended as a deliberate manifestation of *sprezzatura*, translated into Dutch as '*lossigheydt*' (looseness), and Six may well have viewed the painting's fluid brushwork and its *non finito* aspect as the artistic embodiment of this quality.[20]

Although he had begun to work in a loose manner already some three years before, the degree of painterly elegance displayed in the *Portrait of Jan Six* is without parallel, which suggests that Rembrandt himself was aware of the concept of *sprezzatura*, probably from discussions with his patron, and consciously adapted his technique to express it. If Six did indeed alert the artist to Castiglione's discussion of *sprezzatura*, it may have reminded him of Giorgio Vasari's famous pronouncement on Titian's late style, which had been paraphrased in Dutch by Karel van Mander in 1604.[21] Vasari praised Titian's rough manner, which he described as being 'executed with bold strokes and dashed off with a broad and even coarse sweep of the brush', because it made his works seem to have been 'painted with great art, but conceals the labour'.[22] The deceptive ease of Titian's late manner resulted, according to Vasari, in a number of clumsy pictures executed by his imitators and Van Mander advised young artists not to attempt it before having practised the 'fine' style for some time.[23] The dissimulation of effort and artistry recognised by Vasari in Titian's late paintings is the very definition of *sprezzatura*;[24] the English poet John Elsum, in his epigram on 'An Old Man's Head, by Rembrant' published in 1700, recognised the same quality in the Dutch artist's late manner:

> What a coarse rugged Way of Painting's here,
> Stroaks upon Stroaks, Dabbs upon Dabbs appear.
> The Work you'd think was huddled up in haste,
> But mark how truly ev'ry Colour's plac'd,
> With such Oeconomy in such a sort,
> That they each mutually support.
> Rembrant! thy Pencil plays a subtil Part
> This Roughness is contriv'd to hide thy Art.[25]

Whether or not Castiglione's concept of *sprezzatura* played a role in determining the technique of the *Portrait of Jan Six*, Vasari's praise of the dissemblance of hard work in Titian's late paintings would have provided an impetus for Rembrandt's development of his own rough manner. Other positive notions associated with this loose manner were probably also influential. The appeal to the viewer's imagination in 'finishing' works of this sort has already been mentioned. Another effect of Titian's late style, according to Vasari, was that it made his pictures 'seem alive'. This allusive quality was also attributed to Frans Hals's work by some of his admirers, who described his paintings as having 'such force and life' that they seem 'to challenge nature herself', that they 'impart breath and life', or that 'not even life itself seems to be lacking in them'.[26] De Piles later claimed the same by stating that the rough manner in general 'gives life to work'.[27] Yet another positive feature of works executed in the rough manner was that they were closer to the artist's inspiration and imagination. Vasari again had something to say on this matter, not in his *Life* of Titian, but in a discussion of the merits of the rough manner in various media:

> it also appears that very often in these sketches, born in a moment from the fire of art, a man's conception is expressed in a few strokes, while, on the contrary, effort and too great diligence sometimes rob men of their force and judgement, if they never know when to take their hands off the work that they are making.[28]

In a passage that was repeated verbatim by Van Hoogstraten, Pliny the Elder informs us that the last works of the Ancient Greek painters, and those left

Details from *The Apostle Bartholomew* (cat. 108)

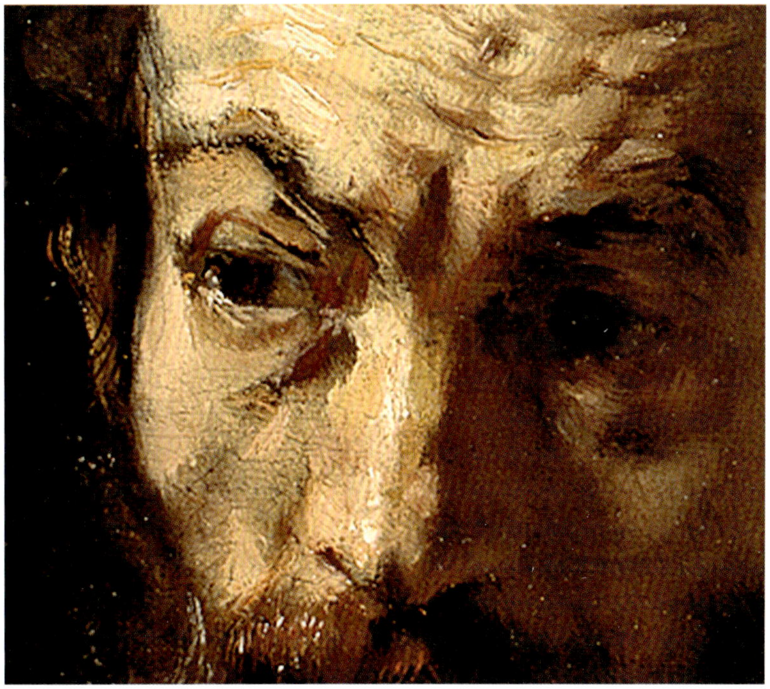

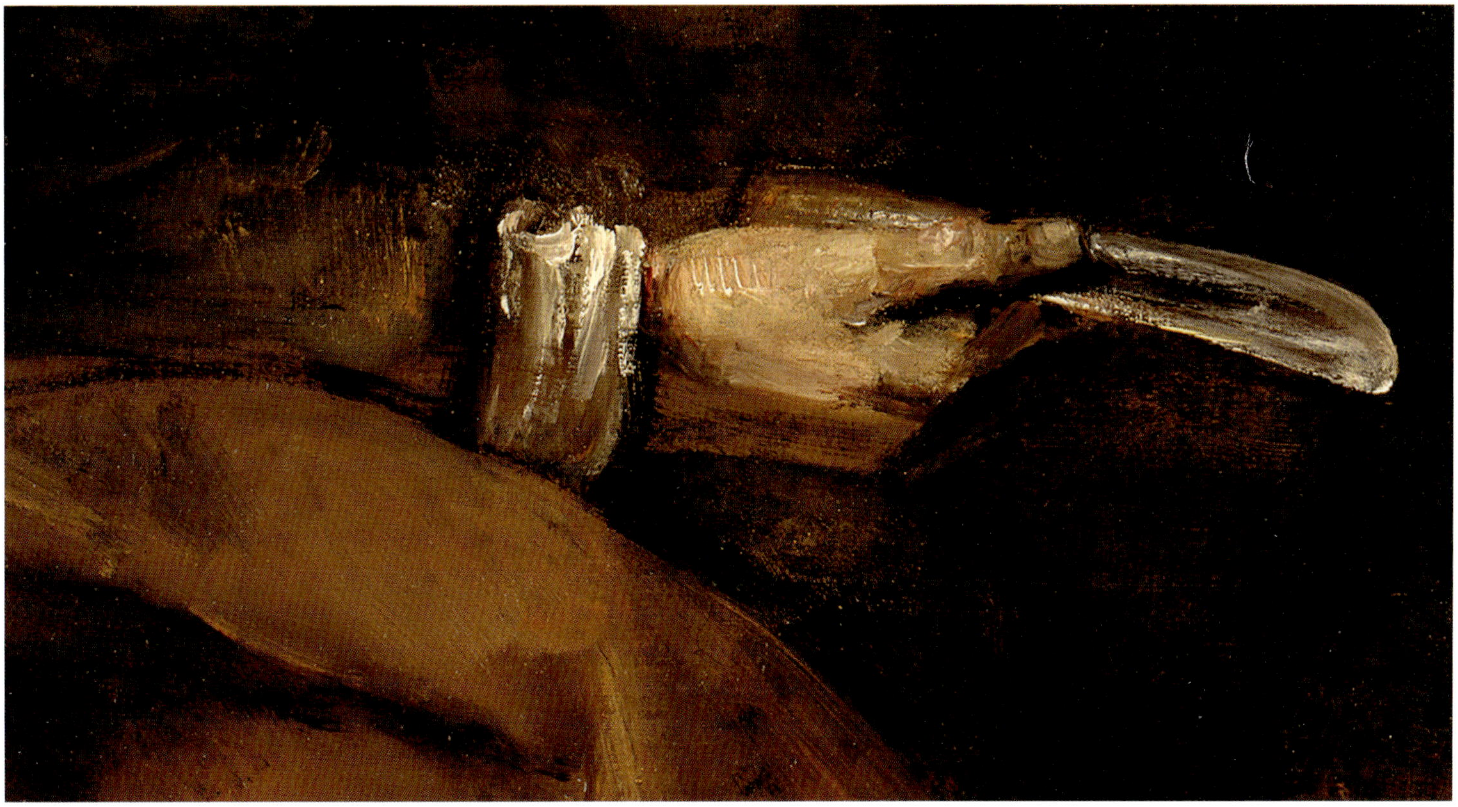

FIG. 53
TITIAN (died 1576)
The Flaying of Marsyas,
about 1570–6
Oil on canvas, 212 × 207 cm
Palace of the Archbishop of
Zámek a Zahrady, Kroměříž

unfinished at the time of their deaths, were 'more admired than those which they finished, because in them are seen the preliminary drawings left visible and the artists' actual thoughts'.[29] The praiseworthy concepts associated with the rough manner were probably not only written about in the seventeenth century, but avidly discussed in artists' workshops and amongst connoisseurs, and it can be assumed that Rembrandt would have been well aware of them.

The question arises of whether the actual work of the artists to whom these positive notions were assigned had any influence on Rembrandt's late technique. Although he could not have seen paintings by the Ancient Greeks, he did have easy access to those of Frans Hals, and he may have known at least one late Titian, *The Flaying of Marsyas* (fig. 53) of about 1570–6, which was in the United Provinces from the late 1640s until sometime in the 1660s as part of the collection owned by the widow of Thomas Howard, Earl of Arundel.[30] A prime example of Titian's late *pittura di macchia* (painting with blotches), the sketchy technique of the *Flaying of Marsyas* can be compared, at least superficially, with certain passages in a number of Rembrandt's late pictures, including the Washington *Lucretia* (cat. 115), the *Portrait of a Lady with Lap Dog* (cat. 42) and the *Portrait of a Family* (cat. 94). Also reminiscent of Titian's late manner is Rembrandt's use of the dry brush, as, for example, in the ermine cloak and left sleeve of the Hammer Museum's *Juno* (cat. 21), which is remarkably close to Titian's handling in his *Portrait of Nicolò Zen* of around 1560.[31] In both works, the loosely painted garments and hands contrast with the more detailed rendering of the faces. On the other hand, the flowing, wet-in-wet brushwork and abbreviated forms in, for example, the *Portrait of Jan Six*, more readily recall Hals's supple style. But the aspect of Hals's technique that may have exerted the most influence on Rembrandt was his frequent use of the underlying layers in the final design of his paintings, as, for instance in his *Portrait of a Man* of around 1635 (fig. 54, detail), where much of the pinkish-beige priming layer was left exposed in the collar, the sleeve of the shirt and the cuffs.

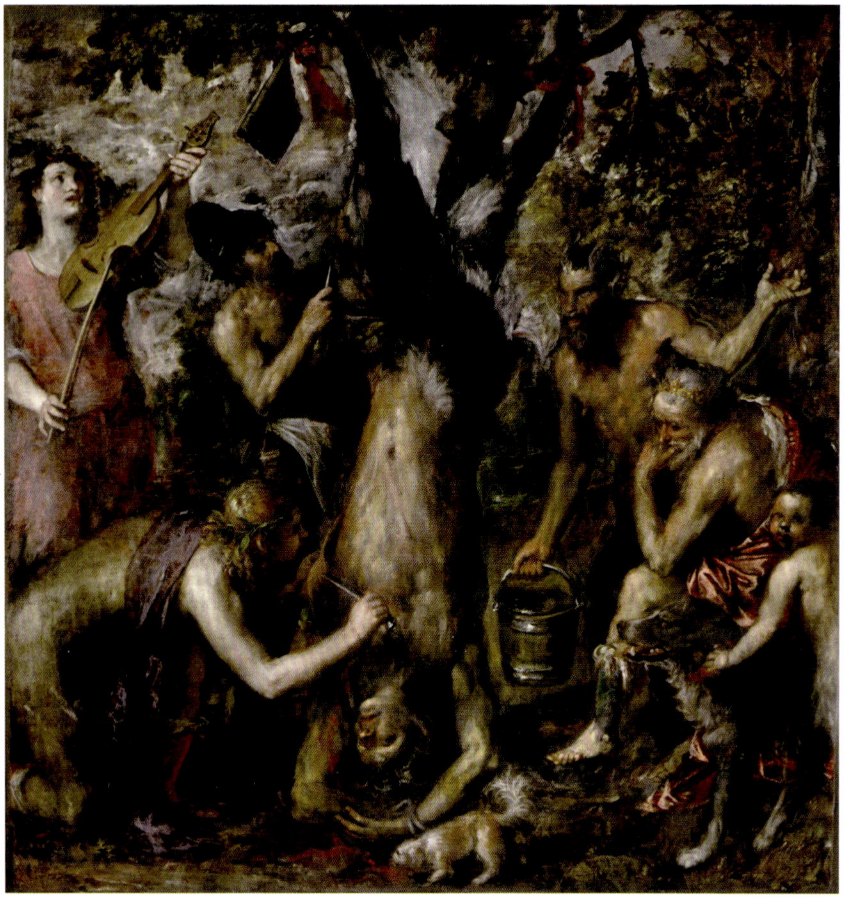

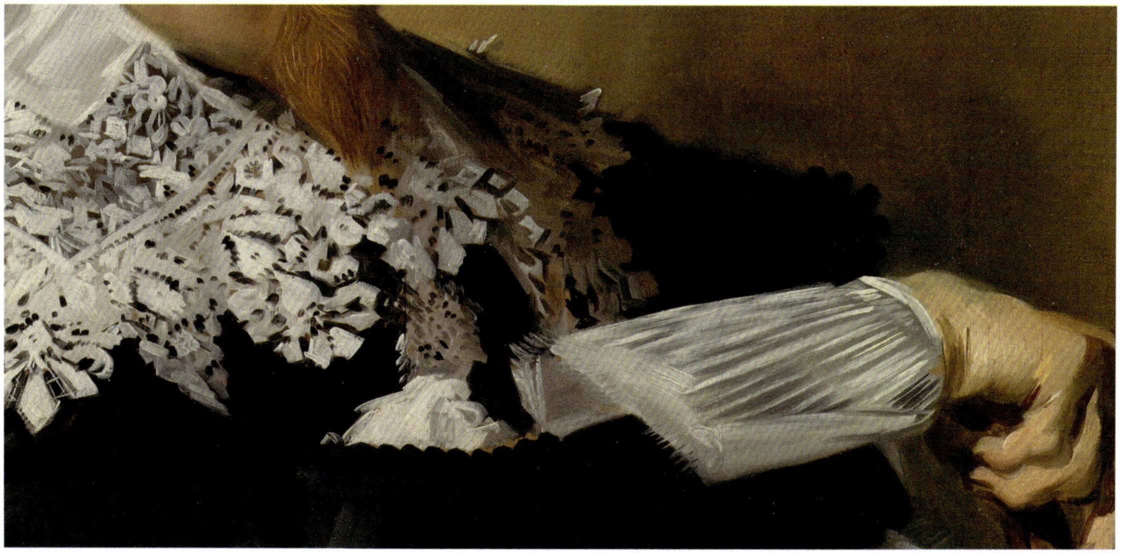

FIG. 54
Detail from
FRANS HALS (1582/3–1666)
Portrait of a Man, about 1635
Oil on canvas, 79.5 × 66.5 cm
Rijksmuseum, Amsterdam.
Gift of Jonkheer J.S.R. van de Poll, Arnhem

Titian's legend, if not his actual paintings, has been viewed as being paradigmatic for one feature of Rembrandt's late technique in particular: the making of revisions during the painting process.[32] Indeed, as modern imaging tools such as X-radiography, infrared reflectography and scanning macro X-ray fluorescence analysis (MA-XRF) have revealed, the Dutch master sometimes altered his late paintings considerably.[33] One composition that underwent radical changes was *'The Syndics'* (cat. 56, p. 129), Rembrandt's 1662 portrait of the five sampling officials and the steward of the Amsterdam Drapers' Guild. Three pen-and-wash preparatory drawings for the portrait have survived (cats 54–5, 68), including a sheet in Berlin, probably a fragment of an entire compositional sketch that in its present state only shows the three figures on the left (cat. 68). The poses in the painting initially followed those in the Berlin drawing quite closely, but the head of the chairman (the seated figure with the open book before him) was subsequently tried out in another position before it was finalised (fig. 55). An even greater, compositionally more significant change was made to the syndic to the left of the chairman. His static standing pose was replaced by an active one, raising himself from his chair. The fragmentary state of the Berlin drawing is regrettable, especially because the missing right side would have included the original position of the figure with which Rembrandt struggled the most, the steward Frans Hendricksz Bel. Recognisable as the steward because, unlike the sampling officials, he wears a skull cap instead of a hat, Bel's figure occupied at least three different positions in the painting before being placed in its current position, behind the two syndics in the centre of the composition. This information has been known for some time from the X-radiograph.[34] What has become apparent from the recently made infrared reflectogram and macro-XRF scans is that the figure of Bel was fully painted in two of his former locations, on the far right and the higher of the two positions between the sampling officials on the right (fig. 56).[35] Even more important than what can be seen in the infrared reflectogram and macro-XRF scans is what cannot be seen: the figure of Bel in the lower position between the two sampling officials is not visible, which suggests that he was first placed there and then completely painted out before being repainted higher up. Unfortunately none of the imaging techniques is capable of indicating Bel's initial location in the composition, but based on the placement of the servant in most corporate group portraits, one assumes he began on the far right. While the pose of the second sampling official from the left was apparently altered in order to enliven the composition, the reason why Bel was moved around so much probably had to do with the painting's unusual perspective.

If we can believe Houbraken, Rembrandt's tendency to constantly revise his paintings went hand in hand with his leaving 'many things only half finished', and was thus another consequence of his impulsive artistic temperament. Houbraken provides two anecdotes about works Rembrandt fundamentally altered as a result of his insistence on being the only person capable of determining when a picture was completed, one concerning the

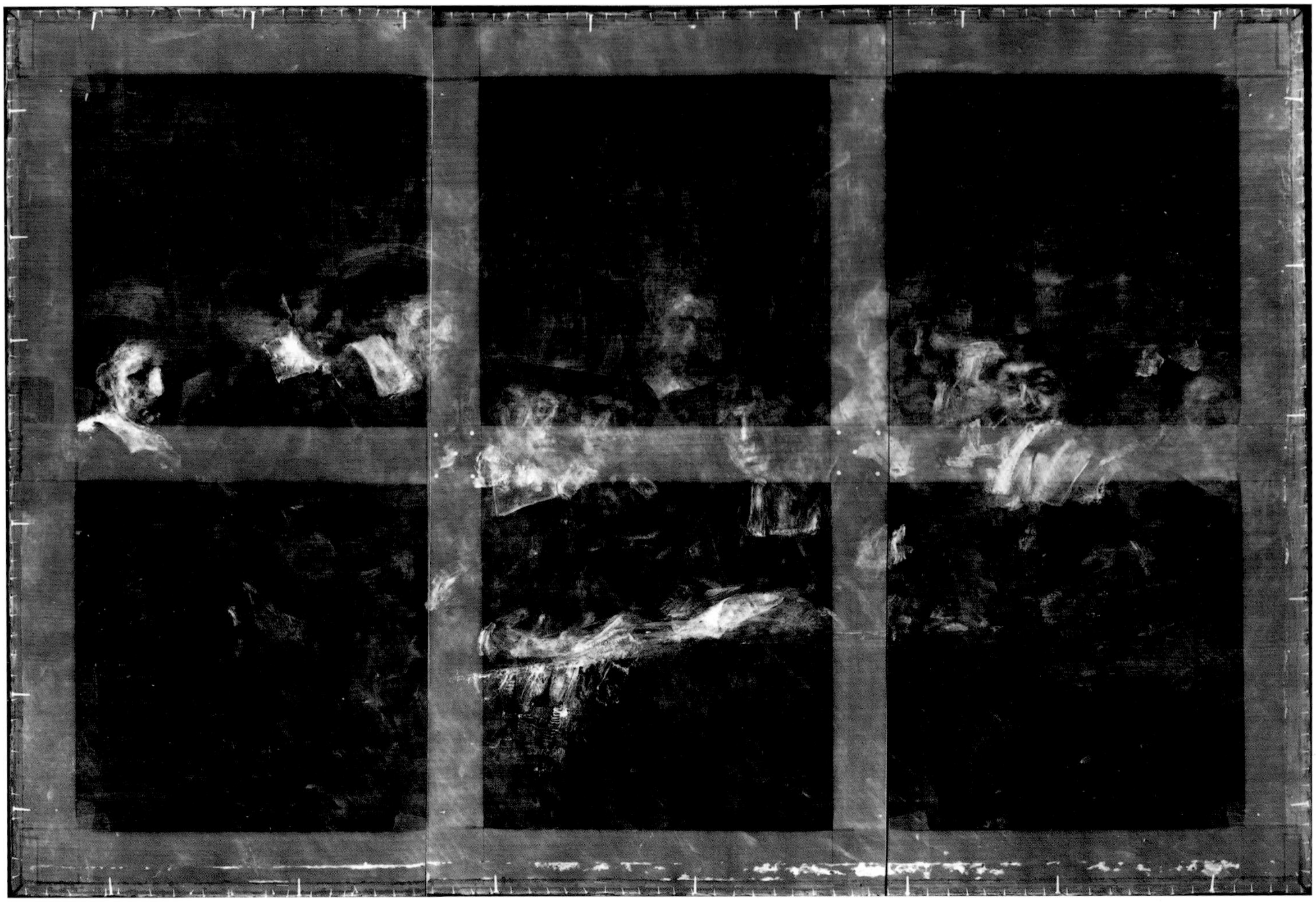

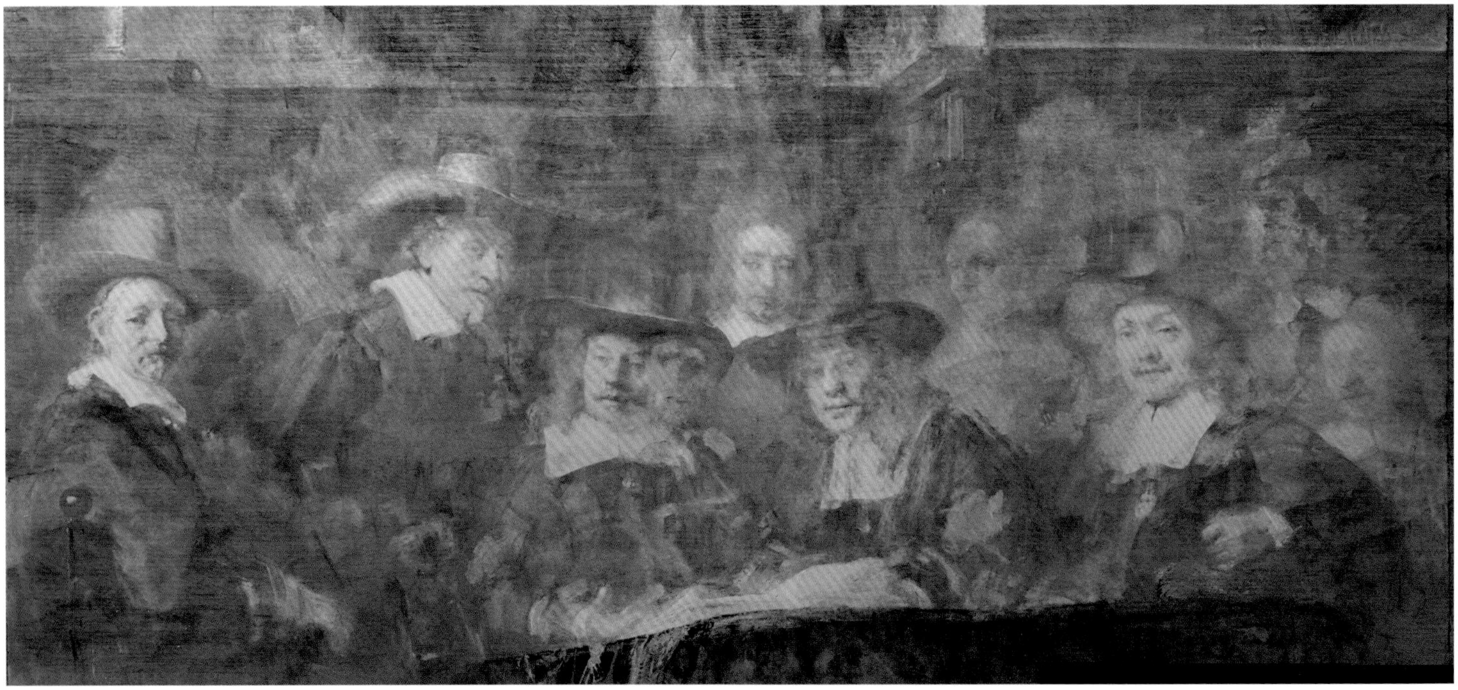

FIG. 55
X-radiograph of *The Sampling Officials of the Amsterdam Drapers' Guild*, known as '*The Syndics*' (cat. 56)

FIG. 56
Macro-XRF lead map of *The Sampling Officials of the Amsterdam Drapers' Guild*, known as '*The Syndics*'

painting over of a beautiful Cleopatra in order to give full effect to a single pearl, and the other the addition of his own suddenly deceased pet monkey to a commissioned family portrait (the latter alteration, of course, to the great consternation of the sitters).[36] Although these stories and the paintings that are mentioned in them obviously came from Houbraken's imagination, they do seem to support the physical evidence of the late paintings that have come down to us. The *Self Portrait with Two Circles* (cat. 58), for example, may owe its apparent lack of finish to the changes that were made to the position of the torso and arms;[37] dissatisfied with the pose as it was, Rembrandt added a few quick, broad brushstrokes to realise his intentions.

The *Juno* (cat. 21) is another example of a late painting with significant changes that some scholars have considered to be unfinished. The lack of detail in the figure's left sleeve and hand have been viewed in the light of a statement made by the picture's probable first owner, Harmen Becker, who in the spring of 1664 reportedly declined to accept repayment of a loan he had made to Rembrandt with the words 'Let Rembrandt first complete the "Juno"'.[38] One wonders, however, whether this painting might be an instance of deliberate *non finito*, and whether Rembrandt had difficulties producing it because he was contemplating the important modifications described above (pp. 77–80) in order to transform an anonymous figure into the majestic goddess.[39] Whatever his reasons for making these particular revisions, they cannot be viewed solely as an aspect of the artist's late work since similar revisions are evident in paintings from all periods of his career. Therefore, the hypothesis that this feature of Rembrandt's technique was based on Titian's example, whether his actual paintings or written and oral descriptions of his working methods, is not very convincing.

While some aspects of Rembrandt's late handling can be compared to – and were perhaps derived from – the methods employed by Titian at the end of his career, and by Hals already from early on in his development, there are three techniques for creating textural effects that are almost completely unique to Rembrandt. Houbraken is at his most facetious when discussing one of them: 'It is also maintained that he once painted a portrait in which the paint had been applied so thickly that one could lift the picture from the ground by the nose'.[40] He goes on to report that there are 'also precious stones and pearls, on brooches and turbans that are painted with so much relief by him that they appear to be moulded',[41] a passage that immediately brings to mind the thickly painted jewels in his *Portrait of a Lady with an Ostrich-Feather Fan* (cat. 38 and detail, p. 147). But Rembrandt did not limit this technique of sculpting with paint to noses and jewellery, as is apparent, for example, in the flowers in the basket in the *Portrait of a Family* (cat. 94), executed with raised ridges of yellow and white paint. This method of using rich impasto to render objects in three dimensions has been likened to the *pastiglia* (pastework) technique employed by fourteenth- century Italian painters, and was probably developed in Leiden by Rembrandt's fellow townsman and friend Jan Lievens in the early 1620s.[42] Rembrandt soon adopted it and used it off and on throughout his career. It reaches a high point both literally and figuratively in Isaac's wide golden sleeve in '*The Jewish Bride*' (cat. 92 and detail, p. 146), where the remarkable plasticity is accentuated by being in close proximity to the flattest area in the painting, namely the brown collar of the cape, which consists mostly of the exposed ground layer.[43]

Another technique Rembrandt frequently applied in his late work, also used at the very beginning of his

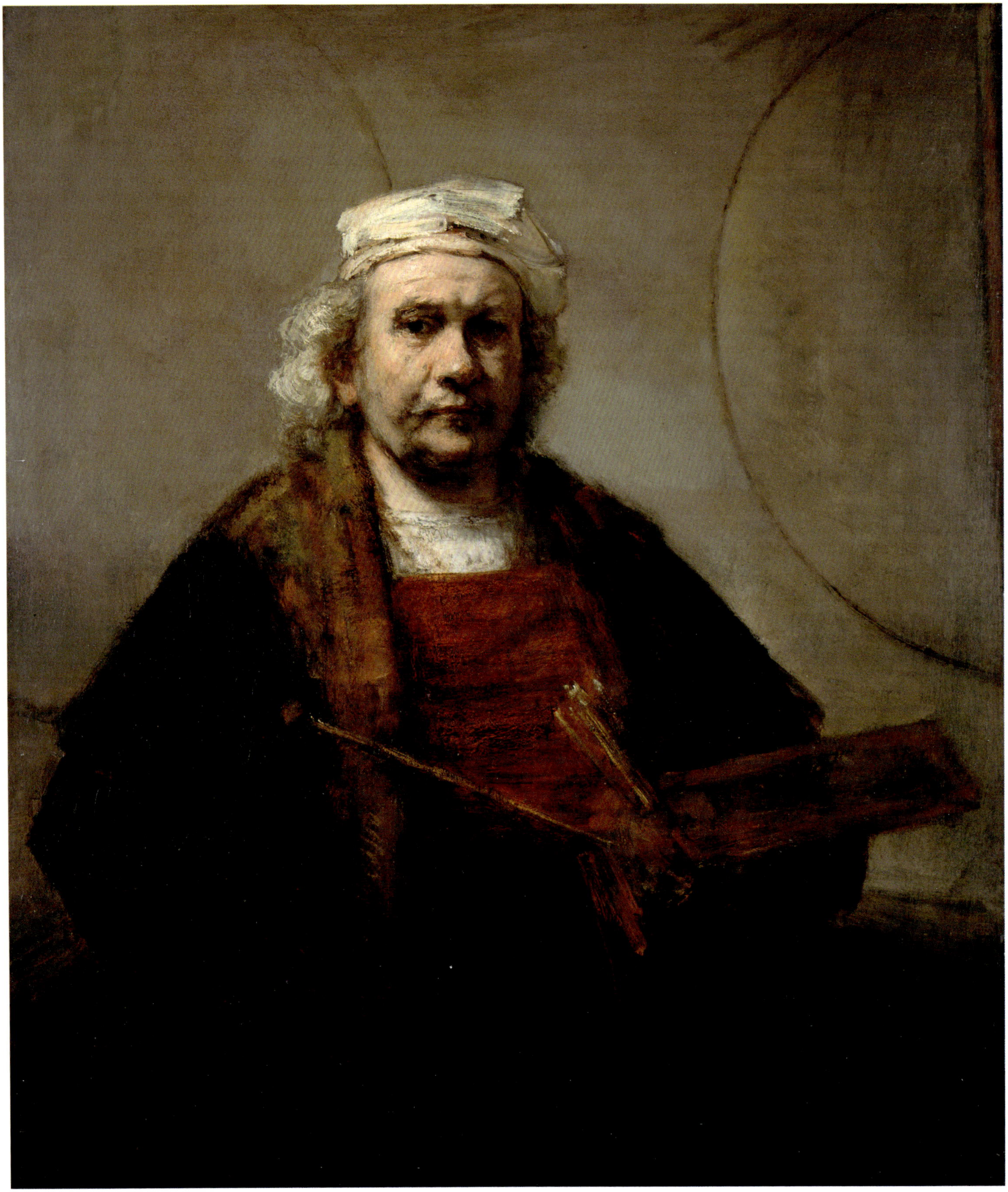

58
Self Portrait with Two Circles,
about 1665–9
Oil on canvas, 116.3 × 97.2 cm
Kenwood House, London,
The Iveagh Bequest

career, is scratching into the wet paint with the butt-end of the brush, a stylus or some other sharp instrument. Houbraken relates that this was one of the methods his friend Arent de Gelder had learned from Rembrandt during his apprenticeship in the early 1660s, and that the former pupil used it, for example, to replicate the embroidery patterns and fringes on the exotic rags that he, like his teacher, collected.[44] Examples of incised fabric patterns in Rembrandt's late oeuvre include the lace collar in the *Portrait of Gerard de Lairesse* (fig. 51) and the decorated edge of the shirt in the *Self Portrait with Two Circles* (cat. 58), while the gloves held by the sampling official on the far right of '*The Syndics*' (cat. 56) may well be the only instance of its use in a fringe. But all manner of objects in Rembrandt's late work display scored lines, including not infrequently head hair (for example, *Portrait of a Lady with an Ostrich-Feather Fan*, cat. 38; *Portrait of an Elderly Man*, cat. 102; *Portrait of a Blond Man*, cat. 52) and occasionally facial hair (*Portrait of an Elderly Man* and *Self Portrait with Two Circles*), as well as for the edges of the leaves of a book ('*The Syndics*'; *Matthew and the Angel*, fig. 72), a wrinkle in the flesh above an eye socket (*Self Portrait with Two Circles*) or the folds in a neck (Washington *Lucretia*, cat. 115).

It is not only the assortment of surfaces to which this technique was applied, but the variety in quantity and type that makes Rembrandt's use of scratch marks in his late work so captivating. In the *Aristotle with a Bust of Homer* (fig. 69, p. 216), for example, only a couple of long, relatively thick lines have been scored into the figure's left sleeve at the shoulder, whereas very thin incised lines are found throughout the costume worn by Isaac in '*The Jewish Bride*', indicating, among other things, zigzag patterns in the cape and the pleating of the skirt of his jerkin. Few paintings from the late period exhibit as much scratching as '*The Jewish Bride*', while there are quite a number in which the technique was used very sparingly or not at all. The Timken Museum *Apostle Bartholomew* (cat. 108 and details, p. 139), for example, has few scratch marks, only a couple of squiggles in the lower left part of the drapery and one solitary line demarcating the tip of the thumb.

Hals's occasional use of the technique, and Rembrandt's in his early work, have been described as timesaving devices, shortcuts to achieving a given effect employed in their most swiftly executed paintings.[45] However, the scratched lines in the foliage and the braiding of the doublet in the 1630 *Jeremiah lamenting the Destruction of Jerusalem* (Rijksmuseum, Amsterdam) – one of Rembrandt's most meticulously rendered early works – suggests that there was something more at play than speed alone.[46] While there is an undeniable element of spontaneity in the apparently haphazard application of the scratch marks in the late work, some of them at least seem to suggest that their maker was striving to imitate nature quite literally, by creating an actual wrinkle, for example, or the minute difference in the level of a thumbnail and its nail bed. One can hardly imagine that such tiny details are perceptible from a normal viewing distance. But just as the eye has the power to meld unmodulated colours together and to complete a face made up of just a few bold brushstrokes, perhaps it is also capable of registering on some level even these infinitesimal variations in depth, and, more importantly, of tricking the mind into believing that it is looking at the actual thing rather than a painted imitation.

Unlike the techniques of sculpting with paint and scratching into the wet surface, which Rembrandt did not invent and which he already employed at the beginning of his career, that of manipulating the paint with a palette

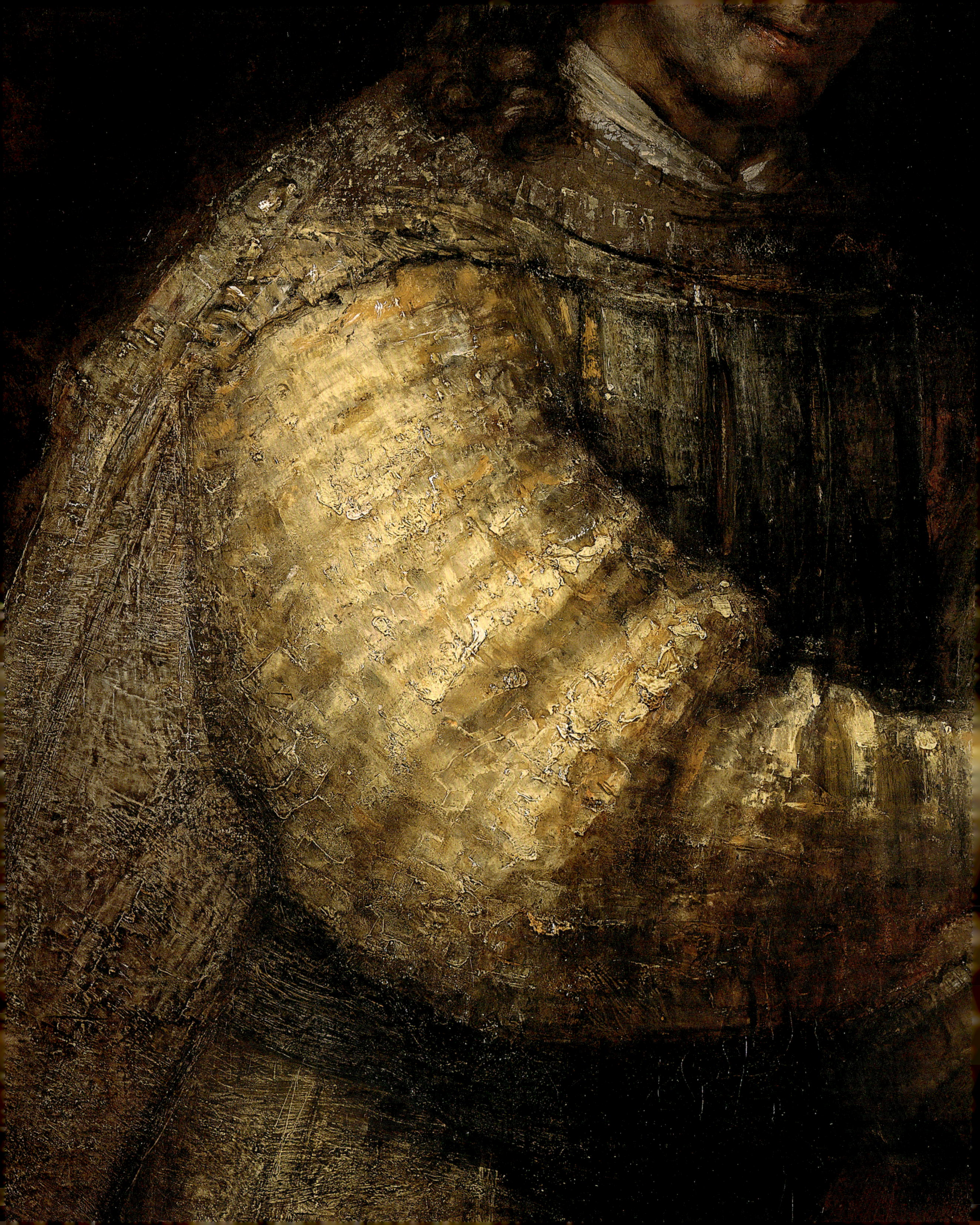

knife or comparable tool appears to have been discovered by Rembrandt and used by him only in his late paintings. Houbraken may have been referring to this technique when he made his remark about Rembrandt's paint appearing to be smeared on with a bricklayer's trowel. Be this as it may, he does state explicitly that it was another of the techniques that Arent de Gelder learned from his teacher.[47] Traditionally, the palette or tempering knife was used to transfer oil paint to and mix colours on the palette.[48] As an English painters' manual of 1692 indicates, there was more than one type of knife: 'You ought to have two Tempering Knives, one broader for the greater quantitys of Colours, the other Narrower and coming Taper toward the end for the smaller'.[49] Rembrandt would also have had a variety of other 'knives' at his disposal in his studio, such as the small ones with which brushes were cleaned, and possibly priming knives for applying ground layers to canvases.[50] Another tool, the so-called 'voider', was often made of horn or wood and is described in another English painting manual as 'about three Inches one Way, and four the other; this Voider is to clear off the Colours from the stone when ground, and also to keep them together in the Time of Grinding, when it spreads too much'.[51] It has not been possible to determine precisely what kind of knives Rembrandt used, and it cannot be excluded that in some instances he simply picked up an odd piece of wood that was lying around.

Some critics, such as Joshua Reynolds in his annual Discourse given at the Royal Academy in London in 1784, believed that Rembrandt made extensive use of the palette knife in his late paintings.[52] There are, however, only a handful of works from the 1650s and early 1660s in which the characteristic straight ridges and perfectly flat paint surfaces produced by this tool can be found, and in those works it was employed only locally and quite sparingly. An early but unusual example of its use is in *Titus at his Desk* of 1655 (cat. 99 and detail, p. 150), where a creamy beige pigment was smeared across the desk with a couple of vertical strokes of a broad, flat knife. Some of the long black lines in this beige layer were carved by flecks of dry paint or perhaps dirt that had become stuck to the blade. A much narrower tool was used to produce the more common rectangular marks with raised ridges, such as in the tablecloth and some of the drapery in *The Conspiracy of the Batavians* of about 1661–2 (cat. 72), as well as at the shoulder of the gold costume in the *Homer* (fig. 71, p. 219), painted in 1663. A few more examples of this economical

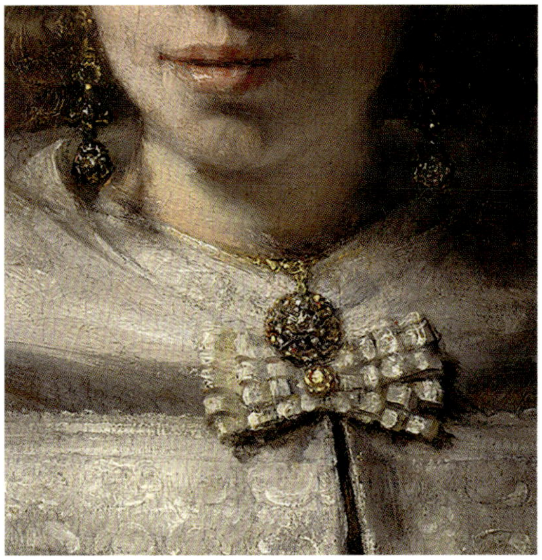

Detail from *Portrait of a Lady with an Ostrich-Feather Fan* (cat. 38)

Detail from *Self Portrait with Two Circles* (cat. 58)

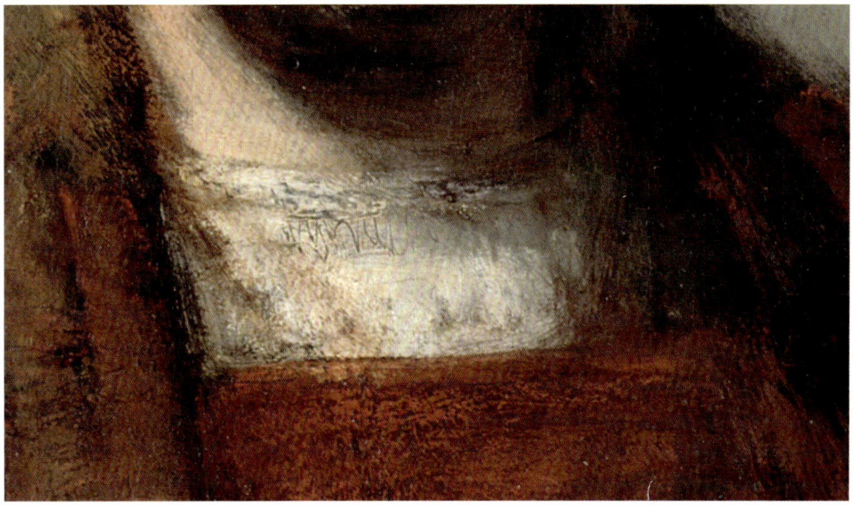

Detail from *Portrait of a Couple as Isaac and Rebecca*, known as '*The Jewish Bride*' (cat. 92)

OVERLEAF
Detail from *Portrait of a Family* (cat. 94)

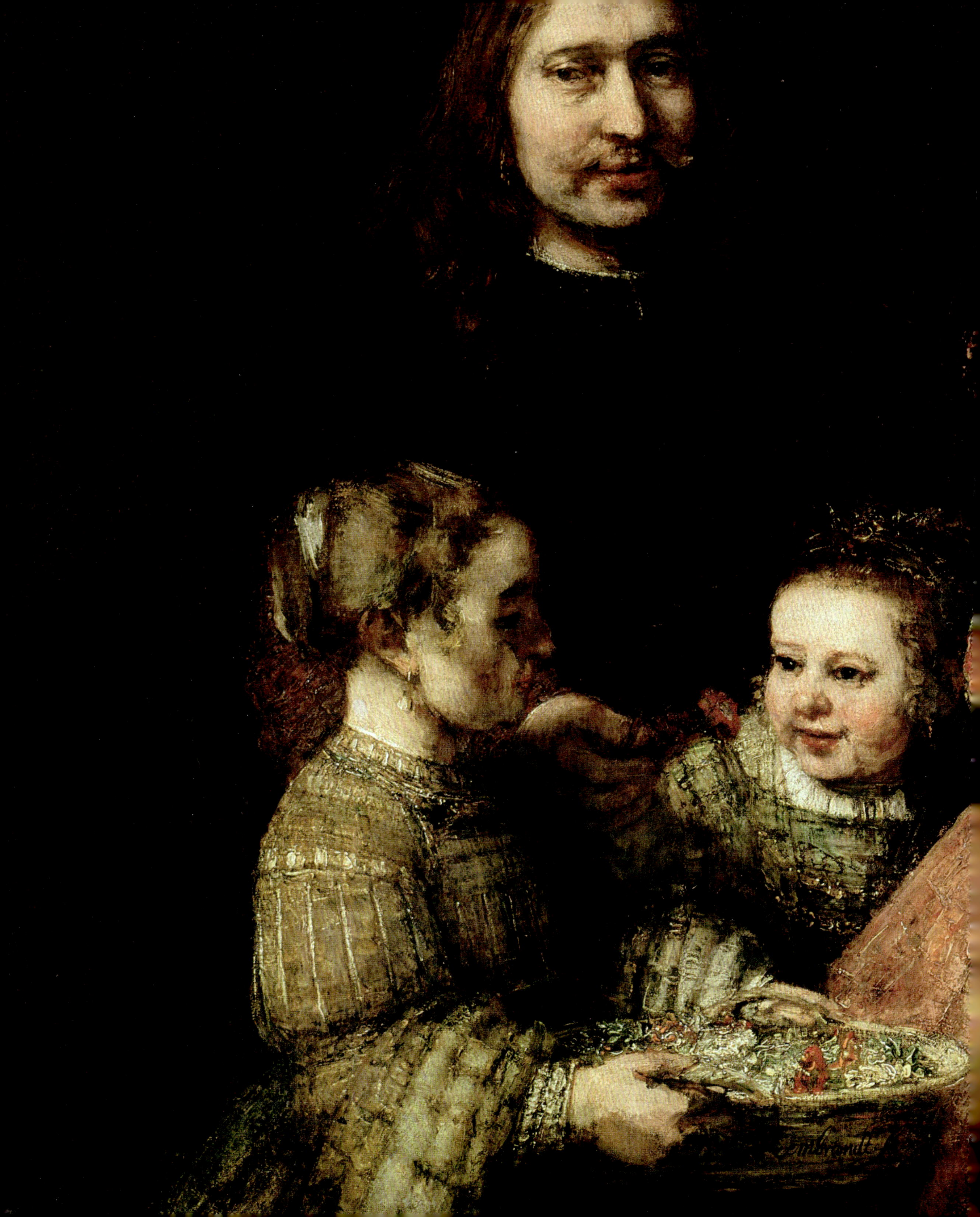

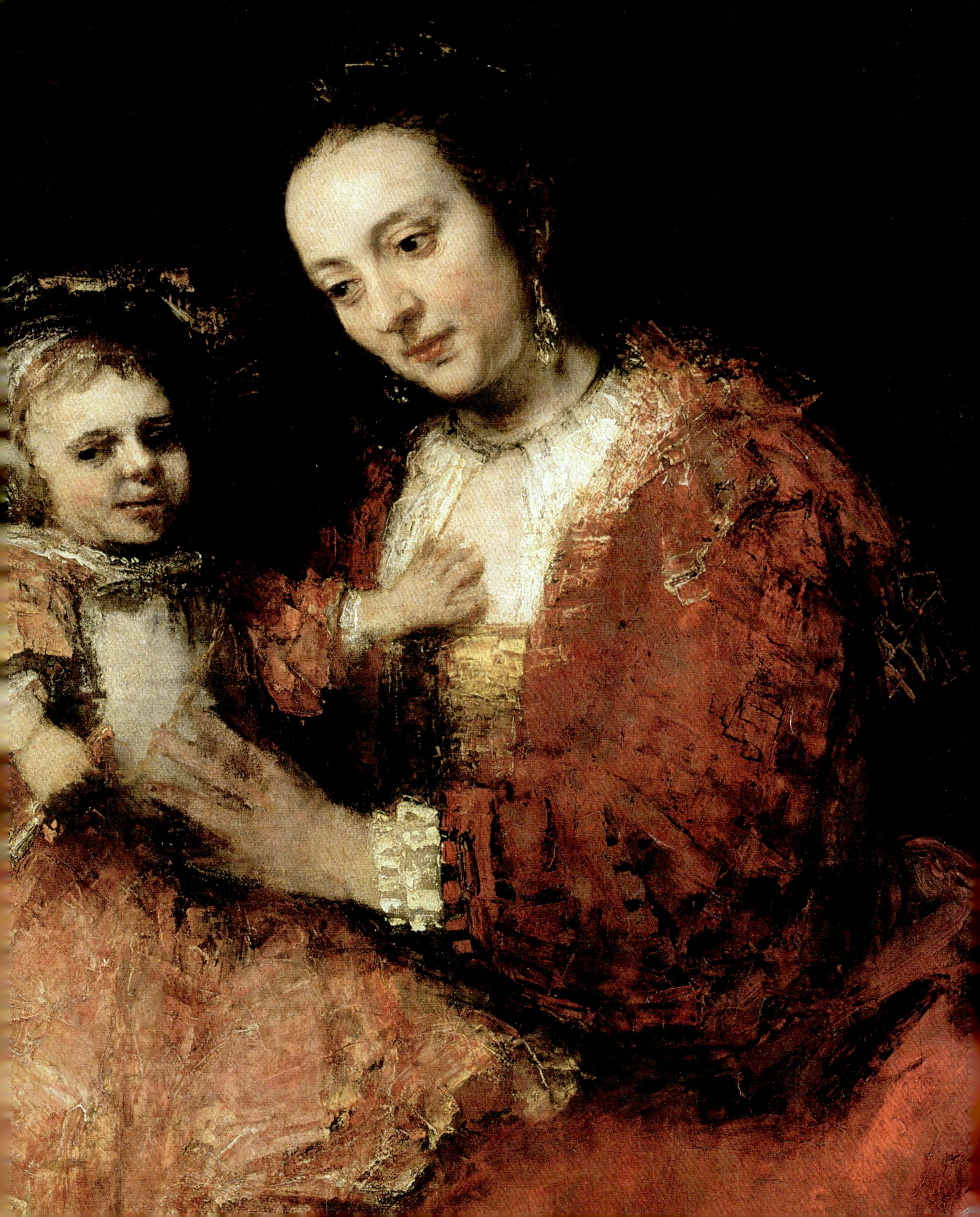

use of the palette knife could be given, but what is apparent is that Rembrandt only employed this technique extensively in three paintings, all of them dating to around the middle of the 1660s: '*The Jewish Bride*', the *Portrait of a Family* and *Lucretia*. In '*The Jewish Bride*' (cat. 92), it appears in Isaac's cape, the lower part of his sleeve and in the middle and right side of Rebecca's dress. The tell-tale markings of the palette knife can also be seen in the wide, red sleeve of the 'Venetian' jacket worn by the mother in the *Portrait of a Family* (cat. 94 and detail, p. 148). Here a black glaze was applied with the knife on top of the red paint in the centre of the sleeve, leaving only dark rectangular outlines. The skirt of the baby boy exhibits an even more exciting use of the palette knife, with white and pink painted wet-in-wet over a dried layer of yellow applied with this tool.

The palette knife was also used liberally in *Lucretia* (cat. 57), in the lower part of the white chemise and both of the exposed white sleeves. Also mostly applied in this manner is the yellow paint forming the underlayer of the brown and the bluish-green garments covering the upper part of the figure's proper right arm. A translucent brown glaze was added with the knife on top of this yellow layer to create the brown fabric, and more opaque blues, greens and greys were painted with the brush over the yellow underlayer at the figure's shoulder. The white chemise at the lower part of the arm was also executed in this fashion, with a dark brown glaze over a white

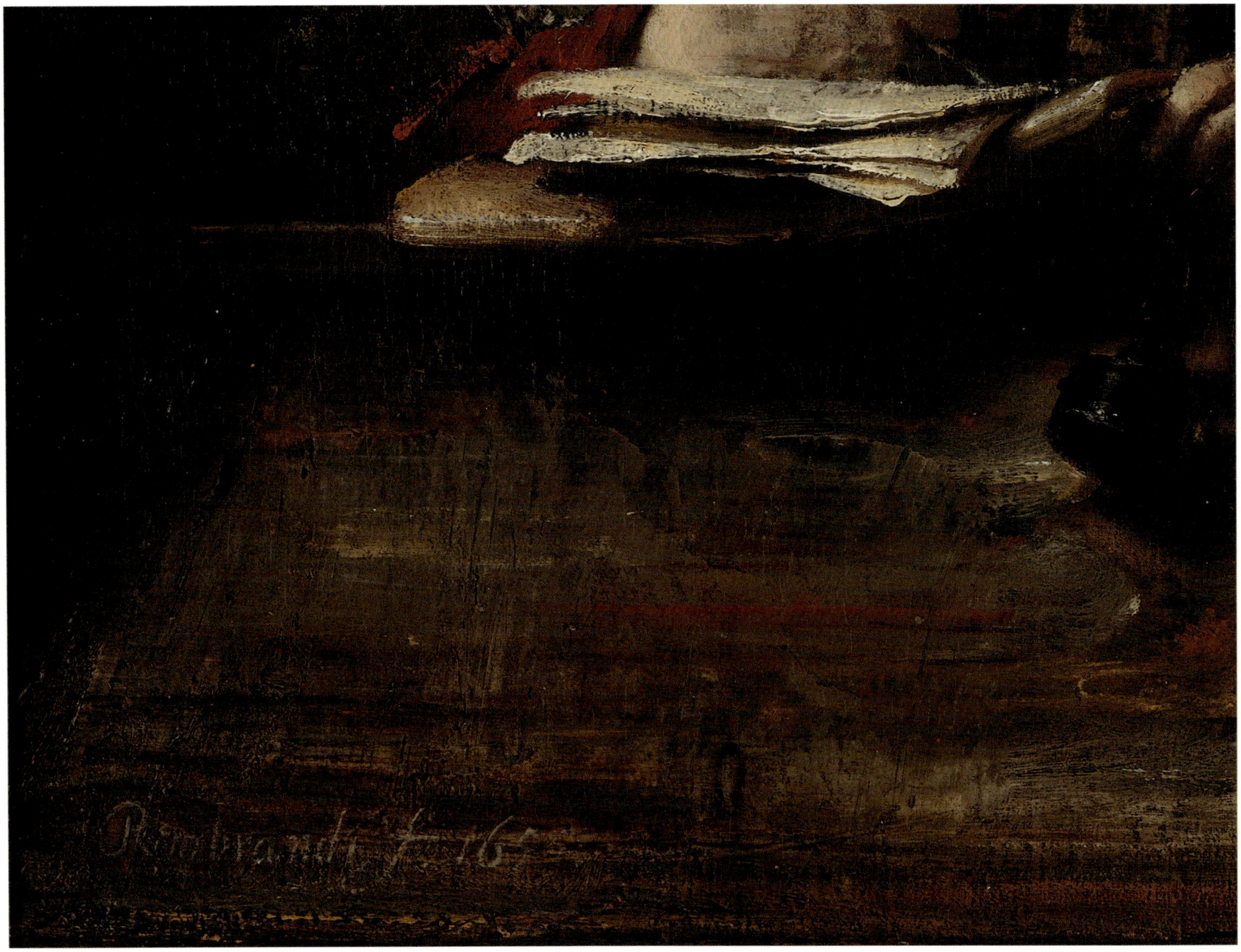

Detail from *Titus at his Desk* (cat. 99)

FIG. 57
X-radiograph of *Lucretia*
(cat. 57)

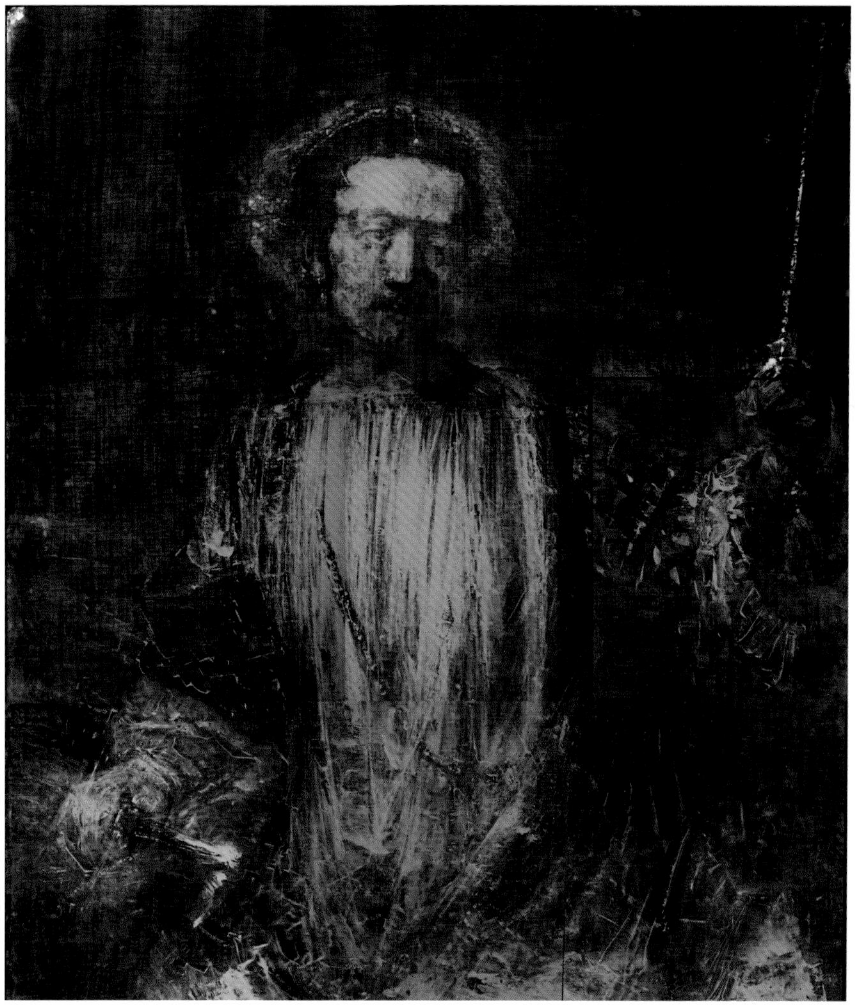

underlayer applied in part with a palette knife. While the rough manner of execution of this painting seems to give the impression that it was dashed off in a matter of hours, several days would have been necessary for the underlying layers applied with the palette knife to dry before another layer could be applied with the knife. If the underlying layer was not dry, the ridges would have been smoothed out by the knife when the next layer was added. The raised, light-reflecting ridges produced by the knife are visible in the painting itself where they have not been covered, but can be seen to much greater advantage in the X-radiograph (fig. 57), which also reveals that even the first lay-in of the figure's proper right hand was made with this tool.[53]

After discussing an aspect of Titian's late working method in his 1678 treatise, Van Hoogstraten ascribed the use of the rough manner by some elderly artists to their physical decline: 'I have also witnessed painters who as the evening of old age darkened their eyes began to wield their brush with ever increasing boldness.'[54] Given the astonishing innovativeness and freedom in Rembrandt's handling of paint in his final years, one can hardly imagine that Van Hoogstraten would have been thinking of his former teacher when he made this disparaging remark. In Rembrandt's case, failing eyesight had little or nothing to do with it, as demonstrated by comparing the relatively fine execution of the *Portrait of Catrina Hooghsaet* (cat. 41) with the quite loose and open manner of the Timken Museum *Apostle Bartholomew*, both painted in 1657. The fact that he did not pioneer all the methods employed in his late work, and had already made use of a number of them at the very onset of his career, does not disqualify Rembrandt's final years from being his most experimental. It was then that he employed his full arsenal of techniques for the first time, and constantly sought new ways to apply them, dramatically varying his approach from one painting to the next.

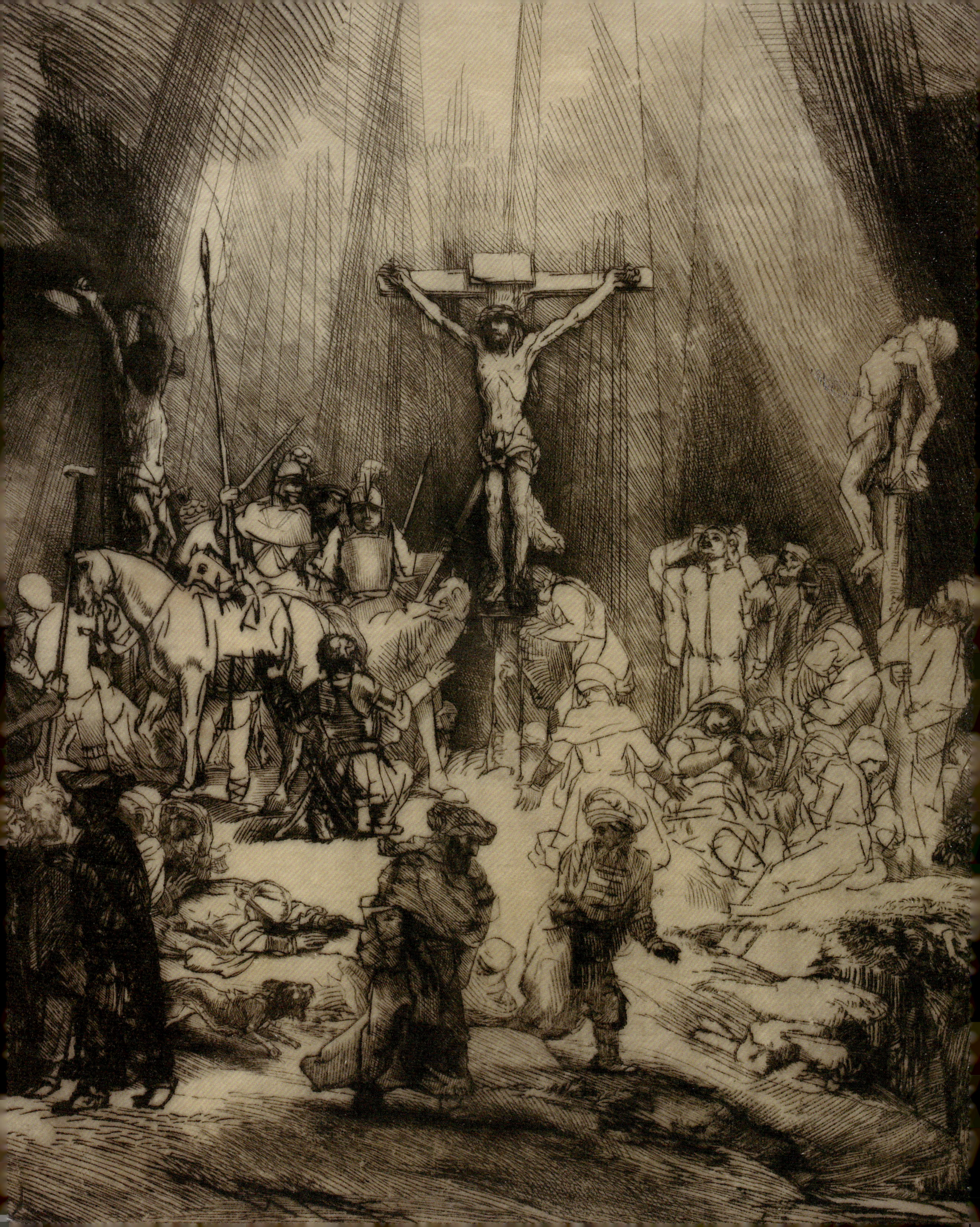

EXPERIMENTAL TECHNIQUE

THE ETCHINGS

Erik Hinterding

LIKE HIS PAINTINGS and drawings, Rembrandt's etchings become noticeably coarser after 1651. This was directly related to his use of drypoint, which became increasingly important in his later prints. Drypoint is a variant of the traditional etching technique. Instead of drawing the lines in the wax of the etching ground and then biting them out with acid, the artist scratches them directly in the copper plate. The metal that is scraped away heaps up along the edges of the lines, creating a burr. The degree of burr depends on the amount of force exerted on the etching needle and the angle with which the incisions are made. A drypoint line is easily recognisable, because some ink is always left behind along the burr, which gives the line a fuzzy, velvety appearance in the print. Another feature of drypoint lines is that they are almost always a little stiffer and more angular than etched or engraved lines, because it is more difficult to control a needle scratching in a copper surface than one that glides through the softer wax of the etching ground.

The drypoint technique was far from new in Rembrandt's day. As early as the fifteenth century it was being used to draw the initial design of a composition in the plate, which was then worked up with the burin.[1] Rembrandt, too, was familiar with drypoint long before 1652, although at that time he was still using it in the traditional way, as an auxiliary technique. In his early etchings he regularly made his final corrections and minor adjustments by scratching directly into the plate.[2] In that period, though, drypoint played hardly any role at all, and the lines have very little burr. That changed around 1639, when he deliberately started seeking out the velvety effect that burr can give to a line and utilised it as an attractive stylistic device. He did this by deliberately pressing the needle harder into the copper to create much more burr. One famous example from the period before 1652 in which he exploited the potential of the technique in all its glory is *Christ healing the Sick*, better known as *The Hundred Guilder Print*, which Rembrandt finished in 1648 (fig. 58).[3] It is a large sheet that encapsulates the most important events from chapter 19 of Saint Matthew's Gospel.[4] The figures entering through the gateway on the right and walking towards Christ, in particular, have been worked up with drypoint into a wide and differentiated spectrum of tints that Rembrandt had never equalled before, ranging from a deep velvet black through pale grey to almost white.[5]

The way in which Rembrandt deployed drypoint to achieve tonal, almost painterly effects was utterly novel. No other artist had done this, and people were well aware of it. Within a few years impressions of *Christ healing* were changing hands for 100 guilders,[6] which was an exorbitant price for a print and a clear sign that its extraordinary qualities were greatly admired.[7] This was confirmed in 1718 by Rembrandt's biographer Arnold Houbraken, who wrote: 'particularly in the so-called hundred-guilder print ... at the treatment of which we can only wonder, because we cannot understand how he could have worked this up from what was originally nothing but a rough sketch.'[8]

Never before in his career as a printmaker had Rembrandt so closely approached an almost photo-realist reproduction of reality with the aid of a highly innovative technique. At the same time, it seems to have marked the culmination of a development, because, strikingly, he then embarked on a coarser, more draughtsman-like style. That new departure is well illustrated by *Clump of Trees with a Vista* of 1652 (cats 59–60). The location has never been identified but it must have been a favourite spot, because the farmhouse with its outbuilding was

Detail from *The Three Crosses* (cat. 62)

also depicted by several of Rembrandt's followers.[9] The print was executed in drypoint alone. The full, velvety lines give the scene a sketchy character and are less suited for fine details than are etched lines, and as a result the composition is primarily an interplay of light and shade. Nevertheless, it gives a convincing picture of a landscape on a sun-drenched summer's day.

The later period of Rembrandt's graphic output cannot be discussed without reference to the support on which he printed his impressions. It was all ordinary western paper until the late 1640s, but after then he increasingly favoured other types of paper and even parchment, and these experiments typify his later manner. For example, several impressions of *A Scholar in his Study* ('*Faust*') (cat. 61) of around 1652 are on cartridge paper, a kind of wrapping paper with coarse, dark fibres that give impressions a lively structure.[10] The oriental paper on which Rembrandt now began printing more of his etchings was even more innovative.[11] This has a very regular, almost silk-like texture, and is yellower than western paper, although the shades can vary quite considerably from ivory to a deep yellowish brown. Most sheets have been identified as being made from the fibres of the *gampi* plant, which identifies them as coming from Japan.[12] A thinner, pale yellow variant is commonly called 'Chinese' but is in fact probably *gasenshi* paper, a Japanese imitation of Chinese calligraphy paper.[13]

Rembrandt must have paid quite a large sum for these exotic papers.[14] The plant that provided the raw material for *gampi* paper could not be cultivated but had to be harvested in the wild. This made the paper extremely expensive, even in Japan,[15] so impressions on oriental paper really were '*éditions de luxe*', even though Rembrandt was primarily interested in the technical printing properties of the paper. Unlike western types, Japanese paper does not absorb ink well, so that it lies on the surface of the sheet and usually runs a little as well. This effect, combined with the drypoint lines, gives superb results. In addition, the warm, yellowish colour of the sheets softens the contrasts and creates attractive tonal effects , which Rembrandt often enhanced by printing the impressions with carefully applied surface tone.[16] The results can be admired in impressions on Japanese paper of *Saint Jerome reading in an Italianate Landscape* of about 1653 (see cat. 23), and in the first state of *Christ at Emmaus: the Larger Plate* of 1654, which is

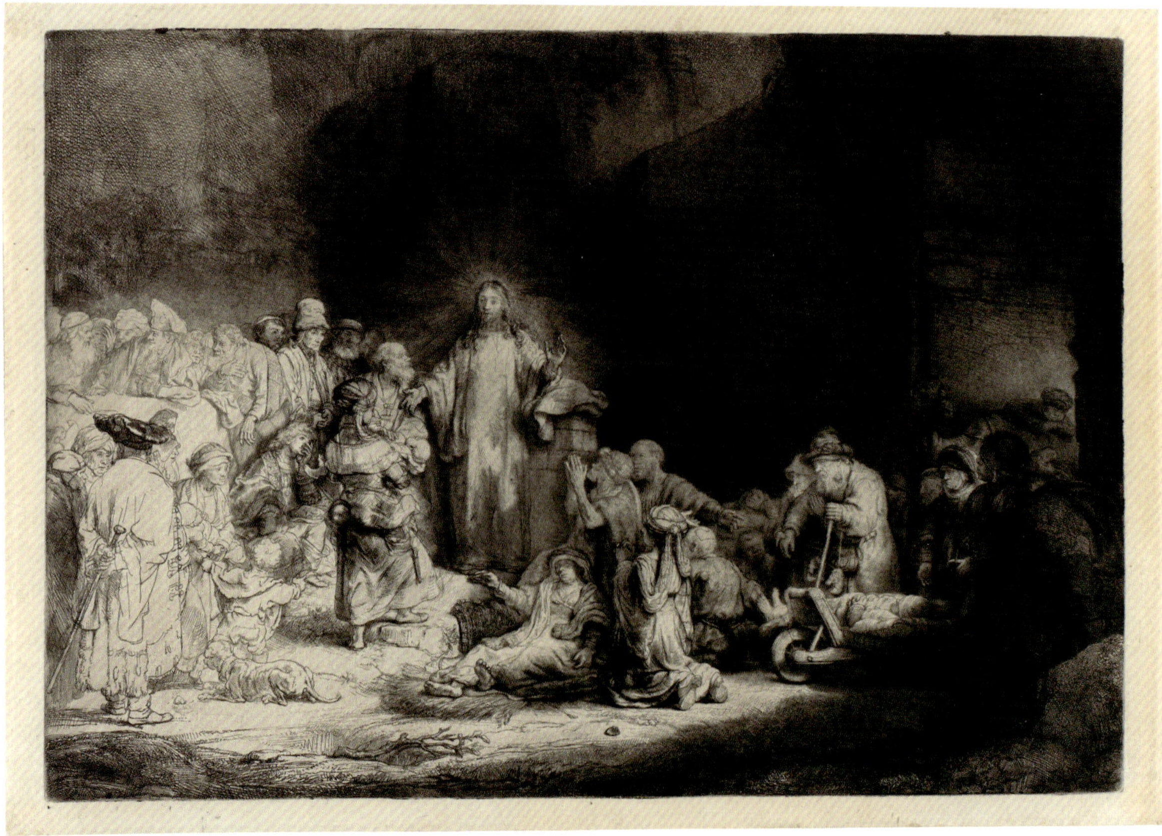

FIG. 58
Christ healing the Sick
(*The Hundred Guilder Print*),
about 1648
Etching with drypoint
and burin, 27.8 × 38.8 cm
Rijksmuseum, Amsterdam.
Bequest of Mr and Mrs
De Bruijn-van der Leeuw,
Muri, Switzerland

59
Clump of Trees with a Vista, 1652
Drypoint, 15.6 × 21.1 cm
First state of two
Rijksmuseum, Amsterdam
(RP-P-OB-454)

60
Clump of Trees with a Vista, 1652
Drypoint, 12.4 × 21.1 cm
Second state of two
Rijksmuseum, Amsterdam
(RP-P-OB-455)

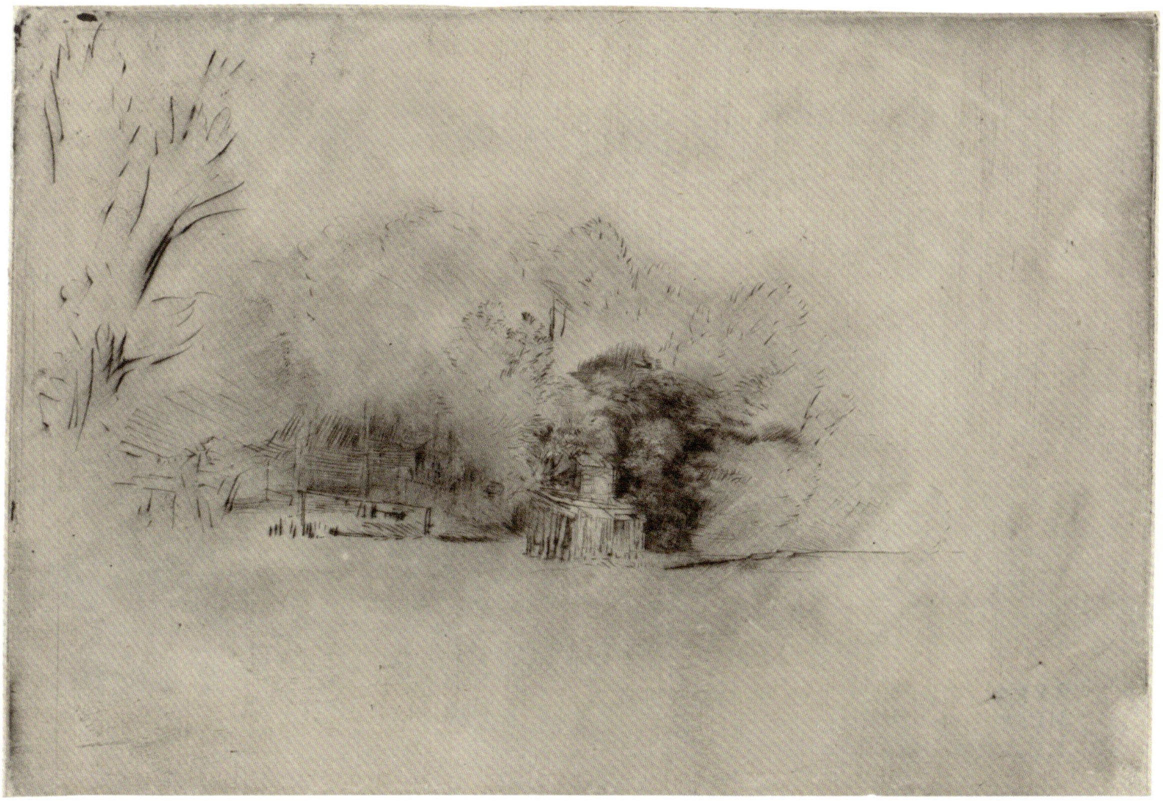

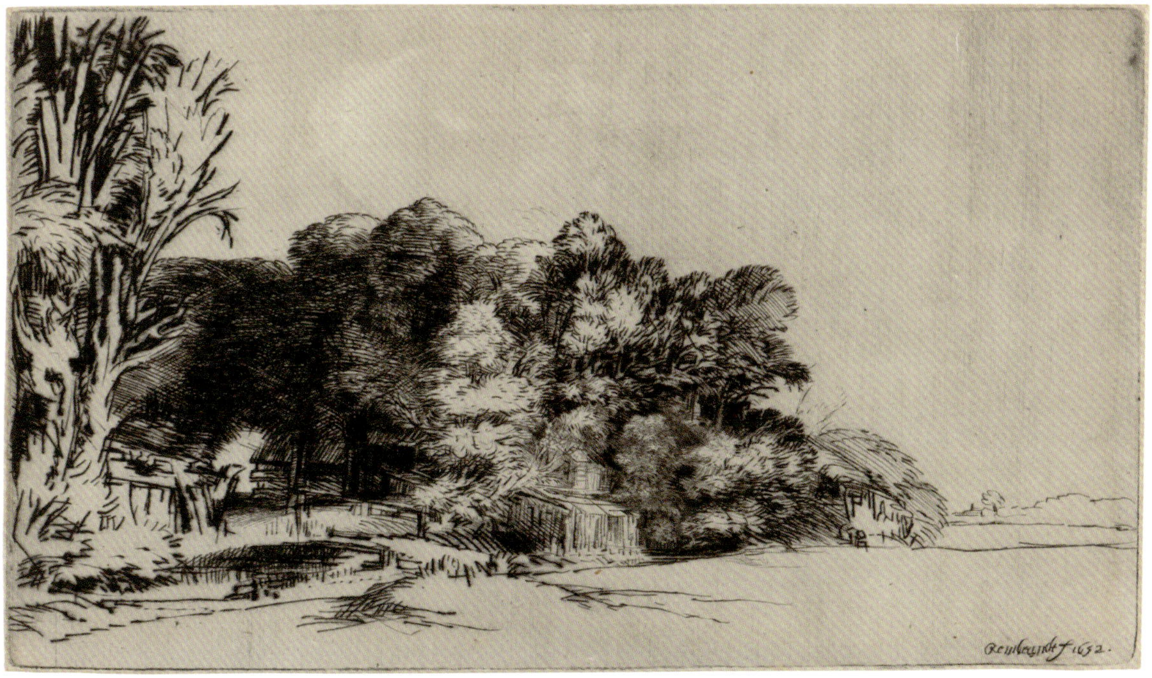

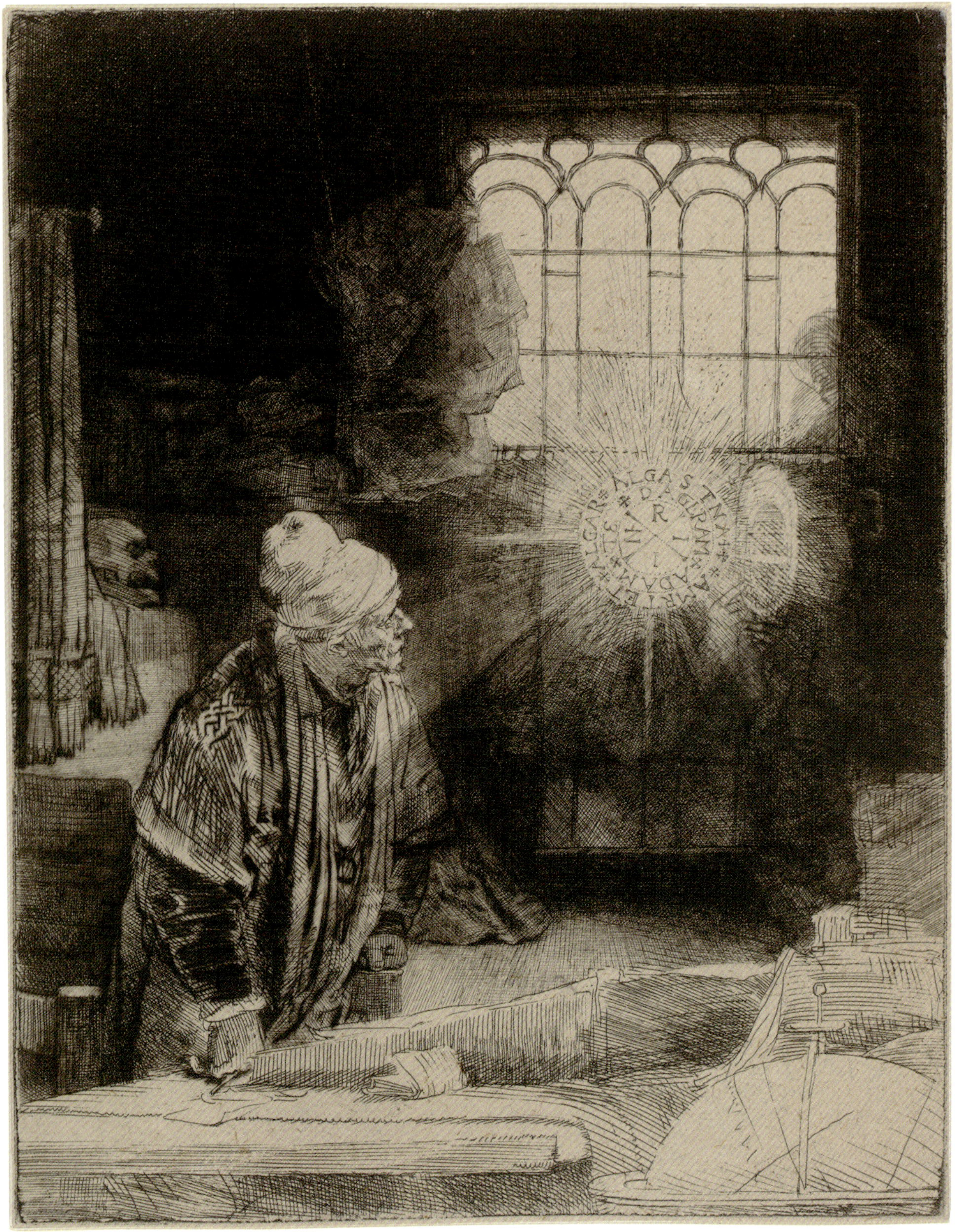

61
A Scholar in his Study ('Faust'), about 1652
Etching, engraving and drypoint, 21 × 16 cm
First state of seven
Graphische Sammlung Albertina, Vienna
(DG1926/429)

often found on Chinese paper (cat. 82, although this is on Japanese paper).

The artistic merits of such papers are obvious enough, so it is not surprising that impressions on oriental paper were already being regarded as among the most desirable of Rembrandt's etchings in the seventeenth century.[17] But it is important to realise that the use of that paper was just one element in a working method that was highly unusual for the period. From the very start of his career as an etcher, Rembrandt had become accustomed to working up a scene on the copper plate itself rather than using a preparatory drawing.[18] One result of this approach was that he usually needed many states to bring a composition to fruition. These trials document the intermediate stages in the genesis of an etching, the purpose of which was to assess the progress of the work on the plate. Impressions of the separate states from Rembrandt's early years are not only rare, but in theory they were not even for sale, although there would always have been collectors who were interested in them.[19]

In the early 1650s it seems that Rembrandt deliberately set about cultivating that interest. Not only did he start working up his plates in more stages than before, but he also began printing more and more of the early states as de luxe editions on oriental paper, often with carefully measured surface tone in order to heighten the tonal effects even further.[20] There can be no doubt, then, that although those impressions may have been an intermediate stage in the genesis of the print, Rembrandt very definitely intended them for sale. That, too, was completely new at the time: no other printmaker did so.[21] The idea that Rembrandt used the early states for commercial purposes is borne out by the fact that he printed many of them in considerable quantities. For example, *Christ at Emmaus: the Larger Plate* was completed in two stages. There are no fewer than 25 impressions of the first, unfinished state, 12 of them on Chinese paper and 5 on Japanese.

Another example that is very typical of Rembrandt's output in the early 1650s is *The Entombment* of around 1654 (cats 80–1). The print went through four stages and was worked up in a procedure that Rembrandt usually followed at the time: the scene was first laid down on the plate as an etching and then given detail with the drypoint. It shows Christ's body being laid in the tomb provided by Joseph of Arimathea.[22] In the first state the entire scene was on the plate in the form of a pure etching in a loose, open style with a lot of parallel hatching. Twenty-four impressions of this state have been traced, all with negligible surface tone, but no fewer than 15 on Chinese and four on Japanese paper.[23] In the second state Rembrandt used drypoint and burin to turn the image into a true nocturnal scene, with the only pool of light being around Christ's body in the lower right corner. The dramatic darkening was intensified in the impressions by printing many of the sheets with variable surface tone (cat. 80).[24] There are 21 known impressions, four of them on costly parchment and seven on Japanese paper.[25] However, Rembrandt evidently felt that he had now made the scene too dark, because in the third state he burnished several passages to bring them back into the light, most notably the alcove at the back with the two skulls on a ledge. That being said, most of the impressions of this state were also printed with heavy surface tone (cat. 81). There are 23 of these, of which only three are on Japanese paper and two on parchment.[26] In the fourth and final state it is mainly the low wall half-way up the right side that has been darkened with additional lines. The early impressions of this state were also printed with much surface tone, but not one of them is on an oriental type of paper or parchment.[27]

62
The Three Crosses, 1653
Drypoint, 38.5 × 45 cm
First state of five
Rijksmuseum, Amsterdam
(RP-P-1961-1196A)

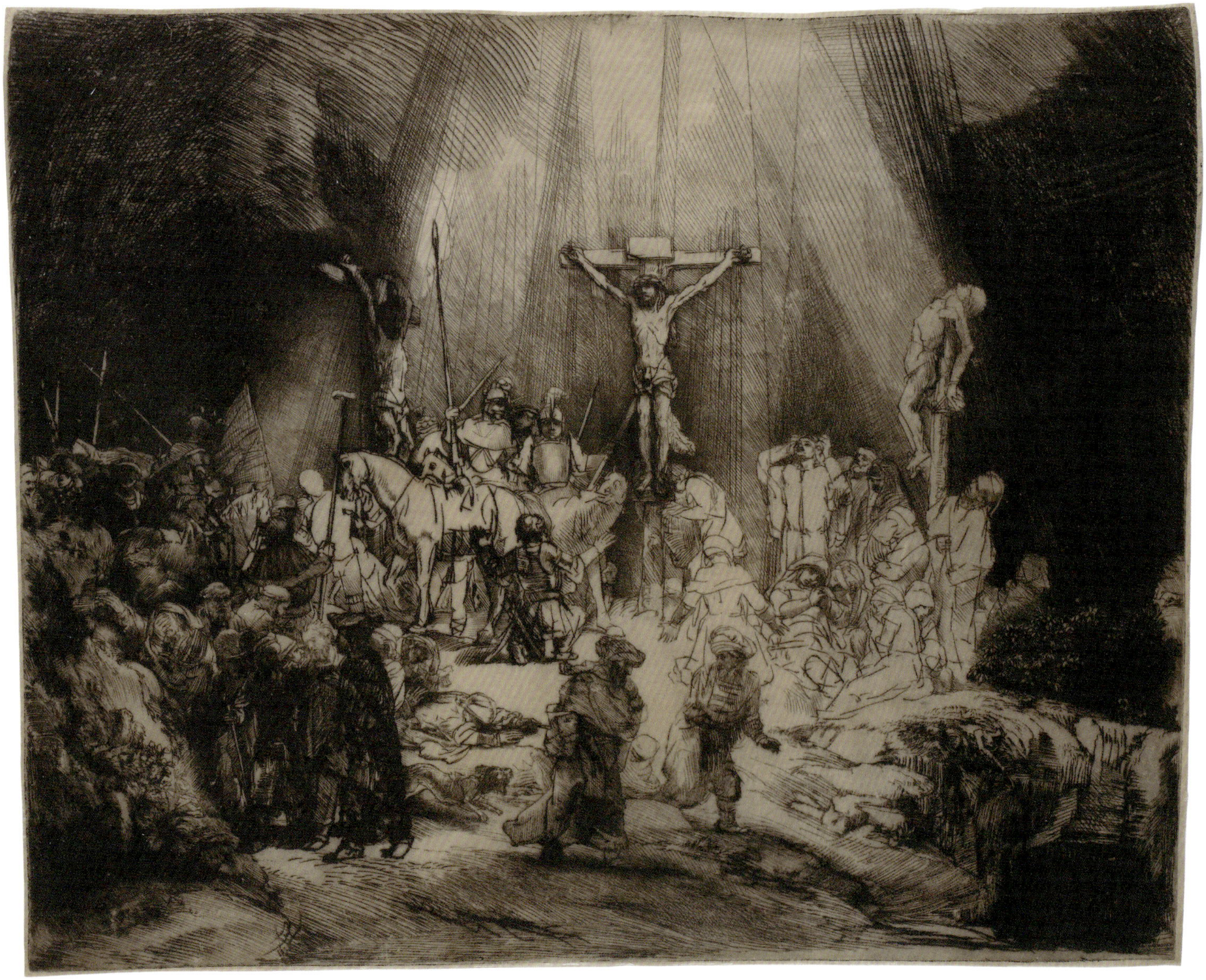

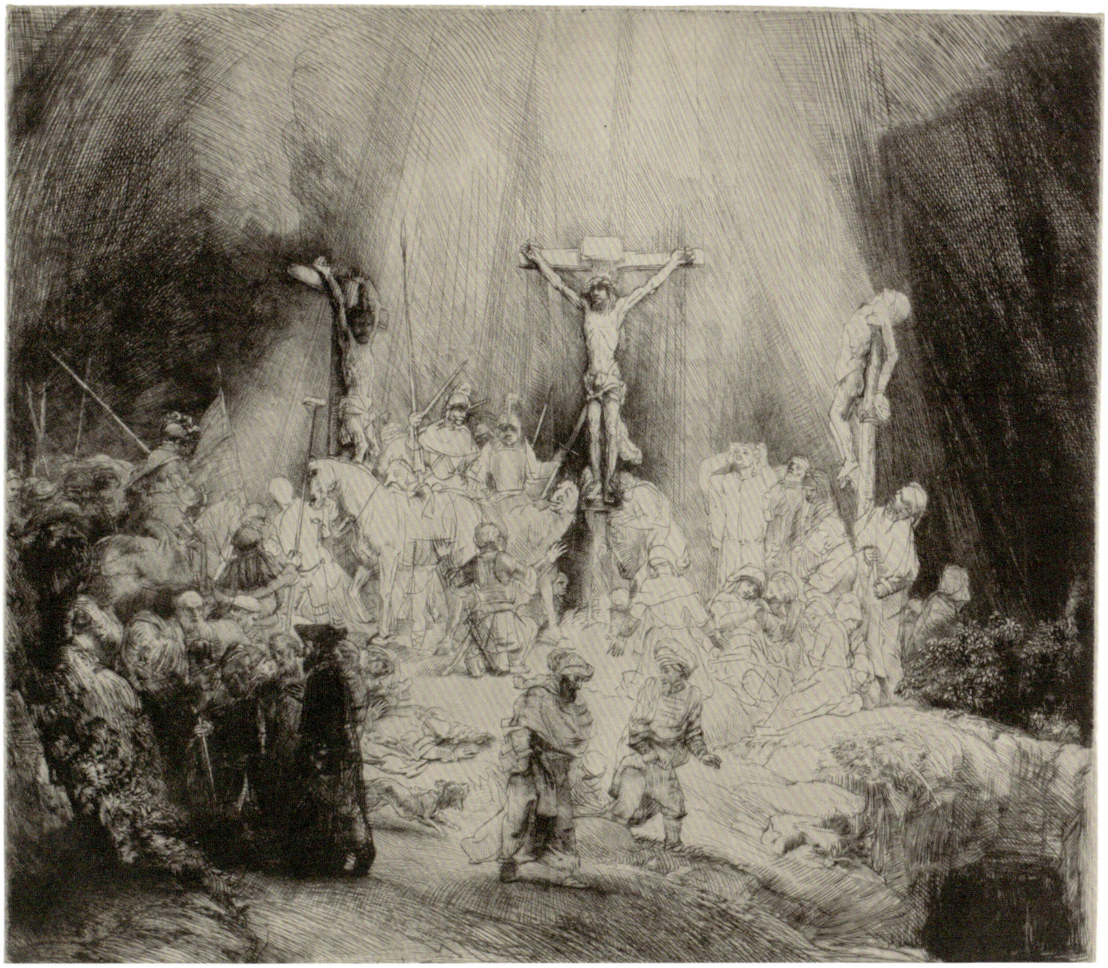

63
The Three Crosses, 1653
Drypoint, 38.5 × 45 cm
Third state of five
Rijksmuseum, Amsterdam
(RP-P-OB-617)

64
The Three Crosses, 1653
Drypoint, 38.5 × 45 cm
Fourth state of five
The Victoria and Albert
Museum, London (CAI.637)

Despite the great graphic potential of drypoint, it has one major drawback: the burr that gives the impressions their distinctive velvety look is fragile and soon wears away, so that only between 50 and 75 impressions can be printed before the plate becomes completely worn out.[28] In 1653 Rembrandt made *The Three Crosses* (cats 62–4), in which he introduced a completely new solution to the problem of wear. This monumental print is one of the highlights of his etched oeuvre and a key point in the history of the graphic arts, for never before had such a large print been executed in drypoint alone. Given the fragility of the technique, it is not surprising that Rembrandt took the greatest care over the impressions from the very outset. There are five known states of the print, but it was already finished in the first one. Of the 21 impressions of the first state that have been traced, no fewer than 17 are on parchment, a support that is far more exclusive than ordinary paper.[29] The second version differs from the first in one minimal correction: the profile of the face of the man on the far right has been

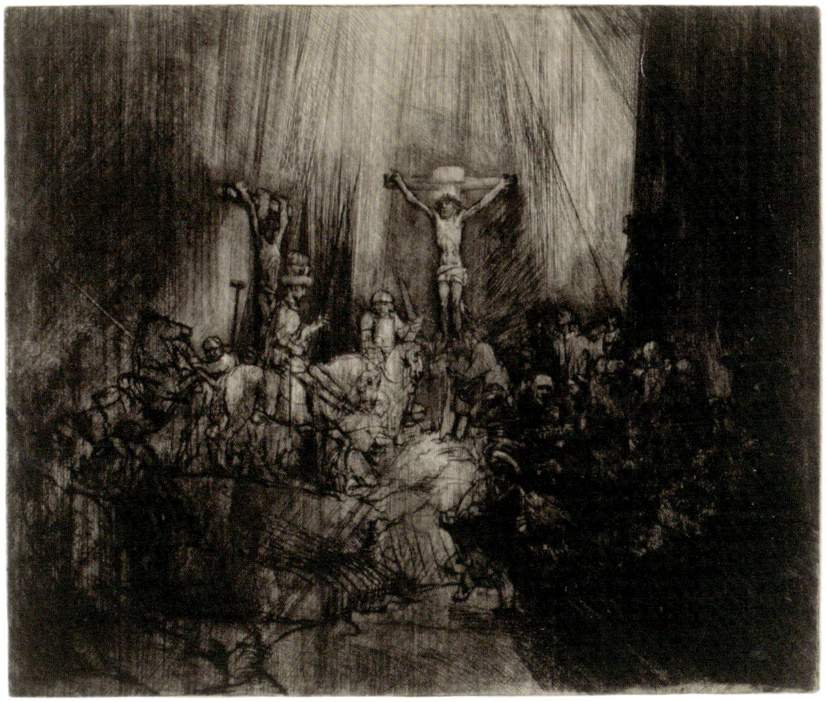

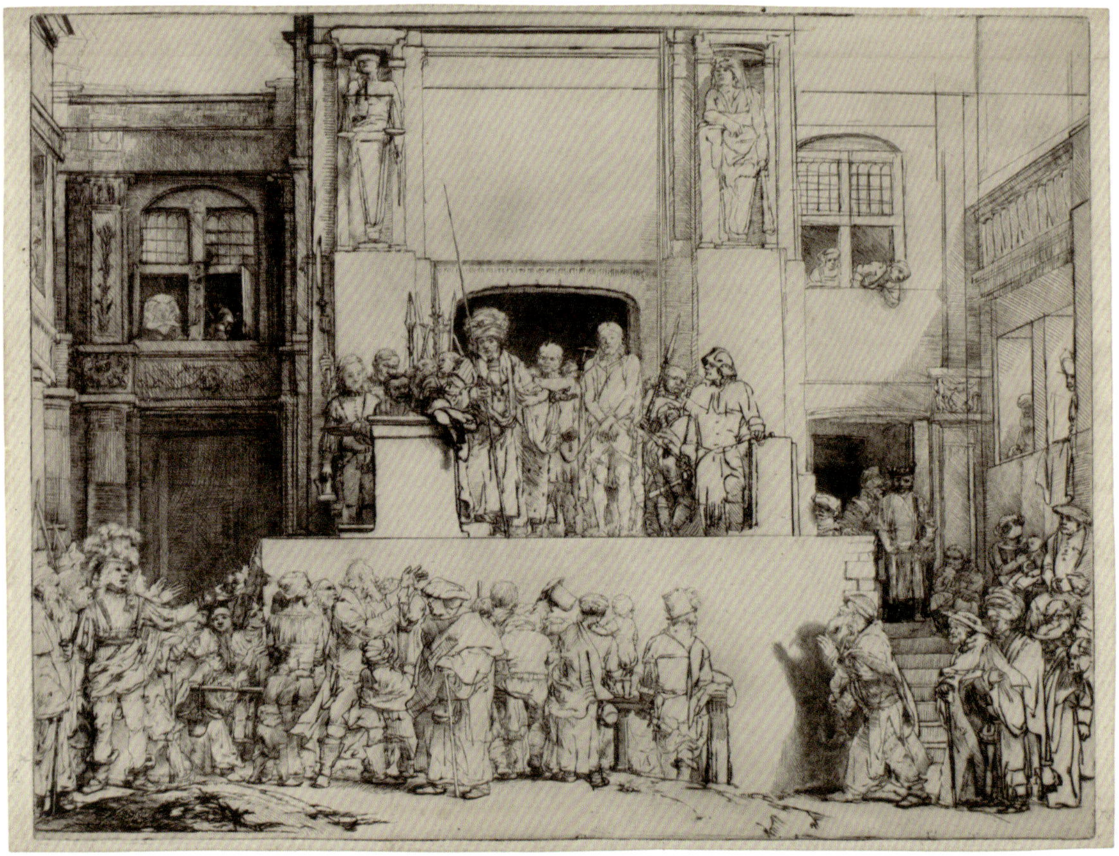

65
Christ presented to the People (Ecce Homo), 1655
Drypoint, 35.8 × 45.5 cm
Fifth state of eight
Rijksmuseum, Amsterdam
(RP-P-OB-610)

Detail from *The Three Crosses* (cat. 64)

darkened even further. There are ten known impressions of this state, all of them printed with the greatest of care on western paper.[30] They are already showing wear in the burr, making the passages on the left and right sides lighter. In the following stage Rembrandt restored these contrasts by hatching them again with the drypoint. He also signed the plate 'Rembrandt.f.1653', indicating that he now regarded the scene as finished (cat. 63). There are 22 impressions of the third state, two of them on parchment. It can be seen in the later impressions of this state that the burr was again beginning to wear, making it look grey and dry, with the result that the composition was becoming lighter once more.[31]

Rembrandt completely transformed the composition in the fourth state (cat. 64), redefining Christ on the cross, replacing many of the bystanders with other figures and darkening the passages on either side of the cross to such an extent that they can barely be made out in some impressions. It was assumed until recently that Rembrandt's modifications were prompted by a reappraisal of the subject around 1661, years after the first state.[32] However, that hypothesis has been demolished by research on the watermarks in the paper Rembrandt used, which has shown that all four states of *The Three Crosses* not on parchment were printed on the same paper.[33] This is common with Rembrandt's prints, and indicates that the states were made in quick succession.[34] When combined with the total of at least 53 impressions of the first three states, this sheds a revealing light on the fourth state. An edition of 53 impressions would not have been much for a pure etching, which could easily run to an edition of 200 or more, but it is certainly a large number for a print executed solely with the drypoint, the more so in this case in that the burr had already vanished from large areas of the plate in later impressions of the third state. The fact that the fourth state of *The Three Crosses* was not made in 1661 but immediately after the others in 1653 shows that the reworking should be seen as as an ingenious way of making new impressions from a worn plate. And this he certainly did: there are no fewer than 78 impressions of the fourth state, this time with three on Japanese paper.[35]

This example can serve as a model for the way in which Rembrandt then went on to rework several other prints. He ran into exactly the same problem with *Christ presented to the People (Ecce Homo)* (cat. 31). This, too, is

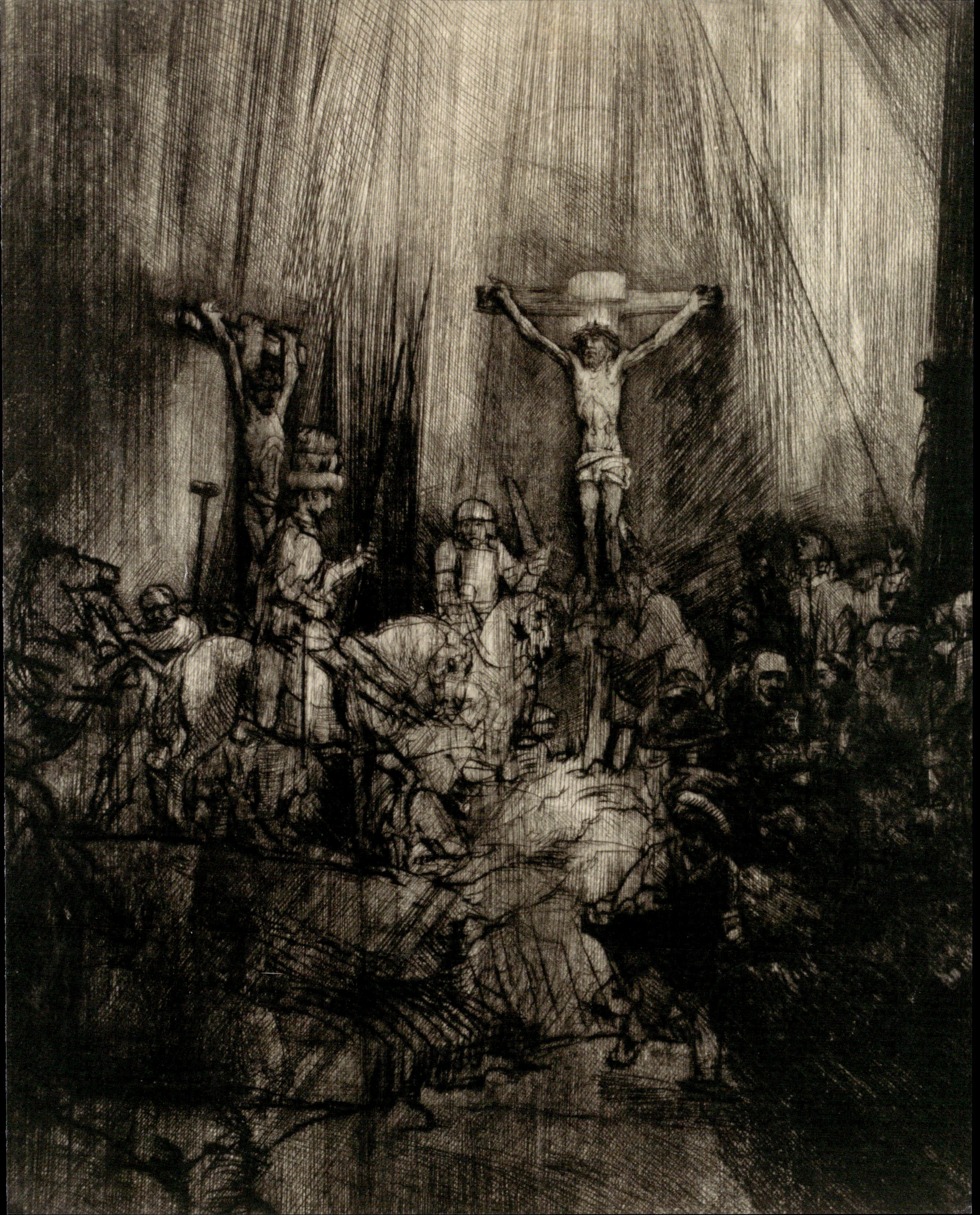

a very large composition executed entirely in drypoint and printed mainly on expensive kinds of oriental paper, starting with the very first impression. By the fifth state, when 71 impressions had already been printed, the plate had become so worn that Rembrandt combined a three-stage repair operation with a total reworking of the scene (cat. 65).

He adopted the same tactic again later, for example in his *Woman sitting half-dressed beside a Stove* of 1658 (cats 14–16). There are no fewer than seven known states of this print, and not all of them intended solely to develop the image. The composition is almost complete in the rare first state, but the background is still too light and looks grey and dingy, probably because the copper plate did not take up the ink properly. In addition, the niche in the wall on the left behind the woman is still not clearly defined. This is essentially a proof state, although Rembrandt would have sold impressions of it. The four known impressions all have surface tone and are on Japanese paper.[36] In the second state, which is also rare, having only five known impressions, Rembrandt simply strengthened the shaded passages on the woman's torso. It was not until the third state (cat. 15) that he turned his attention to the other areas.[37] He clarified the shape of the niche, made the wall darker, hatched the woman's skirt again, did the same to the stove, and worked up other details. The scene was now firmly on the plate, and it is clear that Rembrandt considered it finished from the sizeable number of impressions – at least 37 of them, seven on Japanese paper and nine on Chinese.[38] It was undoubtedly wear to the copper plate that then forced him to work on it further, but as in the case of *The Three*

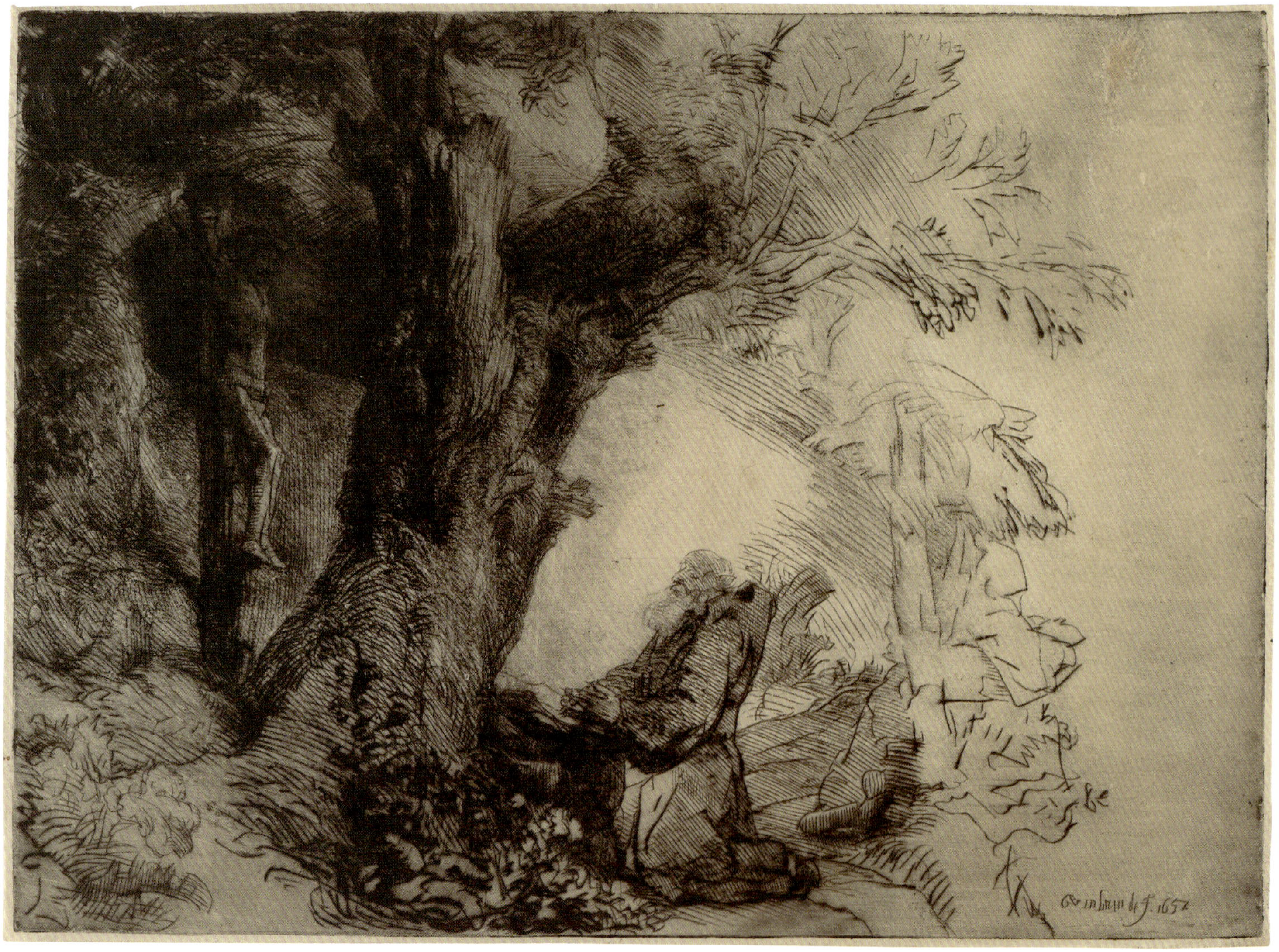

66
Saint Francis beneath a Tree, praying, 1657
Drypoint, 18 × 24.4 cm
First state of two
Rijksmuseum, Amsterdam
(RP-P-OB-171)

Crosses he did not limit himself to repairs alone. He enlivened the scene in the fourth state, which survives in just a single impression, by inserting a damper in the flue of the stove; in the fifth state he added new lines to the woman's skirt to darken it again.[39] He left the background untouched, and as a result it is often possible to see the worsening wear there. The seven impressions of this state that have been catalogued are nevertheless all on Japanese paper.[40] Finally, in the sixth version (cat. 16), which is only occasionally found on oriental paper, he removed the model's white cap, so there is less of a contrast between her head and the dark background.[41]

No one else worked like this in the late seventeenth century. It is important to realise that Rembrandt did not develop all his prints in so many stages, although even then he experimented with the technique. For example, *Saint Francis beneath a Tree, praying* of 1657 was completed in only two stages. The first, a proof state sketched with the drypoint alone (cat. 66), is almost finished on the left but not across the rest of the scene. There are five known impressions of this state, all of them printed with variable surface tone on Japanese paper or parchment.[42] Rembrandt then etched the plate in the second state in order to complete the composition; this was a very unusual sequence and one that he never repeated.[43] The leaves in the lower left corner are far more deeply bitten than the lines of the small church in the top right corner, which could be a sign that Rembrandt bit the plate more than once (cat. 67).[44] This state, too, was regularly printed with surface tone on oriental types of paper, although there are also early impressions on western types.[45]

67
Saint Francis beneath a Tree, praying, 1657
Drypoint and etching,
18 × 24.4 cm
Second state of two
Rijksmuseum, Amsterdam
(RP-P-1962-92)

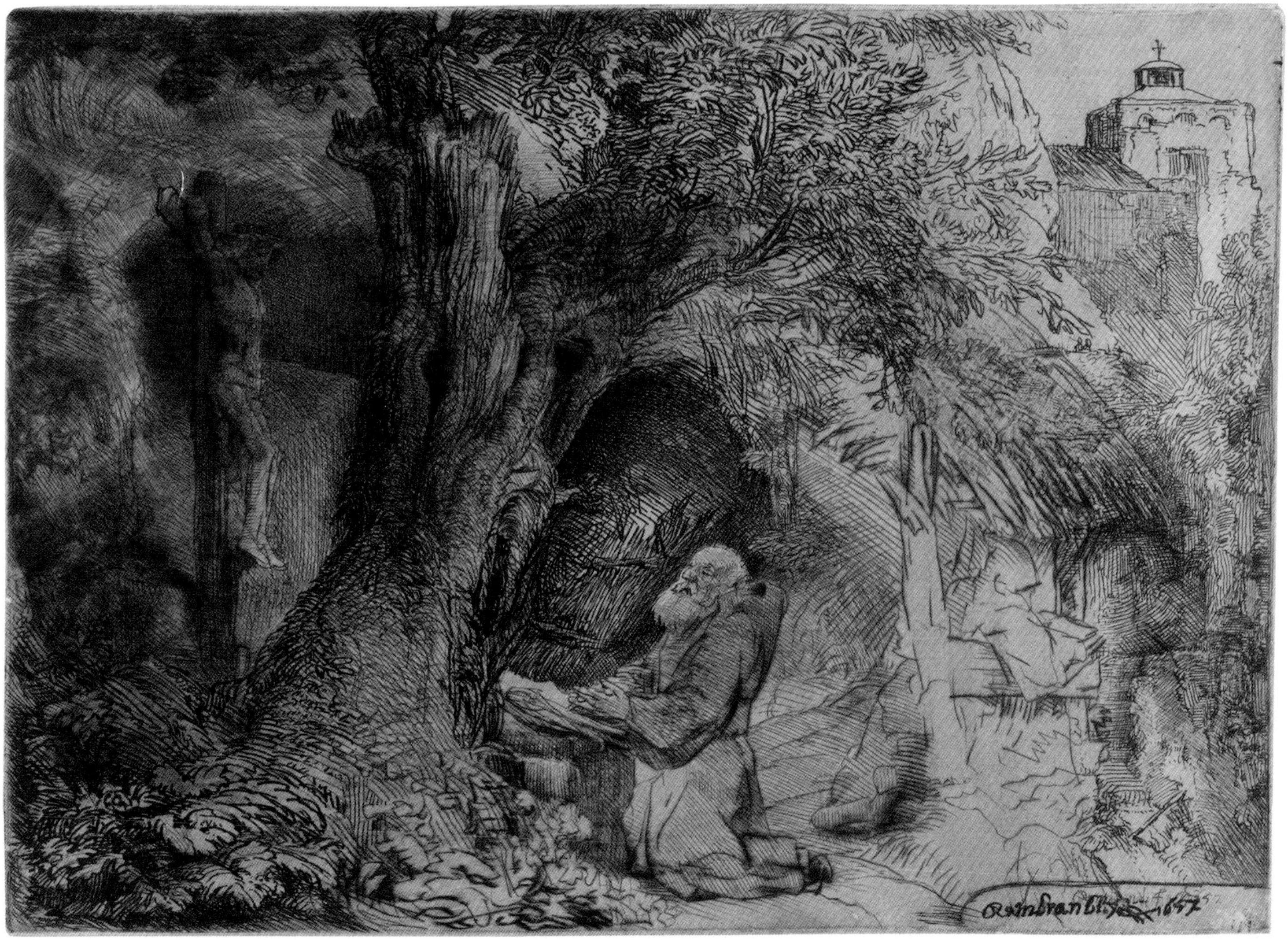

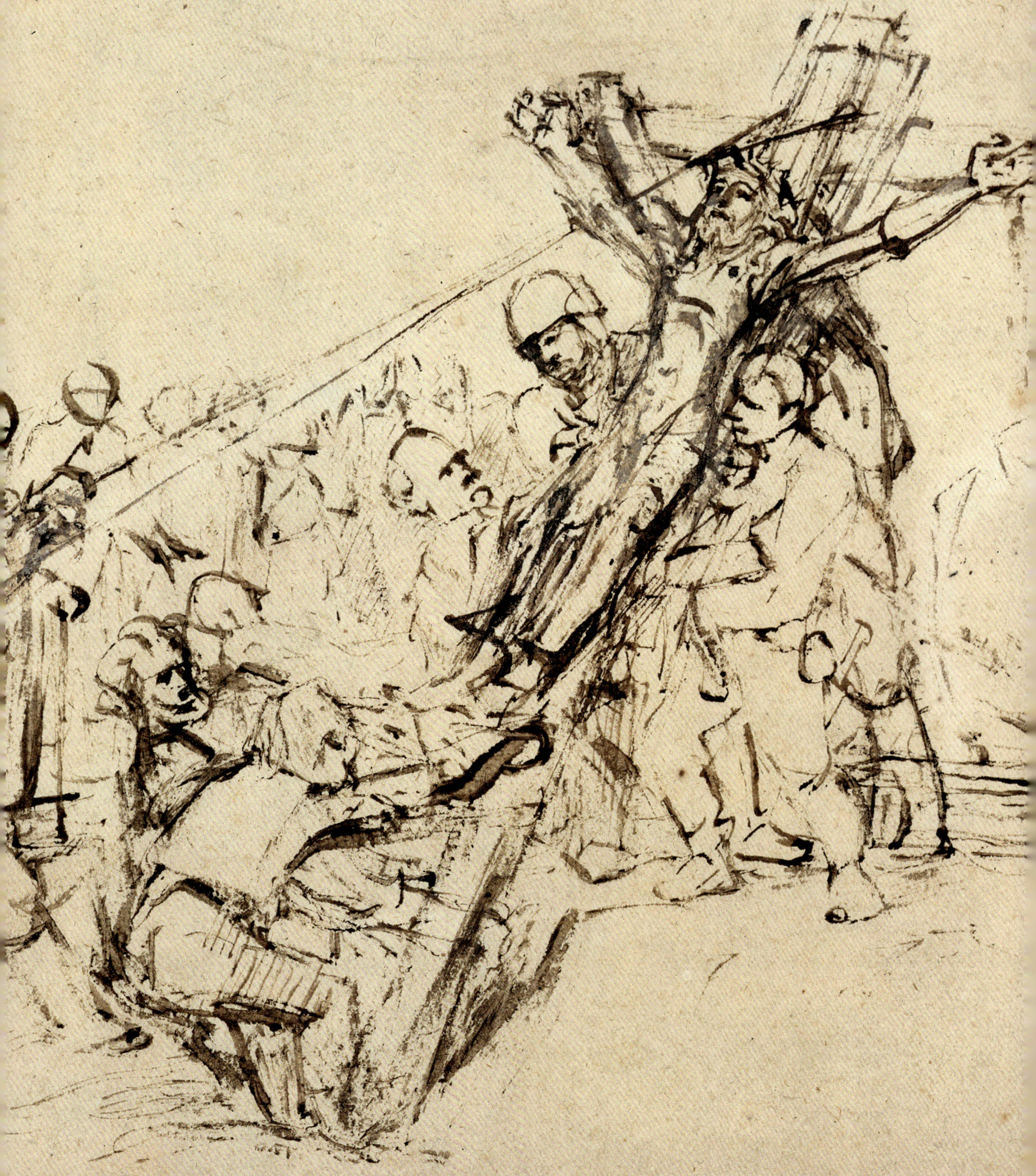

EXPERIMENTAL TECHNIQUE
THE DRAWINGS

Marijn Schapelhouman

THERE IS ONE GREAT difference between Rembrandt's paintings and etchings on the one hand and his drawings on the other: the paintings and prints were merchandise, but with few exceptions the drawings were not made for sale. They were not seen by the public at large, which may be why so little is said about them in the earliest biographies of the artist. One exception is Filippo Baldinucci – not, as it happens, an unquestioning admirer of Rembrandt's work – who reported that a drawing 'in which little or nothing could be seen'[1] fetched what he considered to be far too high a price at auction. But what did the Italian author, who was generally so well informed and described what seems to be Rembrandt's late painting style so vividly, mean by a drawing 'in which little or nothing could be seen'? This phrase recalls the discussion of works considered 'only half finished', the '*manière grossière*', as noted above with respect to the paintings (see p. 133). Was it a cursory sketch, or a sheet so heavily reworked that it was hard to make out what the actual subject was? One finds both in Rembrandt's late drawings.

But to start with the basics. A pen, usually a reed pen, very occasionally a quill, a half-dry brush or a smeared finger and, almost inevitably, white gouache for making corrections – this was Rembrandt's arsenal when he set to work on a drawing in the last two decades or so of his life. His materials had been more varied in his earlier career. He had sometimes used black or red chalk, or a combination of the two, and very occasionally he reached for an implement that was tricky to handle and was probably regarded as hopelessly outdated even in his own day, the silverpoint, which could only be used on prepared cardboard or vellum.

Before analysing Rembrandt's late drawing techniques further, however, it is necessary to determine exactly which works we are talking about. The best place to begin is with the drawings that are unquestionably by the master himself, either because they are signed or because they are inextricably linked to one of his autograph paintings or etchings.[2] It is not a long list, no more than 14 works, but all the same it is impossible to analyse them all within the space of this essay, so the following is a small sample.

There is Rembrandt's eyewitness record on paper, signed and dated 9 July 1652. Two days after the fire that destroyed Amsterdam's old Town Hall he depicted the blackened ruins in a carefully detailed, almost dispassionate record (see fig. 20, p. 59).[3] Such 'journalistic' drawings by Rembrandt are few and far between. In addition to this one, there are only two others from the late period, both from 1664, of Elsje Christiaens, the Danish girl who was found guilty of the brutal murder of her landlady, hanging on the gallows (cats 5–6, p. 58).

Two other drawings with undeniably autograph signatures, also dated 1652, are *Homer reciting Verses* (cat. 25, p. 83) and *Minerva in her Study*. The function of these two is very much clearer: both are in the *Pandora* album, an *album amicorum* that Jan Six must have used from 1647 to 1686, to judge from the dates of the contributions. The *Homer* is dedicated 'Rembrandt aen Joanus Six' ('Rembrandt to Jan Six'). Although their purpose – as gifts for a friend – is plain, that observation raises all sorts of new questions. Why did Rembrandt make two drawings for Six in the same year, and why do they differ so much in style? *Homer reciting Verses* is a spartan, precisely delineated sketch of an ambitious, multi-figured composition, and it seems to cry out that 'this is just the start; the rest will follow'. *Minerva*, on the other hand, is exceptional for Rembrandt in that it is a painstaking, almost affected demonstration of how to wield a brush.

Detail from *The raising of the Cross* (cat. 69)

Or is that the point: to show that he was able to supply everything, from a rapid sketch, an initial idea for a complex composition, to a delicately finished drawing that was a work of art in its own right?

Rembrandt made one more contribution to a friendship book, that belonging to Jacob Heyblocq (1623–1690), theologian, classicist, literary scholar and teacher at one of the two Latin schools in Amsterdam, of which he was later headmaster (cat. 123). The fact that Rembrandt made a drawing for Heyblocq's album does not mean that there was a close bond between them. Heyblocq collected celebrities and tried to fill his book with as many great names as possible. Rembrandt's small drawing, which is signed and dated 1661, is an odd piece of work, not because of the subject, which fits perfectly within Rembrandt's standard repertoire, but above all because of its style. Is this what Baldinucci meant when he spoke of a drawing in which there was little or nothing to be seen? Terse in the extreme, the three figures are executed with thin lines of the pen, together with a few parallel hatchings and a couple of licks of the brush. Apart from that there are a number of dashes and dabs that may have been applied with a finger to suggest a rather vague, indeterminate space. The Christ Child is no more than a schematic shape, and is barely recognisable as a child.[4] Baldinucci would probably have branded this as the work of someone who could not draw.

The drawings for Six and Heyblocq were intended for a public, albeit a small and select one. Almost all the others that belong to the core group of Rembrandt's late drawings were working material, and were for his eyes alone. In the first place there are the sheets made in preparation for a painting one way or another, or during the painting process. The one that appeals most to the imagination is the composition sketch for Rembrandt's grandest failure, *The Conspiracy of the Batavians under Claudius Civilis* (cats 71–2).[5] Its functionality is typical of Rembrandt. It is not an initial idea for the painting but was made as part of the creative process, when Rembrandt began having doubts about his initial design and decided to make several changes to the composition. This was a method he employed on several other occasions: if he did not know what to do next, he started drawing in order to collect his thoughts. Among the cluttered, not to say messy drawings that Rembrandt made from time to time in his closing years, the sketch for *The Conspiracy of the Batavians under Claudius Civilis* is almost a miracle of equilibrium and calm. The complicated central group of Claudius Civilis and his companions has been jotted down in a kind of shorthand, with thin flourishes of the pen. The setting, a high, vaulted hall with views of trees on either side, is rendered with thicker lines. Rembrandt very cunningly used thinned ink to make the area around the central group a little darker, and subtly tinted some of the figures with the brush, with the result that the untouched parts of the paper light up brightly, as if the principal characters in the scene are caught in the glare of a searchlight.

Three preparatory drawings have survived for Rembrandt's last group portrait, '*The Syndics*' (cat. 56), which is more than for any other painting. The complex genesis of this work and the part played in it by the three drawings are discussed above (see pp. 131, 141), but the one in Berlin (cat. 68) may be taken as an example of his late drawing style. This shows three of the five syndics, but the sheet has clearly been trimmed on the right: the brim of a hat and part of a shoulder are still visible, so it seems fairly safe to assume that all five syndics were present before the sheet was damaged. This is a work in progress, a drawing as construction site. It is as if

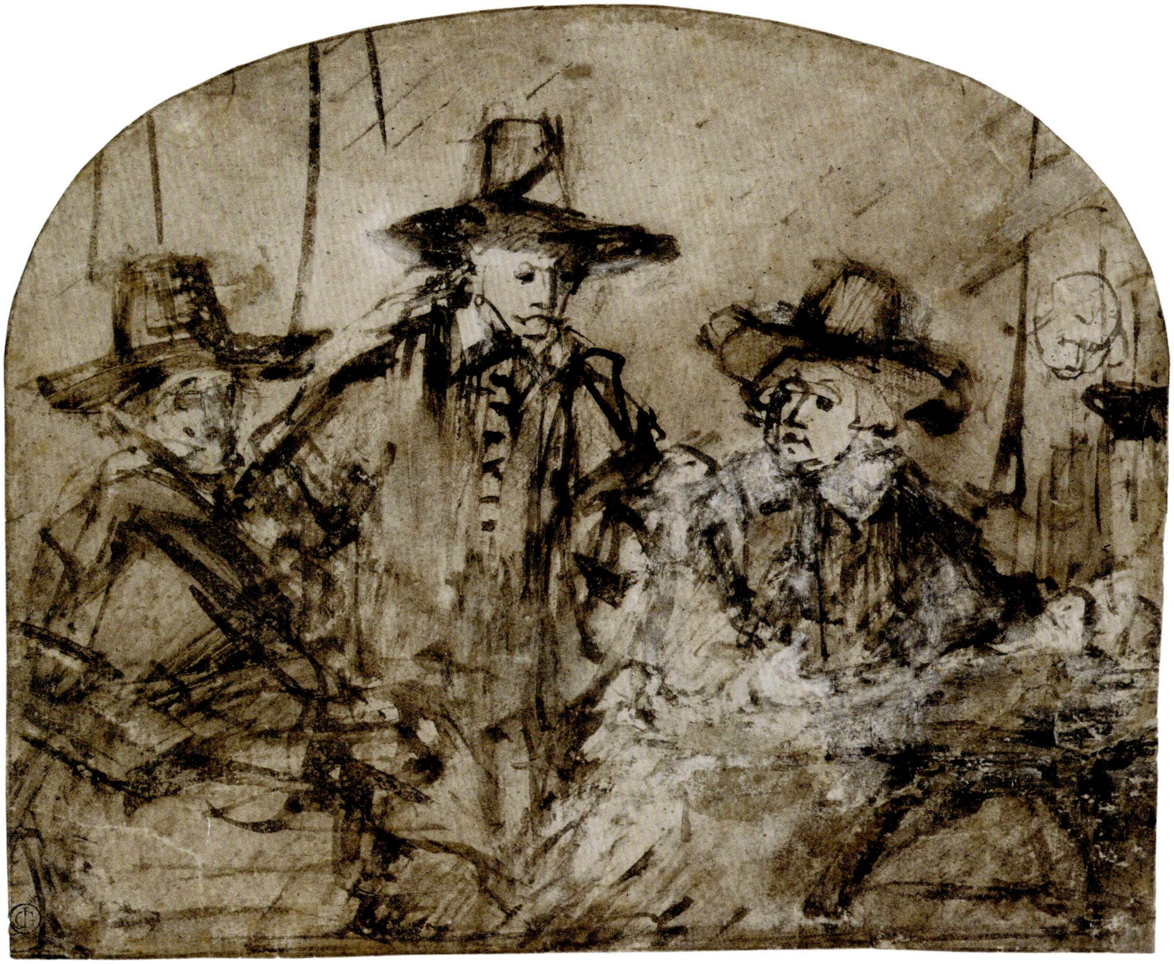

68
Three Syndics, about 1661–2
Reed pen and brown ink with brown wash and white bodycolour, 17.3 × 20.5 cm
Staatliche Museen zu Berlin, Kupferstichkabinett

Rembrandt was jabbing at the paper with his reed pen and regularly using his fingers to clarify his meaning. Time and again he used white gouache to make corrections: some of this has worn off over the years, and the surface of the drawing has taken on a lumpy, smudged look here and there. While a study like this offers precious little aesthetic pleasure, that is hardly the point: this is simply the work of someone frantically searching for the right form, the right position. It is an aid, a means, not an end.

The same is true of the sketch for the small etched portrait of Lieven van Coppenol of around 1658, but here the result is much more pleasing. In fact, this is also more interesting from an artistic point of view than the rather uninspiring print (cats 50–1).

The result of such a brief exploration of some of the drawings from Rembrandt's late period that can reasonably be regarded as autograph is not entirely reassuring. They do not provide an unambiguous picture. It is as if Rembrandt keeps slipping out of our grasp, as if he is showing a different face each time. There is no type of drawing more inextricably bound up with Rembrandt as an artistic personality than the '*historien uyt de geest*' (histories from the imagination), as they were called in the seventeenth century. These are biblical or other narrative scenes that the artist was expected to conjure up in his mind's eye and capture on paper 'from the imagination'. The *Homer* and *Minerva* in Jan Six's album, and *Simeon in the Temple* in Heyblocq's, are rare examples of signed and dated '*historien uyt de geest*'; most other drawings of this kind have neither signature nor year. In Berlin there is a small sketch of the blind Belisarius receiving alms, which, although neither signed nor dated, was annotated by Rembrandt (cat. 121).[6] This is a very rapidly dashed-off little sketch, a jotting that took just a couple of minutes. It does have great evocative force, though, and the seated Belisarius in particular is characterised very succinctly with a few bold strokes of

FIG. 59
HANS WITDOECK
(about 1615–after 1642) after
PETER PAUL RUBENS
(1577–1640)
The raising of the Cross, 1638
Engraving, 61.4 × 46.4 cm
Central plate of three
Rijksmuseum, Amsterdam

69
The raising of the Cross,
about 1655–8
Pen and brown ink, partly
wiped with a finger or dry
brush, white bodycolour,
17.9 × 21.1 cm
Staatliche Museen zu Berlin,
Kupferstichkabinett

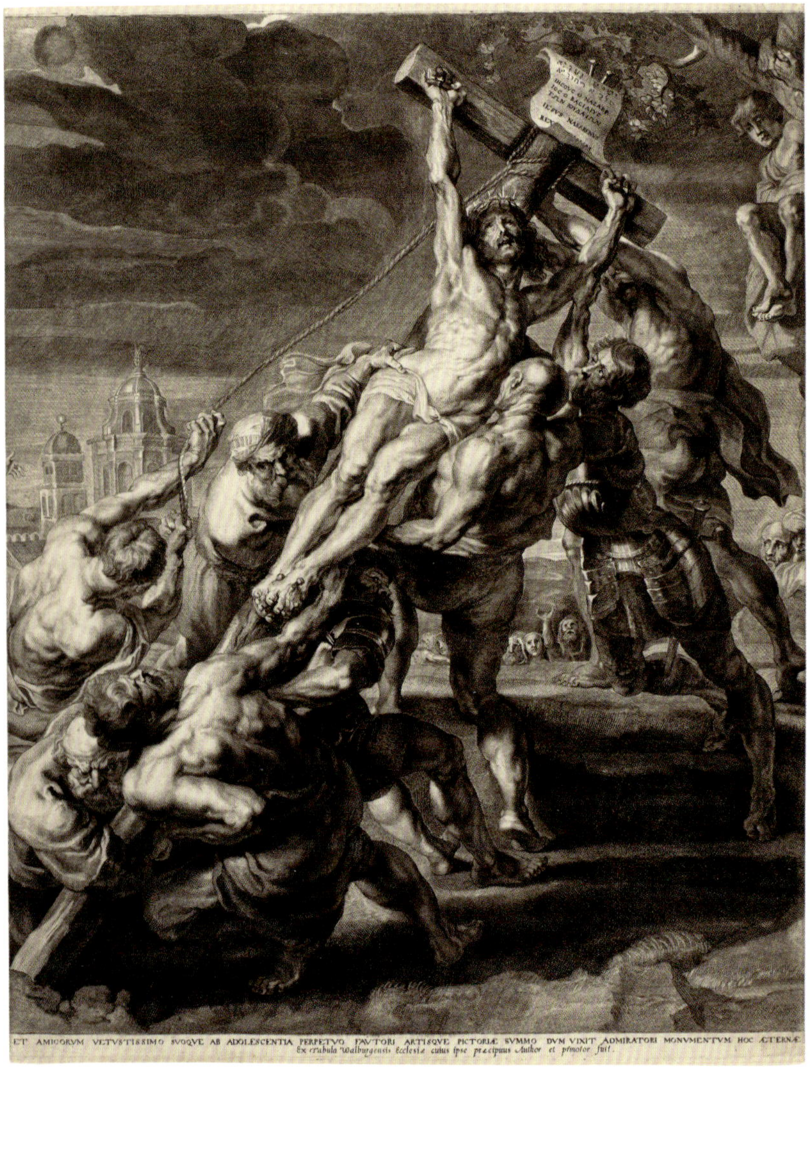

the reed pen. But apart from that, the scene looks rather chaotic. The right arm of the woman giving Belisarius alms is partly hidden by the gouache and her face is a shapeless blob: it looks as if the artist has pressed his thumb into the wet ink. In short, this sketch is a reminder, intended for Rembrandt's eyes alone.

The raising of the Cross (cat. 69) is quite another matter.[7] This is what one would call a real 'history from the imagination' – a masterly composition with many figures, a deeply moving Passion play on paper. The drawing must have been larger originally, for there is an early copy with a Roman officer on horseback on the right. Rembrandt borrowed all sorts of elements from a large painting by Peter Paul Rubens, a triptych that he probably never saw with his own eyes but could very well have known from a spectacular three-plate engraving by Hans Witdoeck (about 1615– after 1642) of 1638 (fig. 59).[8] The soldiers straining with all their might to set the cross upright, the man in the hole at the foot, who is hanging with his full weight on the wood of the cross, and the man who has looped a long rope around the cross are all motifs that recur in Rubens's painting, but Rembrandt has paraphrased them in his very own, extraordinarily practical way. Take the man with the rope. In Rubens's picture he is an idealised youth who is making an elegant gesture as if he is about to wrap the rope around his wrist: he has not yet begun heaving on it. In such cases as this Rembrandt seems to be asking himself how it would have looked in real life. His rope-tugger is a bald, fat man balancing on one leg and letting his heavy body fall backwards to aid his efforts. It is not just this narrative device that is typical of Rembrandt. The draughtsmanship completely matches what we have learned down the years to regard as being characteristic

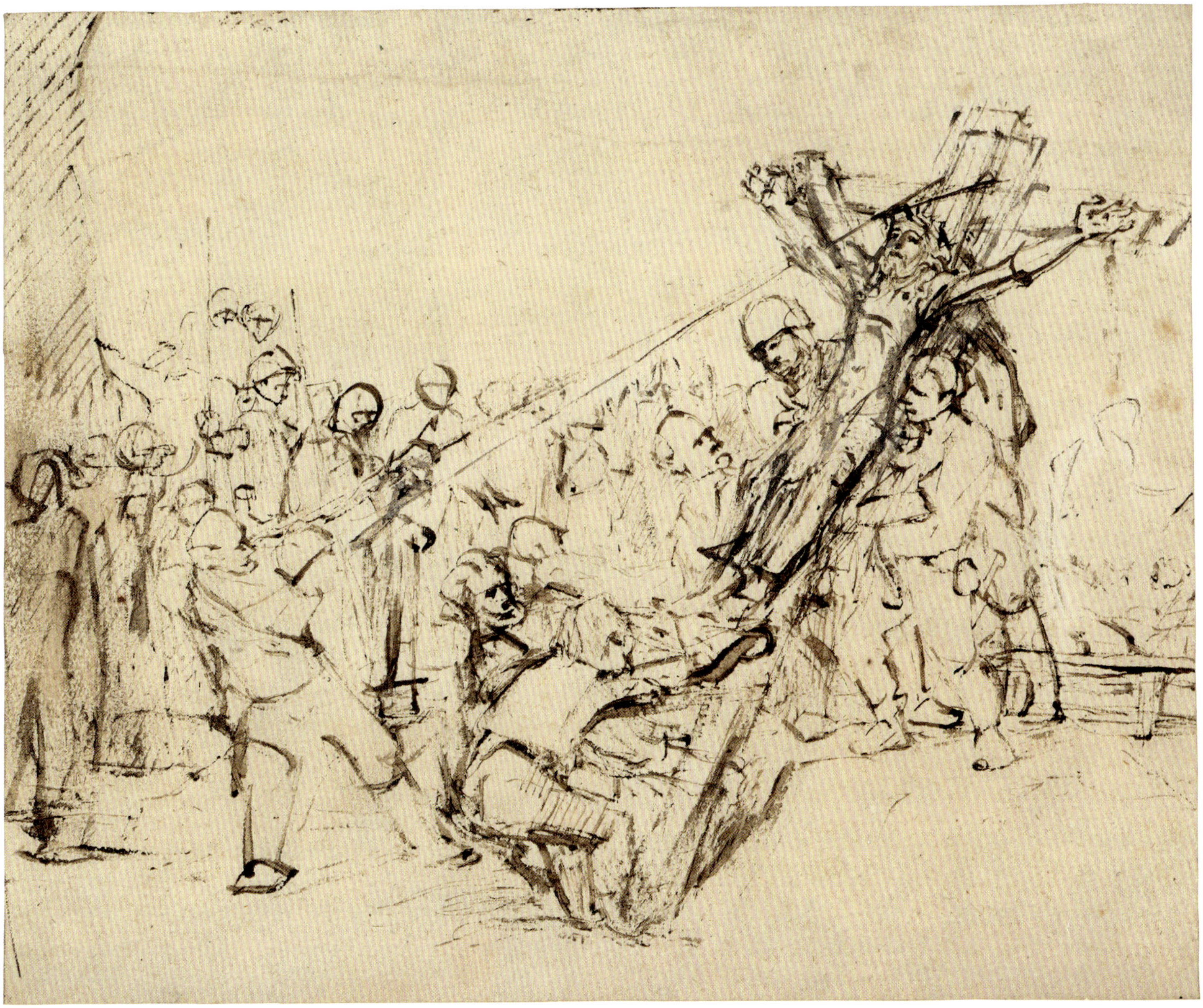

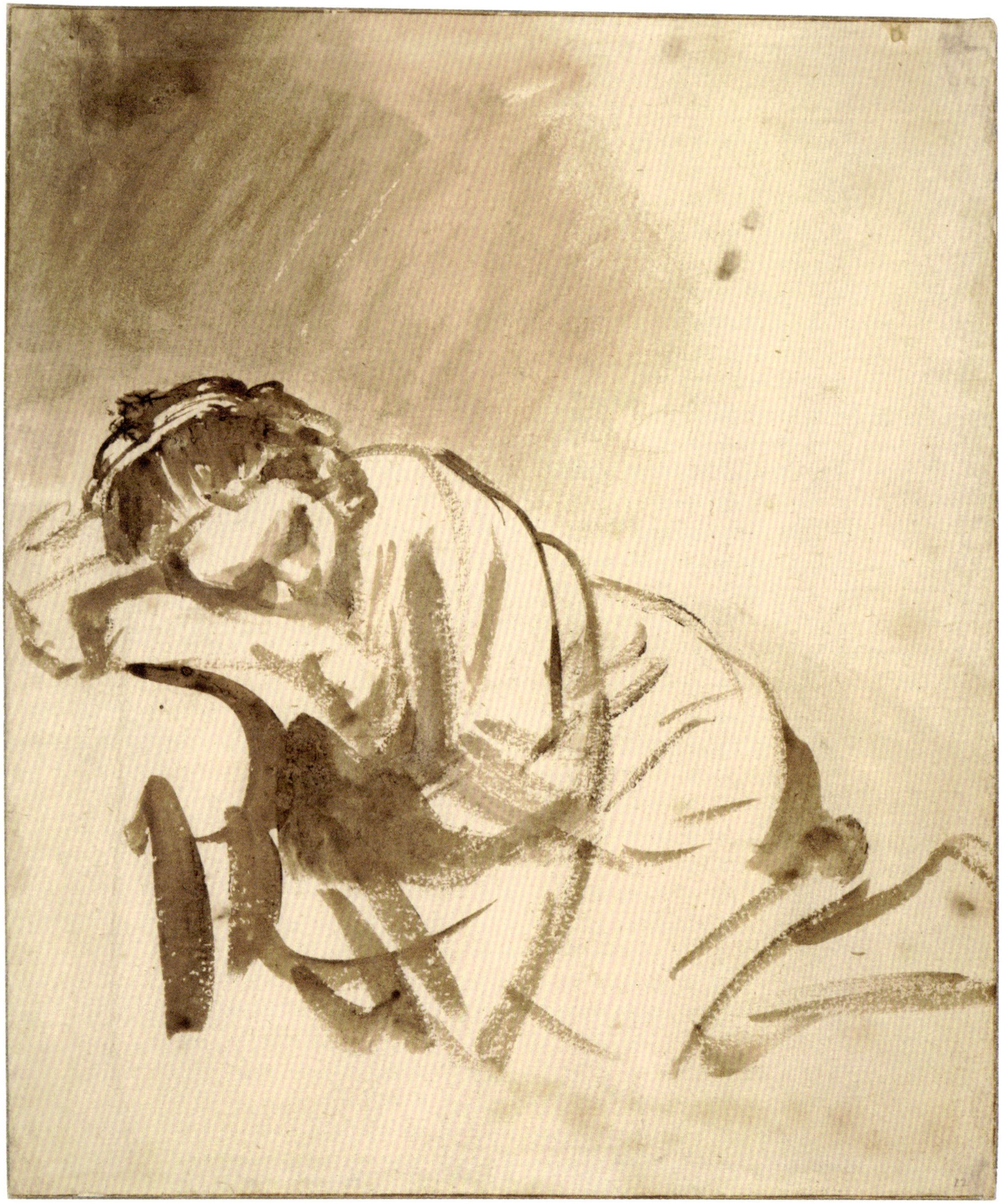

70
A Young Woman sleeping (Hendrickje Stoffels?), about 1654
Brush and brown wash with some white bodycolour; ruled framing lines in pen and brown ink, 24.6 × 20.3 cm
The British Museum, London

of his late style: angular, reducing the forms to an almost schematic simplicity, and playing endlessly with the effect of more, or in fact less, ink on the tip of the reed pen. This is the aged Rembrandt at his best: no doubts have ever been expressed about the authorship of this drawing. Yet it is not signed and cannot be related to any work by Rembrandt in another medium, so one has to fall back on patient observation and comparison with the secure drawings. In the case of *The raising of the Cross* this does not create any major problems, because sketches like the *Homer* in Jan Six's album and the sketch for the portrait of Lieven van Coppenol offer points of reference.

Sometimes, though, a drawing defies all comparison. One such example is *A Young Woman sleeping* (cat. 70), one of the greatest treasures of the British Museum print room.[9] A miracle has taken place here. Rembrandt drew it with the brush alone, which he handled as if he were a Japanese calligrapher. If he wanted to indicate shadows, he dipped his brush deep into the ink and then dragged it sideways across the paper. For the half-tints he allowed the almost dry brush to just graze the surface. A look at this drawing shows that it leaves nothing to be desired. Every loop, curl and streak is exactly where it should be. This is illusion at its most perfect. But still, methodical perfectionists could say that there is nothing in Rembrandt's known drawn oeuvre that can be compared to this drawing, and they would be right. There is some circumstantial evidence: most scholars believe that the young woman here is Hendrickje Stoffels, Rembrandt's last love, and if that is true it is indeed hard to conceive that such an intimate drawing could have been made by anyone other than Rembrandt himself. But perhaps there is something to clutch at for those who cannot accept even that conclusion. X-ray examination of the paper of Rembrandt's etchings has yielded remarkable results in the past few years, and it looks as if the moment is not so far off when we will be able to match pieces of paper digitally. If it can ever be established for certain that drawing A is on paper from the same batch as drawing B, that could lead to some surprising conclusions, but experience teaches that technical examination does not hold the answer to every art-historical question.

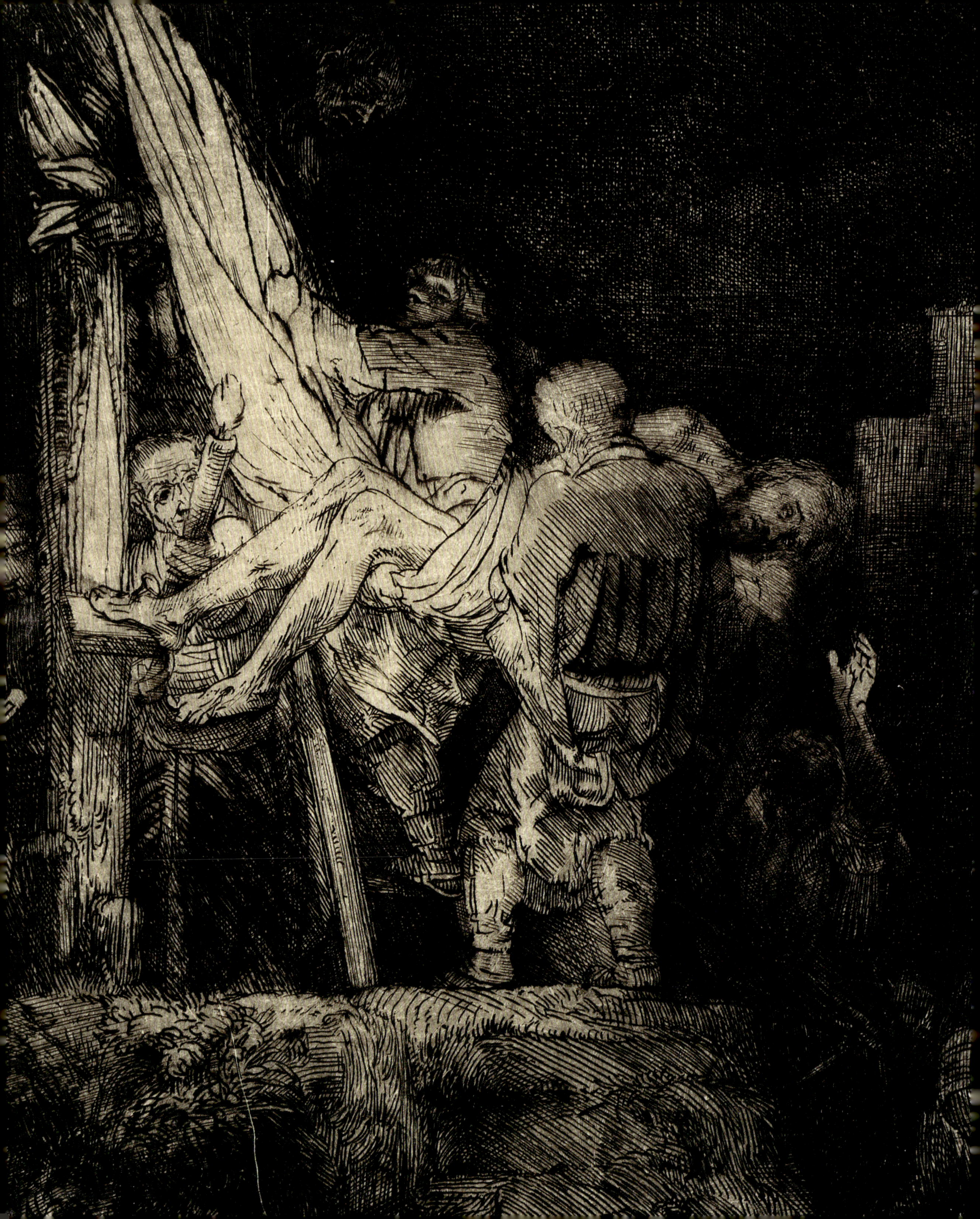

LIGHT

Erik Hinterding

FROM THE VERY START of his career Rembrandt was fascinated by the way in which colour and deliberate contrasts between light and dark could be used to structure a picture, focus attention on certain parts of the composition and increase the sense of depth. He was to cultivate this intense interest throughout his life, as is evident not just from his paintings, but also from his etchings and drawings.[1] His exceptional skill in rendering the effects of light was widely recognised and appreciated, even in his own day, by commentators and fellow artists such as Joachim von Sandrart, Samuel van Hoogstraten and others. In 1685 the French theorist André Félibien praised the well-considered placement of different tonal values and the exceptional understanding of light and dark in Rembrandt's paintings,[2] while a year later the Italian Filippo Baldinucci, referring to his etchings in particular, described 'a bizarre technique he invented with copper plates engraved using acid … thus giving everything a deep chiaroscuro and great force and a picturesque look down to the last mark'.[3] In 1699 Roger de Piles enthused, 'He had a supreme understanding of light and dark',[4] and in 1744 the Parisian art dealer Edmé-François Gersaint wrote:

> There has never been an artist so adept at using light and dark: his touch, both in his paintings and in his prints, was very skilled; his style was free and effortless; his colours deep and forceful.… his reputation is entirely due to his genius, his reflections and his continuous study of the effects of light in nature, which he portrayed with a surprising exactitude and force.[5]

Rembrandt was not the first artist to have a particular interest in strong lighting effects: in the Baroque era Caravaggio (1571–1610) was famously fascinated by theatrical lighting, and his followers, known as the Caravaggisti, included Dutch artists Hendrick ter Brugghen (about 1588–1629) and Gerard van Honthorst (1592–1656). But Rembrandt's methods of achieving and using these effects were highly innovative for his time. For example, he used colours in such a way that they intensified the effect of light within a scene, choosing bright colours with a naturally light tone (such as cream) in well-lit sections and darker tones (such as brown) for areas in shadow. *Jacob blessing the Sons of Joseph* (cat. 120) is a good example of this approach. The painting shows the Old Testament figure of Jacob, close to death, giving his blessing to Ephraim and Manasseh, the children of his son Joseph (Genesis 48: 11–22). The off-white colour of Jacob's clothing is similar in tone to his grey beard, the fur hanging from his shoulder, Ephraim's jacket in front of him and Joseph's turban next to him. Joseph's jacket is in almost the same colour, but darkened by Jacob's shadow, thus forming a transitional area towards the deeper colours around the edge of the composition. It is here that Joseph's wife Asenath stands; it is no coincidence that she wears dark brown clothes that are barely distinguishable from the shadows surrounding her.

Rembrandt's use of light, shadow and colour in this painting was commented on as early as 1675 by Joachim von Sandrart: 'in his work, our artist showed little light except in the main area of interest, around which he skilfully combined light and shadow'.[6] Three years later Rembrandt's pupil Samuel van Hoogstraten wrote at some length on the subject, remarking: 'We will disregard what the philosophers have to say about lux and lumen, and just discuss light and lighting as they concern our art'.[7] He then added to Von Sandrart's comments:

Detail from *The Descent from the Cross by Torchlight* (cat. 78)

> let your strongest light areas be accompanied with gentle, duller light areas as I assure you this will make them appear even brighter; surround your deepest shadows with clear brown tints so that they are even more effective in showing up the force of the light. *Rembrandt* excelled in this skill and was a master in combining companion colours.[8]

Thus Rembrandt kept the composition of his paintings focused by grouping objects according to tone rather than having a disorganised jumble of light and shadow. This concept of companion colours (*'bevriende verwen'*) is closely linked to another idea which is particularly important for our understanding of how he used light and colour and what he was aiming for. This is the concept of 'relationships' (*'houding'*), or the combination of different colours to create a sense of depth. Warm colours appear closer to the viewer while cool colours seem further away, but only if they are slightly impure and not too bright. A natural effect and a feeling of depth can be achieved by softening harsh, bright, strong colours by mixing or, in the Dutch term of the day, *'breken'* (breaking them up).[9] Colours and contrasts are similarly toned down for those parts of the composition that are further in the distance. This is also termed 'aerial perspective'.[10]

This approach to combining colours, tones and contrasts can be seen in Rembrandt's painting of the officials of the Amsterdam Drapers' Guild, known as *'The Syndics'* (cat. 56). The group is lit from the window on the left; as a result, the area of the composition directly under the window is darker than that to the right. Apart from this, the use of contrasts is restrained: only the gentlemen's white collars stand out rather sharply against their black clothing, while their figures blend harmoniously with the brown panelling behind them. Above the panelling can be seen a greyish-brown wall in a somewhat cooler hue. In contrast, the cloth on the table behind which the officials sit is almost red, a warm colour that appears closer to the viewer, and therefore strengthens the impression of depth. Rembrandt further reinforced this effect by making the collars slightly greyer on the figures further back in the composition. This can be seen most clearly on the hatless steward at the back. The same subtle atmospheric effect can be observed in the faces. Von Sandrart commented on Rembrandt's expert use of colour and contrast as

> what we call 'Hauding' in Dutch [*houding*: relationships]. This is an essential observation but is not widely acknowledged. And we can learn from this … in particular from the diligent and extremely skilled Rembrandt: who … produced a miracle, as it were, and consistently observed true harmony without the impediment of unusual colours according to the rules of light.[11]

Rembrandt's use of reflection also merits attention. In art, the term 'reflection' refers not so much to the specular reflection of a light source off a shiny surface as to the light bouncing from one object onto another, and onto that part of the object lying in the shadow, providing an indirect form of lighting. This can be clearly seen in *An Old Woman reading* (cat. 98), where the subject sits in a chair, wrapped in a dark red velvet cloak over a white undergarment that is highlighted by the light source at top left. Her book is also directly illuminated, and in turn functions as an indirect source of light that intensifies the white of her garment; but its effect is particularly clear in the shadow of her hood over her eyes.[12] This approach brought Rembrandt high praise.

Von Sandrart admired his use of reflected light, remarking on his: 'well-measured reflection, so that he lets light give way to shadow with excellent judgement,... great ability in everything',[13] to which Van Hoogstraten added: 'Our Rembrant [acquitted himself] wonderfully in reflections; indeed, it seemed as if he was in his element in choosing to have light reflected back.'[14]

The concepts of '*bevriende verwen*' (companion colours), '*houding*' (relationships) and '*reflectie*' (reflection) in art, all of which originated in the seventeenth century, are crucial to understanding Rembrandt's treatment of light, shadow and colour. Perhaps the most impressive example of a painting demonstrating his fascination for these elements during his late period is *The Conspiracy of the Batavians under Claudius Civilis* (cat. 72) of about 1661–2. This was Rembrandt's most important commission in his later years and the largest he ever produced. It was commissioned by Amsterdam City Council for the gallery in the new Town Hall on Dam Square. The Town Hall was built after the Peace of Münster (1648), which ended the Eighty Years' War (the Dutch revolt against the Spanish). Designed on a monumental scale, it radiated prosperity, demonstrating Amsterdam's renewed self-confidence and pride in itself as a city.[15] The plan for the building's decoration included a series of 12 colossal paintings depicting the revolt of the Batavians, a people living in the area roughly corresponding to the modern Netherlands during the Roman era. The choice of this subject was no coincidence: the rebellion of the Batavians against the Romans was seen as a harbinger of the revolt of the Dutch against the Spanish oppressors, and their eventual victory.[16] Initially, Rembrandt's former pupil Govert Flinck had been commissioned to paint the entire series, but when he died prematurely, Rembrandt was among the artists engaged to provide the individual paintings.[17] The story is taken from the Roman historian Tacitus: in AD 69 the Batavian Claudius Civilis called the tribal leaders and fiercest men among his people to meet with him in a sacred wood, supposedly for a feast. When the hour was late and he judged that the mood was right, he began a speech proclaiming the glory of his people and denouncing the wrongs they had suffered at the hands of the Romans. The crowd eagerly responded to his call to arms, whereupon he required all those present to swear an oath of loyalty to him.[18]

Rembrandt's finished composition is now lost to us: the painting as it stands is only a fragment of the original, which must have measured about 5.5 metres square like the others in the series (figs 6–8).[19] However, a surviving drawing by Rembrandt (cat. 71) gives an idea of the completed composition.[20] He situated the Batavian banquet in a huge vaulted hall, the forest visible between the open arches in the background. The guests sit round a table on an elevated podium approached by broad steps, with a tapestry hung on the wall behind. The remaining fragment of the painting reveals that Rembrandt's interpretation of the story was both unusual and impressive. Claudius Civilis, standing behind the table, wears a tall, exotic headdress.[21] Breaking with tradition, Rembrandt depicts the Batavian leader in frontal view, which clearly shows that he is missing an eye, a historic detail usually glossed over in the past by showing the figure in profile.[22] He was also breaking new ground by showing the Batavians taking the oath not by shaking hands but by ceremonially touching their swords together.[23] But it is the light that really makes the picture spectacular. The event took place at the dead of night and Rembrandt came up with a brilliant trick to show this: he hid the light source behind the figures on the viewer's side of the table. Not only does this give off a glow that lights up

71
The Conspiracy of the Batavians under Claudius Civilis, about 1661
Pen and brown ink with brown wash and white bodycolour, 19.6 × 18 cm
Staatliche Graphische Sammlung, Munich

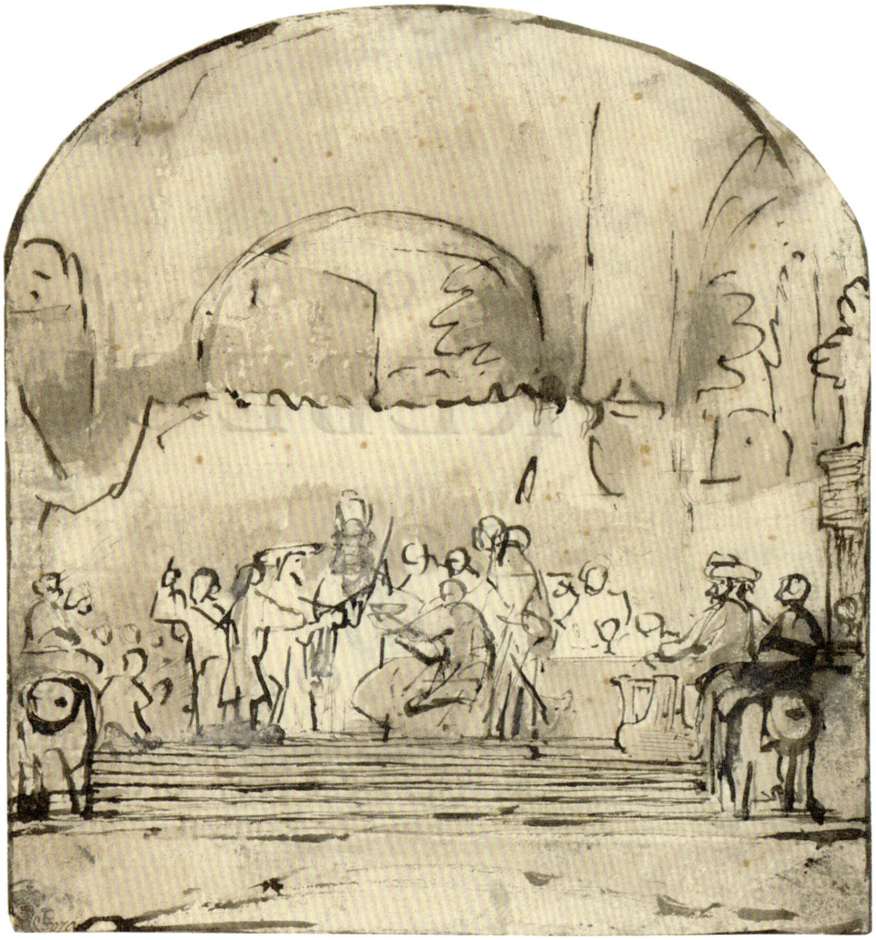

the guests, it also reflects off the tablecloth to illuminate all the figures from below, to a greater or lesser extent. This effect is reinforced by the use of companion colours, in this case various shades of yellow and red, with the occasional hint of green for the illuminated sections and brown hues for the areas in shadow. The area on the right is markedly warmer in tone than that on the left of the table, the result of Rembrandt's addition of greyish-blue colours, in particular, when painting the figure of Claudius Civilis. Not only does he tower over the other men at the banquet, but our attention is also drawn to him because he is depicted in slightly cooler colours. The suggestion of depth is emphasised by the contrast Rembrandt has introduced between these tints and a distinctly warm accent in the foreground: the man in front of the table walking towards Civilis wears a red coat. Such use of a red accent in the foreground, to make it appear closer to the viewer, was a familiar and popular tactic in Rembrandt's day for creating depth within a picture.

The effect of the light is further enhanced in this painting by the rough, impasted application of paint: it is so thickly and unevenly applied to the canvas that it glistens unpredictably when light shines across the surface. Rembrandt used this technique frequently – although seldom so audaciously – in this later, experimental period, for example in '*The Jewish Bride*' (cat. 92).[24]

In his etchings, too, Rembrandt showed a particular fascination for light. This is evident in his use of sharp contrasts as a means of structuring his compositions, as well as in his portrayal of unusual light effects. However, his rendering of light in this medium is inevitably different from that in his paintings. Rembrandt used colour in his paintings to enhance the effect of the light, for example convincingly differentiating daylight, which is cool in colour, from candlelight or torchlight, which radiate a more orange glow. This is of course impossible in prints, where the image is created solely through the interplay of black lines. In this medium he expressed his fascination for light primarily in a continual quest for tonality, and how to achieve intermediate tones that convincingly create a transition from the black of the printer's ink to the white of the paper.

Rembrandt's ability to obtain impressive results in graphic works even in his earlier years is demonstrated by his famous print of Jan Six (fig. 68) of 1647, which employs both etching and drypoint. This was not his first picture with unusual tonal effects, but it was the first time he went so far in depicting an interior illuminated by the light from a window; indeed, it demonstrates that he sometimes took the light effects he used in his paintings and tried them out in his etchings. Although the interior is dark, the details can still be made out.[25] The manuscript that Six peruses is actually one of the sources of light in the picture: the page is lit directly by the light from outside, and reflects that light onto his face, which is therefore lighter than might be expected given the tonal values of the room around him.[26] Rembrandt used similar reflections again in 1656 in his *Portrait of Arnout Tholinx*. The etching shows the physician and inspector, wearing a hat with a wide brim, sitting behind a table with an open book. In the first state of the print (cat. 43) there is too much reflection around the subject's eyes, over-illuminating that section of the image. For the second state (cat. 44) Rembrandt tempered this effect by adding cross-hatching to Tholinx's forehead, although the reflection still intrudes on the shadow under the brim of the hat.

In his later, experimental years Rembrandt continued to show an interest in the question of how to depict light and tonal effects in his etchings, but now he used a completely different approach to reinforce these effects.

72
The Conspiracy of the Batavians under Claudius Civilis, about 1661–2
Oil on canvas, 196 × 309 cm
The Royal Academy of Fine Arts, Sweden

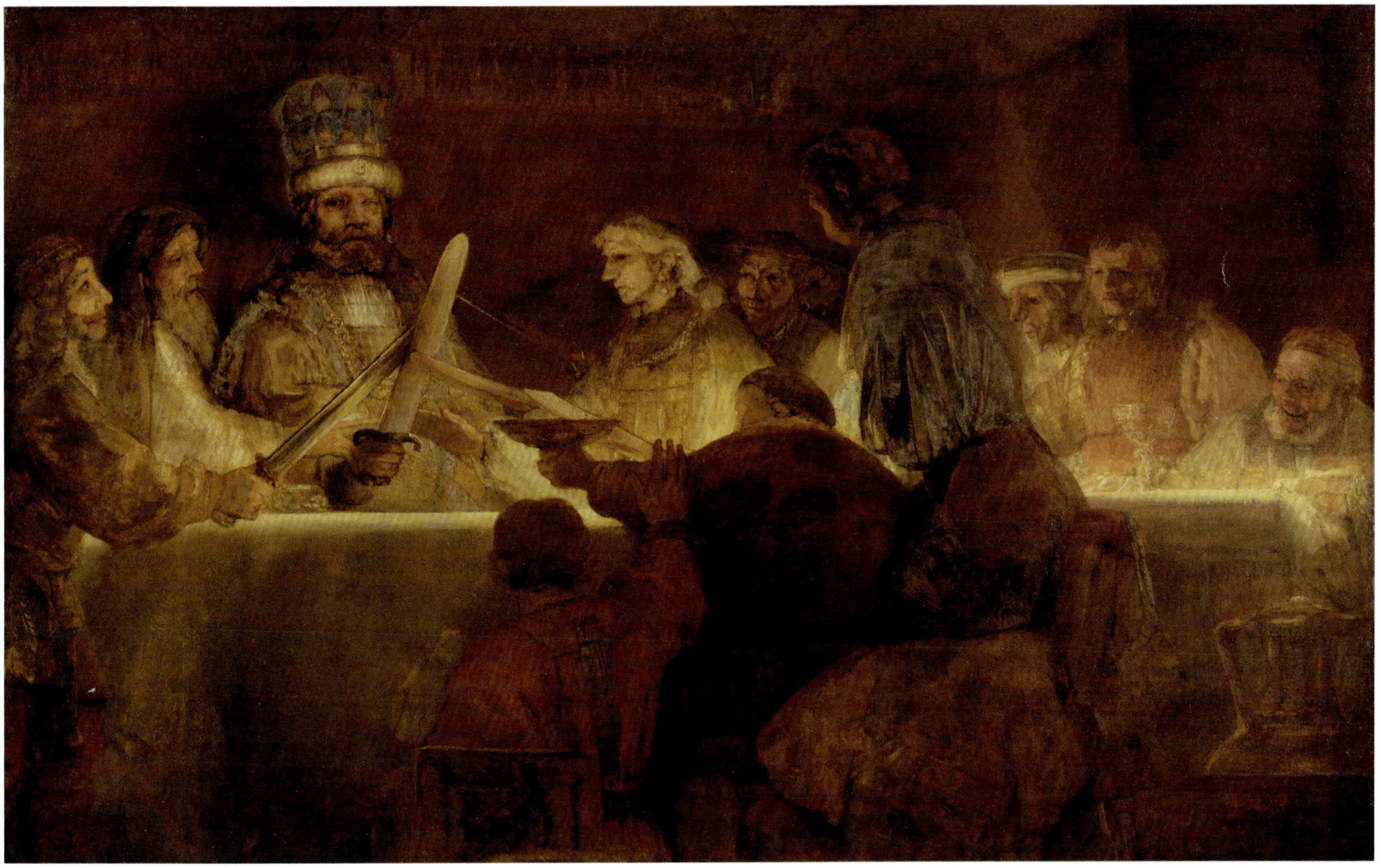

73
Adoration of the Shepherds at Night, about 1657
Etching, engraving and drypoint, 14.8 × 19.8 cm
First state of eleven
The British Museum, London (1848,0911.25)

He increasingly printed on non-standard paper to enhance the graphic effects and tonal qualities of his prints, employing oatmeal paper, which was used as wrapping paper, or tinted, silky oriental paper, or even parchment.[27] He augmented the effects of these different surfaces by leaving a thin layer of ink on certain areas when inking his copper plates; these then left a dark surface tone on the printed sheet. Whereas Rembrandt's various print editions for the market had previously been fairly uniform, these innovations now led him to turn each print into a unique piece or 'printing variant' (not so far removed from 'monotype').

The *Adoration of the Shepherds at Night* of around 1657 (cats 73–6) offers a good example of how Rembrandt created and printed his most tonal prints during this period. Joseph can be seen in the gloom of the stable on the far right, reading a book by the light of a lantern. He looks up at the approaching shepherds. Next to him lies Mary, curled up under the blankets that she pushes to one side to see who is coming; the infant Jesus lies tucked up between them. The bearded man leading the group of shepherds carries a second lantern, lifting his hat in respect as he approaches the holy family. In the first state of the print (cats 73–4) the lantern by which Joseph is reading, although hidden from view, is the most important light source in the picture: it illuminates not only the area around Mary, causing a shadow to fall over Jesus's face, but also the face of the woman behind the standing shepherd with the lantern. The shepherd's lamp is a secondary source of light, illuminating his right hand and revealing the contours of the three oxen on the left.

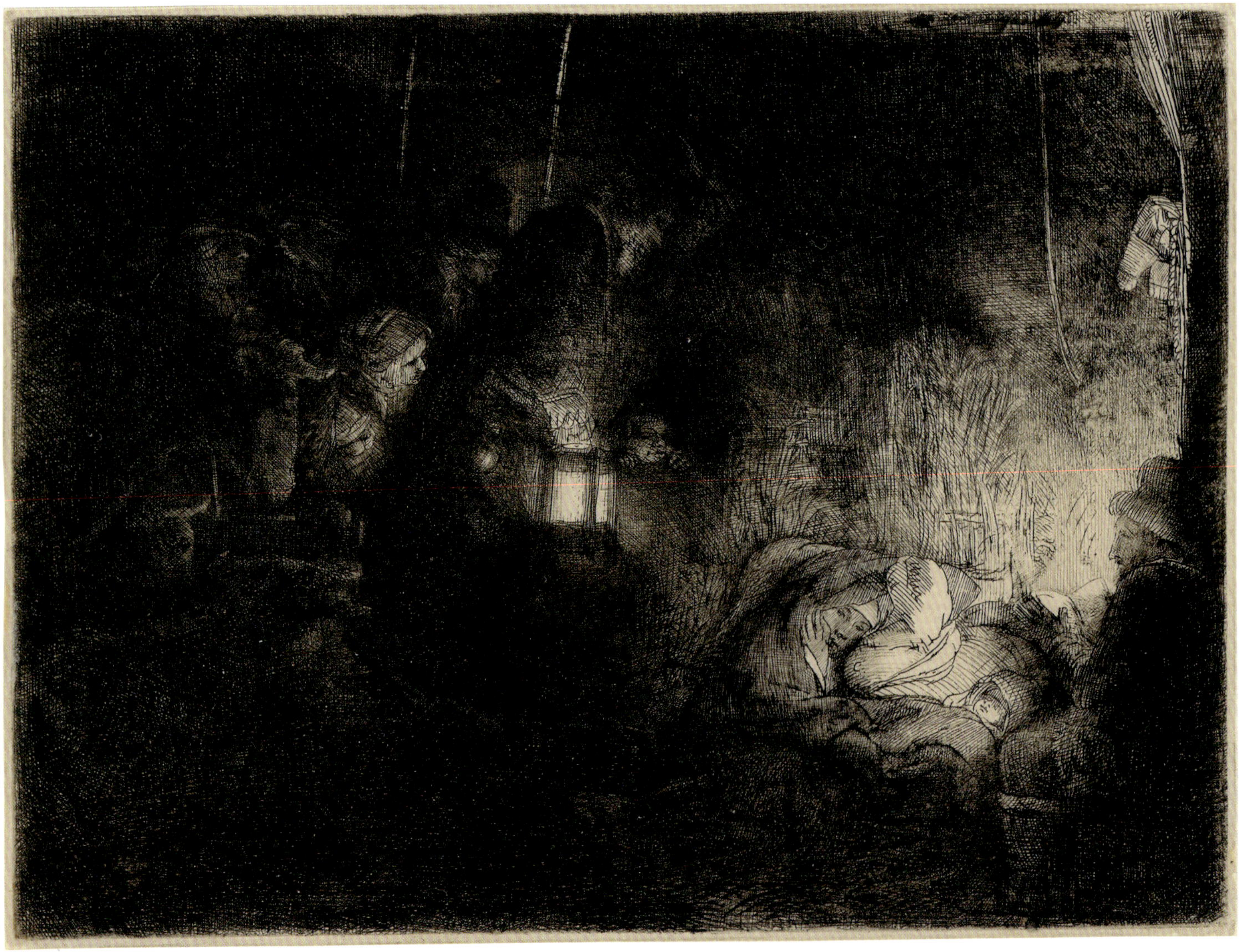

74
Adoration of the Shepherds at Night, about 1657
Etching, engraving and drypoint, 14.8 × 19.8 cm
First state of eleven
Rijksmuseum, Amsterdam (RP-P-1962-22)

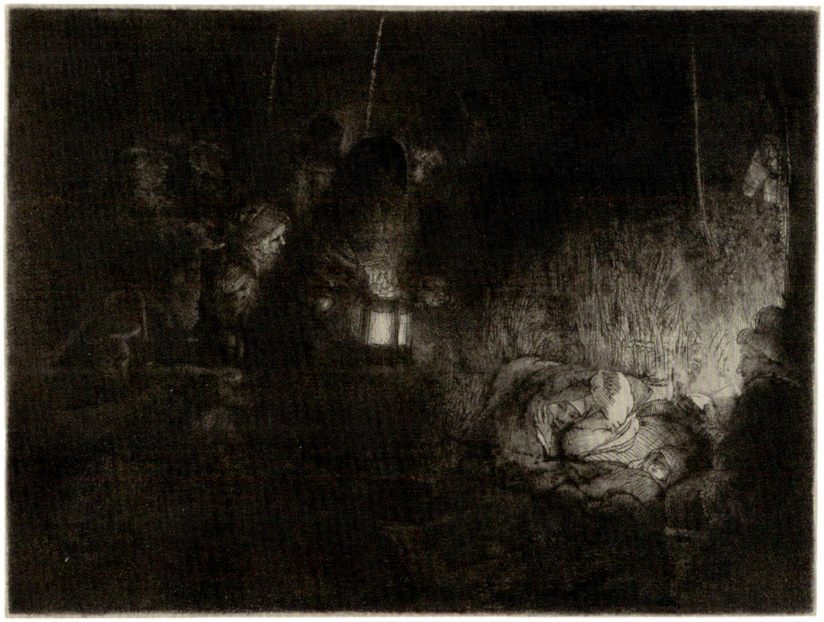

75
Adoration of the Shepherds at Night, about 1657
Etching, engraving and drypoint, 14.8 × 19.8 cm
Fifth state of eleven
The British Museum, London (1848,0911.27)

76
Adoration of the Shepherds at Night, about 1657
Etching, engraving and drypoint, 14.8 × 19.8 cm
Sixth state of eleven
The British Museum, London (F,4.86)

In the subsequent states (cats 75–6) Rembrandt successively reduced the light further until the contours were virtually the only things still visible. At the time, achieving such a convincing optical effect with etching and drypoint was unprecedented.[28] Incidentally, it is striking how many differences can be seen even between impressions from the same state. For example, the ink in the impression from the first state in London (cat. 73) is more sparse than that in the Amsterdam impression (cat. 74), as a result of which far more detail can be seen on the right-hand side. These effects are due to differences in the application of the ink, which Rembrandt amplified in later states by printing with a variable surface tone. But he also influenced the results through his use of different types of paper. For instance, the impressions on Japanese paper are somewhat warmer in tone than those on western paper, while the impressions on Chinese paper are particularly clear and distinct.

Rembrandt's depiction of light and shadow also plays a key – if varying – role in four episodes from the life of Christ etched in around 1654. These are of identical size and were produced using similar techniques, which is

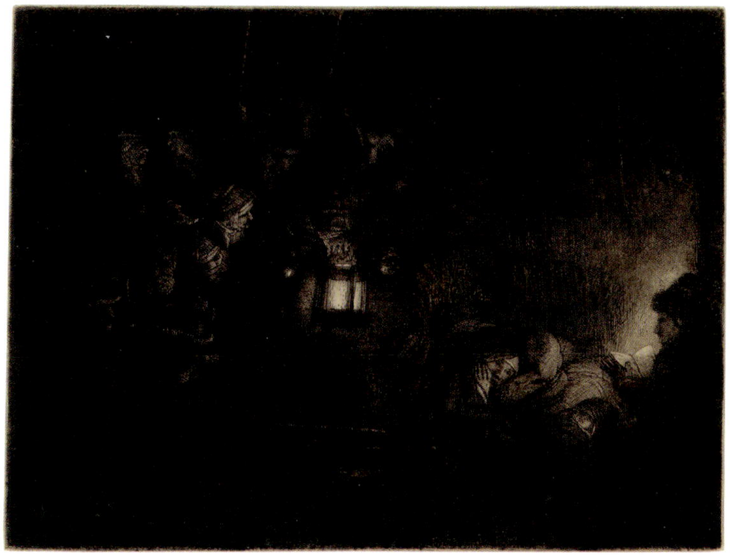

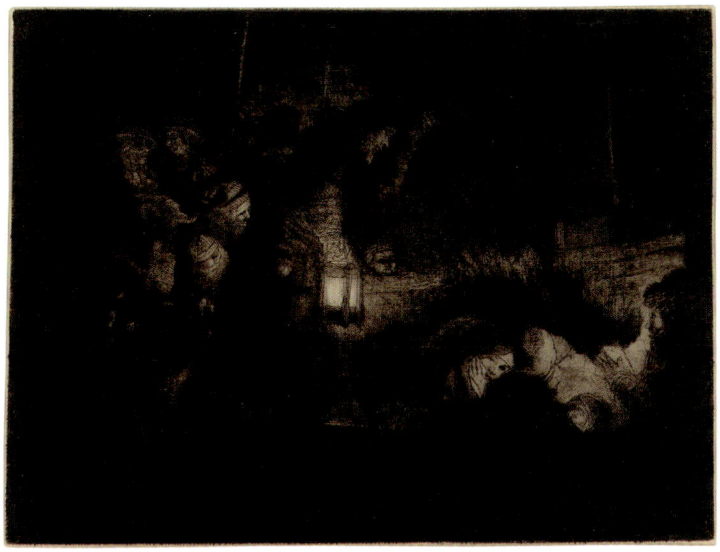

77
The Presentation in the Temple, in the Dark Manner, about 1654
Etching and drypoint,
21 × 16.2 cm
Only state
Rijksmuseum, Amsterdam
(RP-P-1962-27)

why they are commonly bracketed together as a series.[29] *The Presentation in the Temple* (cat. 77) shows Joseph and Mary arriving to present their first-born son to God in the temple. Here they meet old Simeon, the holy man who has received a promise from God that he will not die before he has seen the Messiah. Upon recognising Jesus as the anointed one, he blesses the holy family and gives praise to the Lord (Luke 2: 22–40). The main figures in the scene are delineated in firmly etched lines, the white of the paper showing through them to create light and produce bright highlights. The dark interior of the temple has been more extensively filled in, with finer lines and gradual shifts in tonal value. Only one state of the etching survives, but the individual impressions differ enormously as a result of the variable surface tone Rembrandt applied. The impressions on Japanese paper exude a warmer glow than those on western paper, and some are just as dimly lit as *The Adoration of the Shepherds at Night*.

The next episode from the series, *The Descent from the Cross* (cats 78–9), also takes place in the dark, by the light of a torch. The foot of the cross can be seen in the top left of the picture, with at least five figures gathered around; having unfastened Christ from the cross, they are now carefully lowering him. Rembrandt has indicated the direct glow around the torch by using simple contour lines to draw the shapes there, with almost no shadow. But the further away a shape is from the source of light, the deeper the shadows, which are often depicted using a dramatic series of close parallel lines. The bright light on the eye socket of the man up the ladder is particularly well executed, as is the detail of the raised hand next to Christ's head. The stretcher with the shroud in the foreground also functions as a light source in the composition, although its distance from the torch means that its brightness is muted. Rembrandt achieves this with delicate shading using thinner lines. The linear nature of an etching means that it can never reproduce the warm colour of torchlight at night, but Rembrandt got remarkably close to this effect by printing the etching on orange-yellow Japanese paper (cat. 79). However, he was much more restrained in his use of surface tone compared with the previous etching, possibly because the use of very subdued light effects was incompatible with the glow from a directly visible source of light.

It is certainly noticeable that Rembrandt used a great deal of surface tone in *The Entombment* (cats 80–1), the third print this series. Here the light source is completely hidden by the figure standing on the right in the foreground, in front of Christ, and we only see its glow illuminating Christ and the men occupied with lowering him into the grave. Mary grieving on the left and Joseph of Arimathea behind her can only be discerned from muted highlights. In some versions Rembrandt reinforced this effect by darkening the print through the liberal application of surface tone to such an extent that these details are almost impossible to make out.

Christ at Emmaus: the Larger Plate (cats 82–3) is the last print from this series. Although it is the same size as the others, it appears at first glance to have been produced using a different technique. However, its style is quite similar to the first state of *The Entombment* (cat. 80), which suggests that *Christ at Emmaus* only differs from the former in that in this final plate

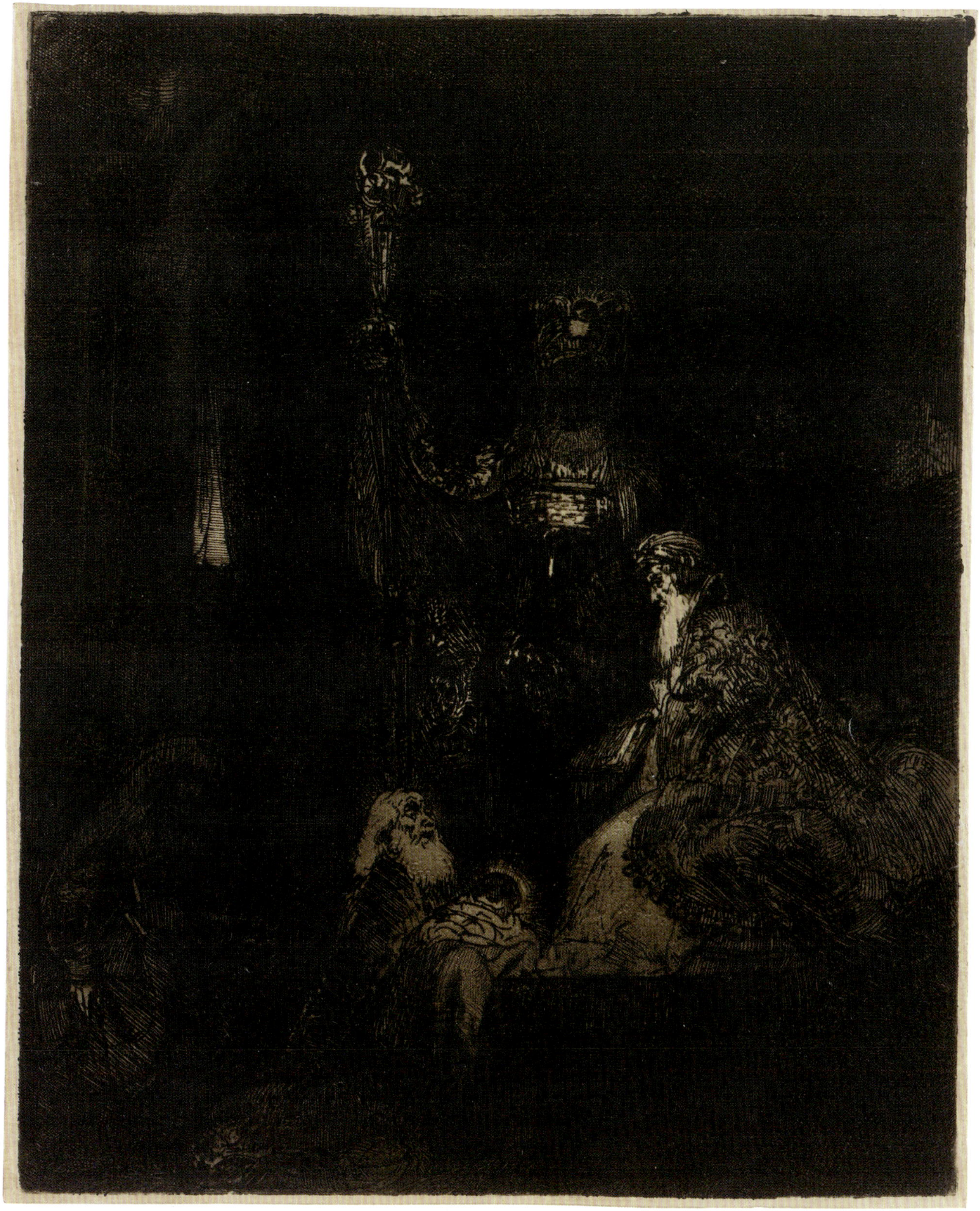

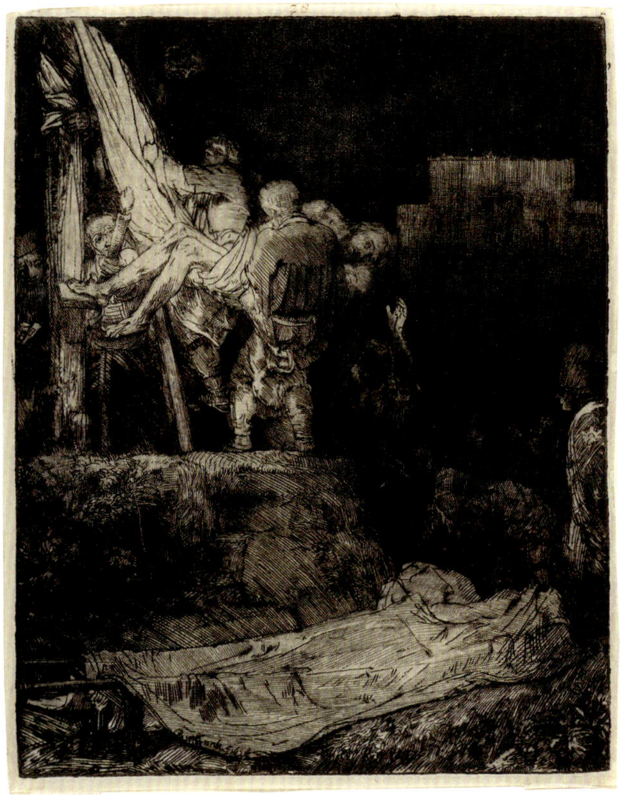

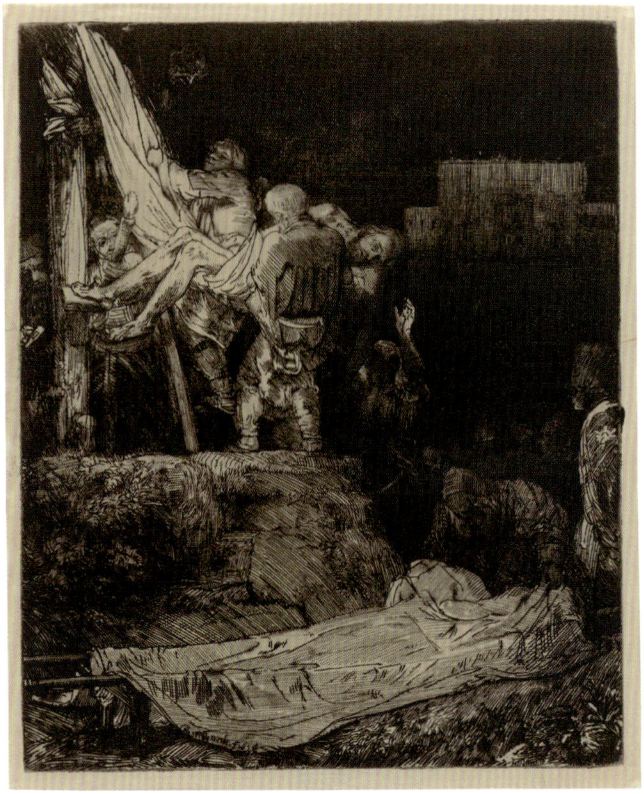

78
The Descent from the Cross by Torchlight, about 1654
Etching and drypoint,
21 × 16.1 cm
First state of four
The Fitzwilliam Museum, Cambridge (AD.12.39-28)

79
The Descent from the Cross by Torchlight, about 1654
Etching and drypoint,
21 × 16.1 cm
First state of four
Rijksmuseum, Amsterdam (RP-P-OB-147)

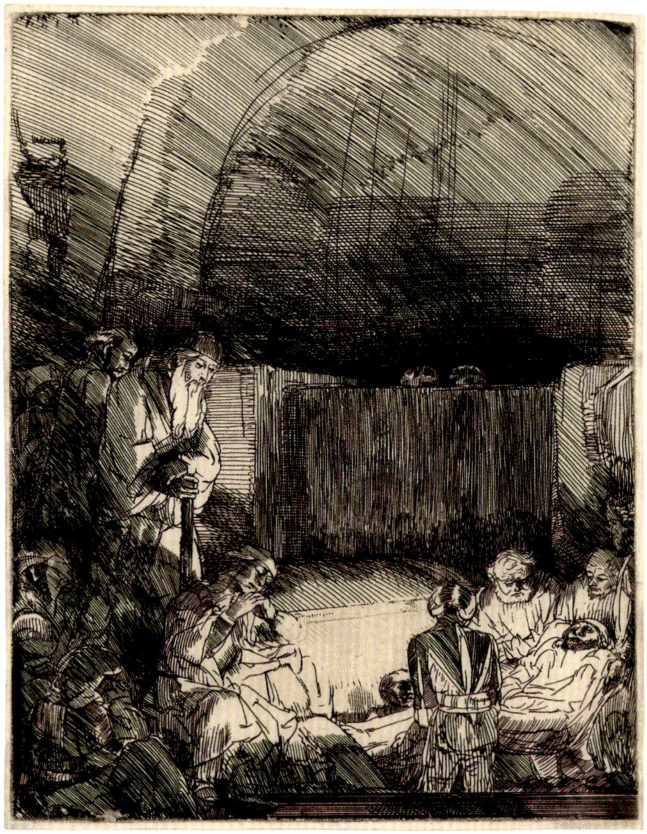

80
The Entombment, about 1654
Etching and drypoint,
21.1 × 16.1 cm
First state of four
The British Museum, London (1910,0212.360)

81
The Entombment, about 1654
Etching and drypoint,
21.1 × 16.1 cm
Third state of four
The British Museum,
London (1843,0513.249)

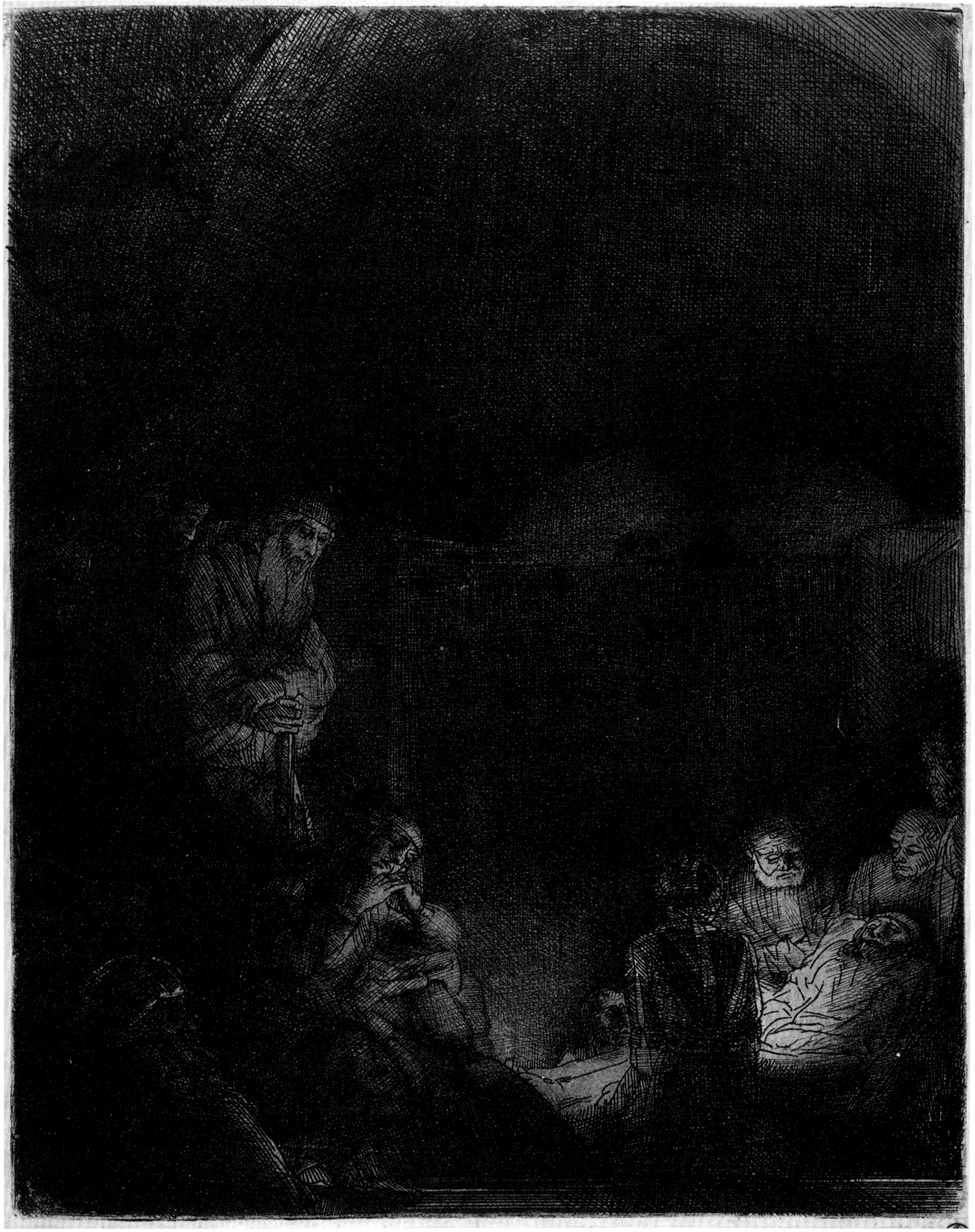

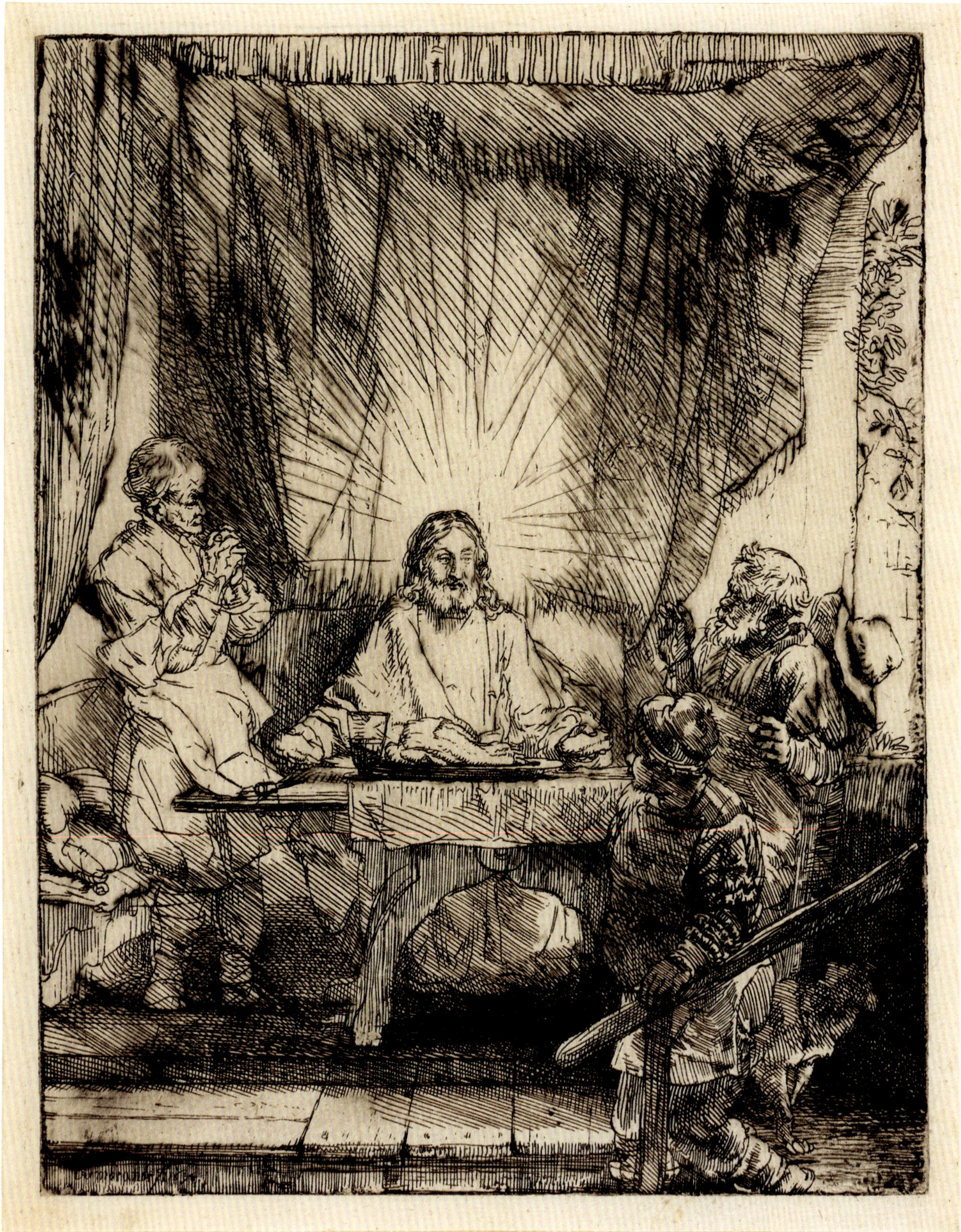

82
Christ at Emmaus: the Larger Plate, 1654
Etching and drypoint, 21.1 × 16 cm
Second state of five
The Fitzwilliam Museum, Cambridge (AD.12.39-46)

83
Christ at Emmaus: the Larger Plate, 1654
Etching and drypoint, 21.1 × 16 cm
First state of five
Rijksmuseum, Amsterdam (RP-P-1962-46)

Rembrandt did not subsequently reduce the amount of light in the initial design for the composition. Its lighter appearance is perhaps appropriate, as the image portrays not just daylight, but also heavenly light. The scene depicts the moment when, three days after the resurrection of Christ, two of his disciples finally realise the identity of their travelling companion, whom they met earlier that day at Emmaus and with whom they are now sharing a meal (Luke 24: 13–31). The action takes place under a kind of canopy, lit from the right, where the outdoors is visible through an archway. Christ's halo also seems to emanate light, illuminating the canopy behind him. It is not entirely clear whether his halo also casts a visible glow on the disciples and the innkeeper descending the steps in the foreground. The disciple standing on the left seems to be completely in the light, either from Christ's halo or the daylight filtering in from the right. The other disciple is also touched by the light emitted by Christ, although his figure is significantly in shadow. Overall, however, the picture is radiant and saturated in light, something Rembrandt emphasised by frequently printing it on bright yellow Chinese paper; there are also some impressions on Japanese paper (cat. 83), which has a warmer tone.[30]

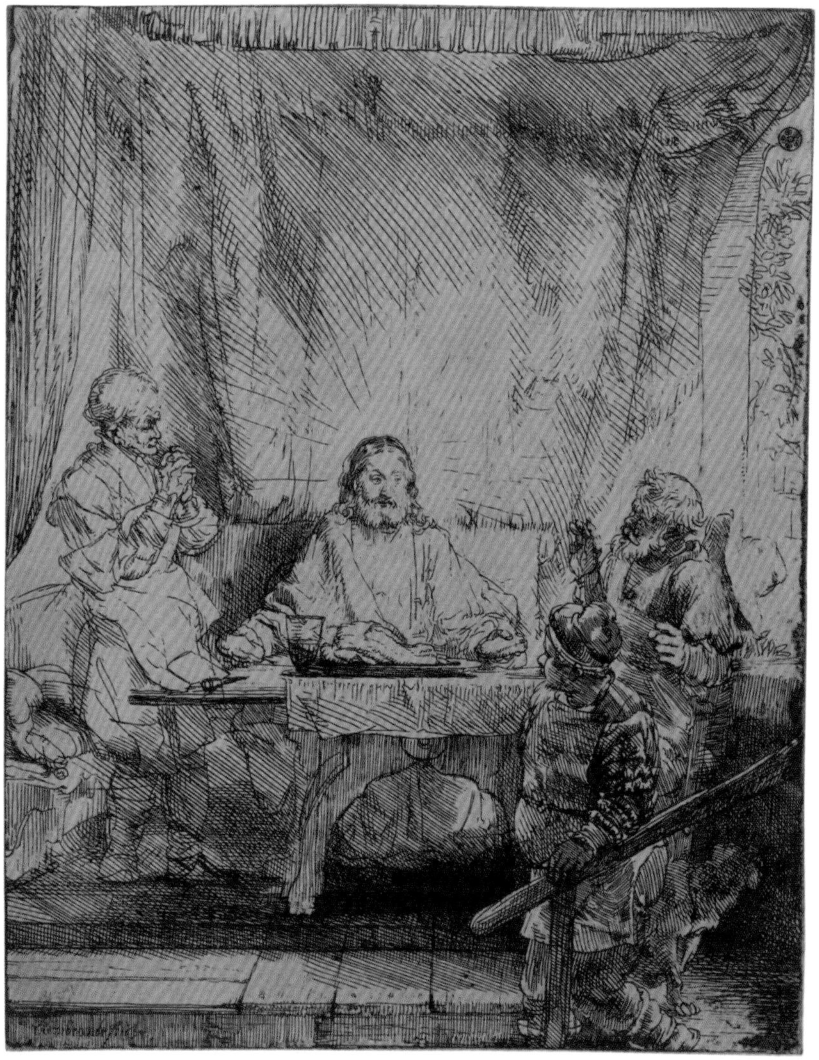

In around 1657 Rembrandt produced *Christ preaching* (*'La petite Tombe'*) (cat. 26), but already in 1654 he had produced six small engravings in the same open style, with firmly etched lines and shading mainly in the form of close parallel lines. These pictures show scenes from Christ's childhood and are also treated as a loosely associated series: *The Adoration of the Shepherds, with the Lamp*; *The Circumcision in the Stable*; *Virgin and Child with the Cat and the Snake*; *The Flight into Egypt, crossing a Brook*; *Christ disputing with the Doctors*; and *Christ returning from the Temple with his Parents* (cats 84–9). Although they are stylistically similar, the lighting varies considerably from one print to the next. For instance, despite the loose style of *The Adoration of the Shepherds*, the artist is still able to portray the glow from the oil lamp very accurately. Mary sits directly beneath the lamp with the baby on her lap, so the two figures are drawn using contour lines only. Joseph, on the other hand, is mainly in the shadows, with only a narrow band of light picking out the front of his face, arm and leg. The same effect can be seen with the shepherds on the left, the bagpipe player and the woman behind him. A striking feature is the umbra caused by the light of the lamp behind the two oxen in the stall on the right. In the other stable scene in this series, *The Circumcision*, the light is much more diffuse and the location of its source is unclear.

Rembrandt's approach to printing these etchings was very different from that taken in the life of Christ series discussed above: the majority were printed on standard western paper, although there are notable differences between the individual impressions. For example, *The Adoration of the Shepherds* was regularly printed on Japanese or Chinese paper, and even the impressions on western paper often incorporated a carefully measured application of surface tone designed to amplify the light effects in the picture. There are also plenty of examples of *Christ returning from the Temple with his Parents* on warm yellow Japanese paper, which enhances the effect of the light in the picture, but they rarely show much evidence of surface tone. This is the only image in the series in which Rembrandt used drypoint to any great extent, and the velvety burr lets him create a sharp contrast between the light and shadow, increasing the impression of a bright, sunny day – which no doubt explains why Joseph needed his broad-brimmed hat.[31] In contrast, the sober style of *Christ disputing with the Doctors* recalls

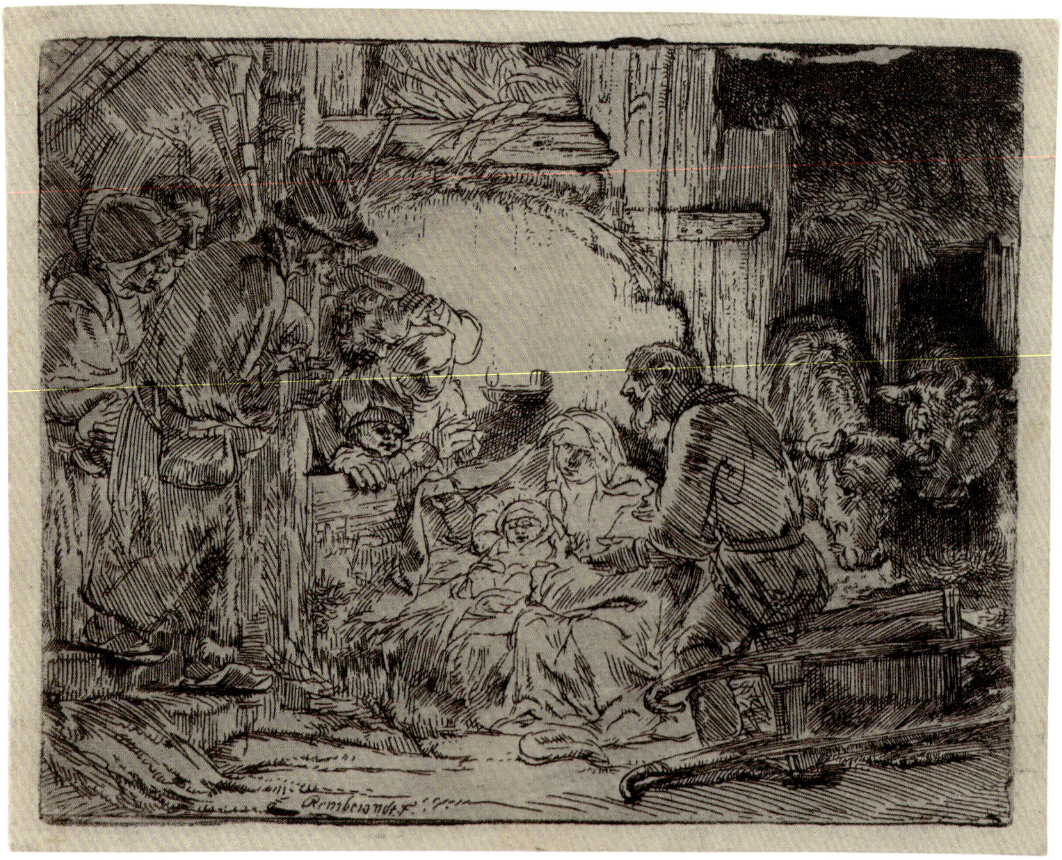

84
The Adoration of the Shepherds, with the Lamp, about 1654
Etching, 10.5 × 12.9 cm
First state of three
Rijksmuseum, Amsterdam
(RP-P-OB-87)

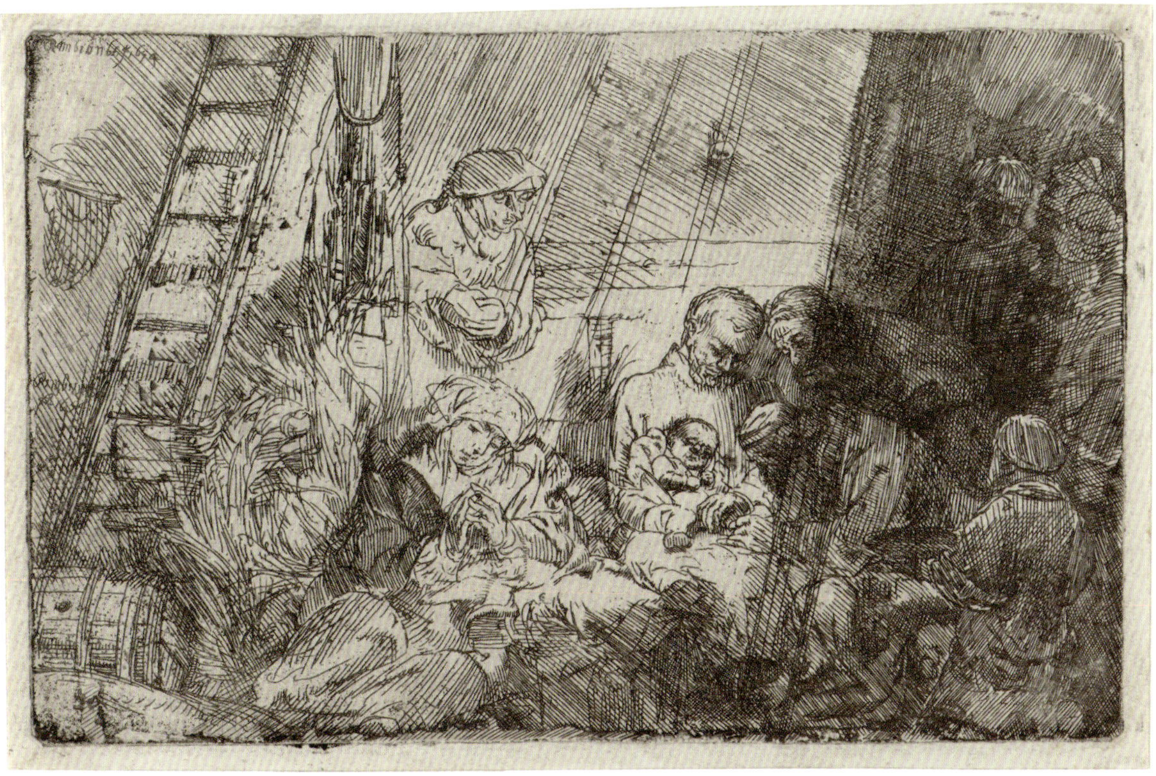

85
The Circumcision in the Stable, 1654
Etching, 9.4 × 14.4 cm
Second state of five
Rijksmuseum, Amsterdam
(RP-P-OB-299)

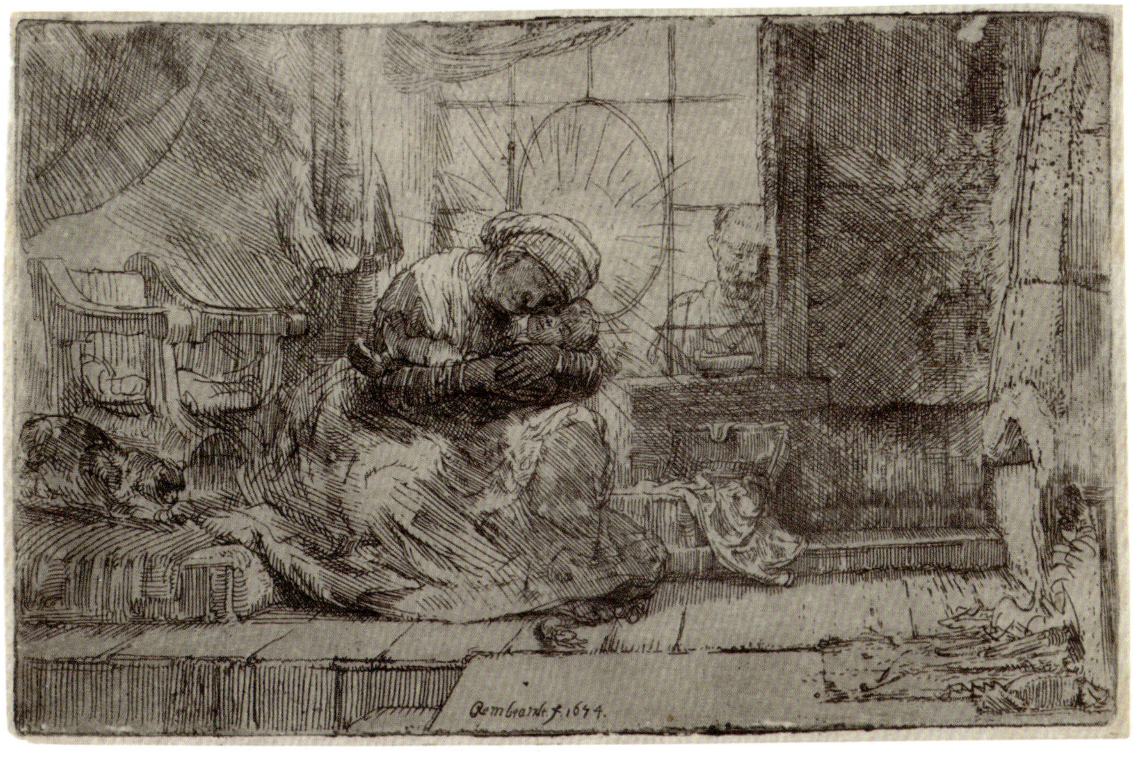

86
Virgin and Child with the Cat and the Snake, 1654
Etching, 9.5 × 14.5 cm
First state of four
Rijksmuseum, Amsterdam
(RP-P-1962-33)

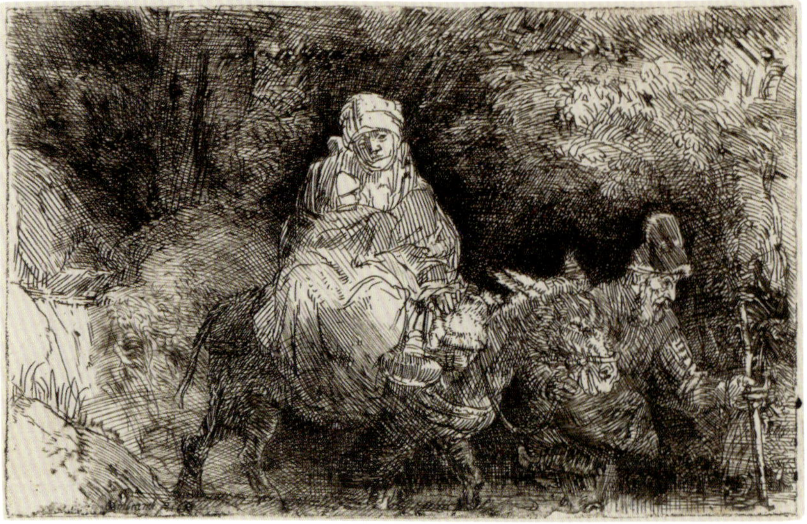

87
The Flight into Egypt, crossing a Brook, 1654
Etching, engraving and drypoint, 9.3 × 14.4 cm
Only state
Rijksmuseum, Amsterdam
(P-P-OB-113)

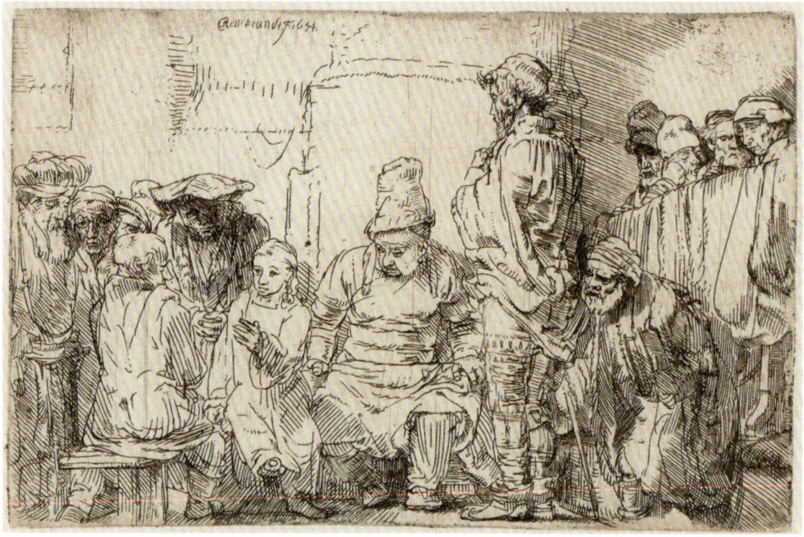

88
Christ disputing with the Doctors, 1654
Etching, possibly with touches of drypoint, 9.5 × 14.4 cm
Only state
Rijksmuseum, Amsterdam
(RP-P-OB-125)

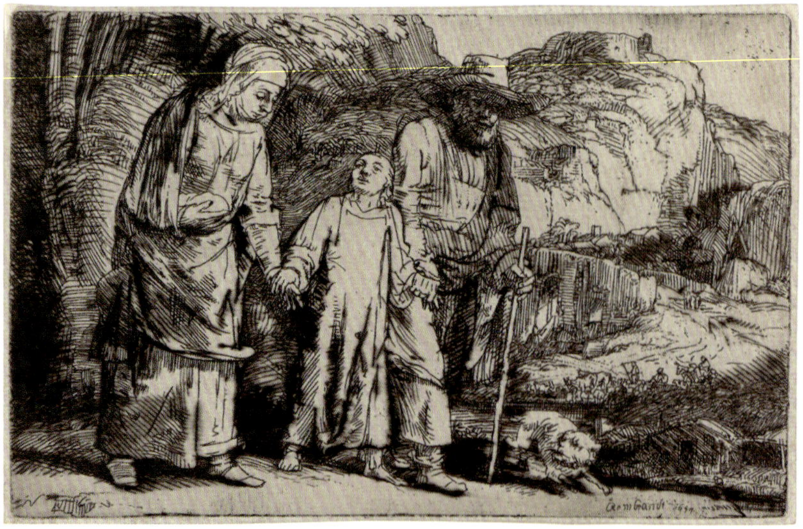

89
Christ returning from the Temple with his Parents, 1654
Etching and drypoint, 9.5 × 14.4 cm
Only state
Rijksmuseum, Amsterdam
(RP-P-1962-32)

Detail from *The Adoration of the Shepherds, with the Lamp* (cat. 84)

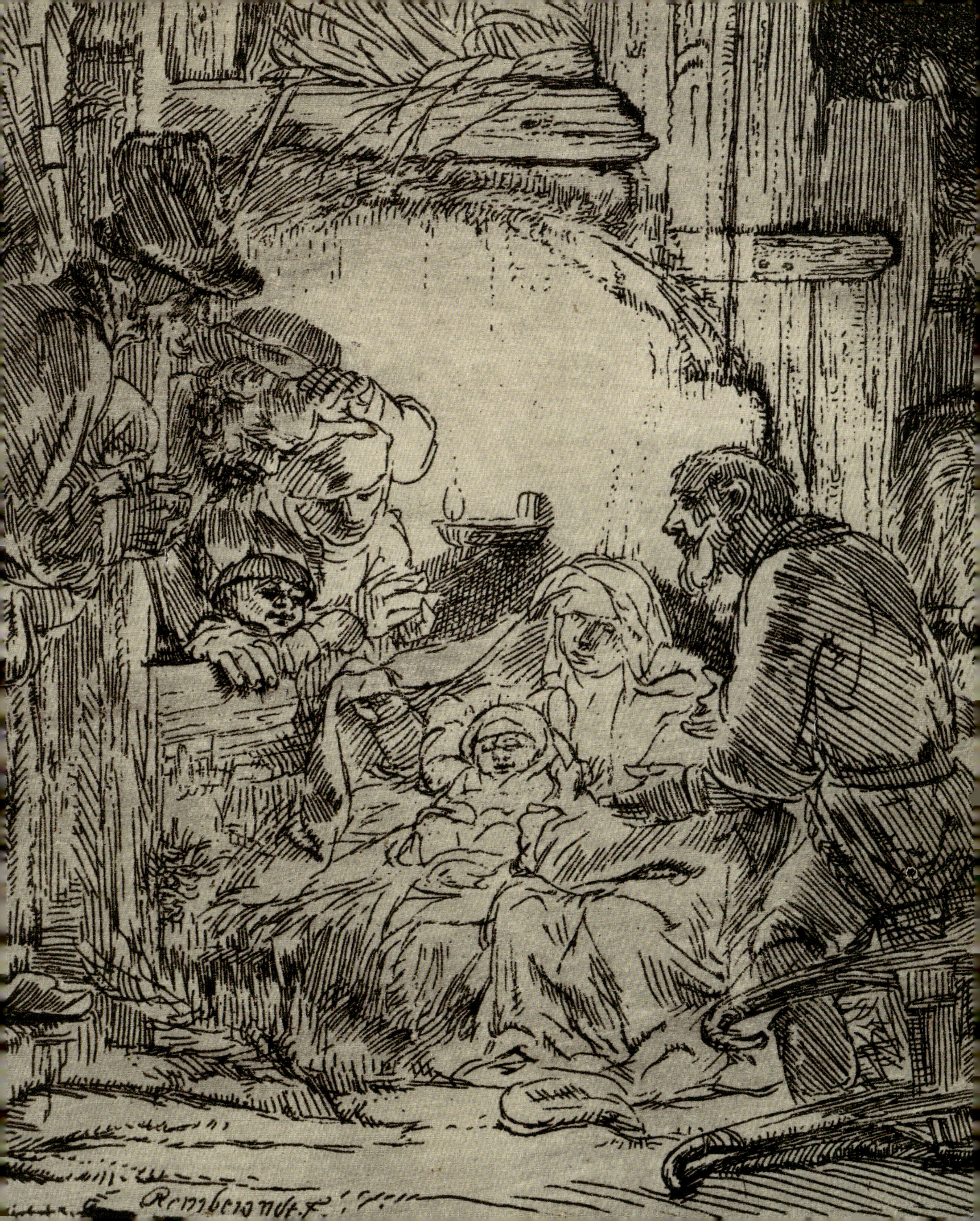
Rembrandt f.

90
Christ disputing with the Doctors, 1652
Etching and drypoint, 12.6 × 21.4 cm
First state of two
Rijksmuseum, Amsterdam
(RP-P-1962-34)

FIG. 60
Christ appearing to the Apostles, 1656
Etching, 16.2 × 21.1 cm
Rijksmuseum, Amsterdam
(RP-P-OB-160)

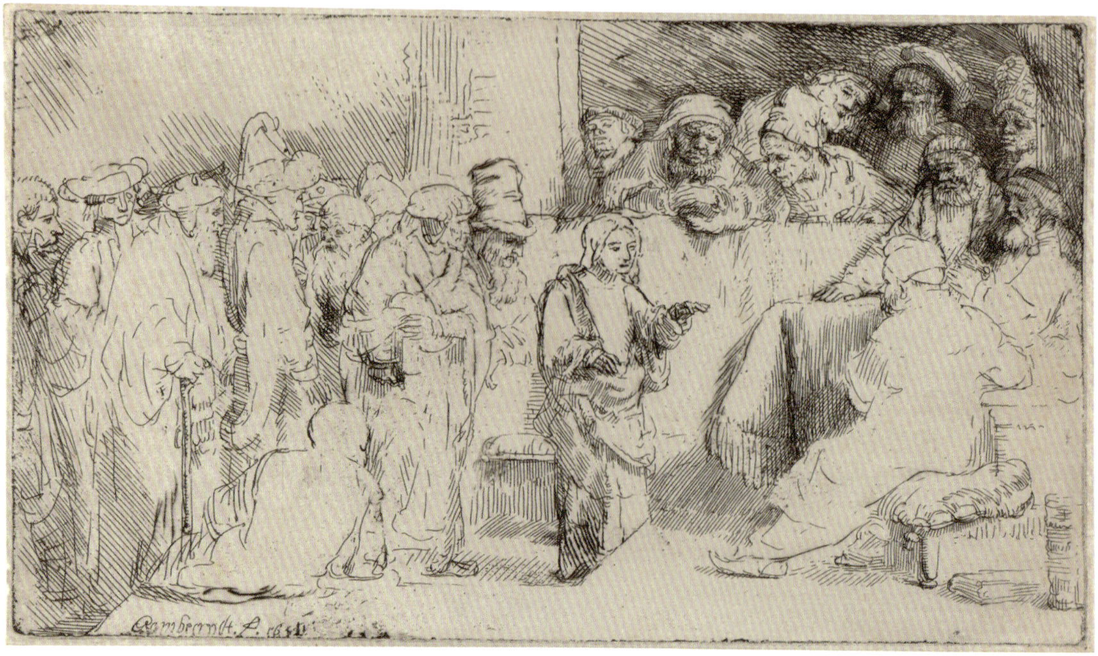

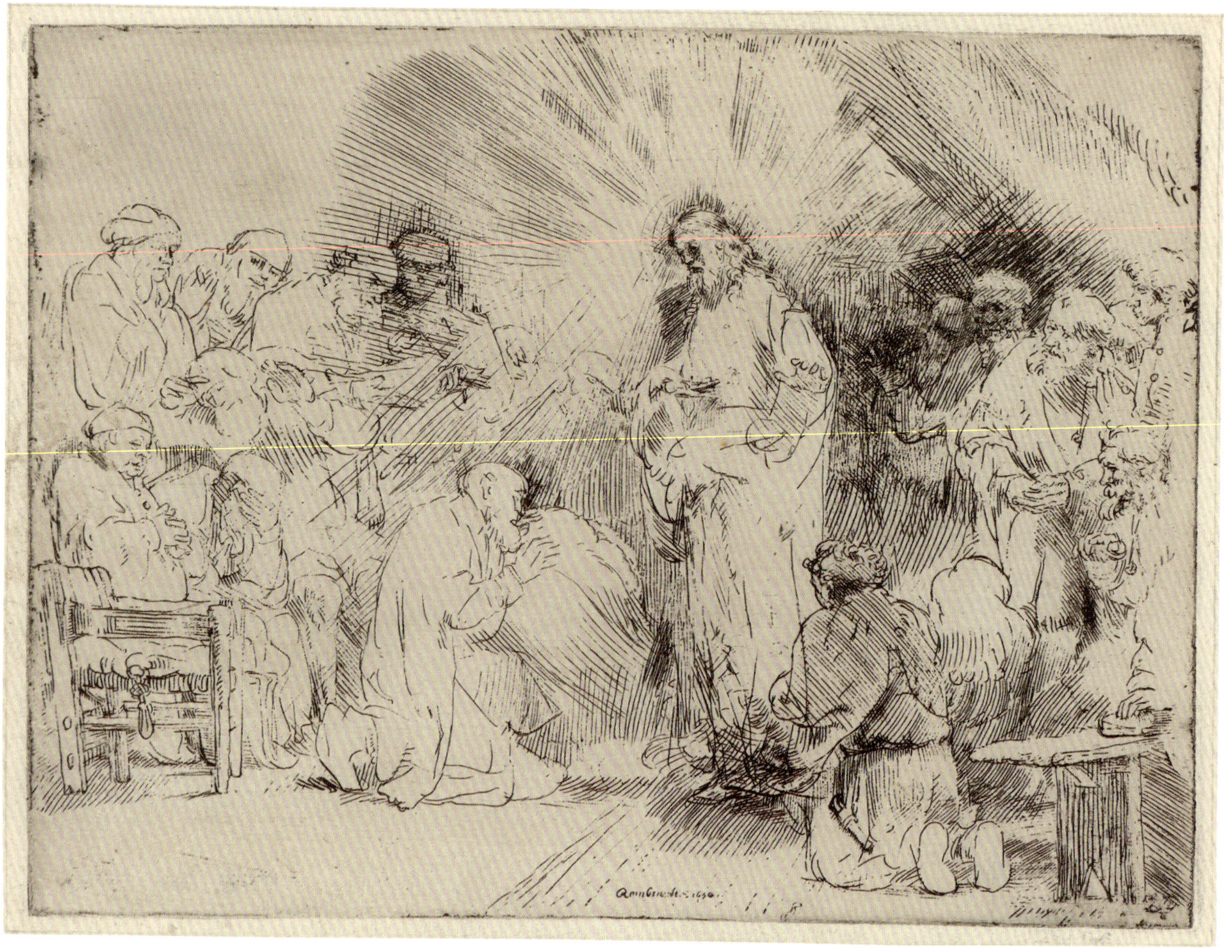

Rembrandt's approach in his etching of the same subject of 1652 (cat. 90), although the style of the earlier version was much more sketchy. In both cases the setting and many of the people present are depicted with little more than a few rough contour lines.

Rembrandt used a similarly economical approach on other occasions in this period, such as in his *Christ appearing to the Apostles* (fig. 60) of 1656. This etching displays rather an uncomfortable form of *non finito*, which, although it could be interpreted as the result of bright light flooding the scene, prompts the question of whether it has actually been finished. This was already an issue in Rembrandt's time. For instance, his biographer Arnold Houbraken wrote: '… one complaint that can be made is that he was so quick to make changes, or driven to do something different, that he only did many things by half, both in his paintings and, even more so, in his etchings'.[32] He tempered this immediately, however, by reporting Rembrandt's reply: 'and he resisted all attempts to alter this, arguing in his defence *that a work is complete if in it the master's intentions have been realised*'.[33]

So Rembrandt himself did not consider such a sketchy work to be unfinished. That puts an interesting perspective on *A Scholar in his Study* ('*Faust*') from about 1652 (cat. 91). This dramatic image shows a man looking up at a circle containing letters and radiating light while a hand just below and to the right points to a sketchily drawn mirror. The iconography of the etching has been the subject of much speculation, but it is probably an allegory of the Christian faith based on Paul's first letter to the Corinthians, in which he compares the contrast between the limits of human knowledge and the perfection of divine knowledge to seeing 'through a glass darkly'.[34] The technique used to produce this print is as striking as the image itself. The background around the window is indicated through subtle shifts in tonal value, and so dark that the contents of the shelf above the skull are suggested rather than portrayed. This is in sharp contrast to the foreground, where the table and globe are merely sketched in. Rembrandt used the same kind of tonal contrast in *Saint Jerome reading in an Italianate Landscape* (cats 22–3), where it certainly enlivens the composition, even if it is not quite clear what the source is of the bright light in the foreground.

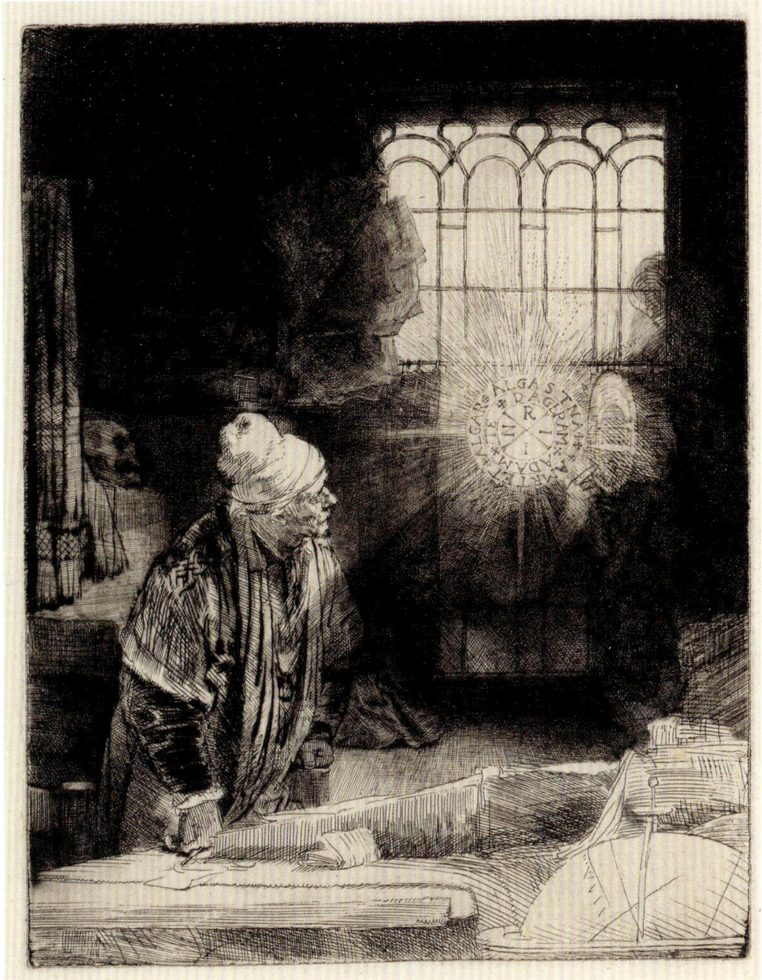

91
A Scholar in his Study ('*Faust*'), about 1652
Etching, engraving and drypoint, 21 × 16 cm
First state of seven
The Fitzwilliam Museum, Cambridge
(AD.12.39-185)

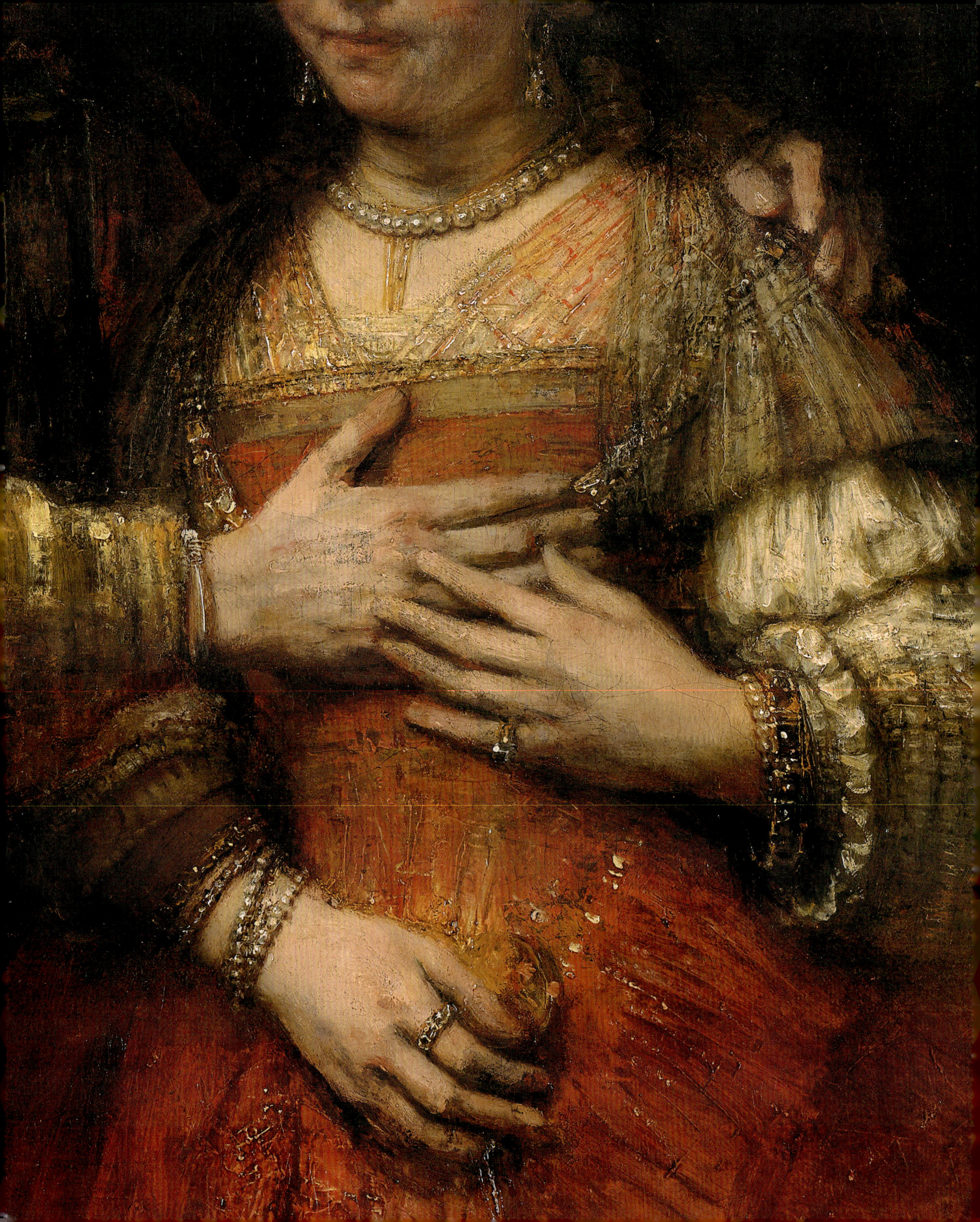

INTIMACY

Jonathan Bikker

UPON VIEWING REMBRANDT'S so-called *'Jewish Bride'* (cat. 92) for the first time in 1885, Vincent van Gogh confessed to a friend that he would gladly give up ten years of his life to be able to sit in front of the painting for a fortnight with only a crust of dry bread to eat.[1] The couple's extraordinarily moving embrace and their loving glances must have been key in eliciting this extreme reaction from the great Post-Impressionist artist, for he exclaimed in a letter to his brother Theo: 'What an intimate, what an infinitely sympathetic painting'.[2] Intimacy is the defining characteristic of many of Rembrandt's most engaging late history paintings and etchings, as well as some of his late portraits and a few works that appear to combine genres, such as *'The Jewish Bride'* and the *Portrait of Abraham Francen, Apothecary* (cat. 103). In the case of the enigmatic *Woman bathing in a Stream* (cat. 95), the quality of intimacy may provide the key to unravelling the painting's iconography. Remarkable features of this and several other works discussed here are the innovative vantage points Rembrandt chose, and the special role he assigned to the beholder.

The physical and emotional core of *'The Jewish Bride'* is formed by the couple's hand gestures: the man holds his right hand lovingly to the woman's bosom and she returns his affection by gently caressing it with her left hand. This tender motif is framed, as it were – and thereby emphasised – by the placement of the man's other hand on his companion's shoulder and the woman's right hand at her midriff. A couple fondly embracing in more or less the same pose appears in a sketch that must have been preparatory to the painting (cat. 93).[3] Other aspects of this drawing's composition, such as the balustrade with a pot plant on the right and the architectural background, can also be found in the painting. But not every element was adopted; noticeably lacking is the face of the man furtively peering at the couple from a balcony at the upper right of the drawing. This figure is the clue to the subject of the composition. According to the Book of Genesis, during a famine God sent Isaac and his wife Rebecca to the Philistine land of Gerar, which was ruled by King Abimelech. Fearful that he would be murdered by the men who desired his beautiful wife, Isaac pretended to be her brother rather than her husband. One day, however, Abimelech looked out of a window and discovered them 'sporting' with one another, as only a married couple does (Genesis 26: 6–8).[4] Nevertheless, the story has a happy ending, as Abimelech merely reprimanded Isaac for his deception, and ordered the Philistines not to lay a hand on the foreigners.

A significant difference between Rembrandt's painting and his preparatory sketch is that in the latter Rebecca sits on Isaac's lap. Based on an engraving by Sisto Badalocchio (1585– after 1621?; fig. 61), this motif was also initially planned for the canvas, as the X-radiograph makes clear, but later expunged.[5] In one of the few other seventeenth-century Dutch treatments of this biblical episode, a 1696 print by Matthijs Pool (1676–1740) after a now lost painting by Barend Graat (1628–1709; fig. 62), the pose in Badalocchio's engraving is retained, except for the fact that it is Isaac who has a bare leg sprawled over Rebecca's instead of the other way around. Graat further heightened the scene's erotic aspect by exposing Rebecca's breasts. Rembrandt, on the other hand, obviously chose this episode for its potential to illustrate a much more profound form of intimacy.

Rembrandt's less sexual interpretation of the story is in line with a note in the official Dutch Bible, the *Statenbijbel* (authorised by the States-General and

Detail from *Portrait of a Couple as Isaac and Rebecca*, known as *'The Jewish Bride'* (cat. 92)

92
Portrait of a Couple as Isaac and Rebecca, known as *'The Jewish Bride'*, about 1665
Oil on canvas, 121.5 × 166.5 cm
Rijksmuseum, Amsterdam

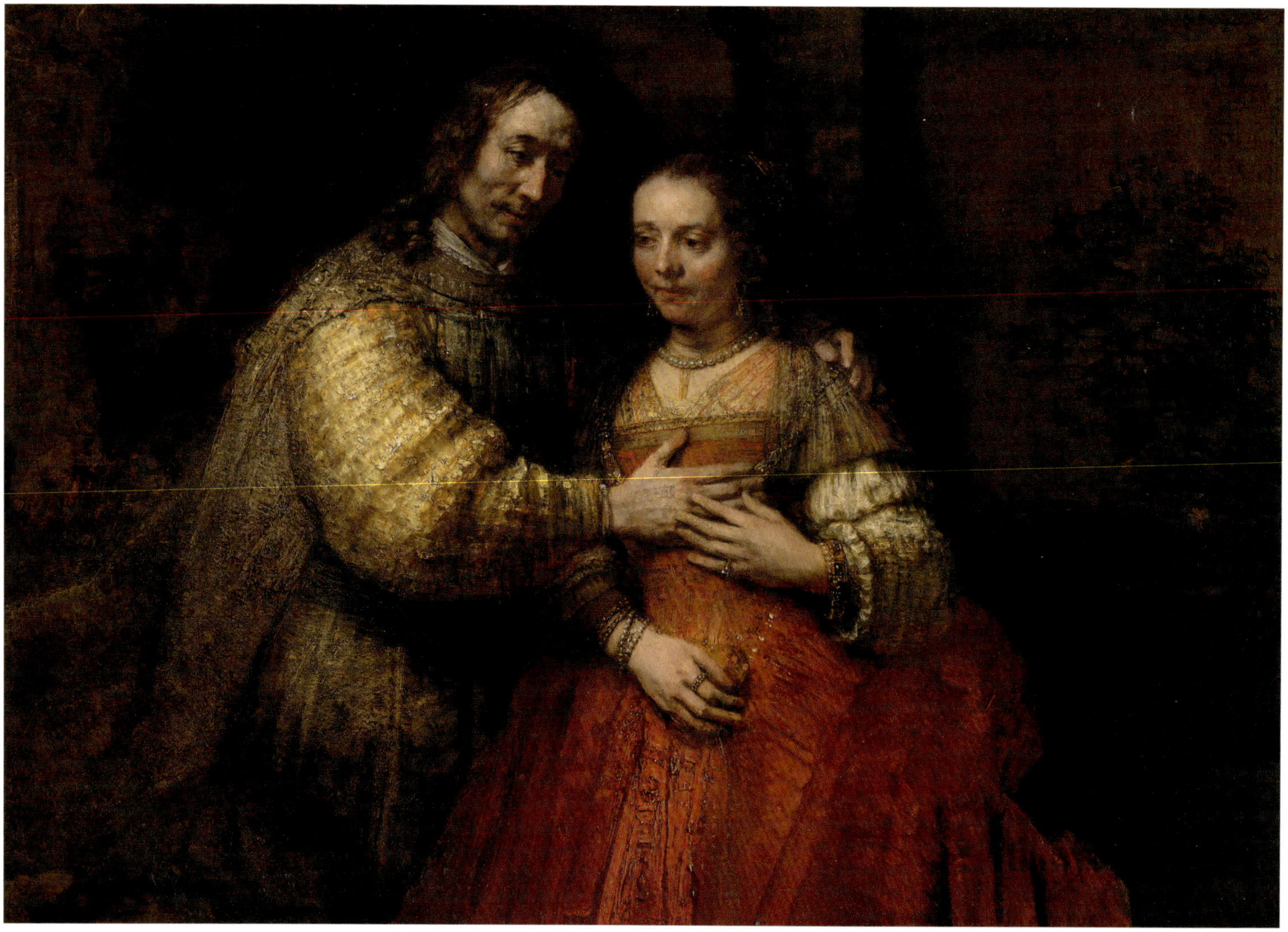

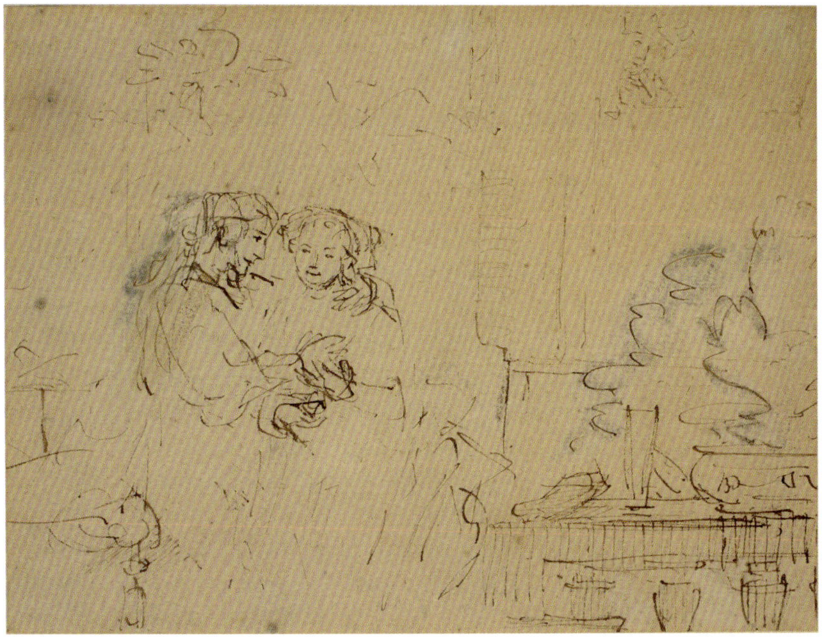

93 and detail
Isaac and Rebecca spied upon by Abimelech, about 1665
Pen and brown ink heightened with white gouache, 14.5 × 18.5 cm
Private collection, USA

published in 1637), clarifying that Isaac and Rebecca were 'employing some intimate yet honourable gestures' when Abimelech discovered that they were man and wife.[6] But this rather sterile description of the couple's actions, and the biblical text itself, do not seem enough to explain the intensity of their affection for one another as Rembrandt depicted it. Another written source, Jacob Cats's monumental *Trou-ringh* (*Wedding Ring*), a book on love and marriage also published in 1637, gives a better sense of the profundity of Isaac's emotion by describing Rebecca as '… his delight, his comfort and life itself. She has brought new youth to his heavy heart. She is so close covenanted with his inner desire that never did she find another woman on his bed.'[7] The last sentence, which Cats repeats further on in his text, is significant: Isaac's father, Abraham, and his brothers were adulterers, but Isaac alone had only one wife and no concubines.

The description of Isaac's deep love of Rebecca in Cats's *Trou-ringh* – one of the most widely read books in the northern Netherlands in the seventeenth century – was, perhaps, also one of the reasons why the couple often featured in Dutch pamphlets occasioned by weddings and on medals intended as engagement or wedding presents.[8] Other reasons would have been the fact that Rebecca was, as the Bible tells us, a beautiful virgin when she married Isaac, and, according to some Dutch theologians, a model of subservience.[9] Rembrandt's former pupil Ferdinand Bol is known from a document to have portrayed his own second wife and her first husband in the guise of Isaac and Rebecca, and

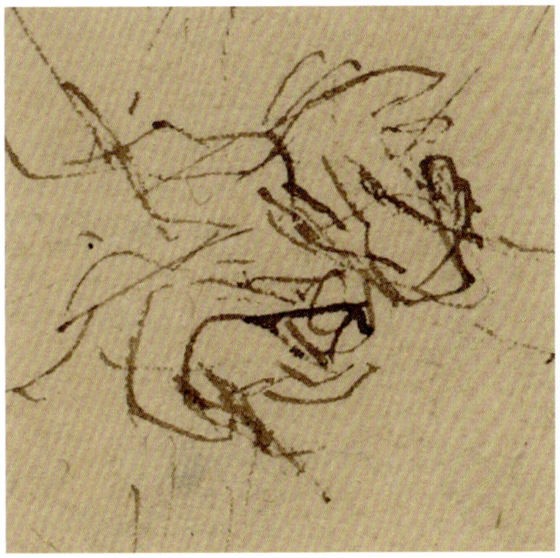

there are a few surviving pictures of the biblical pair by other former pupils that may also be *portraits historiés*.[10] The individualised features of the figures in '*The Jewish Bride*' indicate that it, too, possibly falls under this category of portraiture. Significantly, none of the paintings of Isaac and Rebecca by his former pupils shows the episode of the story chosen by Rembrandt. He alone seems to have realised its potential for conveying the biblical couple's profound love, and perhaps also that of a living couple. Although chaste by comparison with Barend Graat's interpretation, Isaac does have his hand on Rebecca's breast, and the question arises whether, if the painting does indeed double as a portrait, this motif would have been counter to the prevailing sense of decorum. Although we might be inclined to think that it would not have been permissible in the Protestant-dominated

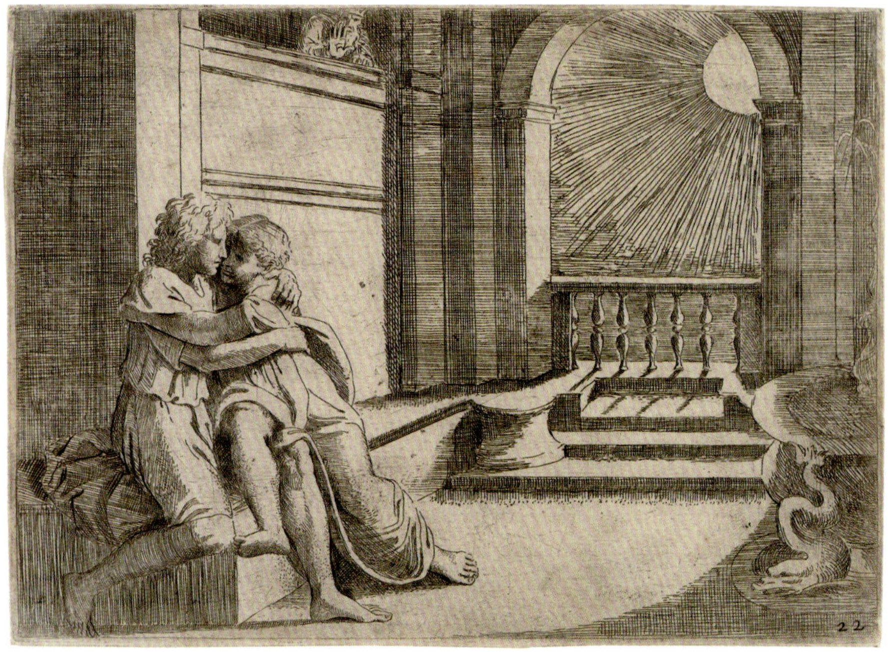

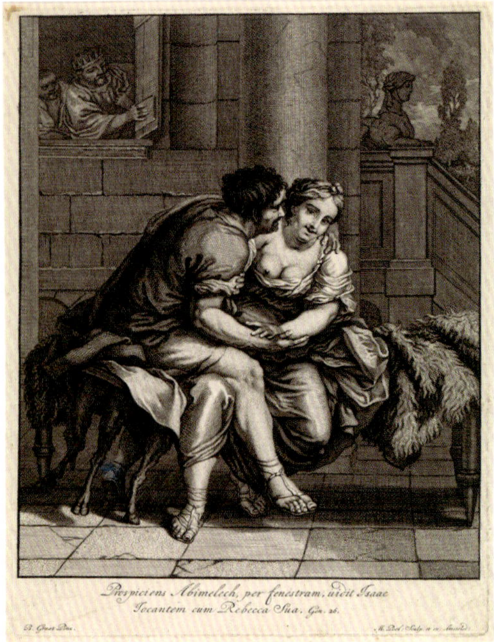

FIG. 61
SISTO BADALOCCHIO
(1585–after 1621?)
after GIULIO ROMANO
(1499?–1546)
Isaac and Rebecca spied upon by Abimelech, 1607
Engraving, 13.2 × 17.8 cm
Rijksmuseum, Amsterdam.
Gift of G.C.M. Luijten, Paris

FIG. 62
MATTHIJS POOL
(1676–1740)
after BAREND GRAAT
(1628–1709)
Isaac and Rebecca spied upon by Abimelech, 1696
Engraving and etching,
30 × 22.3 cm
Rijksmuseum, Amsterdam

culture of the northern Netherlands of the seventeenth century, our modern notions of what was acceptable have recently come under scrutiny as a result of the identification of the couple who sat for a *portrait historié* in which the woman is shown as a bare breasted Venus; the couple in question belonged to the strict Calvinist segment of Dutch society.[11]

The possible function of '*The Jewish Bride*' as a portrait might explain the missing figure of Abimelech. His presence was not necessary because the sitters would have determined with Rembrandt the biblical roles that they enacted, and therefore would have known which scene was depicted. The possibility also exists that the painting originally followed the format of the drawing, but was subsequently cut down on the right, where, also as in the drawing, the figure of Abimelech had been placed. However, the presence of the crack pattern made by the original strainer on all four sides of the canvas suggests that its size has not been significantly altered.[12] It is also important to note that the pot plant and pilaster situated on the right in the drawing have been placed much closer to Isaac and Rebecca in the painting. One suspects, therefore, that Rembrandt intentionally left Abimelech out of the picture, and not merely because the sitters would have considered his presence unnecessary to identify the biblical subject. Not only does Abimelech's absence allow a more concentrated focus on the emotional core of the story, the couple's profound love, it reinforces the fact that the viewer, as witness to that love, performs the same role as the biblical king.

'*The Jewish Bride*' is possibly the only *portrait historié* Rembrandt ever executed.[13] His only certain family portrait, cat. 94, is also from the late period. As in '*The Jewish Bride*', to which it is related stylistically, the figures in the *Portrait of a Family* are dressed in fanciful clothing based on fifteenth- and sixteenth-century pictorial models, although they have not been cast in the roles of biblical figures. By the mid-1660s, when Rembrandt executed *Portrait of a Family*, a number of other artists, including Jürgen Ovens (fig. 63), had already portrayed families in historicising or exotic costumes. While Rembrandt cannot be seen as the initiator of the fancy-dress family portrait, his painting in this genre surpasses the others through the warm interaction of its sitters. The strikingly intimate gesture in '*The Jewish Bride*' has also been put to use in *Portrait of a Family*, but here it is a baby who touches his mother's bosom. In order to accentuate the impact of this tender gesture, Rembrandt devised a chemise with an opening so that the baby's hand has contact with his mother's flesh.[14]

Like the couple in '*The Jewish Bride*', the young woman in a 1654 painting by Rembrandt (cat. 95) is fully immersed in her own world. Having draped her robe over a stone embankment behind her, she is dressed only in a white shift, which she pulls up as she wades into a shallow pool. Alone in a completely private setting, the

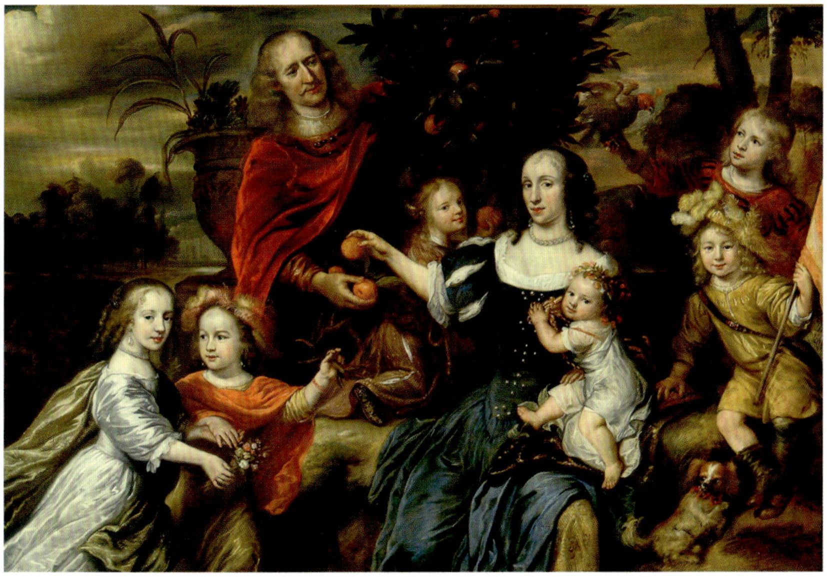

FIG. 63
JÜRGEN OVENS (1623–1678)
Portrait of a Family, 1658
Oil on canvas, 155 × 215.5 cm
Frans Hals Museum, Haarlem

94
Portrait of a Family, about 1665
Oil on canvas, 126 × 167 cm
Herzog Anton Ulrich
Museum, Braunschweig

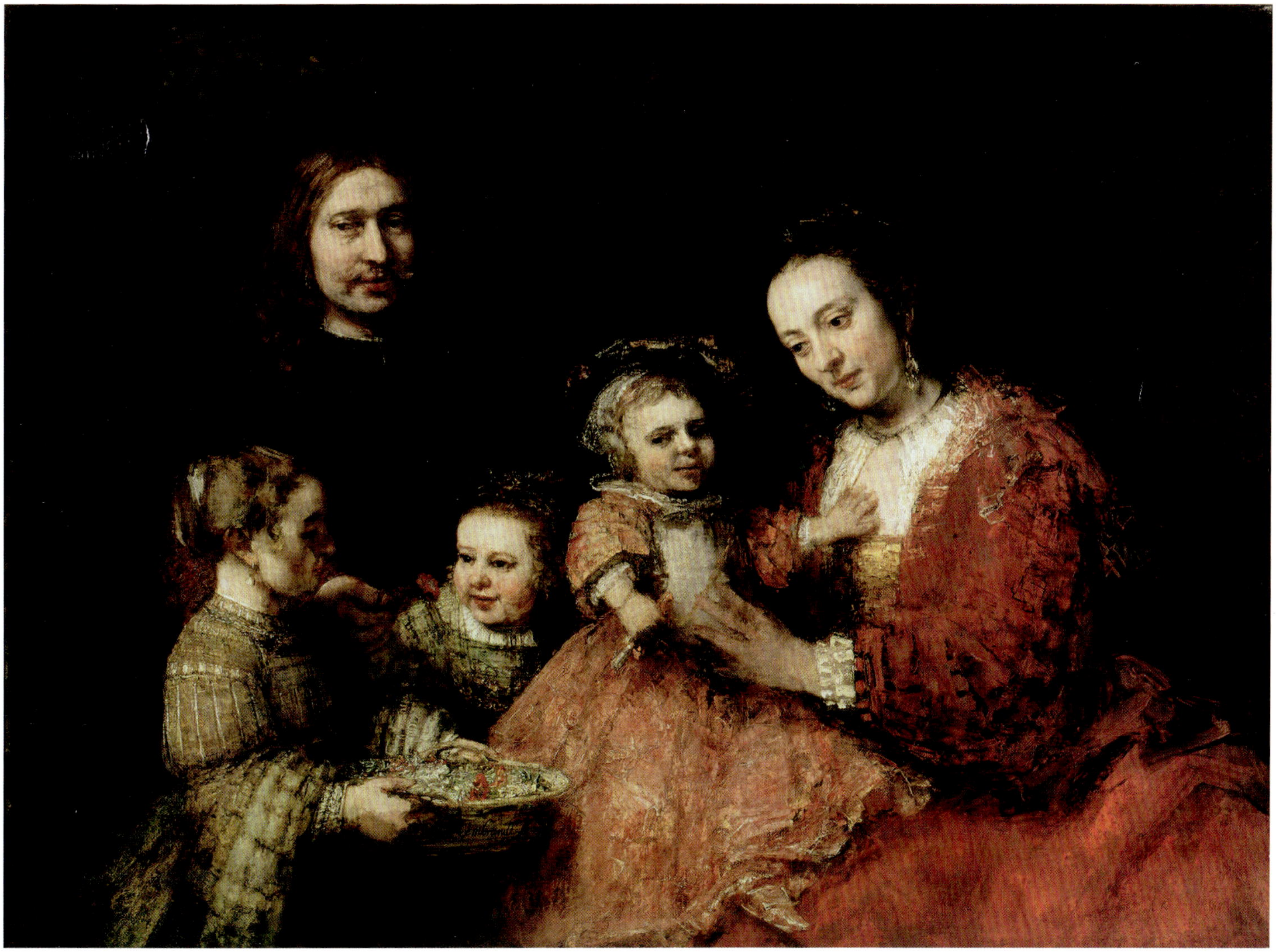

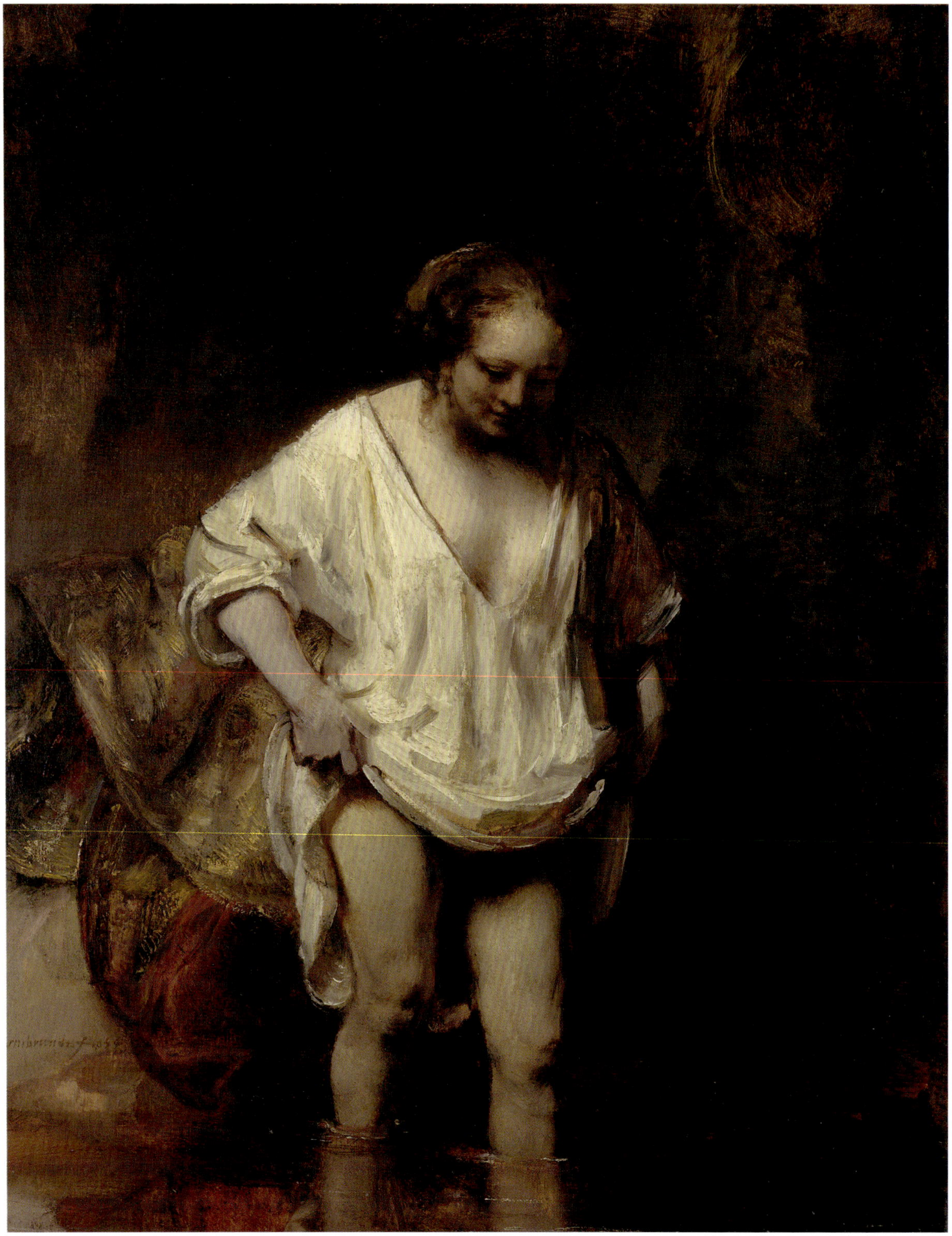

95
A Woman bathing in a Stream, 1654
Oil on panel, 61.8 × 47 cm
The National Gallery, London

woman's gaze is directed downward at the water rather than at another figure outside the painting, or at the viewer. This intensely intimate scene casts the viewer in the role of a voyeur who is permitted a clandestine glimpse of the unsuspecting woman's partially exposed breasts, her thighs and even her sex.

Although this has been considered simply a genre painting in the past, the robe of rich brocade in the background indicates that the woman is more likely to be a mythological, allegorical or biblical figure. Among the identifications that have been put forward, only one, the Old Testament heroine Susanna, fits the intimate tenor of the scene.[15] While there are episodes in the stories of the mythological Diana and Callisto that centre around bathing and contain an element of voyeurism, there is no element of intimacy.[16] Diana was not alone, but with her nymphs, when Actaeon stumbled upon their secret cave and caught sight of them bathing. Callisto, one of Diana's warriors, was resting from her hunting when Jupiter saw and raped her. Her resulting pregnancy was discovered by Diana and the other nymphs when, on a very hot day, they decided to bathe in a brook. Wary that this band of avowed virgins would discover her 'crime', Callisto was reluctant to join in, prompting the others to forcibly remove her tunic, thus revealing her swollen belly. Rather than being simply a case of Rembrandt isolating the main protagonist in a story, as has been argued, if the figure in this painting were indeed Callisto he would have invented a scene for which there is no basis either in the story itself or in the pictorial tradition.[17] Unlike his *Bathsheba with King David's Letter* (cat. 112), also painted in 1654, or '*The Jewish Bride*' (cat. 92), it is not enough to merely imagine the presence of one or more figures in his *Woman bathing in a Stream* in order to make an episode of Callisto's story complete. Furthermore, she was not wading into a pool when Jupiter came across her: it was her very reluctance to bathe that led to the discovery of her pregnancy, and of course she was not alone when this occurred.[18]

The Old Testament stories of Bathsheba (2 Samuel 11: 2) and Susanna (Daniel 13: 19–21) both revolve around the dramatic consequences ensuing from one or more men spying on a beautiful woman, who is married to someone else, as she bathes. A significant difference between the two episodes is that King David is simply reported to have caught sight of Bathsheba one evening while he was walking on the roof of his house, whereas the Bible explicitly states that Susanna was alone when the Elders saw her bathing, for she had sent her maids to fetch oil and ointments. In many depictions of Bathsheba, including Rembrandt's 1654 painting, one or more maids are present. An essential element of Susanna's story, on the other hand, is that no witnesses were present when the two Elders approached her. The Elders were judges who gathered at the house of Susanna's rich husband to hear cases. After secretly watching her for some time, they discovered that they both lusted after her and decided to hide themselves in her garden until they could catch her alone. When the opportunity arose, they pounced on Susanna, giving her the choice to submit to them or be accused in public of having an affair with a young lover.

Some scholars have argued against the possibility that the *Woman bathing in a Stream* depicts Susanna, since in Rembrandt's two earlier paintings of *Susanna and the Elders*, from 1636 (fig. 65) and 1647, the beautiful protagonist is startled: in the first, because she senses the presence of the Elders, and in the second because they grab hold of her.[19] This dramatic moment in the story was the one most artists chose to represent, but

FIG. 64 and detail
LUCAS VAN LEYDEN
(1494–1533)
Susanna and the Elders,
about 1506–10
Engraving, 19.9 × 14.7 cm
Rijksmuseum, Amsterdam

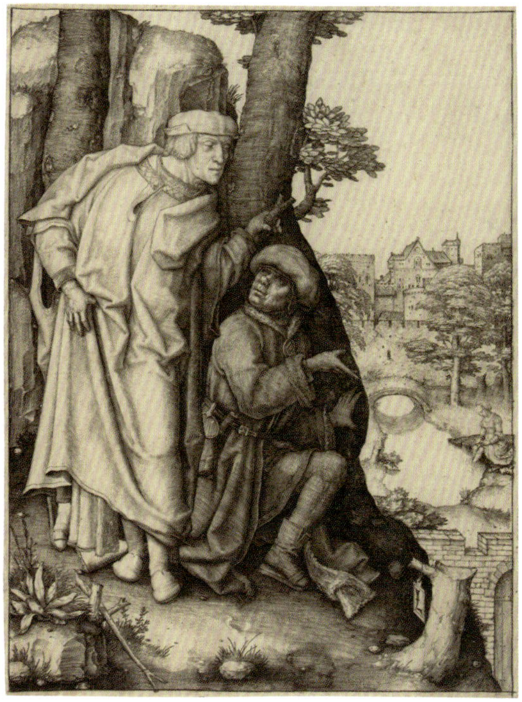

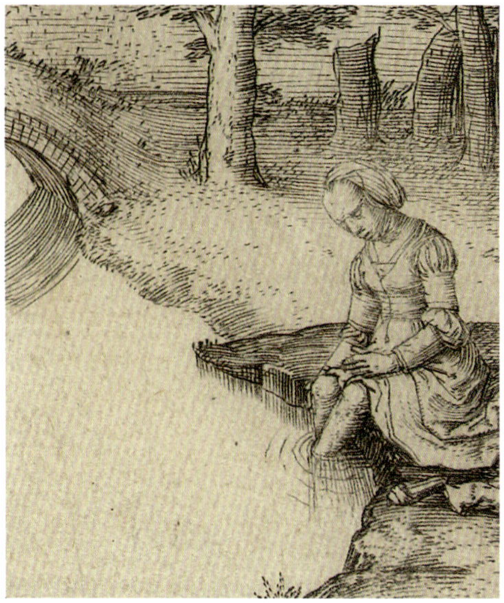

there was also a tradition of illustrating the moment before the Elders made their assault. Examples from the seventeenth century include works by the Italian masters Guercino (1591–1666) and Massimo Stanzione (1586–1656), the Dutch artist Jan Both (about 1618/22–1652), and a painting attributed to Rembrandt's former pupil Govert Flinck.[20] While most of these works were probably unknown to Rembrandt, he is likely to have owned a copy of Lucas van Leyden's highly inventive print of the subject (fig. 64) executed at the beginning of the sixteenth century.[21] In Lucas's extraordinary solution the Elders are shown in the foreground, spying on their unwitting victim, who sits at the edge of a stream in the distant background. Fully clothed, she looks at the water wistfully as she pulls her skirt up to just above her knees. The similarities to Rembrandt's bathing woman, in both gesture and sense of intimacy, are striking: and whereas in Lucas's print the viewer looks on with the Elders, in Rembrandt's painting the viewer quite possibly takes their place. This substitution is already anticipated in Rembrandt's 1636 painting of *Susanna and the Elders*, where the faces of the Elders can only be made out with difficulty in the bushes on the right. If the *Woman bathing* is indeed Rembrandt's third painted depiction of Susanna, it is also his most powerful since it alone forces the viewer to experience the desire felt by the Elders when they spied on her as she bathed. The illicit nature of our gaze and the anticipation that the woman will reveal more as she continues into the water add to the erotic charge. Although the viewer is cast in the role of the voyeur, Susanna's plight is made all the more tangible because in the next moment her privacy – which the viewer knows to be illusory, but she does not – will be violated.

The model for the *Woman bathing in a Stream* and numerous other depictions of women by Rembrandt from the 1650s and 1660s has often been identified as the artist's mistress Hendrickje Stoffels, and the subject matter of these works has been related to events in her personal life. For example, the scholar who identifies the figure as Callisto also suggests, albeit tentatively, that the painting is a comment on Hendrickje's pregnancy out of wedlock in 1654, the year it was made, and her consequent summons before the church council.[22] However, this event can just as easily be tied to the interpretation of the subject as Susanna, for the church elders charged Hendrickje with harlotry, the same accusation as the biblical Elders made to Susanna when they failed to have their way with her.[23] Be this as it may, there is good reason to question the notion that Rembrandt's common-law wife posed for this painting. In the first place, there are no documented portraits of Hendrickje Stoffels, and the women in Rembrandt's drawings, etchings and paintings from this period who have come to be known as 'Hendrickje' show a wide variety of facial features. More to the point, it is unlikely that Rembrandt

FIG. 65
Susanna and the Elders, 1636
Oil on panel, 47.4 × 38.6 cm
Royal Picture Gallery
Mauritshuis, The Hague

would have had his common-law wife pose in such a compromising state of undress; modelling in the nude was considered immoral in seventeenth-century Amsterdam, necessitating artists to pay prostitutes to perform this task.[24]

The existence of drawings of the same model executed by various hands and from different angles, as well as documentary evidence, indicate that artists organised group life-drawing sessions.[25] One of these, involving Rembrandt and at least one of his pupils, resulted in his last-known etching of a woman, a seated nude viewed from behind executed in 1661 (cat. 96). Rembrandt probably etched the figure directly onto the copper plate while his pupil drew her in the same pose, but from two different angles, on paper.[26] When compared to the two drawings, both of which are attributed to the obscure Johannes Raven (1634–1662), it becomes apparent that Rembrandt transformed studio props and accoutrements to produce an intimate history piece.[27] The white cap worn by the model became a classicising coiffure and headdress, while the chair on which she is seated and the curtain backdrop are metamorphosed into what appears to be a curtained bed, or the inside of a tent. The sling or rope used by the model to support her strenuous pose with her arm in the air takes the shape of an arrow in the etching. Close inspection reveals the head of a boy lurking in the shadows of the left background in the print. This motif was probably also inspired by the

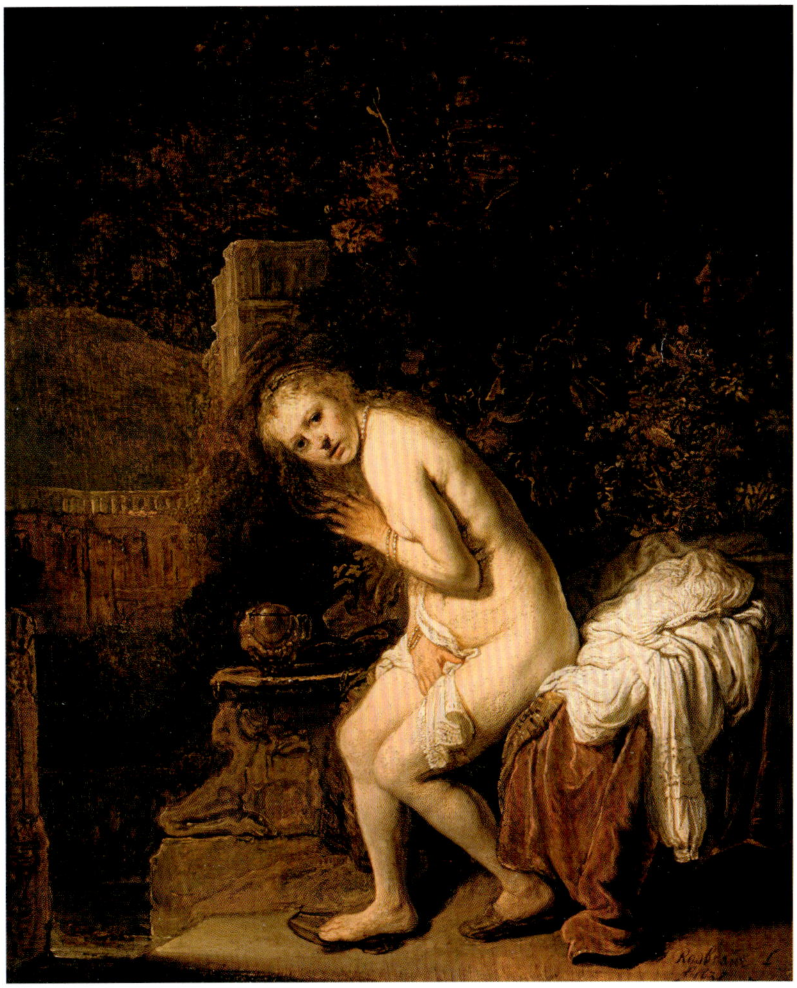

actual studio set-up, the head of one of his pupils intensely observing the model from the front finding its way on to Rembrandt's copper plate. The subject of the etching is probably Venus and Cupid, but it seems very evident that Rembrandt came up with the iconography on the spur of the moment, while working directly from the model.[28]

A similarly haphazard approach is apparent in a 1658 etching of a nude woman (cat. 97).[29] She appears at first glance to be seated on a chair in an interior just like Rembrandt's other etched nudes of the same year (see cats 14–16). Yet there is foliage in the background and the woman's legs are cut off just above the ankles, suggesting that her feet are submerged under water. Here again, it seems that Rembrandt did not have a clear subject in mind before he began drawing on the plate from the model. As in the *Woman bathing in a Stream*, the solitary subject of the etching may be a single-figure Susanna and the Elders, with the viewer assuming the role of the latter. At any rate, with her face averted and in shadow, the impression that we are illicitly viewing the woman during a private moment is equally strong. The question remains as to whether, as in the genesis of their iconographies, the sense of intimacy in these two

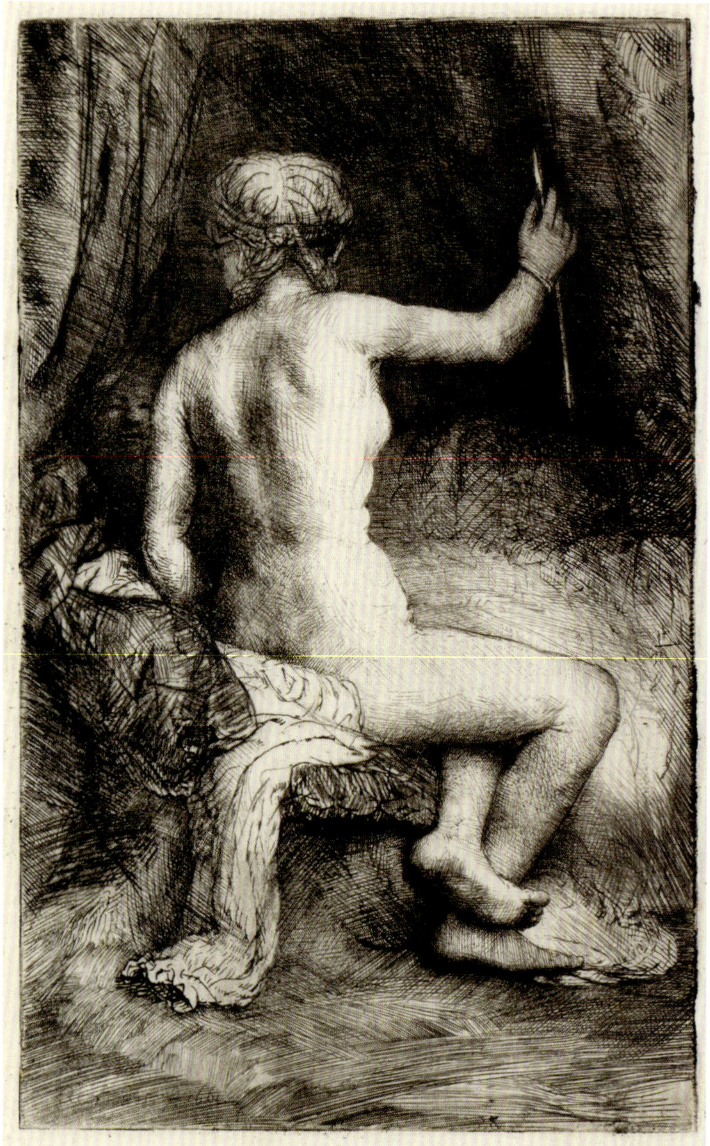

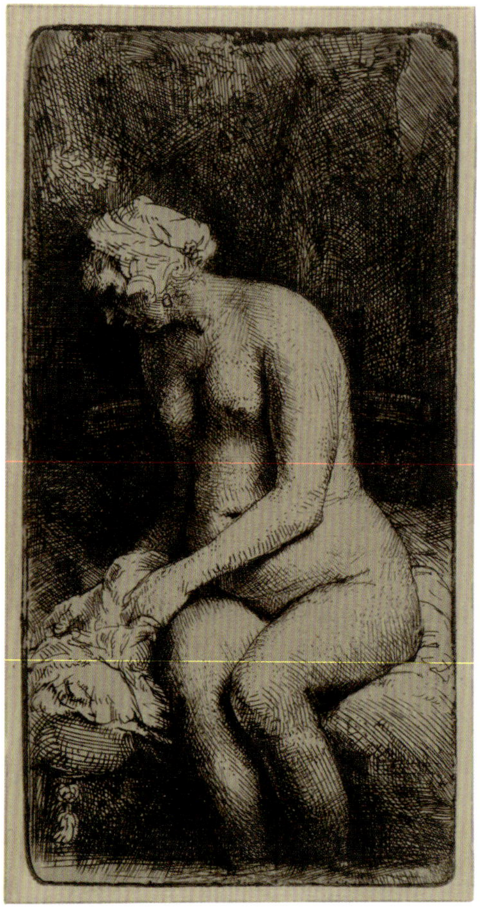

96
Woman with the Arrow, 1661
Etching and drypoint,
20.5 × 12.3 cm
Second state of three
The Fitzwilliam Museum,
Cambridge (AD.12.39-153)

97
Woman bathing her Feet at a Brook, 1658
Etching and drypoint,
16 × 8 cm
First state of two
Rijksmuseum, Amsterdam
(RP-P-OB-263)

prints was not planned from the start, but only arose, perhaps even instinctually, while Rembrandt worked from the nude model.

It is tempting to imagine that Rembrandt's most tender evocation of intimacy, his 1655 *Titus at his Desk* (cat. 99), came about in a similar manner: the artist saw his young son daydreaming as he was writing or drawing, and seized his brushes to record the moment.[30] Another painting from the same year, *An Old Woman reading* (cat. 98), also gives the impression of being a spontaneous, direct study from daily life. However, in both instances this is the result of a masterful illusion. Thoroughly engrossed in their own thoughts – the boy in his reverie, the woman in the words she is reading – the figures are seen extremely close at hand, lending them a powerful sense of immediacy. In the painting of his son, the front of the desk is flush with the picture plane, causing the sheaf of papers, Titus's left hand and his leather pen holder and inkwell to seem to protrude into our space. In the other work, the old woman's cloaked body fills the entire bottom of the composition, extending beyond the edges of the painting. Her hands have been made so large in relation to her torso and head that they and the upper edge of the book similarly appear to emerge from the canvas.

Rembrandt made use of *trompe-l'œil* devices earlier in his career, but he had never before applied such illusionistic tricks to a depiction of a meditative figure. The resulting images are radically innovative, something that a modern audience, accustomed to extreme close-ups made with telephoto lenses, can easily overlook. The very thing that makes the young boy and the old woman appear so real, and their interiority seem almost palpable, never occurs in reality, as it is simply impossible to get this close to someone facing you without them noticing. That said, the subject matter of both paintings is not without precedent. Jan Lievens, who had painted a solitary old woman reading more than once in the early 1620s, can be credited with introducing the theme into Dutch painting. But Rembrandt, in his 1631 painting (fig. 66), made one of the most captivating versions of it.[31] Based in part upon her fanciful costume and the pseudo-Hebraic text in the book, a good case has been made for identifying Rembrandt's subject here as the prophetess Anna, the 84-year-old widow who 'departed not from the temple, but served God with fastings and prayers night and day' (Luke 2: 37).[32] In the *Old Woman reading* of 1655, however, the text is not visible, and the woman does not share the profile pose of a late sixteenth-century engraving of the prophetess that has been seen as the direct model for Rembrandt's earlier painting.[33] Other interpretations for the subject of Rembrandt's later painting are possible, therefore, including the Cumaean Sibyl, who was often shown in sixteenth-century prints as an old woman holding a book; or she may have been conceived simply as an embodiment of exemplary widowhood.[34] According to Jacob Cats's influential *Houwelyck* (*Marriage*), published in 1625, the pious widow has 'A heart that is uplifted by reading in God's book'.[35] While at least the general theme of both these paintings by Rembrandt is the same, they differ enormously from one another as far as scale, pose and style are concerned. The meticulously painted figure in the 1631 work is shown in profile and at nearly full length, whereas in the later painting she is frontal, half-length and rendered with broad, suggestive

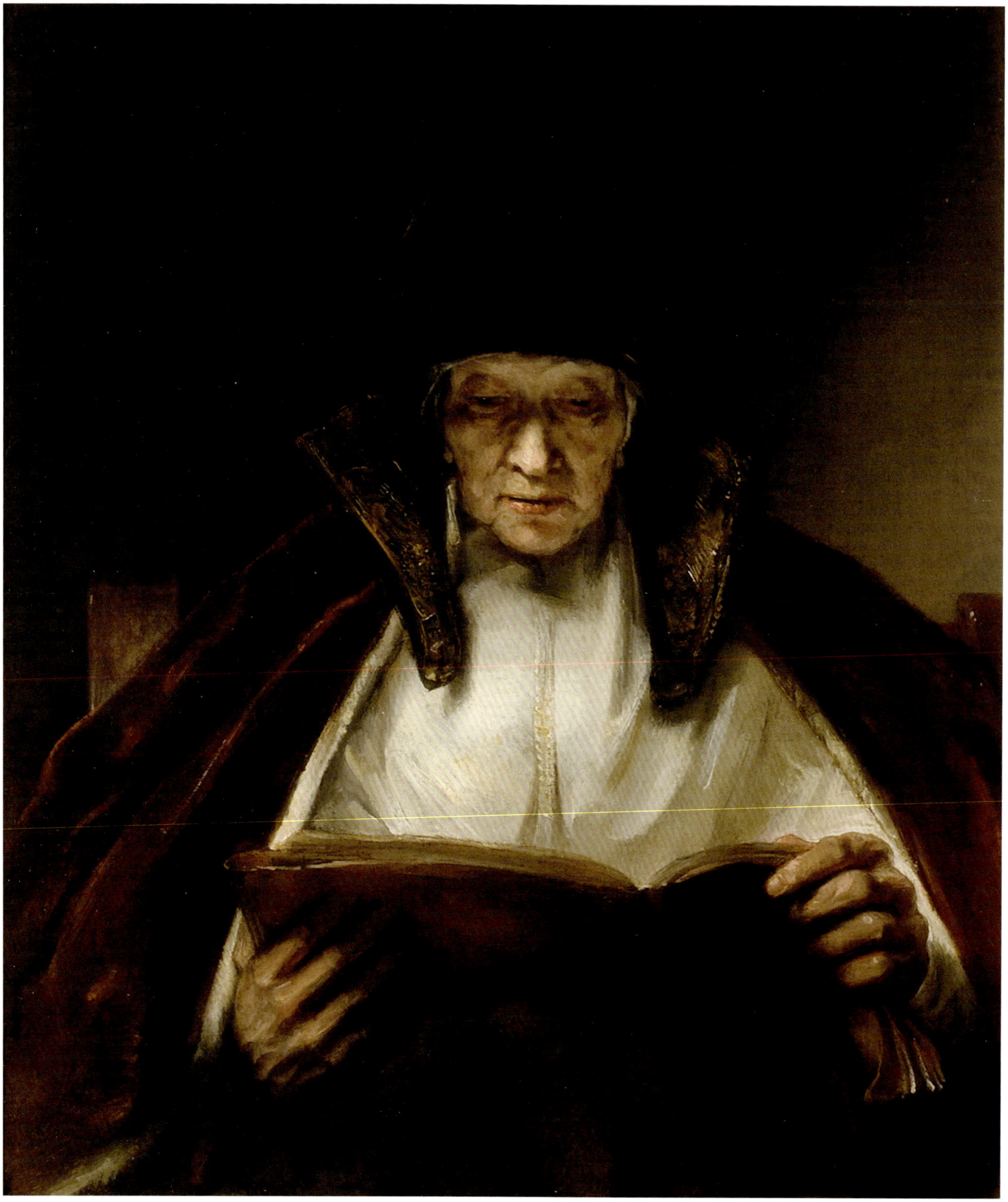

brushstrokes. Nevertheless, in both pictures the word of God – assuming that the woman in the 1655 painting is also reading a religious text – is presented as a source of illumination. In the earlier work the light is concentrated on the open pages of the book, while in the later one the old woman's white robe and face are brilliantly lit as if from light emanating from the book.

Unlike the 1655 *Old Woman reading*, in which Rembrandt appears to have revisited an artistic problem that had concerned him almost a quarter century earlier, his *Titus at his Desk* may have been a response to the challenge set by a work by one of his former pupils, Samuel van Hoogstraten's *Self Portrait writing or drawing at a Window* (fig. 67) of around 1647. This earlier depiction of a boy staring into space while drawing, or more likely writing, probably set an example not only for the theme of Rembrandt's masterpiece, but also for its *trompe-l'œil* aspect. Yet Rembrandt eschewed the rather insipid window frame motif with which Van Hoogstraten positions his figure in the viewer's space, and concentrated more on the boy, bringing him much closer to the spectator. Despite taking up more than a third of the composition, the desk in Rembrandt's painting is unobtrusive, its subtly variegated surface complementing the boy's wistful state of mind.

Both Van Hoogstraten and Rembrandt's paintings were probably conceived as representations of the theme of *Study*, described in Cesare Ripa's much-consulted iconographical handbook as 'A Youth, with a pale Countenance; in a modest Garb; sitting down; his left Hand on a Book, lying open, on which he is very intent; a Pen in his right; a Lamp, and a Cock, on each side'.[36]

98
An Old Woman reading, 1655
Oil on canvas, 78.7 × 66 cm
Duke of Buccleuch and Queensberry, KBE

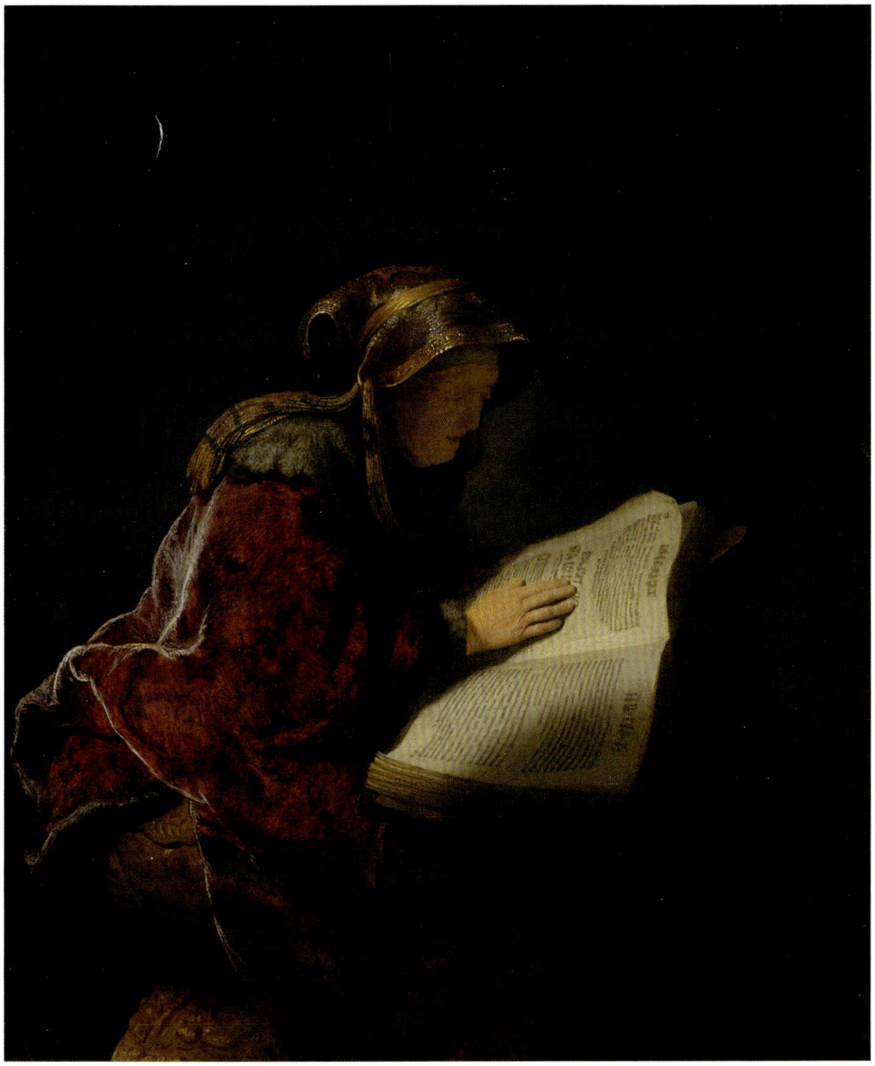

FIG. 66
An Old Woman reading, 1631
Oil on panel, 60 × 48 cm
Rijksmuseum, Amsterdam

99
Titus at his Desk, 1655
Oil on canvas, 77 × 63 cm
Museum Boijmans
Van Beuningen, Rotterdam

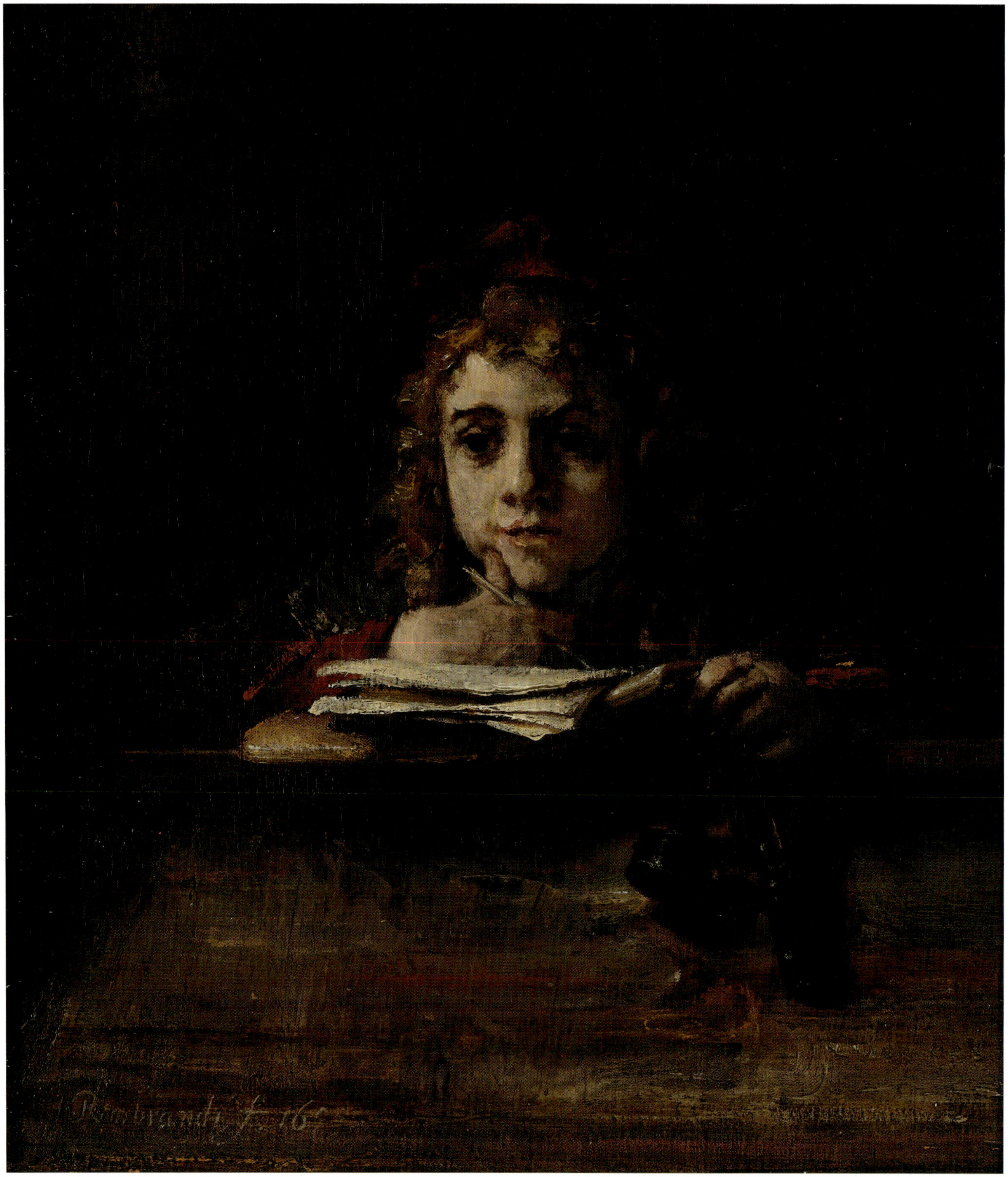

Obviously neither artist followed Ripa's text literally, but the complexion of Rembrandt's boy is distinctly pale.[37] His model for this painting has been commonly identified as his only surviving child with Saskia Uylenburgh, Titus, who was born in 1641 and would have been 13 or 14 years old at the time. As with Hendrickje Stoffels, there are no documented portraits of Titus, and some scholars have strongly argued that the child in the picture is too young to be him. However, estimating the age of the boy in the painting is a tricky business and the possibility cannot be ruled out that Rembrandt either used a sketch made at an earlier date or deliberately made Titus appear younger, for effect. Certainly the use made by Dutch painters of their wives, maidservants and family members as models in such a way that they could be identified in their paintings was a practice that the classicist theoretician Gerard de Lairesse later found supremely irritating.[38]

The same boy who modelled for Rembrandt's 1655 painting, but now with a conspicuously bulbous nose, appears to be the subject of a small etching made around the same time (cat. 100). The copper plate for this print may have been the one listed as '*Titus conterfeytsel*' (portrait of Titus) in the 1679 inventory of the estate of the publisher Clement de Jonghe.[39] The pensive expression suggested by the boy's downcast eyes and the dark shadow on the right side of his face, as well as his

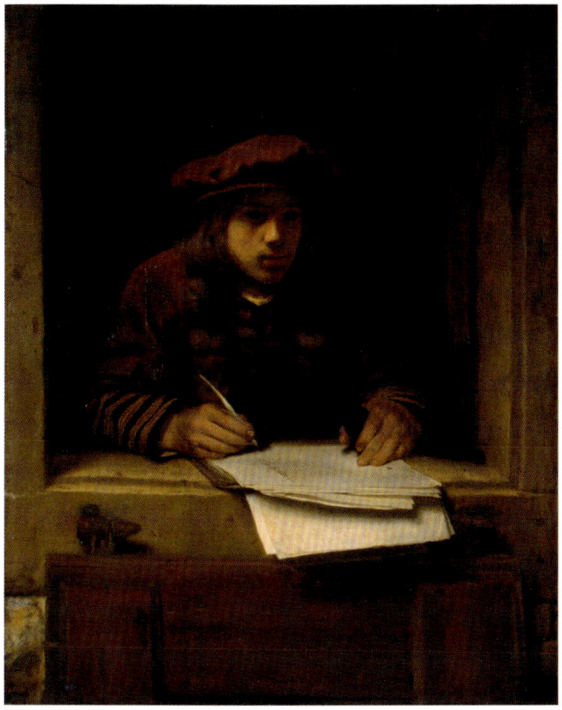

FIG. 67
SAMUEL VAN HOOGSTRATEN (1627–1678)
Self Portrait writing or drawing at a Window, about 1647
Oil on canvas, 102 × 79 cm
The State Hermitage Museum, St Petersburg

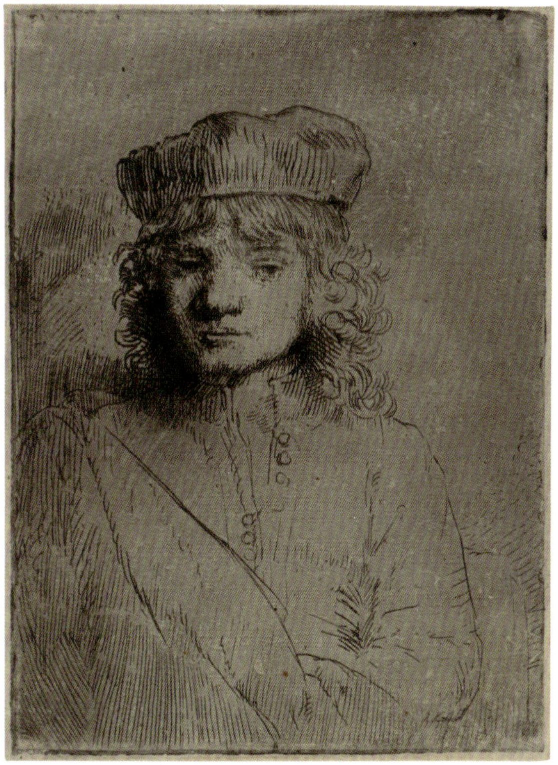

100
The Artist's Son, Titus, about 1656
Etching, 9.9 × 7 cm
Only state
Rijksmuseum, Amsterdam
(RP-P-OB-22)

informal attire – his partly unbuttoned doublet and heavy cloak casually draped over his shoulder – are elements that impart a sense of intimacy to this delicate etching.

Casualness of dress and informal poses are also features of a number of Rembrandt's late commissioned portraits, including his most spectacular one, the *Portrait of Jan Six* (cat. 101), which, according to a verse composed by the sitter, was executed in 1654.[40] Often mistaken by scholars in the past for formal attire, it has been established recently that the sitter's grey knee-length coat and his striking red cloak with gold braid nonchalantly hanging from his left shoulder are typical seventeenth-century riding clothes.[41] Six is shown, therefore, in a moment of leisure, but dressed for a pastime that was the preserve of the elite. Emerging from an impenetrably dark background, the three-quarter-length, life-size figure looks directly into the eyes of the beholder from a slightly elevated position, the shadow cast by his black hat upon his brow and eyes suggesting a serious, thoughtful personality. He tugs distractedly on the gauntlet of one of his riding gloves, rendered with fluid, luscious brushstrokes that brilliantly evoke the suppleness of the leather. The loose application of the paint here and the almost sculptural white cuffs underlines the fleetingness of Six's action, which adds to the portrait's powerful sense of immediacy. The portrait's vivacity and directness afford the viewer an intimate encounter with one of the most effortlessly sophisticated figures of the seventeenth century.

The sitter in the 1667 *Portrait of an Elderly Man* (cat. 102) cuts a similarly nonchalant figure, his hat tipped to one side, his jacket unbuttoned and collar open, its tasselled band strings hanging down on his chest. He is slouched in a chair that hardly seems sturdy enough to carry his weight, his rotund belly protruding out of the picture plane and into the beholder's space. This effect is accentuated by his over-sized hands, the cursory handling of which marvellously suggests their fleshiness,

Detail from *Portrait of Jan Six* (cat. 101)

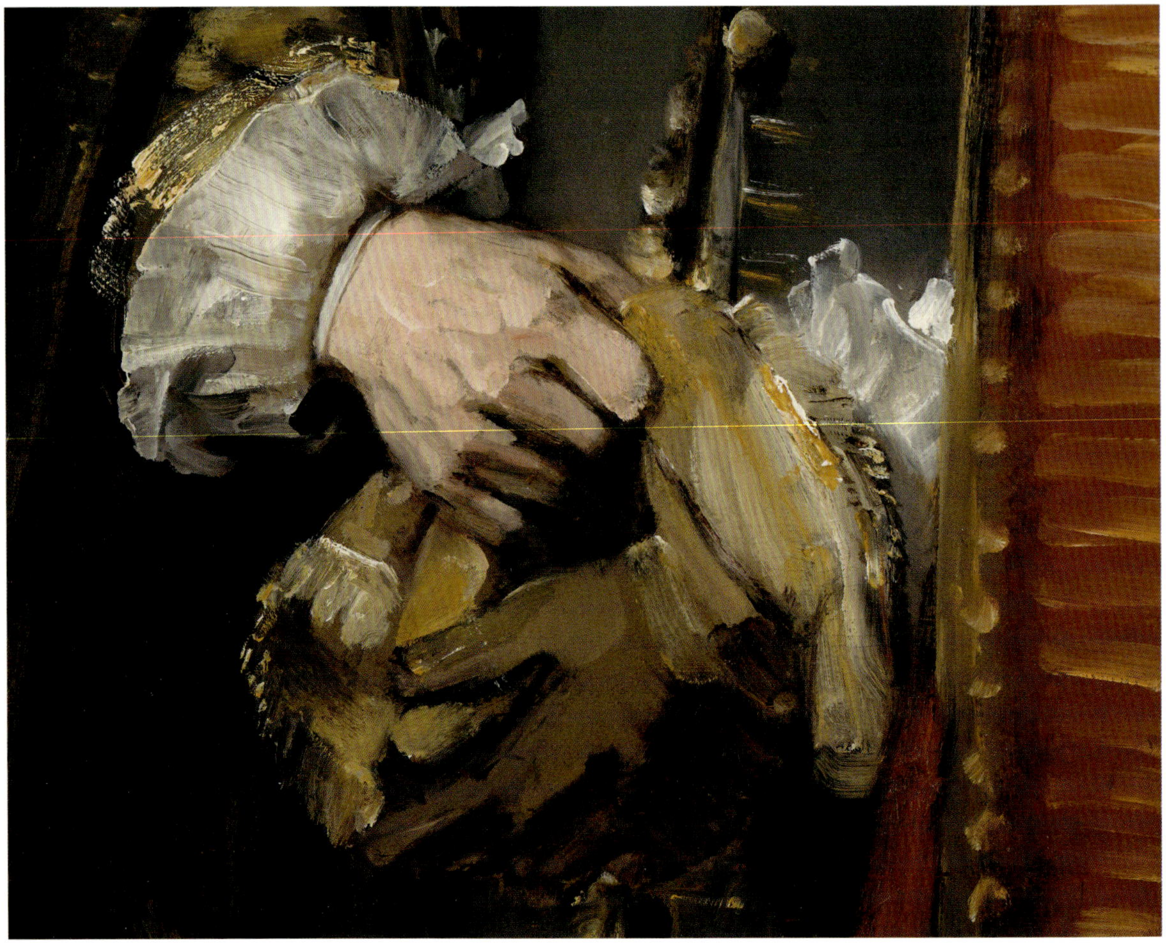

Detail from *Portrait of an Elderly Man* (cat. 102)

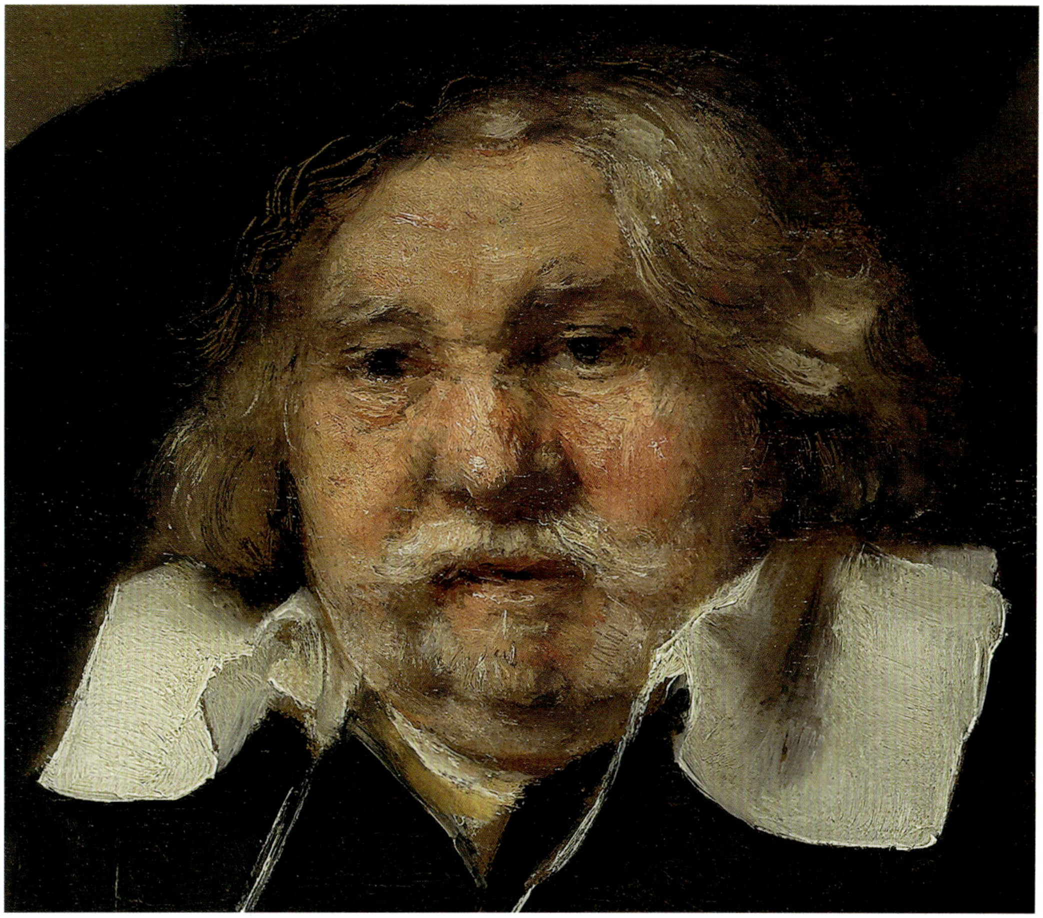

and by the deliberate cropping of the image. The figure's proper left arm and his proper right hand have been cut off, not as the result of the painting having been trimmed at a later date, but intentionally by Rembrandt, who also deliberately limited the amount of space at the top of the composition.[42] The figure's extraordinary presence is further enhanced by the bold and broad execution, which clearly defines the forms and yet remains obstinately legible as individual brushstrokes and scratch marks (the latter in the figure's hair and doublet). The unabashed naturalism of the portrait is also striking: rather than slimming him down a little, making his nose rather less bulbous, ironing out a few of his wrinkles and the crease at the bridge of his nose, and repairing a few of the broken capillaries in his face, Rembrandt offers the sitter up apparently as he was, thereby deliberately turning his back on the distancing effect of idealisation.

Obviously not an official portrait, the informal character of the *Portrait of an Elderly Man* has led scholars to search Rembrandt's own inner circle of intimates for the sitter. The merchant and connoisseur Lodewijck van Ludick has been put forward as the most likely candidate, among other reasons because he was 60 or 61 years old in 1667, an age that seems to match that of the portrayed man.[43] Van Ludick had also been a widower since the year before the date on the portrait, which would explain why it does not have a companion piece. Indeed, the inclination of the sitter's body to his right indicates that a female pendant, which would have hung to the man's left, was never planned. Van Ludick had had dealings with Rembrandt since the 1640s, and in 1666 was recorded living on Rozengracht, the canal where the artist resided from about 1658 until his death.[44] In 1662 Rembrandt had even renewed a promise to paint a portrait of Van Ludick. Taken out of context, these isolated facts would appear to reinforce his candidacy as the sitter in the 1667 portrait, but when the whole story is told, the hypothesis becomes problematic. In 1653 Van Ludick guaranteed a loan of 1,000 guilders made to the artist by Jan Six.[45] Six later transferred the promissory note to a merchant, Gerbrand Ornia (1627–1692), who in 1657 demanded and received payment from Van Ludick, Rembrandt

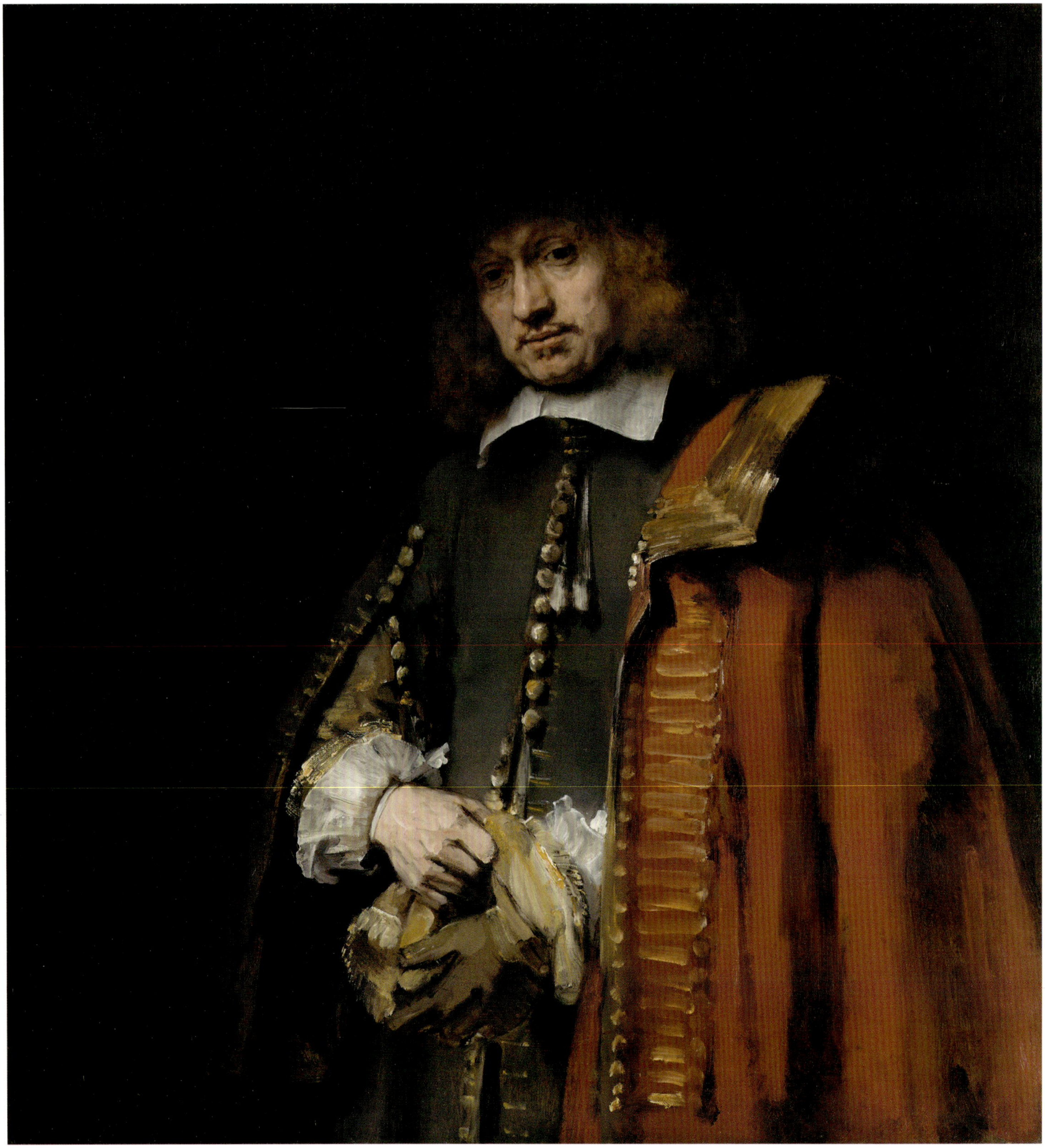

101
Portrait of Jan Six, about 1654
Oil on canvas, 112 × 102 cm
Six Collection, Amsterdam

102
Portrait of an Elderly Man, 1667
Oil on canvas, 81.9 × 67.7 cm
Royal Picture Gallery
Mauritshuis, The Hague

himself not being able to come up with the funds because of his *cessio bonorum*. The portrait Rembrandt was obliged to paint of, or possibly for, Van Ludick (the original wording is vague) appears to have been part of the agreement renegotiated in 1662 to repay the loan that Ornia had taken over from Six. But Van Ludick never received his money from Rembrandt and in 1664 his own financial problems necessitated passing the loan on to Harmen Becker, at a substantial loss. A year later Van Ludick had to sell his house on Warmoesstraat and move to what must have been humbler, rented accommodation in the street where Rembrandt also lived. The questions arise, therefore, of whether the artist would have made good the more than five-year-old promise to portray Van Ludick, to whom he no longer owed money, and whether the merchant would have had enough friendly feelings for the artist in 1667 to commission a portrait from him.

The identity of the sitter in another intimate portrait by Rembrandt, that of the Amsterdam apothecary Abraham Francen, from around 1657 (cats 103–4), stands on firmer ground: it is confirmed by a seventeenth-century inscription on an impression of the etching in the British Museum and was already published in 1700.[46] In the entry on the etching in his 1751 catalogue raisonné of Rembrandt's prints, Edmé-François Gersaint (1694–1750), who probably had the information from his Dutch contacts, tells us of Francen's '*extrême passion*' for prints and how, not being a rich man, he would scrimp on food

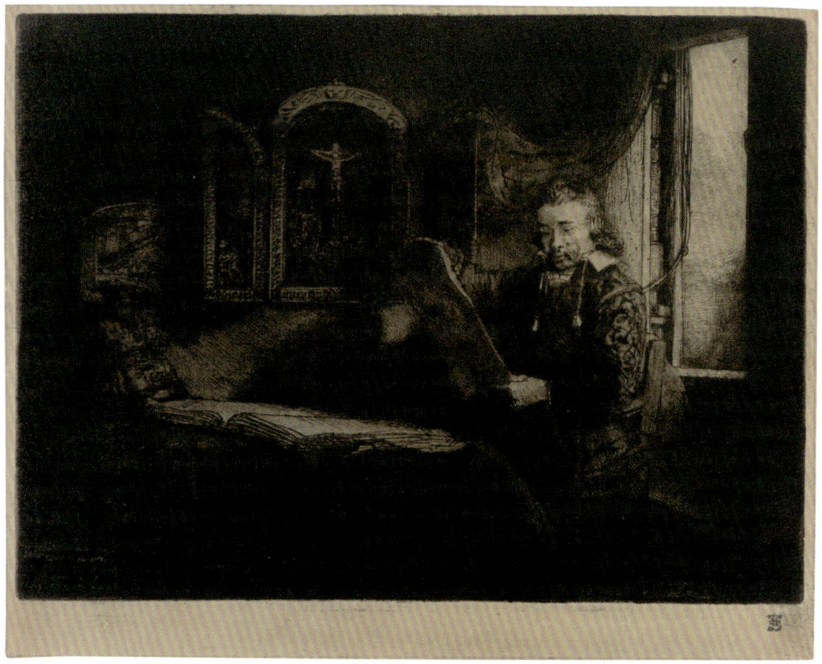

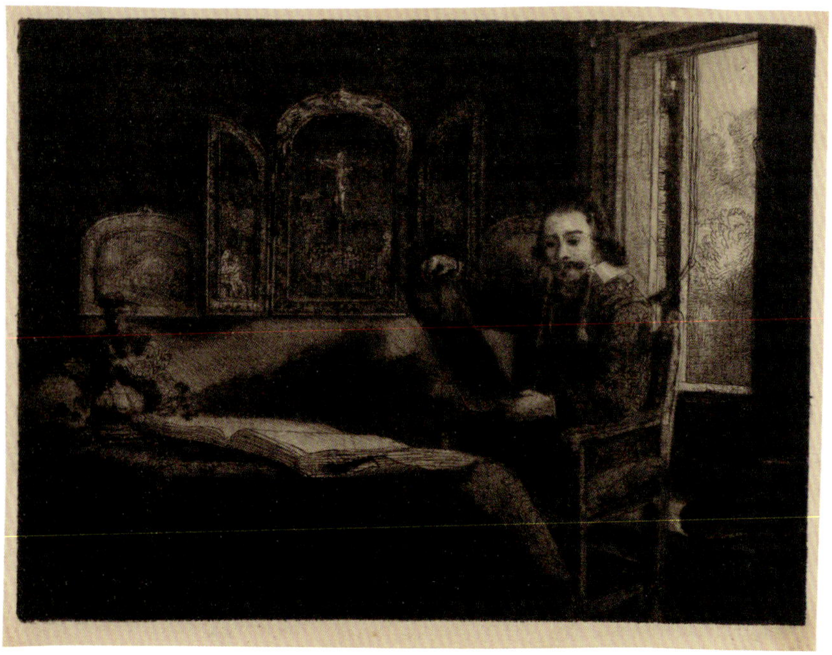

103
Portrait of Abraham Francen, Apothecary, about 1657
Etching, engraving and drypoint, 15.8 × 20.8 cm
Second state of twelve
Rijksmuseum, Amsterdam
(RP-P-1962-34)

104
Portrait of Abraham Francen, Apothecary, about 1657
Etching, engraving and drypoint, 15.8 × 20.8 cm
Sixth state of twelve
Rijksmuseum, Amsterdam
(RP-P-1961-1150)

and drink in order to be able to indulge in his hobby.[47] His first recorded contact with Rembrandt dates to 1653, and they appear to have had a close friendship.[48]

Francen was portrayed by Rembrandt in his art cabinet, thoroughly engrossed in the study of a print or drawing. A large, open album, a Taoist sculpture, a lidded ceramic pot and a skull are displayed on the table before him.[49] His treasures also include a triptych, the central panel of which represents the Crucifixion, hanging on the wall and flanked by one (first and second states), or two (third and fourth states) other paintings of indeterminate subject matter. The intimacy of Francen's deeply shaded study, and the sitter's own interiority, are contrasted with and emphasised by the glimpse of the outside world through the open window. As in the *Portrait of an Elderly Man*, Francen wears an unbuttoned doublet and open collar. In the first two states of the etching the sense of informality is enhanced by the sitter's cloak, which appears to have been casually discarded behind him, and a curtain nonchalantly draped over a wing of the triptych. All told, the portrait etching has much of the character of a genre scene, and has been rightfully compared to the solitary letter readers and writers painted by Johannes Vermeer (1632–1675) and Gerard ter Borch (1617–1681) in the same period.[50]

In theme and composition the portrait of *Abraham Francen, Apothecary* is closely related to Rembrandt's 1647 etched *Portrait of Jan Six in his Study* (fig. 68), and strictly speaking, therefore, the reflective mood of this quiet image cannot be viewed as an innovation of Rembrandt's late period. Nonetheless, the majority of the nine portrait etchings Rembrandt executed between 1651 and the end of his life are imbued in one way or another with the quality of intimacy. For example, in the portrait of Thomas Jacobsz Haringh (cats 45–6) this is a result of the domestic interior setting, veiled in darkness and created exclusively in drypoint, and the almost vulnerable facial expression of the sitter. In the case of the portrait of Johannes Lutma (cats 47–8) this quality comes particularly from the candid portrayal of the 72-year-old silversmith's failing eyesight and the absent gaze of his half-closed eyes.[51] The function of these portrait prints allowed for such an intimate approach; they were made in small editions for distribution among the sitter's circle of friends and acquaintances.[52] That circle in some cases would have included Rembrandt. Francen's friendship with the artist has already been mentioned. Thomas Haringh, who coordinated and acted as the auctioneer of the forced sales of Rembrandt's possessions from the autumn of 1656 to December 1658, was a collector of prints.[53] Another sitter, Dr Arnout Tholinx (cats 43–4), was a son-in-law of Dr Nicolaes Tulp, who commissioned Rembrandt's first group portrait, as well as the brother-in-law of the artist's patron and friend Jan Six.[54] The artist's relationship with some of these men may well have contributed to the intimate nature of their portraits.

Rembrandt's intimate etched portraits, especially that of Jan Six, have been viewed in the context of the increasing popularity of the private study in the homes of seventeenth-century Dutch scholars, teachers, professionals and collectors. While the private study provided a refuge where men could be alone to read, write and quietly reflect, the substantially increased size of urban houses and the concurrent rise in the number of country estates afforded more space for solitary activities and privacy in general.[55] It is tempting to imagine that Rembrandt's own large house on Breestraat would have contributed to the development of intimacy as a defining quality in his work. One thinks of his drawing *Interior with Saskia in Bed* (Institut Néerlandais, Fondation Custodia, Paris) of the early 1640s, for example, in which the artist's first wife is shown sleeping in a box bed in one of the rooms of that house.[56] In addition to the new spaciousness of city dwellings, numerous other aspects of seventeenth-century Dutch life, such as the Protestant encouragement of a personal relationship with God and the so-called 'civilising process' that Dutch society underwent in the second half of the century, form the cultural background to Rembrandt's intimate scenes.[57] But while this background should not be overlooked, we should not minimise Rembrandt's genius in discerning intimacy in Dutch life, and, especially in his late work, giving it pictorial form.

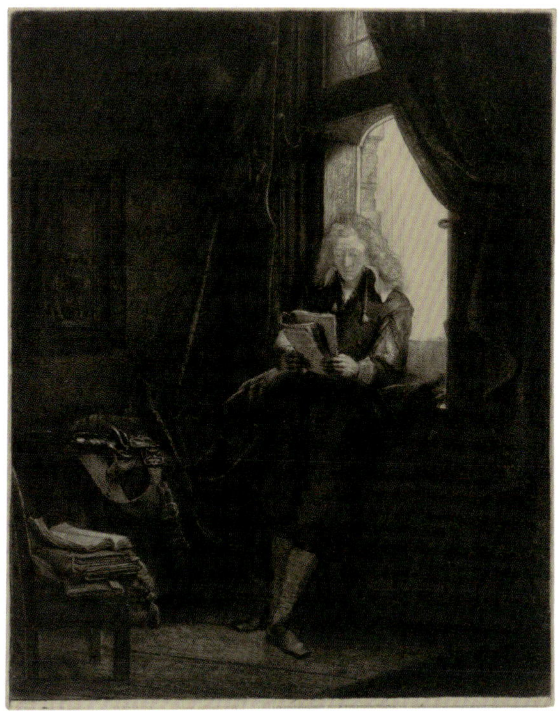

FIG. 68
Portrait of Jan Six in his Study, 1647
Etching, drypoint and burin, 24.6 × 19.1 cm
First state of five
Rijksmuseum, Amsterdam

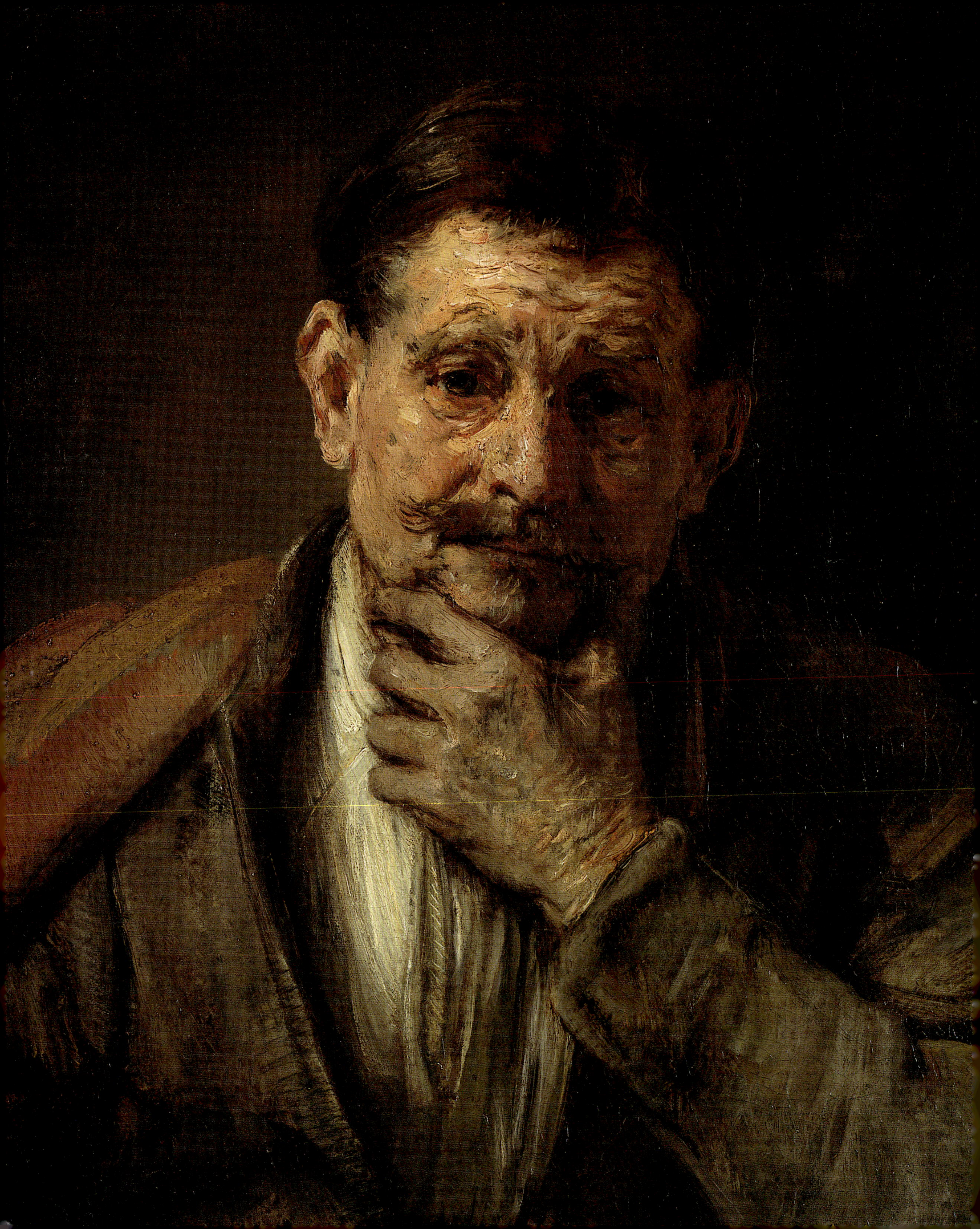

CONTEMPLATION

Jonathan Bikker

IN THE RENAISSANCE and Baroque eras intellectual activity was often associated with melancholy, an imbalance in the four 'humours' that were believed to determine a person's character. The melancholic temperament was associated particularly with creative and learned individuals.[1] As the late sixteenth-century French physician Andreas Laurentius (1558–1609) explained, 'when this humour groweth hot, by the vapours of the blood, it causeth as it were, a kinde of divine ravishment, commonly called *Enthousiasma*, which stirreth men up to plaie the Philisophers, Poets and also to prophesie: in such manner, as it may seeme to containe some divine parts'.[2] In addition to causing *Enthousiasma*, the dry and cold melancholic temperament was closely identified with old age. It is tempting, therefore, to view Rembrandt's preoccupation with contemplative, often elderly men in his late period as a logical by-product of his own senescence.[3] Yet to do so would overlook the fact that he had already depicted brooding philosophers, prophets and apostles during the first decades of his career. With a few exceptions, these early works depict full-length figures on panels of modest dimensions (see, for example, *Jeremiah lamenting the Destruction of Jerusalem*, 1630; Rijksmuseum, Amsterdam). By contrast, the solitary thinkers in his late work are all shown at half or three-quarter length on canvases of significantly greater size, whereby the expressive possibilities of the figures' faces were increased dramatically. Rembrandt's late contemplative figures come in a variety of types, including a philosopher, a poet, a warrior, a monk and several saints; but whatever role they fulfil, they are all shown in the throes of the 'divine ravishment' described by Dr Laurentius.

In the summer of 1654 a crate from Amsterdam arrived in Messina, Sicily, destined for the nobleman Don Antonio Ruffo. It contained the greatest portrait of a philosopher ever made, Rembrandt's *Aristotle with a Bust of Homer* (fig. 69).[4] Although the painting is better documented than most of the artist's late works, it is not known when exactly he received the commission, nor whether he was given any particular instructions. Based on the surviving correspondence concerning other works commissioned by Ruffo, and the confusion about the subject of Rembrandt's painting when it was first recorded in the Sicilian nobleman's accounting books in 1654, it seems safe to assume that the artist himself determined its theme.[5] It has been suggested that Rembrandt simply believed that a subject from Antiquity would be appropriate and cast about his own collection for inspiration, his eyes falling on the busts of Aristotle and Homer.[6] But this is not the first large-scale painting of a scholar in Rembrandt's oeuvre: that distinction belongs to the 1634 *Scholar seated at a Table with Books* (fig. 70), now in Prague, its impressive size suggesting that it may have been a commissioned work.[7] Thus Rembrandt may have been following a familiar pattern in his decision to supply the image of a scholar to his Sicilian patron.

With his hand held to his chin and a furrowed brow, the *Scholar* looks out of the picture plane as if the viewer has interrupted his contemplation of the weighty material contained in the book before him. His identity, if in fact he was intended to have one, is no longer known. Painted nearly twenty years later, Rembrandt's *Aristotle with a Bust of Homer* of 1653 takes the theme much further, not only representing a contemplative thinker but conjuring up the inner workings of the inspired mind. The rather obvious hand gesture denoting thought in the earlier image is not used. Nor does Rembrandt's Aristotle rest his weary head on his

Detail from *The Apostle Bartholomew* (cat. 109)

hand, the traditional gesture signifying melancholy made famous by Dürer's print *Melencholia I*, from which Rembrandt himself frequently drew in his earlier work.[8] Instead, Aristotle rests his right hand on a bust of Homer, his left on his hip and the magnificent chain of honour draped diagonally across his torso. His black apron concentrates our attention on his illuminated face, animated by flickering shadows; these, together with his preoccupied stare, suggest his immense intellect in action. The ethereal lighting cascading into the room from the left, and the intentionally blurred contours of the bust of Homer, Aristotle's proper right sleeve and his right hand, all add to the mysterious atmosphere. The bust – the source of the sage's inspiration – is painted in earth tones with ruddy accents and appears to be made up of an admixture of marble and living flesh. The much smaller medallion bust of a man wearing a helmet suspended from Aristotle's chain of honour has been identified as the great Macedonian king Alexander the Great, who was tutored by the philosopher in his youth.[9] The two men shared a profound admiration for Homer, who had lived some four hundred years before them. Aristotle, for example, makes numerous references in his *Poetics* to Homer, who 'surpassed all others in expression and thought', and to his principal works, the *Iliad* and the *Odyssey*. Alexander is reported to have carried with him at all times a copy of the *Iliad* edited by Aristotle.[10]

Relying heavily on a romanticised reading of the circumstances of Rembrandt's life after he completed *Aristotle with a Bust of Homer*, the most widely accepted interpretation of the painting (put forward by Julius Held) is anecdotal and negative. Aristotle has been

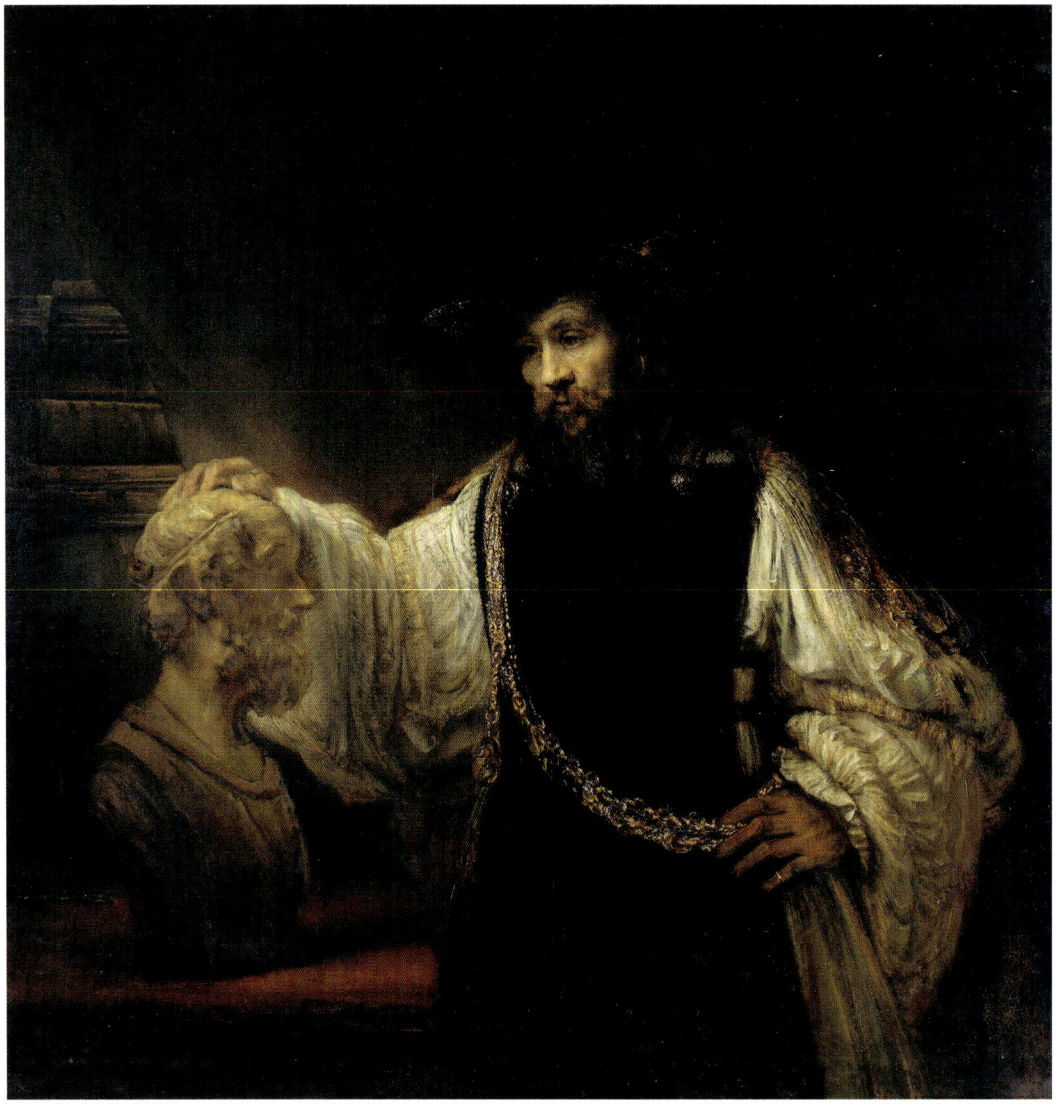

FIG. 69
Aristotle with a Bust of Homer, 1653
Oil on canvas, 143.5 × 136.5 cm
The Metropolitan Museum of Art, New York

described as weighing the enduring values of literature, art and knowledge represented by the bust of Homer against the 'mere secular and transitory awards' symbolised by the sumptuous golden chain he received from his former pupil, Alexander.[11] It seems highly doubtful, however, that Rembrandt's patron Don Antonio Ruffo, himself a nobleman and in a position to bestow such honours, would have understood the chain as anything other than a princely reward for outstanding service.[12] Nor should the painting's sombre mood be construed as a reflection of Aristotle's supposedly dark thoughts. Instead, his dark clothing and surroundings, as well as the shadows cast over his brow and across the sleeve of his shirt, can be viewed in terms of the 'divine ravishment' or '*Enthousiasma*' that, according to Dr Laurentius, was caused when the melancholic humour (black bile) grew hot and induced philosophers to philosophise, poets to versify and prophets to prophesy.

Laurentius was just one of many scholars to subscribe to this popular theoretical explanation of intellectual inspiration, which was first advanced at the end of the fifteenth century by the Florentine humanist philosopher Marsilio Ficino (1433–1499).[13] Significantly, Ficino's theory was predicated on a text attributed to Aristotle, *Problema* XXX from his *Problemata* (*Problems*), a fact acknowledged by Laurentius and other scholars, such as the sixteenth-century German writer and theologian Heinrich Cornelius Agrippa (1486–1535).[14] *Problema* XXX was the first text to link melancholy, hitherto viewed in purely medical terms, to brilliance in philosophy, statesmanship, poetry and the arts. If the black bile was either too cold or too hot it could cause all sorts of

FIG. 70
A Scholar seated at a Table with Books, 1634
Oil on canvas, 145 × 134.9 cm
Národní Galerie, Prague

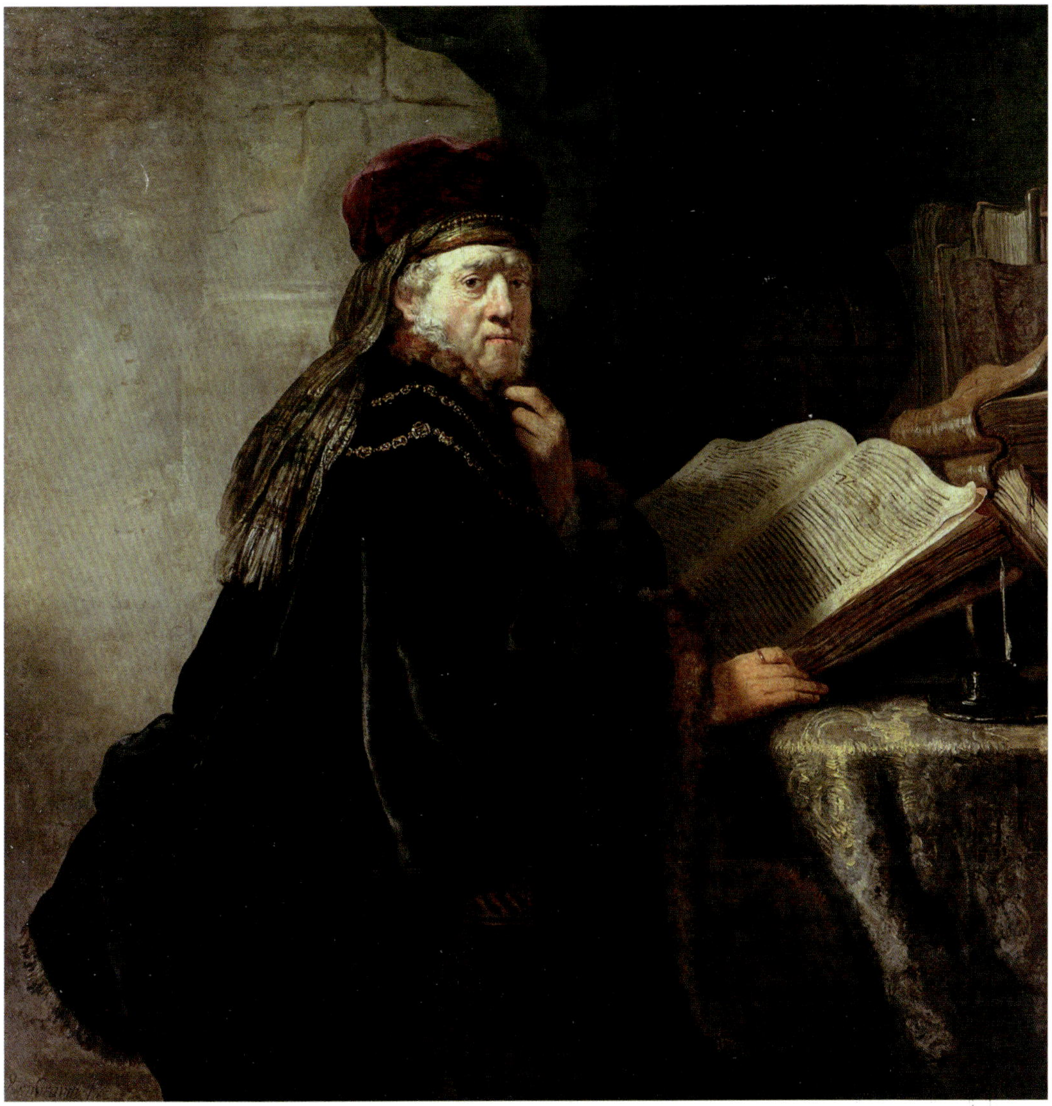

105
The Blind Homer, dictating to a Scribe, about 1663
Pen and brush in brown, white bodycolour, with additions by a later hand in grey and brown wash, 14.8 × 17 cm
Nationalmuseum, Stockholm

ailments, including insanity, but 'Those ... in whom the black bile's excessive heat is relaxed towards a mean, are melancholy, but they are more rational and less eccentric and in many respects superior to others either in culture or in the arts or in statesmanship'.[15] *Aristotle with a Bust of Homer* can be viewed as the pictorial equivalent of Ficino's theory explaining philosophical inspiration. Not only did a text attributed to Aristotle form the basis for this theory, but in Agrippa's version of it, both Homer and Aristotle himself are proffered as examples of geniuses in whom the 'frenzy which leads to wisdom and revelation' was generated by melancholy.[16] Rembrandt may have included the golden chain with the portrait medallion of Alexander the Great in his painting not only to illustrate the philosopher's just rewards, but also because, according to *Problema* XXX, outstanding statesmen as well as poets and philosophers owed their brilliance to the black bile coursing through their bodies at just the right temperature.

The two figures present in effigy in this painting, Alexander the Great and Homer, formed the subjects of two additional paintings Rembrandt sent to Don Antonio Ruffo seven years later, in 1661.[17] The *Alexander* was a finished work but the *Homer* was only half finished: it was sent to Messina for the patron's approval, which it was given. The work was returned to Rembrandt for completion, which according to the date on the fragment preserved in the Mauritshuis (fig. 71), occurred in 1663. It was finally returned to Messina on 20 May 1664. In its present form *Homer* includes only the half-length figure of the blind classical bard, but a preparatory drawing in Stockholm (cat. 105) also shows a young scribe at the lower right. Before it was cut down, presumably after being damaged in a fire,[18] the painting itself must have included not one but two additional figures, as it was recorded in Ruffo's account book as 'Homer, seated, instructing two pupils, half-figure, life-size'.[19]

The entry in Ruffo's account book demonstrates that, as in the case of the *Aristotle*, Ruffo did not fully understand the subject of the *Homer*. The work's genesis makes clear that the 'pupils' were actually scribes writing down Homer's verses as he composed them.[20] Rembrandt derived the subject of his 1663 painting from a sketch he had made in 1652 for Jan Six's *album amicorum* (cat. 25), which in turn was loosely based on the left side of Marcantonio Raimondi's engraving after Raphael, *Apollo and the Muses on Mount Parnassus* (fig. 36).[21] Rembrandt took Raimondi's motif of a scribe recording Homer's

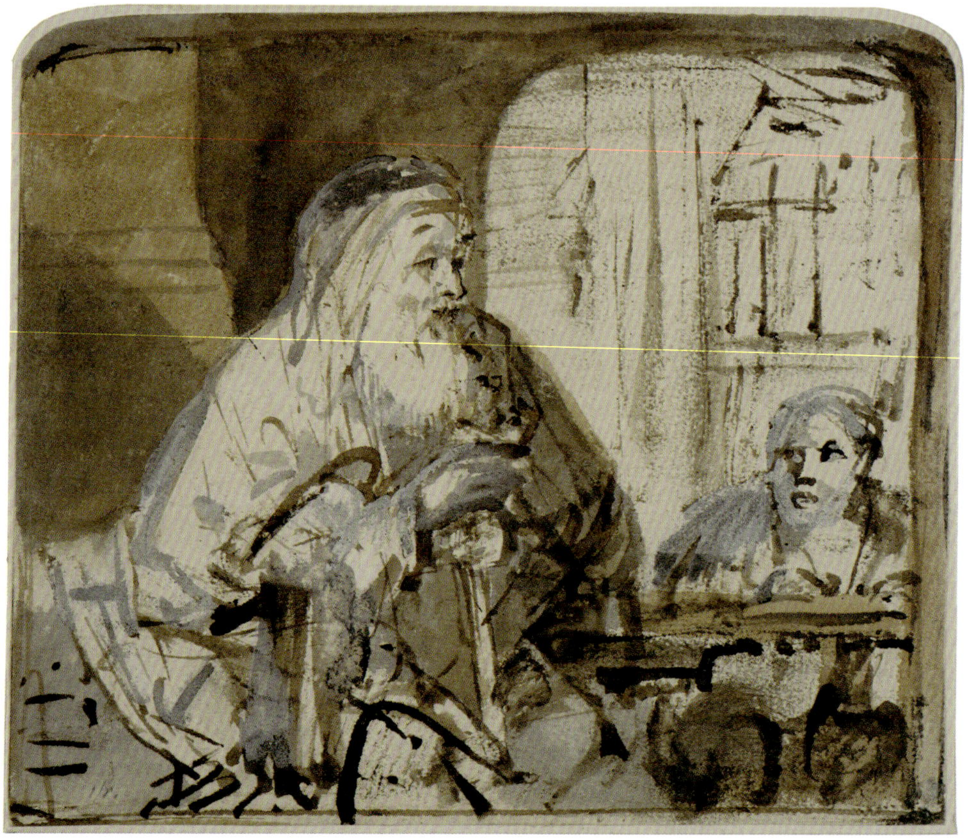

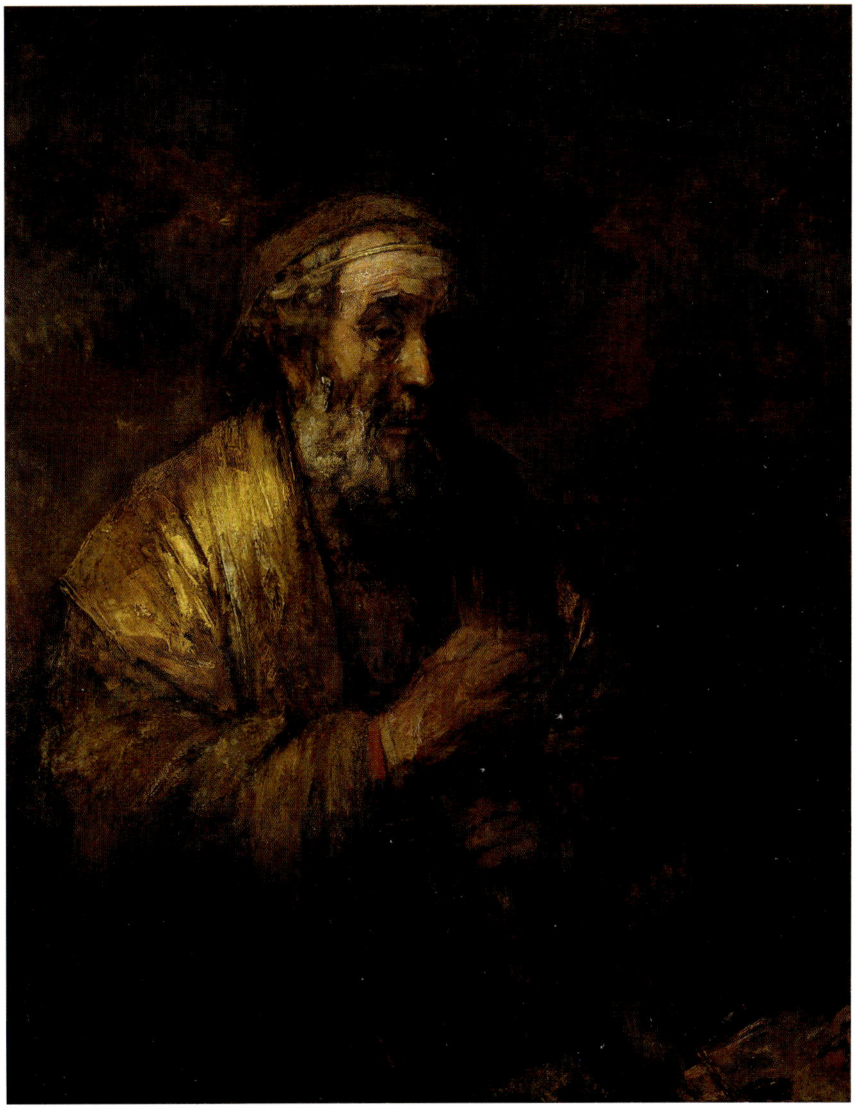

FIG. 71
Homer, 1663
Oil on canvas, 108 × 82.4 cm
Royal Picture Gallery
Mauritshuis, The Hague

recitation of a poem and expanded it into a composition with Homer in the centre, reciting verses before an enthusiastic audience. The scribe sitting to the left of the bard in the engraving was retained, but now sits at the poet's feet on the right side of the composition. For the drawing in Stockholm Rembrandt only kept the poet and the scribe, adding a second scribe to the painting he executed for Ruffo. Homer's pose in the painting, with one hand holding a cane and the other raised in either a declamatory gesture or one that keeps the rhythm of his verse, is also similar to the 1652 sketch. Like the *Aristotle with a Bust of Homer* painted a decade earlier, Rembrandt's *Homer* reciting his verses depicts a genius in a moment of inspired creation. The poet's unseeing eyes reinforce the notion that his verses come from deep inside, while his feeble, almost ingenuous facial expression makes one wonder whether Rembrandt knew Agrippa's assessment of him in his discussion of the effects of the '*humor melancholicus*' on genius: 'We often see uneducated, foolish, irresponsible melancholics (such as Hesiod, Ion, Tynnichus of Chalcis, Homer, and Lucretius are said to have been) suddenly seized by this frenzy, when they change into great poets and invent marvellous and divine songs which they themselves scarcely understand…'.[22]

The painting of *Alexander the Great* sent with the unfinished *Homer* to Messina in 1661 was identified in the past by some scholars as the *Man in Armour* now in Glasgow (cat. 106).[23] However, it has recently come to light that the *Alexander* was still in the Ruffo collection – together with the *Aristotle* and the *Homer* – in 1783,[24] while it is known from the inscription on a reproductive engraving by Johann Gottfried Haid (1710–1776) that the Glasgow painting was in the collection of Sir Joshua Reynolds by 1764. It cannot, therefore, have been the picture owned by the Sicilian nobleman.[25] Nonetheless, the half-length figure probably also represents Alexander the Great. The stylised owl decorating his helmet is the attribute of Pallas Athena, but there can be little doubt that the warrior is a man. By the time of the Italian Renaissance Alexander had been given the attributes of the Greek goddess as the result of the misinterpretation of a common ancient coin which showed her helmeted head in profile on one side and the Macedonian king's name inscribed on the other.[26] The fact that the Glasgow figure is also shown in profile betrays its origin in the numismatic iconography of Alexander the Great – and also lends the picture an Antique flavour. The warrior has a contemplative demeanour, the dark and shadowed aspect of which is made all the more dramatic through contrast with the bright reflections on his breastplate and helmet. Indeed, the figure exemplifies the concentrated

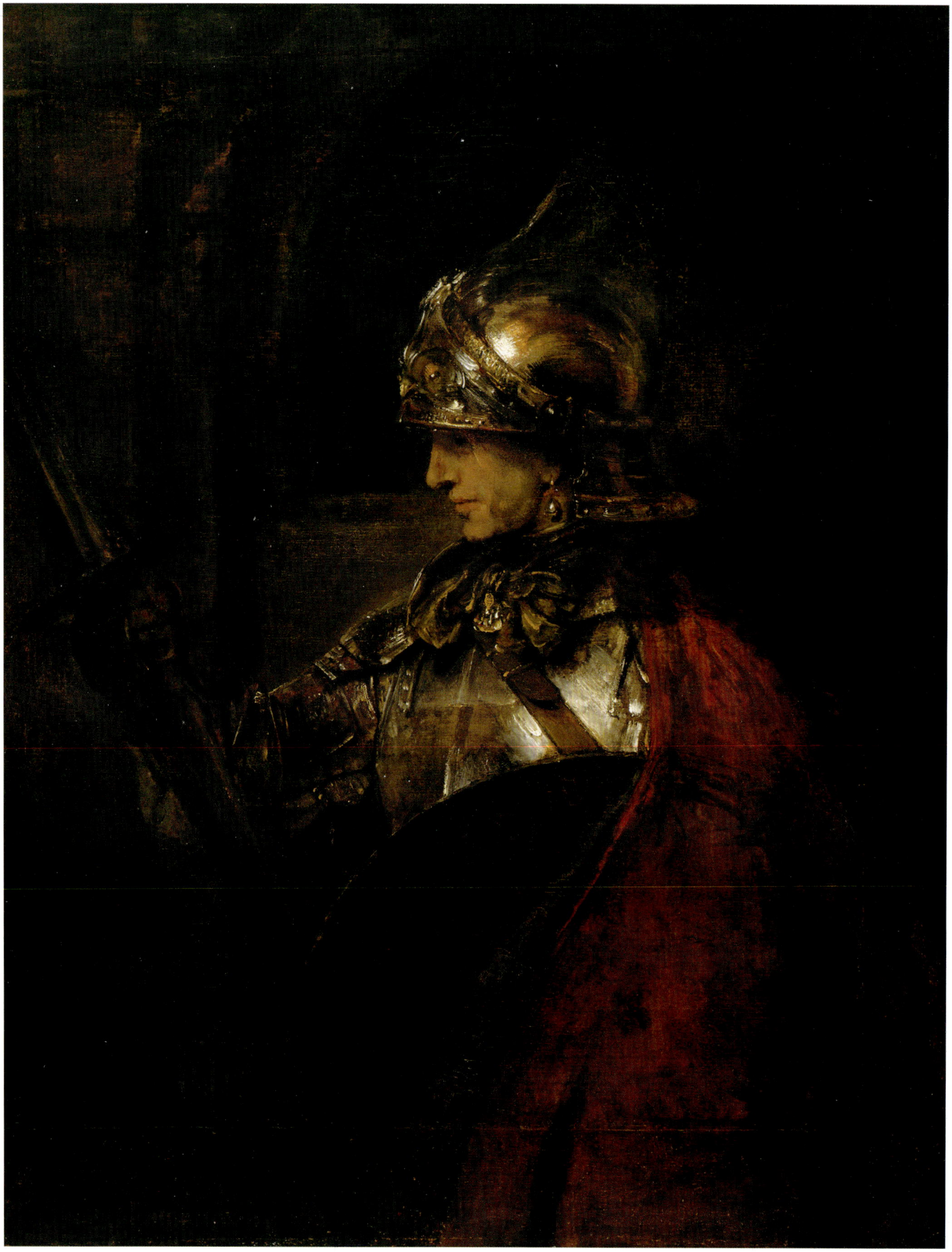

106
A Man in Armour
(Alexander the Great?), 1655
Oil on canvas,
137.4 × 104.4 cm
Kelvingrove Art Gallery and
Museum, Glasgow

107
Titus in Monk's Habit, 1660
Oil on canvas, 79.5 × 67.7 cm
Rijksmuseum, Amsterdam

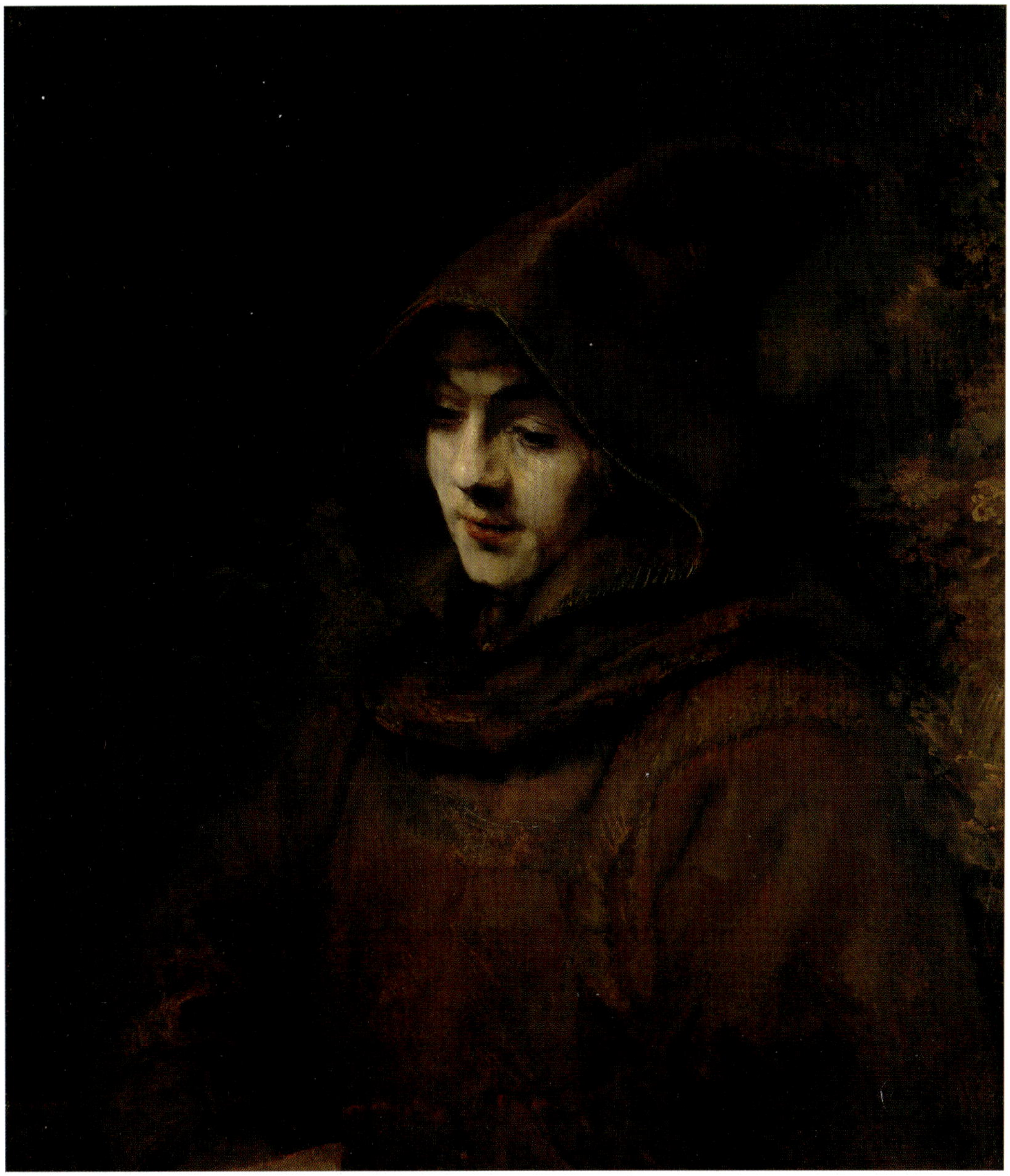

determination of the great military commander who, undefeated in battle, created one of the largest empires of the Ancient world. If the *Alexander* Rembrandt delivered to Ruffo in 1661, now lost, was conceived in a similar, contemplative vein, the commission in its entirety would have formed a trilogy of creative melancholy.[27]

Titus in Monk's Habit (cat. 107), painted in 1660, is the polar opposite of the military persona presented in the Glasgow painting. This figure is as introspective as any of Rembrandt's late scholars, yet he is not an intellectual but rather a mystic, lost to the world in an abyss of inner serenity. He wears the brown habit and peaked cowl of the Franciscan order of the Observants, the crudely stitched, coarse fabric of which underlines the rule of the Friars Minor to serve God in poverty and humility.[28] Against a backdrop of green and brown vegetation, the young man's pale countenance and dark, long-lashed eyes are cast downward in soulful meditation. The visible markings left by the bristles of a broad brush give the face a soft and blurred appearance, suggestive of the monk's trance-like state. At less than half-length, the figure has been deliberately cropped at the bottom to lend the image a palpable sense of immediacy.[29]

An important aspect of the Franciscan way of life is the solitary retreat into nature for prayer and recollection.[30] Even before he officially abandoned his worldly life in

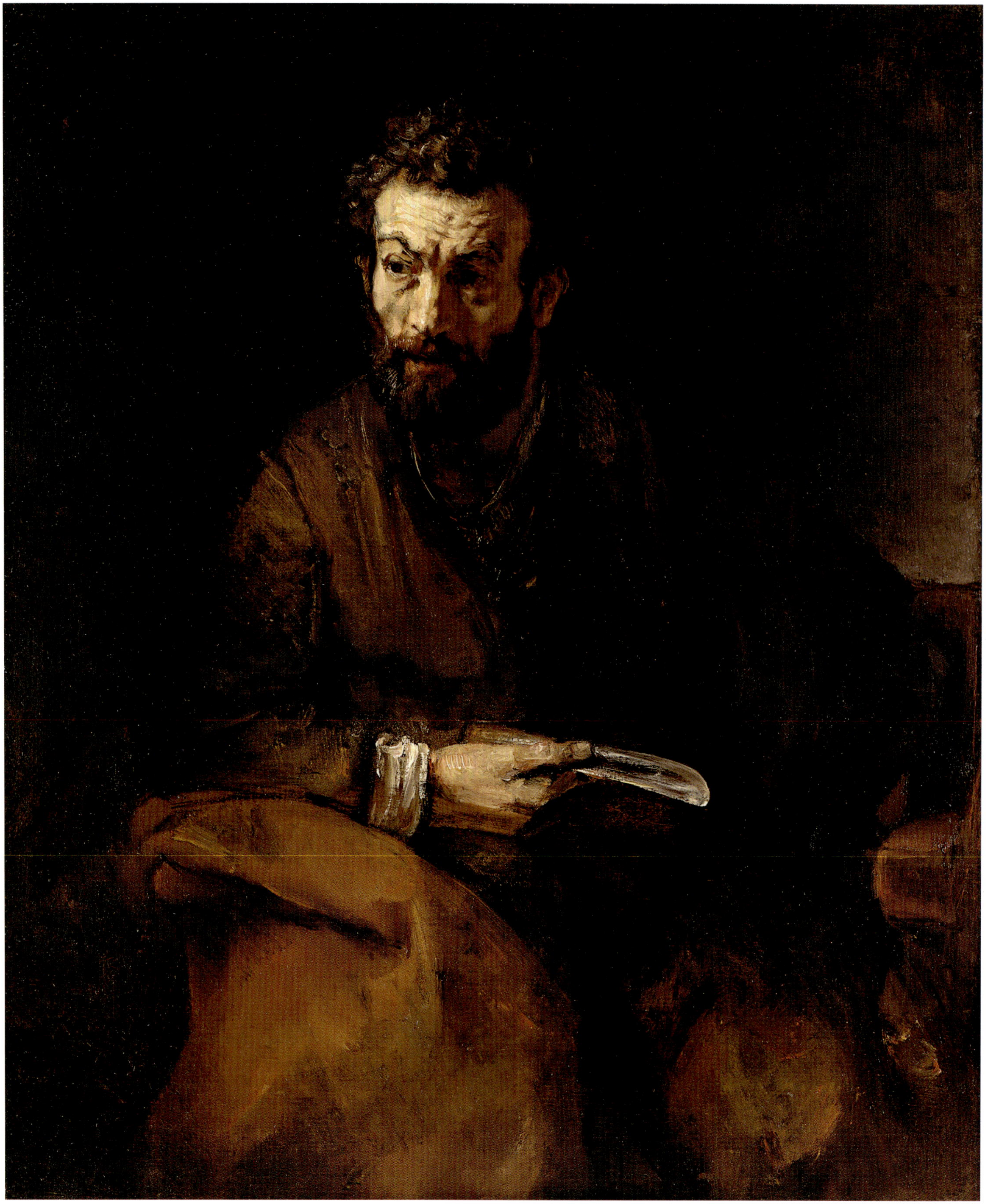

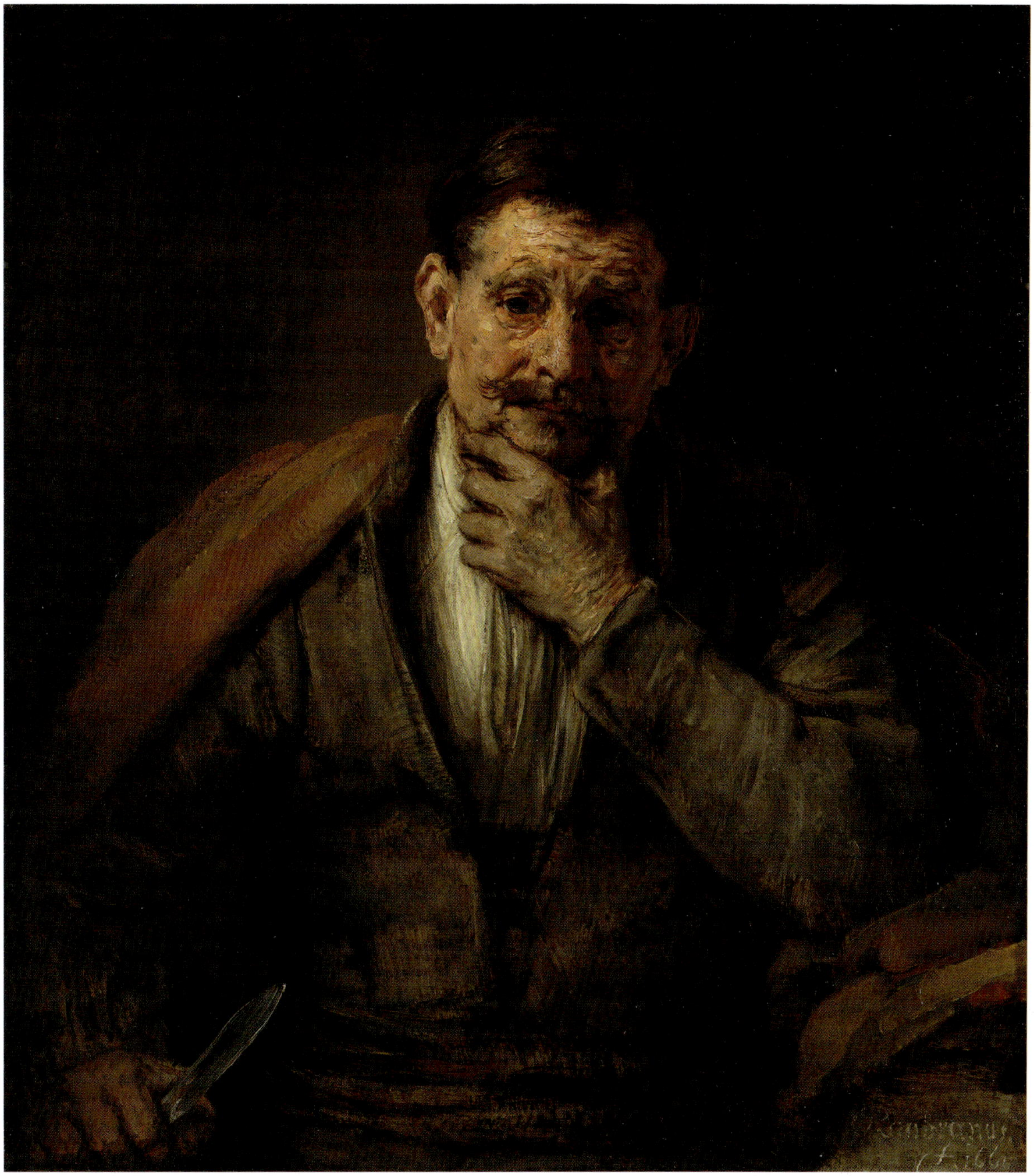

108
The Apostle Bartholomew, 1657
Oil on canvas, 122.7 × 99.7 cm
Timken Museum of Art,
San Diego

109
The Apostle Bartholomew, 1661
Oil on canvas, 86.7 × 75.6 cm
The J. Paul Getty Museum,
Los Angeles

Detail from *Titus in Monk's Habit* (cat. 107)

1206, Saint Francis made periodic retreats in a cave outside Assisi. This seeking out of secluded grottoes and caves reflected not only the Franciscan vow of poverty – as Francis himself said, 'from a hovel one ascends more quickly to heaven than from a palace' – but also the belief that the divine spirit permeated all creation.[31] Saint Francis had a deep love of nature and animals, and, according to an early source, he spoke to the latter 'with a great inner and exterior joy, as if they had been endowed by God with feeling, intelligence, and speech'.[32] It was at the desolate mountain retreat of La Verna in Tuscany in 1224 that, while meditating intensely on the mystery of the cross, Saint Francis received a vision of Christ and had the stigmata impressed upon his body. The moment just prior to this miracle is the subject of a 1657 etching by Rembrandt (cat. 66), in which the forest growth almost subsumes the saint and his constant companion Brother Leo, slumbering in the distance.

It is tempting to connect the younger monk in *Titus in Monk's Habit* with an earlier episode of Francis's imitation of Christ related in the most popular account of the saint's life, the fourteenth-century *Little Flowers of Saint Francis* (*Fioretti di San Francesco*). Around the year 1211, Francis fasted for a period of forty days and forty nights in total isolation on an uninhabited island, just as Christ had done in the desert after his baptism. The *Fioretti* describes how

> Saint Francis being left alone, and there being no dwelling in the island in which he could take shelter, entered into a thick part of the wood all overgrown with brambles and other creeping plants, and forming as it were a kind of hut, there he began to pray and enter into the contemplation of divine things.[33]

The identification of the young monk in Rembrandt's painting as Francis himself has to remain speculative however, as the saint's attributes, the stigmata, are not present.[34]

Although there are no documented portraits of Titus, most scholars agree that he served as the model for this painting.[35] The only writer to disagree considered 'The idea that Rembrandt should have asked a Franciscan monk to let him have a cowl as a masquerade costume for Titus … an altogether modern and sentimental whim'.[36] It seems highly unlikely, however, that Rembrandt made this work for his own pleasure, or as a *portrait historié* of his 19-year-old son. Given the painting's Roman Catholic subject matter, it could have been produced for a foreign client, but this need not be the case either. Despite the fact that Catholicism had been officially forbidden in Amsterdam since 1580, many remained faithful to the Roman Catholic Church. Two of the numerous so-called 'hidden' churches in Amsterdam where they congregated belonged to the Franciscan order. Significantly, both of these churches were located on Sint Anthonisbreestraat, only a stone's throw away from the house where Rembrandt lived between 1639 and 1658.[37] One of the parishioners of those churches may very well have commissioned the painting from him.

Titus in Monk's Habit is only one of a number of single-figure religious paintings Rembrandt executed during the latter part of his career. Quite a number of these works show apostles, the earliest signed and dated example of which is *The Apostle Bartholomew* in San Diego (cat. 108) of 1657. With a furrowed brow, cocked eyebrow and slightly parted lips, the three-quarter-length figure leans forward on his right elbow into the light, as if in animated discussion with someone outside the picture plane. The vigorous champion of Christianity

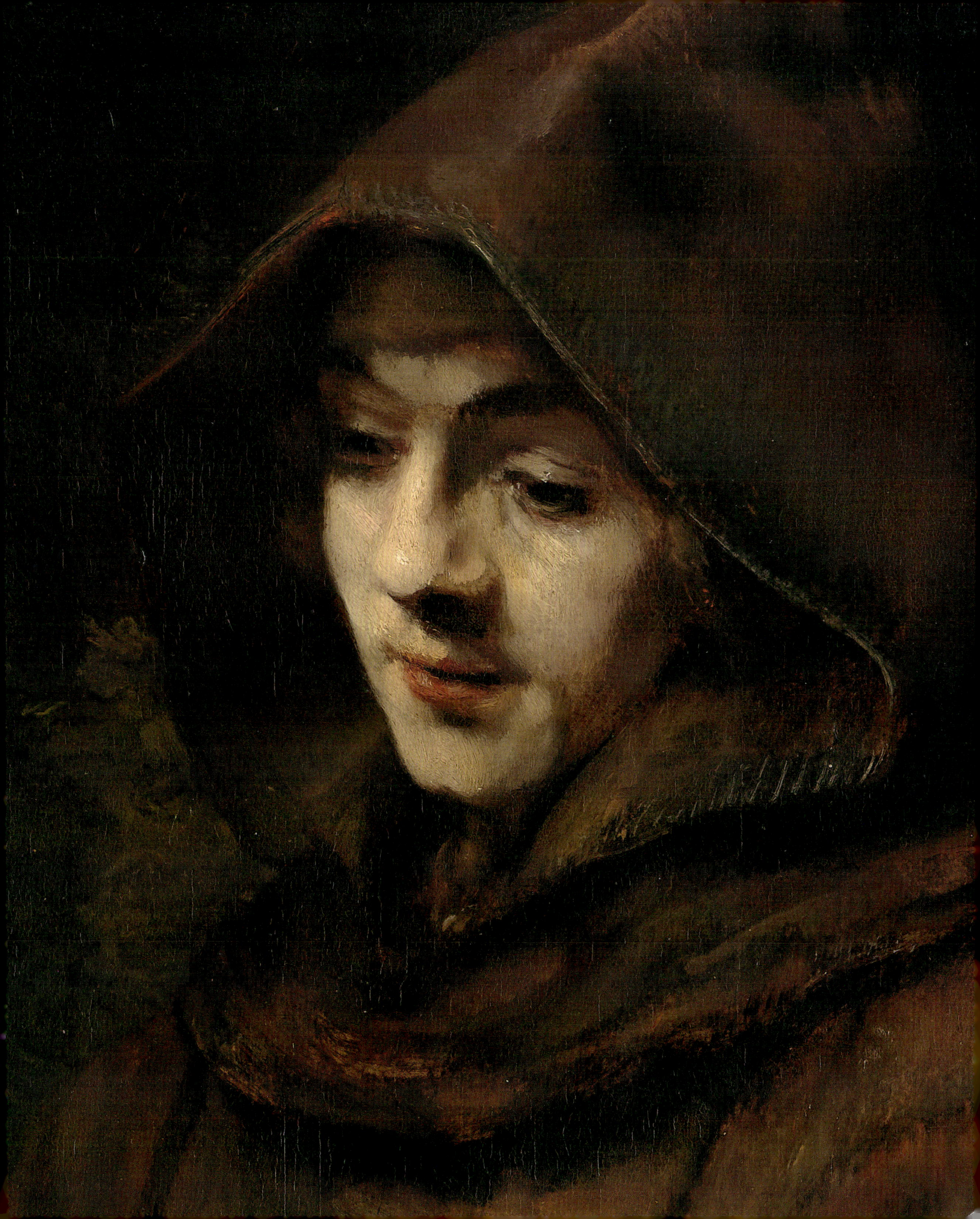

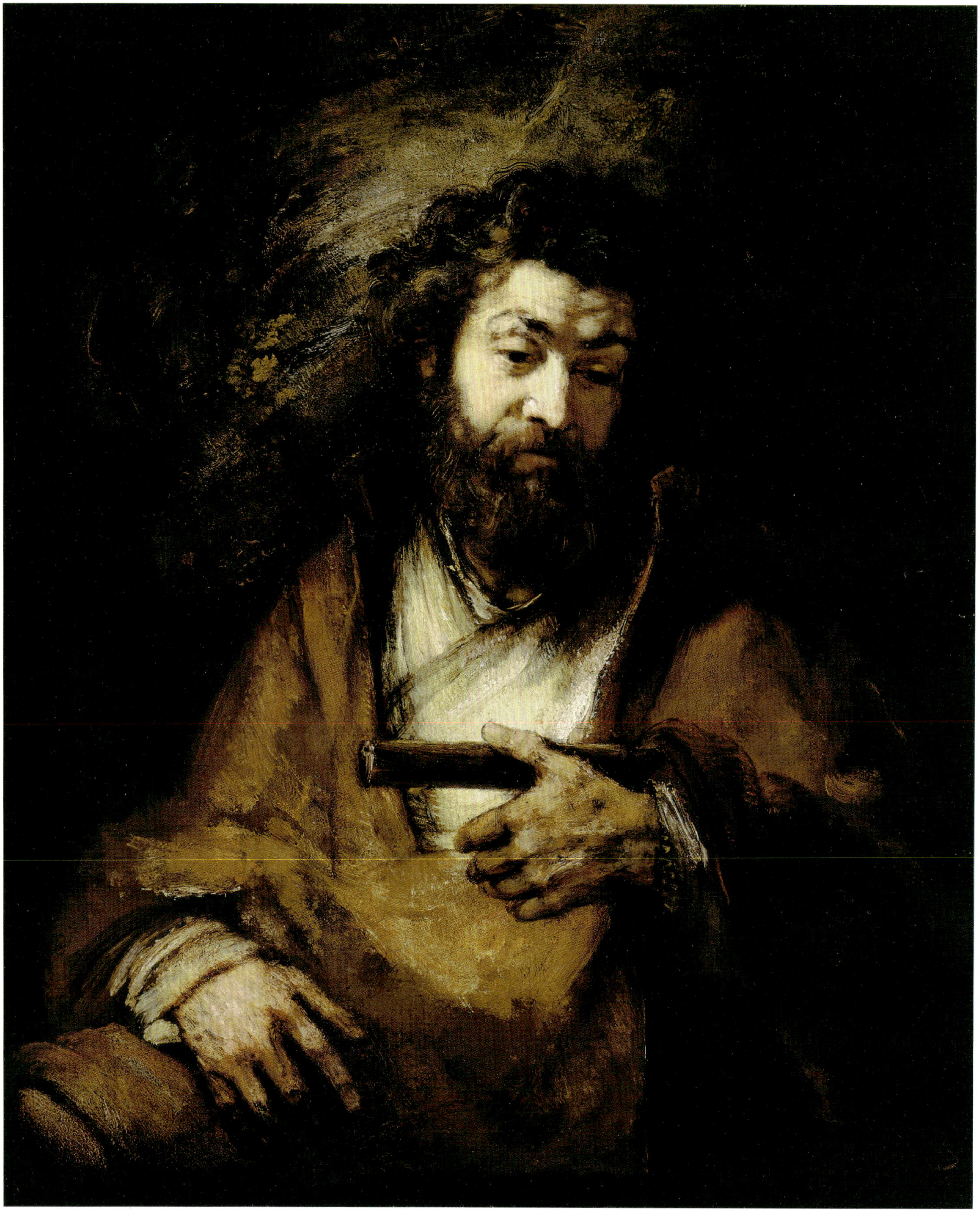

110
The Apostle Simon, 1661
Oil on canvas, 98.3 × 79 cm
Kunsthaus Zürich,
Ruzicka-Stiftung

holds the instrument of his ghastly martyrdom, the knife, with a matter-of-factness that renders it a mere everyday utensil.

Four years later Rembrandt painted another *Apostle Bartholomew* (cat. 109), now in the Getty Museum, but in that work the saint directly engages the viewer. His chin in his left hand and the knife firmly grasped in the other, he ponders his impending death with steadfast fortitude. Alternating short and long, unblended strokes of bulky paint describe the sagging flesh of his face, with its astonishingly realistic drooping jowls and puffy bags under the eyes, as well as the left hand with its greyish pallor of death. The skin of both his face and hand appears almost to be detached from the bones underneath, as if the saint's flaying had already taken place.

Another of the apostles painted in 1661, *The Apostle Simon* in Zurich (cat. 110), conspicuously avoids any direct engagement with the viewer, but the figure is every bit as pensive as the Getty *Apostle Bartholomew*. The thumb of his left hand hooked over the horizontal handle of the cross saw with which he was martyred, Simon looks downward with a slightly squinting gaze redolent of pious resignation.

Although he had portrayed himself in historicising costume on many occasions throughout his career, Rembrandt's first undisputed self portrait in the guise of an historical character and his only one as a biblical figure is the 1661 *Self Portrait as the Apostle Paul* (cat. 111).[38] The hilt of a sword projecting from the saint's cloak alludes to his martyrdom by beheading in AD 69, and possibly to the 'sword of the spirit' mentioned in one of his epistles (Ephesians 6: 17).[39] His other traditional attribute is represented by the manuscript, the back cover of which is folded over in accordance with the 'back-to-front' way in which traditional Hebrew texts are read. The indistinct lettering also appears to be Hebraic rather than Roman, as some scholars have argued.[40] Offered for the viewer's scrutiny, the manuscript is likely meant to be one of the epistles written by the apostle while under house arrest in Rome. This prison setting is indicated by the barred window in the upper right background of the painting. Paul was incarcerated a total of four times, a fact to which he often refers in his letters, sometimes metaphorically by calling himself a 'prisoner of Jesus Christ'.[41] Like the setting, the strong lighting shining down on the apostle from above may also have a symbolic meaning: the concept of light bringing spiritual enlightenment occurs a number of times in the epistles, for example in 2 Corinthians 4: 6: 'For God, who commanded the light to shine out of darkness, hath shined in our hearts, to *give* the light of the knowledge of the glory of God in the face of Jesus Christ.'[42] The intense light focused on Paul's head also recalls the saint's own spiritual enlightenment, namely his conversion on the road to Damascus when 'suddenly there shined round about him a light from heaven: /And he fell to the earth, and heard a voice saying unto him, Saul, Saul, why persecutest thou me?' (Acts 9: 3–4). It may have been in order to accentuate this light that Rembrandt showed himself wearing a turban, an accessory that was not part of the pictorial tradition for the saint – or, indeed, the artist's own earlier depictions of the apostle. Painted wet-in-wet with long, thick, flowing brushstrokes that masterfully evoke the tautly wrapped fabric, the turban is a *tour de force* that may have actually disguised a feature that Rembrandt had in common with the biblical figure: a less than full head of hair.[43] As in the Getty *Apostle Bartholomew*, the saint in the self portrait directly engages the viewer, in this instance with a thoughtful, inquisitive, yet meek expression.

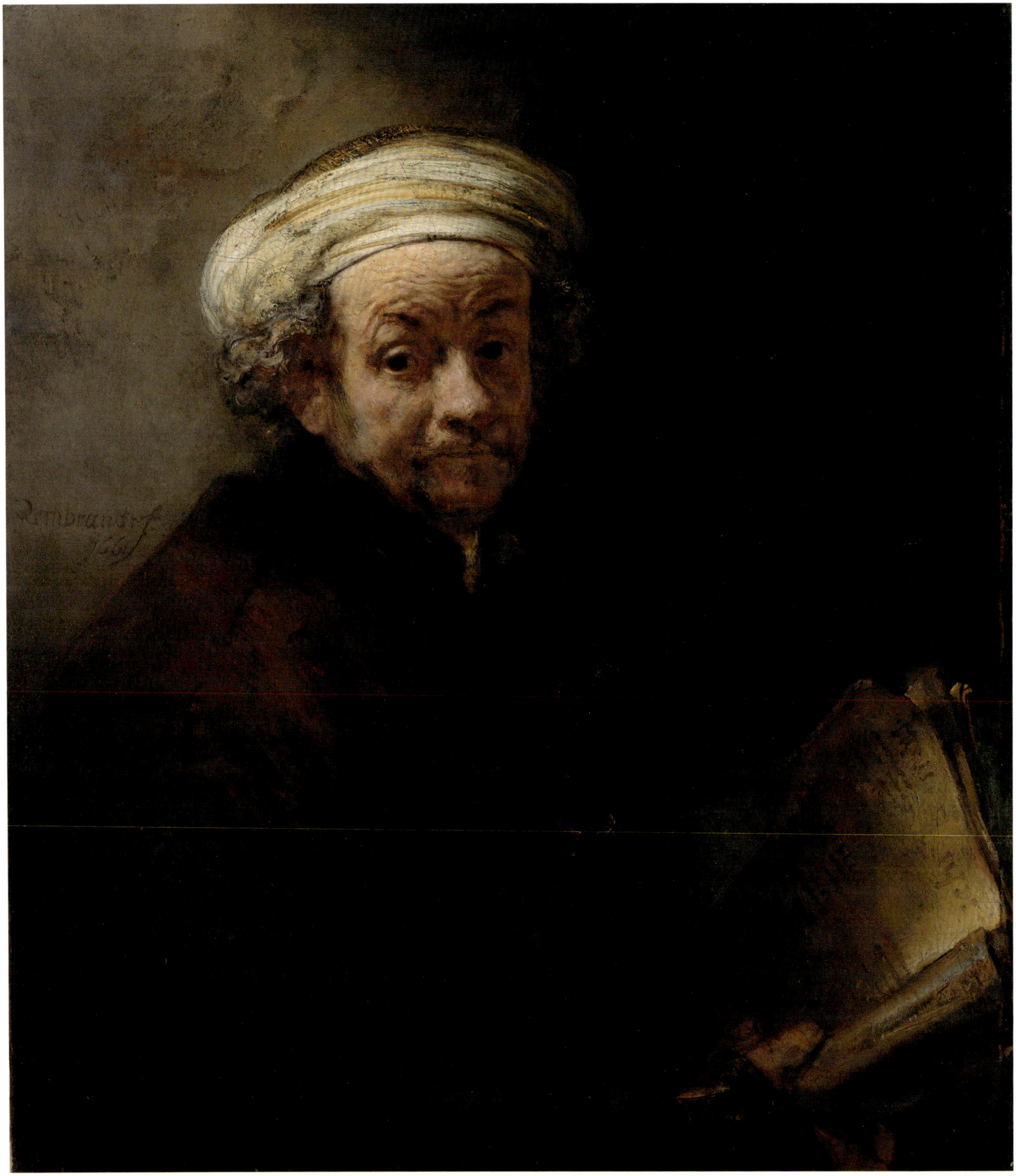

111
Self Portrait as the Apostle Paul, 1661
Oil on canvas, 91 × 77 cm
Rijksmuseum, Amsterdam

Among the apostles from 1661 discussed here, the *Matthew and the Angel* (fig. 72) is the odd man out, as no allusion is made in the painting to the saint's martyrdom. Instead he is shown as one of the four Evangelists. The manuscript of his Gospel lying open before him, he holds a quill in his sinewy right hand and strokes his beard with his left. The latter gesture, which is not unlike that of the Getty *Apostle Bartholomew*, was previously used in the Prague *Scholar seated at a Table with Books* (fig. 70) from 1634; but it can be traced back even further in Rembrandt's oeuvre to his 1627 *Saint Paul in Prison* (Staatsgalerie, Stuttgart).[44] In addition to this gesture, the thickly painted furrows of Matthew's glistening brow and the contracted skin around his eyes suggest the saint's intense concentration on the words of his Gospel. These are being whispered into his ear by an angel, whose hand gently rests on the Evangelist's shoulder. A 1656 composition (fig. 73) by Barent Fabritius (1624–1673), an artist from Rembrandt's circle, probably provided the inspiration for this tender motif.[45] Unlike this possible prototype, however, Rembrandt's angel has neither wings nor a halo, which, together with the unabashed coarseness of Matthew's features, gives his scene a more naturalistic appearance. Rembrandt's flesh-and-blood angel appears real to the viewer, but not to Matthew, who – unlike Fabritius's Matthew – is completely unaware of his presence. The incomparable poignancy of Rembrandt's depiction derives from the fact that while the saint believes he is listening to truths coming from within himself, the viewer realises that he is listening directly to the word of the Lord by way of his messenger, the very real angel whispering into his ear.

A nagging question concerning the apostles painted by Rembrandt in 1661 is whether they were conceived as independent works or as a series, perhaps, considering their number, one that was never completed.[46] The most recent proposal contends that the Getty *Apostle Bartholomew*, the Zurich *Apostle Simon*, the Rijksmuseum *Self Portrait as the Apostle Paul* and the Louvre *Matthew and the Angel* were conceived as a series, together with a *Saint James Major* now in a private collection and *Christ with a Pilgrim's Staff* in the Metropolitan Museum of Art, which has also been interpreted as a depiction of the apostle James the Less.[47] Part of the argument is that a framing device was used for all six paintings, scratched lines in the case of the Rijksmuseum painting and painted black borders in the case of the other five works.[48] It has also been claimed that the size of the images within these borders all correspond, and that all six works were executed in the same style.[49] However, the case is far less cut and dried than this proposal suggests. For example, examination of the Getty painting has revealed that it does not in fact have a painted black border.[50] Moreover, the use of such framing lines is not enough in itself to prove that the other apostles painted in 1661 belong to a series, as Rembrandt also used this device in his 1669 *Self Portrait* in the Mauritshuis (cat. 4).[51] There are also considerable discrepancies in both the sizes of the paintings and the sizes of the images within the painted borders (where they are in fact present), which one would not expect to find in pictures conceived as part of a series executed at the same time.[52] It should also be pointed out that the attribution to Rembrandt himself of the *Christ with a Pilgrim's Staff* in New York is not universally accepted.[53] However, questions of attribution cannot be used as evidence against the series hypothesis, as the supposed series could have been a collaborative studio effort. A more important question is whether the six works have the iconographic unity required of a series. The identification of the figure in the

FIG. 72
Matthew and the Angel, 1661
Oil on canvas, 96 × 81 cm
Musée du Louvre, Paris

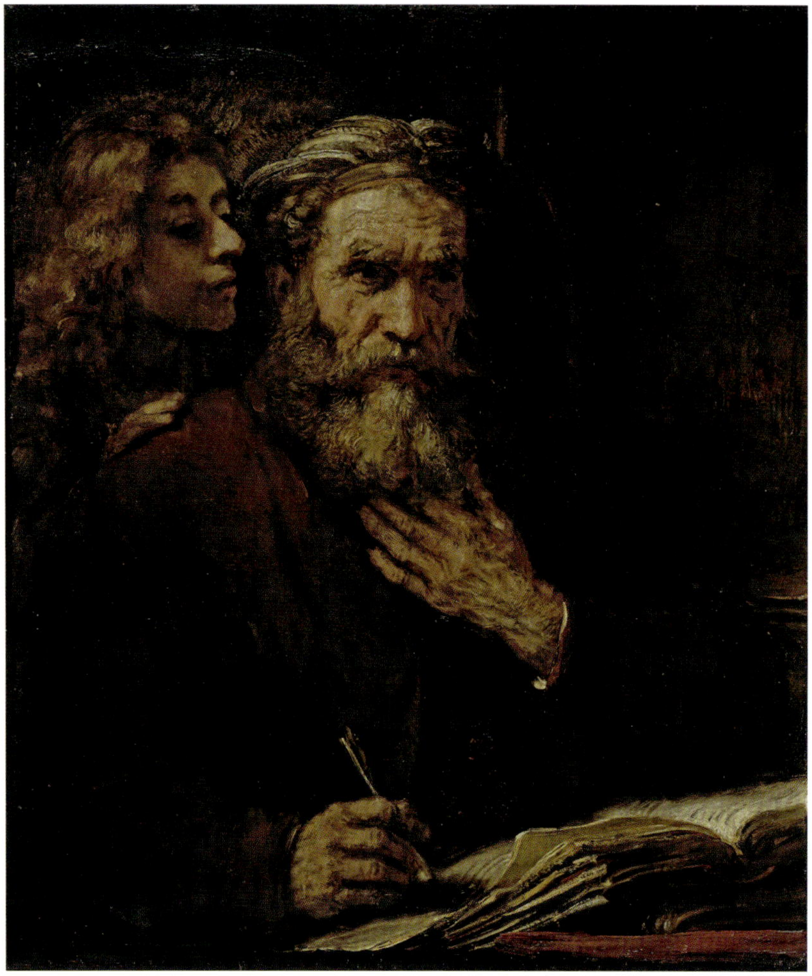

New York painting as Saint James the Less, instead of Christ, is not convincing; and, as already noted above, Saint Matthew is depicted in the Louvre picture in his role as the Evangelist writing his Gospel, whereas in other series of the apostles he is shown with the instrument of his martyrdom.[54] It also seems unlikely that Rembrandt, master of the expressive gesture, would have used almost the same pose of a hand held to the chin in two paintings in the same series – the Getty *Bartholomew* and the *Matthew* in the Louvre.

Unfortunately there is no information on the early provenances of most of these paintings that would shed light on the question of whether or not they were conceived as a set. The *Self Portrait as the Apostle Paul* is the only depiction of an apostle or evangelist by Rembrandt and his circle from this late period that can be traced back to a seventeenth-century collection. This painting has been linked to a description in the 1696 posthumous inventory of the French banker, merchant, collector and art dealer Everhard Jabach: 'Portrait of Rembrandt, with a white cloth around his head, half-length figure large as life, by himself'.[55] Hitherto unpublished evidence that the entry does in fact refer to the *Self Portrait as the Apostle Paul* can be found on the back of the stretcher, where the painted number '123' appears. This was the number of the painting in Jabach's inventory.[56] Although not documented, the possibility exists that Jabach was the original owner of this painting: he had extensive contacts in Amsterdam and important ties to artistic circles there,[57] and could easily have met Rembrandt on a number of occasions, perhaps through the art dealer Gerrit Uylenburgh.[58]

It has been speculated that Rembrandt's late apostle paintings were executed for a Catholic or Mennonite client.[59] Certainly, given the Calvinist ban on images of the saints in houses of worship, Rembrandt's apostles would not have been exhibited in a Reformed church. Private consumption, however, was another matter,

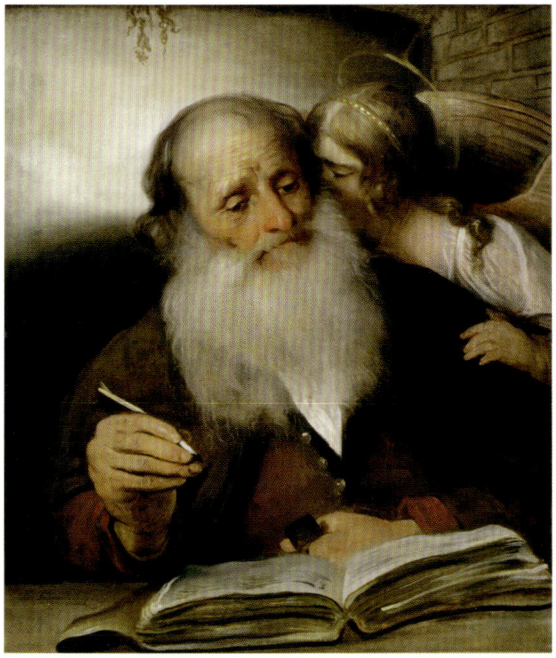

FIG. 73
BARENT FABRITIUS
(1624–1673)
Matthew and the Angel, 1656
Oil on canvas, 76.9 × 63.9 cm
The Montreal Museum of Fine Arts, Montreal.
Gift of Mr and Mrs Michal Hornstein in honour of Frederik J. Duparc

and individual paintings of apostles are mentioned in a number of seventeenth-century probate inventories of adherents of the Reformed Church, including some in Rembrandt's milieu. For example, Jacob Trip (1604–1677), the son of Rembrandt's patrons Jacob Trip and Margaretha de Geer (cats 39–40), owned a painting of the apostle Paul by an unspecified artist.[60]

While loathing the widespread idolatry of the saints and rejecting the role they had been given by the Catholic Church as intermediaries between man and God, Protestants of all denominations revered the apostles as important role models. The Reformers sought a return to the purity of the primitive church, based on the teachings of Christ and the apostles. The most important Protestant doctrine, justification by faith alone (*Sola Fide*), was formulated on the basis of Saint Paul's epistles.[61] For Martin Luther this doctrine, which held that man is saved not by his own righteous actions but by faith in Christ, was the chief article of Christianity. As a Lutheran, Jabach, if he was indeed the original owner of the *Self Portrait as the Apostle Paul*, would have appreciated the significance of this saint as the authority upon which his faith was founded. John Calvin was also a proponent of the *Sola Fide* doctrine, and pointed out that Paul's own conversion exemplified grace received independently of merit. It was also their deaths by martyrdom that made the apostles important role models for seventeenth-century Dutch Protestants.[62] In the certainty of their future salvation and the realisation that they were surrendering themselves as sacrifices to God, the apostles were completely prepared and willing to suffer horrific fates. Not only was their faith unshakable even in the face of death, but their martyrdoms were also viewed as 'proof' of the truth of their Evangelical teachings.

One of the most popular books in the Northern Netherlands in the seventeenth century was *The History and Death of the Pious Martyrs* (*De geschiedenis ende den doodt der vromer martelaren*) by Adriaen van Haemstede (about 1525–1562/3), which was first published in 1559 and went through a number of updated editions until well into the nineteenth century.[63] Van Haemstede's book begins with the lives and deaths of Jesus and the apostles and ends with those of the Protestant martyrs of the sixteenth century. Other Reformed martyrologies were written in the seventeenth century, attesting to the importance of this genre of Protestant literature in general.[64] Leading Calvinist thinkers such as Josephus Justus Scaliger (1540–1609) and Gijsbertus Voetius (1589–1676) encouraged the faithful to read the lives of the saints presented in these works and to follow the apostles' example.

The role of the apostles as exemplars of faith in Protestant culture may explain why Rembrandt depicted his martyred saints as unidealised, real people, who contemplate their fates with steadfast equanimity. Indeed, they are the very opposite of the heroic patriarchs, endowed with powerful physiques and superior wisdom, envisioned by Peter Paul Rubens in his Counter-Reformation series of the apostles painted around 1610–12 (fig. 74). Significantly, a number of scholars have voiced the opinion that two of Rembrandt's late apostles were conceived as *portraits historiés*. While the *Elderly Man as Saint Paul* (fig. 75) from around 1659 does in fact have a pronounced portrait-like quality, one wonders whether it was Rembrandt's refusal to translate his models into types that has deceived some modern viewers into believing that the Getty *Apostle Bartholomew* also falls into this category.[65]

If the *Elderly Man as Saint Paul* was conceived as a *portrait historié*, the man who commissioned and sat for it no doubt felt a powerful connection to the saint. The *Self Portrait as the Apostle Paul* has also often been read as a testament of Rembrandt's own deeply personal identification with the biblical figure. It has been claimed, for example, that by portraying himself as Paul, Rembrandt acknowledged the imperfection of his own life and his dependence on God's mercy, or that the artist viewed his role as 'explicator of the Bible as akin to Paul's searching mission'.[66] Rembrandt's legal difficulties – the Church's reprimand of Hendrickje Stoffels for her illegitimate pregnancy in 1654 and the artist's bankruptcy in 1656 – as well as his posthumous reputation as 'the first heretic of painting' have also been put forward as reasons for the artist's supposed personal identification with the apostle who placed the grace of God above the law.[67]

However, while such highly personal psychological interpretations cannot be proven one way or the other – and seem to fit the age of Romanticism better than the seventeenth century – they also turn a blind eye to the probable function of Rembrandt's *Self Portrait as the Apostle Paul*.[68] Unlike the *portrait historié*, which was most often exhibited in the sitter's home, the self portrait *historié* was more likely to be executed for sale or to be given away rather than hanging in the house of the portrayed artist. Significantly, the inventory of Rembrandt's stock drawn up in 1656 does not mention a single self portrait, although he executed more than any artist before him.[69] Whether the *Self Portrait as the Apostle Paul* was painted on speculation or as a commissioned work, the question arises of whether the patron would have had the intimate knowledge of Rembrandt's life and mind necessary to divine the psychological affinity he may have had with the saint. Would the patron even have had an interest in Rembrandt's personal life and psyche? Furthermore, while for the modern art historian Rembrandt may hold more significance than Saint Paul, it is doubtful that this was the case for the artist's seventeenth-century client. Therefore, instead of asking the question of what using his own likeness here says

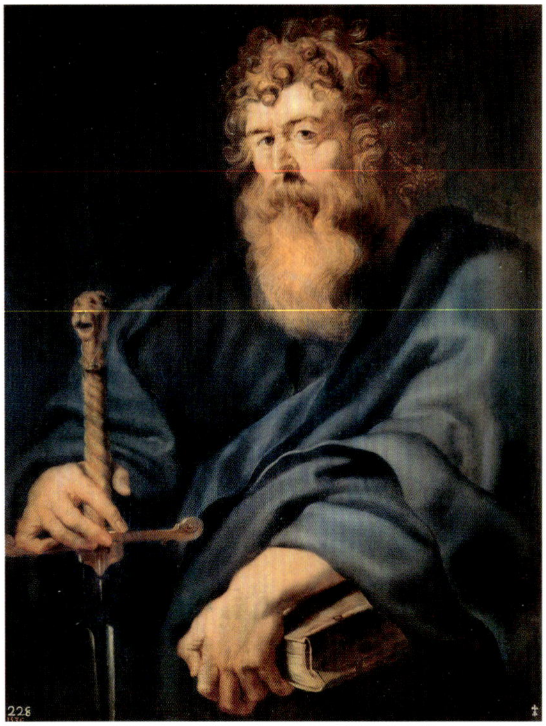

FIG. 74
PETER PAUL RUBENS
(1577–1640)
The Apostle Paul, about 1610–12
Oil on panel, 108 × 84 cm
Museo del Prado, Madrid

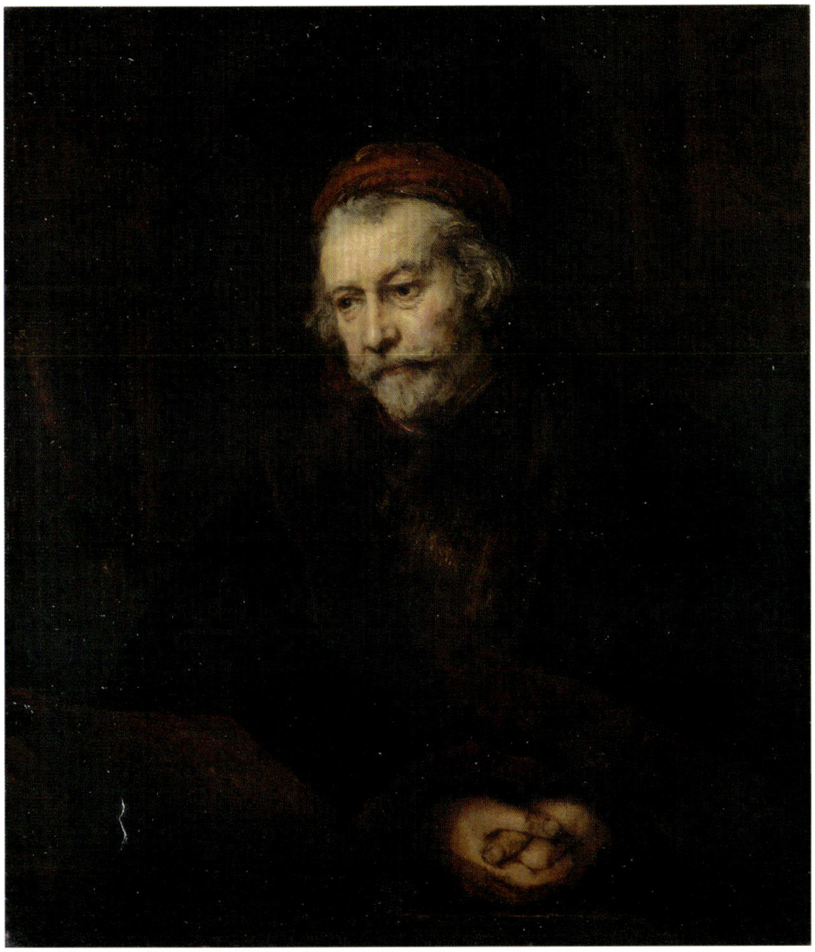

FIG. 75
An Elderly Man as Saint Paul, about 1659
Oil on canvas, 102 × 85.5 cm
The National Gallery, London

about Rembrandt, the question of what it says about Saint Paul should, perhaps, be raised.

The alternative suggestions, that Rembrandt simply used himself as a model, or was offering his patron not only a portrait of a celebrated artist but also a specimen of the reason for his fame, also seem to fall short of the mark.[70] His motivation for using his own likeness should, perhaps, be considered in the light of the apostles' importance as role models for the Protestant faithful. By taking on the role of Saint Paul, Rembrandt suggests that he is committed to following the saint's example; because the artist is a surrogate for the viewer, we are encouraged to do the same. With his quizzical expression Paul seems to be asking the viewer to accept him as a role model, for as Paul himself said, 'Be ye followers of me, even as I also [am] of Christ' (1 Corinthians 11: 1). The function of Rembrandt's likeness in this painting may be similar to that of the artist's insertion of his own likeness in *The raising of the Cross* (Bayerische Staatsgemäldesammlungen, Alte Pinakothek, Munich) of around 1633.[71] Commissioned by Constantijn Huygens for Stadtholder Frederik Hendrik, there can be little doubt that the work's original audience would have recognised Rembrandt's features in the figure wearing a beret at the centre of the composition. By actively participating in the elevation of the cross, Rembrandt makes plain his own responsibility as a sinner for Christ's death.[72] But, as was most likely the case with his *Self Portrait as the Apostle Paul*, the artist did not paint this work for his own pleasure, and self-castigation is not the reason for assigning himself this culpatory role. Rembrandt's own convictions and beliefs are of no importance: what is important is that the viewer forms a personal engagement with the scene. His self portrait, whether in *The raising of the Cross* or as the apostle Paul, is only the vehicle through which this engagement is realised. As such, it is a brilliant device that can be seen as the culmination of his preoccupation with the representation of contemplation; not only did he paint the intangible thought processes of his figures, he summoned up those of his audience as well.

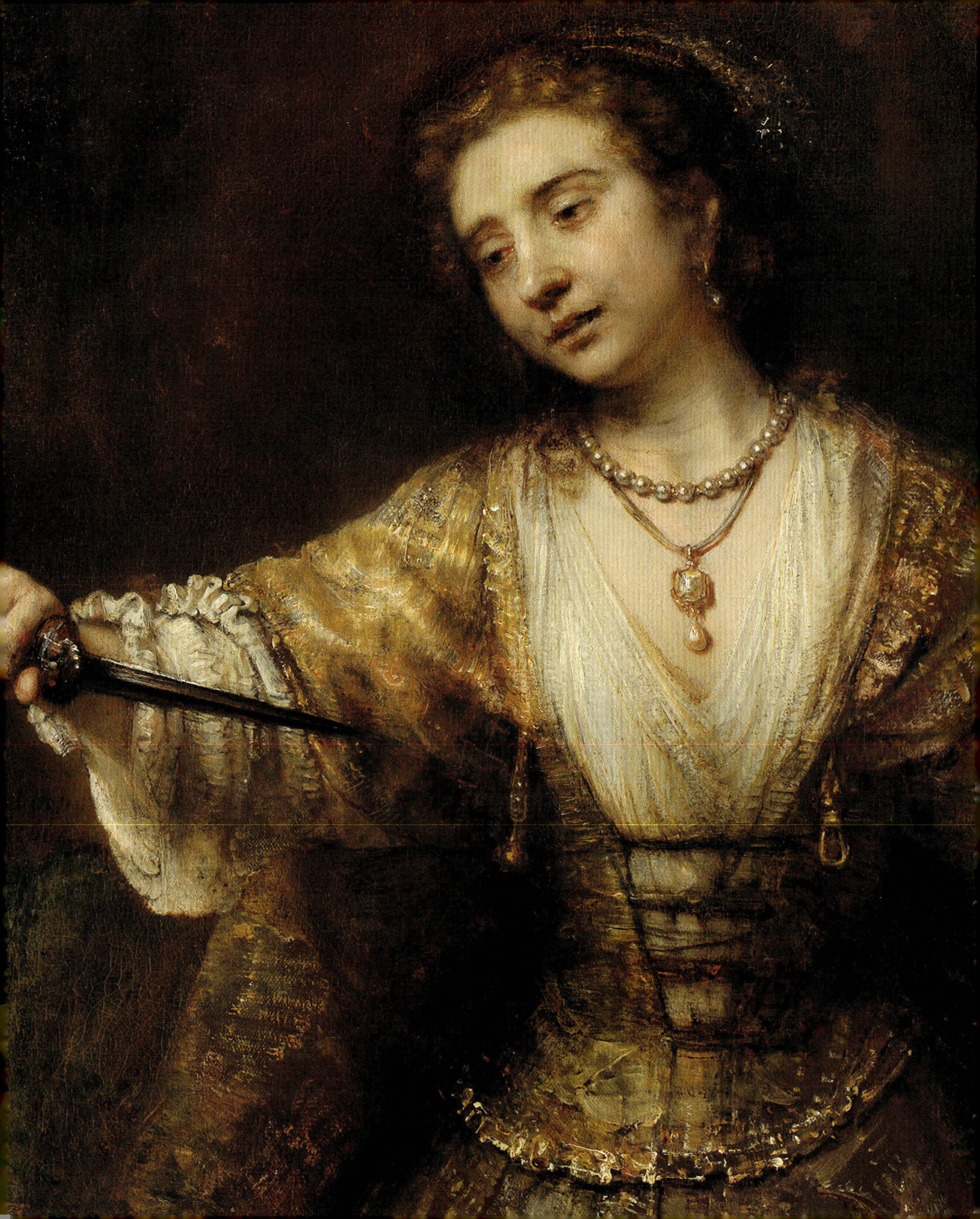

INNER CONFLICT

Gregor J. M. Weber

IN HIS LATER WORKS Rembrandt frequently depicted single figures in contemplative poses, whether they are known personages (for example, specific apostles) or anonymous characters.[1] Such contemplative figures take on a deeper quality in narrative contexts, where they provide introspective depth linked to the specific story of a key figure, their fate, their affliction or their spiritual conflict.

The biblical story of King David and Bathsheba tells of one such conflict. As David's troops were defending Israel against the Ammonites, he spied a woman bathing from the roof of his palace in Jerusalem. This was Bathsheba, the exceptionally beautiful wife of the warrior Uriah. He sent messengers to fetch her; she came and he slept with her (2 Samuel 11: 3). When she became pregnant, David arranged for Uriah to be brought back from the battlefield and ordered him to go home to Bathsheba. In this way he hoped to cover up the fact that the pregnancy was adulterous. But Uriah would only sleep in front of the door to his house as he felt he owed this to his comrades who were still fighting. So David came up with a different ruse: he arranged for Uriah to fight on the front line, which led to him being killed, as expected. When Bathsheba heard of Uriah's death, she mourned for her husband. After the period of mourning, she became David's wife (2 Samuel 11: 1–27). This tale offered plenty of material for an artist to depict actions and passions. Bathsheba was traditionally shown bathing, attended by one or more serving girls, with David watching from a distance in his palace. More dynamic action could be introduced by having his message passed to her verbally, or by showing a letter being delivered or read. The covetous look of the voyeur and Bathsheba being surprised offered opportunities for further embellishment of the story (see fig. 76).

The concept of making contemplation and introspection the dominant themes of his compositions led Rembrandt to an innovative solution. His new approach involved packing the psychological power of the entire story into a single person. In his painting *Bathsheba with King David's Letter* (cat. 112) of 1654 Rembrandt focuses on Bathsheba's emotional situation: he portrays her isolated against a dark background, withdrawn and pensive.[2] The closest thing to visible activity is the female servant on the far left washing Bathsheba's feet. Yet Rembrandt goes to great lengths to play down even this minor action: he immerses the servant almost entirely in shadow and cuts her off at the edge of the painting.[3] This focuses all the attention on the brightly illuminated figure of the seated Bathsheba. Rembrandt emphasises the private and intimate character of the scene by placing her body parallel to the picture plane (only her chest is turned slightly towards the viewer). An X-radiograph of the painting has revealed that Rembrandt originally planned to depict Bathsheba with her head raised and a shocked expression on her face.[4] But then he decided to leave the figure in solitude and express her mental conflict through her quiet, contemplative figure, rather than any dynamic actions.

The pictorial design of the work supports this concept: Rembrandt has created an introspective composition as a vehicle for Bathsheba's contemplative moment. Her eyebrows slightly raised, her eyelids somewhat lowered, she broods over the message she has just read in David's letter, which she still holds in her hand. So this contemplative pose conceals a specific inner conflict: should she obey the king's order or should she remain faithful to her husband? Bathsheba's internal struggle over this moral dilemma can only be

Detail from *Lucretia* (cat. 115)

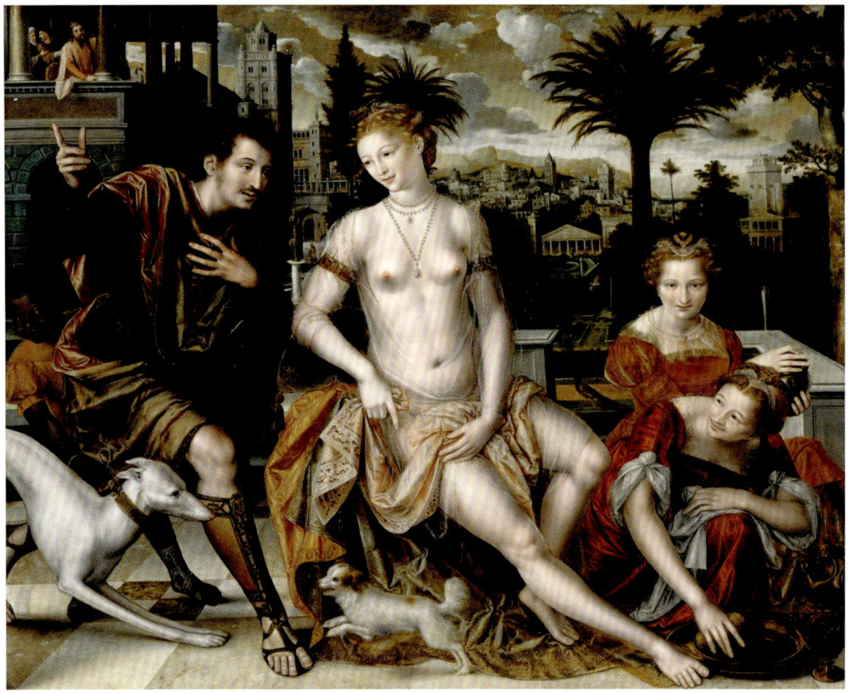

FIG. 76
JAN MASSYS (1509–1575)
David and Bathsheba, 1562
Oil on panel, 162 × 197 cm
Musée du Louvre, Paris

presented covertly, projected as it were by the viewer who knows about the conflict.

It has been frequently pointed out that Rembrandt found inspiration for this composition in a classical relief that François Perrier (1590–1650) had published in a copperplate engraving in 1645 (fig. 77).[5] In this scene the main figure covers her face with a cloth – a sign since classical times of a grief so intense that it cannot possibly be portrayed. For instance, the classical author Pliny mentions a painting by Timanthes of the doomed Iphigenia, in which the artist could only show Iphigenia's father veiled as his grief surpassed what could be shown in paint.[6] The highest degree of grief could not be represented: it could only be envisaged in the mind of the viewer. Perhaps what fascinated Rembrandt about this print was not just the composition, but also the challenge of giving a face to the veiled figure while still requiring the viewers to do their part through the act of projection. We will return to this question later.

This abandonment of the external expression of passions in favour of inner emotion is one of the most striking features of Rembrandt's late works. In doing this, he was turning from the proven methods that by his day had long been the guideline for representing historical subjects.[7] All such stories were accounts of fate and the consequences of actions and passions. Like a dramatist in the theatre, an artist had to have mastered the representation of human gestures and facial expressions, as it would otherwise be impossible to give a credible portrayal of the story. This was why the study of the body in motion (*moti corporis*) was such an important part of an artist's training, as was to an even greater degree the study of changes in the state of the soul (*moti animae*), in other words the passions of the soul (*passiones animae*, in Dutch '*hartstochten*', '*lydingen*'). Indeed, in 1604 Karel van Mander even termed the representation of the passions the 'soul of art', and just a hundred years later François de Kaarsgieter used the

112
Bathsheba with
King David's Letter, 1654
Oil on canvas, 142 × 142 cm
Musée du Louvre, Paris

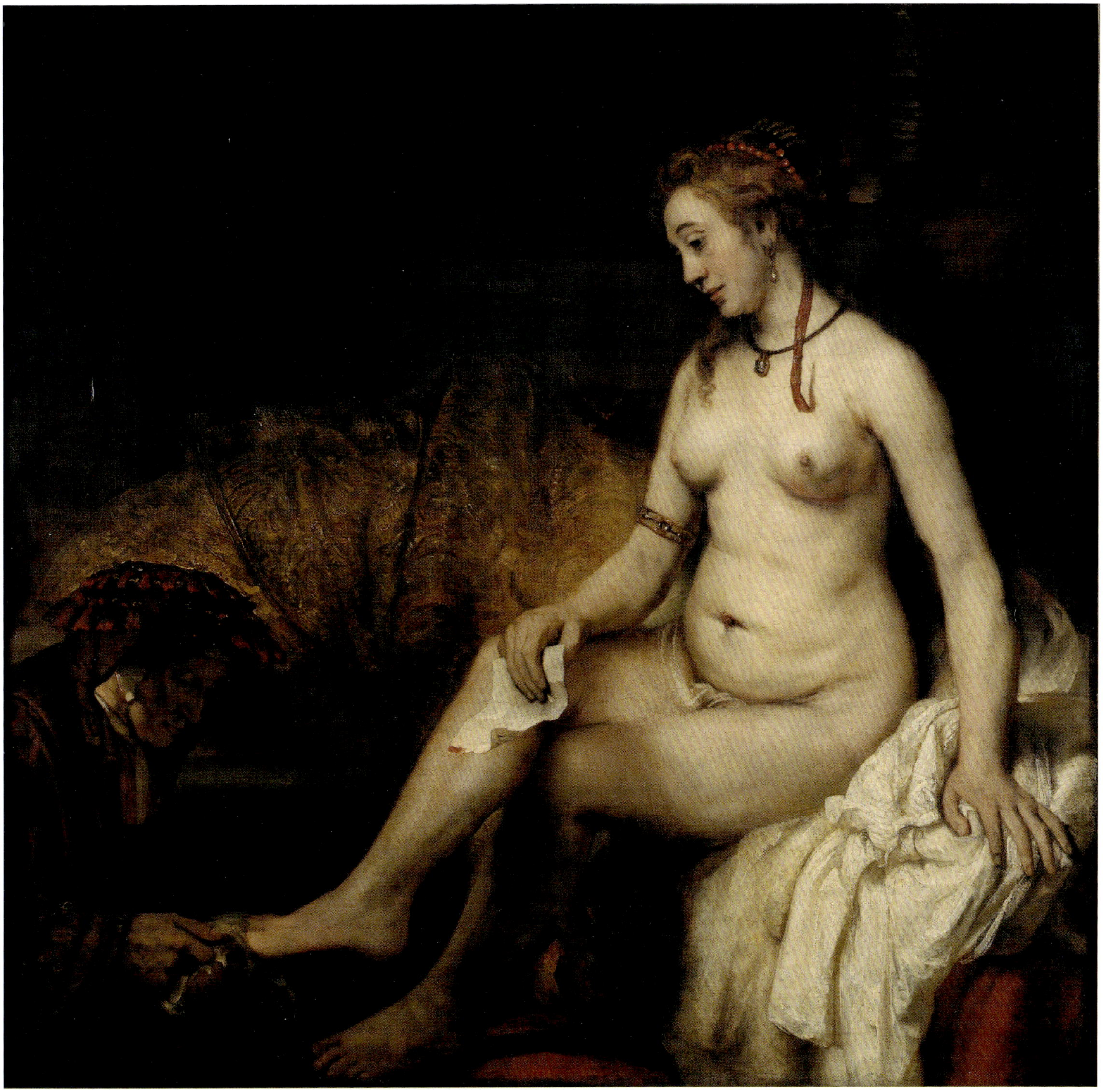

FIG. 77
FRANÇOIS PERRIER
(1590–1650)
'Antique Relief'
Engraving in *Icones et segmenta illustrium e marmore tabularum quae Romae adhuc extant delineata incisa et ad antiquam formam … restituta … Romae*, Rome 1645, plate 50.
Rijksmuseum Library, Amsterdam

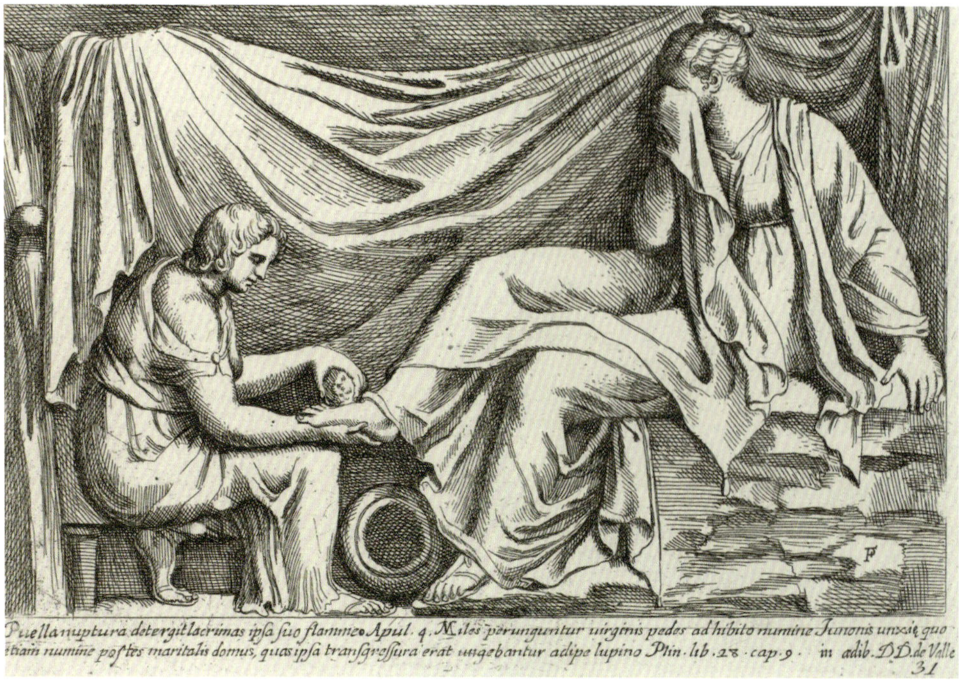

same term in his translation of Charles le Brun's work on the representation of the passions, talking of 'the soul of art' which 'seems to give life to its lifeless figures'.[8] In any event, detailed knowledge of the passions of the soul was an important part of medicine and ethics at that time. The moral philosophers of the day sought to understand the passions so that they could be controlled – this would help people to stop being the passive victims of their passions, but instead able to guide them to be beneficial. René Descartes' *Les Passions de l'Âme*, which first appeared in 1649, is the best-known of a multitude of treatises on the subject of the passions (the first Dutch edition was published in Amsterdam in 1659).[9] Descartes distinguishes between the passions, which are always aroused in response to an external stimulus, and the inner emotions, which are formed in the soul itself through the workings of the imagination and reflection.[10] He makes a clear-cut distinction between the passions that are suffered and the emotions that are produced through contemplation.[11]

The young Rembrandt's approach was perfectly in keeping with these expressions of physical and spiritual stirrings when, in a letter to Constantijn Huygens (1596–1687) dated 12 January 1639, he said he had used 'the greatest and most natural movements' in his paintings for Stadtholder Frederik Hendrik (1584–1647).[12] This was also why Huygens was so enthusiastic about Rembrandt's early painting *Judas returning the Thirty Pieces of Silver* (fig. 78) that he praised it in great detail in his *Autobiography*, written in about 1630:

> … the gesturing of this Judas, … he hurries, whimpers, begs forgiveness without daring to hope for it while his facial features still express that hope, for Judas with his wild face, his unkempt hair, his torn clothes, wringing his hands, painfully digging his fingers in, as he throws himself onto his knees in a blind impulse while his body trembles with uncontrolled pain … I say this with admiration – look at what this young man has packed into a single figure and has expressed as one whole.[13]

Judas had betrayed Christ for a reward of 30 pieces of silver but then regretted what he had done. When he failed in his attempt to undo his deed, he hanged himself in despair (see Matthew 27: 3–5). The young Rembrandt offers sufficient visible clues for the dramatic reading of the figure given by Huygens, such as the convulsive hand-wringing and the face contorted with pain. This representation of highly expressive external reactions is a constant feature of Rembrandt's early work.

The representation of intense passions, their rapid changes and the struggle between them, was a popular topic in literature and art of this period. The best way to portray the conflict between opposing values – virtue and vice, good and evil – was through the fluctuations of the feelings, encapsulated in passions such as revenge and mercy, love and hatred. Played out in the inner struggle of the soul (the *psychomachia*), these form the basic elements for dramas of all kinds: stories, plays and even moralising texts.[14]

One of the struggles of the soul that received most attention was the conflict between chastity and lust. Joost van den Vondel (1587–1679) made this the subject of his *Stryd of kamp tusschen kuyscheyd en geylheid* (*Battle between Chastity and Lust*), in which he considered exemplary figures from history who experienced this conflict, including Susannah, Joseph and Lucretia.[15] The opposing feelings of Joseph and his temptress were also taken as the subject of a poem by Jacob Cats (1577–1660), under the significant title *SELF-STRYT, dat is, krachtighe bewegingh e van VLEES ende GHEEST, Poetischer wijse voorghestelt, inde persoon … van IOSEPH …* (*Inner conflict, that is the powerful movements of the flesh and the spirit, presented in a poetic manner in the person … of Joseph …*) (fig. 79).[16] An essential element for the didactic purpose of these texts was that the inner conflict should take place within a single individual, and that the various performers represent nothing more than the different forces fighting one another within that individual, 'as if the same struggle between spirit and flesh had only taken place within Joseph; as we also know that this conflict is being shown to us through God's word as being located in one and the same person'.[17]

FIG. 78
Judas returning the Thirty Pieces of Silver, 1629
Oil on panel, 79 × 102.3 cm
Private collection

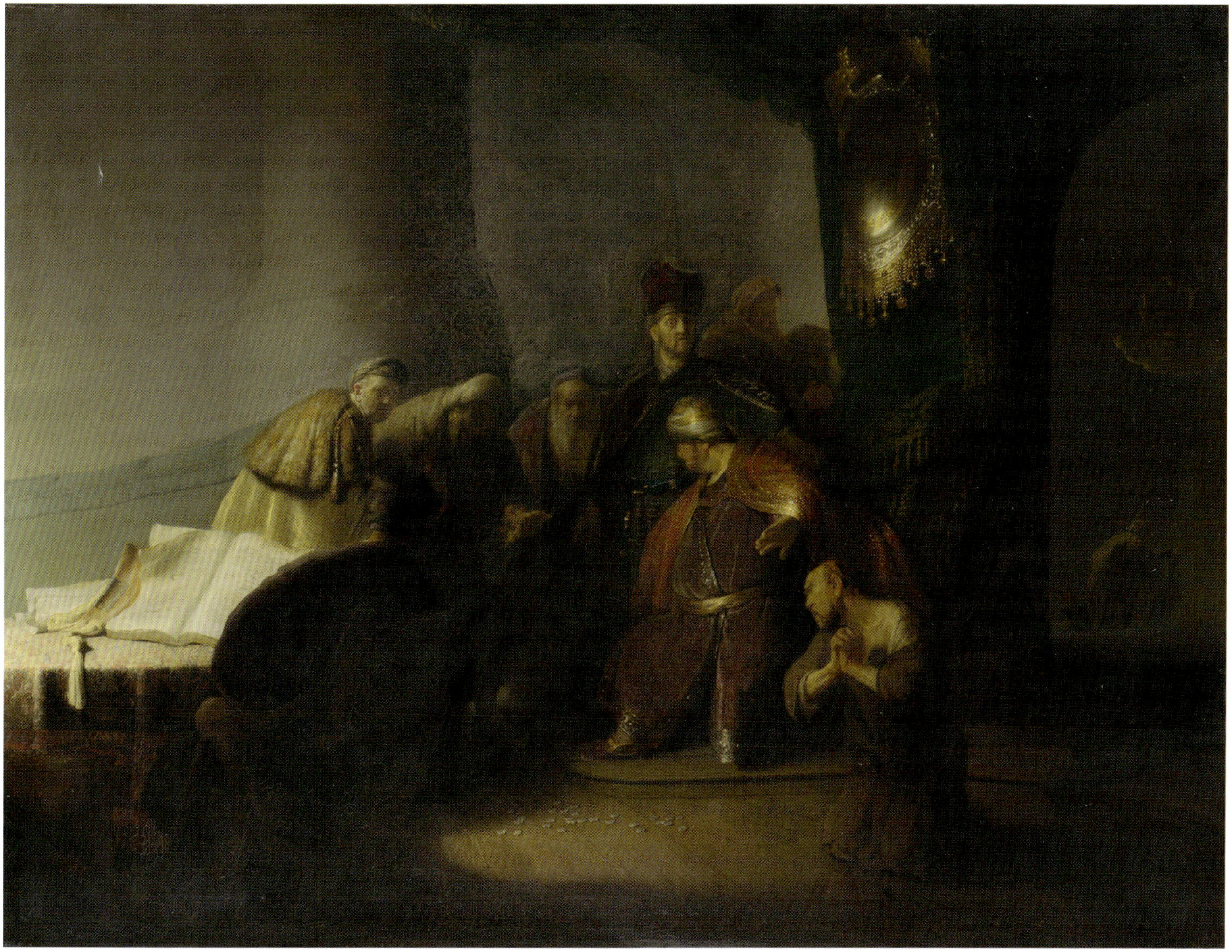

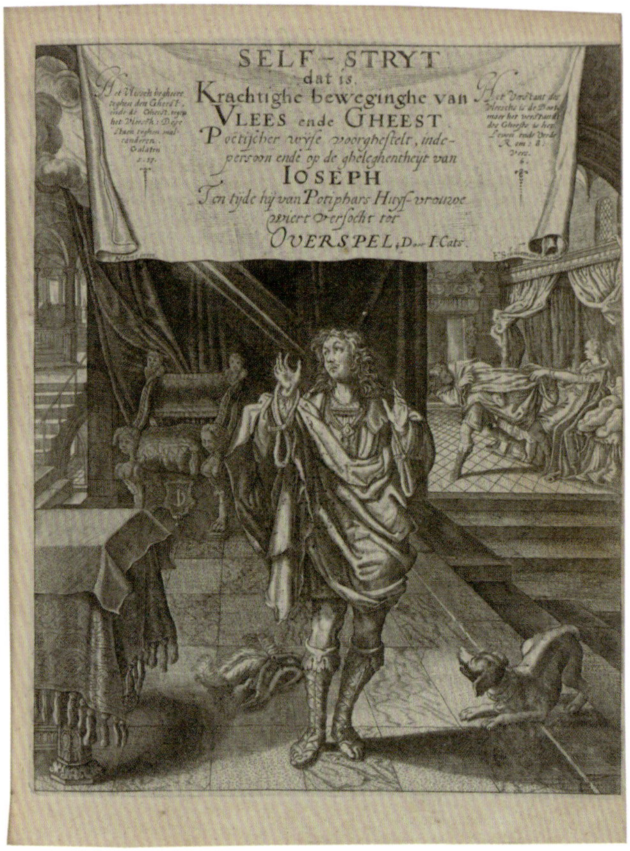

FIG. 79
ADRIAEN VAN DE VENNE
(1589–1662)
Frontispiece to Jacob Cats, *Self-stryt, dat is, krachtighe beweginghe van vlees ende gheest, Poetischer wijse voorghestelt, inde persoon … van Joseph … ten tijde hy van Potiphars huysvrouwe wert versocht tot overspel*, Middelburg 1625
Rijksmuseum Library, Amsterdam

The Old Testament narrative of Joseph in Egypt during his period as a slave in the house of Potiphar, an officer of the pharaoh, was particularly well suited to such 'inner conflicts'. Potiphar's wife, Jempsar, had deliberately waited for her husband to be away in order to seduce Joseph in her bedchamber, but he did not succumb to her wiles. As Joseph fled the scene, Jempsar kept hold of his coat. Later, when Potiphar returned, she showed him the coat as proof of her deceitful accusation that Joseph had tried to seduce her (Genesis 39: 7–19). The Amsterdam poet Jan Vos (1610–1667), who was a theatre director for many years, described such a scene between Joseph and Jempsar in an ekphrastic poem (inspired by a painting) in which the poet himself is torn between the visualised passions of lust and chastity:

> Now, when I see her sheen, desire rages through me.
> When I consider his fidelity, I am gripped by chastity.
> I burn and quiver at the same time. Lust makes me glow.
> Chastity makes me cold. How he flees from these hurdles![18]

Jan Vos belonged to a generation of poets and playwrights who presented the most vehement passions on the stage, in accordance with the dramatic theories of Seneca and Scaliger (see p. 268), and enjoyed great success in doing so.[19] Echoing the struggle of the *psychomachia*, the spectators became caught up in a maelstrom of passions that the actors expressed in rapid succession.

In the 1630s Rembrandt adopted the same principles, looking for scenes with intense outbursts of passion and clearly visible evidence of his figures' inner moods as subjects for his work. For example, in an etching of 1634 he gave a particularly impassioned portrayal of the scene of Jempsar's seduction (fig. 80). Filled with lust and with her private parts laid bare, she turns in her bed towards Joseph, who tries to flee as he vehemently fends her off. The two movements of desire and aversion could scarcely be portrayed in greater opposition.

Rembrandt returned to the subject of Joseph's seduction more than twenty years later, in a work of 1655, but with a very different approach (cat. 113). His interest was now in a scene centred on the spoken word: when Potiphar returned, Jempsar told him of Joseph's supposed attempt to seduce her (Genesis 39: 17–19; Flavius Josephus, *Antiquities of the Jews*, 11: 4, 5). Rembrandt depicts her with her legs nonchalantly crossed, sitting in front of the white bed, one foot on Joseph's coat, which lies on the floor. She points at the alleged offender with a scornful gesture while he, devoid of all hope, surrenders to his fate: a prison sentence. The figure of Joseph with his arm raised immediately calls to mind the figure on the title page of Jacob Cats's *Self-Stryt* (see fig. 79).[20] The conflict between chastity and lust, which was traditionally portrayed as a clearly visible contrast between vehement passions, has now become the confrontation between innocence and slander within a *spoken* line of argument. A variant of Rembrandt's composition was produced in his studio in the same year, 1655 (fig. 81). He gave the unknown artist of this painting quite a free hand, although it may be assumed that the variants were discussed between the two artists.[21] Interestingly, it is the figure of Joseph that has changed most in this version: instead of the gesture with the raised arm and eyes looking towards heaven, he now stands behind the bed, absorbed by his thoughts, with his head bent. In this way, the level of his passions is reduced further to one of inner composure. In both versions Jempsar's falsehood, her protestation of innocence, takes centre stage – although by definition this cannot be read purely from her superficial facial expressions and gestures.

In this psychomachian conflict, Potiphar's wife is given the role of 'lust', which also referred to women's power to obtain their objectives through their powers of seduction. Medieval iconography included the theme of 'the power of women', a collective term for the stories of women who use their wiles to overpower men.[22] Examples from the Old Testament include Judith, who won the confidence of the enemy general Holofernes and beheaded him after spending an evening with him (Judith 12: 10–20; 13: 1–10); Delilah, who cut off her husband Samson's hair while he was sleeping, thus robbing him of his strength so that he could be imprisoned and blinded (Judges 16: 16–21); and Jael, who brought the fleeing captain of the Canaanites to her tent, gave him milk to drink and then killed him as he slept by driving a tent spike into his head (Judges 4: 18–22). These acts are viewed in a positive light – in the case of Judith, for example, as a heroic deed that saved her people. On the other hand, Jael's action was also seen as treacherous in the context of womanly wiles.[23] Rembrandt repeatedly tackled these tales of female power and betrayal: in the case of the story of Samson and Delilah, this even resulted in his most gruesome and violent painting, the 1636 *Blinding of Samson* (Städelsches Kunstinstitut, Frankfurt).[24] In 1657–9 he tackled the subject of Jael, presenting the story in a pen-and-ink

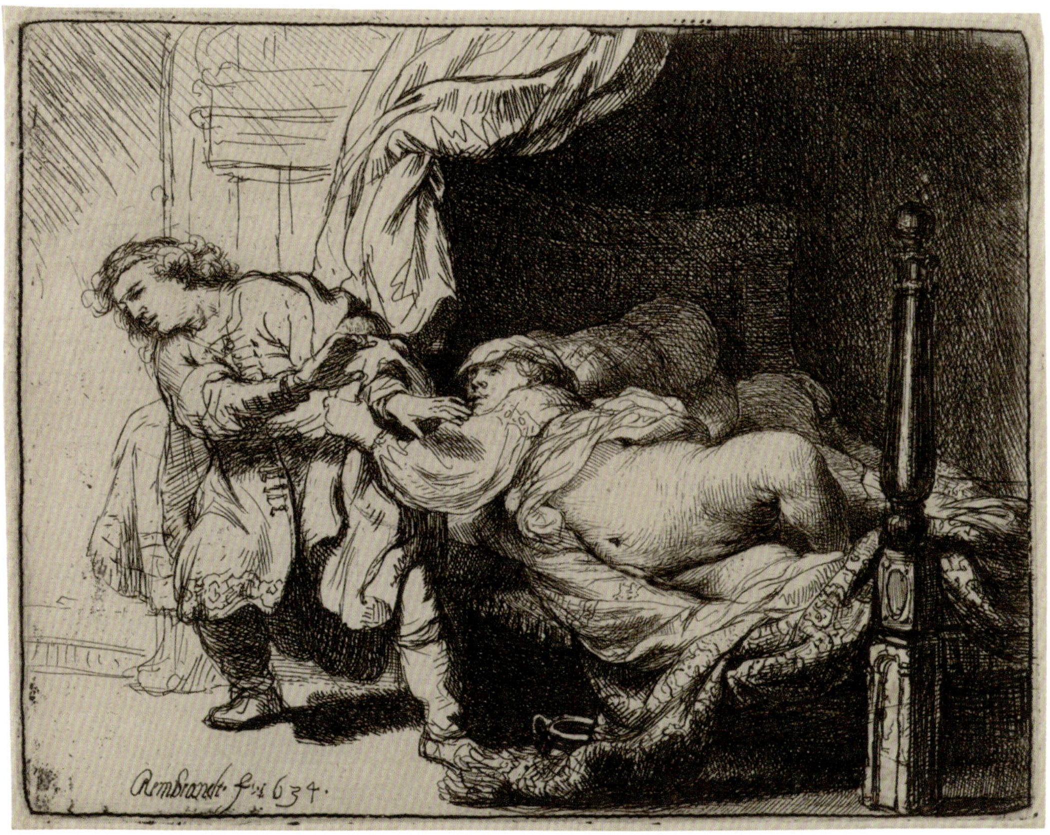

FIG. 80
Joseph and Potiphar's Wife, 1634
Etching, 9.2 × 11.4 cm
Rijksmuseum, Amsterdam

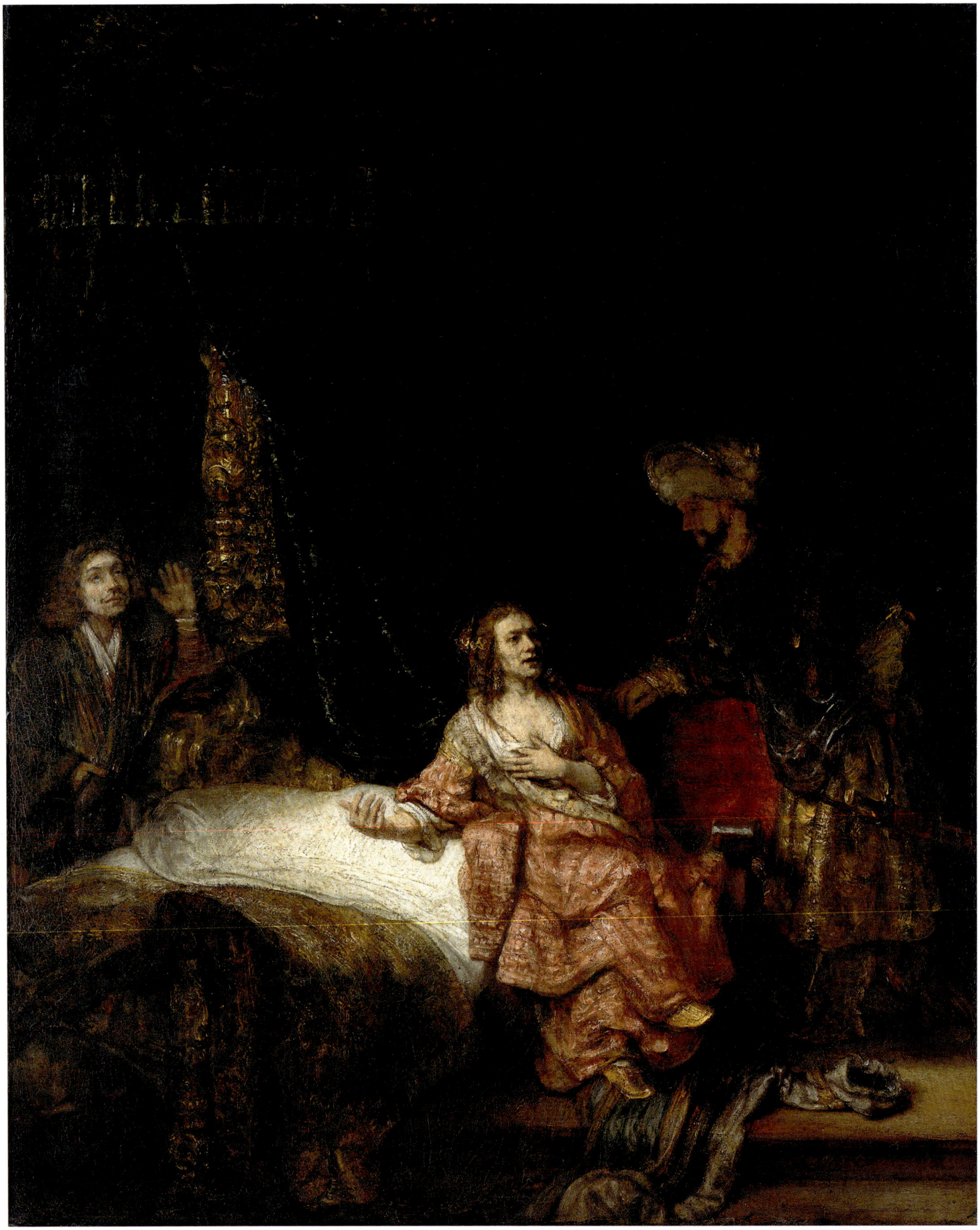

113
Joseph and Potiphar's Wife, 1655
Oil on canvas, 113.5 × 90 cm
Staatliche Museen zu Berlin-Preußischer Kulturbesitz, Gemäldegalerie, Berlin

FIG. 81
WORKSHOP OF REMBRANDT
Joseph accused by Potiphar's Wife, 1655
Oil on canvas, 105.7 × 97.8 cm
National Gallery of Art, Washington (Andrew W. Mellon Collection)

drawing in a very traditional manner (cat. 114). Here he may once again have been prompted by his admiration for Lucas van Leyden, who had portrayed the scene in very similar fashion in a woodcut in the *Small Consequences of the Power of Women* (a series that included the *Fall of Man* and *Samson and Delilah*) in 1517.

It is not known why Rembrandt made the drawing of *Jael killing Sisera* – was it the start of a new interest in the question of what drives a woman to commit such a deed? The inner conflict at the heart of his painting of Bathsheba in 1654 could also be the theme in his pictures of Judith or Jael, as it was in the treatment of these figures by other artists. For example, Peter Paul Rubens showed conflicting emotions of disgust and pride in Judith's face in his painting of the beheading of Holofernes (fig. 82). In this painting the main theme is now the heroine's different emotions rather than the physical act of the beheading. A similar mix of revulsion and courage can also be seen reflected in the face of Jael in a painting by Salomon de Bray (1597–1664; fig. 83). Other artists chose to depict Jael as the embodiment of *psychomachia*, rising triumphantly from committing the horrific murder.[25]

The idea of focusing on a single figure in the throes of inner conflict is one that Rembrandt put into practice very expertly in depicting the fate of another woman, Lucretia, described by Livy as the wife of the Roman nobleman Collatinus. When some men went on a drinking bout, a dispute arose as to whose wife was the most virtuous. They paid a surprise visit to the women, of whom Lucretia alone was occupied with her needlework until deep into the night. One of the men, Tarquinius Sextus, the son of the tyrannical king Tarquinius Superbus, was so provoked both by her beauty and her chastity that he decided to assault her. Some days later he visited Lucretia and threatened her

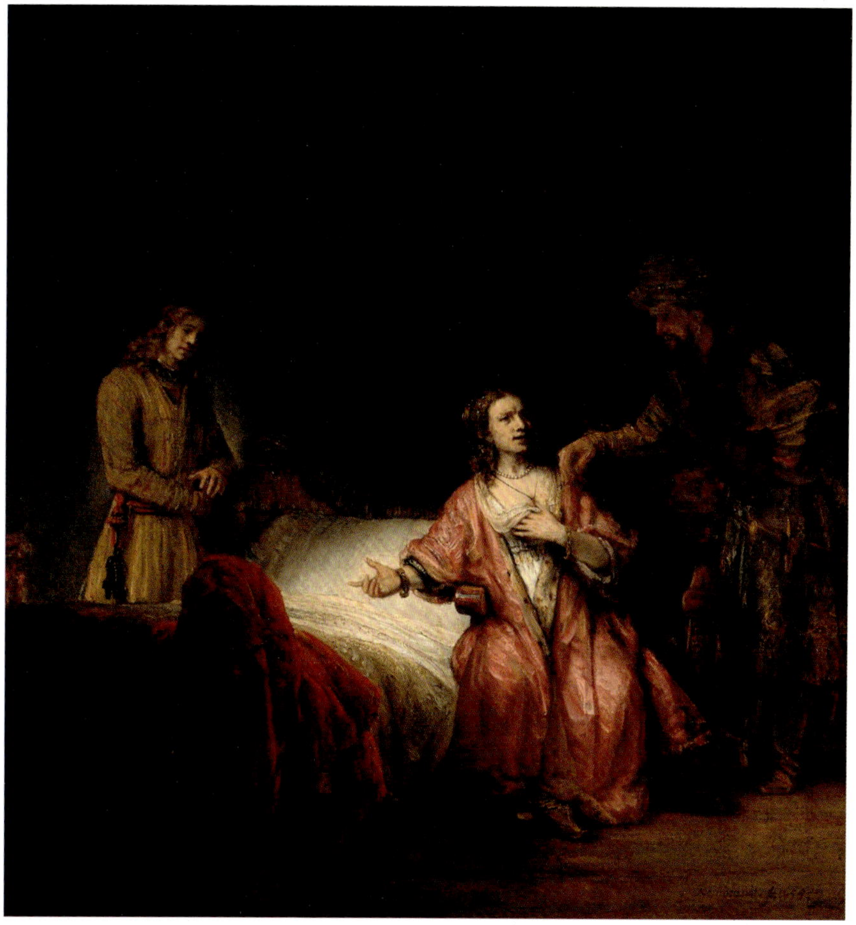

114
Jael killing Sisera, 1657–9
Pen and brown ink with white bodycolour, 19.2 × 17.4 cm
Rijksmuseum, Amsterdam

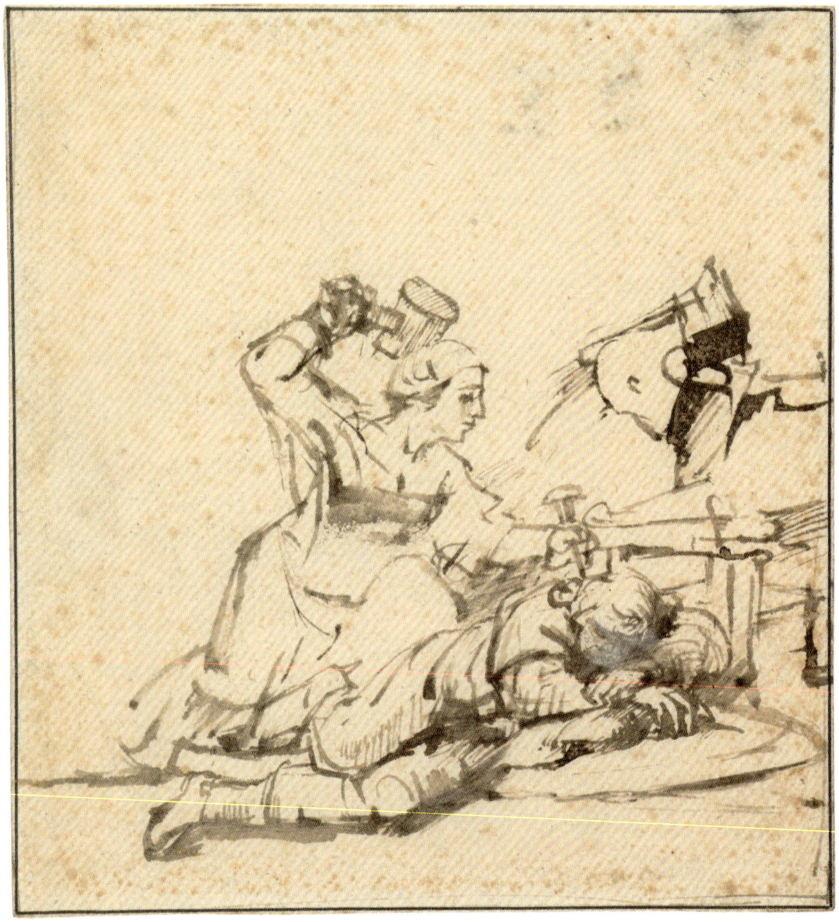

with his sword if she did not submit, but she remained firm, prepared to die to preserve her honour. Tarquinius Sextus then resorted to blackmail, vowing to put a murdered naked slave next to her corpse so that it would appear as if she had been caught in the act of adultery. 'With this threat, lust finally overcame stubborn chastity', as the classical text of Livy put it. On the morning after the rape, distraught Lucretia summoned her father, her husband and several of their friends to tell them what had happened. Although none of those present blamed her for the rape, she could not bear the ignominy and killed herself with a dagger. She would prefer to die than live on in dishonour.[26] Lucretia's suicide sparked a rebellion against the tyrant, and ultimately led to the foundation of the Roman Republic. As a result, Lucretia – like Judith and Jael – had been held up since the sixteenth century as an example of virtue, in particular that of the faithful wife.[27]

This story offers plenty of opportunities for the visualisation of intense passion. Once again, Jan Vos serves as an example, with his highly passionate ekphrastic poem *Lukretia deursteekt zich, door G.F. geschildert* (*Lucretia stabbing herself, painted by G.F.*),[28] which presents the tragedy sympathetically by calling on all the participants:

> Stay calm, Lucretia, stay calm. Would you be your own murderer?
> He who kills himself is spurned by the gods.
> Your innocence can be seen from the tears in your eyes
> … She stabs herself, oh what sorrow! She falls.
> She seems to float in blood.
> Rise, Collatinus, rise, rise, Brutus, Brutus, rise:
> … Destroy the court of Tarquinius with the points of your swords …[29]

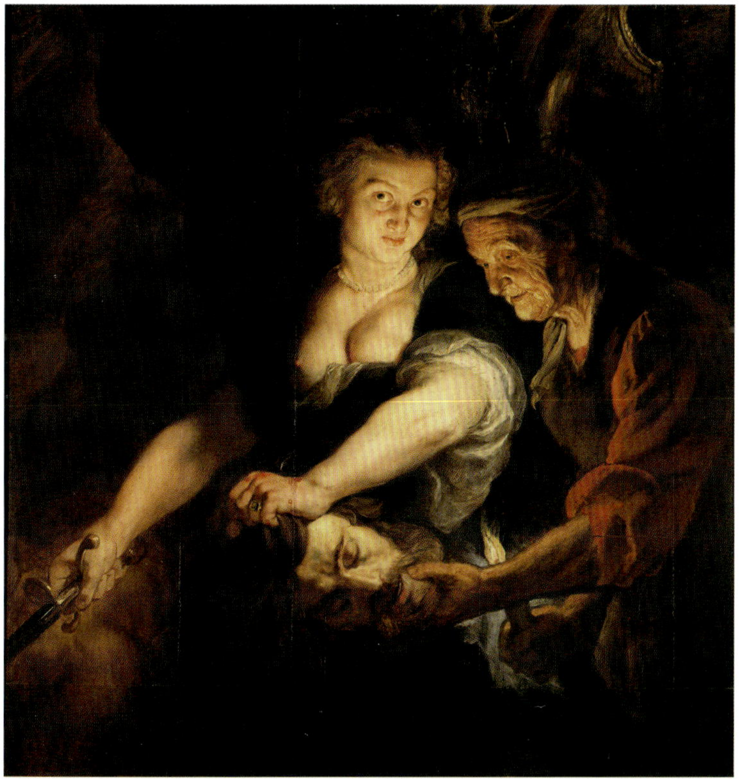

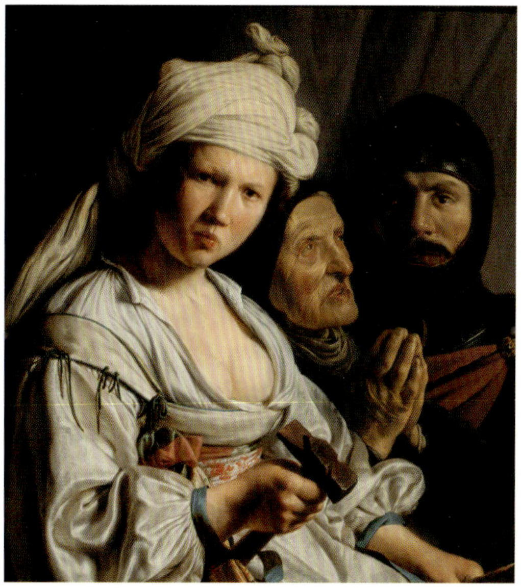

Rembrandt depicted this subject in two impressive paintings, both of which show only the single figure of Lucretia. The earlier of the two works, dated 1664 (cat. 115), shows Lucretia from the front, her arms spread, her left hand raised in accusation while in the right she holds the dagger just before the fatal stab. We see none of the other characters mentioned in the story: all our attention is on Lucretia in her lonely decision. The position of her arms, spread wide as if in a moment of faltering uncertainty, suggest her inner conflict just before her suicide. Yet she is looking at the dagger that will bring her death; she will make her decision at any moment. In Rembrandt's other *Lucretia*, dated 1666 (cat. 57, p. 137), she has already taken this step and her shift below her heart is drenched with blood. The deed has been done and Lucretia lowers her arm with the dagger. Now she looks towards her left, where her other hand pulls the bell rope to call her friends. Only in this detail is there an indication of an 'exterior world', but this is not essential to Rembrandt's picture. Whereas Jan Vos calls on the protagonists in the traditional fashion in his ekphrastic poem, this is not necessary in Rembrandt's painting: he is concerned with portraying a *single* figure, her *inner* conflict and her *lonely* decision.

This concentration on one tragic figure is reminiscent of Rembrandt's early masterpiece *Judas returning the Thirty Pieces of Silver* of 1629 (fig. 78). What Huygens had once praised in the figure of Judas has now been 'distilled' out of the multi-figure scene, and only exists in the mind and projection of the viewer. In contrast to Jan Vos's rather theatrical poetic technique of summoning other personages to represent the various different emotional aspects of the event, Rembrandt now focuses on one figure, one facial expression, one inner weighing up. But while the figure of Judas is still tormented by intense passion, Lucretia has outgrown this stage: she seems quiet, resolute, not passively drifting but carrying out a self-determined act. Her suicide is not an 'act of passion' (as we might say today) but a decision arrived at through an inner assessment of her emotions.[30]

The works by Rembrandt discussed so far deal with conflicts in which a choice had to be made between 'virtue' and 'vice' in the context of sexual temptation. Of course, inner conflict occurs in many other situations in which values involving strong passion and sentiment have to be measured against one another, whether they are associated with fear, despair, uncertainty or another emotion. To take a further example from the Old Testament, Rembrandt was particularly interested in the tumultuous fate of Jacob, one of the patriarchs of Israel, whose life offers an abundance of exemplary, dramatic events. One such is the account of his strange wrestling

FIG. 82
PETER PAUL RUBENS
(1577–1640)
Judith with the Head of Holofernes, about 1617
Oil on panel, 120 × 111 cm
Herzog Anton Ulrich Museum, Braunschweig

FIG. 83
SALOMON DE BRAY
(1597–1664)
Jael, Deborah and Barak, 1635
Oil on panel, 86.5 × 71.5 cm
Museum Catharijneconvent, Utrecht

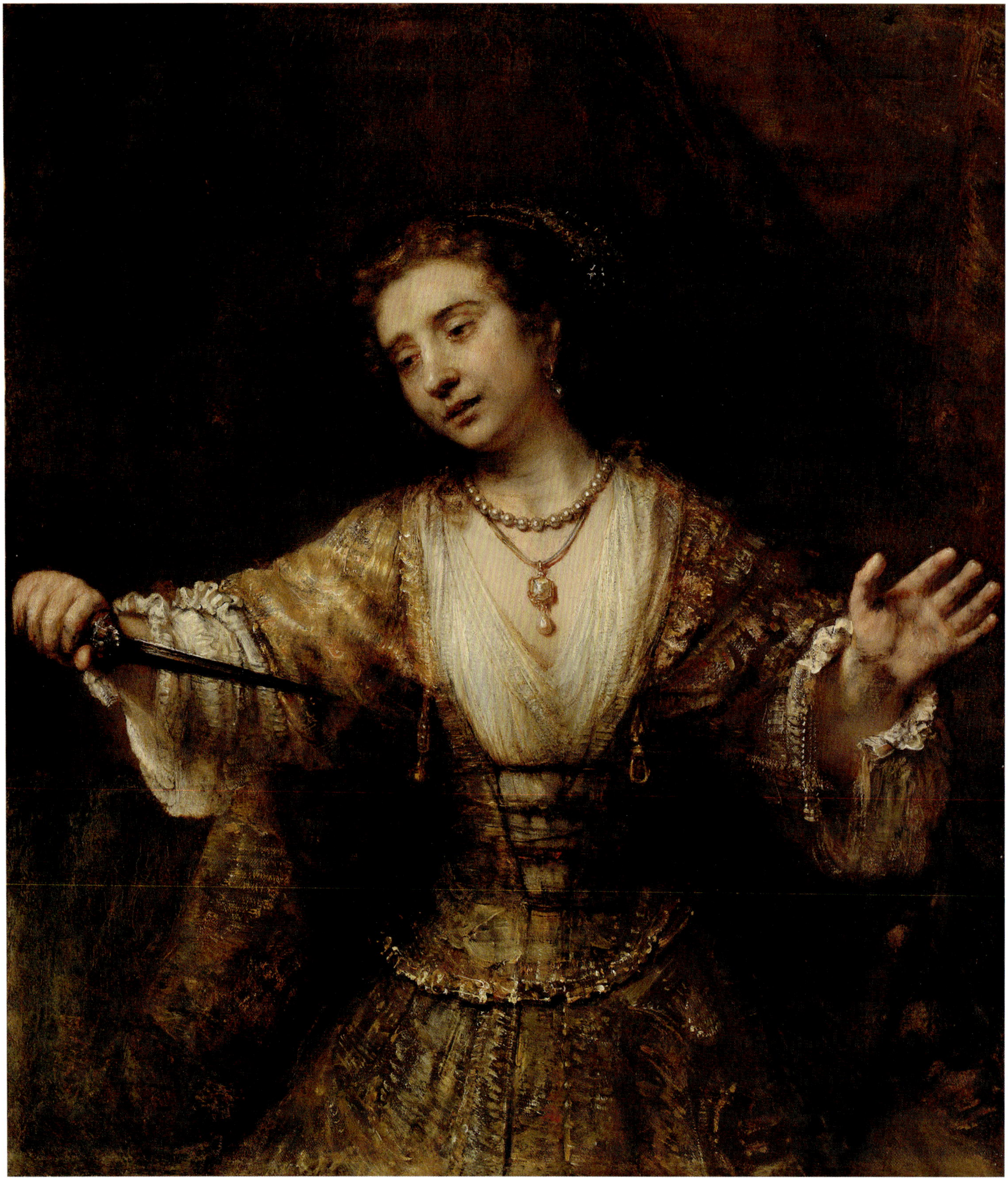

115
Lucretia, 1664
Oil on canvas, 120 × 101 cm
National Gallery of Art, Washington

match with an angel (cat. 118). Jacob had surreptitiously obtained the blessing of his father, Isaac, through a ruse of his mother, although the blessing should rightfully have been given to his elder brother, Esau. Jacob spent twenty years labouring in exile until he was finally able to return home with what was now a large family and his flocks and herds of livestock. However, the hardest part awaited him when he got home – seeing his brother Esau again. His fear of his brother's revenge was immense. That night Jacob beseeched God fervently to spare him and his people: 'Deliver me, I pray thee, from the hand of my brother, from the hand of Esau: for I fear him, lest he will come and smite me, and the mother with the children' (Genesis 32: 11). The same night he divided up his flocks and herds so that he could give Esau a present in reconciliation. Finally, Jacob sent his family to the river Jabbok while he remained behind alone. There he became embroiled in a wrestling match until dawn with a mysterious man and finally had to acknowledge that he was unable to overcome him. The man even put Jacob's hip out of joint, but Jacob kept his grip on the man, and even asked for his blessing. The man – in fact an angel of the Lord – granted him this request and renamed him Israel, 'for as a prince hast thou power with God and with men, and hast prevailed' (Genesis 32: 25–30). After all this hardship, a joyful reconciliation with Esau took place the next day.

This subject had not often been depicted previously: two of the rare examples in the northern Netherlands are paintings by Moyses van Uyttenbroeck (about 1595–before 1647) of 1629 and Bartholomeus Breenbergh (1598–1657) of 1639.[31] Both these small-figured pictures show the wrestling match in terms of forceful movement, as might be expected. Rembrandt adopts a very different solution in his large painting of about 1659 (cat. 118). The angel holds Jacob almost gently, one hand on his shoulder and the other on his hip. He looks upon Jacob's face with a serene, almost affectionate gaze while Jacob closes his eyes as if in sleep. Nothing draws attention away from the figures: the background has been kept dark and sketchy.[32] Rembrandt has not interpreted the struggle as a physical confrontation but as an emotional one.

The Bible talks of Jacob's great fear, his worries and his prayers leading up to the day on which he would meet his brother, Esau. This is a spiritual struggle *in extremis*, that has assumed visible form in the wrestling with the angel. In the end, Jacob asked his unknown adversary for his blessing, in other words for his support in this daunting and emotionally fraught situation, as he struggled with the uncertainties of the following day.

Seen from this perspective, this story anticipates an account of a similar period of adversity in which an angel also offers the hoped-for support, this time from the New Testament. As Christ prayed alone on the Mount of Olives shortly before his arrest, he already knew what fate awaited him – his Passion and death on the cross – and expressed his fear:

> 'Father, if thou be willing, remove this cup from me: nevertheless not my will, but thine, be done.' And there appeared an angel unto him from heaven, strengthening him. And being in an agony he prayed more earnestly: and his sweat was as it were great drops of blood falling down to the ground.[33]

Rembrandt represented this scene in two drawings and a striking etching of around 1652 (cats 116–17).[34] Here again, the angel supports or even embraces Christ, who is tormented by fear and foreboding, offering him assistance and comfort as he deals with his inner conflict.[35] In all three works the building blocks of the visual narrative

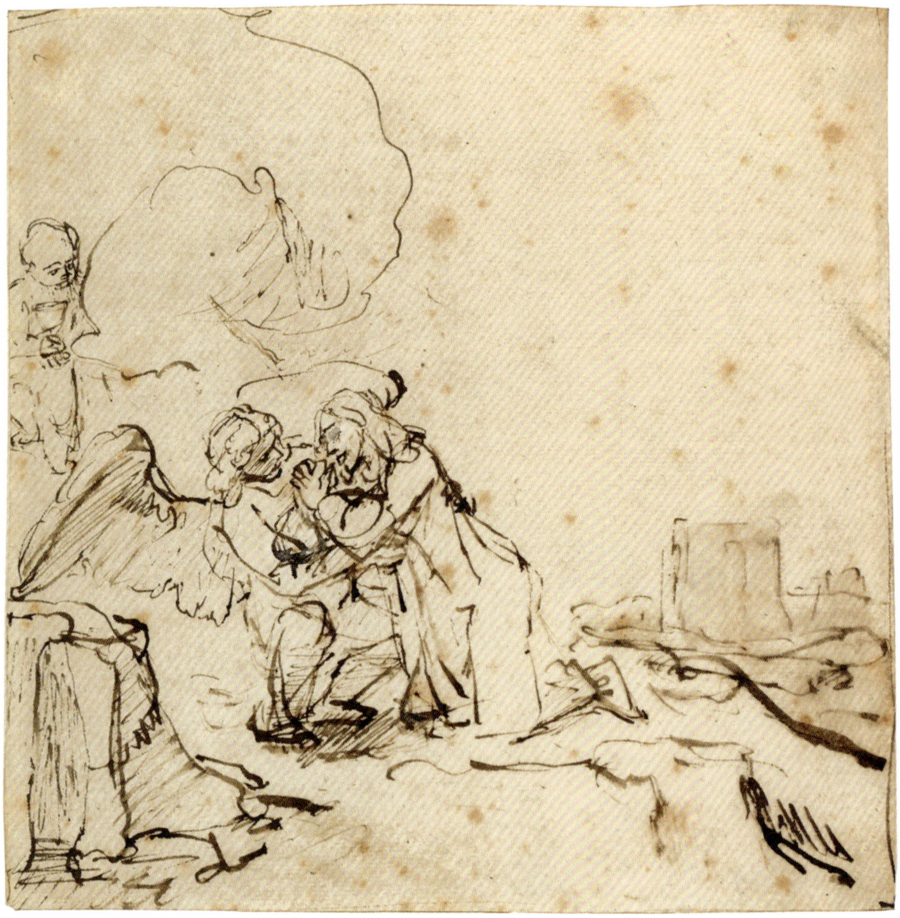

118
Jacob and the Angel, about 1659
Oil on canvas, 137 × 116 cm
Staatliche Museen zu
Berlin-Preußischer
Kulturbesitz,
Gemäldegalerie, Berlin

116
The Agony in the Garden,
about 1648–55
Pen and brown ink,
brown wash, 19.6 × 19 cm
The Fitzwilliam Museum,
Cambridge

117
The Agony in the Garden,
about 1652
Etching and drypoint,
11.1 × 8.4 cm
First state of three
Ashmolean Museum,
Oxford (WA 1855.400.1)

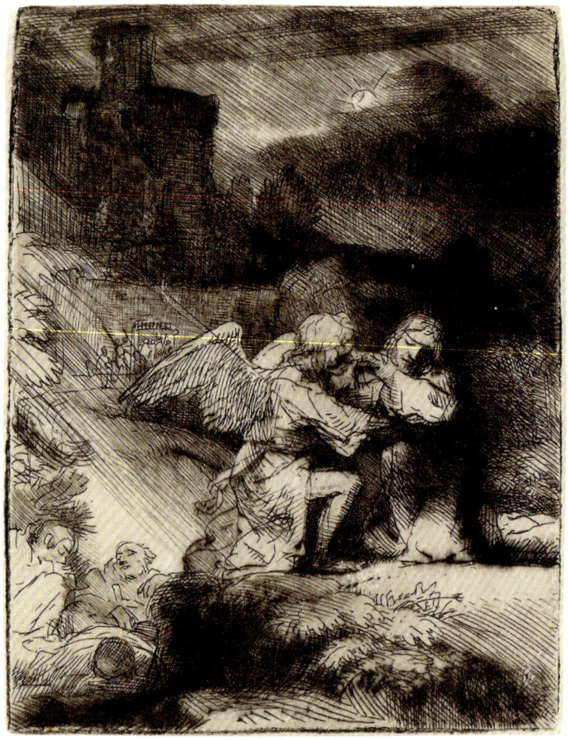

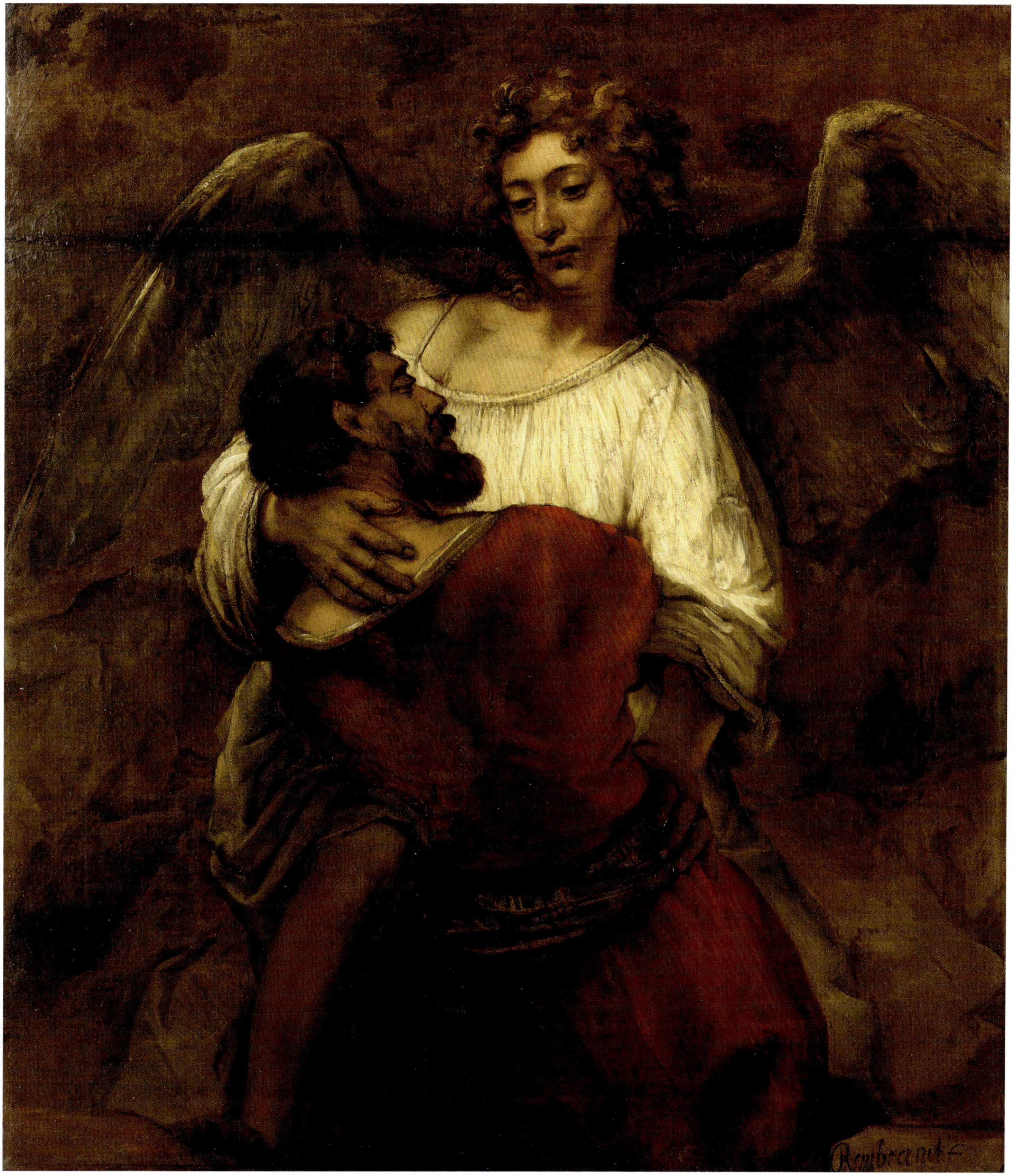
Rembrandt f.

closely resemble those of the Old Testament story of Jacob's wrestling match. For both biblical subjects Rembrandt uses the artistic concept of '*self-stryt*' or inner conflict, which Jacob Cats defined as being 'located in one and the same person', even if several people are present. The closed eyes of both Jacob and Christ clearly emphasise the 'interiority' of their struggle in adversity.

Rembrandt's later work clearly reveals his desire to avoid presenting superficially visible passions and actions. His painting of *Ahasuerus and Haman at the Feast of Esther* (fig. 84) of 1660 shows just how far he could deviate from accepted iconographic tradition. Esther had learnt that Haman, the favourite of the Persian king Ahasuerus, planned to destroy the Jews. During a feast she exposed Haman, who was subsequently sentenced to death for his perfidy by an angry Ahasuerus (Esther 7). Once again, Jan Vos wrote a poem explicitly about Rembrandt's painting:

> Here we see Haman feasting with Ahasuerus
> and Esther.
> But it is futile, inside he is full of woe and pain.
> He bites into Esther's food, but even deeper into
> her heart.
> The king is seized by revenge and fury.
> The wrath of a ruler is awful when he is enraged ...[36]

But whereas Vos talks about intense passions (such as revenge, fury and wrath), Rembrandt's painting shows an almost ossified group at the table. Vos was quite clearly following the rules of poetry, which were admittedly entirely in keeping with the more theatrical paintings of this subject that emphasise the passions. The disparity between such artworks and Rembrandt's painting of 1660 is once again the fact that he is more interested in the inner, emotional conflicts of his protagonists. Wherever possible, he pushes the other characters or motifs in the story into the background, which allows him to transfer the essence of the narrative to these isolated figures and their emotional situation.

The pictorial concept of inner conflict takes on a new form and meaning in Rembrandt's late work. In a sense he reduces the factual information that is important in 'reading' the story being presented: the number of figures is limited to just a few individuals (frequently only a single person) and he also minimises their gestures and facial expressions, even going so far as to depict Jacob with closed eyes. But the less information is incorporated in a picture, the more open it is to projection by the viewer. The formal, stylistic aspects of this effect have frequently been described – in Rembrandt's later work he is no longer mired in the meticulous representation of tiny details; instead he is able to create the desired illusion with just a few brushstrokes (see p. 134). As a result, the viewer assumes more information than has actually been depicted.[37] The same approach applies to the 'reading' of inner emotions: their representation necessarily introduces an element of ambiguity that is absent when relying on forceful actions and passions. Quite apart from anything else, this approach to representing emotions gives the viewer a greater role, even projecting his own emotions onto the figures as they follow their fate.

FIG. 84
Ahasuerus and Haman at the Feast of Esther, 1660
Oil on canvas, 73 × 94 cm
The Pushkin State Museum of Fine Arts, Moscow

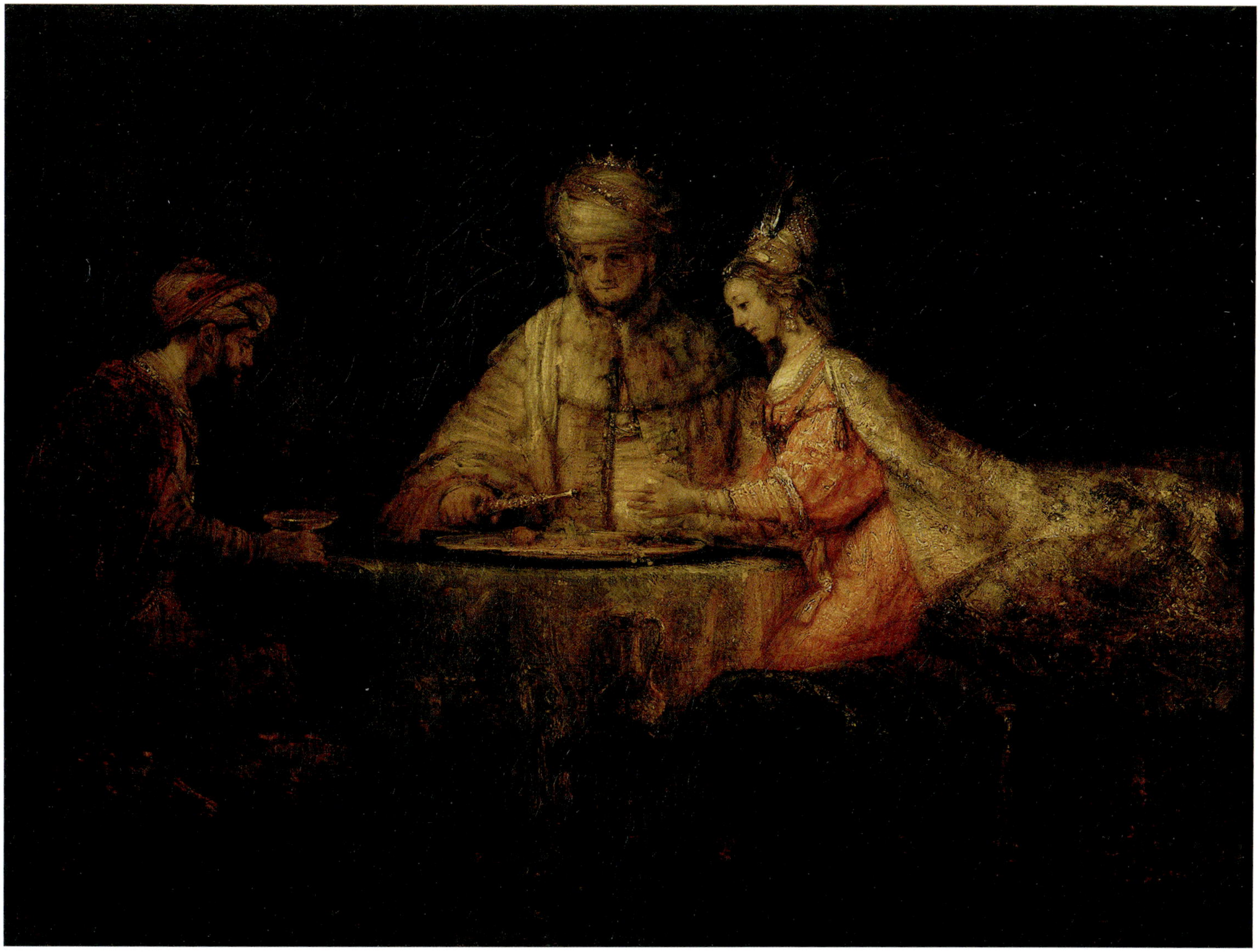

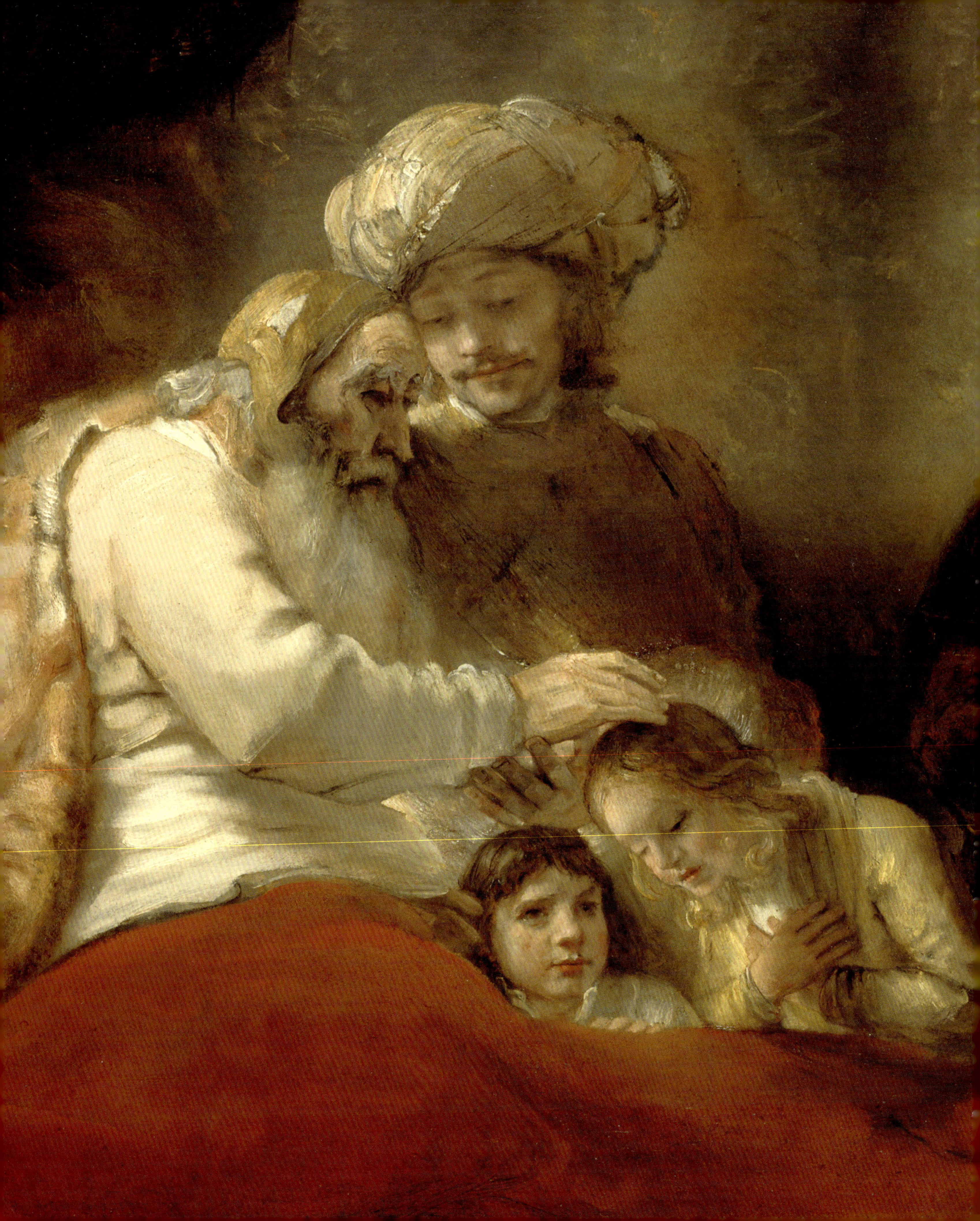

RECONCILIATION

Gregor J. M. Weber

THE DRAMATIC STORIES that Rembrandt chose to represent as an 'inner conflict' embodied by the main protagonists belong to the general category of history paintings, whose subjects derive from literary, mythological, biblical and historical sources. Such stories tend to be rather long and complicated, and in the course of art's history various conventions have emerged in answer to the problem of how best to convey them, particularly in relation to which scenes are most appropriate for representation in the visual arts. After all, while a poet can relate a story as it unfolds in time, a painter is only able to portray a single moment and his figures can only appear once if he is not to undermine the illusion of a credible scene. However, he does have the option of choosing a particularly *significant* moment that embodies a crucial change in the course of events, while also suggesting in this one climactic moment the premonitions and consequences, the before and the after. By the seventeenth century this had become a popular convention: selecting such a 'decisive moment' in the story had proven advantages in the practice of history painting; if nothing else, it ensured the plausibility of the scene being depicted.[1]

Countless history paintings therefore focus on the intense moment in which fate turns: miracles, conversions, acts of redemption, deliverance or condemnation, discoveries or other decisive events. This can be clarified by considering one popular theme: the Old Testament story of the sacrifice of Isaac, in which God commanded Abraham to sacrifice his only son. This sorely tested Abraham's faith in God, but, resolute in his belief, he took the young boy to the sacrificial altar. Abraham duly drew his knife to kill his beloved child, but at that very moment an angel of the Lord called down from heaven, telling Abraham to stay his hand and not to sacrifice Isaac. He realised that Abraham was such a God-fearing man that he was even willing to sacrifice his only son. Then Abraham caught sight of a ram nearby that had become entangled by its horns in a thicket; he took the ram and offered it as a sacrifice in the place of his son (Genesis 22: 1–13). It was precisely this intervention by the angel that Rembrandt chose as the highly dramatic moment for a painting of 1635; he returned to the subject for an etching in 1655 (cat. 119).[2] This last-minute rescue is the climax of the episode. In Rembrandt's print Abraham holds the knife ready in one hand while he covers the boy's eyes with the other hand. But the angel grabs hold of both Abraham's arms, thus forestalling this terrible deed. This device enables the viewer to take in both the imminent, horrific murder and the sudden rescue in a single glance. In temporal terms, there can only be a brief moment of transition in which the intervention of the angel changes the fate of the protagonists from one of misfortune to one of good fortune: in the very next moment they would have changed their positions, postures, gestures and facial expressions.

Rembrandt's etching is entirely conventional as regards the chosen moment and the motifs. On the right he hints at the lead-up to the event with the ascent to the mountain on which the sacrificial altar stands. On the slope can be seen the two men accompanying Abraham and Isaac, whom Abraham had left behind with his ass at the foot of the mountain (Genesis 22: 5). Yet Rembrandt also considered pictorial solutions – particularly in his later work – that are detached from the crucial turning point in the sequence of events. This gave the opportunity to convey a longer moment in an arrested portrayal, with a more static picture.

In the early sixteenth century Lucas van Leyden (Rembrandt's great role model from his home town of

Detail from *Jacob blessing the Sons of Joseph* (cat. 120)

Leiden) had portrayed similarly atypical moments in his paintings and prints. One characteristic feature of their narrative structure was that he looked for scenes that took place shortly before or after the significant moment, and that could consequently look forward or backward to the dramatic climax.[3] For example, he selected a scene from the story of the sacrifice of Isaac that takes place while father and son are walking to the place of sacrifice (fig. 85). The unsuspecting boy asks his father, 'Behold the fire and the wood: but where is the lamb for a burnt offering?' Abraham replies evasively that God himself would provide a lamb for the offering (Genesis 22: 7, 8). Lucas showed the story's denouement in a small scene in the distance on the top of the mountain, portraying the main characters twice in order to take this step into the future. This print must have fascinated Rembrandt; in his own version of 1645 he had concentrated entirely on the quiet conversation between father and son, but now standing at the sacrificial altar (fig. 86). Rembrandt based the relocation of this scene from the walk to the place of sacrifice in the description by Flavius Josephus in *Antiquities of the Jews* (1: 13, 2ff.). According to this text, Abraham openly told his son about the Lord's command, to which Isaac replied that he was prepared to submit entirely to God's will. In this way, both Abraham and his son were examples of firmness in their belief and faith.[4]

Artists also portrayed the moment *after* the rescue by the angel: in his 1642 publication *Lof der Schilder-Konst* (*In Praise of the Art of Painting*), Philips Angel mentions a grisaille by Jan Lievens in which the sacrifice is depicted

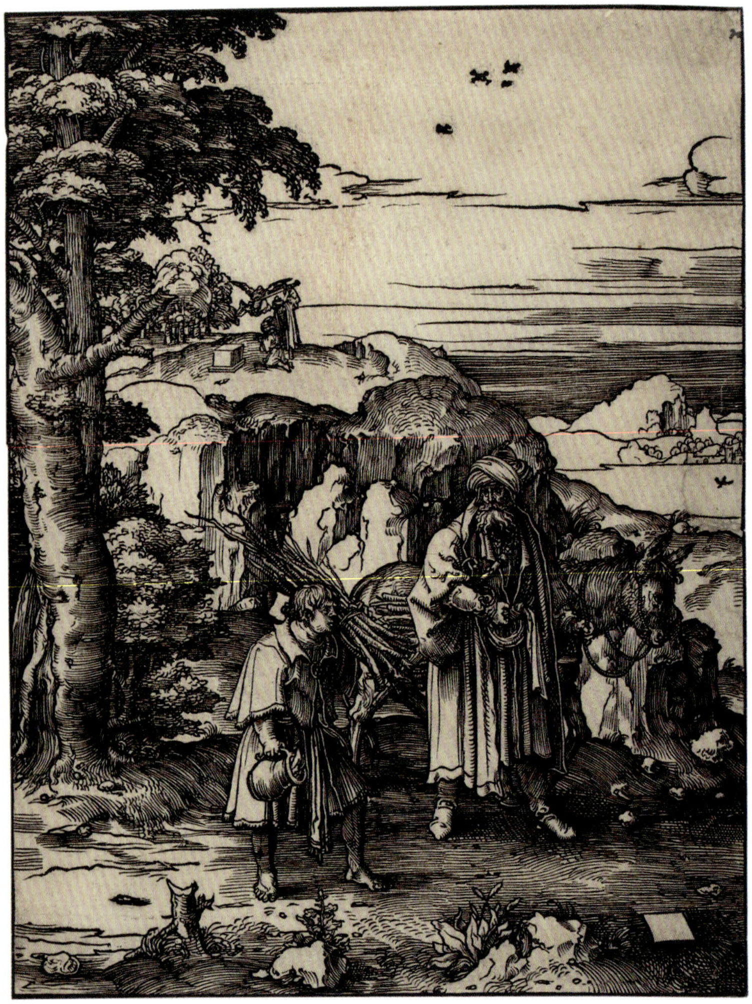

FIG. 85
LUCAS VAN LEYDEN
(died 1533)
Abraham and Isaac, about 1517
Woodcut, 28.5 × 21.2 cm
Rijksmuseum, Amsterdam

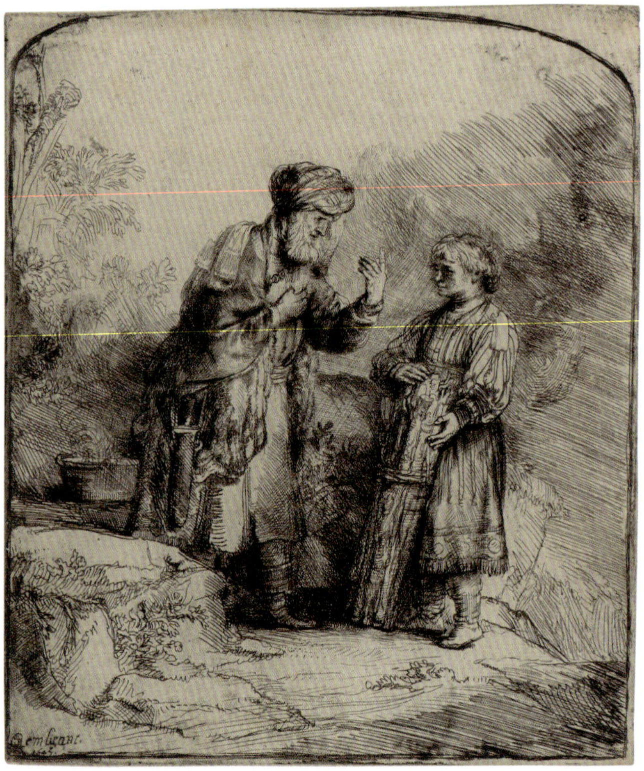

FIG. 86
Abraham and Isaac, 1645
Etching and drypoint,
15.7 × 13 cm
Rijksmuseum, Amsterdam.
Bequest of Mr and Mrs
De Bruijn-van der Leeuw,
Muri, Switzerland

119
Abraham's Sacrifice, 1655
Etching and drypoint,
15.6 × 13.1 cm
Only state
The Fitzwilliam Museum,
Cambridge (AD.12.39-58)

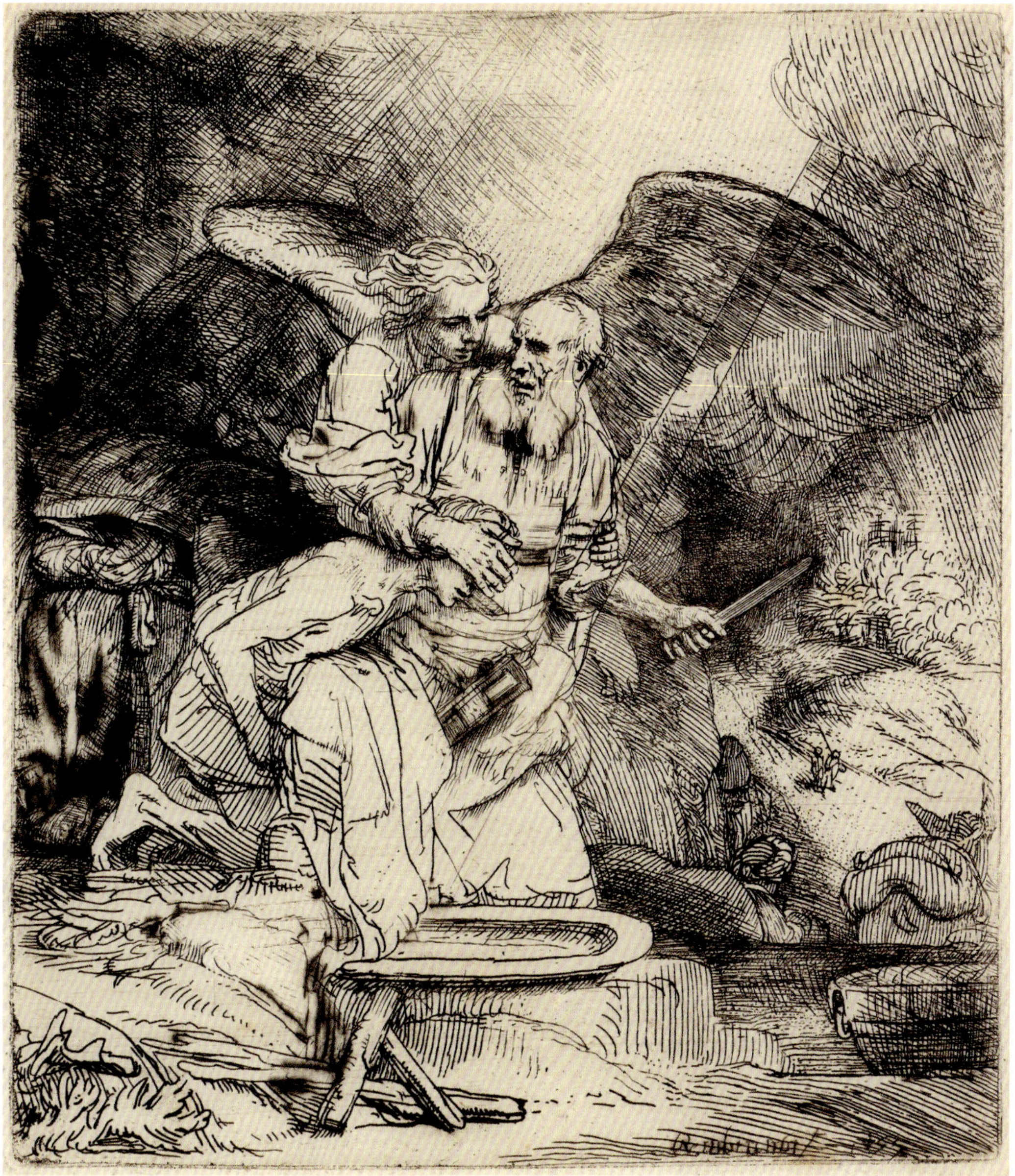

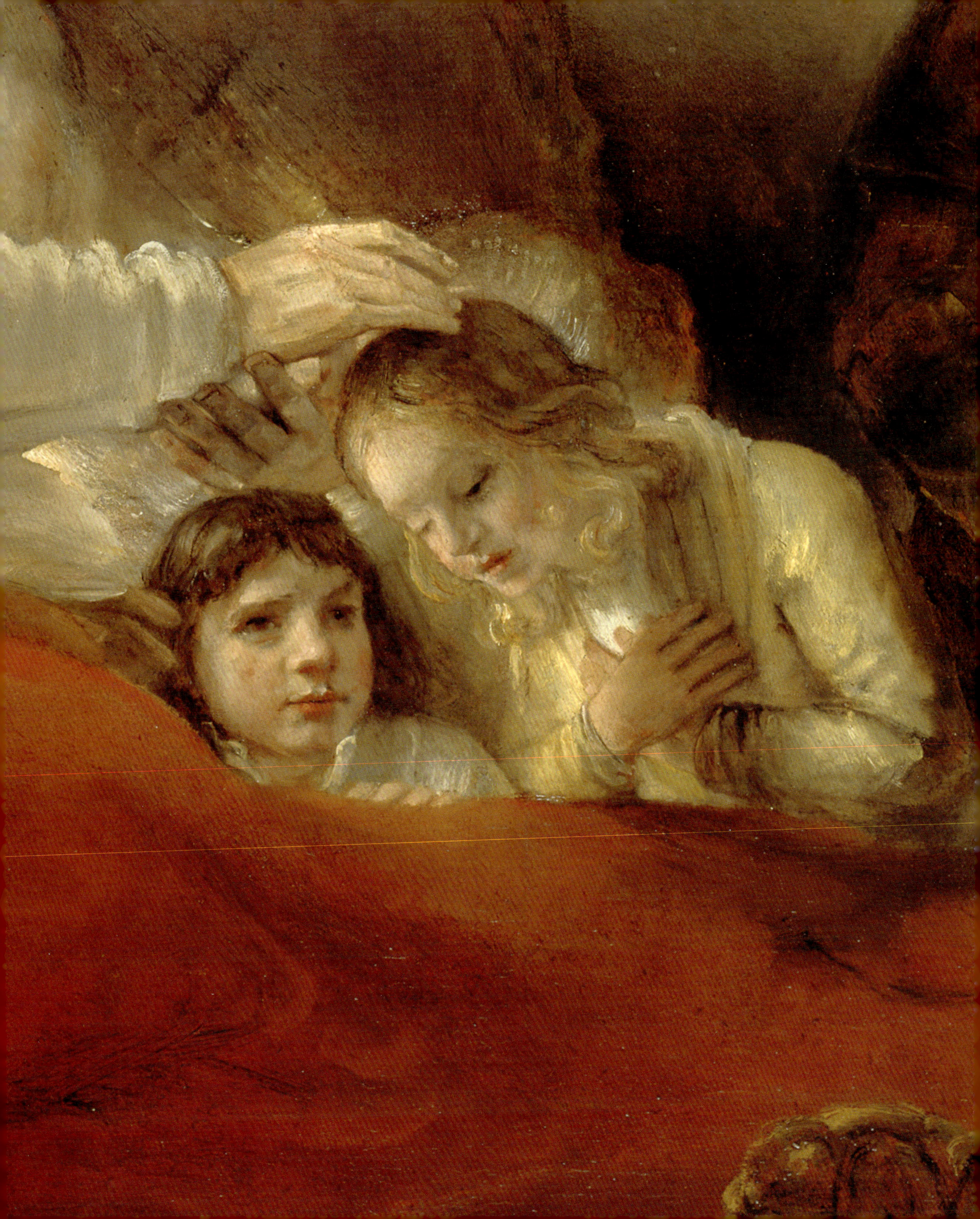

'quite unconventionally and equally idiosyncratically' as the father and son 'embraced each other (as if they had rediscovered one another) and kissed'. Angel also refers to the text by Flavius Josephus as the written source for this, as it continues beyond the biblical version to describe how the two embraced and were full of joy.[5] The grisaille has not survived, but a large painting by Lievens of this same scene has (fig. 87).[6] Abraham and Isaac are in each other's arms and raise their eyes in gratitude towards heaven. The skin of the sacrificial ram lying covered in blood on the ground is a reminder of their narrow escape from tragedy. But this is no longer a depiction of brief, intense movement signifying a sudden change in the characters' feelings; instead, the scene is imbued with the sustained harmony of inner emotions. According to the 1656 inventory of his possessions, Rembrandt owned a painting by Jan Lievens on the subject of the sacrifice of Isaac, but unfortunately it is not known which this was.[7] Nevertheless, he would have been aware of and would have appreciated Lievens's approach in this work: it was in line with the artistic concept of portraying contemplative figures with introspective emotions that he himself prioritised in his later work.

In 1656 Rembrandt took on the subject of Jacob's blessing, and we are able to follow his considerations step by step as he decides to focus on a scene *after* the moment of conflict (cat. 120). The Bible states (Genesis 48) that the patriarch Jacob had become old and sick in Egypt. When his son Joseph heard this, he took his sons Manasseh and Ephraim to see their grandfather. 'Israel', the name Jacob had acquired after wrestling with the angel (cat. 118), sat up in bed and said to Joseph that he wished to adopt the two grandchildren as his own sons, ordering Joseph to bring them to him so that he could give them his blessing:

> Now the eyes of Israel were dim for age, so that he could not see.... And Joseph took them both, Ephraim in his right hand toward Israel's left hand, and Manasseh in his left hand toward Israel's right hand, and brought them unto him. And Israel stretched out his right hand, and laid it upon Ephraim's head, who was the younger, and his left hand upon Manasseh's head, guiding his hand wittingly ... And when Joseph saw that his father laid his right hand upon the head of

FIG. 87
JAN LIEVENS (1607–1674)
The Sacrifice of Isaac, about 1638
Oil on canvas, 180 × 136 cm
Herzog Anton Ulrich Museum, Braunschweig

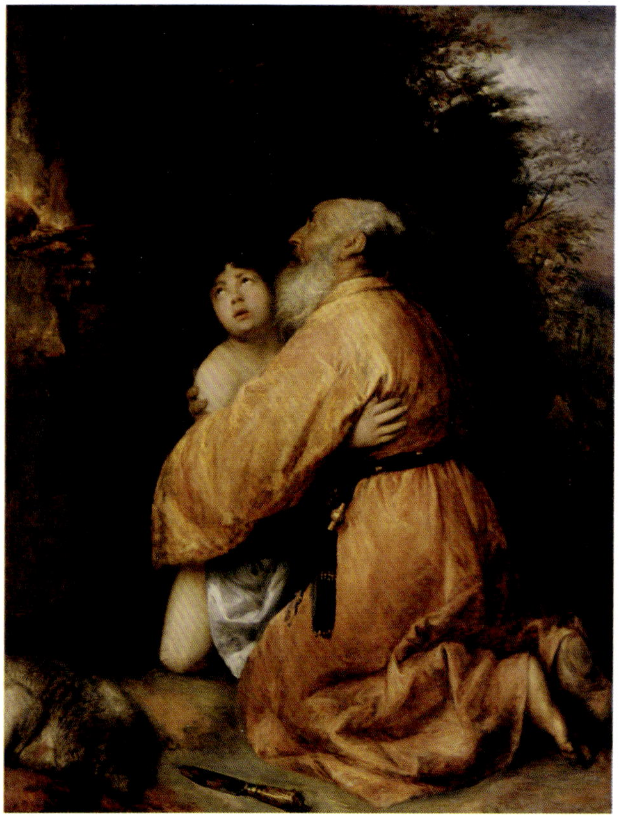

Detail from *Jacob blessing the Sons of Joseph* (cat. 120)

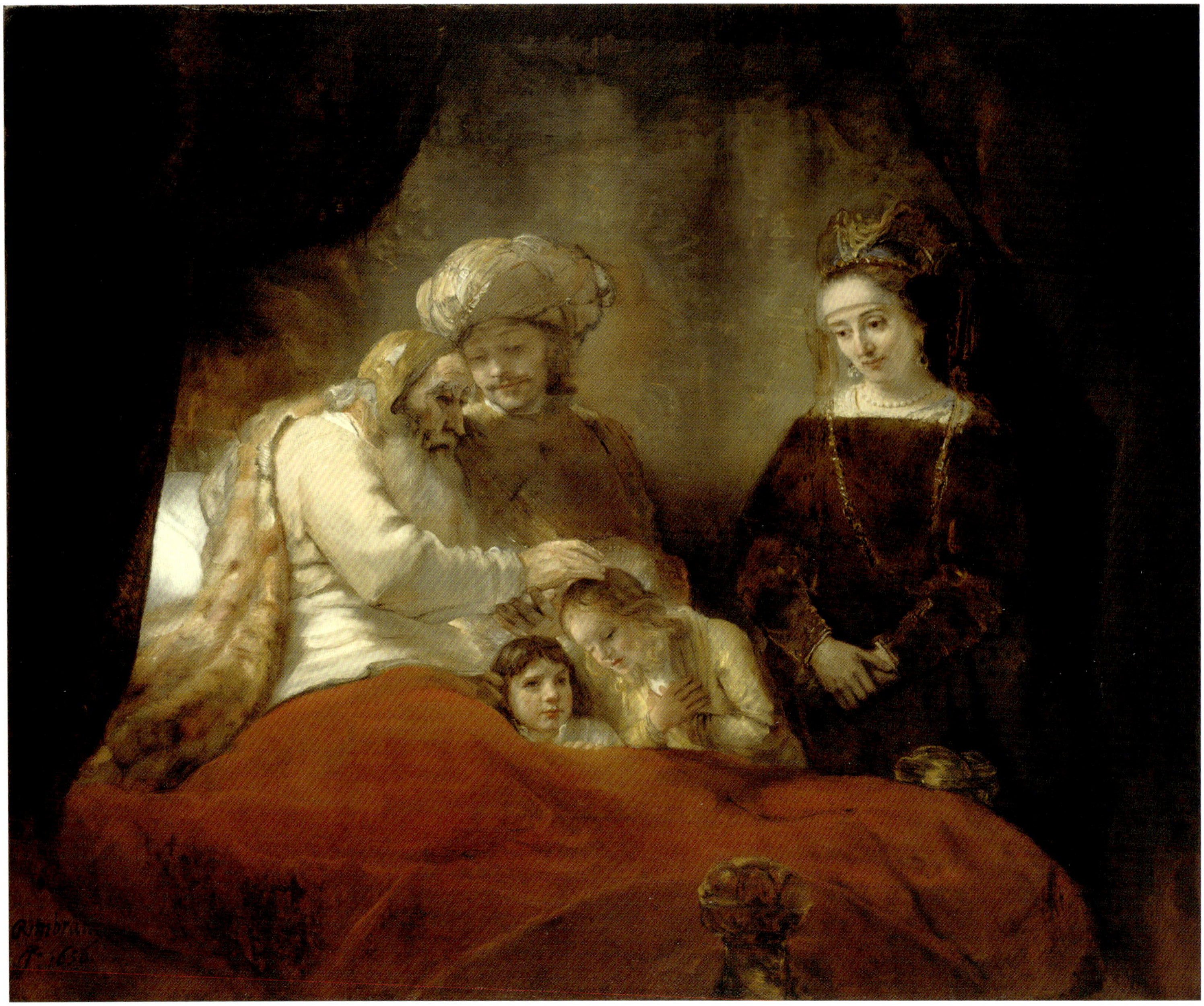

120
Jacob blessing the Sons of Joseph, 1656
Oil on canvas, 173 × 209 cm
Museumslandschaft Hessen Kassel, Gemäldegalerie Alte Meister

Ephraim, it displeased him: and he held up his father's hand to remove it from Ephraim's head unto Manasseh's head. And Joseph said unto his father, Not so, my father: for this is the firstborn; put thy right hand upon his head. And his father refused, and said, I know it, my son, I know it: he also shall become a people, and he also shall be great: but truly his younger brother shall be greater than he, and his seed shall become a multitude of nations.

Biblical scholars have interpreted this as a prophecy of the coming of Christendom, equating Manasseh with Judaism. Consequently, according to artistic tradition Ephraim is usually depicted as blond, while his elder brother is portrayed with dark hair.[8]

The Dutch *Statenbijbel* (completed in 1637) states that Jacob guided his hands *'verstandelijk'*, meaning deliberately or consciously (Genesis 48: 14); the King James Authorised Version (cited above) uses the term 'wittingly'. The early Christian and medieval concordances used the translation 'while he crossed his arms'; this can still be read today in some Catholic versions.[9]

Maarten van Heemskerck (1498–1574) depicted the scene thus in 1549 (fig. 88); as a result, the disregard for the rights of the firstborn becomes clear immediately as the viewer is confronted with the oddness of such a blessing. The viewer is indeed witnessing a struggle, a conflict between the father and the son, who is extremely displeased with this error and (literally) tries to take matters into his own hands. The reversal in the order of precedence of Manasseh and Ephraim is traditionally pictured as a dramatic scene full of passion.

In 1636, twenty years before his large painting, Rembrandt recorded this dispute in a drawing that is now lost (fig. 90).[10] Here Joseph approaches his father directly, his eyes narrowed and his mouth fiercely open as he corrects Jacob. He gestures wildly with one hand in front of his father's face, while taking hold of his arm roughly with the other hand to prevent the (in his view) erroneous blessing. The action centres on an openly staged conflict rather than the blessing. Pupils of Rembrandt such as Jan Victors (1619–1676 or later) also portrayed this scene in a similar fashion.[11] Rembrandt himself also initially returned to his old drawing for his 1656 version of the picture: an X-radiograph (fig. 89)

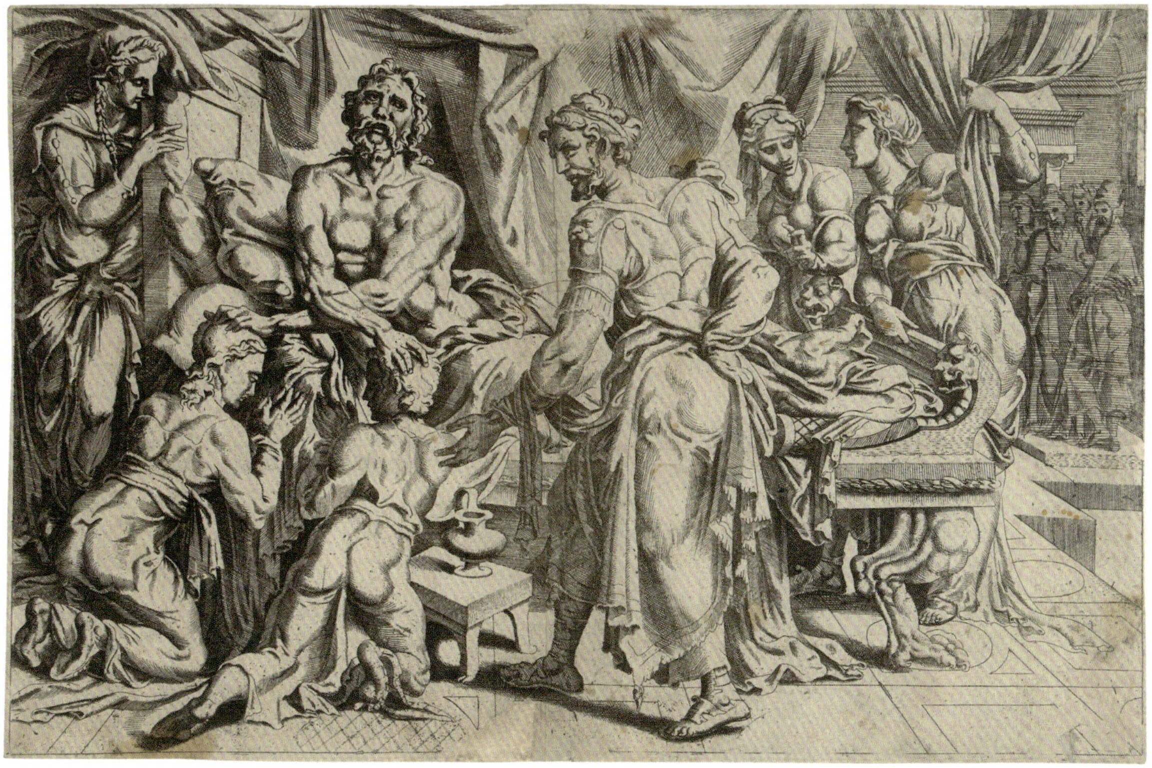

FIG. 88
DIRCK VOLKERTSZ COORNHERT (1522–1590) after MAARTEN VAN HEEMSKERCK (1498–1574)
Jacob blessing Ephraim and Manasseh, about 1549
Etching, 24.8 × 37.2 cm
Rijksmuseum, Amsterdam

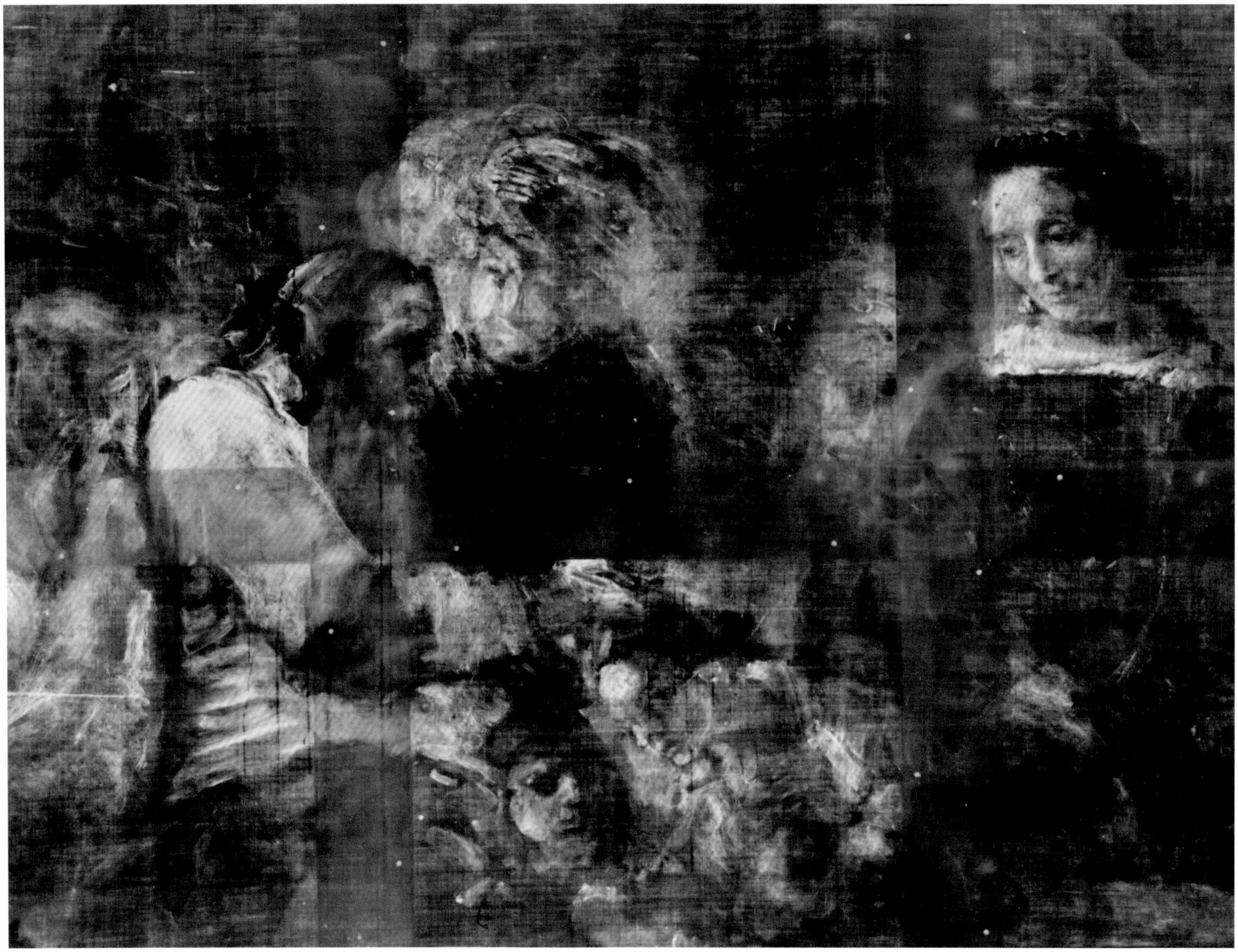

FIG. 89
X-radiograph of the central part of *Jacob blessing the Sons of Joseph* (cat. 120)

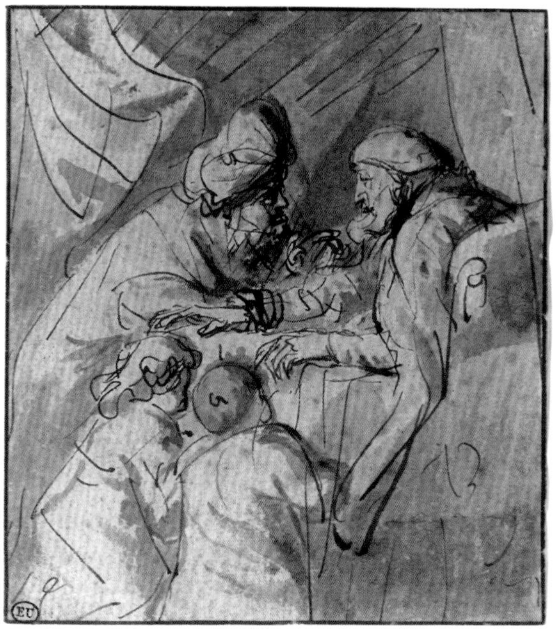

FIG. 90
Jacob blessing Ephraim and Manasseh, about 1636
Pen and brown ink with grey wash, 10.7 × 11.3 cm
Present whereabouts unknown (formerly B. Houthakker collection, Amsterdam)

reveals that he planned a symmetric positioning of the old man Jacob with his son directly opposite him (Joseph's head is only shown to the left of the shoulder of the woman, who was added later). Thus he used a mirror image of the composition in the drawing, and also moved the two children to behind the bed. In a subsequent stage he decided to shift Joseph closer to his father, although in a stance that deviates considerably from the one visible today: Joseph looked directly into Jacob's face and his facial features clearly appeared hostile. Rembrandt is concerned in this phase of the picture's production only with the portrayal of the quarrel, as depicted in the older examples from the artistic tradition.

Finally, Rembrandt made a further modification before arriving at the solution that makes his painting so exceptional even today: he inclined Joseph's head towards his father, so that they are almost cheek by jowl and appear to merge together. Joseph's eyes are now directed at his father's hand, which he gently supports with his fingertips. It is no longer possible to speak of a conflict, as neither the facial expressions nor the gestures betray any signs of a quarrel. Joseph has realised that his father deliberately positioned his hands in this way. Now it is the blessing itself that takes up all the attention and is completed by the old man laying his hand on Ephraim's head. Reflected light sparkles around the head of Ephraim as he bows forward devotedly – Rembrandt knows how to use light to stage a scene. Those present are witnessing a significant action, that of the blessing, which exudes peace. Although she is not mentioned in the biblical story, Rembrandt has included Joseph's Egyptian wife, Asenath, on the right; she observes the event from behind the bed, just as the viewer observes from the front of the bed. She completes the composition not only from a formal point of view, but also in terms of the subject, as she completes the family. Rembrandt may have added her by arrangement with the unknown person who commissioned the painting.[12]

So Rembrandt was now tackling this subject anew and using a completely different design, abandoning the traditional representation of a passionate struggle, portraying instead the peaceful concord of the emotions of all the participants. The choice of the moment after the quarrel between Joseph and Jacob brings to mind the picture by Jan Lievens of Abraham and Isaac after the rescue by the angel (fig. 87). In both cases, the shift in the moment being portrayed leads to a scene of reconciliation and peace.

Thus a further theme is added to the pictorial concepts that characterise Rembrandt's later work: the search for moments following a conflict, in other words, quiet moments in which the mood of the scene is one of calm and reconciliation. This does not require a happy denouement: once accepted, even an unhappy fate can result in spiritual peace. The neo-Stoic Justus Lipsius (1547–1606) prized spiritual constancy as an ethical goal, to be freed 'from the yoke of the passions and fate' and able to cope serenely with all hardships like a 'bastion of calm'.[13]

Rembrandt is therefore interested in fate, which permits reflection on past conflicts and the vagaries of fortune. A significant example in this context is a drawing in which he summarises the fate of the Byzantine general Flavius Belisarius (about AD 505–565), a story he had evidently not previously known about. Indeed, representations of the story were quite rare in Rembrandt's time. Belisarius was one of the most successful military commanders serving the Emperor Justinian, and was awarded the highest offices and honours. However, when he fell from grace he was blinded as a punishment and discharged from military service.[14] Rembrandt's interest is less concerned with the process of Belisarius' downfall than with the fate of the once-great general who is now a beggar, scraping a living on the streets, his lowly status warning those who recognise him of the mutability of fortune. Rembrandt noted the following on his drawing of this subject (cat. 121): 'Take pity on poor Belisarius, who once enjoyed great esteem because of his valiant deeds and now has been robbed of his sight through jealousy'. In 1636 he had portrayed the blinding of Samson as a most horrific event, the victim positioned right in the foreground of the painting; with Belisarius, he depicts a similar tale long after the event, eliciting sympathy for a poor beggar after his blinding. Yet Belisarius himself does not complain: he is not the vehicle for the passion of the painting, for he has accepted his fate. Rather, it is the other figures who find this spectacle distressing.

Rembrandt's words 'Take pity' could also be the subtitle of an impressive painting that was certainly produced in his studio and according to his design, even if it was not painted entirely by him. This picture, *Haman recognises his Fate* (fig. 91), shows the precipitous fall from grace suffered by one of the favourites of King Ahasuerus, but does so very unconventionally

121
The Blind Belisarius receiving Alms, about 1656–60
Pen and brown ink with corrections in lead white, 16.7 × 12.1 cm
Staatliche Museen zu Berlin, Kupferstichkabinett

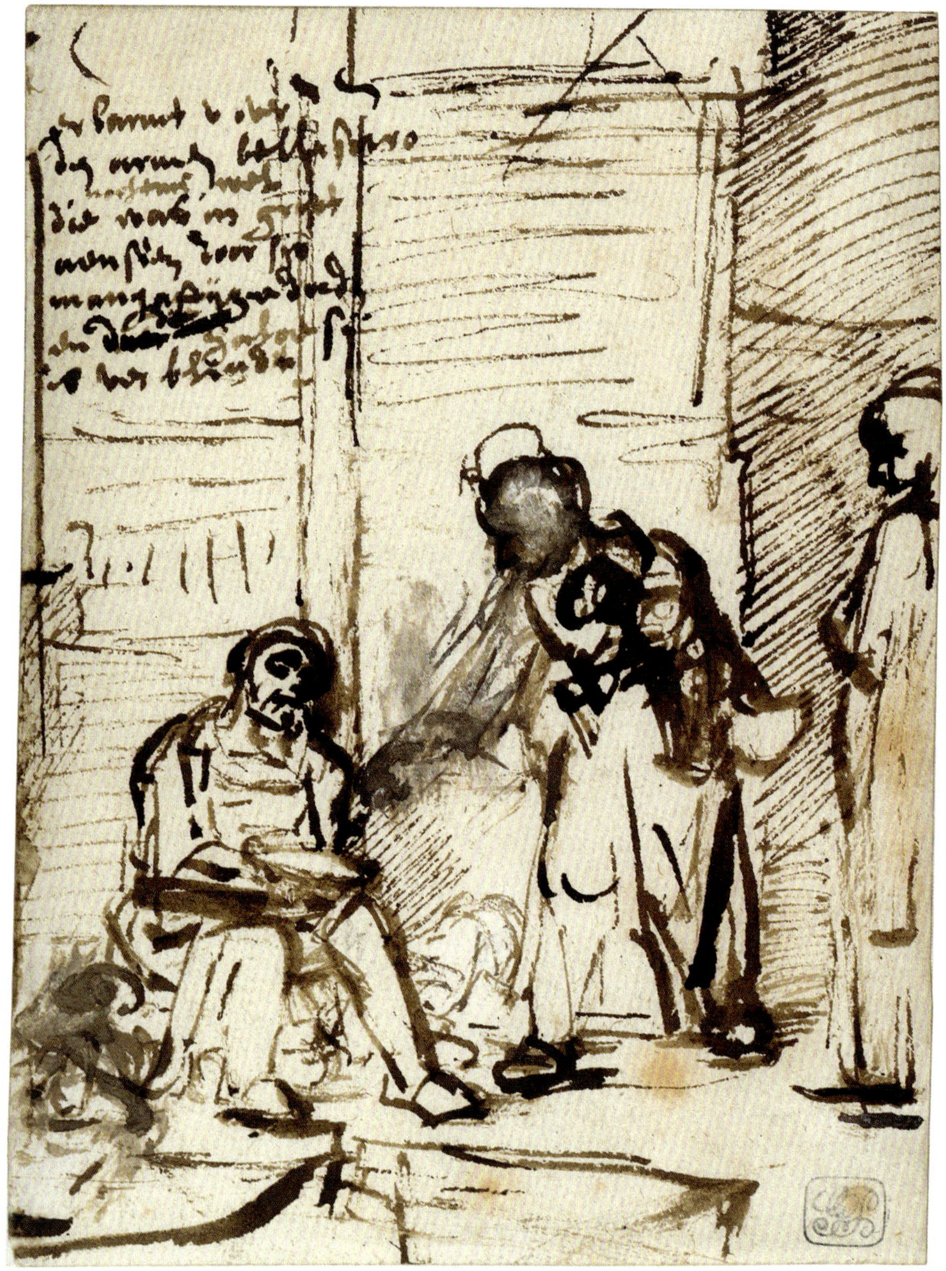

FIG. 91
REMBRANDT
and WORKSHOP
Haman recognises his Fate,
about 1666–9
Oil on canvas, 127 × 117 cm
The State Hermitage Museum,
St Petersburg

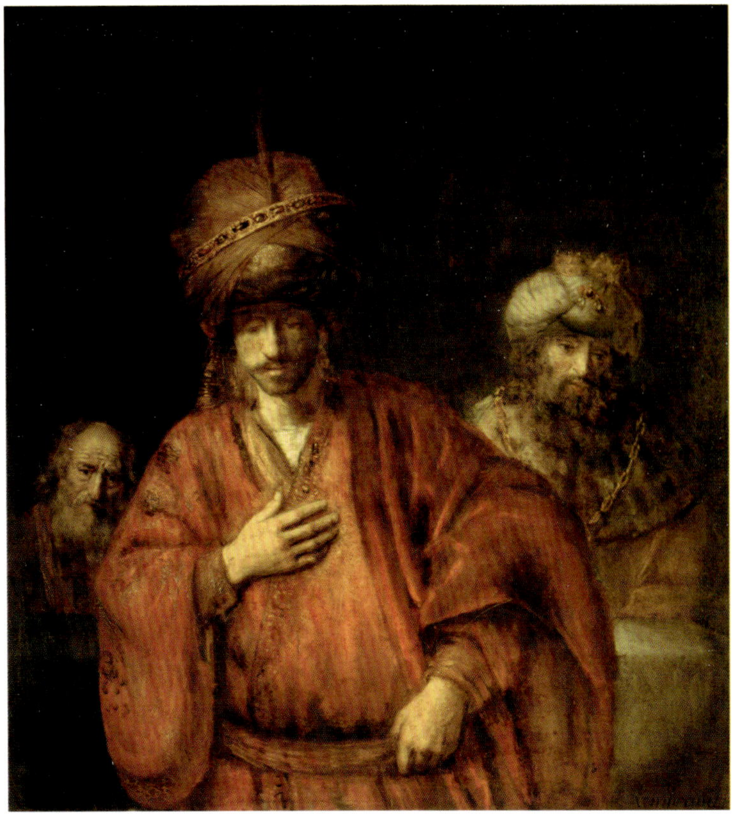

by concentrating on one main figure. Haman devised a plan to kill all the Jews in the Persian kingdom in a single night. The Jew Mordecai, an exemplary supporter of the king, had not received any proper recognition for an earlier act of deliverance. When Ahasuerus, who still knew nothing about the plot to annihilate the Jews, asked Haman what should be done with a man whom the king wished to honour, Haman thought the king was referring to him and so he recommended a procession in royal garments on a royal horse. But he was then given the order to honour his enemy Mordecai in this manner (Esther 6: 6–10; Flavius Josephus, *Antiquities of the Jews*, XI: 6, 10). Rembrandt depicts Haman having just received the king's order; he is quiet and pensive while Mordecai watches him. Yet Haman is in the foreground, very close to the picture's edges and walking towards us as he looks downwards, his hand on his heart. He no longer appears as a corrupt courtier, but as a man whose fate it is to become the guilty one. According to the doctrine of predestination, an individual's own ruin could be predetermined: he may only then be saved if he acknowledges God's decision and hopes for his grace. Haman does not rebel against his fate; instead, he understands that there is nothing more he can do (Esther 6: 12–13). He has accepted his fate.[15]

Another work created in Rembrandt's studio at the same period, around 1666–9, is *The Return of the Prodigal Son* (fig. 92), the largest painting produced in the final years of his life. This could just as easily be entitled 'Pity' or 'Reconciliation'. Christ himself told this parable of two sons. One of them asked his father to pay him his inheritance, then went into the wide world and squandered his wealth on riotous living, until he was eventually reduced to living amongst swine. Full of remorse, he returned home and was welcomed back joyfully by his father (Luke 15: 14–32). Once again, the viewer is confronted with the action head-on. The son, dressed in rags, is on his knees in front of his father; one shoe has slipped off his foot to reveal dirt and calluses. The father leans over his son and gently embraces him with both hands. Visually, his arms form a diamond shape framing the head of his son. The reactions of the figures gathered around are calm and thoughtful. The figure on the far right is possibly the Prodigal's brother; in the parable he responds with jealousy to his brother's return, but here his face – like those of the other two men – is calm and thoughtful, even serene. The face of the prodigal son himself is barely visible. Once again, the viewer is being invited to project his own understanding of the emotions in the scene (see p. 250 above). There is no sign here of

FIG. 92
REMBRANDT
and WORKSHOP
The Return of the Prodigal Son,
about 1666–9
Oil on canvas, 262 × 206 cm
The State Hermitage Museum,
St Petersburg

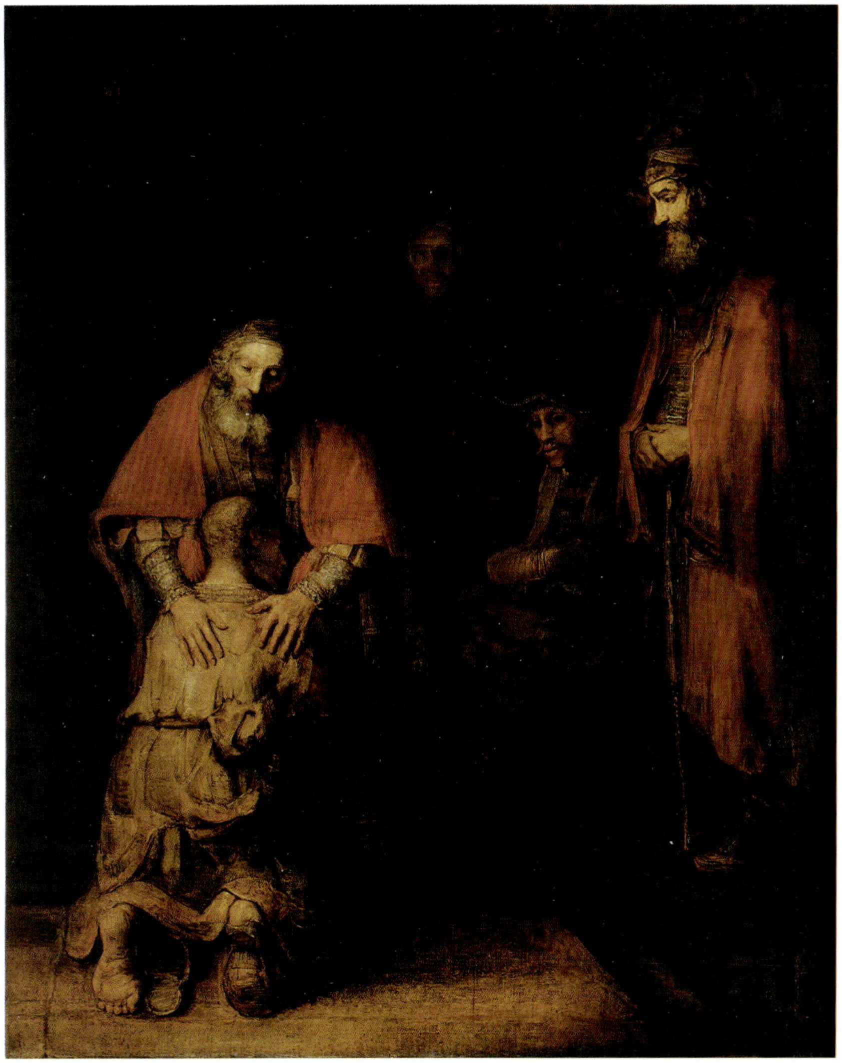

any sudden transition from misfortune to good fortune: the father does not rush to meet the son, nor does the son beg first for forgiveness (Luke 15: 20ff.). Instead, the gentle act of reconciliation exudes permanence – there is nothing to disturb this enduring scene.

This concept – of presenting moments of reconciliation or emotional peace beyond the critical moment – is demonstrated perhaps in its most far-reaching form in Rembrandt's final depiction of the presentation of Jesus in the temple (cat. 122). Since 1627 he had created several versions of this biblical story in paintings and prints, including his impressive etching of 1654 (cat. 77). Saint Luke's Gospel relates that the holy family set off for the temple in Jerusalem to dedicate Jesus to God in accordance with Jewish custom, and to obtain redemption by offering a sacrifice. In the temple they meet Simeon, an elderly and devout man, to whom it had been foretold that he would only die once he had seen the Messiah. Simeon recognises the child as the Messiah, takes him in his arms and gives thanks to God: 'Lord, now lettest thou thy servant depart in peace, according to thy word: for mine eyes have seen thy salvation, which thou hast prepared before the face of all people; a light to lighten the Gentiles, and the glory of thy people Israel' (Luke 2: 25–33). The etching from 1654 shows Simeon's eulogy during the presentation of Jesus in the Temple. Simeon is kneeling – his eyes closed against the bright light – in front of the imposing high priests, who look down on him without really understanding.

Rembrandt chose to give Simeon a similarly introspective look in a small drawing in Jacob Heyblocq's *album amicorum*, which he dated 1661 (cat. 123). Here, for the first time, he restricted the scene to the three half-figures of Simeon, Mary and Joseph, creating a much more intimate atmosphere. All the attention is

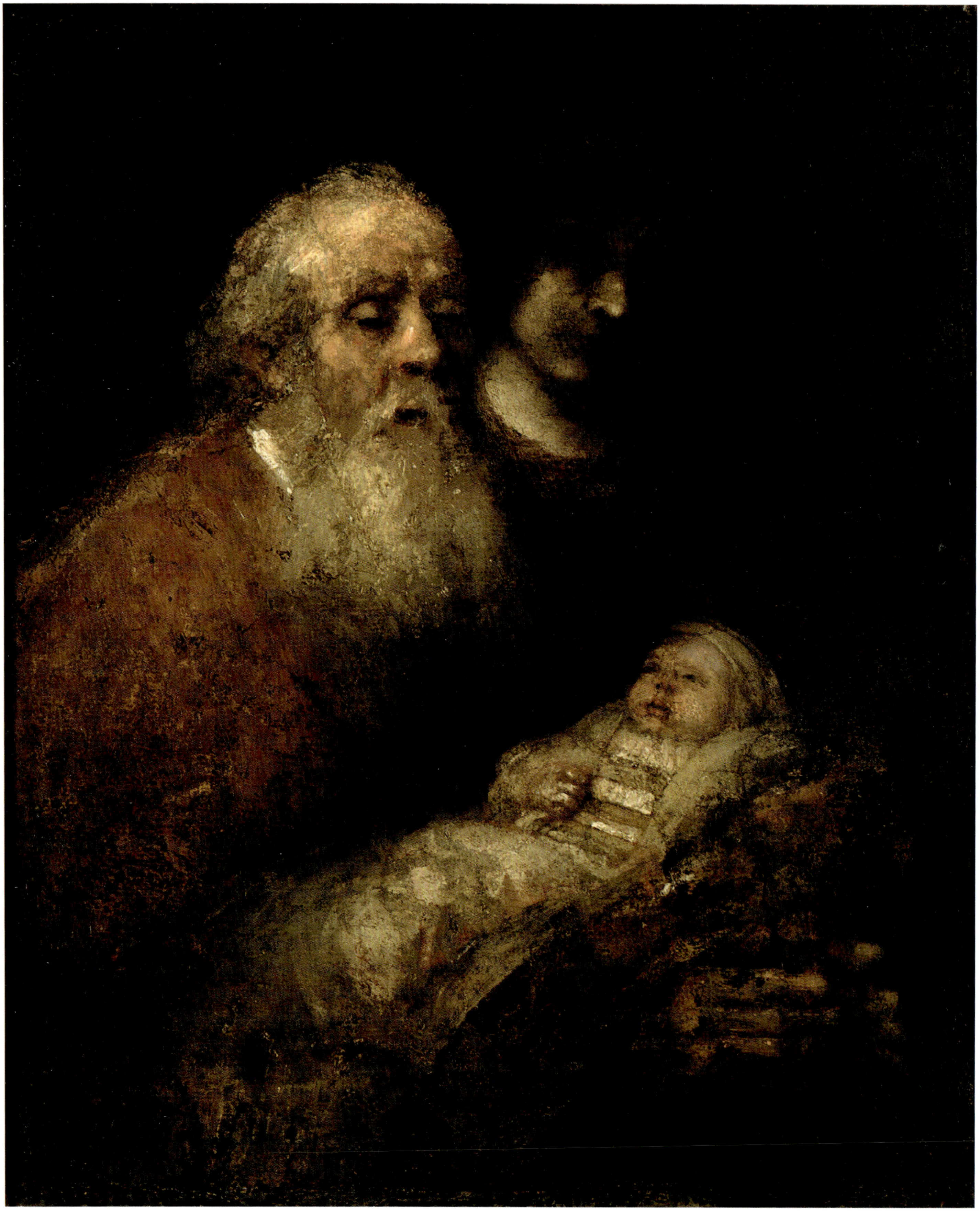

122
Simeon with the Infant Christ in the Temple, about 1669
Oil on canvas, 98.5 × 79.5 cm
Nationalmuseum, Stockholm

FIG. 93
JÜRGEN OVENS (1523–78)
Simeon in the Temple, 1651
Oil on canvas, 113.5 × 101 cm
Kunsthalle, Kiel

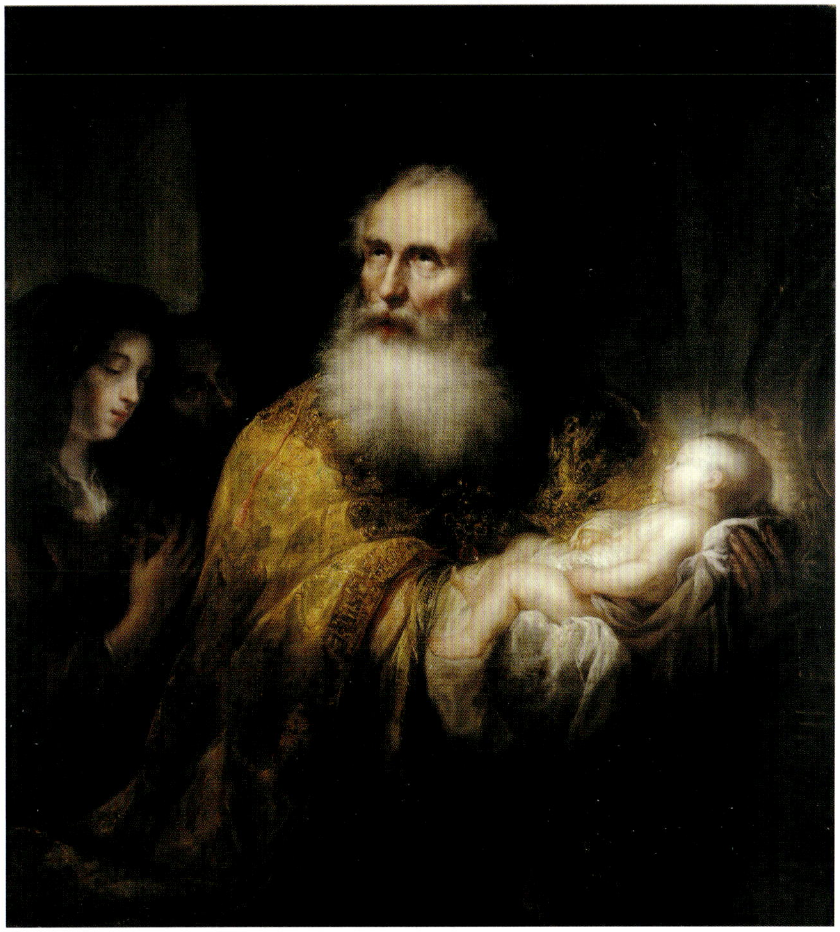

drawn to the old man talking as he holds the child in his arms. The painting of the subject (cat. 122) remained unfinished in Rembrandt's studio, where it was remarked upon by visitors only a few months before the artist's death in October 1669.[16] As in the Heyblocq drawing, Rembrandt reduced the scene to half-length figures. The painting's poor condition does not allow us to draw any conclusions about the figure of Mary in the background; Rembrandt probably only sketched the outline, to be completed by another artist.[17] Simeon carries the infant Jesus in his arms, but without holding him properly: he stretches his hands out in front stiffly. It seems as if he does not dare touch the child, or as if his hands are about to close in prayer. Once again, Simeon's eyes are almost shut while his mouth is slightly open: it is his inner vision that causes him to utter his words of praise. He knows that the Messiah has arrived and now he can 'depart in peace', in the words of the Bible.

We know that this painting was commissioned, so the choice of subject should not be interpreted as a 'personal testimonial' by Rembrandt, a kind of final statement of his belief. Furthermore, the pictorial solution of creating a 'close-up' with the half-figure of Simeon was far from unknown. This compositional format apparently enjoyed a certain popularity among clients in Utrecht, as it was utilised in their interpretations of the subject by several artists: Paulus Moreelse (1571–1638) in 1614, Jan van Bijlert (1598–1671) around 1625–35 and Hendrick Bloemaert (about 1601–1672) around 1635–40.[18] Rembrandt's pupils also took this approach in paintings of the subject: for instance, Jürgen Ovens created an impressive version in 1651 (fig. 93). However, all show Simeon looking towards heaven with his eyes open – they lack the timid attitude and introspective look that Rembrandt gave him.[19]

The rejection of intense external and visible passions in favour of introspective moods is clearly evident in Rembrandt's history paintings in the period 1654–69. Was he going his own way here, or was there a parallel development in debates about dramatic theory around

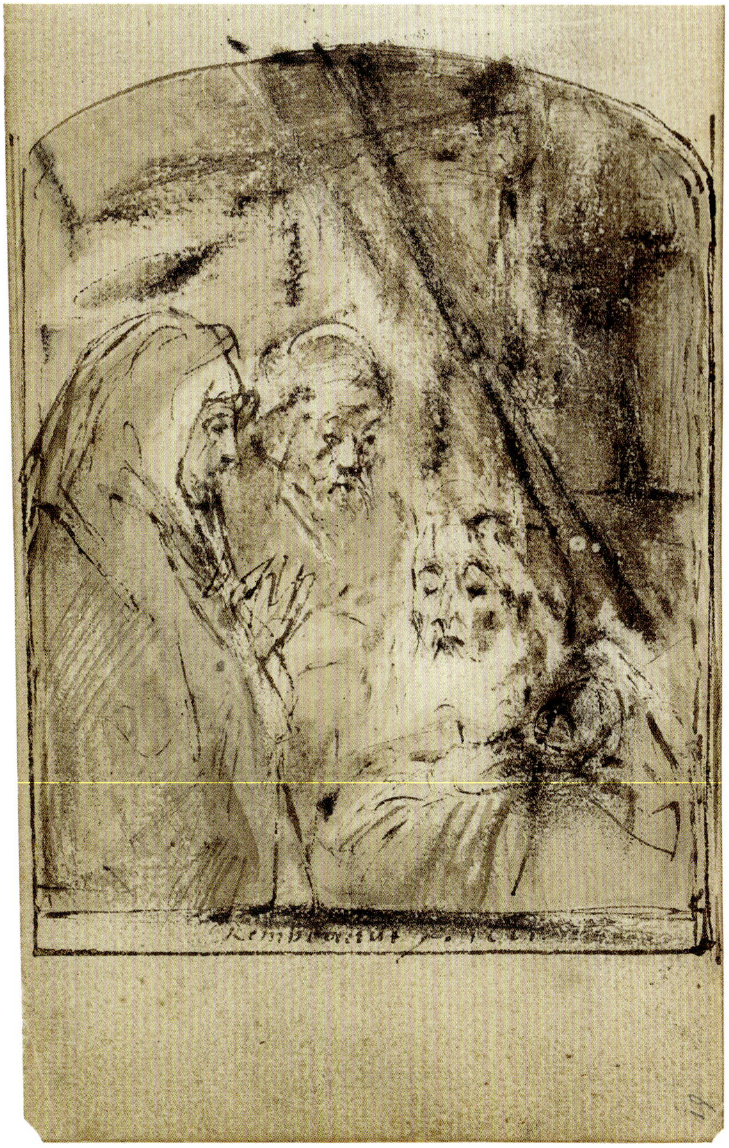

123
Simeon in the Temple
(*Album Amicorum Jacob Heyblocq*, fol. 61r), 1661
Pen and brush and brown ink with white bodycolour, 12 × 8.9 cm
Koninklijke Bibliotheek, National Library of the Netherlands, The Hague

that time in Amsterdam?[20] In the first half of the seventeenth century, the defining form in theatre was that advocated by Seneca (about 3 BC to AD 65) and Julius Caesar Scaliger (1484–1558), in which intense passions and twists of fate were presented in quick succession on the stage. The audience experienced the same passions as the protagonists as they witnessed the spectacle and atrocities being enacted; they were affected directly as they were caught up in the performance.[21] The successful tragedies of Jan Vos are eloquent proof of this: he was the very same author who verbalised strong passions in his poems about history paintings, passions that – in the case of a painting by Rembrandt of 1660 that is the subject of one of his poems – are not actually represented at all (see fig. 84).

An alternative dramatic theory based on Aristotle (384–322 BC) was formulated by Joost van den Vondel in his preface to his play *Jeptha* in 1659. He had already observed these principles in his translation of *Electra* by Sophocles (about 497–407 BC).[22] Fear and sympathy are aroused in the spectators through the unfolding of the narrative, in the course of which the protagonists experience countless passions. In the preface to *Electra*, Van den Vondel states: 'Many passions swirl through this tragedy: anger, boldness, fear, grief, hatred and love, fidelity and infidelity, sadness and joy, each in their most intense form.'[23] The conflict finally reaches a climax in the actions, Aristotle's *peripeteia* (which Vondel translates as '*staetveranderinge*', or change of state), which marks a turning point in the fate of the heroes. This climactic moment should preferably coincide with the 'discovery' ('*anagnorisis*', or '*herkennis*' in Dutch), which generally means the moment when insight into the true state of affairs is attained.[24]

There is a certain parallel here with the history paintings, in which Rembrandt no longer portrays the conflict as a clearly visible and impassioned dispute, but instead repositions the conflict in the realm of the internalised feelings of the participants. In doing so, he places the onus of envisaging the conflict on the viewer, who of course needs to be familiar with the story in order to do so. Yet he also seeks to avoid the turning point in the action, the *peripeteia*, looking instead for moments of reflection. The conflict is observed by looking back at it, by reflecting on the experience of fate. This is not something mentioned by Vondel, who still takes plays full of '*hartstoghten*' (passions) and '*woelingen*' (turmoil) as his starting point. In this respect, Rembrandt was indeed exploring new avenues.

It seems that Rembrandt came up with a new idea during this period, of how (and whether) he could achieve the '*naetuereelste beweechgelickheijt*' (most natural movement) of actions and passions in his paintings.[25] As he evidently realised, pictures are by their very nature static, so this movement cannot be achieved in a fixed and immobile image that at the same time attempts to represent a dynamic process. It is more logical to imbue the static picture with emotions that do *not* change abruptly and visibly. In the realm of affection this means not showing passions, which are by definition aroused by an external sensory stimulus, but instead inner emotions, formed within the mind by reflecting on values and on what has happened. Consequently these emotions may only be portrayed in a subdued manner, indeed often merely being suggested – and this is what Rembrandt expresses so eloquently in his late works.

We actually know very little about Rembrandt's reasons for selecting one pictorial solution rather than another – we can only analyse the body of pictures that he produced. We do not even know to which specific religious denomination he belonged, nor whether he was interested in the ethical writings of thinkers such as Lipsius, Cats or Descartes.[26] However, when we consider these highly diverse texts together, a common objective does emerge clearly: to strive for contentment and assurance in life, and peace of mind. It seems as if these ideals were the inspiration for Rembrandt in his choice of subjects and pictorial compositions towards the end of his creative life.

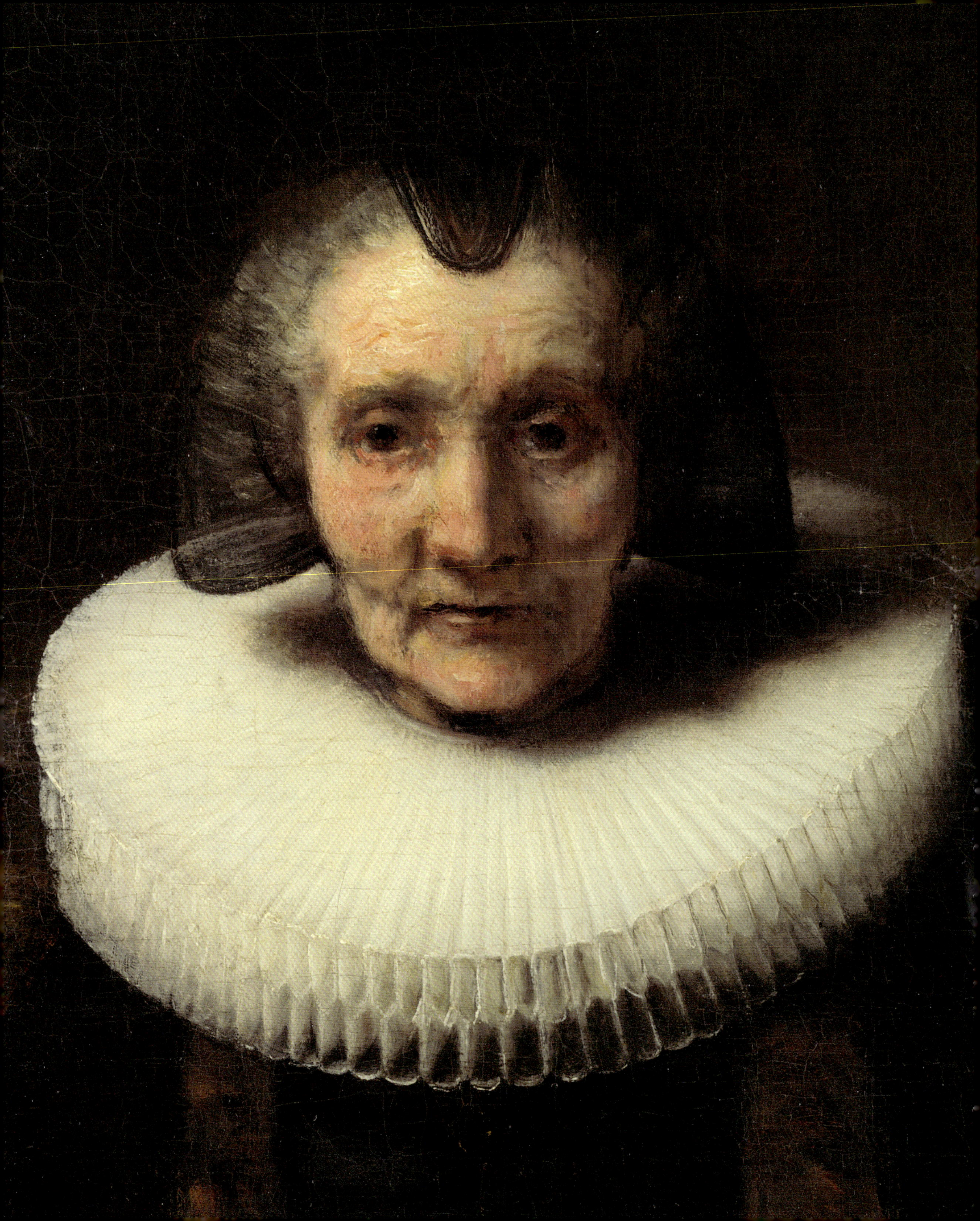

NOTES

EXPLAINING LATE REMBRANDT

1 Lairesse 1707, p. 324, quoted in Van de Wetering 1997/2009, p. 156.
2 As pointed out by Gerson 1968, p. 104. See also Van de Wetering in Amsterdam 2006b, pp. 52, 117; Van de Wetering in *Corpus* v, p. 115.
3 For Rembrandt's introspective single-figure paintings, see the chapter 'Inner Conflict'. For the artist's use of drypoint see the chapter 'Experimental Technique: The Etchings'.
4 De Piles 1699, p. 95. For the source for De Piles's theory, see Sohm 2007, p. 8.
5 De Piles 1699, pp. 259–60.
6 Vasari 1568 (1979), vol. 3, pp. 1981–2. At the end of his *Life* of the artist, however, Vasari contradicts himself by claiming that Titian damaged his own reputation by continuing to paint after he was no longer physically capable.
7 Van Mander 1604, fols 174v–177v.
8 Van Mander 1604, fols 48r–v.
9 Von Sandrart 1675, vol. 1, p. 72.
10 As in the distinction made by Raupp 1993, p. 94, referring to the critical evaluation of Homer since Aristotle: the *Iliad* is considered a dramatic, youthful work full of feeling, whereas the *Odyssey* is seen as an epic, solemn late work by Homer. On this subject, see Aristotle, *Poetics* 1459, b 14; Pseudo-Longinus, *On the Sublime* 9, 13–15.
11 Quintilian, *Institutio oratoria* v 1, 2. 8–10.
12 Ripa 1644, p. 374; see also ibid., p. 258.
13 Janssen 2007, p. 24. The often reported claim that in the early modern period one would have been lucky to live beyond the age of 35 does not take into consideration the high infant mortality rate. See ibid., p. 25. On the average ages of artists at the time of their deaths in the seventeenth century, see Held 1987, pp. 132–3; Sohm 2007, pp. 14–15.
14 For Poussin's trembling hands, see Friedländer 1962, p. 250.
15 See Van de Wetering in *Corpus* v, p. 117, and p. 151 in the chapter 'Experimental Technique: The Paintings'.
16 See, in particular, Brinckmann 1925; Pinder 1926; Lützeler 1934. Cf. Von Einem 1973; Rosand 1987; Raupp 1993.
17 Neumann 1902; Simmel 1916.
18 See, for example, Simmel 1916, p. 123; Pinder 1943, p. 106; Neumann 1902, p. 503.
19 Neumann 1902; Simmel 1916, esp. pp. 533–7. See further Tietze 1944; Gantner 1965; Von Einem 1973.
20 Munsterberg 1983; Raupp 1993, pp. 96, 97 note 86, refers to research on the psychology of creativity.
21 See Sohm 2007 on Italian artists 1500–1800.
22 Schmidt-Degener 1906, p. 5.
23 Schmidt-Degener 1906, p. 75.
24 Van de Wetering in Amsterdam 2006b, pp. 50–6, 108–15.
25 Houbraken 1718–21, vol. 1, p. 273, quoted in Ford 2007, p. 94.

LATER LIFE AND CAREER

1 Houbraken 1718–21, vol. 1, p. 272.
2 Von Sandrart 1675 (1925), p. 203. As Slive 1953, p. 93, points out: 'The beginning of the lengthy legend of Rembrandt the slob has its origin in Sandrart'. See also Scheller 1961, pp. 89–91. De Piles 1699, pp. 42–4: '… quand je veux délasser mon esprit, leur dit-il, ce n'est pas l'honneur que je cherche, c'est la liberté.'
3 Von Sandrart 1675 (1925), p. 202. Quoted from Ford 2007, p. 29. Emmens 1979, p. 85, rightly places Von Sandrart's statements on Rembrandt's lowly origins and the low company he kept in the context of the contemporary belief that an artist's life reflects how and what he paints.
4 Bartsch 19. Houbraken 1718–21, vol. 1, p. 272.
5 On Geertje Dircks, see, among others, Vis 1965; Wijnman 1968; Van Deursen in Berlin, Amsterdam and London 1991a, pp. 47–8.
6 Dudok van Heel in Berlin, Amsterdam and London 1991a, p. 60.
7 Strauss and Van der Meulen 1979, pp. 318–20, doc. nos 1654/11, 1654/12, 1654/14, 1654/15. See Roodenburg 1990, pp. 230, 233, for the explanation of the Church's charge against Hendrickje.
8 Dudok van Heel in Berlin, Amsterdam and London 1991a, p. 54. On Flinck's advantageous marriages, see Dudok van Heel 1982, p. 71; for Bol's, see Blankert 1982, pp. 22–24; Bok and Van der Molen 2009, p. 65.
9 For the first suggestion, see Dudok van Heel in Edinburgh and London 2001, p. 25, and for the second, Crenshaw 2006, p. 60.
10 The painting is in the Musée Jacquemart-André, Paris. Bredius and Gerson 1969, no. 281.
11 On the ethical judgement of insolvency and bankruptcy in the seventeenth century, see Roodenburg 1990, pp. 377–81, and Dudok van Heel in Berlin, Amsterdam and London 1991a, p. 61.
12 Strauss and Van der Meulen 1979, pp. 345–7, doc. no. 1656/10.
13 Baldinucci 1686, p. 80. Crenshaw 2006, p. 89, misreads this passage to say that it was Rembrandt's collecting in general.
14 On the effects of the war on artists' livelihoods, see Bok 1994.
15 Dudok van Heel 1997 points out that Rembrandt overpaid for the house.
16 See Dudok van Heel in Berlin, Amsterdam and London 1991a, p. 60, and Crenshaw 2006, p. 48.
17 Rembrandt borrowed 4,180 guilders from Cornelis Witsen, 1,000 from Jan Six and 4,200 from Isaack Hertsbeeck. See Strauss and Van der Meulen 1979, p. 297, doc. no. 1653/5; p. 302, doc. nos 1653/11, 1653/12; and Crenshaw 2006, pp. 51–6.
18 Strauss and Van der Meulen 1979, p. 343, doc. no. 1656/8.
19 For these sales, see Van Eeghen 1969d.
20 Van Eeghen 1969a.
21 Dudok van Heel in Berlin, Amsterdam and London 1991a, p. 61; Crenshaw 2006, p. 78.
22 Crenshaw 2006, p. 76.
23 Van Eeghen 1969e.
24 Dudok van Heel 1982.
25 Strauss and Van der Meulen 1979, pp. 305–6, doc. no. 1653/17; pp. 328–31, doc. no. 1655/6; pp. 333–4, doc. no. 1655/8; pp. 342–3, doc. no. 1656/7; pp. 393–4, doc. no. 1656/19; pp. 533–4, doc. no. 1664/6; pp. 546–7, doc. no. 1665/9; pp. 554–5, doc. no. 1665/17; Hofstede de Groot 1906, pp. 370–1, doc. no. 311.
26 See pp. 211–12 in the chapter 'Intimacy'.
27 Van Eeghen 1969a, p. 174.
28 Although Dusart's profession is frequently listed as painter in contemporary documents, his extant oeuvre is exceedingly small. His address is given in a number of documents as Prinsengracht. He probably lived in the house that his father-in-law, the painter Abraham de Verwer (1585–1650), purchased in 1641. On this house, see Blaauw 2005, p. 80. Dusart also lived in The Hague from 1664 to 1666. On Dusart, see also Briels 1997, p. 323.
29 For the documents involving Dusart and Rembrandt, see Strauss and Van der Meulen 1979, pp. 532–3, doc. no. 1664/4; p. 563, doc. no. 1666/4; pp. 576–7, doc. no. 1668/5; pp. 586–9, doc. no. 1669/5.
30 See pp. 209, 211 in the chapter 'Intimacy'.
31 See also Dudok van Heel 2006, p. 215, where the inhabitants of the Jordaan neighbourhood are considered to be the 'ordinary folk' mentioned by Houbraken.
32 Strauss and Van der Meulen 1979, pp. 462–5, doc. no. 1660/20.
33 Hinterding 2006, vol. 1, p. 124.
34 Hinterding 2006, vol. 1, pp. 148–9.

35 Von Sandrart 1675 (1925), p. 203. Quoted from Ford 2007, p. 30.
36 For a list of probable Rembrandt pupils and the likely dates when they studied with him, see Liedtke 2004a, p. 68.
37 Houbraken 1718–21, vol. I, p. 256.
38 Strauss and Van der Meulen 1979, pp. 410–13, doc. no. 1658/3.
39 Heppner 1935. For Bol's *Moses descends from Mount Sinai*, about 1663 (Royal Palace [formerly Town Hall], Amsterdam; oil on canvas, 423 × 284 cm), see Blankert 1982, pp. 109–10, no. 47.
40 See Brown in Berlin, Amsterdam and London 1991a, p. 274. The painting's size also makes it unlikely that it served as a demonstration piece, as Wheelock has suggested (in Washington and Los Angeles 2005, p. 35 note 8).
41 Houbraken 1718–21, vol. II, p. 22. Quoted from Schwarz 1985, p. 282.
42 Strauss and Van der Meulen 1979, p. 451, doc. no. 1659/21. Dudok van Heel 1969a identified the painting in question with the full-length portrait of a man in Kassel (Gemäldegalerie Alte Meister, Staatliche Museen, Kassel, inv. GK 239). This identification is not endorsed in *Corpus* III, pp. 297–304, no. A 129. See also Weber in Kassel 2006, pp. 195–201, no. 27. This is also discussed in the chapter 'Artistic Conventions', see p. 274 note 7.
43 Von Sandrart 1675 (1925), p. 203; Slive 1953, pp. 92–3.
44 Dudok van Heel 1982, p. 75; Schwartz 1985, p. 318.
45 Van Eeghen 1956. The drawing was made when Rembrandt was considering making changes to the composition. See Haak 1969; Schatborn in Berlin, Amsterdam and London 1991b, p. 130.
46 Bille 1956a; Bille 1956b.
47 Strauss and Van der Meulen 1979, pp. 499–502, doc. no. 1662/6, where the English translation mistakenly implies that the painting was not yet installed in the Town Hall. Quoted, therefore, from Buchbinder-Green 1974, p. 204.
48 This hypothesis was proposed by Franken 2004, who also demonstrated that the changes to the painting were made before it was installed in the Town Hall.
49 Van de Waal 1952, vol. I, p. 233; Van de Waal 1974, p. 35. See also p. 73 in the present volume.
50 Blankert 1975, p. 27. See also Blankert 1982, p. 45.
51 Strauss and Van der Meulen 1979, pp. 531–2, doc. no. 1664/3, pp. 533–4, doc. no. 1664/6.
52 Strauss and Van der Meulen 1979, p. 505, doc. no. 1662/9.
53 Houbraken 1718–21, vol. I, p. 269.
54 For this and the following observations, see the graphs published in Bok and Van der Molen 2009.
55 For Rihel's biography, see Van Eeghen 1958. For Jacob Trip and Margaretha de Geer, see Dudok van Heel 1979.
56 See Dudok van Heel 1969b, pp. 234–5.
57 On Hinlopen's familial ties, see Dudok van Heel 1969b, p. 233; Schwartz 1985, pp. 272–3.
58 For *The Anatomy Lesson of Dr Nicolaes Tulp* see *Corpus* II, pp. 172–89, no. A 51.
59 As pointed out by Van Eeghen 1957, p. 80.
60 Rembrandt received a 75-guilder advance for a portrait in 1654, but the total price is not known; Strauss and Van der Meulen 1979, pp. 310–11, doc. no. 1654/4.
61 Strauss and Van der Meulen 1979, pp. 499–502, doc. no. 1662/6.
62 Wheelock 1995, pp. 270–6, esp. p. 273. See also *Corpus* V, pp. 647–58, no. V 30.
63 The commission is discussed in more detail on pp. 215 and 218 in the present volume.
64 The present whereabouts of the modelli is not known. On this commission, which only recently came to light, see Magnani 2007.
65 See Sluijter 2008, pp. 13–16, for Rembrandt's frequent attempts to get the highest prices possible for his work.
66 Hoogewerff 1919, pp. 66–7.
67 *Corpus* IV, pp. 583–4. The painting entered the collection of Cardinal Leopoldo de' Medici around 1671–2; see Rutgers 2008, p. 21, who argues against the hypothesis that Cosimo de' Medici acquired the *Self Portrait*.
68 See p. 230 in the present volume.
69 On these relations, see Lammertse in London and Amsterdam 2006, p. 273.
70 Lammertse in London and Amsterdam 2006, pp. 108, 270.
71 For the mention in the 1683 inventory, see Brejon de Lavergnée 1987, p. 336, no. 318. Hulftegger 1954–5, p. 134, suggests that the *Self Portrait at the Easel* had been among the works purchased for the king's collection from a certain M. de la Feuille in 1671. Vittet 2004, pp. 59–60, has shown that this was not the case. The notion that Jabach sold the painting to the king first proposed by Foucart 1982, p. 72, and endorsed by, among others, Vittet 2004, p. 60, and Ducos and Mottin in Cincinnati 2008, p. 73, assume that the self portrait by Rembrandt mentioned in Jabach's 1696 inventory was a copy of the one now in the Louvre. The painting mentioned in Jabach's inventory, however, was much more likely the Rijksmuseum *Self Portrait as the Apostle Paul*. See p. 230 in the present volume. Nevertheless, because of his connections with the Amsterdam art world, Jabach may very well have been responsible for bringing the Louvre *Self Portrait* to France.
72 Strauss and Van der Meulen 1979, pp. 310–11, doc. no. 1654/4. See Van der Veen in Melbourne and Canberra 1997, p. 77, for the possible identification of the young woman who sat for Rembrandt. See Houbraken 1718–21, vol. II, pp. 276–7, for a delightful story about a client's accusation against Nicolaes Maes that he had failed to render a satisfactory likeness. The painting is also discussed on pp. 101 and 104 in the present volume.
73 Giltaij 1999, pp. 53–4. See also Sluijter 2008, pp. 14–15, where the attitudes of other artists who worked for Ruffo are also considered.
74 Bok 2004, pp. 170–8; Crenshaw 2006, pp. 110–35.
75 Van der Helst and Lievens are examples of other Dutch artists who estimated their work higher than their patrons were willing to pay. See, for the Van der Helst case, Sluijter 2008, pp. 12–13; Van Gent 2011, p. 33. For Lievens's case, see Wheelock in Washington, Milwaukee and Amsterdam 2008, p. 24.
76 Strauss and Van der Meulen 1979, p. 561, doc. no. 1666/2.
77 Hofstede de Groot 1906, p. 381, doc. no. 315.

THE LATE SELF PORTRAITS

1 Nor is this a modern compulsion: artists' biographers such as Vasari and Karel van Mander routinely make a point of identifying (self) portraits in the works they describe.
2 As Van de Wetering has observed (in *Corpus* IV, p. 133), '[the] habit of treating Rembrandt's self-portraits as a separate category of works has undoubtedly helped to reinforce the tendency to see these as a kind of autobiography'.
3 Van de Wetering in *Corpus* IV, p. 133.
4 On this tradition, see Raupp 1984; and, specifically with reference to how Rembrandt's self portraits fit into this tradition, Manuth in London and The Hague 1999, pp. 40–57.
5 Chapman 1990; Chapman in Cincinnati 2008, pp. 17–49; Chapman in Dickey and Roodenburg 2010, esp. pp. 235–9.
6 Van de Wetering in London and The Hague 1999, pp. 8–37; Van de Wetering 2002; Van de Wetering in *Corpus* IV, pp. 89–317; Van de Wetering in Cincinnati 2008, pp. 51–71. Other writers who have focused on different aspects of the 'marketability' of Rembrandt's self portraits include De Jongh (1991) and Alpers (1988). De Vries (1989) considered the self portraits as '*tronies*', or character heads, in which the identity of the model is of minimal importance, although he subsequently withdrew that opinion (per Van de Wetering in *Corpus* IV, p. 173 note 227). Hirschfelder 2008, p. 169, has concluded that none of the self portraits from Rembrandt's late period can properly be described as *tronies*.
7 As Chapman has noted, most recently in Cincinnati 2008, pp. 19–20, and in Dickey and Roodenburg 2010, pp. 235–9.
8 On Montaigne's influence in the seventeenth-century Netherlands, see Smith and Enenkel 2007. See also Taylor 1989, esp. pp. 143–58.
9 Among others, Manuth in London and The Hague 1999, p. 44.
10 For an overview of these theories as they relate to Rembrandt's work, see Labouvie-Vief 1997.
11 As noted by (among others) Van de Wetering in London and The Hague 1999, p. 28.
12 Van de Wetering in *Corpus* IV, pp. 117–32, 143–4.
13 De Winkel in *Corpus* IV, pp. 45–87.
14 Liedtke 2011, p. 24.
15 For a discussion of Rembrandt's depiction of human passions and emotions, see the chapters 'Inner Conflict' and 'Reconciliation' in the present volume.
16 See most recently Nicolaisen in Fritzsche, Leonhard and Weber 2013, pp. 281–304.
17 Van Hoogstraten 1678, pp. 109–10; see further Chapman in Dickey and Roodenburg 2010, p. 252, and Weststeijn in Fritzsche, Leonhard and Weber 2013, p. 326.
18 Koerner 1986, p. 9, similarly notes the importance of the element of time in Rembrandt's self portraits, transforming physiognomic studies into true expressions of character by investing them with 'a depth of experience beyond any sign of a particular emotion'.

19 See Van de Wetering in Amsterdam 2006b, pp. 106–23, and in Berlin 2006, pp. 90–101.
20 Raupp 1984, esp. pp. 36–44.
21 As Van de Wetering has also noted (in *Corpus* IV, p. 290), the portraits in which Rembrandt depicted himself as a painter at work – including those from which he ultimately chose to eradicate any overt references to his profession – show a greater degree of reworking than other self portraits, suggesting that he was especially concerned with the way in which he represented his relationship to his profession.
22 See Chapman 1990, pp. 49f.; De Winkel in *Corpus* IV, pp. 62f.
23 On the costume in this portrait, see De Winkel in *Corpus* IV, pp. 57, 88.
24 See Raupp 1984, p. 180; and De Winkel in *Corpus* IV, pp. 59–60.
25 Chapman 1990, p. 94. A poem by Rembrandt's friend Jeremias de Decker (published posthumously in *Hollandsche Parnas*, 1667) praised him as 'the Apelles of our day'.
26 Houbraken wrote that Rembrandt proclaimed 'that a work is complete if in it the master's intentions have been realised.' (Houbraken 1718–21, vol. 1, p. 259).
27 X-radiograph reproduced in *Corpus* IV, p. 499.
28 Ten '*mansmutsen*' (men's caps) are listed in the 1669 inventory of Rembrandt's estate; see Strauss and Van der Meulen 1979, p. 587, doc. no. 1669/5; and De Winkel 2006, p. 160.
29 X-radiographs reproduced in *Corpus* IV, pp. 519, 571 and 589, respectively.
30 X-radiographs reproduced in *Corpus* IV, p. 509.
31 This painting is discussed in greater detail on p. 71 in the present volume.
32 A possible earlier self portrait *historié* is the '*Self Portrait' as the Prodigal Son in the Tavern*, about 1635 (Staatliche Kunstsammlungen, Gemäldegalerie Alte Meister, Dresden; *Corpus* III, no. A III), although the identification of the man in the painting with Rembrandt himself is questionable.
33 On this powerful and intriguing series (including cats 108–10 and fig. 72), see Washington and Los Angeles 2005; see also the chapter 'Contemplation' in the present volume, which examines *Self Portrait as the Apostle Paul* in a different context.
34 Wheelock in Washington and Los Angeles 2005, p. 109.
35 De Winkel in *Corpus* IV, p. 73.
36 Rembrandt wears a gold chain in several other self portraits: see *Corpus* I, nos A 20 (1629) and A 33 (1630); *Corpus* II, nos A 71 and A 72 (both 1633); and *Corpus* IV, nos 1 (1642), 2 (about 1640), 9 (1654) and 28 (1669).
37 The painting's radical technique is discussed further on pp. 134, 137, 143 and 145 in the present volume.
38 Bryant 2003, p. 70, is surely wrong to suggest that in making this change Rembrandt was 'correcting his mistake': through his work as a printmaker he was intimately familiar with issues of reversal. He seems to have made a direct transcription of reality and then – similar to the development of a print through successive states – made such adjustments as were needed to bring it in line with his vision for the finished result.
39 On the concept of the 'viewer's share' and the awareness of this concept in the seventeenth century, see p. 134 and the references cited there; see also Van de Wetering in *Corpus* IV, pp. 303, 305.
40 Joshua Reynolds described the painting in 1781 as '... in a very unfinished manner, but admirable for its colour and effect; his pallet [*sic*] and pencils and maulstick are in his hand, if it may so be called; for it is so slightly touched, that it can scarce be made out to be a hand'. Reynolds (1824), p. 198.
41 Broos 1971, esp. pp. 177–82.
42 As concluded by Bryant 2003, p. 72; Buijsen in London and The Hague 1999, p. 220; and Brown in Berlin, Amsterdam and London 1991a, p. 286.
43 A similar point is made by Liedtke 2011, p. 27.
44 The Uffizi painting is undated, but was probably acquired by (and possibly painted for) Cosimo de' Medici in 1669; see *Corpus* IV, pp. 582–6 (with additional references).
45 De Winkel in *Corpus* IV, pp. 76–8.
46 See Noble 2009, p. 136.

OBSERVATION OF EVERYDAY LIFE

1 In addition to the two drawings reproduced here, there is another in the Staatliche Graphische Sammlung, Munich; see especially Munich and Amsterdam 2001, nos 34, 35, p. 47, figs 1, 2. A fourth sheet in Cambridge is an eighteenth-century copy of the Havemeyer drawing (cat. 5).The attribution of cat. 6 (Robert Lehmann Collection) has recently been questioned; see Vienna 2004, pp. 140–1, no. 53.
2 Strauss and Van der Meulen 1979, pp. 349–88, doc. no. 1656/12.
3 Sluijter 2006, pp. 195–219; Bakker 2011; Felfe in Fritzsche, Leonhard and Weber 2013.
4 Blankert in Paris 2007, pp. 85–6; Weber 2007, pp. 12–13; Paris, Philadelphia and Detroit 2011, nos 30, 35, 39, 40, 41 and others.
5 This is essentially what Samuel van Hoogstraten calls the '*kenlijkheyt*' of painting; see Van de Wetering 1997/2009, pp. 182–4.
6 Amsterdam 1976, pp. 117–19.
7 See Lugt 1915; Amsterdam and Paris 1998.
8 The Frick Collection, New York, inv. 13.3.25. See Amsterdam and Paris 1998, p. 344, fig. 6.
9 Hinterding 2008, no. 106.
10 See e.g. Emmens 1979, pp. 152–66; Weber 1991, pp. 130–6; Bakker 1995; Sluijter 2006, pp. 208–9; Van de Wetering in *Corpus* V, pp. 133–5.
11 Bakker 1995, p. 152 (trans. M. Hoyle); Bredero (ed. Stuiveling) 1975, pp. 17–18.
12 Bakker 1995, p. 152; Bredero (ed. Stutterheim) 1974, p. 133.
13 Alsteens and Buijs 2008, p. 357. The term 'picturesque' has taken on a more limited meaning in current usage.
14 See Pels 1681, p. 36.
15 De Bisschop 1671, introduction, quoted in Bakker 1995, pp. 156–7 (trans. M. Hoyle); cf. Emmens 1979, pp. 69–76.
16 See Lairesse (1707) 1740, vol. 1, pp. 418–34.
17 Bartsch 159; see also p. 92 in the present volume.
18 De Bisschop 1671, introduction, quoted in Bakker 1995, pp. 156–7 (trans. M. Hoyle); cf. Emmens 1979, p. 71; Sluijter 2006, p. 198.
19 Sluijter 2006, pp. 319–27.
20 Bartsch 202.
21 See Schatborn 1987; Manuth in Edinburgh and London 2001, pp. 48–53.
22 '[He] found out everything by himself'. See note 25, below.
23 See Von Sandrart 1675 (1925), p. 203, quoted in Bakker 1995, p. 155 (trans. M. Hoyle).
24 See Von Sandrart 1675 (1925), p. 202.
25 Houbraken 1718–21, vol. 1, p. 268. Cf. Van de Wetering in *Corpus* V, p. 130.
26 See Emmens 1979, p. 90, for this phrase from Andries Pels.
27 Houbraken 1718–21, vol. 1, p. 267.
28 See Van Mander 1604, fol. 131 (appendix), note to fol. 68v, line 47. See Blankert 1973, note 23, for this source.
29 Blankert 1973; London and The Hague 1999, pp. 216–19, no. 82; *Corpus* IV, no. 25.
30 Mai in Dordrecht and Cologne 1998, pp. 99–109; Dordrecht and Cologne 1998, pp. 174–5, no. 22 B.
31 Most recently, Van de Wetering in Amsterdam 2011, pp. 20–5.

EMULATION

1 For Rembrandt's collection, see Scheller 1969 and Amsterdam 1999.
2 De Piles 1699 (1706), p. 317.
3 See Broos in Amsterdam 1999, p. 138.
4 Broos 1977.
5 The National Gallery, London (NG 1944).
6 The relationship of Rembrandt's 1639 and 1640 self portraits to the '*Ariosto*' is discussed by, among others, De Jongh 1969, pp. 49–67, and Chapman 1990, pp. 72–8. For the *Flora*, see, among others, Golahny 1984, pp. 181–5, and Liedtke 2007, pp. 661–9, esp. p. 665 note 5, with regard to Rembrandt's earlier use of this prototype.
7 See, among others, De Jongh 1969, pp. 49–67, and Chapman 1990, pp. 72–8.
8 See Wheelock 1995, pp. 262–4.
9 The source for the pose is pointed out by MacLaren 1960, p. 318.
10 For an explanation of neutron activation autoradiography, see Ainsworth et al. 1982, pp. 9–12.
11 The Metropolitan Museum of Art, New York; Bredius 1935, no. 326. See Liedtke 2007, p. 693.
12 For the provenance of '*La Schiavona*', see Wethey 1969–75, vol. 2, p. 139, no. 95.
13 As pointed out by Lloyd Williams in Edinburgh and London 2001, p. 240, who mentions Paris Bordone's work in this context.
14 This was suggested by Held 1969, p. 97 (fig. 11). The painting was part of the collection of the J. Paul Getty Museum until 1992. See also Golahny 1984, pp. 207–8.
15 The X-radiograph and an explanation for the changes are discussed in Held 1991, pp. 200–1.
16 Strauss and Van der Meulen 1979, pp. 554–5, doc. no. 1665/17. For a discussion of this document, see Held

1969, pp. 85–9. A *Juno* by Rembrandt as well as one by an unidentified artist are listed in Becker's posthumous estate inventory drawn up between 19 October and 23 November 1678; see Bredius 1910, pp. 195–201.

17 On seventeenth-century Dutch collections with substantial holdings of Italian paintings, see Van Veen in Amsterdam 1992, pp. 102–16, and Meijer 2000, with further literature.

18 See Schneider in Washington 1990, pp. 156–60, nos 38–9. Bevers 2006, p. 204, however, assigns one of the copies after Titian, *Mountainous Landscape with a Horse* (Kupferstichkabinett, Staatliche Museen zu Berlin), to the Rembrandt follower Pieter de With (about 1635–after 1689).

19 On the relationship of the drawing to the etching, see, among others, Schatborn in Berlin, Amsterdam and London 1991b, pp. 93–4, no. 25, and White 1999, p. 249.

20 For a discussion of the iconography of the dead tree with living branches in Rembrandt's etchings of Saint Jerome, see Kuretsky 1974.

21 See Ackley in Boston and Chicago 2003, p. 293.

22 Strauss and Van der Meulen 1979, p. 359, doc. no. 1656/12, inv. [109]. This was first proposed by Valentiner 1905, p. 80. See also Tümpel in Berlin 1970, no. 77.

23 Von Sandrart 1675 (1925), p. 202. De Piles 1699 (1706), p. 319.

24 On the duration of Jan Six's grand tour, see De Winkel 2006, p. 289 note 11.

25 Broos in Amsterdam 1985, pp. 72–3, no. 61; Schatborn in Berlin, Amsterdam and London 1991b, pp. 109–12, no. 31 (A); White 1999, pp. 65–6.

26 Van Hoogstraten 1678, p. 193. On the seventeenth-century Dutch theoretical texts concerning emulation, see De Jongh 1969, pp. 54–8; Golahny 1984, pp. 257–60; and Sluijter 2006, pp. 251–65.

27 See especially White 1999, pp. 65–6.

28 Clark 1966, p. 72; Plomp 1997, pp. 307–8, no. 332; Bisanz-Prakken in Vienna 2004, pp. 308–9, no. 149.

29 Plomp 1997, pp. 307–8, no. 332, however, dates the drawing a few years later than the etching.

30 Clark 1966, p. 75.

31 Brown in Berlin, Amsterdam and London 1991a, p. 265. For *The Anatomy Lesson of Dr Nicolaes Tulp*, see *Corpus* II, pp. 172–89, no. A 51.

32 See, among others, Six 1905, p. 38, and Middelkoop 1994, p. 14.

33 This source was first suggested by Six 1905, p. 37.

34 For the comparison of these two works, see Haak 1972, pp. 44–5.

35 '*Een dito* [album] *van Hanibal, Augustijn en Loduwijck Crats, Guwido de Bolonese en Spanjolette*'. Strauss and Van der Meulen 1979, p. 369, doc. no. 1656/12, inv. [209].

36 Strauss and Van der Meulen 1979, p. 373, doc. no. 1656/12, inv. [232].

37 For other Dutch examples of its use, see Sluijter 2006, pp. 305–6.

38 Quoted from Ford 2007, p. 45.

39 Quoted from Cornelis and Filedt Kok 1998, p. 43, where a similar comment by Samuel van Hoogstraten is also cited.

40 Strauss and Van der Meulen 1979, p. 367, doc. no. 1656/12, inv. [193]; p. 369, doc. no. 1656/12, inv. [198]. See also Cornelis and Filedt Kok 1998, p. 46.

41 For discussions of the influence of Lucas van Leyden on Rembrandt, see, among others, Wheelock in Logan 1983, pp. 291–6, and Scallen in Dixon 1998, pp. 135–49.

42 Quoted from Broos in Amsterdam 1985, p. 55.

43 As pointed out by Broos in Amsterdam 1985, p. 55, and Hinterding in Amsterdam and London 2000, p. 317, where on p. 321 the first state of the print is illustrated in reverse.

44 See Clark 1966, p. 90, for the suggestion that Marcantonio Raimondi's *The Martyrdom of Saint Lawrence* after Baccio Bandinelli was Rembrandt's source for the architecture and symmetry in his *Christ presented to the People*.

45 See on this point especially Hinterding in Amsterdam and London 2000, pp. 314–15.

46 As pointed out by Wheelock in Logan 1983, p. 296.

47 This source was first proposed by Stone-Ferrier in Lawrence, New Haven and Austin 1983, pp. 53–5, no. 5.

48 On these copies and the Mughal originals, see Schatborn 1985, pp. 126–31; Royalton-Kisch 1992, pp. 141–3; and Slive 2009, pp. 173–4.

49 Strauss and Van der Meulen 1979, p. 369, doc. no. 1656/12, inv. [203].

50 Slatkes 1983.

51 One of Rembrandt's copies featuring such items of clothing is *Two Mughal Noblemen* in the British Museum (1895,0915.1281).

ARTISTIC CONVENTIONS

1 Baldinucci 1686, p. 79, quoted and discussed in Slive 1953, pp. 111–12. See also Sluijter 2006, p. 297.

2 Sluijter 2006, pp. 299–302.

3 On the woman's race, see White 1999, pp. 204–6; Lloyd Williams in Edinburgh and London 2001, p. 229; Rassieur in Boston and Chicago 2003, pp. 286–7; Sluijter 2006, pp. 298–300; Kolfin 2013.

4 Rembrandt's early contributions to the 'tradition of originality' in Amsterdam portraiture is discussed in Ekkart 2009.

5 For a discussion of this phenomenon, see Van der Veen in Melbourne and Canberra 1997, esp. pp. 73–9.

6 Rembrandt's patrons and early collectors of his work are discussed on pp. 28–32 in the present volume.

7 Complaint of Diego d'Andrade, 23 February 1654; Strauss and Van der Meulen 1979, pp. 310–11, doc. no. 1654/4. See also Crenshaw 2006, pp. 120–5. The final outcome of the dispute is not known. In 1642 Rembrandt had clashed with the powerful burgomaster Andries de Graeff over the value of a painting De Graeff had commissioned from the artist; soured relations may well have prejudiced future potential patrons. The disputed painting may have been the full-length portrait of a man dated 1639, convincingly identified as De Graeff, now in the Gemäldegalerie Alte Meister, Staatliche Museen, Kassel. The contested valuation – 500 guilders – would not have been inconceivable for a portrait of this size (Strauss and Van der Meulen 1979, p. 451, doc. no. 1659/21). For the identification of the portrait with the Kassel picture, see Dudok van Heel 1969; this is rejected in *Corpus* III, p. 302, but convincingly upheld by (among others) Weber in Kassel 2006, pp. 195–201.

8 Kok 2013. Rembrandt's patronage during the latter part of his career is discussed on pp. 25–32 in the present volume.

9 Houbraken 1718–21, vol. 2, pp. 273–4.

10 Although the man's gesture is similar, the relationship between Rembrandt's sitters could not be more different from that evoked in Frans Hals's cheerfully affectionate portraits of Stephanus Geraerdts (Koninklijk Museum voor Schone Kunsten, Antwerp) and Isabella Coymans (private collection) of about 1650–2, which are so thoroughly united by gaze and gesture.

11 See MacLaren and Brown 1991, vol. 1, pp. 350–1. For the portraits by Jacob Gerritsz and Aelbert Cuyp, see Chong 1992, pp. 337, 540–2; for those by Maes, see Krempel 2000, pp. 282, 287, 296, 300, 357; Németh 1996, pp. 79–84.

12 See Rüger in London and The Hague 2007, pp. 204–5.

13 As first suggested by Van Eeghen in Meischke and Reeser 1983, p. 72.

14 De Winkel 2006, pp. 79–85; for an opposing view, see Dickey 1995.

15 The X-radiograph is published in London 1988, rev. edn 2006, p. 175.

16 A codicil to Catrina's will, drawn up in December 1657, mentions 'the portraits of the testatrix and her deceased brother' but there is no indication that the brother's portrait was by Rembrandt; see Strauss and Van der Meulen 1979, p. 405, doc. no. 1657/9. See also Lloyd Williams in Edinburgh and London 2001, p. 214; Wijnman 1959, p. 37.

17 De Winkel 2006, pp. 15–16; Wijnman 1959, p. 33.

18 On Rembrandt's portrait prints in general, see Amsterdam 1986; and especially Dickey 2004.

19 The painted portrait, dated 1656, is in the Musée Jacquemart-André, Paris (oil on canvas, 76 × 63 cm).

20 Ekkart in Amsterdam 1986, p. 17.

21 The mezzotint was introduced to The Netherlands by Wallerant Vaillant (1623–1677) in the mid-1660s, but there is no evidence that Rembrandt used the technique. See Wuestman 1995, p. 66.

22 Luijten in Amsterdam and London 2000, p. 332; Ackley in Boston and Chicago 2003, p. 159 note 2.

23 Coppenol may have approached Rembrandt for the commission on the recommendation of his niece, Catrina Hooghsaet (cat. 41).

24 The Metropolitan Museum of Art, New York (50.145.33); see Liedtke 2007, vol. 2, pp. 679–86. The painting depicts Coppenol with quill pen in his left hand to account for the reversal of the printing process.

25 For a medical analysis of Lairesse's features, see Johnson 2004, pp. 301–3.

26 Rembrandt's portrait of Jeremias de Decker (The State Hermitage Museum, St Petersburg, inv. 748) and the *Portrait of an Elderly Man* (cat. 102), both regarded as 'friendship portraits', are decidedly more modest and informal.

27 Lairesse 1707 (1740), vol. 1, p. 325. Translation from Slive 1953, p. 164.

28 For a discussion of this painting, see pp. 208–11 in the present volume.

29 There is no evidence that the canvas has been significantly trimmed along this edge; see Blankert in Melbourne and Canberra 1997, p. 180 note 1.
30 The portrait has been said to be signed and dated 1663 (see MacLaren and Brown 1991, vol. 1, p. 358), but although traces of a signature are found just below the hoof of the horse's right foreleg, a date is not visible with infrared reflectography or any other means.
31 Rembrandt's '*Polish Rider*' (fig. 99; The Frick Collection, New York) is more an allegory than a portrait. The other life-sized Dutch equestrian portrait is Paulus Potter, *Equestrian Portrait of Dirck Tulp*, 1653 (Six Collection, Amsterdam). It is possible that Rembrandt may have begun the Rihel commission with a very different composition in mind: X-radiographs show that underneath the present painting is a horizontally orientated full-length image of a man standing in what appears to be a landscape setting. See Wieseman 2010, pp. 96–111.
32 For example: Titian, *Equestrian Portrait of Charles V*, 1548 (Museo del Prado, Madrid); Peter Paul Rubens, *Modello for Equestrian Portrait of the Duke of Buckingham*, 1625 (Kimbell Art Museum, Fort Worth); Peter Paul Rubens, *Equestrian Portrait of Cardinal Infante Ferdinand of Austria*, about 1636 (Museo del Prado, Madrid); Anthony van Dyck, *Equestrian Portrait of Charles I*, about 1637–8 (The National Gallery, London); Diego Velázquez, *Equestrian Portrait of Philip IV*, 1635–6 (Museo del Prado, Madrid).
33 This painting is discussed in greater detail on pp. 86–8 in the present volume.
34 Riegl 1931/1999, esp. pp. 282–90; Haak 1972.
35 See also the discussion of this painting on p. 141 in the present volume.
36 Van Mander 1604, fol. 281r.
37 Lairesse 1707 (1740), vol. 2, p. 5.

EXPERIMENTAL TECHNIQUE THE PAINTINGS

1 Houbraken 1718–21, vol. 1, p. 269.
2 Félibien 1685, p. 150.
3 Félibien 1685, p. 150.
4 Houbraken 1718–21, vol. 1, p. 259.
5 Félibien 1685, p. 151.
6 Gombrich 1960, p. 193.
7 Houbraken 1718–21, vol. 1, p. 269.
8 Van Hoogstraten 1678, p. 235. See Van de Wetering in *Corpus* V, p. 117.
9 Van Hoogstraten 1678, p. 27. See esp. Gombrich 1960, pp. 181–202 on this phenomenon, which he refers to as 'the beholder's share'. See also Van de Wetering in Amsterdam 2006b and Berlin 2006, pp. 117–23; Weststeijn 2008, p. 230.
10 De Piles 1699, pp. 69–70. Quoted from De Piles 1699 (1706), p. 51.
11 De Piles 1708, p. 258. Quoted from De Piles 1708 (1743), p. 156.
12 Houbraken 1718–21, vol. 1, p. 258.
13 Houbraken 1718–21, vol. 1, p. 259.
14 In certain cases, such as *Moses breaking the Tablets of the Law* (fig. 3), a painting's condition needs to be taken into account before declaring it unfinished (as in Van de Wetering 1997, pp. 207–11).
15 Pliny (1952), pp. 319–20 (bk XXXV, 80).
16 Van Hoogstraten 1678, p. 321. Quoted from Weststeijn 2008, p. 239.
17 Castiglione 1528, bk 1, unpaginated.
18 Van Hoogstraten 1657. For Van Hoogstraten's friendship with Lambert van den Bos, the translator of Castiglione's book, see Roscam Abbing 1993, p. 51, where Van Hoogstraten's dependence on Castiglione's *Il libro del cortegiano* for his book is pointed out, and where it is suggested that he executed the title page of Van den Bos's translation.
19 For the listings of the book in Six's 1706 inventory, see De Winkel 2006, p. 298 note 150.
20 This notion was first entertained by De Jongh 1985, p. 67.
21 Van Mander 1604, fols 48r–v, 176v–177r.
22 Vasari 1568 (1979), vol. 3, pp. 1981–2.
23 Van Mander 1604, fol. 48v.
24 The term *sprezzatura* itself, as well as the concept, was applied by various sixteenth- and seventeenth-century critics to Titian's late work. See Pousão-Smith 2003, pp. 262–3, with further literature.
25 Quoted from Slive 1953, p. 147.
26 Schrevelius 1648, p. 383; De Bie 1661, p. 282. For the appreciation of Hals's handling, see Broos 1978–9, pp. 121–2.
27 De Piles 1708, p. 258. Quoted from De Piles 1708 (1743), p. 156.
28 Vasari 1568 (1979), vol. 1, p. 332.
29 Pliny (1952), p. 367 (bk XXXV, 145); Van Hoogstraten 1678, p. 360.
30 On the peregrinations of Titian's painting, see Meijer 2000, pp. 392–4.
31 Kingston Lacy, The Bakes Collection, Dorset / The National Trust (1257086). Rembrandt, however, could not have known this specific work by Titian as it was in Italy in the seventeenth century.
32 Van de Wetering in Berlin, Amsterdam and London 1991a, pp. 21–2; Van de Wetering 1997, pp. 165–9.
33 X-radiography is a method of looking through the layers of a painting. Some pigments, especially those containing lead, such as lead white and lead tin yellow, strongly absorb X-rays. Infrared reflectography (IRR) registers pigments containing carbon, mostly black pigments. Scanning Macro X-ray fluorescence spectrometry (MA-XRF) can identify and map the distribution of elements present in the pigments that make up the paint by briefly exposing the painting to X-rays and analysing the emitted fluorescence radiation.
34 For interpretations of the X-radiographs, see Van Schendel 1956; Brown in Berlin, Amsterdam and London 1991a, pp. 281–2.
35 The infrared reflectogram was made and analysed by Ige Verslype in September 2010; see Verslype in Rutgers and Rijnders 2014, p. 250. The macro-XRF scans were made by Geert van der Snickt (University of Antwerp), Anna Krekeler and Lisette Vos (Rijksmuseum) in April 2013 as part of the 'ReVisRembrandt' project co-funded by the Netherlands Organisation for Scientific Research (NWO) and the National Science Foundation (NSF), and headed by Joris Dik (Delft University of Technology), Petria Noble (Royal Picture Gallery Mauritshuis) and Koen Janssens (University of Antwerp).
36 Houbraken 1718–21, vol. 1, p. 259.
37 For a discussion of the X-radiograph of this painting, see *Corpus* IV, pp. 564, 565.
38 This was suggested by Held 1969, p. 94, before an X-radiograph of the work had been made. See also Lloyd Williams in Edinburgh and London 2001, p. 242. For the 29 August 1665 document, see Strauss and Van der Meulen 1979, pp. 554–5, doc. no. 1665/17.
39 As Held 1991, p. 201, concluded after seeing the X-radiograph.
40 Houbraken 1718–21, vol. 1, p. 269.
41 Houbraken 1718–21, vol. 1, p. 269.
42 Van de Wetering in Berlin, Amsterdam and London 1991a, pp. 26–9; Von Sonnenburg in New York 1995, vol. 1, p. 78; Van de Wetering 1997, pp. 173–8. That Lievens indeed took the lead in the development of this technique can be confirmed by its application already in the fringe of the headscarf in the *Old Woman reading*, about 1624–5 (Rijksmuseum, Amsterdam, inv. SK-A-4702).
43 With thanks to Ige Verslype for establishing this.
44 Houbraken 1718–21, vol. 3, p. 207.
45 Groen and Hendriks in Washington, London and Haarlem 1989, p. 120; Van de Wetering in *Corpus* I, p. 31. Examples of paintings by Hals where the technique of scratching was used are *Young Man holding a Skull*, about 1626–8 (The National Gallery, London, NG 6458) and '*The Merry Drinker*', about 1628–30 (Rijksmuseum, Amsterdam, inv. SK-A-135).
46 Rijksmuseum, Amsterdam, inv. SK-A-3276.
47 Houbraken 1718–21, vol. 3, p. 207.
48 For a seventeenth-century description of how to use the palette knife, see De Piles 1684, p. 101.
49 Smith 1692, p. 385. Palette knives are illustrated in Jan Miense Molenaer's *Studio Scene*, 1631 (Gemäldegalerie, Berlin, inv. 873) and Michiel van Musscher's *Painter at Work*, about 1665–70 (Liechtenstein Museum, Vienna, inv. GE 2397).
50 For these other types of 'knife', see Kirby Talley 1981, pp. 218, 263–4; Kleinert 2006, pp. 50, 52, 57.
51 Smith 1676, p. 3.
52 Reynolds (1975), p. 223.
53 The hand was extensively overpainted at a later date, possibly because the use of the palette knife made it appear unfinished.
54 Van Hoogstraten 1678, p. 242.

EXPERIMENTAL TECHNIQUE THE ETCHINGS

1 See Landau and Parshall 1994, p. 54; Luijten 1998; New Hollstein Dutch (hereafter NHD) (Lucas van Leyden), p. 9, fig. 1; NHD (The Muller Dynasty), vol. 2, nos 1, 56, 59, 60, 62, 63, 77, 79; Stijnman 2012, pp. 161–2; Amsterdam 1985; TIB (Dürer) 21, 43, 59.
2 See NHD (Rembrandt), pp. liii–liv, and under nos 1–109; Hinterding 2012, pp. 2–5.
3 White and Boon 1969, no. 74 (NHD [Rembrandt] 239).
4 The literature on this print is vast. For a representative selection see under NHD (Rembrandt) 239.
5 Hinterding 2011, pp. 180–1.
6 See Vanden Bussche 1880.
7 Most prints cost a few stuivers at the time, although large sheets could easily top 1 guilder. On this see Amsterdam

1988, pp. 119–22; Hinterding 2006, vol. I, pp. 59–65; Laurentius 2010, pp. 81–4.
8 Houbraken 1718–21, vol. I, p. 258, and on p. 271 he described Rembrandt's unusually velvety shadows as 'tender, flickering shadows … and treated as finely and softly as can be done with the art of scraping'.
9 For a list, see Hinterding 2008, pp. 412–13.
10 See Washington 1977, pp. 9, 13. Cf. Amsterdam and Paris 1998, p. 227, and Giltaij 1988b, no. 27.
11 See White 1999, pp. 9–11.
12 See Biörklund 1968, pp. 170–9, esp. p. 171; Van Breda 1997, pp. 25–38.
13 See Van Breda 1997, pp. 28–9.
14 See Biörklund 1968, p. 173; Hinterding 2006, vol. I, pp. 112–14.
15 See Biörklund 1968, pp. 170–1; Van Breda 1997, p. 28.
16 These are precisely the characteristics that struck the English traveller Edward Browne when he visited Amsterdam in 1668: 'Here is a strange variety of excellent prints … Here are divers good ones of Rembrandt and some upon Indian paper that look like washing, though scratched after his manner.' See Van Strien 1993, p. 255.
17 See De Piles 1699, p. 434.
18 White 1999, *passim.*
19 Hinterding 2006, vol. I, pp. 119–21.
20 Hinterding 2011, pp. 186–7.
21 Only Ferdinand Bol appears to have followed his master's example, and then only on a small scale. See Hollstein (Ferdinand Bol), vol. 3, nos 2, 15, 18.
22 For this procedure, see Morse 1966; White 1999, pp. 5–8.
23 See NHD (Rembrandt) 284, with a list of impressions. One that is not mentioned there is in Pasadena (Norton Simon Museum), on Chinese paper.
24 See Boston and New York 1969, no. 18.
25 See note 23.
26 See note 23.
27 See note 23.
28 See Van der Linden 1979, p. 118; Morse 1966, p. 100; Stijnman 2012, pp. 332–3.
29 Parchment was far more expensive than paper. Twelve sheets cost the same as 500 sheets (a ream) of paper. See Voet 1969–72, vol. 2, p. 45; Thijs 1993, pp. 138–9; Hinterding 2006, vol. I, p. 185 note 388. See also NHD (Rembrandt) 274i, with a list of impressions; this does not include impressions on parchment in Berlin, Cambridge (Pepys Library) and a private collection. One impression on western paper that is not listed is in a private collection in the United States.
30 NHD (Rembrandt) 274ii, with a list of impressions. One that is not listed there is in a private collection in the United States.
31 NHD (Rembrandt) 274iii, with a list of impressions. For three more see Hinterding 2006, vol. I, p. 186 note 391.
32 Musper 1935, a view still found in White 1969, pp. 99–103.
33 Hinterding 2006, vol. I, pp. 128–9.
34 Hinterding 2006, vol. I, pp. 21–7 and *passim.*
35 NHD (Rembrandt) 274iv, with a list of impressions. For one on Japanese paper not mentioned there, see Hinterding 2006, vol. I, p. 186 note 396.
36 See NHD (Rembrandt) 307, with a list of impressions.
37 See note 36.
38 See note 36.
39 See note 36.
40 See note 36.
41 See note 36. Later impressions of this state have an unintentional scratch above the woman's left breast. This was removed in the seventh state, but not by Rembrandt. See NHD (Rembrandt) 307vii.
42 NHD (Rembrandt) 299i, with a list of impressions.
43 Middleton-Wake (1878, no. 252), considered this procedure so odd that he assumed Rembrandt used a separate plate for the second state, which he therefore thought was printed from two plates.
44 White 1999, p. 251.
45 NHD (Rembrandt) 299i, with a list of impressions.

EXPERIMENTAL TECHNIQUE THE DRAWINGS

1 Ford 2007, p. 44.
2 Schatborn 2011; Royalton-Kisch and Schatborn 2011; Schatborn and Dudok van Heel 2011.
3 Royalton-Kisch and Schatborn 2011, p. 334, no. 68, fig. 139.
4 It is true that the drawing is described here in rather bald, some might say crude, terms. One can approach it in a far loftier way, as Robinson does in his fine entry in Los Angeles 2009, pp. 234–5.
5 Royalton-Kisch and Schatborn have included this drawing in their *Core List*, but with the caveat that Royalton-Kisch had 'some reservations' about doing so. Here they are breaking their own fourth commandment, that 'the drawing must be accepted as authentic by both of us without reservation'. See Royalton-Kisch and Schatborn 2011, p. 344, no. 73, and p. 323.
6 Bevers 2006, pp. 177–9, no. 52.
7 Bevers 2006, pp. 167–70, no. 49. The copy after this drawing is discussed on p. 167 and reproduced on p. 168.
8 Hollstein, vol. 53, pp. 100–7, no. 5. Rubens's painting is now in the Onze-Lieve-Vrouwekathedral in Antwerp.
9 London 1992, no. 58.

LIGHT

1 See Van de Wetering in Vienna 2004, pp. 27–40.
2 Félibien 1685, pp. 151–2.
3 Baldinucci 1686, p. 79.
4 De Piles 1699, pp. 437–8.
5 Gersaint 1744, pp. 65–6.
6 Von Sandrart 1675 (1925), p. 327. For a discussion of the comments by both Von Sandrart and Van Hoogstraten, see Van de Wetering 1997, pp. 187–8; Van Eikema-Hommes and Van de Wetering in Amsterdam 2006a, pp. 164–79; Van de Wetering in *Corpus* V, pp. 3–140, esp. pp. 71–80, 103–12, 125–8. See also Van de Waal 1974, pp. 12–27.
7 Van Hoogstraten 1678, p. 257. See Bohlmann, Fink and Weiss 2008 and Kassel 2011 for the scientific and philosophical interest in light in the seventeenth century. See also Weststeijn 2008, *passim.*
8 Van Hoogstraten 1678, p. 306.
9 Van Eikema-Hommes and Van de Wetering in Amsterdam 2006a, pp. 177–8.
10 Van Hoogstraten called it 'the thickness of the air' (*'de dikheit der lucht'*); Van Hoogstraten 1678, pp. 264–5.
11 Von Sandrart 1675 (1925), p. 83. On the subject of relationships (*'houding'*), see Taylor 1992 and Van de Wetering 1997, pp. 150–2, 255–6.
12 Van de Wetering in Vienna 2004, p. 34. See also Van Eikema-Hommes and Van de Wetering in Amsterdam 2006a, p. 176; van de Wetering in *Corpus* V, pp. 73–80.
13 Von Sandrart 1675, p. 327.
14 Van Hoogstraten 1678, p. 273.
15 Fremantle 1959.
16 Van de Waal 1952, pp. 215–38; Blankert 1975; Goossens 1996.
17 See Schwartz 2006, pp. 178–83; Amsterdam 2011.
18 Tacitus, pp. 201–2. See also Golahny 2003, pp. 187–91.
19 Van der Coelen in Roscam Abbing 2006, vol. I, pp. 31–56.
20 Benesch 279; Munich and Amsterdam 2001, no. 37; Van de Wetering in *Corpus* V, pp. 24–5.
21 See De Winkel 2006, p. 209, on the subject of Civilis' attire.
22 Van de Waal 1974, pp. 28–43; Van der Coelen in Roscam Abbing 2006; Blanc 2009.
23 Van der Coelen in Roscam Abbing 2006, vol. I, pp. 33–45; see also Smith 1995.
24 See Van Eikema-Hommes and Van de Wetering in Amsterdam 2006a, p. 178. See also Van de Wetering in *Corpus* V, pp. 117–19.
25 Preliminary sketches were made in preparation for the print. See Amsterdam and London 2000, no. 57.
26 Van de Wetering in Vienna 2004, p. 34.
27 On this subject, see the chapter 'Experimental Technique: The Etchings' in the present volume, esp. p. 154.
28 See Hinterding 2012.
29 Von Seidlitz 1922, no. 50; Van de Wetering in Amsterdam and London 2000, pp. 44–7; Hinterding 2001, pp. 137–9.
30 NHD (Rembrandt) 283, with a list of examples.
31 See NHD (Rembrandt) 276–81 for an overview of the impressions and the type of paper used.
32 Houbraken 1718–21, vol. I, p. 258.
33 Houbraken 1718–21, vol. I, p. 259.
34 I Corinthians 13: 12. For a summary of the debate about the meaning of this print, see Hinterding 2008, no. 198.

INTIMACY

1 Van Gogh-Bonger 1953, p. 94.
2 Jansen, Luijten and Bakker 2009, no. 534, dated about 10 October 1885.
3 Valentiner 1923–4, pp. 17–22, was the first scholar to recognise that this was the preparatory drawing for *'The Jewish Bride'*. The correct identification of the subjects of the drawing and the painting as Isaac and Rebecca was first made by Müller-Hofstede in Valentiner 1925–34, vol. I, p. 478, no. 243.

4 'Sporting' is the word used in the King James Bible.

5 It was Müller-Hofstede's recognition of this model that led to his correct identification of the subject of the drawing and painting. Müller-Hofstede in Valentiner 1925–34, vol. I, p. 478, no. 243. The painting was given the title '*The Jewish Bride*' in 1833 by its then owner, Adriaan van der Hoop. For a discussion of other interpretations of the painting, see Bikker 2013, pp. 25–8.

6 *Biblia* 1637.

7 Cats 1637, p. 14.

8 On the popularity of *Trou-ringh*, see Schenkeveld 1991, p. 31.

9 See De Jongh in Haarlem 1986, pp. 319–20; Bleyerveld 2000–1, pp. 246, 248.

10 The document is transcribed in Blankert 1982, p. 82. Blankert 1982, p. 23, identified the painting as *Portrait of a Couple in a Landscape* (Dordrechts Museum, Dordrecht, inv. DM/948/126, on loan from the Cultural Heritage Agency of the Netherlands, NK 2435). The painting in Dordrecht, however, appears to be a fragment of a larger painting that included *Portrait of a Young Man as a Shepherd*, now in the Musée des Beaux-Arts, Lyon, inv. A213; see Bruyn 1994. For the paintings of Isaac and Rebecca by Rembrandt's former pupils, see Broos 1993, pp. 113–20.

11 The painting is Ferdinand Bol's 1656 *Portrait of Wigbold Slicher and Elisabeth Spiegel as Venus and Paris with Cupid*, 1656 (Dordrechts Museum, Dordrecht, inv. DM/953/471, on loan from the Cultural Heritage Agency of the Netherlands, NK 1701). For the identification and its significance for our understanding of seventeenth-century Dutch decorum, see Ekkart 2002.

12 See Kloek and Jansen 1993, unpaginated.

13 Rembrandt's self portraits *historiés* form a category apart. The possibility exists that the *Jacob blessing the Sons of Joseph* (cat. 120) is also a *portrait historié*, although the identification of the supposed sitters proposed by Schwartz 1985, pp. 269–71, is highly speculative.

14 With thanks to Bianca du Mortier for pointing this out to me.

15 MacLaren 1960, p. 313, was the first scholar to suggest that the painting might be a study for a Susanna and the Elders. See also Bauch 1966, p. 15, no. 278; Van Thiel in Amsterdam 1969, p. 74, no. 14. The fact that the picture is signed and dated indicates that Rembrandt thought of it as a finished painting rather than an oil sketch. The bevelling on all sides of the reverse of the panel rules out the possibility that it is a fragment. See London 1988, p. 96.

16 Diana (Ovid, *Metamorphoses* III: 165–205) is suggested as one of the possible subjects in London 1988, p. 96. For the identification as Callisto (Ovid, *Metamorphoses* II: 405–531) see Leja 1996; Van de Wetering in *Corpus* V, p. 530, where the figure is identified as the disgraced Callisto in the wilderness as described in Karel van Mander's '*Wtlegghingh*' (Commentary) on Ovid's *Metamorphoses*.

17 Nor is the identification of the scene as the disgraced Callisto in the wilderness (as Van de Wetering has proposed) feasible, as neither Van Mander nor Ovid make any mention of bathing.

18 The painting has also been viewed as an allegory of indecency based on the superficial resemblance of the woman's pose to that of an antique statue known as the *Mulier Impudica* (*Shameless Woman*), which Rembrandt could have known from an engraving. This was first suggested by Van der Waals in Amsterdam 1988, pp. 63–4, and extensively argued by Colenbrander in Roscam Abbing 2006, vol. I, pp. 57–73. However, as pointed out by Van de Wetering in *Corpus* V, p. 526, it is doubtful whether the woman is smiling and therefore shameless. This hypothesis also neglects the vantage point and intimate mood of the painting.

19 This objection was first made by Tümpel 1986, p. 405, no. 122. Rembrandt's 1647 *Susanna and the Elders* is in the Staatliche Museen, Gemäldegalerie, Berlin, inv. 828E.

20 Guercino, *Susanna and the Elders*, 1617 (Museo del Prado, Madrid, inv. P00201); Massimo Stanzione, *Susanna and the Elders*, about 1631–7 (Joslyn Art Museum, Omaha, inv. 1983.27); Jan Both, *Susanna and the Elders*, before 1642 (private collection); attr. Govert Flinck, *Susanna and the Elders* (Staatliche Museen, Gemäldegalerie, Berlin, inv. 813B).

21 On Rembrandt's interest in Lucas van Leyden's work, see p. 92 in the present volume.

22 Leja 1996, p. 327. The child, Cornelia, was baptised on 30 October 1654; see Strauss and Van der Meulen 1979, p. 321, doc. no. 1654/18.

23 Strauss and Van der Meulen 1979, pp. 318, 320, doc. nos 1654/11, 1654/12, 1654/14 and 1654/15.

24 For these objections to the identification of the model in these works as Hendrickje Stoffels, see Manuth in Edinburgh and London 2001, p. 50; Sluijter 2006, pp. 327–31. On the use of prostitutes as models, see Manuth in Edinburgh and London 2001, pp. 51–3.

25 See Manuth in Edinburgh and London 2001, pp. 47, 49–50, with further literature.

26 The drawings are in the Rijksmuseum and the British Museum. They are illustrated together with Rembrandt's print in Edinburgh and London 2001, p. 233.

27 See Rassieur in Boston and Chicago 2003, p. 290.

28 For this interpretation of the iconography and a discussion of other subjects that have been proposed, see Ackley in Boston 1981, p. 249, and Hinterdng 2008, pp. 366–7.

29 See especially Hinterding in Amsterdam and London 2000, p. 353.

30 Giltaij in Frankfurt 2003, p. 162, suggests that the painting is a realistic record of Rembrandt's observation of his son writing or sketching.

31 Lievens's earliest *Old Woman reading* is in the Philadelphia Museum of Art (487) and dates to around 1621–3; see De Witt in Washington, Milwaukee and Amsterdam 2008, pp. 82–3, no. 1. Lievens's *Old Woman reading* in the Rijksmuseum, inv. SK-A-4702, can be dated to about 1624–5.

32 See Tümpel 1971, p. 32; Bruyn in *Corpus* I, pp. 355–6.

33 The print that likely served as a model for the Rijksmuseum painting is by Karel van Mallery (1571–1645) after a design by Maerten de Vos (1532–1603) from around 1590–5, and was one of a series of prints of 15 prominent women from the New Testament (*Icones illustrium feminarum novi testamenti*). This model was first pointed out by Campbell 1971, p. 152; see also Tümpel 1971, p. 32.

34 On exemplary widowhood, see especially Franits 1993, pp. 172–8. See also Lloyd Williams in Edinburgh and London 2001, p. 212.

35 Cats 1625, p. 55.

36 Ripa 1593 (1709), p. 73. See also Kelch in Berlin, Amsterdam and London 1991a, p. 257, where the *Titus at his Desk* is discussed in terms of the related concept of creative melancholy. According to Giltaij in Frankfurt 2003, p. 164, the painting falls into the category of the 'pupil' or 'young scholar'.

37 The notion entertained by Ernst van de Wetering (recorded in Giltaij 1988a, p. 72) that the boy represents Saint John writing his Gospel cannot be substantiated because the painting does not include the saint's attribute, an eagle.

38 As noted by De Vries 1989, p. 197.

39 De Hoop Scheffer and Boon 1971, p. 13, no. 58; Ackley in Boston and Chicago 2003, p. 303.

40 See Six 1893, p. 156.

41 See De Winkel 2006, pp. 93–132.

42 Slatkes 1992, p. 277, no. 179, assumes that the painting was cut down. Based on Michiel Franken's examination of the X-radiograph, Blankert and Blokhuis in Melbourne and Canberra 1997, p. 183, countered this notion. See also Duparc in Broos et al. 2004, p. 215, and Noble's technical description of the painting in Broos et al. 2004, p. 220.

43 This identification was tentatively put forward and elucidated by Duparc in Broos et al. 2004, p. 219. It had been earlier stated as a fact, without argumentation, by Dudok van Heel in Edinburgh and London 2001, p. 26.

44 For Van Ludick's biography, see Van Eeghen 1969a, p. 172; Van der Veen in Amsterdam 1999, p. 143; Duparc in Broos et al. 2004, p. 219.

45 For a discussion of this loan with references to the relevant documents, see Crenshaw 2006, pp. 83–6.

46 Le Comte 1700, vol. 3, p. 283. As pointed out by Hinterding 2008, vol. 2, p. 486, the impression in the British Museum is inv. no. 1844,0625.19 and the inscription reads '*jan francen Apotheker kunstbeminaer*'. See Van Eeghen 1969a, p. 173; Van der Veen in Amsterdam 1999, p. 142; Gersaint 1751, pp. 199–200, no. 253. It has also been suggested that the etching was begun as a portrait of Otto van Cattenburch (1612–1665) and only later came to represent Abraham Francen; see, among others, Six 1908, p. 64; Van Eeghen 1969a, p. 175; Crenshaw in Chong and Zell 2002, p. 169. Dickey 2004, p. 148, argues that Abraham Francen's richer brother Daniel is a more likely candidate for the sitter.

47 Gersaint 1751, p. 199.

48 On this relationship, see pp. 23–4 in the present volume.

49 Hinterding in Amsterdam and London 2000, pp. 337–40, no. 84.

50 See Dickey 2004, p. 146, where the etching is compared to Johannes Vermeer's *Girl reading a Letter at an Open Window*, about 1657–9 (Gemäldegalerie

Alte Meister, Dresden, inv. 1336) and Gerard ter Borch's *Lady reading a Letter*, about 1665 (The Wallace Collection, London, inv. P236).

51 On these two etchings, see especially Luijten in Amsterdam and London 2000, pp. 326–8, no. 81, pp. 332–7, no. 83.

52 Ekkart in Amsterdam 1986, pp. 5, 13.

53 On Haringh, see Van Eeghen 1969b, pp. 74–8.

54 For Tholinx's biography, see Van Tol 1983.

55 Westermann in Denver and Newark 2001, pp. 69–72.

56 Institut Néerlandais, Fondation Custodia, Paris, inv. 226. For the identification of the room in Rembrandt's house on Breestraat, see Schatborn in Berlin, Amsterdam and London 1991b, p. 80.

57 These aspects of seventeenth-century Dutch culture have been applied mostly to developments in genre painting. See, among others, Salomon in Gaskell and Jonker 1998, pp. 309–25; Franits 2004, pp. 96–7; Wieseman in Cambridge 2011, p. 31.

CONTEMPLATION

1 The standard work on melancholy is Klibansky, Panofsky and Saxl 1964. See also Wittkower 1969, pp. 102–7 and, for the Dutch context, Chapman 1990, pp. 26–32.

2 Laurentius 1597 (1599), pp. 85–7.

3 On the relationship of melancholy to old age, see, among others, Janssen 2007, pp. 71–5.

4 For a discussion of the history of the commission, see Giltaij 1999, pp. 43–5, with earlier literature.

5 The painting was recorded as a depiction of Aristotle or Albertus Magnus. See Held 1969, pp. 12–13; Giltaij 1999, p. 44; Liedtke 2007, vol. II, p. 633.

6 Giltaij 1999, p. 81.

7 It is suggested in *Corpus* II, pp. 516–18, that the 1634 Prague painting is identical to the 'Paracelsus' in the 1676 sale of Reynier van der Wolff's collection, and that it may have been made for his father-in-law, the Rotterdam brewer Dirck Jansz Pesser and his wife, Haesje Jacobsdr van Cleyburg, whose portraits Rembrandt executed in the same year. The *Portrait of Dirck Jansz Pesser* is in the Los Angeles County Museum of Art (inv. M.69.16) and that of Haesje Jacobsdr van Cleyburg in the Rijksmuseum, Amsterdam (inv. SK-A-4833). See *Corpus* II, pp. 558–64, no. A 102; pp. 565–70, no. A 103. However, a document discovered by, and analysed in, Rutgers 2008, p. 26 note 121, casts serious doubt on whether Van der Wolff's 'Paracelsus' is in fact the painting now in Prague.

8 For example, the etching *A Student at a Table by Candlelight* from around 1642 (Rijksmuseum, Amsterdam, inv. RP-P-OP-234).

9 For the identification of the medallion, see Kraft 1965, p. 12.

10 Held 1969, p. 33.

11 Held 1969, p. 40. See also Liedtke 2004b, p. 74, where the 'period flavour of Held's study' is considered to be 'most evident in his assumption that the *Aristotle* can be understood as the painter's own manifesto'.

12 As pointed out in Liedtke 2007, vol. II, p. 636, where, however, Held's interpretation of Aristotle's thoughts is supported. The fact that Rembrandt's *Scholar seated at a Table with Books* in Prague (fig. 70) also wears a chain suggests that the artist himself did not attach a negative meaning to such princely gifts.

13 Klibansky, Panofsky and Saxl 1964, p. 259.

14 Laurentius' account of the effects of melancholy on geniuses and its roots in Aristotle's *Problema* XXX was also quoted in Robert Burton's immensely popular *Anatomy of Melancholy*, first published in 1621: Burton 1621 (1638), p. 192.

15 Quoted from Klibansky, Panofsky and Saxl 1964, pp. 24–5. Held 1969, p. 31, also points out that the text attributed to Aristotle was the basis for Ficino's theory of melancholy, but only emphasises its negative aspects.

16 For the translation of Agrippa's text, see Klibansky, Panofsky and Saxl 1964, pp. 355–6.

17 For a discussion of the history of the commission of these two works, see Giltaij 1999, pp. 50–5, with earlier literature.

18 Hoogewerff 1917, p. 135 note 1; De Vries, Tóth-Ubbens and Froentjes 1978, pp. 172 and 177 note 20; Broos 1993, p. 276.

19 Ruffo 1916, p. 318, no. 223; Giltaij 1999, pp. 55, 156, no. 23.

20 The interpretation of Homer as a teacher was accepted, however, by De Vries, Tóth-Ubbens and Froentjes 1978, p. 174.

21 On the relationship of the 1652 drawing to the drawing in Stockholm and the 1663 painting, see, among others, Broos 1993, pp. 271–4.

22 Quoted from Klibansky, Panofsky and Saxl 1964, p. 356.

23 This was first proposed by Hoogewerff 1917, p. 142, and most extensively argued by Brown and Roy 1992. The hypothesis was rejected by Giltaij in Melbourne and Canberra 1997, pp. 134–7, no. 15, and Giltaij 1999, pp. 55–60.

24 For the entries in the inventory made in that year, see De Gennaro 2001, p. 214, nos 59, 63, 76. See also Giltaij in Cavallino and Salerno 2005, pp. 51–63, and Giltaij 2005.

25 White et al. in New Haven 1983, p. 18, no. 4. Nor can the *Figure in Armour* in the Museu Calouste Gulbenkian in Lisbon, which Brown and Roy (1992, p. 288 note 18), Giltaij (1999, pp. 60–2) and Liedtke (2007, vol. II, p. 645 note 37) assign to a Rembrandt follower, be identified with Ruffo's painting, as it was recorded in the collection of Count Silvain-Raphaël Baudouin in Paris in 1780; see the transcription of Baudouin's catalogue in Dijon 2003, p. 230, no. 25.

26 Kraft 1965, pp. 11–12. See also Held 1969, p. 17, and Brown in Berlin, Amsterdam and London 1991a, p. 260.

27 Ruffo's *Alexander* is described as seated in his account books; see Giltaij 1999, pp. 55, 156, no. 22. See also Giltaij 1999, pp. 63–5, for the suggestion that a Rembrandt school drawing of a contemplative young man seated at a table is a record of the no longer extant painting.

28 The precise order to which the habit belongs was identified by Hedquist 1994, p. 24.

29 Cusping is present on all sides of the canvas, although less deep on the left side and at the bottom than on the right side and at the top.

30 On this subject, see, for example, Sorrell 1988 and Thompson 2012, pp. 54–8.

31 Quoted from Englebert 1965 (2013), p. 79.

32 Quoted from Sorrell 1988, p. 42.

33 Quoted from Hudleston 1930, p. 23.

34 Writing before the painting was restored in 1990, Tümpel (1986, p. 400, no. 91) mistakenly believed that the stigmata are present.

35 As well as for paintings in Vienna (Bredius and Gerson 1969, no. 122), London (Bredius and Gerson 1969, no. 123) and Paris (Bredius and Gerson 1969, no. 126) that show the same model.

36 Valentiner 1956, p. 400.

37 See Hedquist 1994, pp. 26–7.

38 The notion that Rembrandt represented himself in the so-called *Prodigal Son in the Tavern* of about 1635 (Staatliche Kunstsammlungen, Gemäldegalerie, Dresden, inv. 1559) is a matter of contention, as is the biblical interpretation of the painting's subject matter. On the identity of the models, see *Corpus* III, 1989, pp. 134–47, no. A 111, esp. p. 146.

39 This possibility was pointed out by Buijsen in London and The Hague 1999, p. 213.

40 Van Thiel 1969, p. 1b, interpreted the last letters of the first word at the top of the page as 'SIS' and thought the full word read 'EFESIS' (Ephesus).

41 See e.g. Philemon 1: 9.

42 See also Buijsen in London and The Hague 1999, p. 213, where Ephesians 5: 8–14 is cited.

43 While none of Rembrandt's late self portraits shows the artist bare-headed, nor do any of them show hair peeking out on his forehead from under the headgear – a conspicuous contrast to his early self portraits. For the biblical description of Paul's physical appearance, see Réau 1955–9, vol. III, p. 1038. Buijsen (in London and The Hague 1999, p. 213) considers the turban a reference to the Middle East of the Bible in general, while Van Thiel (1969, p. 1a) suggests that it may be an allusion to the apostle's place of birth, Tarsus in present-day Turkey.

44 Staatsgalerie, Stuttgart, inv. 746. *Corpus* I, pp. 143–9, no. A 11.

45 This source was first pointed out by Sumowski 1959, p. 290.

46 Schmidt-Degener 1919, p. 266, was first to propose that these works were conceived as a series. His series was later augmented in Valentiner 1920 and Benesch 1956. See also Tümpel 1986, p. 399, under no. 83, and p. 400, under no. 88.

47 This is essentially the series proposed by Schmidt-Degener in 1919, with the omission of the *Virgin Mary* in Épinal (Musée départemental d'art ancien et contemporaine, oil on canvas, 107 × 81 cm, inv. 1828.37; Bredius 1935, no. 397) and with the addition of *The Apostle Simon* (cat. 110), which only came to light later and was first published in Münz 1948. Wheelock (in Washington and Los Angeles 2005, p. 29) ambiguously defines these works as the 'core group', while Van de Wetering (in *Corpus* IV, p. 548) elevates them to the status of a series. See also Van de Wetering in Amsterdam 2006b and Berlin 2006, p. 396. For the *Saint James Major* in a private collection, see Wheelock in Washington and Los Angeles 2005,

pp. 102–5, no. 9. For the *Christ with a Pilgrim's Staff* (The Metropolitan Museum of Art, New York, The Jules Bache Collection, inv. 49.7.37; oil on canvas, 95.3 × 82.6 cm), see Liedtke 2007, vol. II, pp. 766–71, no. 174.

48 This was first claimed by Wheelock in Washington and Los Angeles 2005, pp. 29, 106, 136 note 4.

49 Van de Wetering in *Corpus* IV, p. 548, and Van de Wetering in Berlin 2006, p. 396.

50 The painting was examined by Anna Krekeler and the present author on 12 September 2013.

51 On the painted black borders in this work, see Noble in Broos et al. 2004, p. 224.

52 The *Apostle Simon* in Zurich, which only has painted borders on the sides and at the bottom, is the tallest of these works at 98.3 cm, while the length of the Getty *Apostle Bartholomew* measures only 86.7 cm. Wheelock (in Washington and Los Angeles 2005, p. 106) suggests that the missing border at the top of the Zurich painting may in fact indicate that it was cut down in this dimension. At 82.6 cm, the *Christ with a Pilgrim's Staff* in The Metropolitan Museum of Art is the widest of the paintings, while the *Saint James Major* in a private collection is the narrowest at 72 cm. This measurement of the width of the *Saint James Major* does not include the approximately 4 cm strip attached to the left side of the painting, which, according to Martin Bijl's technical examination published in the catalogue for the Sotheby's auction held on 25 January 2007 (lot 74), is a later addition. Also according to Bijl, the original canvas could not have measured much more than 72 cm.

53 See especially Liedtke 2007, vol. II, pp. 766–71, no. 174, with earlier literature. The present author agrees with the attribution of this painting to a Rembrandt follower. Liedtke (1998, p. 313) also questions the attribution of the *Saint James Major* to Rembrandt. See Wheelock in Washington and Los Angeles 2005, p. 29, for an analysis of the subtle differences in technique among the accepted apostles from 1661.

54 The identification of the figure in the New York painting as Saint James the Less was first suggested in Von Bode and Hofstede de Groot 1897–1905, vol. VI (1901), p. 9, no. 417, and accepted by, among others, Tümpel 1986, p. 400, no. 86, and Sutton in Washington and Los Angeles 2005, pp. 111–12, no. 12.

55 For the transcription of the inventory, see De Grouchy 1894, pp. 249–92, esp. p. 255. Manuth in London and The Hague 1999, p. 51, was the first scholar to suggest that the entry in Jabach's inventory may refer to the Rijksmuseum *Self Portrait*.

56 Although the present stretcher only dates to 1936, the conservator who relined the painting carefully preserved the provenance information on the back of the original canvas and stretcher. In addition to the painted number '123', a wax seal and a handwritten label were transferred. Such painted numbers have also been found on a few of the panel paintings owned by Jabach. See Grossmann 1951, p. 19 notes 49, 50.

57 On Jabach, see e.g. Schnapper 1994, pp. 267–82; Lammertse in London and Amsterdam 2006, pp. 270–4.

58 For Jabach's dealings with Gerrit Uylenburgh, see Lammertse in London and Amsterdam 2006, pp. 108, 270.

59 For the argument that these paintings were executed for a Catholic client, see Valentiner 1920–1, p. 222. The notion that Mennonites may have been the patrons of these works is suggested in Valentiner 1956, p. 400; Wheelock in Washington and Los Angeles 2005, pp. 23–5, and Woollett in Washington and Los Angeles 2005, p. 101.

60 Getty Provenance Index, archival inventory N-1578, 2 June 1678.

61 The importance of the apostle Paul for Protestants has been pointed out in an art historical context by, among others, Halewood 1982, pp. 4–10; Chapman 1990, pp. 122–3; Manuth in Washington and Los Angeles 2005, p. 46.

62 See Exalto 2005, esp. pp. 93–109.

63 The full title reads *De geschiedenis ende den doodt der vromer martelaren, die om het getuyghenisse des evangeliums haer bloedt ghestort hebben, van den tijden Christi af totten Jare MDLIX*. On this book's popularity, see Heijting 1997, pp. 284, 285, 290.

64 For an overview of this literature, see Van Eijnatten and Van Lieburg 2006, p. 228.

65 For the London *Saint Paul* as a *portrait historié*, see, for example, MacLaren 1960, p. 319, and Wheelock in Washington and Los Angeles 2005, p. 82. On the Getty *Bartholomew* and other apostles as possible *portraits historiés*, see Sutton in Washington and Los Angeles 2005, p. 65.

66 For the first interpretation, see Tümpel 1986, p. 367, and Chapman 1990, pp. 120, 127. The quotation is taken from Chapman 1990, p. 126. Schwartz 2006, pp. 353–4, also suggests that Rembrandt viewed his role as an artist as being similar to Paul's as an explicator of the Gospel.

67 Chapman 1990, pp. 125–6; Wheelock in Washington and Los Angeles 2005, p. 109.

68 De Vries 1989, p. 197, was first to caution against projecting these Romantic notions onto the seventeenth-century mentality.

69 As pointed out by Van de Wetering in London and The Hague 1999, p. 28.

70 De Vries 1989, p. 196, claims that Rembrandt used himself in his self portraits simply as a convenient model. For the dual function of all of Rembrandt's self portraits as examples of his amazing artistic capabilities and portraits of the person who could achieve them, see Van de Wetering in London and The Hague 1999, esp. p. 30; Manuth in London and The Hague 1999.

71 Bayerische Staatsgemäldesammlungen, Alte Pinakothek, Munich, inv. 394. *Corpus* II, pp. 311–12, no. A 69.

72 See Tümpel 1986, p. 136; Chapman 1990, p. 113; P.J.J. van Thiel in Berlin, Amsterdam and London 1991a, p. 160.

INNER CONFLICT

1 See pp. 215–33 in the present volume.

2 Adams 1998; Sluijter 2006, pp. 333–68.

3 See Sluijter in Jensen Adams 1998, pp. 51–7, on the artistic tradition of Bathsheba's old serving woman.

4 See Berlin, Amsterdam and London 1991a, p. 242, fig. 39b.

5 Berlin, Amsterdam and London 1991a, pp. 244–5, fig. 39e; Sluijter in Jensen Adams 1998, pp. 74–5, fig. 23.

6 Pliny, *Natural History* XXXV: 73; Cicero, *Orator* XXII: 74; Quintilian, *Institutio oratoria* II, XIII: 12. This story became a stock theme in the literature on art, see for example Van Hoogstraten 1678, p. 110.

7 See Dickey and Roodenburg 2010.

8 Miedema 1973, vol. I, fol. 27r (p. 175); Le Brun 1703, in the preface 'Aan den Leezer' by the translator. On Le Brun's *Conférence sur l'expression…*, see Montagu 1994.

9 Amongst others, Levi 1964; James 1996; Gaukroger 1998; Dickey and Roodenburg 2010, intro., pp. 7–16.

10 Descartes (1649) 1984, art. 29, 91, 147: '… that our good and evil depend mainly on the inner excitations [*emotiones interieures*] that are aroused in the soul only by the soul itself. They are distinguished in this way from the passions, which always depend on a movement of the animal spirits.'

11 This does not mean that this distinction was common in everyday language; this is simply the distinction that Descartes made between the two phenomena of passions and emotions. Van Mander preferred the term 'affect' for passion, while Van Hoogstraten used '*hartstocht*' or '*lijding*'. Franciscus Junius spoke of '*roersel*' or '*ontroeren*', '*beroeren*'. See Weststeijn in Dickey and Roodenburg 2010, pp. 264–5.

12 Strauss and Van der Meulen 1979, pp. 161–2, doc. no. 1639/2. Van de Wetering in Amsterdam 2006b and Berlin 2006, pp. 83–4. Roodenburg in Dickey and Roodenburg 2010, pp. 307–18.

13 Huygens and Heesakkers 1994, p. 86.

14 For *psychomachia* as a medieval visualisation of the struggle of the soul in moralising texts, see Norman 1988; O'Reilly 1988.

15 Vondel (1927–40), vol. 2, pp. 486–94; Porteman 1986, pp. 309–11.

16 See Porteman 1986, pp. 311–14. Cats's poems were published in more than twenty editions between 1620 and 1650.

17 Preface to 1621 edn of Cats's poems (see note 15), unpaginated.

18 Vos 1662–71, pp. 569–71; Weber 1991, p. 219. 'Jempsar' is also the name given to Potiphar's wife in Joost van den Vondel's play *Joseph in Egypten* (*Joseph in Egypt*), Amsterdam 1640, although she is not named in the Bible. On the popular literary genre of epigrams to paintings, see Schenkeveld 1991, pp. 127–30.

19 Buitendijk 1975; Konst 1993, pp. 31–46, 163–78. See p. 268 in the present volume.

20 The Rembrandt Research Project has cast doubt on whether the figure of Joseph was painted by Rembrandt himself. Even if painted by another artist, it was certainly produced in Rembrandt's studio and under his supervision. See Berlin 2006, pp. 366–7, no. 62.

21 For the differences, see the excellent analysis by Van de Wetering in Berlin 2006, pp. 229–33.

22 See Bleyerveld 2000.

23 Amsterdam 1991b, pp. 66–7.

24 Städelsches Kunstinstitut, Frankfurt, inv. 1383. Kassel 2005, pp. 43–58, no. 5.

25 Düsseldorf and Darmstadt 1995, pp. 232, 234.

26 Livy, *Historiae* I: 57–8.
27 Düsseldorf and Darmstadt 1995, pp. 294–313.
28 It is not clear whether 'G.F.' refers to Govert Flinck.
29 Vos 1662–71, p. 550; Weber 1991, p. 191.
30 Descartes also distinguishes between the passions of the spirit and the acts of will, 'which one could denote the emotions of the spirit'. Descartes (1649) 1984, art. 29.
31 See Amsterdam 1991b, p. 225.
32 The background appears to be incomplete. The canvas could well once have been bigger; the piece of canvas that has been inserted with the signature on the bottom right may have been part of this previous, larger version.
33 Luke 22: 42–4.
34 The second drawing is in the Hamburger Kunsthalle, inv. 22413. See Benesch 899; Hamburg 2011, no. 852.
35 Tümpel 1986, p. 296.
36 Vos 1662–71, p. 565; Weber 1991, p. 202; Sluijter in Dickey and Roodenburg 2010, p. 300; Geerdink 2012, pp. 114–15. On the subject of Haman, see also pp. 250, 262–4 in the present volume.
37 Van de Wetering in Amsterdam 2006b and Berlin 2006, pp. 96–101, describes the 'beholder's share' with reference to remarks by Samuel van Hoogstraten about the sketchiness of his drawings. On this subject, see Gombrich (1960) 1977, part 3, pp. 154–244.

RECONCILIATION

1 Blankert in Washington, Detroit and Amsterdam 1980, pp. 26–7; Blankert 1982, pp. 34–6; Weber 1991, pp. 191–211; Sluijter in Dickey and Roodenburg 2010, pp. 285–305.
2 For this large painting (The State Hermitage Museum, St Petersburg, inv. 92) and a version made by a pupil in 1636 (Alte Pinakothek, Munich, inv. 438), see Dekiert 2004.
3 Parshall 1978.
4 See Tümpel in Berlin 2006, pp. 105–8. Rembrandt owned a German edition of Flavius Josephus with illustrations by Tobias Stimmer; Strauss and Van der Meulen 1979, p. 379, doc. no. 1656/12, no. 284.
5 Angel 1642, p. 48: '*gansch onghemeen, en evenwel eygentlic*', '*sy malkanderen (als van nieuw ghevonden) ombelsden, en kuste ...*'
6 Kassel 2005, no. 18, and pp. 32–9.
7 Strauss and Van der Meulen 1979, p. 361, doc. no. 1656/12: '*122 Een Abrahams offerhande van Jan Lievensz*' ('122 An Abraham's sacrifice by Jan Lievensz').
8 See Von Erffa 1989–95, vol. 2, p. 459; Bar-Efrat 1987; Zell 2002, pp. 166 ff.; Kassel 2005, p. 71.
9 For details of this translation problem, see Bar-Efrat 1987, p. 594.
10 There are several versions of this drawing, the original of which may perhaps be the one formerly in the Houthakker collection: Benesch 130 A, fig. 155 (about 1636); sale Amsterdam (Sotheby's/Mak van Waay), 17–18 November 1975, lot 190 (collection B. Houthakker, Amsterdam; buyer unknown). Copies are in the collections of L. Grassi, Florence (1924), and Rijksmuseum, Amsterdam; see Schatborn 1985, pp. 162 ff., nos 74, 75.
11 See Jan Victors's versions of the painting of about 1645–50 in the Szépművészeti Múzeum, Budapest; of 1650–2 in the Muzeum Narodowe, Warsaw; and of after 1660 in Kursk State Art Gallery. Kassel 2005, figs 43, 48, 54.
12 This large painting, produced in the year of Rembrandt's bankruptcy, is unlikely to have been painted without a commission. Schwartz 1984, p. 271, suspects that it may be a *portrait historié* of an actual family (as an overmantel painting of the Schrijver-de Graeff family). However, the argument for this seems too speculative; see also Zell 2002, pp. 163–4.
13 Lipsius (1584) 1948, p. 20. This work, which was originally written in Latin, was published in around fifty editions in the seventeenth century in various translations, e.g. by François van Hoogstraten, Rotterdam 1675.
14 Belisarius became a subject for artists primarily through Jean-François Marmontel's novel *Bélisaire* (1767). Earlier writings were, of necessity, based on the *Historia arcana* (*Secret History*) by Procopius (about 490–562). One of the rare early examples of a portrayal of this subject is a painting by Mattia Preti in the Museum Boijmans Van Beuningen, Rotterdam (3245).
15 Tümpel 1986, p. 316.
16 The artists Allaert and Cornelis van Everdingen state this; it was intended for Dirck van Cattenburgh. Copenhagen 2006, p. 209, no. 19; p. 287, with literature.
17 See Tümpel 1986, p. 398.
18 See De Jonge 1938, no. 240; Huys Janssen 1998, nos 18, 19; Roethlisberger and Bok 1993, no. H 63.
19 According to an erroneous medieval interpretation of the scene, Simeon was considered to be the high priest performing the purification at the Presentation in the Temple, which is why he wears the costly robes of priests in these pictures, something that Rembrandt has corrected. See Tümpel in Berlin 2006, pp. 109, 127 note 21.
20 Discussed by Sluijter in Dickey and Roodenburg 2010.
21 Smits-Veldt 1991, chaps III, IV; see also pp. 236–43 in the present volume.
22 Sluijter in Dickey and Roodenburg 2010, pp. 294–5.
23 Vondel (1927–40), vol. 3, p. 641. See also the preface to *Jeptha* (Jephthah), Vondel (1927–40), vol. 8, p. 777.
24 In the '*hartstoghten*' (passions) and emotional '*woelingen*' (turmoil) cited by Vondel, Sluijter sees the 'inner conflict' of the protagonists, which no longer takes place suddenly and no longer consists of an instantaneous movement: 'We observe protagonists who seem to recognise and realise their tragic circumstances, and we feel that we are witnessing the *woelingen* which troubles the protagonists' mind'. Sluijter in Dickey and Roodenburg 2010, p. 296.
25 See Van de Wetering in Berlin 2006, pp. 44, 96; Van de Wetering in *Corpus* V (2011), p. 135.
26 Van de Wetering in Berlin 2006, p. 31; Manuth in Berlin 2006, pp. 51–63.

BIBLIOGRAPHY

AINSWORTH ET AL. 1982
M.W. Ainsworth et al., *Art and Autoradiography: Insights into the Genesis of Paintings by Rembrandt, Van Dyck, and Vermeer*, New York 1982

ALPERS 1988
S. Alpers, *Rembrandt's Enterprise: The Studio and the Market*, Chicago 1988

ALPERS 1993
S. Alpers, 'Rembrandt's *Claudius Civilis*', in *Rembrandt and his Pupils* (papers given at a symposium at Nationalmuseum, Stockholm, 2–3 October 1992), ed. G. Cavalli-Björkman, Stockholm 1993, pp. 14–30

ALSTEENS AND BUIJS 2008
S. Alsteens and H. Buijs, *Paysages de France. Dessinés par Lambert Doomer et les artistes hollandais et flamands des XVIe et XVIIe siècles*, Paris 2008

AMSTERDAM 1898
Rembrandt: schilderijen bijeengebracht ter gelegenheid van de inhuldiging van Hare Majesteit Koningin Wilhelmina, exh. cat., Stedelijk Museum, Amsterdam 1898

AMSTERDAM 1969
P.J.J. van Thiel, L.C.J. Frerichs and P. Schatborn, *Rembrandt 1669/1969*, exh. cat., Rijksmuseum, Amsterdam 1969

AMSTERDAM 1976
E. de Jongh, *Tot Lering en Vermaak*, exh. cat., Rijksmuseum, Amsterdam 1976

AMSTERDAM 1985
B.P.J. Broos, *Rembrandt en zijn voorbeelden / and his sources*, exh. cat., Museum Het Rembrandthuis, Amsterdam 1985

AMSTERDAM 1986
R.E.O. Ekkart and E. Ornstein-van Slooten, *Oog in oog met de modellen van Rembrandts portret-etsen / Face to Face with the Sitters for Rembrandt's Etched Portraits*, exh. cat., Museum Het Rembrandthuis, Amsterdam 1986

AMSTERDAM 1988
J. van der Waals, *De prentschat van Michiel Hinloopen: een reconstructie van de eerste openbare papierkunstverzameling in Nederland*, exh. cat., Rijksmuseum, Amsterdam 1988

AMSTERDAM 1991a
B. Meijer, *Rondom Rembrandt en Titiaan*, exh. cat., Museum Het Rembrandthuis, Amsterdam 1991

AMSTERDAM 1991b
C. Tümpel et al., *Het Oude Testament in de Schilderkunst van de Gouden Eeuw*, exh. cat., Joods Historisch Museum Amsterdam, Zwolle 1991

AMSTERDAM 1992
E. Bergvelt and R. Kistemaker (eds), *De wereld binnen handbereik: Nederlandse kunst- en rariteitenverzamelingen, 1585–1735*, exh. cat., Amsterdams Historisch Museum, Zwolle 1992

AMSTERDAM 1999
B. van den Boogert et al., *Rembrandts schatkamer*, exh. cat., Museum Het Rembrandthuis, Amsterdam 1999

AMSTERDAM 2006a
D. Bull et al., *Rembrandt / Caravaggio*, exh. cat., Rijksmuseum, Amsterdam 2006

AMSTERDAM 2006b
E. van de Wetering et al., *Rembrandt: Quest of a Genius*, exh. cat., Museum Het Rembrandthuis, Amsterdam, Zwolle 2006 [also shown at Gemäldegalerie, Staatliche Museen zu Berlin, with different catalogue; see Berlin 2006]

AMSTERDAM 2011
M. van der Zwaag (ed.), *Opstand als opdracht. Flinck, Ovens, Lievens, Jordaens, De Groot, Bol en Rembrandt in het Paleis*, exh. cat., Koninklijk Paleis, Amsterdam 2011

AMSTERDAM AND LONDON 2000
E. Hinterding, G. Luijten and M. Royalton-Kisch, *Rembrandt the Printmaker*, exh. cat., Rijksmuseum, Amsterdam and The British Museum, London 2000

AMSTERDAM AND PARIS 1998
B. Bakker et al., *Landscapes of Rembrandt: His Favourite Walks*, exh. cat., Gemeentearchief, Amsterdam and Institut Néerlandais, Paris, Bussum 1998

AMSTERDAM AND ROTTERDAM 1956
A. van Schendel et al., *Rembrandt: tentoonstelling ter herdenking van de geboorte van Rembrandt op 15 juli 1606: schilderijen*, exh. cat., Rijksmuseum, Amsterdam and Museum Boymans, Rotterdam 1956

AMSTERDAM AND WASHINGTON 1981
P. Schatborn, *Dutch Figure Drawings from the Seventeenth Century*, exh. cat., Rijksmuseum, Amsterdam and National Gallery of Art, Washington, The Hague 1981

ANGEL 1642
P. Angel, *Lof der schilder-konst*, Leiden 1642

ANON. 1761
[R. and J.D. Dodsley], *London and its Environs described*, 6 vols, London 1761

ANON. 1827
A Concise Description of Bury Saint Edmund's, and its environs…, London 1827

BAKKER 1995
B. Bakker, '*Schilderachtig*: discussions of a seventeenth-century term and concept', *Simiolus* 23 (1995), pp. 147–62

BAKKER 2011
B. Bakker, '*Au vif – naar 't leven – ad vivum*: The Medieval Origin of a Humanist Concept', in *Aemulatio. Imitation, emulation and invention in Netherlandish art from 1500 to 1800. Essays in honor of Eric Jan Sluijter*, eds A. Boschloo et al., Zwolle 2011, pp. 37–52

BALDINUCCI 1686
F. Baldinucci, *Cominciamento e progresso dell'arte dell'intagliare in rame, colle vite di molti de' più eccelenti Maestri della stessa Professione…*, Florence 1686

BAR-EFRAT 1987
S. Bar-Efrat, 'Some remarks on Rembrandt's "Jacob blessing Ephraim and Manasseh"', *The Burlington Magazine* 129 (1987), pp. 594–5

B./BARTSCH
A. Bartsch, *Catalogue raisonné de toutes les estampes qui forment l'oeuvre de Rembrandt…* Vienna 1797

BAUCH 1966
K. Bauch, *Rembrandt Gemälde*, Berlin 1966

BEN./BENESCH
O. Benesch, *The Drawings of Rembrandt*, 6 vols, London 1954–7; 2nd edn, rev. and enlarged by E. Benesch, London 1973

BENESCH 1956
O. Benesch, 'Worldly and Religious Portraits in Rembrandt's Late Art', *The Art Quarterly* 19 (1956), pp. 335–55

BERLIN 1930
M.J. Friedländer, *Rembrandt-Ausstellung*, exh. cat., Preussische Akademie der Künste, Berlin 1930

BERLIN 1970
C. Tümpel, *Rembrandt legt die Bibel aus. Zeichnungen und Radierungen aus dem Küpferstichkabinett der Staatlichen Museen Preussischer Kulturbesitz Berlin*, exh. cat., Küpferstichkabinett, Staatliche Museen zu Berlin 1970

BERLIN 2006
K. Bahre et al., *Rembrandt: Genie auf der Suche*, exh. cat., Gemäldegalerie, Staatliche Museen zu Berlin 2006 [also shown at Museum Het Rembrandthuis, Amsterdam, with different catalogue; see Amsterdam 2006b]

BERLIN, AMSTERDAM AND LONDON 1991a
C. Brown, J. Kelch and P. van Thiel, *Rembrandt: The Master & his Workshop*, vol. 1: *Paintings*, exh. cat., Altes Museum, Gemäldegalerie, Staatliche Museen zu Berlin; Rijksmuseum, Amsterdam and The National Gallery, London 1991

BERLIN, AMSTERDAM AND LONDON 1991b
H. Bevers, P. Schatborn and B. Welzel, *Rembrandt: The Master & his Workshop*, vol. 2: *Drawings & Etchings*, exh. cat., Altes Museum, Kupferstichkabinett, Staatliche Museen zu Berlin; Rijksmuseum, Amsterdam; and The National Gallery, London 1991

BEVERS 2006
H. Bevers, *Rembrandt: Die Zeichnungen im Berliner Kupferstichkabinett: kritischer Katalog, Berlin, Kupferstichkabinett*, Staatliche Museen zu Berlin, Berlin 2006

Biblia 1637
Biblia, dat is: De gantsche H. Schrifture, vervattende alle de canonijcke Boecken des Ouden en des Nieuwen Testaments, Leiden 1637

DE BIE 1661
C. de Bie, *Het gulden cabinet vande edel vry schilder-const*, Antwerp 1661

BIKKER 2013
J. Bikker, *The Jewish Bride*, Amsterdam 2013

BILLE 1956a
C. Bille, 'Rembrandt's *Claudius Civilis* at Amsterdam in 1734', *Konsthistorisk Tidskrift* 25 (1956), pp. 25–30

BILLE 1956b
C. Bille, 'Rembrandt's *Claudius Civilis* and its owners in the 18th century', *Oud Holland* 71 (1956), pp. 54–9

BIÖRKLUND 1968
G. Biörklund, with the assistance of O.H. Barnard, *Rembrandt's Etchings True and False: A Summary Catalogue in a distinctive chronological Order and completely illustrated*, 2nd edn, Stockholm, London and New York 1968

DE BISSCHOP 1671
J. de Bisschop, *Paradigmata variorum artificum, voor-beelden der teken-konst van verscheyde meesters*, The Hague 1671

BLAAUW 2005
A. Blaauw, 'Over de Waterlands doopsgezinde schilder Abraham de Verwer van Burchstaete', *Doopsgezinde Bijdragen* 31 (2005), pp. 75–91

BLANC 2009
J. Blanc, 'Rembrandt and the historical construction of his *Conspiracy of Claudius Civilis*', in *Myth in History, History in Myth*, eds L. Cruz and W. Frijhoff, Leiden 2009, pp. 237–53

BLANKERT 1973
A. Blankert, 'Rembrandt, Zeuxis and Ideal Beauty', in *Album Amicorum J.G. van Gelder*, eds J. Bruyn et al., The Hague 1973, pp. 32–9

BLANKERT 1975
A. Blankert, *Kunst als regeringszaak in Amsterdam in de 17e eeuw: rondom schilderijen van Ferdinand Bol*, Lochem 1975

BLANKERT 1982
A. Blankert, *Ferdinand Bol (1616–1680): Rembrandt's Pupil*, Doornspijk 1982

BLEYERVELD 2000
Y. Bleyerveld, *Hoe bedriechlijck dat de vrouwen zijn. Vrouwenlisten in de beeldende kunst in de Nederlanden circa 1350–1650*, Leiden 2000

BLEYERVELD 2000–1
Y. Bleyerveld, 'Chaste, obedient and devout: Biblical women as patterns of female virtue in Netherlandish and German graphic art, ca. 1500–1750', *Simiolus* 28 (2000–1), pp. 219–50

VON BODE AND HOFSTEDE DE GROOT 1897–1905
W. von Bode and C. Hofstede de Groot, *Rembrandt: Beschreibendes Verzeichnis seiner Gemälde mit den heliographischen Nachbildungen, Geschichte seines Lebens und seiner Kunst*, 8 vols, Paris 1897–1905 [English edn trans. F. Simmonds, Paris 1897–1906]

BOHLMANN, FINK AND WEISS 2008
C. Bohlmann, T. Fink and P. Weiss (eds), *Lichtgefüge des 17. Jahrhunderts: Rembrandt und Vermeer, Spinoza und Leibniz*, Munich 2008

BOK 1990
M.J. Bok, 'Kunstbezit in de Amsterdamse familie Van Ceulen: op zoek naar twee schilderijen van Rembrandt', *Jaarboek van het Centraal Bureau voor Genealogie en het Iconographisch Bureau*, 44 (1990), pp. 149–59

BOK 1994
M.J. Bok, *Vraag en aanbod op de Nederlandse kunstmarkt, 1580–1700*, Ph.D. dissertation, Utrecht 1994

BOK 2004
M.J. Bok, 'Rembrandt's Fame and Rembrandt's Failure: The Market for History Paintings in the Dutch Republic', in *Rembrandt and Dutch History Painting in the 17th Century*, ed. A. Kofuku, Tokyo 2004, pp. 159–78

BOK AND VAN DER MOLEN 2009
M.J. Bok and T. van der Molen, 'Productivity Levels of Rembrandt and His Main Competitors in the Amsterdam Art Market', *Jahrbuch der Berliner Museen* 51 (2009), special issue, *Rembrandt – Wissenschaft auf der Suche*, pp. 61–8

BOSTON 1981
C.S. Ackley, *Printmaking in the Age of Rembrandt*, exh. cat., Museum of Fine Arts, Boston, 1981

BOSTON AND CHICAGO 2003
C.S. Ackley et al., *Rembrandt's Journey: Painter, Draftsman, Etcher*, exh. cat., Museum of Fine Arts, Boston and The Art Institute of Chicago, 2003

BOSTON AND NEW YORK 1969
F. Stampfle et al., *Rembrandt: Experimental Etcher*, exh. cat., Museum of Fine Arts, Boston and The Pierpont Morgan Library, New York, Greenwich, Conn. 1969

BRAUNSCHWEIG 2006
Silke Gatenbrocker, *Familienglück: Rembrandt und sein Braunschweiger Meisterwerk*, exh. cat., Herzog Alton Ulrich-Museum, Braunschweig 2006

VAN BREDA 1997
J. van Breda, 'Rembrandt etchings on oriental papers: Papers in the collection of the National Gallery of Victoria', *Art Bulletin of Victoria* 38 (1997), pp. 25–38

BREDERO (ed. Stutterheim) 1974
G.A. Bredero, *Spaanschen Brabander, met fragmenten uit Lazarus van Tormes*, ed. C.F.P. Stutterheim, Culemborg 1974

BREDERO (ed. Stuiveling) 1975
G.A. Bredero, *Boertigh, amoreus, en aendachtigh groot liedboeck*, ed. G. Stuiveling, Culemborg 1975

BREDIUS 1909
A. Bredius, 'Uit Rembrandts laatste levensjaar', *Oud Holland* 26 (1909), pp. 238–40

BREDIUS 1910
A. Bredius, 'Rembrandtiana', *Oud Holland* 28 (1910), pp. 193–204

BREDIUS 1935
A. Bredius, *Rembrandt Gemälde*, Vienna 1935 [English edn *The Paintings of Rembrandt*, 2 vols, London 1937]

BREDIUS AND GERSON 1969
A. Bredius, *Rembrandt: The Complete Edition of the Paintings*, rev. H. Gerson, London 1969

BREJON DE LAVERGNÉE 1987
A. Brejon de Lavergnée, *L'Inventaire Le Brun de 1683. La collection des tableaux de Louis XIV*, Paris 1987

BRIELS 1997
J. Briels, *Vlaamse schilders en de dageraad van Hollands Gouden Eeuw 1585–1630*, Antwerp 1997

BRINCKMANN 1925
A.E. Brinckmann, *Spätwerke grosser Meister*, Berlin 1925

BROOS 1971
B.P.J. Broos, 'The "O" of Rembrandt', *Simiolus* 4 (1971), pp. 150–82

BROOS 1977
B.P.J. Broos, *Index to the Formal Sources of Rembrandt's Art*, Maarssen 1977

BROOS 1978–9
B.P.J. Broos, 'Review of S. Slive, *Frans Hals*, 3 vols, London 1970/1974', *Simiolus* 10 (1978–9), pp. 115–23

BROOS 1993
B.P.J. Broos, *Intimacies & Intrigues: History Painting in the Mauritshuis*, Ghent 1993

BROOS ET AL. 2004/2005
B.P.J. Broos et al., *Portraits in the Mauritshuis 1430–1790*, ed. Q. Buvelot, The Hague and Zwolle 2004 (2nd edn 2005)

BROUN 1987
F.J.P. Broun, 'Sir Joshua Reynolds' Collection of Paintings', 3 vols, dissertation, Princeton (Princeton University) 1987

BROWN AND ROY 1992
C. Brown and A. Roy, 'Rembrandt's "Alexander the Great"', *The Burlington Magazine* 134 (1992), pp. 286–97

BRÜCKNER 1997
Christel Brückner, *Rembrandts Braunschweiger 'Familienbild': Seine thematische Figuren und Farbkomposition und die Kunst Italiens*, Hildesheim, Zürich, New York 1977

LE BRUN 1703
Charles le Brun, *Afbeelding der Hertstogten, of Middelen om dezelve volkomen te leeren afteekenen … vertaalt door F. de Kaarsgieter …*, Amsterdam 1703

BRYANT 2003
J. Bryant, *Kenwood, Paintings in the Iveagh Bequest*, New Haven 2003

BUCHANAN 1824
W. Buchanan, *Memoirs of Painting with a Chronological History of the Importation of Pictures by the Great Masters into England since the French Revolution*, 2 vols, London 1824

BUCHBINDER-GREEN 1974
B.J. Buchbinder-Green, 'The Painted Decorations of the Town Hall of Amsterdam', dissertation, Northwestern University, Chicago 1974

BUITENDIJK 1975
W.J.C. Buitendijk, *Jan Vos. Toneelwerken …*, Assen and Amsterdam 1975

BURTON 1621/1638
R. Burton, *The Anatomy of Melancholy: What it is With all the kinds causes symptomes prognostickes & severall cures of it*, Oxford 1621 (rev. edn 1638)

VANDEN BUSSCHE 1880
E. Vanden Bussche, 'Un évèque bibliophile. Notes sur la bibliothèque et le cabinet de gravures de Charles Vanden Bosch, neuvième évèque de Bruges; ses relations avec Elzévirs, Meyssens, etc.', *La Flandre: Revue des Monuments d'histoire et d'antiquités* 13 (1880), pp. 345–63

CAMBRIDGE 2011
M.E. Wieseman, H.P. Chapman and W.E. Franits, *Vermeer's Women: Secrets and Silence*, exh. cat., The Fitzwilliam Museum, Cambridge 2011

CAMPBELL 1971
C.G. Campbell, *Studies in the Formal Sources of Rembrandt's Figure Compositions*, Ph.D. dissertation, University of London 1971

CARROLL 1986
M.D. Carroll, 'Civic ideology and its subversion: Rembrandt's *Oath of Claudius Civilis*', *Art History* 9 (1986), pp. 10–35

CASTIGLIONE 1528
B. Castiglione, *Il Cortegiano*, Venice 1528

CATS 1625
J. Cats, *Houwelyck, dat is de gantsche gelegentheyt des echten-staets*, Middelburg 1625

CATS 1637
J. Cats, *'s Werelts begin, midden, eynde, besloten in den trou-ringh met den proefsteen van den selven*, Dordrecht 1637

CAVALLI-BJÖRKMAN 2005
G. Cavalli-Björkman, *Nationalmuseum Stockholm. Dutch and Flemish Paintings*, vol. II: *Dutch Paintings c.1600–c.1800*, Stockholm 2005

CAVALLINO AND SALERNO 2005
M.A. Pavone and A.L. Giannone, *Percosi d'arte: Tra vestigia dei Messapi il collezionismo dei Ruffo e l'evoluzione pittorica di Mino delle Site*, exh. cat., Convento di S. Domenico, Cavallino and Pinacoteca Provinciale, Salerno 2005

CHAPMAN 1990
H.P. Chapman, *Rembrandt's Self-Portraits: A Study in Seventeenth-Century Identity*, Princeton 1990

CHONG 1992
A.D. Chong, *Aelbert Cuyp and the Meanings of Landscape*, Ph.D. dissertation, New York University 1992

CHONG AND ZELL 2002
A. Chong and M. Zell (eds), *Rethinking Rembrandt*, Zwolle 2002

CINCINNATI 2008
H.P. Chapman et al., *Rembrandt: Three Faces of the Master*, ed. B. Leca, exh. cat., Cincinnati Art Museum, Cincinnati 2008

CLARK 1966
K. Clark, *Rembrandt and the Italian Renaissance*, London 1966

LE COMTE 1700
F. Le Comte, *Cabinet des singularitez d'architecture, peinture, sculpture, et gravure ou introduction à la connoissance des plus beaux arts, figurez sous les tableaux, les statuës & les estampes*, 3 vols, Paris 1700

COPENHAGEN 2006
L. Bøgh Rønberg et al., *Rembrandt: The Master and his Workshop*, exh. cat., Statens Museum for Kunst, Copenhagen, 2006

CORNELIS AND FILEDT KOK 1998
B. Cornelis and J.P. Filedt Kok, 'The taste for Lucas van Leyden prints', *Simiolus* 26 (1998), pp. 18–86

Corpus I
J. Bruyn et al., *A Corpus of Rembrandt Paintings*, vol. I: *1625–1631*, trans. D. Cook-Radmore, The Hague, Boston and London 1982

Corpus II
J. Bruyn et al., *A Corpus of Rembrandt Paintings*, vol. II: *1631–1634*, trans. D. Cook-Radmore, The Hague, Boston and London 1986

Corpus III
J. Bruyn et al., *A Corpus of Rembrandt Paintings*, vol. III: *1635–1642*, trans. D. Cook-Radmore, The Hague, Boston and London 1989

Corpus IV
E. van de Wetering et al., *A Corpus of Rembrandt Paintings*, vol. IV: *The Self-Portraits*, trans. J. Kilian, K. Kist and M. Pearson, Dordrecht 2005

Corpus V
E. van de Wetering et al., *A Corpus of Rembrandt Paintings*, vol. V: *Small-Scale History Paintings*, trans. M. Pearson, J. Kilian and K. Kist, Dordrecht 2011

COURTRIGHT 1996
N. Courtright, 'Origins and Meanings of Rembrandt's Late Drawing Style', *The Art Bulletin* 78 (1996), pp. 485–510

CRENSHAW 2006
P. Crenshaw, *Rembrandt's Bankruptcy: The Artist, his Patrons, and the Art World in Seventeenth-Century Netherlands*, Cambridge 2006

DE DECKER 1667
J. de Decker, *Lof der Geldsucht ofte Vervolg der Mijmoeffeningen*, Amsterdam 1667

DEKIERT 2004
M. Dekiert, *Rembrandt: die Opferung Isaaks*, Munich 2004

DENVER AND NEWARK 2001
M. Westermann et al., *Art & Home: Dutch Interiors in the Age of Rembrandt*, exh. cat., Denver Art Museum, Denver and Newark Museum, Newark 2001

DESCARTES 1649 (1984)
René Descartes, *Die Leidenschaften der Seele* (1649), ed. and trans. K. Hammacher, Hamburg 1984

DICKEY 1986
S.S. Dickey, '"Judicious negligence": Rembrandt transforms an emblematic convention', *The Art Bulletin* 68, no. 2 (June 1986), pp. 253–62

DICKEY 1995
S.S. Dickey, '"Met een wenende ziel – doch droge ogen", Women holding handkerchiefs in seventeenth-century Dutch portraits', *Nederlands Kunsthistorisch Jaarboek* 46 (1995), pp. 332–67

DICKEY 2004
S.S. Dickey, *Rembrandt: Portraits in Print*, Amsterdam and Philadelphia 2004

DICKEY AND ROODENBURG 2010
S.S. Dickey and H. Roodenburg (eds), *The passions in the arts of the early modern Netherlands / De hartstochten in de kunst in de vroegmoderne Nederlanden* (*Nederlands Kunsthistorisch Jaarboek* 60), Zwolle 2010

DICKSON, PARMENTIER AND OHLMEYER 2007
D. Dickson, J. Parmentier and J.H. Ohlmeyer (eds), *Irish and Scottish Mercantile Networks in Europe and Overseas in the Seventeenth and Eighteenth Centuries*, Ghent 2007

DIJON 2003
M. Piotrovsky et al., *Rembrandt et son école: Collections du musée de l'Ermitage de Saint-Pétersbourg*, exh. cat., Musée des Beaux-Arts, Dijon 2003

DIXON 1998
L.S. Dixon (ed.), *In Detail: New Studies of Northern Renaissance Art: Essays in Honour of Walter S. Gibson*, Turnhout 1998

DORDRECHT AND COLOGNE 1998
P. Schoon et al., *Arent de Gelder (1645–1727): Rembrandts laatste leerling*, exh. cat., Dordrechts Museum, Dordrecht, and Wallraf-Richartz-Museum, Cologne, Ghent 1998

DUDOK VAN HEEL 1969a
S.A.C. Dudok van Heel, 'Het Macenaat De Graeff en Rembrandt', *Maandblad Amstelodamum* 56 (1969), pp. 150–5

DUDOK VAN HEEL 1969b
S.A.C. Dudok van Heel, 'De Rembrandt's in de verzamelingen "Hinlopen"', *Maandblad Amstelodamum* 56 (1969), pp. 233–7

DUDOK VAN HEEL 1979
S.A.C. Dudok van Heel, 'Het maecenaat Trip: opdrachten aan Ferdinand Bol en Rembrandt van Rijn', *Kroniek van het Rembrandthuis* (1979), pp. 14–26

DUDOK VAN HEEL 1982
S.A.C. Dudok van Heel, 'Het "schilderhuis" van Govert Flinck en de kunsthandel van Uylenburgh aan de Lauriergracht te Amsterdam', *Jaarboek Amstelodamum* 74 (1982), pp. 70–90

DUDOK VAN HEEL 1997
S.A.C. Dudok van Heel, 'Rembrandt doet in 1639 een miskoop: de geschiedenis van Rembrandts huis', *Kroniek van het Rembrandthuis* (1997), pp. 2–13

DUDOK VAN HEEL 2006
S.A.C. Dudok van Heel, *De jonge Rembrandt onder tijdgenoten: godsdienst en schilderkunst in Leiden en Amsterdam*, Rotterdam 2006

DÜSSELDORF AND DARMSTADT 1995
B. Baumgärtel and S. Neysters, *Die Galerie der starken Frauen: Regentinnen, Amazonen, Salondamen*, exh. cat., Kunstmuseum, Düsseldorf and Hessisches Landesmuseum, Darmstadt 1995

EDINBURGH AND LONDON 2001
J. Lloyd Williams et al., *Rembrandt's Women*, exh. cat., National Galleries of Scotland, Edinburgh and Royal Academy of Arts, London 2001

VAN EEGHEN 1956
I.H. van Eeghen, 'Rembrandt's Claudius Civilis and the Funeral Ticket', *Konsthistorisk Tidskrift* 25 (1956), pp. 55–7

VAN EEGHEN 1957
I.H. van Eeghen, 'De Staalmeesters', *Jaarboek Amstelodamum* 49 (1957), pp. 65–80

VAN EEGHEN 1958
I.H. van Eeghen, 'Frederik Rihel, een 17de-eeuwse zakenman en paardenliefhebber', *Maandblad Amstelodamum* 45 (1958), pp. 73–81

VAN EEGHEN 1969a
I.H. van Eeghen, 'Elsje Christiaens en de kunsthistorici', *Maandblad Amstelodamum* 56 (1969), pp. 173–81

VAN EEGHEN 1969b
I.H. van Eeghen, 'Handboogstraat 5', *Maandblad Amstelodamum* 56 (1969), pp. 169–76

VAN EEGHEN 1969c
I.H. van Eeghen, 'Het Amsterdamse Sint Lucasgilde in de 17e eeuw', *Jaarboek Amstelodamum* 61 (1969), pp. 65–102

VAN EEGHEN 1969d
I.H. van Eeghen, '"De Keizerskroon", een optisch bedrog', *Maandblad Amstelodamum* 56 (1969), pp. 162–8

VAN EEGHEN 1969e
I.H. van Eeghen, 'Het huis op de Rozengracht', *Maandblad Amstelodamum* 56 (1969), pp. 180–3

VAN EIJNATTEN AND VAN LIEBURG 2006
J. van Eijnatten and F. van Lieburg, *Nederlandse religiegeschiedenis*, Hilversum 2006

VON EINEM 1973
H. von Einem, 'Zur Deutung des Altersstiles in der Kunstgeschichte', in *Album Amicorum J.G. van Gelder*, eds J. Bruyn et al., The Hague 1973, pp. 88–92

EKKART 2002
R.E.O. Ekkart, 'A *portrait historié* with Venus, Paris and Cupid: Ferdinand Bol and the patronage of the Spiegel family', *Simiolus* 29 (2002), pp. 14–41

EKKART 2009
R.E.O. Ekkart, 'Rembrandt and Innovation in Amsterdam Portraiture', *Jahrbuch der Berliner Museen* 51 (2009), pp. 39–42

EMMENS 1964
J.A. Emmens, *Rembrandt en de regels van de kunst*, dissertation, Utrecht University, Utrecht 1964

EMMENS 1979
J.A. Emmens, *Rembrandt en de regels van de kunst* (*J.A. Emmens, verzameld werk*, vol. 2) (1968), Amsterdam 1979

ENGLEBERT (1965) 2013
O. Englebert, *St Francis of Assisi: A Biography*, trans. E.M. Cooper, Cincinnati 2013

VON ERFFA 1989–95
H.M. von Erffa, *Ikonologie der Genesis: die christlichen Bildthemen aus dem Alten Testament und ihre Quellen*, 2 vols, Munich 1989–95

EXALTO 2005
J. Exalto, *Gereformeerde heiligen: de religieuze exempeltraditie in vroegmodern Nederland*, Nijmegen 2005

FARRER 1908
E. Farrer, *Portraits in Suffolk Houses (West)*, London 1908

FÉLIBIEN 1685
A. Félibien, *Entretiens sur les vies et sur les ouvrages des plus excellens peintres anciens et modernes*, vol. IV, Paris 1685

FOKKENS 1662
M. Fokkens, *Beschrijvinge Der wijdt-vermaarde Koop-stadt Amstelredam*, Amsterdam 1662

FORD 2007
C. Ford, *Lives of Rembrandt by Joachim von Sandrart, Filippo Baldinucci and Arnold Houbraken*, London 2007

FOUCART 1982
J. Foucart, *Les peintures de Rembrandt au Louvre*, Paris 1982

FOUCART 2009
J. Foucart, *Catalogue des peintures flamandes et hollandaises du musée du Louvre*, Paris 2009

FRANITS 1993
W.E. Franits, *Paragons of Virtue: Women and Domesticity in Seventeenth-Century Dutch Art*, Cambridge, MA 1993

FRANITS 2004
W.E. Franits, *Dutch Seventeenth-Century Genre Painting: Its Stylistic and Thematic Evolution*, New Haven and London 2004

FRANKEN 2004
M. Franken, 'Changing Direction: The Reconstruction of the Genesis of Rembrandt's *Conspiracy of the Batavians under Claudius Civilis* Reconsidered', *Art Bulletin of Nationalmuseum Stockholm* 11 (2004), pp. 75–82

FRANKEN 2012
M. Franken, 'Schimmen van de Staalmeesters belicht', *RKD Bulletin* 2 (2012), pp. 49–54

FRANKFURT 2003
J. Giltaij, *Rembrandt 'Rembrandt'*, exh. cat., Städelsches Kunstinstitut, Frankfurt am Main 2003

FREMANTLE 1959
K. Fremantle, *The Baroque Town Hall of Amsterdam*, Utrecht 1959

FRIEDLÄNDER 1962
W. Friedländer, 'Poussin's Old Age', *Gazette des Beaux-Arts* 60 (1962), pp. 249–64

FRITZSCHE, LEONHARD AND WEBER 2013
C. Fritzsche, K. Leonhard and G.J.M. Weber (eds), *Ad Fontes!: Niederländische Kunst des 17. Jahrhunderts in Quellen*, Petersberg 2013

GANTNER 1965
J. Gantner, 'Der alte Künstler', in *Festschrift für Herbert von Einem*, eds G. von der Osten and G. Kauffmann, Berlin 1965, pp. 71–6

GASKELL AND JONKER 1998
I. Gaskell and M. Jonker (eds), *Vermeer Studies*, Washington 1998

GAUKROGER 1998
S. Gaukroger (ed.), *The Soft Underbelly of Reason: The Passions in the Seventeenth Century*, London and New York 1998

GEERDINK 2012
N. Geerdink, *Dichters en verdiensten: de sociale verankering van het dichterschap van Jan Vos (1610–1667)*, Hilversum 2012

DE GENNARO 2001
R. de Gennaro, 'Aggiunta alle notizie sulla collezione di Antonio Ruffo. "Nota di quadri vincolati in primogenitura" scampati al terremoto del 5 Febbraio 1783', *Napoli Nobilissima* 5–6 (2001), pp. 211–15

VAN GENT 2011
J. van Gent, *Bartholomeus van der Helst: een studie naar zijn leven en werk*, Zwolle 2011

GERSAINT 1744
E.-F. Gersaint, *Catalogue raisonné des diverses curiosités du Cabinet de feu M. Quentin de Lorangere*, Paris 1744

GERSAINT 1751
E.-F. Gersaint, *Catalogue raisonné de toutes les pièces Qui forment l'Oeuvre de Rembrandt…*, Paris 1751

GERSON 1968
H. Gerson, *De schilderijen van Rembrandt*, Alphen aan den Rijn 1968

GERSZI 2005
T. Gerszi, *17th Century Dutch and Flemish Drawings in the Budapest Museum of Fine Arts: A Complete Catalogue*, Budapest 2005

GILTAIJ 1988a
J. Giltaij, *Een gloeiend palet: schilderijen van Rembrandt en zijn school / A Glowing Palette: Paintings of Rembrandt and his School*, Rotterdam 1988

GILTAIJ 1988b
J. Giltaij, *De tekeningen van Rembrandt en zijn school in het Museum Boymans-van Beuningen / The Drawings by Rembrandt and his School in the Museum Boymans-van Beuningen*, Rotterdam 1988

GILTAIJ 1999
J. Giltaij, *Ruffo en Rembrandt: over een Siciliaanse verzamelaar in de zeventiende eeuw die drie schilderijen bij Rembrandt bestelde*, Zutphen 1999

GILTAIJ 2005
J. Giltaij, 'Nieuws omtrent Ruffo en Rembrandt', *Kroniek van het Rembrandthuis* (2005), pp. 47–9

VAN GOGH-BONGER 1953
J. van Gogh-Bonger (ed.), *Verzamelde brieven van Vincent van Gogh*, vol. 3, Amsterdam and Antwerp 1953

GLASGOW 2012
P. Black and E. Hermans, *Rembrandt and the Passion*, exh. cat., The Hunterian Museum, Glasgow, Munich 2012

GOLAHNY 1984
A. Golahny, *Rembrandt's Paintings and the Venetian Tradition*, Ph.D. dissertation, University of Michigan, Ann Arbor 1984

GOLAHNY 2003
A. Golahny, *Rembrandt's Reading: The Artist's Bookshelf of Ancient Poetry and History*, Amsterdam 2003

GOMBRICH 1960/1977
E.H. Gombrich, *Art and Illusion: A Study in the Psychology of Pictorial Representation*, Princeton 1960 (4th edn 1977)

GOOSSENS 1996
E.J. Goossens, *Treasure Wrought by Chisel and Brush: The Town Hall of Amsterdam in the Golden Age*, Amsterdam 1996

GREGORY AND ZDANOWICZ 1988
J. Gregory and I. Zdanowicz, *Rembrandt in the Collections of the National Gallery of Victoria*, Melbourne 1988

GROSSMANN 1951
F. Grossmann, 'Holbein, Flemish paintings and Everhard Jabach', *The Burlington Magazine* 93 (1951), pp. 16–25

GROUCHY 1894
E.H. de Grouchy, 'Éverhard Jabach: collectionneur parisien (1695)', *Mémoires de la Société de l'Histoire de Paris et de l'Île-de-France* 21 (1894), pp. 217–92

HAAK 1969
B. Haak, 'De nachtelijke samenzwering van Claudius Civilis in het Schakerbos op de Rembrandttentoonstelling te Amsterdam', *Antiek* 4 (1969), pp. 136–48

HAAK 1972
B. Haak, *Regenten en regentessen; overlieden en chirurgijns: Amsterdamse groepportretten van 1600 tot 1835*, Amsterdam 1972

HAARLEM 1986
E. de Jongh, *Portretten van echt en trouw: huwelijk en gezin in de Nederlandse kunst van de zeventiende eeuw*, exh. cat., Frans Halsmuseum, Haarlem 1986

HALEWOOD 1982
W.H. Halewood, *Six Subjects of Reformation Art: A Preface to Rembrandt*, Toronto 1982

HALL ET AL. 1982/2005
M. Hall et al., *Treasures of the Fitzwilliam Museum*, Cambridge 1982 (rev. edn 2005)

HAMBURG 2011
A. Stefes, *Bruegel, Rembrandt & Co: niederländische Zeichnungen 1450–1850*, exh. cat., Hamburger Kunsthalle, Hamburg 2011

HAVERKAMP-BEGEMANN 1973
E. Haverkamp-Begemann, 'Eine unbekannte Vorzeichnung zu Claudius Civilis', in *Neue Beiträge zur Rembrandt-Forschung*, eds O. von Simson and J. Kelch, Berlin 1973, pp. 31–43

HAVERKAMP-BEGEMANN ET AL. 1999
E. Haverkamp-Begemann et al., *The Robert Lehman Collection*, vol. 7: *Fifteenth- to Eighteenth-Century European Drawings*, New York 1999

HdG
C. Hofstede de Groot, *A Catalogue Raisonné of the Works of the Most Eminent Dutch Painters of the Seventeenth Century*, 8 vols, trans. E.G. Hawke, London 1908–27

HEDQUIST 1994
V. Hedquist, 'Rembrandt and the Franciscans of Amsterdam', *Dutch Crossing: A Journal of Low Country Studies* 18 (1994), pp. 20–49

HEIJTING 1997
W. Heijting, 'Protestantse bestsellers in de Republiek rond het midden van de zeventiende eeuw', *De zeventiende eeuw* 13 (1997), pp. 283–92

HELD 1969
J.S. Held, *Rembrandt's* Aristotle *and other Rembrandt Studies*, Princeton 1969

HELD 1977
J.S. Held, 'Rembrandt's *Juno*', *Apollo* 105 (1977), pp. 479–85

HELD 1983
J.S. Held, *Rembrandt-Studien*, Leipzig 1983

HELD 1987
J.S. Held, 'Commentary', *Art Journal* 46 (1987), pp. 127–33

HELD 1991
J.S. Held, *Rembrandt Studies*, Princeton 1991

HEPPNER 1935
A. Heppner, 'Moses zeigt die Gesetztafeln bei Rembrandt und Bol', *Oud Holland* 52 (1935), pp. 241–51

HILLES 1929
F.W. Hilles (ed.), *Letters of Sir Joshua Reynolds*, Cambridge 1929

HINTERDING 2001
E. Hinterding, *Rembrandt als etser. Twee studies naar de praktijk van productie en verspreiding*, Utrecht 2001

HINTERDING 2006
E. Hinterding, *Rembrandt as an Etcher. The Practice of Production and Distribution*, trans. M Hoyle, 3 vols, Ouderkerk aan den IJssel 2006

HINTERDING 2008
E. Hinterding, *Rembrandt etchings from the Frits Lugt collection*, 2 vols, Bussum and Paris 2008

HINTERDING 2011
E. Hinterding, '"The incomparable *Reinbrand*": Rembrandt als onafhankelijk prentmaker in 17e-eeuws Amsterdam', in *Gedrukt tot Amsterdam. Amsterdamse prentmakers en -uitgevers in de Gouden Eeuw*, eds E. Kolfin and J. van der Veen, Amsterdam 2011, pp. 164–99

HINTERDING 2012
E. Hinterding, 'Rembrandt als vernieuwer van de techniek van de droge naald', *Desipientia* 19, no. 1 (2012), pp. 2–6

HIRSCHFELDER 2008
D. Hirschfelder, *Tronie und Porträt in der niederländischen Malerei des 17. Jahrhunderts*, Berlin 2008

HOET 1751
G. Hoet, *Catalogus of naamlyst van schilderyen, met derzelver pryzen*, vol. 1, The Hague 1751

HOFF 1995
U. Hoff, *European Paintings before 1800 in the National Gallery of Victoria*, 4th edn, Melbourne 1995

HOFSTEDE DE GROOT 1906
C. Hofstede de Groot, *Die Urkunden über Rembrandt (1575–1721)*, The Hague 1906

HOFSTEDE DE GROOT 1928
C. Hofstede de Groot, 'De portretten van het echtpaar Jacob Trip en Margaretha de Geer door de Cuyp's, N. Maes en Rembrandt', *Oud-Holland* 45 (1928), pp. 260–4

HOLLSTEIN
F.W.H. Hollstein, *Hollstein's Dutch and Flemish etchings, engravings, and woodcuts, ca. 1450–1700*, 72 vols, Amsterdam, Blaricum, Roosendaal and Rotterdam 1949–2010

HOLLSTEIN (BOL)
F.W.H. Hollstein, *Jan Boeckhorst–Pieter Bruegel de Oude (Dutch and Flemish etchings, engravings and woodcuts ca. 1450–1700*, vol. 3), Amsterdam 1950

HOOGEWERFF 1917
G.J. Hoogewerff, 'Rembrandt en een Italiaansche Maecenas', *Oud Holland* 35 (1917), pp. 129–48

HOOGEWERFF 1919
G.J. Hoogewerff, *De twee reizen van Cosimo De' Medici Prins van Toscane door de Nederlanden (1667–1669): journalen en documenten*, Amsterdam 1919

VAN HOOGSTRATEN 1657
S. van Hoogstraten, *Den eerlyken jongeling*, Dordrecht 1657

VAN HOOGSTRATEN 1678
S. van Hoogstraten, *Inleyding tot de hooge schoole der schilderkonst: anders de zichtbaere werelt*, Rotterdam 1678

DE HOOP SCHEFFER AND BOON 1971
D. de Hoop Scheffer and K.G. Boon, 'De inventaris-lijst van Clement de Jonghe en Rembrandts etsplaten', *Kroniek van het Rembrandthuis* (1971), pp. 1–17

HOUBRAKEN 1718–21
A. Houbraken, *De groote schouburgh der Nederlantsche konstschilders en schilderessen*, 3 vols, Amsterdam 1718–21

HUDLESTON 1930
D.R. Hudleston (trans.), *The Little Flowers of Saint Francis of Assisi*, New York 1930

HULFTEGGER 1954–5
A. Hulftegger, 'Formation des collections de peintures de Louis XIV', *Bulletin de la société de l'histoire de l'art français* (1954–5), pp. 124–34

HUYGENS *Vita*
C. Huygens, *Vita*, n.d., Koninklijk Bibliotheek, The Hague (MS. K.A. XLVIII)

HUYGENS AND HEESAKKERS 1994
C. Huygens, *Mijn Jeugd*, trans. and ed. C.L. Heesakkers, Amsterdam 1994

HUYS JANSSEN 1998
P. Huys Janssen, *Jan Van Bijlert 1597/98–1671: Catalogue Raisonné*, Philadelphia 1998

JAMES 1996
S. James, *Passion and Action: The Emotions in Seventeenth-Century Philosophy*, Oxford 1996

JANSEN, LUIJTEN AND BAKKER 2009
L. Jansen, H. Luijten and N. Bakker (eds), *Vincent van Gogh: The Letters. The Complete Illustrated and Annotated Edition*, 6 vols, Amsterdam 2009; online: *Vincent van Gogh: The Letters* (http://vangoghletters.org/vg)

JANSSEN 2007
A. Janssen, *Grijsaards: de verbeelding van de ouderdom in de Nederlandse prentkunst (1550–1650)*, Zutphen 2007

JENSEN ADAMS 1998
A. Jensen Adams (ed.) *Rembrandt's 'Bathsheba Reading King David's Letter'*, Cambridge and New York 1998

JOHNSON 2004
H.A. Johnson, 'Gerard de Lairesse: Genius among the Treponemes', *Journal of the Royal Society of Medicine* 97, no. 6 (2004), pp. 301–3

DE JONGE 1938
C.H. de Jonge, *Paulus Moreelse: portret- en genreschilder te Utrecht, 1571–1638*, Assen 1938

DE JONGH 1969
E. de Jongh, 'The Spur of Wit: Rembrandt's response to an Italian Challenge', *Delta: A Review of Arts, Life and Thought in the Netherlands* 12, no. 6 (1969), pp. 48–67

DE JONGH 1985
E. de Jongh, 'Review of B. Haak, *Hollandse schilders in de gouden eeuw*, Amsterdam 1984', *Simiolus* 15 (1985), pp. 65–8

DE JONGH 1991
E. de Jongh, 'De mate van ikheid in Rembrandts zelfportretten', *Kunstschrift* 6 (1991), pp. 13–23

KASSEL 2005
G.J.M. Weber, *Rembrandt im Kontrast: Die Blendung Simsons und Der Segen Jakobs*, exh. cat., Gemäldegalerie Alter Meister, Staatliche Museen Kassel and Schlossmuseum Wilhelmshöhe, Kassel, Munich 2005

KASSEL 2006
G.J.M. Weber, *Rembrandt-Bilder: Die historische Sammlung der Kasseler Gemäldegalerie*, exh. cat. Gemäldegalerie Alte Meister, Staatliche Museen, Kassel 2006

KASSEL 2011
C. Bohlmann et al., *Lichtgefüge: das Licht im Zeitalter von Rembrandt und Vermeer*, exh. cat., Schlossmuseum Wilhelmshöhe, Kassel 2011

KIRBY TALLEY 1981
M. Kirby Talley, *Portrait Painting in England: Studies in the Technical Literature before 1700*, London 1981

KLEINERT 2006
K. Kleinert, *Atelierdarstellungen in der niederländischen Genremalerei des 17. Jahrhunderts*, Petersberg 2006

KLIBANSKY, PANOFSKY AND SAXL 1964
R. Klibansky, E. Panofsky and F. Saxl, *Saturn and Melancholy: Studies in the History of Natural Philosophy, Religion and Art*, London 1964

KLOEK AND JANSEN 1993
W.T. Kloek and G.M.C. Jansen, *Rembrandt in nieuw licht: presentatie van zeven gerestaureerde schilderijen van Rembrandt*, Amsterdam 1993

KOERNER 1986
J.L. Koerner, 'Rembrandt and the Epiphany of the Face', *RES: Anthropology and Aesthetics* 12 (1986), pp. 5–32

KOK 2013
E.E. Kok, *Culturele ondernemers in de Gouden Eeuw: De artistieke en sociaal-economische strategieën van Jacob Backer, Govert Flinck, Ferdinand Bol en Joachim von Sandrart*, Ph.D. dissertation, University of Amsterdam 2013

KOLFIN 2013
E. Kolfin, 'Rembrandt's *Reclining Nude* Reconsidered', *Print Quarterly* 30 (2013), pp. 39–43

KONST 1993
J. Konst, *Woedende wraakghierigheid en vruchtelooze weeklachten. De hartstochten in de Nederlandse tragedie van de zeventiende eeuw*, Assen and Maastricht 1993

KRAFT 1965
K. Kraft, 'Der behelmte Alexander der Grosse', *Jahrbuch für Numismatik und Geldgeschichte* 15 (1965), pp. 7–32

KREMPEL 2000
L. Krempel, *Studien zu den datierten Gemälden des Nicolaes Maes (1634–1693)*, Petersberg 2000

KRUSE 1909
J. Kruse, 'Eine neuentdeckte Homerus-Zeichnung von Rembrandt im Nationalmuseum zu Stockholm', *Oud Holland* 27 (1909), pp. 221–8

KURETSKY 1974
S.D. Kuretsky, 'Rembrandt's Tree Stump: An Iconographic Attribute of St Jerome', *The Art Bulletin* 56 (1974), pp. 571–80

L./LUGT
F. Lugt, *Les Marques de Collections de dessins et d'estampes*, Amsterdam 1921; Supplement, The Hague 1956 (http://www.marquesde-collections.fr/)

LABOUVIE-VIEF 1997
G. Labouvie-Vief, 'Psychological Transformations and Late-Life Creativity', *Rembrandt and Late-Life Creativity* 11 [1994–6], 1997, pp. 71–83

LAIRESSE 1707 (1740)
G. de Lairesse, *Groot Schilderboek*, 2 vols in one, 1st edn 1707, 2nd edn Haarlem 1740 (repr. Soest 1969)

LAIRESSE 1707
G. de Lairesse, *Groot Schilderboek, Waar in de Schilderkonst in al Haar Deelen Grondig werd onderweezen, ook door Redeneeringen en Printverbeeldingen verklaard*, Amsterdam 1707

LANDAU AND PARSHALL 1994
D. Landau and P. Parshall, *The Renaissance Print*, New Haven 1994

LAURENTIUS 1597 (1599)
A. Laurentius, *A Discourse of the Preservation of the Sight; of Melancholic Diseases; of Rheumes, and of Old Age*, trans. R. Surphlet, London 1599

LAURENTIUS 2010
F. Laurentius, *Clement de Jonghe (ca. 1624–1677). Kunstkoper in de Gouden Eeuw*, Houten 2010

LAWRENCE, NEW HAVEN AND AUSTIN 1983
L.A. Stone-Ferrier, *Dutch Prints of Daily Life: Mirrors of Life or Masks of Morals*, exh. cat., Spencer Museum of Art, University of Kansas, Lawrence; Yale University Art Gallery, New Haven; and Huntington Gallery, University of Texas, Austin 1983

LEJA 1996
J. Leja, 'Rembrandt's *Woman Bathing in a Stream*', *Simiolus* 24 (1996), pp. 321–7

LEVI 1964
A. Levi, SJ, *French Moralists: The Theory of the Passions 1585–1649*, Oxford 1964

LIEDTKE 1998
W. Liedtke, 'Review of A. Blankert et al., *Rembrandt: A Genius and his Impact*, National Gallery of Victoria, Melbourne, and National Gallery of Australia, Canberra, 1997–8', *Simiolus* 26 (1998), pp. 312–17

LIEDTKE 2004a
W. Liedtke, 'Rembrandt's "Workshop" revisited', *Oud Holland* 117 (2004), pp. 48–73

LIEDTKE 2004b
W. Liedtke, 'The Meaning of Rembrandt's Aristotle with a Bust of Homer', in V. Manuth and A. Rüger (eds), *Collected Opinions: Essays on Netherlandish Art in Honour of Alfred Bader*, London 2004, pp. 72–87

LIEDTKE 2007
W. Liedtke, *Dutch Paintings in The Metropolitan Museum of Art*, 2 vols, New Haven and London 2007

LIEDTKE 2011
W. Liedtke, 'Rembrandt at Work: Some Late Self-Portraits', *Kroniek van het Rembrandthuis* (2011), pp. 20–7

VAN DER LINDEN 1979
F. van der Linden, *De grafische technieken*, De Bilt 1979

LIPSIUS 1584 (1948)
J. Lipsius, *Twee Boecken van de Stantvasticheyt* (*Two books of constancy*), trans. J. Mourentorf (1584), Antwerp 1948

LOGAN 1983
A.-M.S. Logan (ed.), *Essays in Northern European Art presented to Egbert Haverkamp-Begemann on his Sixtieth Birthday*, Doornspijk 1983

LONDON 1938
Seventeenth-Century Art in Europe, exh. cat., Royal Academy of Arts, London 1938

LONDON 1988/2006
D. Bomford et al., *Art in the Making: Rembrandt*, exh. cat., The National Gallery, London 1988 (rev. edn 2006)

LONDON 1992
M. Royalton-Kisch, *Drawings by Rembrandt and his Circle in the British Museum*, exh. cat., The British Museum, London 1992

LONDON 1995
A. Laing, *In Trust for the Nation: Paintings in National Trust Houses*, exh. cat., The National Gallery, London 1995

LONDON AND AMSTERDAM 2006
F. Lammertse and J. van der Veen, *Uylenburgh & zoon: kunst en commercie van Rembrandt tot De Lairesse, 1625–1675*, exh. cat., Dulwich Picture Gallery, London, and Museum Het Rembrandthuis, Amsterdam, Zwolle 2006

LONDON AND THE HAGUE 1999
C. White and Q. Buvelot (eds), *Rembrandt by Himself*, exh. cat., The National Gallery, London and Royal Cabinet of Paintings Mauritshuis, The Hague 1999

LONDON AND THE HAGUE 2007
R.E.O. Ekkart and Q. Buvelot, *Dutch Portraits: The Age of Rembrandt and Frans Hals*, trans. B. Jackson, exh. cat., The National Gallery, London, and Royal Picture Gallery, Mauritshuis, The Hague, London 2007

LOS ANGELES 2009
H. Bevers et al., *Drawings by Rembrandt and His Pupils: Telling the Difference*, exh. cat., J. Paul Getty Museum, Los Angeles 2009

LUGT 1915
F. Lugt, *Wandelingen met Rembrandt in en om Amsterdam*, 2nd edn Amsterdam 1915

LUIJTEN 1998
[G. Luijten], 'Keuze uit de aanwinsten', *Bulletin van het Rijksmuseum* 46 (1998), pp. 321–2

LUTTERVELT ET AL. 1956
R. Luttervelt et al., *Konsthistorisk Tidskrift* (special issue devoted to *The Conspiracy of the Batavians under Claudius Civilis*) 25 (1956)

LÜTZELER 1934
H. Lützeler, *Grundstile der Kunst*, Berlin and Bonn 1934

LYNA 2012
D. Lyna, 'In Search of a British Connection: Flemish Dealers in the London Art Market and the Taste for Continental Painting (1750–1800)', in *Marketing Art in the British Isles, 1700 to the Present*, eds C. Gould and S. Mesplède, Farnham 2012, pp. 101–18

MACLAREN 1960
N. MacLaren, *National Gallery Catalogues: The Dutch School*, London 1960

MACLAREN AND BROWN 1991
N. MacLaren, *National Gallery Catalogues: The Dutch School 1600–1900*, rev. C. Brown, 2 vols, London 1991

MAGNANI 2007
L. Magnani, '1666. Een onbekende opdracht uit Genua voor Rembrandt', *Kroniek van het Rembrandthuis* (2007), pp. 3–17

MAISAK 2008
P. Maisak, 'Von Rembrandts sogenanntem Doctor Faustus zu Goethes *Faust*', *Jahrbuch des Freien Deutschen Hochstifts* 2008, pp. 109–52

VAN MANDER 1604
K. van Mander, *Het Schilder-Boeck waer in Voor eerst de leerlustighe Iueght den grondt der Edel Vry Schilderconsten in verscheyden deelen Wort Voorghedragen*, Haarlem 1604

MARTIN 1967
G. Martin, 'A Rembrandt Self Portrait from his last year', *The Burlington Magazine* 109 (1967), pp. 354–5

MEIJER 2000
B.W. Meijer, 'Italian Paintings in seventeenth-century Holland: Art Market, Art Works and Art Collections', in *L'Europa e l'arte italiana*, ed. M. Seidel, Venice 2000, pp. 377–417

MEISCHKE AND REESER 1983
R. Meischke and H.E. Reeser (eds), *Het Trippenhuis te Amsterdam*, Amsterdam 1983

MELBOURNE AND CANBERRA 1997
A. Blankert et al., *Rembrandt: A Genius and his Impact*, exh. cat., National Gallery of Victoria, Melbourne and National Gallery of Australia, Canberra 1997

MIDDELKOOP 1994
N. Middelkoop, *De anatomische les van Dr. Deyman*, eds M. Jonker and H. Wiggers, Amsterdam 1994

MIDDELKOOP, REICHWEIN AND VAN GENT 2008
N. Middelkoop, G. Reichwein and J. van Gent, *De oude meesters van de stad Amsterdam: schilderijen tot 1800*, Bussum and Amsterdam 2008

MIDDLETON-WAKE 1878
C.H. Middleton-Wake, *A descriptive catalogue of the etched work of Rembrandt van Rhyn*, London 1878

MIEDEMA 1973
H. Miedema, *Karel van Mander: Den grondt der edel vry schilder-const*, 3 vols, Utrecht 1973

MÖLLER 1984
G.J. Möller, 'Het album Pandora van Jan Six (1618–1700)', *Jaarboek van het Genootschap Amstelodamum* 76 (1984), pp. 69–101

MONTAGU 1994
J. Montagu, *The Expression of the Passions: The Origin and Influence of Charles Le Brun's 'Conférence sur l'expression générale et particulière'*, New Haven 1994

MORSE 1966
P. Morse, 'Rembrandt's Etching Technique: An Example', *Smithsonian Institution, United States National Museum Bulletin* 250 (1966), pp. 95–107

DU MOULIN DE JONGE 1688
P. du Moulin de Jonge, *Verhandelinge van den Vrede der Ziele…*, trans. H. Dullaert, Amsterdam 1688

MÜLLER-HOFSTEDE 1952
C. Müller Hofstede, *Rembrandts Familienbild und seine Restaurierung* (Kunsthefte des Herzog Anton Ulrich-Museums, 7), Braunschweig 1952

MÜLLER-SCHIRMER 2008
A. Müller-Schirmer, 'Grenzen im Licht: Über Licht und Schatten in den Zeichnungen von Rembrandt', *Oud Holland* 121 (2008), pp. 56–80

MUNICH AND AMSTERDAM 2001
T. Vignau-Wilberg, with contribution from P. Schatborn, *Rembrandt auf Papier: Werk und Wirkung (Rembrandt and his Followers: Drawings from Munich)*, exh. cat., Staatliche Graphische Sammlung München, Alte Pinakothek, Munich and Museum Het Rembrandthuis, Amsterdam, Munich 2001

MUNSTERBERG 1983
H. Munsterberg, *The Crown of Life: Artistic Creativity in Old Age*, New York 1983

MÜNZ 1948
L. Münz, 'A newly discovered late Rembrandt', *The Burlington Magazine* 90 (1948), pp. 64–7

MUSPER 1935
T. Musper, 'Die Datierung des späten Zustandes der *Drei Kreuze* von Rembrandt', *Kunst- und Antiquitäten-Rundschau* 6 (1935), p. 137

NATTER 2006
B. Natter, '"Het Joodse bruidje". De vroegst bekende duiding opnieuw bekeken', *Bulletin van het Rijksmuseum* 54 (2006), pp. 163–81

NÉMETH 1996
I. Németh, 'De portretten van Jacob Trip en Margaretha de Geer door Nicolaes Maes in Boedapest', *Oud Holland* 110 (1996), pp. 79–84

NEUMANN 1902
C. Neumann, *Rembrandt*, Berlin and Stuttgart 1902

NEW HAVEN 1983
C. White, D. Alexander and E.G. D'Oench, *Rembrandt in Eighteenth-Century England*, exh. cat., Yale Center for British Art, New Haven 1983

NEW YORK 1995
H. von Sonnenburg et al., *Rembrandt/ Not Rembrandt in The Metropolitan Museum of Art: Aspects of Connoisseurship*, 2 vols, exh. cat., The Metropolitan Museum of Art, New York, 1995

NEW YORK, FORT WORTH AND CLEVELAND 1990
G. Luijten and A.W.F.M. Meij (eds), *From Pisanello to Cézanne: Master Drawings from the Museum Boymans-van Beuningen Rotterdam*, exh. cat., The Pierpont Morgan Library, New York, Kimbell Art Museum, Fort Worth and The Cleveland Museum of Art, Rotterdam 1990

NHD (LUCAS VAN LEYDEN)
J.P. Filedt Kok, with the assistance of B. Cornelis and A. Smits, *Lucas van Leyden (The New Hollstein: Dutch & Flemish etchings, engravings, and woodcuts, 1450–1700*, vol. 3), ed. G. Luijten, Rotterdam 1996

NHD (THE MULLER DYNASTY)
J.P. Filedt Kok, H. Stroomberg and E. Hinterding, *Lucas van Leyden (The New Hollstein: Dutch & Flemish etchings, engravings, and woodcuts, 1450–1700*, vol. 7), ed. G. Luijten and C. Schuckman, 3 vols, Rotterdam 1999

NHD (REMBRANDT)
E. Hinterding and J. Rutgers, *Rembrandt (The New Hollstein: Dutch & Flemish etchings, engravings, and woodcuts, 1450–1700*, vols 18–19), ed. G. Luijten, 7 vols, Ouderkerk aan den IJssel 2013

NOBLE 2009
P. Noble et al., *Preserving our Heritage: Conservation, Restoration and Technical Research in the Mauritshuis*, The Hague and Zwolle 2009

NORDENFALK 1982
C.A.J. Nordenfalk, *The Batavians' Oath of Allegiance: Rembrandt's only monumental Painting*, Stockholm 1982

NORMAN 1988
J.S. Norman, *Metamorphoses of an Allegory: The Iconography of the Psychomachia in Medieval Art*, New York 1988

O'REILLY 1988
J. O'Reilly, *Studies in the Iconography of the Virtues and Vices in the Middle Ages*, New York and London 1988

PARIS 2006
S. Renouard de Bussière, *Rembrandt, eaux-fortes*, exh. cat., Petit Palais, Musée des Beaux-Arts de la Ville de Paris, 2006

PARIS 2007
L. Sigal-Klagsbald et al., *Rembrandt et la nouvelle Jérusalem: juifs et chrétiens à Amsterdam au siècle d'or*, exh. cat., Musée d'art et d'histoire du Judaïsme, Paris 2007

PARIS, PHILADELPHIA AND DETROIT 2011
L. DeWitt et al., *Rembrandt et la figure du Christ / Rembrandt and the Face of Jesus*, exh. cat., Musée du Louvre, Paris; Philadelphia Museum of Art, Philadelphia; and Detroit Institute of Arts, Detroit 2011

PARSHALL 1978
P. Parshall, 'Lucas van Leyden's narrative style', *Nederlands Kunsthistorisch Jaarboek* 29 (1978), pp. 185–237

PELS 1681
A. Pels, *Gebruik en misbruik des tooneels*, Amsterdam 1681

PERLOVE AND SILVER 2009
S.K. Perlove and L. Silver, *Rembrandt's Faith: Church and Temple in the Dutch Golden Age*, Pennsylvania 2009

DE PILES 1684
R. de Piles, *Les premiers éléments de la Peinture pratique: enrichis de figures de proportion mesurées sur l'antique*, Paris 1684

DE PILES 1699
R. de Piles, *Abregé de la Vie des Peintres, Avec des réflexions sur leurs Ouvrages*, Paris 1699

DE PILES 1699 (1706)
R. de Piles, *The Art of Painting and the Lives of the Painters*, London 1706

DE PILES 1708
R. de Piles, *Cours de peinture par principes*, Paris 1708

DE PILES 1708 (1743)
R. de Piles, *The Principles of Painting*, London 1743

PINDER 1926
W. Pinder, *Das Problem der Generation in der Kunstgeschichte Europas*, Berlin 1926

PINDER 1943
W. Pinder, *Rembrandts Selbstbildnisse*, Leipzig 1943

PLINY (1952)
Pliny, *Natural History, Books XXXIII–XXXV* (Loeb Classical Library), trans. H. Rackham, Cambridge MA and London 1952

PLOMP 1997
M.C. Plomp, *The Dutch Drawings in the Teyler Museum*, vol. 2: *Artists Born between 1575 and 1639*, Haarlem 1997

PORTEMAN 1986
K. Porteman, 'Vondels gedicht "op een italiaensche schildery van Susanne"', in *'t ondersoeck leert. Studies over middeleeuwse en 17de eeuwse literatuur ter nagedachtenis van Prof. Dr L. Rens*, eds G. van Eemeren and F. Willaert, Leuven and Amersfoort 1986, pp. 301–18

POSTMA 1988
H.J. Postma, 'De Amsterdamse verzamelaar Herman Becker (*c.* 1617–1678); nieuwe gegevens over een geldschieter van Rembrandt', *Oud Holland* 102 (1988), pp. 1–21.

POUSÃO-SMITH 2003
M.-I. Pousão-Smith, '*Sprezzatura, Nettigheid* and the Fallacy of "Invisible Brushwork" in Seventeenth-Century Dutch Painting', in *Virtus: virtuositeit en kunstliefhebbers in de Nederlanden 1500–1700* / Virtue*: virtuoso, virtuosity in Netherlandish art 1500–1700*, ed. J. de Jong (*Nederlands Kunsthistorisch Jaarboek* 54), Zwolle 2003, pp. 259–79

RALEIGH, CLEVELAND AND MINNEAPOLIS 2011
G.S. Keyes, T. Rassieur and D.P. Weller, *Rembrandt in America: Collecting and Connoisseurship*, exh. cat., North Carolina Museum of Art, Raleigh; The Cleveland Museum of Art; and Minneapolis Institute of Arts, New York 2011

RAUPP 1984
H.-J. Raupp, *Untersuchungen zu Künstlerbildnis und Künstlerdarstellung in den Niederlanden im 17. Jahrhundert*, Hildesheim and New York 1984

RAUPP 1993
H.-J. Raupp, 'Der alte Künstler und das Alterswerk', in *Bilder vom alten Menschen in der niederländischen und deutschen Kunst 1550–1750*, eds U. Berger and J. Desel, Herzog Anton Ulrich-Museum, Braunschweig 1993, pp. 87–97

RÉAU 1955–9
L. Réau, *Iconographie de l'art Chrétien*, 6 vols, Paris 1955–9

VAN REGTEREN ALTENA 1950
J.Q. van Regteren Altena, 'Retouches aan ons Rembrandt-beeld, 1. De zoogenaamde voorstudie voor de Anatomische les van Dr Deyman', *Oud Holland* 65 (1950), pp. 171–8

VAN REGTEREN ALTENA 1961
J.Q. van Regteren Altena, 'De tekeningen (uit de schenking De Bruijn)', *Bulletin van het Rijksmuseum* 9 (1961), pp. 68–89

REYNOLDS (1824)
J. Reynolds, 'A Journey to Flanders and Holland', in *The Complete Works of Sir Joshua Reynolds*, vol. 2, London 1824

REYNOLDS (1975)
J. Reynolds, *Discourses on Art, 1769–1799*, New Haven and London 1975

RIEGL (1931) 1999
A. Riegl, *The group portraiture of Holland*, intro. by W. Kemp, trans. E.M. Kain and D. Britt, Los Angeles 1999

RIPA (1593) 1709
C. Ripa, *Iconologia or Moral Emblems*, trans. P. Tempest, London 1709

RIPA 1644
C. Ripa, *Iconologia, of uytbeeldinghe des verstands*, Amsterdam 1644

DE ROBELIN 2012
R. de Robelin, 'On the Provenance of Rembrandt's *The Conspiracy of the Batavians under Claudius Civilis*', *Art Bulletin of Nationalmuseum Stockholm* 19 (2012), pp. 121–6

ROETHLISBERGER AND BOK 1993
M.G. Roethlisberger and M.J. Bok, *Abraham Bloemaert and his Sons: Paintings and Prints*, Doornspijk 1993

ROODENBURG 1990
H. Roodenburg, *Onder censuur: de kerkelijke tucht in de gereformeerde gemeente van Amsterdam, 1578–1700*, Hilversum 1990

ROSAND 1987
D. Rosand, 'Editor's Statement: Style and the Ageing Artist', *Art Journal* 46 (1987), pp. 91–3

ROSCAM ABBING 1993
M. Roscam Abbing, *De schilder en schrijver Samuel van Hoogstraten 1627–1678: eigentijdse bronnen en oeuvre van gesigneerde schilderijen*, Leiden 1993

ROSCAM ABBING 2006
M. Roscam Abbing (ed.), *Rembrandt*, 2 vols, Leiden 2006

ROSENBERG 1909
A. Rosenberg, *Rembrandt: des Meisters Gemälde*, Stuttgart and Berlin 1909

ROTERMUND 1963
H.-M. Rotermund, *Rembrandts Handzeichnungen und Radierungen zur Bibel*, Lahr/Schwarzwald and Stuttgart 1963

ROTTERDAM 1990
G. Luijten and A.W.F.M. Meij, *From Pisanello to Cézanne: Master Drawings from the Museum Boymans Van Beuningen, Rotterdam*, exh. cat., Museum Boymans Van Beuningen, Rotterdam 1990

ROTTERDAM 2006
P. van der Coelen, *Rembrandts passie: het Nieuwe Testament in de Nederlandse prentkunst van de zestiende en zeventiende eeuw*, Museum Boijmans Van Beuningen, Rotterdam 2006

ROYALTON-KISCH 1989
M. Royalton-Kisch, 'Rembrandt's Sketches for his Paintings', *Master Drawings* 27 (1989), pp. 128–45

ROYALTON-KISCH 1992
M. Royalton-Kisch, *Drawings by Rembrandt and his Circle in the British Museum*, London 1992

ROYALTON-KISCH 2010
M. Royalton-Kisch, *Catalogue of the Drawings by Rembrandt and his School in the British Museum*, London 2010

ROYALTON-KISCH AND SCHATBORN 2011
M. Royalton-Kisch and P. Schatborn, 'The Core Group of Rembrandt Drawings, II: The List', *Master Drawings* 49 (2011), pp. 323–36

RUFFO 1916
V. Ruffo, 'Galleria Ruffo nel secolo XVII in Messina (con lettere di pittori ed altri documenti inediti)', *Bolletino d'Arte* 10 (1916), pp. 21–64, 95–128, 165–92, 237–56, 284–320, 369–88

RUTGERS 2008
J. Rutgers, *Rembrandt in Italië: receptie en verzamelgeschiedenis*, dissertation, University of Utrecht 2008

RUTGERS AND RIJNDERS 2014
J. Rutgers and M. Rijnders (eds), *Rembrandt in perspectief: de veranderende visie op de meester en zijn werk*, Zwolle 2014

VON SANDRART 1675
J. von Sandrart, *Teutsche Academie der Edlen Bau- Bild- und Mahlerey-Künste*, Nuremberg 1675

VON SANDRART 1675 (1925)
J. von Sandrart, *L' Academia Todesca della architettura, scultura et pittura, oder Teutsche Academie der edlen Bau-, Bild-, und Mahlerey-Künste* (Nuremberg and Frankfurt am Main 1675), ed. A.R. Peltzer, Munich 1925

SCALLEN 1992
C.B. Scallen, 'Rembrandt's Etching *St Jerome Reading in an Italian Landscape*', *Delineavit et Sculpsit* 8 (1992), pp. 1–11

SCHAEFTER ET AL. 2011
I. Schaefter, K. Pilz, C. von Sint-George, 'Rembrandts "Selbstbildnis als Zeuxis". Neues zum Original, zur Erhaltung und Frage der Restaurierung', *Zeitschrift für Kunsttechnologie und Konservierung* 25, no. 2 (2011), pp. 285–323

SCHAMA 1999
S. Schama, *Rembrandt's Eyes*, New York and London 1999

SCHAPELHOUMAN 2006
M. Schapelhouman, 'Rembrandt als toeschouwer', *Rijksmuseum Kunstkrant* 32 (2006), pp. 10–11

SCHATBORN 1985
P. Schatborn, *Tekeningen van Rembrandt, zijn onbekende leerlingen en navolgers: Catalogus van de Nederlandse tekeningen in het Rijksprentenkabinet / Drawings by Rembrandt, his anonymous pupils and followers: Catalogue of the Dutch Drawings in the Rijksprentenkabinet*, The Hague 1985

SCHATBORN 1987
P. Schatborn, 'Rembrandt's late tekeningen van vrouwelijke naakt-figuren', *Kroniek van het Rembrandthuis* 39 (1987), pp. 28–40

SCHATBORN 2011
P. Schatborn, 'The Core Group of Rembrandt Drawings, I: Overview', *Master Drawings* 49 (2011), pp. 293–322

SCHATBORN AND DUDOK VAN HEEL 2011
P. Schatborn and S.A.C. Dudok van Heel, 'The Core Group of Rembrandt Drawings, III: Supplement', *Master Drawings* 49 (2011), pp. 347–51

SCHELLER 1961
R.W. Scheller, 'Rembrandt's reputatie van Houbraken tot Scheltema', *Nederlands Kunsthistorisch Jaarboek* 12 (1961), pp. 81–118

SCHELLER 1969
R.W. Scheller, 'Rembrandt en de encyclopedische kunstkamer', *Oud Holland* 84 (1969), pp. 81–147

VAN SCHENDEL 1956
A. van Schendel, 'De schimmen van de Staalmeesters: een röntgenologisch onderzoek', *Oud Holland* 71 (1956), pp. 1–23

SCHENKEVELD 1991
M.A. Schenkeveld, *Dutch Literature in the Age of Rembrandt: Themes and Ideas*, Amsterdam and Philadelphia 1991

SCHMIDT-DEGENER 1906
F. Schmidt-Degener, *Rembrandt: een beschrijving van zijn leven en zijn werk*, Amsterdam 1906

SCHMIDT-DEGENER 1915
F. Schmidt-Degener, 'Rembrandt en Homerus', in *Feest-bundel, Dr Abraham Bredius aangeboden den achttienden april 1915*, vol. 1, Amsterdam 1915, pp. 19–22

SCHMIDT-DEGENER 1919
F. Schmidt-Degener, 'Rembrandt en Vondel', *De Gids* 83 (1919), pp. 222–75

SCHNAPPER 1994
A. Schnapper, *Curieux du Grand Siècle; collections et collectionneurs dans la France du XVIIe siècle*, Paris 1994

SCHOLTEN 1904
H.J. Scholten, *Musée Teyler à Haarlem: catalogue raisonné des dessins des écoles française et hollandaise*, Haarlem 1904

SCHREVELIUS 1648
T. Schrevelius, *Harlemias, ofte, om beter te seggen, de eerste stichtinghe der stadt Haerlem*, Haarlem 1648

SCHWARTZ 1984
G. Schwartz, *Rembrandt: zijn leven, zijn schilderijen*, Maarssen 1984

SCHWARTZ 1985
G. Schwartz, *Rembrandt: His Life, His Paintings*, New York 1985

SCHWARTZ 2006
G. Schwartz, *Rembrandt's Universe, His Art, His Life, His World*, London 2006

SCHWARTZ 2007
G. Schwartz, 'Rembrandt Harmensz. van Rijn, "Simeon with the Christ child in his arms, with Mary and Joseph, 1661"', in *In arte venustas: studies on drawings in honour of Teréz Gerszi, presented on her eightieth birthday*, ed. A. Czére, Budapest 2007, pp. 170–2

VON SEIDLITZ 1922
W. von Seidlitz, *Die Radierungen Rembrandts: mit einem kritischen Verzeichnis und Abbildung sämtlicher Radierungen*, Leipzig 1922

SIMMEL 1916
G. Simmel, *Rembrandt: ein kunstphilosophischer Versuch*, Leipzig 1916

SIX 1893
J. Six, 'Iets over Rembrandt', *Oud Holland* 11 (1893), pp. 154–61

SIX 1905
J. Six, 'De ligging van het lijk in Rembrandt's Anatomische les van dr. Deyman', *Oud Holland* 23 (1905), pp. 37–40

SIX 1908
J. Six, 'Rembrandt's voorbereiding van de etsen van Jan Six en Abraham Francen', *Onze Kunst* 14 (1908), pp. 53–64

SIX 1924
J. Six, 'De Pandora van Jan Six', *Haagsch Maandblad* 1, no. 3 (April 1924), pp. 378–92

SLATKES 1983
L. Slatkes, *Rembrandt and Persia*, New York 1983

SLATKES 1992
L. Slatkes, *Rembrandt: Catalogo completo dei dipinti*, Florence 1992

SLIVE 1953
S. Slive, *Rembrandt and His Critics, 1630–1730*, The Hague 1953

SLIVE 2009
S. Slive, *Rembrandt Drawings*, Los Angeles 2009

SLUIJTER 2006
E.J. Sluijter, *Rembrandt and the Female Nude*, Amsterdam 2006

SLUIJTER 2008
E.J. Sluijter, 'Introduction', in A. Tummers and K. Jonckheere (eds), *Art Market and Connoisseurship: A Closer Look at Paintings by Rembrandt, Rubens and their Contemporaries*, Amsterdam 2008, pp. 7–30

SMITH 1676
J. Smith, *The Art of Painting in Oyl*, London 1676

SMITH 1692
M. Smith, *The Art of Painting According to the Theory and Practise of the Best Italian, French, and German Masters*, London 1692

SMITH 1829–42
J.A. Smith, *A Catalogue Raisonné of the Works of the Most Eminent Dutch, Flemish, and French Painters*, 9 vols, London 1829–42; vol. 7 (1836) and supplement vol. 9 (1842)

SMITH 1988
D.R. Smith, '"I Janus": Privacy and the Gentlemanly Ideal in Rembrandt's Portraits of Jan Six', *Art History* 11 (1988), pp. 42–63

SMITH 1995
D.R. Smith, 'Inversion, Revolution and the Carnivalesque in Rembrandt's *Civilis*', *Res: Anthropology and Aesthetics* 27 (1995), pp. 89–110

SMITH AND ENENKEL 2007
P.J. Smith and K.A.E. Enenkel (eds), *Montaigne and the Low Countries (1580–1700)*, Leiden 2007

SMITS-VELDT 1991
M.B. Smits-Veldt, *Het Nederlandse Renaissancetoneel*, Utrecht 1991

SOHM 2007
P. Sohm, *The Artist Grows Old: The Ageing of Art and Artists in Italy 1500–1800*, New Haven and London 2007

SORRELL 1988
R.D. Sorrell, *St Francis of Assisi and Nature: Tradition and Innovation in Western Attitudes toward the Environment*, Oxford 1988

STERLING ET AL. 1998
C. Sterling et al., *The Robert Lehman Collection*, vol. 2: *Fifteenth- to Eighteenth-Century European Paintings*, New York and Princeton 1998

STIJNMAN 2012
A. Stijnman, *Engraving and Etching 1400–2000: A history of the development of manual intaglio printmaking processes*, London and Houten 2012

STOCKHOLM 1992
G. Cavalli-Björkman et al., *Rembrandt och hans tid: människan i centrum / Rembrandt and His Age: Focus on Man*, exh. cat., Nationalmuseum, Stockholm, 1992

STOGDON 2011
N. Stogdon, *A Descriptive Catalogue of the Etchings of Rembrandt in a Private Collection, Switzerland*, n.p. 2011

STRATTON 1986
S. Stratton, 'Rembrandt's Beggars: Satire and Sympathy', *Print Collector's Newsletter* 17 (1986), pp. 78–82

STRAUSS AND VAN DER MEULEN 1979
W.L. Strauss and M. van der Meulen (eds), *The Rembrandt Documents*, New York 1979

VAN STRIEN 1993
C.D. van Strien, *British Travellers in Holland during the Stuart Period: Edward Browne and John Locke as Tourists in the United Provinces*, Leiden 1993

SUMOWSKI 1959
W. Sumowski, 'Review of D. Pont, *Barent Fabritius 1624–1673*, Utrecht 1958', *Kunstchronik* 12 (1959), pp. 287–94

TACITUS
C. Tacitus, uit het Latijn vertaald door V.J.C Hunink, *Historiën*, Amsterdam 2010

TAYLOR 1989
C. Taylor, *Sources of the Self: The Making of the Modern Identity*, Cambridge 1989

TAYLOR 1992
P. Taylor, 'The Concept of *houding* in Dutch Art Theory', *Journal of the Warburg and Courtauld Institutes* 55 (1992), pp. 210–32

VAN THIEL 1969
P.J.J. van Thiel, '*Zelfportret als de apostel Paulus*: Rembrandt van Rijn (1606–1669)', *Openbaar Kunstbezit* 13 (1969), pp. 1a–b

THIJS 1993
A.K.L. Thijs, *Antwerpen, internationaal uitgeverscentrum van devotieprenten 17de–18de eeuw*, Leuven 1993

THOMASSEN 1990
K. Thomassen (ed.), *'Alba Amicorum': Vijf eeuwen vriendschap op papier gezet; Het 'album amicorum' en het poëziealbum in de Nederlanden*, Maarssen 1990

THOMASSEN AND GRUYS 1998
K. Thomassen and J.A. Gruys (eds), *The Album Amicorum of Jacob Heyblocq; with Introduction, Transcriptions, Paraphrases & Notes to the Facsimile*, trans. P. Thomson, Zwolle 1998

THOMPSON 2012
A. Thompson, *Francis of Assisi: A New Biography*, Ithaca 2012

TIB (Dürer)
W.L. Strauss (ed.), *The Illustrated Bartsch*, vol. 10: *Sixteenth-Century German Artists, Albrecht Dürer*, New York 1981

TIETZE 1944
H. Tietze, 'Earliest and Latest Works of Great Artists', *Gazette des Beaux-Arts* 26 (1944), pp. 273–84

VAN TOL 1983
D. van Tol, 'Een portret van dr. Arnout Tholinx (1607–1679)', *Jaarboek van het Centraal Bureau voor Genealogie en het Ikonografisch Bureau* 37 (1983), pp. 139–50

TÜMPEL 1969
C. Tümpel, 'Studien zur Ikonographie der Historien Rembrandt's. Deutung und Interpretation der Bildinhalte', *Nederlands Kunsthistorisch Jaarboek* 20 (1969), pp. 107–98

TÜMPEL 1971
C. Tümpel, 'Ikonographische Beiträge zu Rembrandt, II', *Jahrbuch der Hamburger Kunstsammlungen* 16 (1971), pp. 20–38

TÜMPEL 1986
C. Tümpel and A. Tümpel, *Rembrandt*, Antwerp 1986

VALENTINER 1905
W.R. Valentiner, *Rembrandt und seine Umgebung*, Strasbourg 1905

VALENTINER 1920–1
W.R. Valentiner, 'Die vier Evangelisten Rembrandt', *Kunstchronik und Kunstmarkt* 56 (1920–1), pp. 219–22

VALENTINER 1923–4
W.R. Valentiner, 'Deutung der "Judenbraut"', *Kunst und Künstler* 22 (1923–4), pp. 17–22

VALENTINER 1925–34
W.R. Valentiner, *Rembrandt: Des Meisters Handzeichnungen*, 2 vols, Stuttgart, Berlin and Leipzig 1925–34

VALENTINER 1956
W.R. Valentiner, 'The Rembrandt Exhibitions in Holland', *The Art Quarterly* 19 (1956), pp. 390–404

VASARI 1568 (1979)
G. Vasari, *Lives of the Most Eminent Painters, Sculptors and Architects* (1568), trans. G. du C. de Vere, 3 vols, New York 1979

VERTUE (1934)
'George Vertue's Note-books, III', *The Walpole Society* 22 (1934)

VIENNA 2004
K.A. Schröder and M. Bisanz-Prakken (eds), *Rembrandt*, exh. cat., Graphische Sammlung Albertina, Vienna, Wolfratshausen 2004

VIS 1965
D. Vis, *Rembrandt en Geertje Dircx*, Haarlem 1965

VITTET 2004
J. Vittet, 'Découvertes sur la provenance de plusieurs tableaux célèbres des collections de Louis XIV', *La revue des musées de France* 54 (2004), no. 2, pp. 55–61

VOET 1969–72
L. Voet, *The Golden Compasses: A history and evaluation of the printing and publishing activities of the Officina Plantiniana at Antwerp*, 2 vols, Amsterdam and New York 1969–72

VONDEL (1927–40)
J.F.M. Sterck et al. (eds), *De Werken von Vondel. Volledige en geïllustreerde tekstuitgave*, 10 vols, Amsterdam 1927–40

VOS 1662–71
J. Vos, *Alle de gedichten van den poëet Jan Vos*, 2 vols, Amsterdam 1662–71

DE VRIES 1989
L. de Vries, '*Tronies* and other Single Figured Netherlandish Paintings', *Leids Kunsthistorisch Jaarboek* 8 (1989), pp. 185–202

DE VRIES, TÓTH-UBBENS AND FROENTJES 1978
A.B. de Vries, M. Tóth-Ubbens and W. Froentjes, *Rembrandt in the Mauritshuis*, Alphen aan de Rijn 1978

WAAGEN 1854
G. Waagen, *Treasures of Art in Great Britain: Being an Account of the Chief Collections of Paintings, Drawings, Sculptures, Illuminated MSS*, 3 vols, London 1854

VAN DE WAAL 1952
H. van de Waal, *Drie eeuwen vaderlandsche geschied-uitbeelding 1500–1800: een iconologische studie*, 2 vols, The Hague 1952

VAN DE WAAL 1956
H. van de Waal, 'De Staalmeesters en hun legende', *Oud Holland* 71 (1956), pp. 61–107

VAN DE WAAL 1974
H. van de Waal, *Steps towards Rembrandt: Collected articles 1937–1972*, ed. R.H. Fuchs, trans. P. Wardle and A. Griffiths, Amsterdam 1974

WALKER 1980
J. Walker, *The Armand Hammer Collection: Five Centuries of Masterpieces*, New York 1980

WALTZ 1900
A. Waltz, *Bericht über ein Rembrandt zugeschriebenes Gemälde im Colmarer Museum*, Colmar 1900

WASHINGTON 1977
A. Robison, *Paper in Prints*, exh. cat., National Gallery of Art, Washington 1977

WASHINGTON 1985
G. Jackson-Stops (ed.), *The Treasure Houses of Britain: Five Hundred Years of Private Patronage and Art Collecting*, exh. cat., National Gallery of Art, Washington, New Haven and London 1985

WASHINGTON 1990
C.P. Schneider et al., *Rembrandt's Landscapes: Drawings and Prints*, exh. cat., National Gallery of Art, Washington 1990

WASHINGTON, DETROIT AND AMSTERDAM 1980
A. Blankert et al., *Gods, Saints and Heroes: Dutch Painting in the Age of Rembrandt*, exh. cat. National Gallery of Art, Washington, Detroit Institute of Arts and Rijksmuseum, Amsterdam, 1980

WASHINGTON, LONDON AND HAARLEM 1989
S. Slive et. al., *Frans Hals*, exh. cat., National Gallery of Art, Washington, Royal Academy of Arts, London and Frans Halsmuseum, Haarlem 1989

WASHINGTON AND LOS ANGELES 2005
A.K. Wheelock, Jr, et al., *Rembrandt's Late Religious Portraits*, exh. cat., National Gallery of Art, Washington and The J. Paul Getty Museum, Los Angeles 2005

WASHINGTON, MILWAUKEE AND AMSTERDAM 2008
A.K. Wheelock, Jr, et al., *Jan Lievens: A Dutch Master Rediscovered*, exh. cat., National Gallery of Art, Washington, Milwaukee Art Museum, Milwaukee and Museum Het Rembrandthuis, Amsterdam, 2008

WEBER 1991
G.J.M. Weber, *Der Lobtopos des 'lebenden' Bildes: Jan Vos und sein 'Zeege der Schilderkunst' von 1654*, Hildesheim and New York 1991

WEBER 2007
G.J.M. Weber, 'Sprechende Ähnlichkeit mit geschlossenem Mund. Die Formeln eines Bildgedichts von Jan Vos', *Im Blickpunkt* 3 (August 2007), pp. 10–13

WEGNER 1973
W. Wegner, *Kataloge der Staatlichen Graphischen Sammlung München*, vol. 1: *Die Niederländischen Handzeichnungen des 15.–18. Jahrhunderts*, Berlin 1973

WESENDONCK 1888
O. Wesendonck, *Gemälde-Sammlung von Otto Wesendonck in Berlin*, Katalog A, Berlin 1888

WESTSTEIJN 2008
T. Weststeijn, *The Visible World: Samuel van Hoogstraten's Art Theory and the Legitimation of Painting in the Dutch Golden Age*, trans. B. Jackson and L. Richards, Amsterdam 2008

VAN DE WETERING 1997/2009
E. van de Wetering, *Rembrandt: The Painter at Work*, Amsterdam 1997 (2nd edn 2009)

VAN DE WETERING 2002
E. van de Wetering, 'The various functions of Rembrandt's self-portraits', *Kroniek van het Rembrandthuis* (2002), pp. 27–42

WETHEY 1969–75
H.E. Wethey, *The Paintings of Titian: Complete Edition*, 3 vols, London 1969–75

WHEELOCK 1995
A.K. Wheelock, Jr, *Dutch Paintings of the Seventeenth Century: The Collections of the National Gallery of Art Systematic Catalogue*, Washington 1995

WHEELOCK 2014
A.K. Wheelock, Jr, *Dutch Paintings of the Seventeenth Century*, NGA Online Editions, http://purl.org/nga/collection/catalogue/17th-century-dutch-paintings

WHITE 1999
C. White, *Rembrandt as an Etcher: A Study of the Artist at Work* (1969), 2nd edn, New Haven and London 1999

WHITE AND BOON 1969
C. White and K.G. Boon, *Rembrandt's Etchings: An Illustrated Critical Catalogue*, 2 vols, Amsterdam, London and New York 1969

WIESEMAN 2010
M.E. Wieseman, 'Rembrandt's Portrait(s?) of Frederik Rihel', *National Gallery Technical Bulletin* 31 (2010), pp. 96–111

WIJNMAN 1959
H.F. Wijnman, 'Rembrandt's portret van Catrina Hoogsaet', in *Uit de Kring van Rembrandt en Vondel: verzamelde studies over hun leven en omgeving*, Amsterdam 1959, pp. 19–38

WIJNMAN 1968
H.F. Wijnman, 'Een episode uit het leven van Rembrandt: de geschiedenis van Geertje Dircks', *Jaarboek Amstelodamum* 60 (1968), pp. 103–18

WILSON 1836
T. Wilson, *A Descriptive Catalogue of the Prints of Rembrandt*, London 1836

DE WINKEL 2006
M. de Winkel, *Fashion and Fancy: Dress and Meaning in Rembrandt's Paintings*, Amsterdam and Chicago 2006

WITTKOWER 1969
R. and M. Wittkower, *Born Under Saturn: The Character and Conduct of Artists: A Documented History from Antiquity to the French Revolution* (1963), rev. edn New York and London 1969

WUESTMAN 1995
G. Wuestman, 'The mezzotint in Holland: "easily learned, neat and convenient"', *Simiolus* 23 (1995), pp. 63–89

ZELL 2002
M. Zell, *Reframing Rembrandt: Jews and the Christian image in seventeenth-century Amsterdam*, Berkeley 2002

ZIEGLER 2003
H. Ziegler, 'Wilhelm von Bode et le musée de Colmar', in S. Lecoq-Ramond, *Histoire du musée d'Unterlinden et de ses collections: De la Révolution à la Première Guerre mondiale*, Colmar 2003, pp. 303–6

CHRONOLOGY

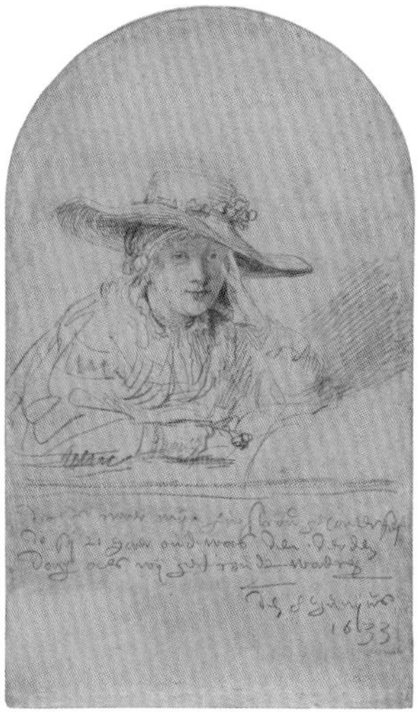

FIG. 94
Portrait of Saskia in a Straw Hat, 1633
Silverpoint on vellum, 18.5 × 10.7 cm
Staatliche Museen zu Berlin, Kupferstichkabinett

1606
Rembrandt Harmensz van Rijn is born in Leiden on 15 July, the ninth child of the miller Harmen Gerritsz van Rijn and his wife, Neeltgen (Cornelia) Willemsdr van Zuytbrouck.

1613–20
Attends the Latin School in Leiden.

About 1620–4/5
Enrols at the University of Leiden in 1620 but never actually studies there. Later that year begins a three-year apprenticeship with the Leiden painter Jacob van Swanenburgh (1571–1638). Also studies with Pieter Lastman (1583–1633) in Amsterdam during this period.

1625–6
By 1625 is working as an independent master in Leiden and makes his earliest-known dated painting, *The Stoning of Saint Stephen* (Musée des Beaux-Arts, Lyon). Begins to make etchings in about 1626.

1628
The Utrecht lawyer Arnold van Buchel (1565–1641) visits Leiden and notes in his diary that 'a miller's son' (Rembrandt) is causing a sensation there as an artist.

Publishes his first etchings and rapidly develops into a gifted graphic artist.

Gerrit Dou (1613–1675) becomes Rembrandt's first pupil.

1629
Makes his earliest dated etched and painted (Alte Pinakothek, Munich) self portraits.

Around 1629 Constantijn Huygens (1596–1687), secretary to Stadtholder Frederik Hendrik, visits Rembrandt and Jan Lievens (1607–1674).

Isaac de Jouderville (1613–1648) becomes Rembrandt's apprentice in 1629/30.

Works include *Judas returning the Thirty Pieces of Silver* (fig. 78), described by Huygens.

1630
Rembrandt's father dies.

1631
Probably towards the end of the year, leaves Leiden for Amsterdam, where he lodges with the art dealer Hendrick Uylenburgh. From 1631–4 is active in Uylenburgh's workshop, painting primarily portraits. Works include *Old Woman reading* (fig. 66), *Portrait of Nicolaes Ruts* (The Frick Collection, New York) and *Seated Female Nude* (etching) (fig. 95).

1632
Completes his first group portrait, *The Anatomy Lesson of Dr Nicolaes Tulp* (fig. 96), for the Amsterdam Guild of Surgeons.

1633
A painted self portrait (Musée du Louvre, Paris) is his first work to bear the signature 'Rembrandt f[ecit]'. From 1633 he signs almost exclusively with his Christian name, undoubtedly in imitation of great Italian painters like Leonardo, Michelangelo, Raphael and Titian.

On 8 June makes a silverpoint drawing on vellum of his fiancée Saskia Uylenburgh (1612–1642) (fig. 94), a burgomaster's daughter from Leeuwarden and cousin of his employer, Hendrick Uylenburgh.

Two paintings by Rembrandt are recorded in the collection of Charles I of England.

1634
Becomes a citizen of Amsterdam and a member of the city's Saint Luke's Guild (guild of painters).

Marries Saskia Uylenburgh.

Works include *A Scholar seated at a Table with Books* (fig. 70) and *Joseph and Potiphar's Wife* (etching) (fig. 80).

1635
Rents a house in Nieuwe Doelenstraat.

A son Rumbartus, named after Saskia's father, is baptised on 15 December but lives only two months.

Works include *Abraham's Sacrifice* (State Hermitage Museum, St Petersburg) and *Belshazzar's Feast* (The National Gallery, London).

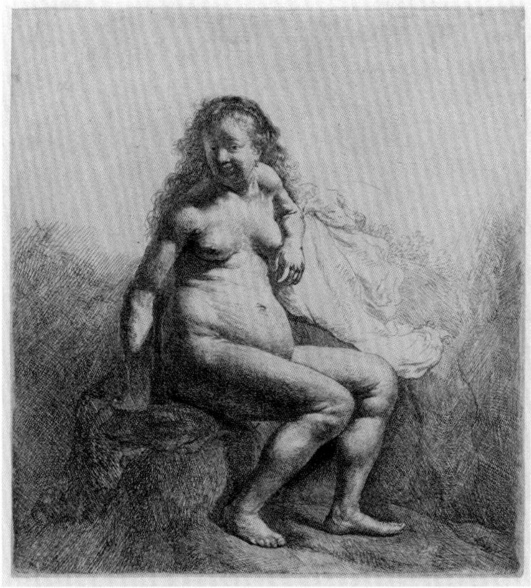

FIG. 95
Seated Female Nude, about 1631
Etching, 17.7 × 16 cm
Rijksmuseum, Amsterdam

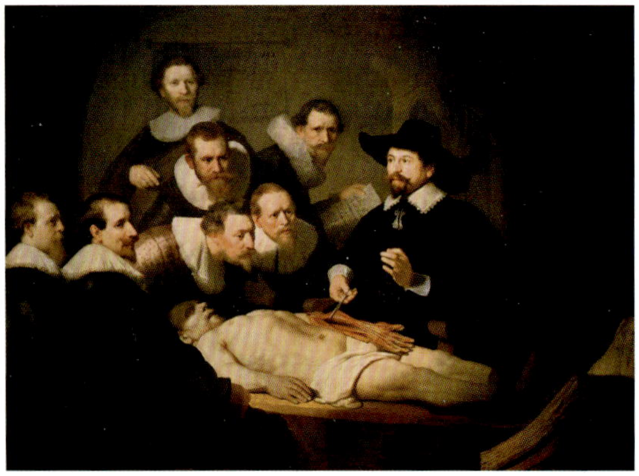 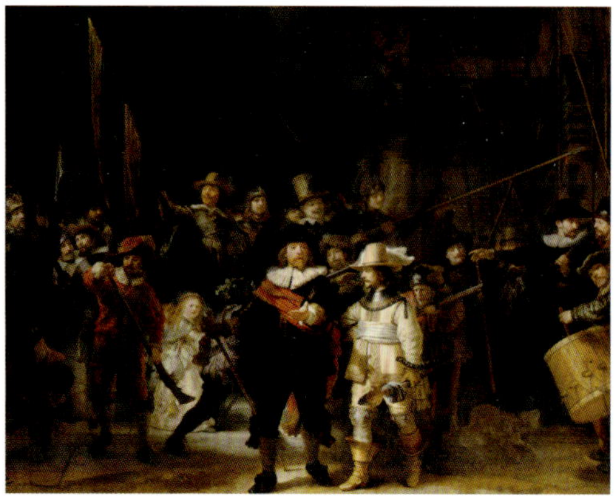

FIG. 96
The Anatomy Lesson of Dr Nicolaes Tulp, 1632
Oil on canvas, 169 × 217 cm
Royal Picture Gallery Mauritshuis, The Hague

FIG. 97
Officers and other Civic Guardsmen of District II in Amsterdam under the Command of Captain Frans Banninck Cocq and Lieutenant Willem van Ruytenburch, known as '*The Night Watch*', 1642
Oil on canvas, 379.5 × 453.5 cm
Rijksmuseum, Amsterdam.
On loan from the City of Amsterdam

Mid-1630s

Rembrandt is now one of the most highly paid painters in Holland. He and Saskia enjoy a rich lifestyle and he begins to amass a vast collection of art and curiosities.

Apparently now working independently of Uylenburgh, takes on numerous pupils, among them Govert Flinck (1615–1660) in about 1635–6; Ferdinand Bol (1616–1680) in about 1636–42; and Gerbrand van den Eeckhout (1621–1674) in about 1635–8/9.

Paints an increasing number of history paintings, including a series of scenes from Christ's Passion for Stadtholder Frederik Hendrik (Alte Pinakothek, Munich). Other works include *Susanna and the Elders*, 1636 (fig. 65) and *The Blinding of Samson*, 1636 (Städel Museum, Frankfurt).

1637

In May Rembrandt and Saskia move to a rented house on Binnen-Amstel (now Zwanenburgerstraat 41).

1638

A daughter, Cornelia, is born, but lives only three weeks.

1639

On 5 January buys a magnificent house in Sint Anthonisbreestraat (today the Rembrandthuis Museum) for 13,000 guilders, mostly financed by loans. Retains the address in Binnen-Amstel until 1 May.

Works include *Self Portrait leaning on a Stone Sill* (etching), inspired by paintings by Raphael and Titian.

1640

On 29 July a second daughter called Cornelia is baptised but lives only a few weeks.

Rembrandt's mother dies.

Paints *Self Portrait at the Age of 34* (fig. 14).

1641

Titus, the only child of Rembrandt and Saskia to survive to adulthood, is baptised on 22 September.

On 18 October the artist Philips Angel (about 1618–1664/5) delivers an address to the members of the Leiden painters' guild in which he praises Rembrandt's 'keen and deep reflection'. The city chronicler Jan Jansz Orlers (1570–1646) publishes a brief biography of the artist, praising him as 'one of the most celebrated painters of this century'.

Carel Fabritius (1622–1654) becomes a pupil.

1642

Saskia dies in June and is buried in the Oude Kerk in Amsterdam. Her will stipulates that Rembrandt is to have the usufruct of her estate, provided he does not remarry.

Geertje Dircks (1610/15–after 1656?) is hired as Titus's nurse. She becomes Rembrandt's mistress.

Completes '*The Night Watch*', a dramatic and highly innovative group portrait of one of Amsterdam's civic guard companies (fig. 97).

Bernhard Keil (1624–1654) probably begins his two-year apprenticeship with Rembrandt. Samuel van Hoogstraten (1627–1678) studies with Rembrandt from around 1642/3 to 1646/7.

1647

The value of Rembrandt's estate, including house and chattels, is estimated at 40,750 guilders at the time of Saskia's death five years earlier.

Hendrickje Stoffels (1626–1663) begins work as Rembrandt's housekeeper, eventually becoming his mistress.

Works include *Portrait of Jan Six in his Study* (etching) (fig. 68).

1648

Geertje Dircks makes a will, leaving all her possessions to Titus van Rijn.

Works include *Self Portrait at the Window, Drawing on an Etching-Plate* (etching) (fig. 15) and *Christ healing the Sick: The Hundred Guilder Print* (etching) (fig. 58).

1649

Geertje Dircks sues Rembrandt for alleged breach of marital promise. In October the Commissioners of the Chamber of Marital Affairs order Rembrandt to pay her alimony of 200 guilders per year.

A number of pupils, including Willem Drost (1633–1659), Nicolaes Maes (1634–1693) and Jacobus Leveck (1634–1675), study with Rembrandt in the late 1640s and early 1650s.

1650

Contrives to have Geertje Dircks committed to the Spinhuis (women's house of correction) in Gouda.

1651

Paints *Young Girl at a Window* (Nationalmuseum, Stockholm) (fig. 1).

1652

Commissioned by the Sicilian nobleman Don Antonio Ruffo (1610/11–1678) to paint a picture; *Aristotle with a Bust of Homer* is completed a year later (fig. 69). Other works of 1652 include two drawings for the friendship album of Jan Six (cat. 25) and *Self Portrait* (Kunsthistorisches Museum, Vienna) (fig. 16).

1653

Ordered to pay 8,470 guilders owing from the purchase of the house in Sint Anthonisbreestraat in 1639. Borrows heavily to pay off the debt but financial problems only worsen.

Works include *The Three Crosses* (etching) (cats 62–4).

1654

Hendrickje is banned from taking Communion by the Reformed Church for 'practising whoredom with the painter Rembrandt'.

Rembrandt and Hendrickje's daughter Cornelia (1654–1685) is born.

Works include *Portrait of Jan Six* of about 1654 (cat. 101), *Woman bathing in a Stream* (cat. 95) and *Bathsheba with King David's Letter* (cat. 112).

1655

Geertje Dircks is released from the Spinhuis, possibly on account of illness.

The 14-year-old Titus van Rijn draws up his will, making his father his universal heir.

In December 1655 and January 1656 Rembrandt auctions works from his own collection.

Works include *Christ presented to the People* (*Ecce Homo*) (etching) (cats 31–2, 65).

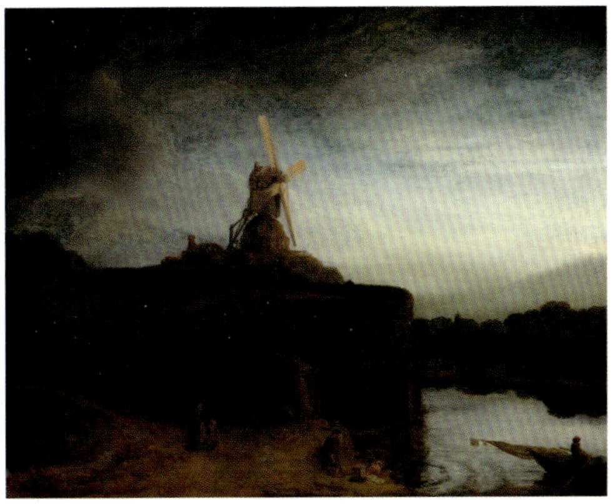

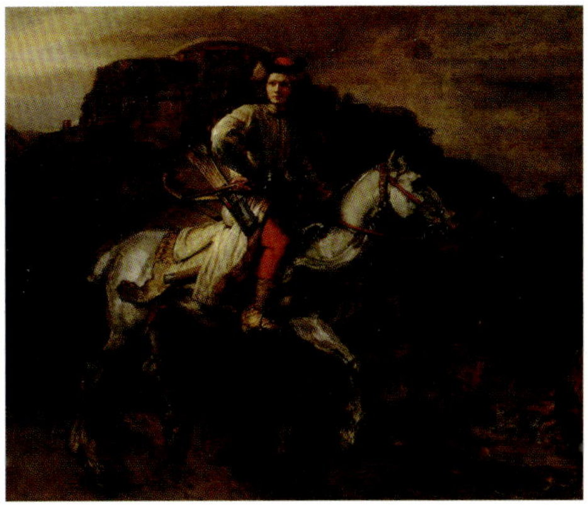

FIG. 98
The Mill, about 1645/8
Oil on canvas, 87.6 × 105.6 cm
National Gallery of Art, Washington, Widener Collection

FIG. 99
The Polish Rider, about 1655
Oil on canvas, 116.8 × 134.9 cm
The Frick Collection, New York, Henry Clay Frick Bequest

1656

Transfers ownership of his house to Titus.

Applies to the High Court of Holland for *cessio bonorum*, a voluntary surrender of possessions to his creditors. Attributes his financial problems to 'losses suffered in business as well as damages and losses at sea'. A detailed inventory is made of Rembrandt's possessions. The letter of cession is awarded in August, and the first of six public auctions takes place before 12 September.

Works include *The Anatomy Lesson of Dr Joan Deyman* (cat. 29) and *Jacob blessing the Sons of Joseph* (cat. 120).

1657

Titus drafts a second will, nominating his half-sister, Cornelia, as his heir. Rembrandt and Hendrickje are to be Cornelia's guardians and Rembrandt is to have the income of Titus's bequeathed possessions and assets for the rest of his life.

Works include *The Apostle Bartholomew* (cat. 108), one of the first in a series of single-figured religious images painted between 1657 and 1661.

1658

Auctions of Rembrandt's possessions continue. The house in Sint Anthonisbreestraat is auctioned.

Some time between 1658 and August 1661 Rembrandt, Hendrickje, Titus and Cornelia move to a rented house on Rozengracht, in Amsterdam's Jordaan district.

Despite reduced circumstances, paints one of the grandest self portraits of his career (The Frick Collection, New York) (fig. 12).

1660

Following the death of his former pupil Govert Flinck (1615–1660), Rembrandt is one of several painters commissioned to complete paintings for Amsterdam's new Town Hall.

His accounts are liquidated and ordered closed. Hendrickje and Titus formally register an art-dealing partnership, relieving Rembrandt of all financial control.

Guercino (Giovanni Francesco Barbieri) paints a now-lost companion piece to Rembrandt's *Aristotle with a Bust of Homer* (fig. 69) for Don Antonio Ruffo. Guercino refers to Rembrandt's painting as 'completely perfect' and adds, 'I sincerely esteem [Rembrandt] as a great virtuoso'.

1661

The biographer Cornelis de Bie (1627–after 1711) praises Rembrandt's paintings ('which enlighten every mind') and etchings ('It is the very soul of life that lives therein').

Hendrickje Stoffels drafts a will on 7 August, declaring her daughter, Cornelia van Rijn, sole beneficiary.

Around 1661, Arent de Gelder (1645–1727) becomes one of Rembrandt's last pupils for a period of two years; he continues to paint in his master's late style into the eighteenth century.

1662

Forced to sell Saskia's grave in the Oude Kerk.

The Conspiracy of the Batavians under Claudius Civilis (cat. 72) is hung in the Amsterdam Town Hall some time before 21 July, but is later replaced by a work by Govert Flinck and Jürgen Ovens (fig. 8).

Other works include *The Sampling Officials of the Amsterdam Drapers' Guild* ('*The Syndics*') (cat. 56).

1663

Hendrickje Stoffels is buried in a rented grave in Amsterdam's Westerkerk on 24 July. The cause of death is unrecorded but was probably the plague.

1665–8

Titus van Rijn applies for legal maturity in 1665 and is awarded full power of attorney over his father's affairs in the following year. Rembrandt falls behind in rental payments for the house on Rozengracht.

In 1667 the Florentine Grand Duke Cosimo de' Medici (1642–1723) visits Rembrandt; a member of the prince's retinue describes him as 'pittore famoso'.

Works include *Lucretia*, 1666 (cat. 57); *Portrait of Gerard de Lairesse* (fig. 51) and *Self Portrait with two Circles* (cat. 58).

1668

Titus marries Magdalena van Loo (1641–1669). He dies seven months later and is buried in the Westerkerk.

1669

Titus and Magdalena's daughter, Titia van Rijn, is born.

Paints *Self Portrait at the Age of 63* (cat. 3) and *Self Portrait* (cat. 4). Other works include *Simeon with the Infant Christ in the Temple* (cat. 122), left unfinished in Rembrandt's studio at his death.

Rembrandt dies on 4 October and is buried four days later in an anonymous rented grave in the Westerkerk.

LIST OF EXHIBITED WORKS

A complete record of works included in the exhibitions at the National Gallery, London and the Rijksmuseum, Amsterdam. Works are listed chronologically. Illustrated works are followed by their catalogue number in square brackets.

Works exhibited in only one venue are indicated by 'London' or 'Amsterdam' beside their catalogue number.

A more extensive scholarly supplement of the exhibited works, compiled by Marjorie E. Wieseman, Jonathan Bikker, Erik Hinterding and Marijn Schapelhouman, with Albert Godycki and Lelia Packer, is available free of charge in a printable format on the website of the National Gallery, London. www.nationalgallery.org.uk/rembrandt/the_late_works/supplement

The Agony in the Garden, about 1648–55
Pen and brush and brown ink, 19.6 × 19 cm
The Syndics of the Fitzwilliam Museum, Cambridge (2140)
[cat. 116]

Christ disputing with the Doctors, 1652
Etching and drypoint, 12.6 × 21.4 cm
FIRST STATE OF TWO
Rijksmuseum, Amsterdam. Bequest of Mr and Mrs De Bruijn-van der Leeuw, Muri, Switzerland (printed with light surface tone, RP-P-1962-34)
[Amsterdam, cat. 90]

The Agony in the Garden, about 1652
Etching and drypoint, 11.1 × 8.4 cm
FIRST STATE OF THREE
Ashmolean Museum, Oxford, Presented by Chambers Hall, 1855 (WA1855.400.1)
[London, cat. 117]
Rijksmuseum, Amsterdam. Bequest of Mr and Mrs De Bruijn-van der Leeuw, Muri, Switzerland (RP-P-1962-38)
[Amsterdam, not illustrated]

Clump of Trees with a Vista, 1652
Drypoint, 15.6 × 21.1 cm (first state); 12.4 × 21.1 cm (second state)
FIRST STATE OF TWO
Ashmolean Museum, Oxford, Presented by Chambers Hall, 1855 (WA 1855.425)
[London, cat. 10]
Rijksmuseum, Amsterdam (RP-P-OB-454)
[Amsterdam, cat. 59]
SECOND STATE OF TWO
The Syndics of the Fitzwilliam Museum, Cambridge (printed with surface tone, AD.12.39-388)
[London, cat. 11]
Rijksmuseum, Amsterdam (printed with irregular surface tone, RP-P-OB-455)
[Amsterdam, cat. 60]

Homer reciting Verses ('Pandora', Album Amicorum Jan Six, fol. 40r), 1652
Pen and brush and brown ink with white bodycolour, 19 × 14 cm
Six Collection, Amsterdam
[Loan decision pending, cat. 25]

Peasant Family on the Tramp, about 1652
Etching, 11.3 × 9.3 cm
FIRST STATE OF THREE
Rijksmuseum, Amsterdam (RP-P-OB-220)
[Amsterdam, cat. 13]

A Scholar in his Study (*'Faust'*), about 1652
Etching, engraving and drypoint, 21 × 16 cm
FIRST STATE OF SEVEN
The Syndics of the Fitzwilliam Museum, Cambridge (AD.12.39-185)
[London, cat. 91]
Rijksmuseum, Amsterdam. Bequest of Mr and Mrs De Bruijn-van der Leeuw, Muri, Switzerland (Japanese paper, RP-P-1962-122)
[Amsterdam, not illustrated]
Graphische Sammlung Albertina, Vienna (cartridge paper, DG1926/429)
[Amsterdam, cat. 61]

Farmhouse on a River, about 1652 or 1653?
Pen and brown ink on brown cartridge paper, 12 × 22.6 cm
Museum Boijmans Van Beuningen, Rotterdam (Koenigs Collection) (R 114)
[cat. 9]

The Three Crosses, 1653
Drypoint, 38.5 × 45 cm
FIRST STATE OF FIVE
The British Museum, London (printed with surface tone on vellum, 1842,0806.139)
[London, not illustrated]
Rijksmuseum, Amsterdam. Bequest of Mr and Mrs De Bruijn-van der Leeuw, Muri, Switzerland (printed with surface tone on vellum, RP-P-1961-1196A)
[Amsterdam, cat. 62]
THIRD STATE OF FIVE
Rijksmuseum, Amsterdam (RP-P-OB-617)
[London, cat. 63]
FOURTH STATE OF FIVE
The Victoria and Albert Museum, London, Ionides Bequest (CAI.637)
[London, cat. 64]

Rijksmuseum, Amsterdam. Bequest of Mr and Mrs De Bruijn-van der Leeuw, Muri, Switzerland (Japanese paper, RP-P-1962-40)
[Amsterdam, not illustrated]

Saint Jerome reading in an Italianate Landscape, about 1653
Etching and drypoint, 25.9 × 21 cm
FIRST STATE OF TWO
Rijksmuseum, Amsterdam (printed with surface tone on Japanese paper, RP-P-OB-184)
[Amsterdam, cat. 22]
SECOND STATE OF TWO
The Syndics of the Fitzwilliam Museum, Cambridge (printed with surface tone on Japanese paper, AD.12.39-376)
[London, cat. 23]
Rijksmuseum, Amsterdam. Bequest of Mr and Mrs De Bruijn-van der Leeuw, Muri, Switzerland (cartridge paper, RP-P-1962-52)
[Amsterdam, not illustrated]

A Woman bathing in a Stream, 1654
Oil on panel, 61.8 × 47 cm
The National Gallery, London (NG 54)
[cat. 95]

Bathsheba with King David's Letter, 1654
Oil on canvas, 142 × 142 cm
Départment des Peintures, Musée du Louvre, Paris (M1957)
[cat. 112]

The Adoration of the Shepherds, with the Lamp, about 1654
Etching, 10.5 × 12.9 cm
FIRST STATE OF THREE
Rijksmuseum, Amsterdam (printed with surface tone, RP-P-OB-87)
[Amsterdam, cat. 84]

The Circumcision in the Stable, 1654
Etching, 9.4 × 14.4 cm
SECOND STATE OF FIVE
Rijksmuseum, Amsterdam (RP-P-OB-299)
[Amsterdam, cat. 85]

Virgin and Child with the Cat and the Snake, 1654
Etching, 9.5 × 14.5 cm
FIRST STATE OF FOUR
Rijksmuseum, Amsterdam. Bequest of Mr and Mrs De Bruijn-van der Leeuw, Muri, Switzerland (printed with surface tone, RP-P-1962-33)
[Amsterdam, cat. 86]

The Flight into Egypt, crossing a Brook, 1654
Etching, engraving and drypoint, 9.3 × 14.4 cm
ONLY STATE
Rijksmuseum, Amsterdam (RP-P-OB-113)
[Amsterdam, cat. 87]

Christ disputing with the Doctors, 1654
Etching, possibly with touches of drypoint, 9.5 × 14.4 cm
ONLY STATE
Rijksmuseum, Amsterdam (RP-P-OB-125)
[Amsterdam, cat. 88]

Christ returning from the Temple with his Parents, 1654
Etching and drypoint, 9.5 × 14.4 cm
ONLY STATE
Rijksmuseum, Amsterdam. Bequest of Mr and Mrs De Bruijn-van der Leeuw, Muri, Switzerland (RP-P-1962-32)
[Amsterdam, cat. 89]

Christ at Emmaus: the Larger Plate, 1654
Etching and drypoint, 21.1 × 16 cm
FIRST STATE OF FIVE
Rijksmuseum, Amsterdam. Bequest of Mr and Mrs De Bruijn-van der Leeuw, Muri, Switzerland
(Japanese paper, RP-P-1962-46)
[Amsterdam, cat. 83]
SECOND STATE OF FIVE
The Syndics of the Fitzwilliam Museum, Cambridge (AD.12.39-46)
[London, cat. 82]
Rijksmuseum, Amsterdam (RP-P-OB-158)
[Amsterdam, not illustrated]

The Ringball Player, 1654
Etching, 9.5 × 14.3 cm
FIRST STATE OF TWO
Rijksmuseum, Amsterdam (RP-P-OB-215)
[Amsterdam, cat. 12]

Portrait of Jan Six, about 1654
Oil on canvas, 112 × 102 cm
Six Collection, Amsterdam (00070)
[Loan decision pending, cat. 101]

The Presentation in the Temple, in the Dark Manner, about 1654
Etching and drypoint, 21 × 16.2 cm
ONLY STATE
The Syndics of the Fitzwilliam Museum, Cambridge (printed with surface tone on Japanese paper, AD.12.39-102)
[London, not illustrated]
Rijksmuseum, Amsterdam. Bequest of Mr and Mrs De Bruijn-van der Leeuw, Muri, Switzerland (printed with heavy surface tone on Japanese paper, RP-P-1962-27)
[Amsterdam, cat. 77]

The Entombment, about 1654
Etching and drypoint, 21.1 × 16.1 cm
FIRST STATE OF FOUR
The British Museum, London (printed with surface tone, 1910,0212.360)
[London, cat. 80]
Rijksmuseum, Amsterdam. Bequest of Mr and Mrs De Bruijn-van der Leeuw, Muri, Switzerland (Japanese paper, RP-P-1962-41)
[Amsterdam, not illustrated]
SECOND STATE OF FOUR
Rijksmuseum, Amsterdam (printed with surface tone on vellum, RP-P-OB-152)
[Amsterdam, not illustrated]
THIRD STATE OF FOUR
The British Museum, London (printed with surface tone on Japanese paper, 1843,0513.249)
[London, cat. 81]
Rijksmuseum, Amsterdam. Bequest of Mr and Mrs De Bruijn-van der Leeuw, Muri, Switzerland (printed with surface tone, RP-P-1961-1032)
[Amsterdam, not illustrated]
FOURTH STATE OF FOUR
Rijksmuseum, Amsterdam. Bequest of Mr and Mrs De Bruijn-van der Leeuw, Muri, Switzerland (RP-P-1962-44)
[Amsterdam, not illustrated]

The Descent from the Cross by Torchlight, about 1654
Etching and drypoint, 21 × 16.1 cm
FIRST STATE OF FOUR
The British Museum, London (printed with surface tone on Japanese paper, F,5.8)
[London, not illustrated]
The Syndics of the Fitzwilliam Museum, Cambridge (printed with surface tone on Chinese paper, AD.12.39-28)
[London, cat. 78]

Rijksmuseum, Amsterdam. Bequest of Mr and Mrs De Bruijn-van der Leeuw, Muri, Switzerland (RP-P-1962-45)
[Amsterdam, not illustrated]
Rijksmuseum, Amsterdam (printed with surface tone on Japanese paper, RP-P-OB-147)
[Amsterdam, cat. 79]

A Young Woman sleeping (Hendrickje Stoffels?), about 1654
Brush and brown wash with some white bodycolour; ruled framing lines in pen and brown ink, 24.6 × 20.3 cm
The British Museum, London (1895,0915.1279)
[cat. 70]

Joseph and Potiphar's Wife, 1655
Oil on canvas, 113.5 × 90 cm
Staatliche Museen zu Berlin-Preußischer Kulturbesitz, Gemäldegalerie, Berlin (828H)
[cat. 113]

A Man in Armour (Alexander the Great?), 1655
Oil on canvas, 137.4 × 104.4 cm
Kelvingrove Art Gallery and Museum, Glasgow, Lent by Glasgow Life (Glasgow Museums) on behalf of Glasgow City Council. Bequeathed by Jane Graham Gilbert, 1877 (601)
[cat. 106]

Titus at his Desk, 1655
Oil on canvas, 77 × 63 cm
Museum Boijmans Van Beuningen, Rotterdam (St. 2)
[cat. 99]

An Old Woman reading, 1655
Oil on canvas, 78.7 × 66 cm
By kind permission of the Duke of Buccleuch and Queensberry, KBE (144)
[cat. 98]

Abraham's Sacrifice, 1655
Etching and drypoint, 15.6 × 13.1 cm
ONLY STATE
The Syndics of the Fitzwilliam Museum, Cambridge (AD.12.39-58)
[London, cat. 119]
Rijksmuseum, Amsterdam (Japanese paper, RP-P-OB-63)
[Amsterdam, not illustrated]

Christ presented to the People (Ecce Homo), 1655
Drypoint, 38.3 × 45.5 cm (first to third states); 35.8 × 45.5 cm (from fourth state)
FIRST STATE OF EIGHT
The British Museum, London (printed with surface tone on Japanese paper, 1848,0911.38)
[London, cat. 31]
THIRD STATE OF EIGHT
Rijksmuseum, Amsterdam. Purchased with the support of the Stichting tot Bevordering van de Belangen van het Rijksmuseum (Japanese paper, RP-P-1975-1)
[Amsterdam, not illustrated]
FIFTH STATE OF EIGHT
Rijksmuseum, Amsterdam (RP-P-OB-610)
[Amsterdam, cat. 65]
SIXTH STATE OF EIGHT
The British Museum, London (printed with surface tone on Japanese paper, 1848,0724.17)
[London, cat. 32]
SEVENTH STATE OF EIGHT
Rijksmuseum, Amsterdam (Japanese paper, RP-P-OB-611)
[Amsterdam, not illustrated]
EIGHTH STATE OF EIGHT
Rijksmuseum, Amsterdam (Japanese paper, RP-P-OB-612)
[not illustrated]

The Goldsmith, 1655
Etching and drypoint, 7.7 × 5.6 cm
FIRST STATE OF THREE
Ashmolean Museum, Oxford, Presented by Chambers Hall, 1855 (Japanese paper, WA1855.349)
[London, cat. 33]
Rijksmuseum, Amsterdam (RP-P-OB-210)
[Amsterdam, not illustrated]

Thomas Jacobsz Haringh ('Old Haringh'), about 1655
Drypoint with touches of burin(?), 19.5 × 15 cm
FIRST STATE OF THREE
Graphische Sammlung Albertina, Vienna (printed with surface tone on Japanese paper, DG1926/445)
[Amsterdam, cat. 45]
THIRD STATE OF THREE
Ashmolean Museum, Oxford. Presented by Chambers Hall, 1855 (WA 1855.288)
[London, cat. 46]
Rijksmuseum, Amsterdam. Bequest of Mr and Mrs De Bruijn-van der Leeuw, Muri, Switzerland (Japanese paper, RP-P-1962-102)
[Amsterdam, not illustrated]

The raising of the Cross, about 1655–8
Pen and brown ink, partly wiped with a finger or dry brush, white bodycolour, 17.9 × 21.1 cm
Staatliche Museen zu Berlin, Kupferstichkabinett (KdZ 12013)
[London, cat. 68]

Jacob blessing the Sons of Joseph, 1656
Oil on canvas, 173 × 209 cm
Museumslandschaft Hessen Kassel, Gemäldegalerie Alte Meister, Kassel (GK249)
[cat. 120]

The Anatomy Lesson of Dr Joan Deyman, 1656
Oil on canvas, 100 × 134 cm
Amsterdam Museum, Amsterdam (C 85)
[cat. 29]

Design for the Frame of 'The Anatomy Lesson of Dr Joan Deyman', about 1656
Reed pen and brown ink, 10.9 × 13.2 cm
Amsterdam Museum, Amsterdam (SK-TA-7395)
[cat. 28]

Abraham entertaining the Angels, 1656
Etching and drypoint, 15.9 × 13.1 cm
ONLY STATE
The Syndics of the Fitzwilliam Museum, Cambridge (printed with surface tone, AD.12.39-71)
[London, cat. 34]
Rijksmuseum, Amsterdam. Purchased with the support of the F.G. Waller Fonds (RP-P-1954-135)
[Amsterdam, not illustrated]

Portrait of Johannes Lutma, 1656
Etching, engraving and drypoint, 19.7 × 15 cm
FIRST STATE OF FOUR
The Syndics of the Fitzwilliam Museum, Cambridge (AD.12.39-428)
[London, cat. 47]
Rijksmuseum, Amsterdam (RP-P-OB-550)
[Amsterdam, not illustrated]
SECOND STATE OF FOUR
The Syndics of the Fitzwilliam Museum, Cambridge (Japanese paper, AD.12.39-419)
[London, cat. 48]
Rijksmuseum, Amsterdam (RP-P-OB-548)
[Amsterdam, not illustrated]

Portrait of Arnout Tholinx, about 1656
Etching, engraving and drypoint, 19.8 × 14.9 cm
FIRST STATE OF TWO
The British Museum, London (F,6.68)
[London, cat. 43]
Département des Arts graphiques, Musée du Louvre, Paris (Collection Edmond de Rothschild) (2502 LR / recto)
[Amsterdam, not illustrated]
SECOND STATE OF TWO
Rijksmuseum, Amsterdam (RP-P-OB-577)
[Amsterdam, cat. 44]

The Artist's Son, Titus, about 1656
Etching, 9.9 × 7 cm
ONLY STATE
Ashmolean Museum, Oxford, Presented by Chambers Hall, 1855 (printed with surface tone, WA1855.278)
[London, not illustrated]
Rijksmuseum, Amsterdam (printed with surface tone on Japanese paper, RP-P-OB-22)
[Amsterdam, cat. 100]

Portrait of a Gentleman with a Tall Hat and Gloves, about 1656–8
Oil on canvas, 99.5 × 82.5 cm
National Gallery of Art, Washington (Widener Collection) (1942.9.67)
[cat. 37]

Portrait of a Lady with an Ostrich-Feather Fan, about 1656–8
Oil on canvas, 99.5 × 83 cm
National Gallery of Art, Washington (Widener Collection) (1942.9.68)
[cat. 38]

The Blind Belisarius receiving Alms, about 1656–60
Pen and brown ink with corrections in lead white, 16.7 × 12.1 cm
Staatliche Museen zu Berlin, Kupferstichkabinett, Berlin (KdZ 5275)
[Amsterdam, cat. 121]

The Apostle Bartholomew, 1657
Oil on canvas, 122.7 × 99.7 cm
Timken Museum of Art, The Putnam Foundation Collection, San Diego (34.19)
[cat. 108]

Portrait of Catrina Hooghsaet, 1657
Oil on canvas, 126 × 98.5 cm
Penrhyn Castle, Gwynedd, The Trustees of the Penrhyn Settled Estates (1420340)
[cat. 41]

Saint Francis beneath a Tree, praying, 1657
Drypoint (drypoint and etching from second state), 18 × 24.4 cm
FIRST STATE OF TWO
Rijksmuseum, Amsterdam (Japanese paper, RP-P-OB-171)
[cat. 66]
SECOND STATE OF TWO
Rijksmuseum, Amsterdam. Bequest of Mr and Mrs De Bruijn-van der Leeuw, Muri, Switzerland (RP-P-1962-92)
[Amsterdam, cat. 67]

Adoration of the Shepherds at Night, about 1657
Etching, engraving and drypoint, 14.8 × 19.8 cm
FIRST STATE OF ELEVEN
The British Museum, London (1848,0911.25)
[London, cat. 73]
Rijksmuseum, Amsterdam. Bequest of Mr and Mrs De Bruijn-van der Leeuw, Muri, Switzerland (RP-P-1962-22)
[Amsterdam, cat. 74]
SECOND STATE OF ELEVEN
Rijksmuseum, Amsterdam (RP-P-1992-14)
[Amsterdam, not illustrated]
FIFTH STATE OF ELEVEN
The British Museum, London (1848,0911.27)
[London, cat. 75]
Rijksmuseum, Amsterdam. Bequest of Mr and Mrs De Bruijn-van der Leeuw, Muri, Switzerland (Chinese paper, RP-P-1961-1007)
[Amsterdam, not illustrated]
SIXTH STATE OF ELEVEN
The British Museum, London (Japanese paper, F,4.86)
[London, cat. 76]
SEVENTH STATE OF ELEVEN
Rijksmuseum, Amsterdam (printed with surface tone on Japanese paper, RP-P-OB-91)
[Amsterdam, not illustrated]

Christ preaching ('La Petite Tombe'), about 1657
Etching and drypoint, 15.5 × 20.7 cm
FIRST STATE OF TWO
The Victoria and Albert Museum, London, Ionides Bequest (CAI 642)
[London, cat. 26]
Rijksmuseum, Amsterdam (Japanese paper, RP-P-OB-130)
[Amsterdam, not illustrated]
Rijksmuseum, Amsterdam. Bequest of Mr and Mrs De Bruijn-van der Leeuw, Muri, Switzerland (RP-P-1962-35)
[Amsterdam, not illustrated]

Portrait of Abraham Francen, Apothecary, about 1657
Etching, engraving and drypoint, 15.8 × 20.8 cm
SECOND STATE OF TWELVE
Rijksmuseum, Amsterdam. Bequest of Mr and Mrs De Bruijn-van der Leeuw, Muri, Switzerland (printed with surface tone on Japanese paper, RP-P-1962-98)
[Amsterdam, cat. 103]
SIXTH STATE OF TWELVE
Rijksmuseum, Amsterdam. Bequest of Mr and Mrs De Bruijn-van der Leeuw, Muri, Switzerland (printed with surface tone on Japanese paper RP-P-1961-1150)
[Amsterdam, cat. 104]

The Entombment of Christ (after Polidoro da Caravaggio), about 1657–8
Pen and brush in brown ink, white heightening, yellow and red chalk on greyish paper in the shape of a lunette; the upper corners added later, 18.1 × 28.4 cm
Teylers Museum, Haarlem (O* 049)
[Amsterdam, cat. 27]

Jael killing Sisera, 1657–9
Pen and brown ink with white bodycolour, 19.2 × 17.4 cm
Rijksmuseum, Amsterdam. Bequest of C. Hofstede de Groot, The Hague (RP-T-1930-8)
[Amsterdam, cat. 114]

Christ and the Woman of Samaria, 1658
Etching and drypoint, 20.5 × 16 cm (first state); 12.6 × 16 cm (from second state)
FIRST STATE OF FIVE
Rijksmuseum, Amsterdam (Japanese paper, RP-P-OB-137)
[Amsterdam, not illustrated]
THIRD STATE OF FIVE
The Syndics of the Fitzwilliam Museum, Cambridge (Japanese paper, AD.12.39-63)
[London, cat. 24]
Rijksmuseum, Amsterdam. Bequest of Mr and Mrs De Bruijn-van der Leeuw, Muri, Switzerland (printed with some surface tone, RP-P-1961-1026)
[Amsterdam, not illustrated]

Self Portrait, drawing on an Etching Plate, 1658
Etching, 11.8 × 6.4 cm
ONLY STATE
Petit Palais, Musée des Beaux-Arts de la Ville de Paris (printed with surface tone on Japanese paper, Dutuit 7681)
[London, not illustrated]
Graphische Sammlung Albertina, Vienna (printed with surface tone on Japanese paper, DG1930/562)
[Amsterdam, cat. 1]

Sketch for the Portrait of Lieven Willemsz van Coppenol ('The Smaller Plate'), about 1658
Pen and brown ink, brown wash, with white heightening, 16.2 × 15.1 cm
Szépművészeti Múzeum / Museum of Fine Arts, Budapest (1570)
[cat. 50]

Portrait of the Calligrapher Lieven Willemsz van Coppenol ('The Smaller Plate'), about 1658
Etching, engraving and drypoint, 25.8 × 19 cm

SECOND STATE OF SEVEN
Rijksmuseum, Amsterdam (RP-P-OB-572)
[Amsterdam, not illustrated]
THIRD STATE OF SEVEN
Ashmolean Museum, Oxford. Presented by Chambers Hall, 1855 (WA1855.289)
[London, cat. 51]

Portrait of the Calligrapher Lieven Willemsz van Coppenol (*'The Large Coppenol'*), 1658
Etching, engraving and drypoint, 34 × 29 cm
SIXTH STATE OF NINE
Rijksmuseum, Amsterdam (with inscription in lower margin in pen and ink by Coppenol, 1661, RP-P-OB-630)
[Amsterdam, not illustrated]
SEVENTH STATE OF NINE
The British Museum, London (with inscription in lower margin in pen and ink by Coppenol, 1664, F,6.65)
[London, cat. 49]

Woman sitting half-dressed beside a Stove, 1658
Etching and drypoint, 22.8 × 18.7 cm
FIRST STATE OF SEVEN
Rijksmuseum, Amsterdam. Bequest of Mr and Mrs De Bruijn-van der Leeuw, Muri, Switzerland (printed with surface tone on Japanese paper, RP-P-1962-73)
[Amsterdam, cat. 14]
THIRD STATE OF SEVEN
The Syndics of the Fitzwilliam Museum, Cambridge (printed with surface tone on Japanese paper, AD.12.39-74)
[London, cat. 15]
Rijksmuseum, Amsterdam (Japanese paper, RP-P-OB-256)
[Amsterdam, not illustrated]
SIXTH STATE OF SEVEN
Rijksmuseum, Amsterdam (RP-P-OB-258)
[cat. 16]

Reclining Female Nude (*'La Négresse couchée'*), 1658
Etching and drypoint, 8.1 × 15.8 cm
SECOND STATE OF SIX
The Syndics of the Fitzwilliam Museum, Cambridge (printed with surface tone on Japanese paper, AD.12.39-163)
[London, cat. 35]
Rijksmuseum, Amsterdam. Bequest of Mr and Mrs De Bruijn-van der Leeuw, Muri, Switzerland (Japanese paper, RP-P-1962-79)
[Amsterdam, not illustrated]

Woman bathing her Feet at a Brook, 1658
Etching and drypoint, 16 × 8 cm
FIRST STATE OF TWO
Rijksmuseum, Amsterdam (printed with surface tone on Japanese paper, RP-P-OB-263)
[Amsterdam, cat. 97]

Woman at the Bath, with a Hat beside her, 1658
Etching and drypoint, 15.6 × 12.9 cm
FIRST STATE OF TWO
The Syndics of the Fitzwilliam Museum, Cambridge (printed with surface tone on Japanese paper, AD.12.39-160)
[London, cat. 17]
Rijksmuseum, Amsterdam (printed with surface tone on Japanese paper, RP-P-OB-261)
[Amsterdam, not illustrated]
SECOND STATE OF TWO
The British Museum, London (1843,0607.127)
[London, not illustrated]
Rijksmuseum, Amsterdam (printed with surface tone on Japanese paper, RP-P-OB-262)
[Amsterdam, cat. 18]

Self Portrait, 1659
Oil on canvas, 84.5 × 66 cm
National Gallery of Art, Washington (Andrew W. Mellon Collection) (1937.1.72)
[cat. 2]

Jupiter and Antiope, 1659
Etching and drypoint, 13.8 × 20.5 cm
SECOND STATE OF THREE
The Syndics of the Fitzwilliam Museum, Cambridge (printed with surface tone on Japanese paper, AD.12.39-159)
[London, cat. 30]
Rijksmuseum, Amsterdam (RP-P-OB-435)
[Amsterdam, not illustrated]
Rijksmuseum, Amsterdam. Bequest of Mr and Mrs De Bruijn-van der Leeuw, Muri, Switzerland (RP-P-1961-1112)
[Amsterdam, not illustrated]

Jacob and the Angel, about 1659
Oil on canvas, 137 × 116 cm
Staatliche Museen zu Berlin-Preußischer Kulturbesitz, Gemäldegalerie, Berlin (828)
[Amsterdam, cat. 118]

Titus in Monk's Habit, 1660
Oil on canvas, 79.5 × 67.7 cm
Rijksmuseum, Amsterdam. Purchased with the support of the Vereniging Rembrandt (SK-A-3138)
[cat. 107]

The Amstelveenseweg outside Amsterdam, about 1660–2
Pen and brush in brown ink on light brown cartridge paper, 13.5 × 20.4 cm
Rijksmuseum, Amsterdam. Bequest of Mr and Mrs De Bruijn-van der Leeuw, Muri, Switzerland (RP-T-1961-85)
[cat. 8]

Recumbent Lion, facing Right, about 1660–5
Pen and brown ink on brown paper, 12.2 × 21.2 cm
Rijksmuseum, Amsterdam. Purchased with the support of the Vereniging Rembrandt (RP-T-1901-A-4524)
[cat. 7]

Self Portrait as the Apostle Paul, 1661
Oil on canvas, 91 × 77 cm
Rijksmuseum, Amsterdam. Bequest of Mr and Mrs De Bruijn-van der Leeuw, Muri, Switzerland (SK-A-4050)
[cat. 111]

The Apostle Bartholomew, 1661
Oil on canvas, 86.7 × 75.6 cm
The J. Paul Getty Museum, Los Angeles (71.PA.15)
[cat. 109]

The Apostle Simon, 1661
Oil on canvas, 98.3 × 79 cm
Kunsthaus Zürich, Ruzicka-Stiftung (R.26)
[cat. 110]

The Conspiracy of the Batavians under Claudius Civilis, about 1661–2
Oil on canvas, 196 × 309 cm
The Royal Academy of Fine Arts, Sweden (NM578)
[cat. 72]

The Conspiracy of the Batavians under Claudius Civilis, about 1661
Pen and brown ink with brown wash and white bodycolour, 19.6 × 18 cm
Staatliche Graphische Sammlung München (1451)
[London, cat. 71]

Simeon in the Temple (*Album Amicorum Jacob Heyblocq*, fol. 61r), 1661
Pen and brush and brown ink with white bodycolour, 12 × 8.9 cm
Koninklijke Bibliotheek, National Library of the Netherlands, The Hague (KB KW 131 H 26)
[cat. 123]

Portrait of Jacob Trip, about 1661
Oil on canvas, 130.5 × 97 cm
The National Gallery, London (NG 1674)
[cat. 39]

Portrait of Margaretha de Geer, Wife of Jacob Trip, about 1661
Oil on canvas, 130.5 × 97.5 cm
The National Gallery, London (NG 1675)
[cat. 40]

Woman with the Arrow, 1661
Etching and drypoint, 20.5 × 12.3 cm
SECOND STATE OF THREE
The Syndics of the Fitzwilliam Museum, Cambridge (printed with light surface tone, AD.12.39-153)
[London, cat. 96]
Rijksmuseum, Amsterdam (printed with surface tone, RP-P-OB-264)
[Amsterdam, not illustrated]

Nude Woman resting on a Cushion, about 1661–2
Pen and brush in brown ink with white bodycolour, 13.6 × 28.3 cm
Rijksmuseum, Amsterdam (RP-T-1917-1)
[cat. 36]

Nude Woman seated by a Stove, about 1661–2
Pen and brush in brown ink with black chalk and white bodycolour on ledger paper, 29.2 × 17.5 cm
Rijksmuseum, Amsterdam (RP-T-00-227)
[cat. 19]

Three Syndics, about 1661–2
Reed pen and brush and brown ink with white bodycolour on brownish paper, 17.3 × 20.5 cm
Staatliche Museen zu Berlin, Kupferstichkabinett, Berlin (KdZ 5270)
[Amsterdam, cat. 68]

Standing Syndic: Volckert Jansz, about 1661–2
Reed pen and brush and brown ink, corrected and heightened with white, on ledger paper, 22.5 × 17.5 cm
Museum Boijmans Van Beuningen, Rotterdam (Koenigs Collection) (R133)
[cat. 54]

Seated Syndic: Jacob van Loon, about 1661–2
Reed pen and brush and brown ink with white bodycolour on ledger paper 19.5 × 16 cm
Rijksmuseum, Amsterdam. Bequest of H.P. Gerritsen, The Hague (RP-T-1896-A-3172)
[cat. 55]

The Sampling Officials of the Amsterdam Drapers' Guild, known as *'The Syndics'*, 1662
Oil on canvas, 191.5 × 279 cm
Rijksmuseum, Amsterdam, on loan from the City of Amsterdam (SK-C-6)
[cat. 56]

Self Portrait as Zeuxis, about 1662
Oil on canvas, 82.5 × 65 cm
Wallraf-Richartz-Museum & Fondation Corboud, Cologne (2526)
[Amsterdam, cat. 20]

Juno, about 1662–5
Oil on canvas, 127 × 123.8 cm
The Armand Hammer Collection. Gift of the Armand Hammer Foundation, Hammer Museum, Los Angeles (AH.90.58)
[cat. 21]

Portrait of a Lady with a Lap Dog, about 1662–5
Oil on canvas, 81.3 × 64.1 cm
Collection Art Gallery of Ontario, Toronto. Bequest of Frank P. Wood, 1955 (54/60)
Frame: Collection Art Gallery of Ontario, Toronto. Gift of an anonymous collector, 1997
[cat. 42]

Portrait of Frederik Rihel on Horseback, about 1663
Oil on canvas, 294.5 × 241 cm
The National Gallery, London. Bought with a special grant and contributions from The Art Fund and The Pilgrim Trust, 1959 (NG 6300)
[cat. 53]

The Blind Homer, dictating to a Scribe, about 1663
Pen and brush in brown, white bodycolour, with additions by a later hand in grey and brown wash, 14.8 × 17 cm
Nationalmuseum, Stockholm (NMH 1677/1875)
[cat. 105]

Lucretia, 1664
Oil on canvas, 120 × 101 cm
National Gallery of Art, Washington (Andrew W. Mellon Collection) (1937.1.76)
[cat. 115]

Elsje Christiaens hanging on the Gibbet, 1664
Pen and brush and brown ink on Japanese paper, 17.2 × 9 cm
Lent by The Metropolitan Museum of Art, New York, H.O. Havemeyer Collection, bequest of Mrs H.O. Havemeyer, 1929 (29.100.937)
[cat. 5]

Elsje Christiaens hanging on the Gibbet, in three-quarter Profile, 1664
Pen and brush and brown ink on Japanese paper, 15.8 × 8.1 cm
Lent by The Metropolitan Museum of Art, New York, Robert Lehman Collection, 1975 (1975.1.803)
[cat. 6]

Portrait of a Family, about 1665
Oil on canvas, 126 × 167 cm
Herzog Anton Ulrich-Museum, Braunschweig (GG 238)
[Amsterdam, cat. 94]

Portrait of a Couple as Isaac and Rebecca, known as '*The Jewish Bride*', about 1665
Oil on canvas, 121.5 × 166.5 cm
Rijksmuseum, Amsterdam, on loan from the City of Amsterdam (A. van der Hoop Bequest) (SK-A-216)
[cat. 92]

Isaac and Rebecca spied upon by Abimelech, about 1665
Pen and brown ink with white gouache corrections, 14.5 × 18.5 cm
Private collection, USA
[Amsterdam, cat. 93]

Self Portrait with Two Circles, about 1665–9
Oil on canvas, 116.3 × 97.2 cm
English Heritage, The Iveagh Bequest (Kenwood, London) (57)
[cat. 58]

Lucretia, 1666
Oil on canvas, 110.2 × 92.3 cm
Lent by the Minneapolis Institute of Arts (The William Hood Dunwoody Fund, Minneapolis) (34.19)
[cat. 57]

Portrait of a Blond Man, 1667
Oil on canvas, 108.9 × 92.7 cm
National Gallery of Victoria, Melbourne, Felton Bequest, 1951 (2372/4)
[cat. 52]

Portrait of an Elderly Man, 1667
Oil on canvas, 81.9 × 67.7 cm
Royal Picture Gallery Mauritshuis, The Hague, acquired with the support of the Friends of the Mauritshuis Foundation, the Ministry of Education, Culture and Science, the National Art Collections Fund, the BankGiro Loterij, the VSB Fund The Hague, the Rembrandt Association, the Prince Bernhard Cultural Fund, the ING Group, Professor A.C.R. Dreesmann, the Dr Hendrik Muller National Fund and private benefactors, 1999 (1118)
[cat. 102]

Self Portrait at the Age of 63, 1669
Oil on canvas, 86 × 70.5 cm
The National Gallery, London (NG 221)
[cat. 3]

Self Portrait, 1669
Oil on canvas, 65.4 × 60.2 cm
Royal Picture Gallery Mauritshuis, The Hague, acquired with the support of the Rembrandt Assocation and private benefactors, 1947 (840)
[cat. 4]

Simeon with the Infant Christ in the Temple, about 1669
Oil on canvas, 98.5 × 79.5 cm
Nationalmuseum, Stockholm. Donated in 1949 by Mr Nils B. Hersloff (4567)
[cat. 122]

PHOTOGRAPHIC CREDITS

AMSTERDAM
© Amsterdam Museum: cats 28, 29; figs 9, 40.

© 2014, Collectie Six, Amsterdam: cats 25, 101.

Museum Het Rembrandthuis © Amsterdam, Rembrandthouse Museum: fig. 20.

Rijksmuseum, Amsterdam © Rijksmuseum, Amsterdam: cats 7, 8, 12, 13, 14, 16, 18, 19, 22, 36, 44, 55, 56, 59, 60, 62, 63, 65, 66, 67, 74, 77, 79, 83, 84, 85, 86, 87, 88, 89, 90, 92, 97, 100, 103, 104, 107, 111, 114; figs 13, 15, 24, 33, 36, 38, 41, 42, 50, 54, 55, 56, 58, 59, 60, 61, 62, 64, 66, 68, 77, 79, 80, 85, 86, 88, 90, 95, 97.

© Royal Palace Amsterdam Foundation / Photo: Erik and Petra Hesmerg: figs 6, 7, 8; © Royal Palace Amsterdam Foundation / Photo: Tom Haartsen: figs 4, 5.

BERGAMO
© Comune di Bergamo – Accademia Carrara: fig. 35.

BERLIN
Gemäldegalerie, Staatliche Museen zu Berlin-Preussischer Kulturbesitz © Scala, Florence / BPK Bildagentur für Kunst, Kultur und Geschichte, Berlin. Photo: Jörg P. Anders: cats, 113, 118; fig. 3.

Kupferstichkabinett, Staatliche Museen zu Berlin-Preussischer Kulturbesitz © Scala, Florence / BPK Bildagentur für Kunst, Kultur und Geschichte, Berlin. Photo: Jörg P. Anders: cats 69, 121.

© Staatliche Museen zu Berlin. Bildarchiv Preussischer Kulturbesitz. Photo: Jörg P. Anders: cat. 68; figs 52, 94.

BRAUNSCHWEIG
Herzog Anton Ulrich Museum Braunschweig, Kunstmuseum des Landes Niedersachsen: © akg-images / André Held: cat. 94; © Photo: Scala, Florence: fig. 82; © The Art Archive / Superstock: fig. 87.

BRUSSELS
Koninklijke Musea voor Schone Kunsten van Belgie, Brussels © Royal Museum of Fine Arts of Belgium, Brussels / Photo: J. Geleyns / Ro scan: fig. 23.

BUDAPEST
© Szépművészeti Múzeum, Budapest: cat. 50; © Szépművészeti Múzeum, Budapest / Scala, Florence: figs 47, 48.

CAMBRIDGE
© Fitzwilliam Museum, Cambridge: cats 11, 15, 17, 23, 24, 30, 34, 35, 47, 48, 78, 82, 91, 96, 116, 119.

CAMBRIDGE, MASSACHUSETTS
Harvard University Art Museums, Cambridge, Massachusetts © Fogg Art Museum, Harvard University Art Museums, USA / The Bridgeman Art Library: fig. 37.

COLOGNE
Wallraf-Richartz-Museum and Fondation Corboud, Cologne © Photo Scala, Florence / BPK, Bildagentur für Kunst, Kultur und Geschichte, Berlin / Photo: Jochen Remmer: cat. 20; © Photo Scala, Florence / BPK, Bildagentur für Kunst, Kultur und Geschichte, Berlin: fig. 21.

EDINBURGH
On loan from a Private Collection to the Scottish National Gallery © National Galleries of Scotland: fig. 17.

FLORENCE
Galleria degli Uffizi, Florence © Photo Scala, Florence – courtesy of the Ministero Beni e Att. Culturali: fig. 28; © Soprintendenza Speciale per il Polo Museale Fiorentino / Scala, Florence: fig. 11.

FRANKFURT AM MAIN
© U. Edelmann – Städel Museum – ARTOTHEK: fig. 27.

GLASGOW
© CSG CIC Glasgow Museums Collection: cat. 106.

HAARLEM
© Teylers Museum, Haarlem, The Netherlands: cat. 27. Haarlem-de Hallen © Frans Hals Museum, Haarlem / Photo: Tom Haartsen: fig. 63.

HAMBURG
© Hamburger Kunsthalle, Hamburg, Germany / The Bridgeman Art Library: fig. 34.

KASSEL
© Museumslandschaft Hessen Kassel, Gemäldegalerie Alte Meister: cat. 120; fig. 89.

KIEL
© Kunsthalle zu Kiel, erworben mit Mitteln der Vereinigung der Freunde der Kunsthalle (Carstens-Gesellschaft) / Photo: Martin Frommhagen: fig. 93.

KROMĚŘÍŽ
Palace of the Archbishop of Zámek a Zahrady © akg-images / Erich Lessing: fig. 53.

LONDON
© Johnny van Haeften Limited (2013), London: fig. 2.

The Iveagh Bequest (Kenwood, London) © English Heritage: cat. 58.

© The Trustees of The British Museum: cats 31, 32, 43, 49, 70, 73, 75, 76, 80, 81; fig. 44.

© The National Gallery, London: cats 3, 39, 40, 53, 95; figs 14, 31, 75.

© Victoria and Albert Museum, London: cats 26, 64.

LOS ANGELES
The Armand Hammer Collection / Straus Center for Conservation © President and Fellows of Harvard College: fig. 32.

The Armand Hammer Collection © Hammer Museum, Los Angeles: cat. 21.

© The J. Paul Getty Museum, Los Angeles, California: cat. 109.

MADRID
© Museo Nacional del Prado, Madrid / Photo AISA / The Bridgeman Art Library, London: fig. 74.

MELBOURNE
© National Gallery of Victoria, Melbourne: cat. 52.

MINNEAPOLIS, MINNESOTA
© The Minneapolis Institute of Arts, Minnesota: cat. 57; fig. 57.

MONTREAL, QUEBEC
© The Montreal Museum of Fine Arts, Denis Farley: fig. 73.

MOSCOW
© Pushkin State Museum, Moscow / Photo: Scala, Florence: fig. 84.

MUNICH
© Staatliche Graphische Sammlung München, Inv. 1451 Z: cat. 71.

NEW YORK
© The Frick Collection: figs 12, 99.

The Metropolitan Museum of Art, New York: © The Metropolitan Museum of Art / Art Resource / Scala, Florence: cats 5, 6; figs 18, 25, 29, 39, 43, 51, 69.

The New York Public Library, New York © Art and Architecture Collection, Miriam and Ira D. Wallach Division of Art, Prints and Photographs, The New York Public Library, Astor, Lenox and Tilden Foundations: fig. 26.

© Otto Naumann, Ltd, New York: fig. 49.

OXFORD
Ashmolean Museum, University of Oxford © Copyright in this Photograph Reserved to the Ashmolean Museum, Oxford: cats 10, 33, 46, 51, 117.

PARIS
Musée du Louvre, Paris © Musée du Louvre, Dist. RMN-Grand Palais / Angèle Dequier: cat. 112; © RMN-Grand Palais (Musée du Louvre) / Gérard Blot: fig. 22; © RMN-Grand Palais (Musée du Louvre) / Hervé Lewandowski: figs 19, 72; © RMN-Grand Palais (Musée du Louvre) / René-Gabriel Ojéda: fig. 76.

PENRHYN
© Trustees of the Penrhyn Settled Estates / Photo: Ashmolean Museum, University of Oxford: cat. 41.

PRAGUE
Národní Gallery, Prague © akg-images: fig. 70.

PRIVATE COLLECTIONS
By kind permission of the Duke of Buccleuch and Queensberry KBE © The Buccleuch Collection: cat. 98.

© Private Collection: fig. 78.

© Photo: Ellen McDermott: cat. 93.

ROTTERDAM
© Museum Boijmans Van Beuningen, Rotterdam. Loan Museum Boijmans Van Beuningen Foundation (Collection Koenigs) / Photo: Studio Tromp, Rotterdam: cats 9, 54; © Museum Boijmans Van Beuningen, Rotterdam. Loan Museum Boijmans Van Beuningen Foundation / Photo: Studio Tromp, Rotterdam: cat. 99.

SAN DIEGO
© Putnam Foundation / Timken Museum of Art, San Diego, CA: cat. 108.

ST PETERSBURG
The State Hermitage Museum, St Petersburg © akg-images: fig. 91; © Photo: Scala, Florence: fig. 92; © The State Hermitage Museum / Photo by Vladimir Terebenin, Leonard Kheifets, Yuri Molodkovets: fig. 67.

STOCKHOLM
Nationalmuseum, Stockholm © Åsa Lunden / Nationalmuseum Stockholm: figs 1, 45, 46; © Photo: Hans Thorwid / Nationalmuseum, Stockholm: cat. 105; © Photo: Eric Cornelius / Nationalmuseum, Stockholm: cat. 122.

The Royal Academy of Fine Arts, Sweden, on loan to the Nationalmuseum Stockholm © Photo: Erik Cornelius / Nationalmuseum, Stockholm: cat. 72.

THE HAGUE
© The Hague, Koninklijke Bibliotheek [131 H 26. Fol. 61]: cat. 123.

© Royal Picture Gallery Mauritshuis, The Hague: cats 4, 102; fig. 71; © Royal Picture Gallery Mauritshuis, The Hague / Photo: The Bridgeman Art Library, London: fig. 65; © Royal Picture Gallery Mauritshuis, The Hague / Photo: Scala, Florence: fig. 96.

TORONTO, ONTARIO
© Art Gallery of Ontario, Toronto: cat. 42.

UTRECHT
© Museum Catharijneconvent. Photo: Ruben De Heer: fig. 83.

VIENNA
Albertina, Vienna © Albertina, Vienna: cats 1, 45, 61.

Graphische Sammlung Albertina, Vienna © White Images / Scala, Florence: fig. 30.

Kunsthistorisches Museum, Vienna © Photo Fine Art Images / Heritage Images / Scala, Florence: fig. 16.

WASHINGTON, DC
National Gallery of Art, Washington © Image courtesy of the Board of Trustees, National Gallery of Art, Washington, DC: cats 2, 37, 38, 115; figs 10, 81, 98.

ZÜRICH
Kunsthaus Zürich, Ruzicka Stiftung © 2014 Kunsthaus Zürich. All rights reserved: cat. 110.

INDEX

All works of art are by Rembrandt unless otherwise stated.
Figures in *italics* refer to illustrations.

We are grateful to the Siebold Stichting Foundation and Fukushima Medical University for their support of the International Conference *Rembrandt Now: Technical Practice, Conservation and Research* and the Public Programme associated with *Rembrandt: The Late Works*.

Siebold
Stichting / Foundation

LIST OF LENDERS

AMSTERDAM
Amsterdam Museum
Collectie Six
Rijksmuseum

BANGOR
The Trustees of the Penrhyn Settled Estates

BERLIN
Staatliche Museen zu Berlin:
 Gemäldegalerie
 Kupferstichkabinett

BRAUNSCHWEIG
Herzog Anton Ulrich-Museum

BUDAPEST
Szépművészeti Múzeum / Museum of Fine Arts

CAMBRIDGE
The Fitzwilliam Museum

COLOGNE
Wallraf-Richartz-Museum & Fondation Corboud

GLASGOW
Glasgow Life (Glasgow Museums) on behalf of Glasgow City Council

HAARLEM
Teylers Museum

KASSEL
Museumslandschaft Hessen Kassel: Gemäldegalerie Alte Meister

LONDON
The British Museum
English Heritage
The National Gallery
Victoria and Albert Museum

LOS ANGELES
The J. Paul Getty Museum
Hammer Museum

MELBOURNE
National Gallery of Victoria

MINNEAPOLIS
Minneapolis Institute of Arts

MUNICH
Staatliche Graphische Sammlung

NEW YORK
Private Collection
Robert Lehman Collection
The Metropolitan Museum of Art

OXFORD
Ashmolean Museum of Art and Archaeology

PARIS
Musée du Louvre
Petit Palais, Musée des Beaux-Arts de la Ville de Paris

ROTTERDAM
Museum Boijmans Van Beuningen

SAN DIEGO
Timken Museum of Art

SELKIRK
The Duke of Buccleuch and Queensberry, KBE

STOCKHOLM
Nationalmuseum
The Royal Academy of Fine Arts, Sweden

THE HAGUE
Koninklijke Bibliotheek
Mauritshuis

TORONTO
Art Gallery of Ontario

VIENNA
Albertina

WASHINGTON DC
National Gallery of Art

ZÜRICH
Kunsthaus Zürich